T0281067

Lecture Notes in Computer Science 14759

The series Lecture Notes in Computer Science (LNCS), including its subseries Lecture Notes in Artificial Intelligence (LNAI) and Lecture Notes in Bioinformatics (LNBI), has established itself as a medium for the publication of new developments in computer science and information technology research, teaching, and education.

LNCS enjoys close cooperation with the computer science R & D community, the series counts many renowned academics among its volume editors and paper authors, and collaborates with prestigious societies. Its mission is to serve this international community by providing an invaluable service, mainly focused on the publication of conference and workshop proceedings and postproceedings. LNCS commenced publication in 1973.

Silvia Bonfanti · Angelo Gargantini ·
Michael Leuschel · Elvinia Riccobene ·
Patrizia Scandurra
Editors

Rigorous State-Based Methods

10th International Conference, ABZ 2024
Bergamo, Italy, June 25–28, 2024
Proceedings

 Springer

Editors
Silvia Bonfanti ⓘ
Department of Management, Information
and Production Engineering
University of Bergamo
Bergamo, Italy

Angelo Gargantini ⓘ
Department of Management, Information
and Production Engineering
University of Bergamo
Bergamo, Italy

Michael Leuschel ⓘ
Institut für Informatik
Heinrich-Heine-Universität
Düsseldorf, Germany

Elvinia Riccobene ⓘ
Dipartimento di Informatica
Università degli Studi di Milano
Milan, Italy

Patrizia Scandurra ⓘ
Department of Management, Information
and Production Engineering
University of Bergamo
Bergamo, Italy

ISSN 0302-9743   ISSN 1611-3349 (electronic)
Lecture Notes in Computer Science
ISBN 978-3-031-63789-6   ISBN 978-3-031-63790-2 (eBook)
https://doi.org/10.1007/978-3-031-63790-2

This Springer imprint is published by the registered company Springer Nature Switzerland AG
The registered company address is: Gewerbestrasse 11, 6330 Cham, Switzerland

Preface

ABZ 2024 - the 10th International Conference on Rigorous State-Based Methods was held in Bergamo, Italy, from June 25–28, 2024.

The ABZ conference series is dedicated to the cross-fertilization of state-based and machine-based formal methods. Abstract State Machines (ASM), Alloy, B, TLA, VDM, and Z are examples of these methods. They share a common conceptual foundation and are widely used in both academia and industry for the rigorous design and analysis of hardware and software systems. The ABZ conferences aim to be a forum for the vital exchange of knowledge and experience among the research communities around different formal methods.

ABZ 2024, which this volume is dedicated to, follows the success of the nine ABZ conferences from its first edition organized in London (UK) in 2008, where the acronym ABZ was invented to merge, into a single event, the ASM, B, and Z conference series. The Alloy community joined the event at the second ABZ 2010 conference, which was held in Orford (Canada). The VDM community joined the event at ABZ 2012, which was held in Pisa (Italy). ABZ 2014, held in Toulouse (France), brought the inclusion of the TLA$^+$ community and the idea of proposing at each ABZ an industrial case study as a common problem for the application of different formal methods. The ABZ 2016 conference was held in Linz, Austria, and ABZ 2018 in Southampton, UK. In 2018 the steering committee decided to retain the acronym ABZ and add the subtitle 'International Conference on Rigorous State-Based Methods' to make more explicit the intention to include all state-based formal methods. The two succeeding ABZ events were organized in Ulm (Germany) as virtual events, while ABZ 2023 was held in Nancy, France.

ABZ 2024 received 47 submissions. At least three program committee members single-blindly reviewed each submission, and 29 papers were accepted for publication in this volume and presentation at the conference: 9 long papers covering a broad spectrum of research, from fundamental to applied work, 12 short papers of work in progress, industrial experience reports and tool development, 2 papers of PhD students working on topics related to state-based formal methods, and 5 papers on the case ABZ 2024 case study, which was dedicated to the specification and analysis of a medical device: the Mechanical Lung Ventilator (MLV), inspired by the Mechanical Ventilator Milano developed during COVID-19. A paper in this volume is dedicated to describing the case study.

The ABZ program included two invited talks: one was given by David Basin from ETH in Zurich (Switzerland) on *Getting Electronic Payments Right*, and one by Maurice ter Beek from ISTI/CNR in Pisa (Italy) on *Formal Methods and Tools applied in the railway domain*. Moreover, a remote invited talk, not included in this volume, was given by Joe Kiniry from Galois in Portland (USA) on *What happens when the Government starts encouraging the use of formal methods?*

ABZ 2024 hosted two workshops, one on the *Rodin Platform*, an Eclipse-based toolset for Event-B, and the other, the *IVOIRE* workshop, on a rigorous model validation process and toolchain based on validation obligations.

Organizing and running this event required a lot of effort from several people. We are grateful to all the authors who submitted their work to ABZ 2024. We wish to thank all members of the Program Committee and all the additional reviewers for their precise, careful evaluation of the papers, and for their availability during the discussion period which considered each paper's acceptance. Furthermore, we thank Claudio Menghi and Alexander Raschke for managing proposals of workshops and tutorials, Philipp Körner and Chiara Braghin for taking care of the doctoral symposium, Atif Mashkoor and Fabian Vu for their valuable work in advertising this event, and finally Andrea Bombarda and Mario Lilli for managing the conference website.

We wish to express our deepest gratitude to the University of Bergamo, which provided all the necessary organizational support, FME (Formal Methods Europe) who partially supported our keynotes, and the Universities of Bergamo and Milan for their financial support.

The conference was managed with EquinOCS Springer Nature, which was a valuable support for the submitting and reviewing process, and for preparing this volume.

For readers of these proceedings, we hope that you find these proceedings useful, interesting, and challenging for future research.

May 2024

Elvinia Riccobene
Michael Leuschel
Silvia Bonfanti
Angelo Gargantini
Patrizia Scandurra

Organization

Program Committee Chairs

Bonfanti, Silvia	University of Bergamo, Italy
Gargantini, Angelo	University of Bergamo, Italy
Leuschel, Michael	Heinrich-Heine-Universität Düsseldorf, Germany
Riccobene, Elvinia	Università degli Studi di Milano, Italy
Scandurra, Patrizia	University of Bergamo, Italy

Program Committee Members

Aït-Ameur, Yamine	IRIT/INPT-ENSEEIHT, France
Aguirre, Nazareno	Universidad Nacional de Río Cuarto, Argentina
André, Ètienne	Université Sorbonne Paris Nord, LIPN, France
Arcaini, Paolo	National Institute of Informatics, Japan
Banach, Richard	University of Manchester, UK
Börger, Egon	University of Pisa, Italy
Bonfanti, Silvia	University of Bergamo, Italy
Braghin, Chiara	Università degli Studi di Milano, Italy
Bryant, Adam	Galois Inc., USA
Butler, Michael	University of Southampton, UK
Campos, José	University of Minho, Portugal
Cristiá, Maximiliano	Universidad Nacional de Rosario, Argentina
Cunha, Alcino	University of Minho, Portugal
Dingel, Juergen	Queen's University, Canada
Dubois, Catherine	ENSIIE-Samovar, France
Ernst, Gidon	LMU Munich, Germany
Ferrarotti, Flavio	Software Competence Center Hagenberg, Austria
Filali Amine, Mamoun	IRIT CNRS, Université Paul Sabatier, France
Frappier, Marc	Université de Sherbrooke, Canada
Gargantini, Angelo	University of Bergamo, Italy
Gervais, Frederic	Université Paris-Est Créteil, LACL, France
Gervasi, Vincenzo	University of Pisa, Italy
Hallerstede, Stefan	Aarhus University, Denmark
Havelund, Klaus	Jet Propulsion Laboratory, USA
Hoang, Thai Son	University of Southampton, UK
Ishikawa, Fuyuki	National Institute of Informatics, Japan

Kouchnarenko, Olga	University of Franche-Comté, France
Körner, Philipp	Heinrich Heine University, Düsseldorf, Germany
Laleau, Régine	Paris-East Créteil University, France
Leuschel, Michael	Heinrich-Heine-Universität Düsseldorf, Germany
Lisitsa, Alexei	University of Liverpool, UK
Mallet, Frederic	Université Côte d'Azur, France
Mammar, Amel	SAMOVAR, Télécom SudParis, Institut Polytechnique de Paris, France
Mashkoor, Atif	JKU Linz, Austria
Menghi, Claudio	University of Bergamo, Italy
Mery, Dominique	Université de Lorraine, LORIA, France
Merz, Stephan	Inria, Villers-lès-Nancy, France
Monahan, Rosemary	Maynooth University, Ireland
Paulweber, Philipp	fiskaly GmbH, Austria
Prinz, Andreas	University of Agder, Norway
Raschke, Alexander	Ulm University, Germany
Riccobene, Elvinia	Università degli Studi di Milano, Italy
Scandurra, Patrizia	University of Bergamo, Italy
Schellhorn, Gerhard	Universität Augsburg, Germany
Schewe, Klaus-Dieter	Zhejiang University, China
Singh, Neeraj	INPT-ENSEEIHT/IRIT, University of Toulouse, France
Voisin, Laurent	Systerel, France
Zimmermann, Wolf	Martin Luther University Halle-Wittenberg, Germany
ter Beek, Maurice	CNR, ISTI, Pisa, Italy

Additional Reviewers

Bombarda, Andrea	University of Bergamo, Italy
Canciani, Andrea	Geckosoft, Italy
Kobayashi, Tsutomu	National Institute of Informatics, Japan
Stock, Sebastian	JKU Linz, Austria

Abstract of Invited Talk

Getting Electronic Payments Right

David Basin ⓘ

ETH Zurich, Zurich, Switzerland
`basin@inf.ethz.ch`

Abstract. EMV is the international protocol standard for smartcard payments and is used in billions of payment cards worldwide. Despite the standard's advertised security, various issues have been previously uncovered, deriving from logical flaws that are hard to spot in EMV's lengthy and complex specification, running over 2,000 pages. We have formalized various models of EMV in Tamarin, a symbolic model checker for cryptographic protocols. Tamarin was extremely effective in finding critical flaws, both known and new. For example, we discovered multiple ways that an attacker can use a victim's EMV card for high-valued purchases without the victim's supposedly required PIN. We report on this, as well as follow-up work with an EMV consortium member on verifying the latest, improved version of the protocol, the EMV Kernel C-8. Overall, our work provides evidence that security protocol model checkers like Tamarin have an essential role to play in developing real-world payment protocols and that they are up to this challenge. This work is in collaboration with Xenia Hofmeier, Ralf Sasse, and Jorge Toro-Pozo.

Keywords: EMV · Electronic Payments · Tamarin Prover

Contents

Short Research Papers

Invited Talk

Formal Methods and Tools Applied in the Railway Domain

Maurice H. ter Beek[(⊠)][iD]

Formal Methods and Tools Lab, CNR–ISTI, Pisa, Italy
`maurice.terbeek@isti.cnr.it`

Abstract. ABZ and other state-based formal methods and tools are successfully applied to the development of safety-critical systems for decades now, in particular in the transport domain, without a single language or tool emerging as the dominant solution for system design. Formal methods are highly recommended by the current safety standards in the railway industry, but railway engineers often lack the knowledge to transform their semi-formal models into formal models, with a precise semantics, to serve as input to formal methods tools. We share the results of performing empirical studies in the railway domain, including usability analyses of formal methods tools involving railway practitioners. We discuss, in particular with respect to railway systems and their modelling, our experiences in applying rigorous state-based methods and tools to a variety of case studies, for which we interacted with a number of companies from the railway domain. We report on lessons learned from these experiences and provide pointers to drive future research towards facilitating further synergies between—on the one hand—researchers and developers of ABZ and other state-based formal methods and tools, and—on the other hand—practitioners from the railway industry.

1 Introduction

For decades now, railways are controlled by real-time computer-based systems. To fulfil stringent safety requirements, railway control systems typically require extensive verification and validation, largely relying on formal methods, as highly recommended by the CENELEC European standards [30,51] for the development of the most critical software for use in the railway industry. This is also witnessed by hundreds of recent projects financed as part of the European Shift2Rail Joint Undertaking[1] and its successor Europe's Rail[2] and as part of related initiatives outside the EU, like the UK Rail Research and Innovation Network (UKRRIN)[3] and the Chinese State Key Laboratory of Rail Traffic Control and Safety[4].

The original version of the chapter has been revised. A correction to this chapter can be found at https://doi.org/10.1007/978-3-031-63790-2_31

[1] https://shift2rail.org/.
[2] https://rail-research.europa.eu/.
[3] https://www.ukrrin.org.uk/.
[4] http://en.bjtu.edu.cn/research/institute/laboratory/16583.htm.

S. Bonfanti et al. (Eds.): ABZ 2024, LNCS 14759, pp. 3–21, 2024.
https://doi.org/10.1007/978-3-031-63790-2_1

We participated in the Shift2Rail projects ASTRail[5] and 4SECURail[6] and in the Italian regional projects TRACE-IT (TRAin Control Enhancement via Information Technology), STINGRAY (SmarT station INtelliGent RAilwaY) and SmaRIERS (Smart Railway Infrastructures: Efficiency, Reliability and Safety). Through these projects we interacted with a number of companies from the railway domain, which allowed us to apply more than three decades of experience with formal methods and tools accumulated in our research lab FMT (Formal Methods and Tools) to a variety of case studies from the railway domain.

The main safety-critical railway signalling systems can be classified in two large classes of applications: train movement and distancing control systems, including the Automatic Train Control (ATC), Automatic Train Operation (ATO), Automatic Train Protection (ATP) and Automatic Train Supervision (ATS) subsystems, and interlocking systems. All these subsystems respect international standards to ensure interoperability between the different subsystems described. These include ERTMS/ETCS (European Rail Traffic Management Systems/European Train Control System), its Chinese counterpart CTCS (Chinese Train Control System), both focusing on interoperability for passenger, high speed and freight lines, and CBTC (Communication-Based Train Control) systems, mainly aimed at the automatic operation of high capacity metro lines.

The aforementioned classes of subsystems have been subject to formal specification and verification for several decades now, as witnessed by the success stories of the application of the rigorous state-based B method to many cases, which include the verification of the ATP system for the RER Line A of Paris [61], the Subway Speed Control System (SSCS) of the Calcutta subway [44], and Line 14 of the Paris Metro [48], as well as derivatives thereof, like line 1 or the NY Canarsie line [50], and the driverless Paris–Roissy Airport shuttle [25]. Moreover, B was also used for an industrial scale analysis of Alstom's U400 system [41], which is in operation in about 100 metro lines worldwide.

Further success stories of applying formal methods and tools to railway systems include the metro control system of Rio de Janeiro, with the support of Simulink/Stateflow [54], the ERTMS/ETCS standard with NuSMV [36] and Hybrid ERTMS/ETCS Level 3 with several formal methods and tools as part of the ABZ 2018 case study [4,7,34,42,47,63,77,88]. Moreover, in [6], the system structure of a movement authority scenario of CTCS Level 3 was modelled in AADL [84] and Hybrid CSP [68], and verified with the Hybrid Hoare Logic Prover [89], an interactive theorem prover based on Isabelle/HOL [92]. Recently, in [21], the autonomous positioning system in development for the Florence tramways was verified with the UPPAAL model-checking toolset [26,46].

In this paper, we first share the results of performing empirical studies in the railway domain, including usability analyses of formal methods tools involving railway practitioners, in Sects. 2 and 3. We then present some applications of formal methods and tools to case studies from the railway domain in Sect. 4, reporting some lessons learned from these experiences and providing some pointers to drive future research in the concluding Sect. 5.

---

[5] http://www.astrail.eu/.

[6] https://www.4securail.eu/.

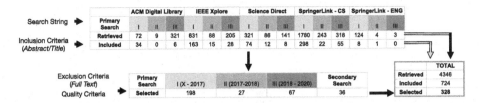

Fig. 1. Process of study selection and numerical results. The value of TOTAL in the bottom-right table is obtained by summing-up the cells in Retrieved, Included and Selected from the other tables. ©2022 ACM. Reprinted (and annotated) with permission from ACM Computing Surveys [52].

2 Systematic Mapping Study

In [52], we presented the first systematic mapping study[7] on formal methods in the railway domain, focusing on railway signalling systems, to complement other empirical studies that we performed, which considered the perspective of stakeholders [15, 22] and surveyed different tools for railway system design [55, 56, 79] (cf. Sect. 3). Starting from the base terms "formal methods" (representing the object of research) and "railways" (representing the domain of application), we used alternative keywords and wildcards to elaborate the following search string:

"formal" OR "model check*" OR "model based" OR "model driven" OR "theorem prov*" OR "static analysis"
AND
"railway*" OR "CBTC" OR "ERTMS" OR "ETCS" OR "interlocking" OR "automatic train" OR "train control" OR "metro" OR "CENELEC"

As shown in Fig. 1, after originally retrieving 4346 studies from four main scientific databases, eventually 328 high-quality studies were selected from the literature from the period 1989–2020. These 328 papers were analysed in detail.

Figure 2 shows that formal methods for railways is a hot topic with a strong industrial focus, given that 143 papers were published solely during the last five years (44% of the total), while no less than 79 papers (24%) involve industry (papers with at least one industrial co-author).

Figure 3 shows that models are at the basis of practically all papers and that formal verification and model checking are the main analysis techniques [9, 39], but also simulation [64], theorem proving [80, 83] and refinement [2, 3, 74] are prominently applied techniques.

In terms of concrete languages and tools, Figs. 4 and 5 illustrate that the landscape is highly diversified, but B (15% in total and 22% of the industrial papers) [1, 8, 25, 41, 59, 63, 67, 76, 87] and ProB (9% in both cases) [1, 41, 63, 67, 76, 87] are among the dominant languages and frequently used tools. However, there are examples also of ASM, VDM, Z, Alloy and TLA+ [35, 57, 70], as well as of Atelier-B and Rodin [4, 40, 41, 65, 82, 88]. Tools of the B family (i.e., ProB, Atelier-B and Rodin) clearly dominate (18% overall and 20% of the industrial papers).

---

[7] A variant of systematic literature reviews aiming at classifying the literature [71, 81].

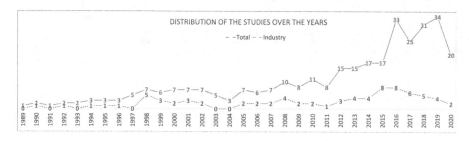

Fig. 2. Studies by year. ©2022 ACM. Reprinted with permission from ACM Computing Surveys [52].

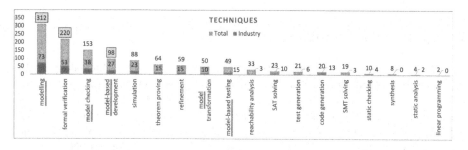

Fig. 3. Techniques. ©2022 ACM. Reprinted (and annotated) with permission from ACM Computing Surveys [52].

Our systematic mapping study shows that the empirical maturity of the field is still limited, as many of the selected papers present only examples or experience reports. We call for more empirical rigor in the field, with case studies, which can leverage the strong link with industries, and for controlled experiments, which can address issues related to the learnability of formal methods and aspects related to human factors. In fact, many papers do not focus on a particular railway system or standard, but we signal an improvement with high-quality papers on the ERTMS/ETCS [28,63], CBTC [41] and CTCS [11] standards. Interlocking is still the most popular subject of study, but other railway subsystems (e.g., ATC, ATO, ATP and ATS) are being considered more frequently in recent years [62,90,91]. ABZ has contributed to this goal with the Hybrid ERTMS/ETCS Level 3 case study at ABZ 2018 [4,7,34,42,47,63,77,88].

Our findings also show that almost all core railway development phases can be addressed with the support of formal methods, which is in line with the recommendations of the norms [30,51]. However, additional effort should be dedicated to the later phases of the development process, in particular testing, implementation and validation, which are currently apparently not sufficiently addressed.

Fig. 4. Modeling language families considered in the studies. ©2022 ACM. Reprinted (and annotated) with permission from ACM Computing Surveys [52].

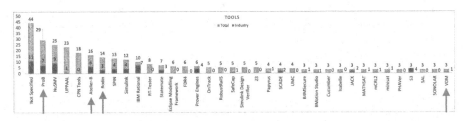

Fig. 5. Tools. ©2022 ACM. Reprinted (and annotated) with permission from ACM Computing Surveys [52].

3   Systematic Evaluation and Usability Analysis

In [55], we presented the first systematic tool evaluation[8] and usability analysis of formal methods tools for railway signalling system design. This complements other empirical studies that we performed, which surveyed various tools for railway system design [56,79] selected based on surveys with stakeholders [22,53] and a literature review [52] (cf. Sect. 2). The 13 selected tools are as follows: SPIN, Simulink, nuXmv, ProB, Atelier-B, UPPAAL, FDR4, CPN Tools, CADP, mCLR2, SAL, TLA+ and UMC (cf. [55] for individual references to these tools[9]).

The research questions (RQs) we posed ourselves in [55] were the following:

RQ1: *Which are the features to consider for evaluating a formal methods tool?*
RQ2: *How do different tools compare with respect to these features?*
RQ3: *How do different tools compare with respect to their usability?*

Table 1 summarises the characteristics and expertise of the participants who evaluated the tools based on direct hands-on experience. Next to the assessors and academic experts (including the authors of [55]), we involved nine railway practitioners as industry experts, who had no prior experience with applying formal methods tools yet more than 10 years of experience in the railway domain.

---

[8] Based on the DESMET methodology for evaluating software engineering tools [72].
[9] In [55], UPPAAL denoted all variants (i.e., UPPAAL 4.0, UPPAAL SMC, UPPAAL Stratego and UPPAAL Tiga), by now integrated in UPPAAL 5: https://uppaal. org/.

Table 1. Characteristics and expertise of the study participants. ©2021 IEEE. Personal use is permitted, but republication/redistribution requires IEEE permission. Reprinted (and adapted) with permission from IEEE Transactions on Software Engineering [55].

ID	Role in Study	Milieu	Main Function	Age	Sex	Years of Experience in		
						Formal Methods (FM)	Railway Industry	FM in Railways
1	assessor	academic	workpackage leader	39	M	>13	3	13
2	assessor	academic	tool developer	62	M	>20	0	9
3	assessor	academic	researcher	36	M	>6	0	4
4	expert	academic	group leader	48	M	>15	0	9
5	expert	academic	project leader	66	F	>30	0	>25
6	expert	academic	professor	65	M	>30	0	>25
7	expert	industry	system engineer	NA	M	0	>10	0
8	expert	industry	system engineer	52	M	0	>10	0
9	expert	industry	system engineer	48	M	0	>10	0
10	expert	industry	software developer	43	M	0	>10	0
11	expert	industry	product manager	NA	M	0	>10	0
12	expert	industry	system engineer	48	M	0	>10	0
13	expert	industry	innovation engineer	NA	M	0	>10	0
14	expert	industry	software developer	45	M	0	>10	0
15	expert	industry	innovation engineer	NA	F	0	3 to 10	0

The systematic feature evaluation was performed by the assessors, after elicitating the features with a collaborative approach inspired by the KJ method [85]. During a 3 h workshop, the assessors, the academic experts and two industry experts came up with 33 features that should be considered when evaluating a formal methods tool for railway system design, hierarchically categorized into functional, expressiveness, and quality features, comprising 8 subcategories. The assessors produced an evaluation sheet for each tool based on the following use:

1. install and run the tool;
2. consult the tool's website for official documentation;
3. search for additional documentation useful to fill the evaluation sheet;
4. consult the 114 papers on formal methods and railways from the literature review [53] to check for the tool's application in railways;
5. perform some trials with the tool to confirm the claims reported in the documentation, and assign the value to those features that required hands-on activity to be evaluated;
6. report the evaluation on the sheet, together with links to the consulted documents and papers, and appropriate notes when the motivation of an assignment needed clarification.

The evaluation sheets were revised after face-to-face meetings to align visions and balance judgments, and reviewed externally as part of a deliverable of the ASTRail project, and they are publicly available for inspection [79]. Figure 6 reports the table resulting from the feature evaluation activity.

Category	Name	SPIN	Simulink	nuXmv	ProB	Atelier B	UPPAAL	FDR4	CPN Tools	CADP	mCRL2	SAL	TLA+	UMC
Development Functionalities	Specification / Modeling	TEXT	GRAPH	TEXTIM	TEXT	TEXT	GRAPH	TEXTIM	GRAPH	TEXTIM	TEXT	TEXTIM	TEXT	TEXT
	Code Generation	NO	YES	NO	NO	YES	NO	NO	NO	YES	NO	NO	NO	NO
	Documentation / Report Generation	PARTIAL	YES	NO	PARTIAL	PARTIAL	PARTIAL	PARTIAL	NO	PARTIAL	PARTIAL	NO	NO	PARTIAL
	Requirements Traceability	NO	YES	NO	NO	NO	NO	NO	NO	NO	NO	NO	NO	NO
	Project Management	NO	YES	NO	YES	YES	NO	NO	NO	NO	NO	NO	NO	NO
Verification Functionalities	Simulation	TEXT	GRAPH	TEXT	MIX	NO	GRAPH	TEXT	GRAPH	TEXT	TEXT	TEXT	NO	TEXT
	Formal Verification	MC-L	MC-O	MC-L,MC-B	MC-L,MC-B,RF	TP	MC-L,RF	RF	MC-B	MC-B,RF	MC-B,RF	MC-L,TP	MC-L,TP	MC-B
	Large-scale Verification Technique	FLY,POR,PAR	BMC	BMC,SYM	SCT	SCT	SMC,SYM	COM,POR	BMC	COM,PAR	COM,PAR	PAR,SCT	SYM,SCT	FLY
	Model-based Testing	NO	YES	NO	YES	NO	YES	NO	NO	YES	NO	YES	NO	NO
Language Expressiveness	Non-determinism	INT	EXT	INT,EXT	INT,EXT	INT,EXT	INT,EXT	INT,EXT	INT	INT,EXT	INT,EXT	INT,EXT	INT	INT
	Concurrency	ASYNCH	NO	SYNCH	NO	NO	SYNCH	ASYNCH	ASYNCH	ASYNCH	ASYNCH	A/SYNCH	ASYNCH	A/SYNCH
	Timing Aspects	NO	YES	YES	NO	NO	YES	YES	YES	NO	YES	YES	NO	NO
	Stochastic or Probabilistic Aspects	NO	NO	NO	NO	NO	YES	NO	NO	NO	YES	NO	NO	NO
	Modularity of the Language	HIGH	HIGH	HIGH	LOW	LOW	MEDIUM	HIGH	HIGH	HIGH	HIGH	MEDIUM	MEDIUM	HIGH
	Supported Data Structures	BASIC	COMPLEX	COMPLEX	COMPLEX	COMPLEX	COMPLEX	COMPLEX	COMPLEX	COMPLEX	COMPLEX	COMPLEX	COMPLEX	COMPLEX
	Float Support	NO	YES	YES	NO	YES	YES	NO	NO	NO	NO	NO	NO	NO
Tool Flexibility	Backward Compatibility	LIKELY	LIKELY	LIKELY	LIKELY	MODERATE	LIKELY	MODERATE	LIKELY	LIKELY	LIKELY	MODERATE	MODERATE	MODERATE
	Standard Input Format	OPEN	PARTIAL	OPEN	OPEN	OPEN	PARTIAL	OPEN	PARTIAL	STANDARD	OPEN	OPEN	OPEN	STANDARD
	Import / Export vs. Other Tools	MEDIUM	LOW	MEDIUM	HIGH	MEDIUM	LOW	MEDIUM	MEDIUM	HIGH	HIGH	MEDIUM	LOW	MEDIUM
	Modularity of the Tool	LOW	HIGH	LOW	HIGH	MEDIUM	HIGH	LOW	LOW	HIGH	MEDIUM	LOW	LOW	MEDIUM
	Team Support	NO	NO	NO	NO	YES	NO	NO	NO	NO	NO	NO	NO	NO
Maturity	Industrial Diffusion	HIGH	HIGH	HIGH	HIGH	HIGH	HIGH	MEDIUM	MEDIUM	MEDIUM	MEDIUM	LOW	MEDIUM	LOW
	Stage of Development	MATURE	MATURE	MATURE	MATURE	MATURE	MATURE	MATURE	MATURE	MATURE	MATURE	MATURE	MATURE	PROTOTYPE
Usability	Availability of Customer Support	PARTIAL	YES	PARTIAL	YES	YES	YES	PARTIAL	PARTIAL	PARTIAL	PARTIAL	PARTIAL	PARTIAL	PARTIAL
	Graphical User Interface	LIMITED	YES	NO	PARTIAL	PARTIAL	YES	LIMITED	PARTIAL	LIMITED	PARTIAL	NO	LIMITED	PARTIAL
	Mathematical Background	MEDIUM	BASIC	MEDIUM	MEDIUM	ADVANCED	MEDIUM	ADVANCED	MEDIUM	ADVANCED	ADVANCED	ADVANCED	ADVANCED	MEDIUM
	Quality of Documentation	GOOD	EXCELLENT	GOOD	GOOD	EXCELLENT	GOOD	EXCELLENT	GOOD	GOOD	GOOD	GOOD	GOOD	LIMITED
Company Constraints	Cost	FREE	PAY	MIX	FREE	FREE	MIX	MIX	FREE	MIX	FREE	FREE	FREE	FREE
	Supported Platforms	ALL	ALL	ALL	ALL	ALL	ALL	ALL	Windows	ALL	ALL	ALL	ALL	ALL
	Complexity of License Management	EASY	ADEQUATE	EASY	EASY	EASY	MODERATE	MODERATE	EASY	MODERATE	EASY	EASY	EASY	EASY
	Easy to Install	YES	YES	YES	YES	YES	YES	YES	YES	PARTIAL	YES	YES	YES	YES
Railway-specific Criteria	CENELEC Certification	NO	PARTIAL	NO	NO	NO	NO	NO	NO	NO	NO	NO	NO	NO
	Integration in the CENELEC Process	MEDIUM	YES	MEDIUM	YES	YES	MEDIUM	MEDIUM	MEDIUM	MEDIUM	MEDIUM	LOW	LOW	MEDIUM
		SPIN	Simulink	nuXmv	ProB	Atelier B	UPPAAL	FDR4	CPN Tools	CADP	mCRL2	SAL	TLA+	UMC

Fig. 6. Evaluation table. ©2021 IEEE. Personal use is permitted, but republication/ redistribution requires IEEE permission. Reprinted (and annotated) with permission from IEEE Transactions on Software Engineering [55].

We note that ProB and Atelier-B stand out for project management and score well on tool flexibility (Atelier-B is the only tool including team support), usability and maturity; TLA+ much less.

We selected a subset of seven tools for the usability evaluation, excluding those requiring advanced mathematical background (except for Atelier-B, since it is one of the few tools used in the development of real-world railway products, cf. "Integration in the CENELEC process" in Fig. 6) and those for which it is known from the literature that they are inadequate for handling industry-size problems. We performed the usability evaluation of the resulting seven tools (SPIN, Simulink, nuXmv, ProB, Atelier-B, UPPAAL and UMC) with railway experts adopting the following methodology.

First, the assessors developed a model of the moving block system for each of the tools. The experts were already familiar with the sample system, which has moreover been used as a reference by other papers in the literature [34,56].

Next, the different characteristics of the tools were illustrated in a 3 h meeting with the experts, using the predeveloped models as reference. The experts were asked to evaluate the usability of each tool based on their first impression. After an introduction, each tool was presented in a 15 min demo, covering the tool's general structure, then opening, navigating and describing the model, followed by a guided simulation and a description and presentation of a formal verification session. After the presentation of each tool, the experts filled a usability questionnaire for the tool.

We used the widely adopted System Usability Scale (SUS) questionnaire of Brooke [31,32], following Brooke's guidelines [31] to calculate the SUS score and

Bangor et al. [10] for the interpretations for the scores: 100 = Best Imaginable; 85 = Excellent; 73 = Good; 52 = OK; 39 = Poor; 25 = Worst Imaginable.

Figure 7 presents the results of the SUS questionnaire. The tool that clearly stands out as being considered the most usable is Simulink (SUS Score = 76.39), with ProB (62.22) as runner-up, whereas Atelier-B (45.56) is considered among the least usable tools, which is attributed to the refinement-based theorem-proving approach that requires mastering advanced skills. Overall, tool usability is acceptable, given the average SUS Score (56.67) between OK and Good.

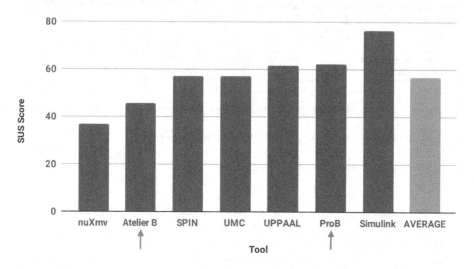

Fig. 7. SUS scores for the different tools. ©2021 IEEE. Personal use is permitted, but republication/redistribution requires IEEE permission. Reprinted (and annotated) with permission from IEEE Transactions on Software Engineering [55].

4   Success Stories

In this section, we briefly discuss some of our experiences in applying rigorous state-based formal methods and tools to case studies that resulted from our participation in European Shift2Rail projects like ASTRail and 4SECURail and Italian regional projects like TRACE-IT, STINGRAY and SmaRIERS with industrial partners from the railway domain.

4.1   Next Generation Railway Signalling Systems

The railway domain is known to be cautious concerning the adoption of technological innovations, in particular when compared with other transport domains. Hence, while satellite-based positioning systems are in use for quite some time now in the avionics and automotive domains, current railway signalling systems

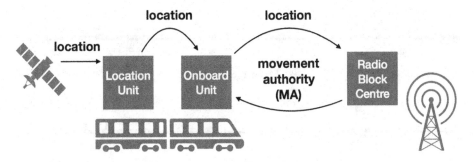

Fig. 8. ERTMS/ETCS Level 3 moving block railway signalling (reprinted from [17]).

still typically use traditional ground-based train detection systems with fixed block distancing. So-called ERTMS/ETCS Level 2 signalling systems make use of trackside equipment like track circuits or axle counters for exact train position detection and train integrity supervision and of fixed blocks starting and ending at signals, with the block sizes being determined by parameters like the speed limit, the train's speed and braking characteristics and the drivers' sighting and reaction times. Yet, the faster trains are allowed to run, the longer their worst-case braking distance, resulting in an increased safety distance and a decreased line capacity. Therefore, to increase the competitiveness, robustness and attractiveness of the railway domain, a recognised challenge consists of transitioning to the next generation of railway signalling system based on effective, precise moving block signalling systems by GNSS-based satellite positioning [58,78].

Such next generation ERTMS/ETCS Level 3 signalling systems no longer rely on trackside equipment for train position detection and train integrity supervision, but an onboard odometry system is responsible for monitoring the train's position and autonomously computing its current speed. This onboard unit frequently sends the train's position to a radio block centre which, in turn, sends each train a movement authority, computed by exploiting its knowledge of the position of the rear end of the train ahead (cf. Fig. 8). The resulting moving block signalling systems allow trains in succession to close up, since a safe zone around the moving trains can be computed, thus considerably reducing headways between trains, in principle to the braking distance (cf. Fig. 9). This allows for more trains to run on existing railway tracks and the removal of trackside equipment moreover results in lower capital and maintenance costs [58].

Starting with our involvement in ASTRail, we contributed to the many experiments and case studies being conducted and validated before actually moving to ERTMS/ETCS Level 3 signalling systems [4,7,12,13,16,28,29,34,42,47,63, 77,88]. In [13,16], we presented Simulink [43] models for a simplified moving block specification with only one train, and used UPPAAL SMC [46] for formal verification and sensitivity analysis based on Statistical Model Checking (SMC) [5,75].

In [17], we presented an extension and refinement of the aforementioned UPPAAL model, consider more trains which concurrently communicate with the

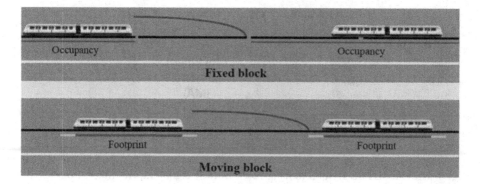

Fig. 9. Safe braking distance between trains for fixed block and moving block signalling (Image courtesy of Israel.abad/Wikimedia Commons distributed under the CC BY-SA 3.0 license).

same (trackside) radio block centre. The movement authority that was previously considered constant, was now computed dynamically according to the traffic on the railway line, and in particular the tail of the train ahead. The physical behaviour of the trains was tuned and validated according to parameters about high-speed trains from the literature [69]. We formally verified the correctness of the function that computes the movement authority, formalised in first-order logic. The concurrent nature of the radio block centre led to the detection and mitigation of corner cases. We also carried out experiments to validate candidate parameter setups to reduce the risk of trains exceeding their movement authority.

4.2   Synthesis of Autonomous Driving Strategies

In [18], we performed the first application of synthesis techniques to autonomous driving for next generation railway signalling systems. As described in the previous section, the Simulink and UPPAAL SMC models from [13,16] offered the possibility to fine tune communication parameters that are fundamental for the reliability of their operational behaviour; however, they did not account for the synthesis of autonomous driving strategies. In [18], we presented a UPPAAL Stratego [45] model (i.e., a stochastic priced timed game) of a satellite-based moving block railway signalling system that does account for autonomous driving. The autonomous driving module was not modelled manually, but it was synthesised automatically as a strategy based on a safety requirement that the model must respect, after which both standard and statistical model checking were applied under the resulting (safe) strategy. We moreover considered reliability aspects, and the autonomous driving strategy also provided guarantees for the minimal expected arrival time. It must be noted that the original model had to be simplified considerably to undergo strategy synthesis and verification, since UPPAAL SMC scales well to large systems by applying simulations rather than full state-space explorations whereas UPPAAL Stratego requires full state-space exploration of the timed game for strategy synthesis.

This was our first experience with strategy synthesis and optimisation of a case study from the railway domain and also with UPPAAL Stratego. This is a very recent formal methods tool which has not been much experimented with. In fact, while developing the model we ran into corner cases that needed interactions with the developers, which led to the release of new versions, with patches fixing the issues discovered through our modelling efforts.

A promising line of future research would be to adapt the statistical synthesis techniques described in [66] to learn safety objectives, thus avoiding the full state-space exploration (as currently performed in UPPAAL Stratego) while guaranteeing the scalability of SMC. This would enable the modelling of more complex case studies from the railway domain.

4.3   Smart Railway Systems and Stations of the Future

Traditionally, railway stations have a private energy distribution and communication system, mainly to ensure uninterrupted power supply and security. However, there are important drawbacks, such as prohibiting proper integration in the smart cities concept by exploiting information between different transport systems (e.g., bike sharing, car sharing, urban transport) and failing to benefit from state-of-the-art energy-saving techniques. In STINGRAY and SmaRIERS, we aimed to enhance the integration of railway stations into smart cities of the future and study advanced energy-saving techniques. In this section, we report work on two project case studies on smart energy consumption.

In [14], we performed a comparison of formal methods tools by experimenting the modelling and analysis features of Möbius [38] and UPPAAL SMC. As in Sect. 3, we applied both tools to the same case study. This time, the features on which we compared them ranged from modelling (e.g., communication primitives and delay distributions) to property specification (e.g., measures of interest) and experiments and presentation of results (e.g., experiment parameter setup). The case study concerns a cyber-physical system from the railway domain, namely a railroad switch heater that is meant to assure the correct operation of switches in case of ice and snow through a central control unit in charge of managing policies of energy consumption while satisfying reliability constraints. It contains physical components (the heater), cyber components (the heating policies and the related coordinator), stochastic aspects (failure events and weather forecasts), and logical/physical dependencies. The models and analyses with stochastic activity networks and Möbius were originally presented in [19], whereas those with stochastic hybrid automata and UPPAAL SMC were originally presented in [20].

To improve their usability, we concluded that Möbius could provide primitive support for non-anonymous replicas and channel communication (a suggestion which has since been implemented by the tool's developers), graphical visualisation of data and primitive support for ordinary differential equations, whereas UPPAAL SMC could provide primitive support for batches of experiments with different parameters (a suggestion which was well received by one of the tool's main developers) and further distribution delays (e.g., deterministic time).

In [24], we addressed the design of future smart station lighting management applications, which aim to reduce station illumination whenever (time) and wherever (space) possible while guaranteeing minimum illumination levels as required by current legislation. The (ceiling) lights (LEDs) along a station's platforms are equipped with a data acquisition module called MADILL. A C-MAD unit collects the messages from each MADILL and it is equipped with brightness sensors and commands to switch lights on, off, or dim them—either individually or for groups of lights.

We considered user-experience related requirements like "passengers should always be able to rely on an illuminated pathway when getting off or on a train, from the main entrance, to the platform", to avoid passengers transiting or waiting in non-illuminated areas, with the associated risks (e.g., theft or injury), or "there should be an illumination level greater than x on platforms where a train is about to arrive, even if the train is late". Such requirements are inherently spatial or spatio-temporal, as they deal with the possibly complex reachability relations and pathways of a train station. We envisioned how to tackle these concretely by applying spatial model-checking techniques and the VoxLogicA tool [27, 37], as illustrated in Fig. 10 through images produced by VoxLogicA.

Fig. 10. Illustration of an experiment aimed at identifying poorly illuminated platform areas. **Top-left:** Pistoia station. Blue squares: a design with MADILL units, clearly insufficient in number. Red squares: some C-MAD units. Green squares: indicate the platforms open to the public. **Top-right:** illumination computed using an attenuation formula with VoxLogicA (overlay is made with an external program). **Bottom-left:** by a threshold on the illumination value, areas that are sufficiently illuminated have been computed (output from VoxLogicA). **Bottom-right:** the parts of the platforms that are not sufficiently illuminated are computed using VoxLogicA (shown in white). (Color figure online, reprinted from [24]).

5   Conclusion

Railway transportation by train, metro or tram is among the most environmentally friendly and energy-efficient means of transportation. In the near future, the railway domain is expected to contribute significantly to the European Green Deal by improved digitalisation and data analytics[10]. Current challenges include the extension of formal methods and tools to cope with AI-based systems, such as equipping verification tools with certificate generation, and their integration into the CENELEC standards [86]. There are, however, several limiting factors.

First, we need to close the gap between semi-formal models that are popular and suitable to communicate with industry and the formal models that are required to apply formal methods tools in safety-critical domains, like railways. Furthermore, each formal methods tool currently requires modelling expertise in a different input language and expert knowledge of different analysis techniques, making it important to pick the right tool based on input from industry and the requirements at hand. While it is no problem, or even a plus, for our FMT lab to host researchers with many different and complementary expertises, in-house expertise on formal methods tools is rare in industry (AWS and ASML are notable exceptions [23]).

Hence, the road to success that we foresee is to start from the basis, i.e., we, together with many experts [60], advocate a prominent role of formal methods in computer science education. First, there is the importance of formal methods *thinking* in computer science education [49], which provides the necessary rigour in reasoning on correctness, and the fundamental skill of abstraction [73]. Then, there is the importance of *knowing* formal methods [33], since the skills and knowledge acquired from studying formal methods provide the indispensable solid foundation that forms the backbone of computer science practice. This is confirmed by the recent increase in *using* formal methods in industry [23,60], not limited to the safety-critical domain.

Acknowledgements. Thanks to all co-authors of the work recollected in this invited contribution: Davide Basile, Vincenzo Ciancia, Felicita Di Giandomenico, Alessandro Fantechi, Alessio Ferrari, Stefania Gnesi, Diego Latella, Axel Legay, Mieke Massink, Franco Mazzanti, and Giorgio Spagnolo.

Competing Interests. The author(s) has no competing interests to declare that are relevant to the content of this manuscript.

References

1. Abo, R., Voisin, L.: Formal implementation of data validation for railway safety-related systems with OVADO. In: Counsell, S., Núñez, M. (eds.) SEFM 2013. LNCS, vol. 8368, pp. 221–236. Springer, Cham (2014). https://doi.org/10.1007/978-3-319-05032-4_17

---

[10] https://transport.ec.europa.eu/system/files/2021-04/2021-mobility-strategy-and-action-plan.pdf.

2. Abrial, J.: Refinement, decomposition and instantiation of discrete models. In: Proceedings of the 12th International Workshop on Abstract State Machines (ASM 2005), pp. 17–40 (2005)
3. Abrial, J.: Modeling in Event-B: System and Software Engineering. Cambridge University Press, Cambridge (2010). https://doi.org/10.1017/CBO9781139195881
4. Abrial, J.: The ABZ-2018 case study with Event-B. Int. J. Softw. Tools Technol. Transf. **22**(3), 257–264 (2020). https://doi.org/10.1007/s10009-019-00525-3
5. Agha, G., Palmskog, K.: A survey of statistical model checking. ACM Trans. Model. Comput. Simul. **28**(1), 6:1–6:39 (2018). https://doi.org/10.1145/3158668
6. Ahmad, E., Dong, Y., Larson, B.R., Lü, J., Tang, T., Zhan, N.: Behavior modeling and verification of movement authority scenario of Chinese train control system using AADL. Sci. China Inf. Sci. **58**(11), 1–20 (2015). https://doi.org/10.1007/s11432-015-5346-2
7. Arcaini, P., Kofroň, J., Ježek, P.: Validation of the hybrid ERTMS/ETCS level 3 using SPIN. Int. J. Softw. Tools Technol. Transf. **22**(3), 265–279 (2020). https://doi.org/10.1007/s10009-019-00539-x
8. Badeau, F., Amelot, A.: Using B as a high level programming language in an industrial project: Roissy VAL. In: Treharne, H., King, S., Henson, M., Schneider, S. (eds.) ZB 2005. LNCS, vol. 3455, pp. 334–354. Springer, Heidelberg (2005). https://doi.org/10.1007/11415787_20
9. Baier, C., Katoen, J.P.: Principles of Model Checking. MIT Press, Cambridge (2008)
10. Bangor, A., Kortum, P.T., Miller, J.T.: An empirical evaluation of the system usability scale. Int. J. Hum. Comput. Interact. **24**(6), 574–594 (2008). https://doi.org/10.1080/10447310802205776
11. Bao, Y., Chen, M., Zhu, Q., Wei, T., Mallet, F., Zhou, T.: Quantitative performance evaluation of uncertainty-aware hybrid AADL designs using statistical model checking. IEEE Trans. Comput. Aided Des. Integr. Circuits Syst. **36**(12), 1989–2002 (2017). https://doi.org/10.1109/TCAD.2017.2681076
12. Bartholomeus, M., Luttik, B., Willemse, T.: Modelling and analysing ERTMS hybrid level 3 with the mCRL2 toolset. In: Howar, F., Barnat, J. (eds.) FMICS 2018. LNCS, vol. 11119, pp. 98–114. Springer, Cham (2018). https://doi.org/10.1007/978-3-030-00244-2_7
13. Basile, D., ter Beek, M.H., Ciancia, V.: Statistical model checking of a moving block railway signalling scenario with UPPAAL SMC. In: Margaria, T., Steffen, B. (eds.) ISoLA 2018. LNCS, vol. 11245, pp. 372–391. Springer, Cham (2018). https://doi.org/10.1007/978-3-030-03421-4_24
14. Basile, D., ter Beek, M.H., Di Giandomenico, F., Fantechi, A., Gnesi, S., Spagnolo, G.O.: 30 years of simulation-based quantitative analysis tools: a comparison experiment between Möbius and Uppaal SMC. In: Margaria, T., Steffen, B. (eds.) Leveraging Applications of Formal Methods, Verification and Validation: Verification Principles. ISoLA 2020. LNCS, vol. 12476, pp. 368–384. Springer, Cham (2020). https://doi.org/10.1007/978-3-030-61362-4_21
15. Basile, D., et al.: On the industrial uptake of formal methods in the railway domain. In: Furia, C.A., Winter, K. (eds.) IFM 2018. LNCS, vol. 11023, pp. 20–29. Springer, Cham (2018). https://doi.org/10.1007/978-3-319-98938-9_2
16. Basile, D., ter Beek, M.H., Ferrari, A., Legay, A.: Modelling and analysing ERTMS L3 moving block railway signalling with Simulink and UPPAAL SMC. In: Larsen, K.G., Willemse, T. (eds.) FMICS 2019. LNCS, vol. 11687, pp. 1–21. Springer, Cham (2019). https://doi.org/10.1007/978-3-030-27008-7_1

17. Basile, D., ter Beek, M.H., Ferrari, A., Legay, A.: Exploring the ERTMS/ETCS full moving block specification: an experience with formal methods. Int. J. Softw. Tools Technol. Transf. **24**(3), 351–370 (2022). https://doi.org/10.1007/S10009-022-00653-3
18. Basile, D., ter Beek, M.H., Legay, A.: Strategy synthesis for autonomous driving in a moving block railway system with UPPAAL STRATEGO. In: Gotsman, A., Sokolova, A. (eds.) FORTE 2020. LNCS, vol. 12136, pp. 3–21. Springer, Cham (2020). https://doi.org/10.1007/978-3-030-50086-3_1
19. Basile, D., Chiaradonna, S., Di Giandomenico, F., Gnesi, S.: A stochastic model-based approach to analyse reliable energy-saving rail road switch heating systems. J. Rail Transp. Plan. Manag. **6**(2), 163–181 (2016). https://doi.org/10.1016/j.jrtpm.2016.03.003
20. Basile, D., Di Giandomenico, F., Gnesi, S.: Statistical model checking of an energy-saving cyber-physical system in the railway domain. In: Proceedings of the 32nd Symposium on Applied Computing (SAC 2017), pp. 1356–1363. ACM (2017). https://doi.org/10.1145/3019612.3019824
21. Basile, D., Fantechi, A., Rucher, L., Mandò, G.: Analysing an autonomous tramway positioning system with the UPPAAL Statistical Model Checker. Form. Asp. Comput. **33**(6), 957–987 (2021). https://doi.org/10.1007/s00165-021-00556-1
22. ter Beek, M.H., Borälv, A., Fantechi, A., Ferrari, A., Gnesi, S., Löfving, C., Mazzanti, F.: Adopting formal methods in an industrial setting: the railways case. In: ter Beek, M.H., McIver, A., Oliveira, J.N. (eds.) FM 2019. LNCS, vol. 11800, pp. 762–772. Springer, Cham (2019). https://doi.org/10.1007/978-3-030-30942-8_46
23. ter Beek, M.H., et al.: Formal methods in industry. Form. Asp. Comput. (2024)
24. ter Beek, M.H., Ciancia, V., Latella, D., Massink, M., Spagnolo, G.O.: Spatial model checking for smart stations: Research challenges. In: Lluch Lafuente, A., Mavridou, A. (eds.) Formal Methods for Industrial Critical Systems. FMICS 2021. LNCS, vol. 12863, pp. 39–47. Springer, Cham (2021). https://doi.org/10.1007/978-3-030-85248-1_3
25. Behm, P., Benoit, P., Faivre, A., Meynadier, J.-M.: Météor: a successful application of B in a large project. In: Wing, J.M., Woodcock, J., Davies, J. (eds.) FM 1999. LNCS, vol. 1708, pp. 369–387. Springer, Heidelberg (1999). https://doi.org/10.1007/3-540-48119-2_22
26. Behrmann, G., et al.: UPPAAL 4.0. In: Proceedings of the 3rd International Conference on the Quantitative Evaluation of SysTems (QEST 2006), pp. 125–126. IEEE (2006). https://doi.org/10.1109/QEST.2006.59
27. Belmonte, G., Ciancia, V., Latella, D., Massink, M.: VoxLogicA: a spatial model checker for declarative image analysis. In: Vojnar, T., Zhang, L. (eds.) TACAS 2019. LNCS, vol. 11427, pp. 281–298. Springer, Cham (2019). https://doi.org/10.1007/978-3-030-17462-0_16
28. Berger, U., James, P., Lawrence, A., Roggenbach, M., Seisenberger, M.: Verification of the European rail traffic management system in real-time Maude. Sci. Comput. Program. **154**, 61–88 (2018). https://doi.org/10.1016/j.scico.2017.10.011
29. Biagi, M., Carnevali, L., Paolieri, M., Vicario, E.: Performability evaluation of the ERTMS/ETCS - level 3. Transp. Res. C-Emerg. **82**, 314–336 (2017). https://doi.org/10.1016/j.trc.2017.07.002
30. Boulanger, J.L.: CENELEC 50128 and IEC 62279 Standards. Wiley, Hoboken (2015)
31. Brooke, J.: SUS: a 'quick and dirty' usability scale. In: Jordan, P.W., Thomas, B., Weerdmeester, B.A., McClelland, I.L. (eds.) Usability Evaluation in Industry, chap. 21, pp. 189–194. CRC press (1996). https://doi.org/10.1201/9781498710411

32. Brooke, J.: SUS: a retrospective. J. Usability Stud. **8**(2), 29–40 (2013). https://doi.org/10.5555/2817912.2817913
33. Broy, M., et al.: Does every computer scientist need to know formal methods? Form. Asp. Comput. (2024)
34. Butler, M., Hoang, T.S., Raschke, A., Reichl, K.: Introduction to the special section on the ABZ 2018 case study: hybrid ERTMS/ETCS level 3. Int. J. Softw. Tools Technol. Transf. **22**(3), 249–255 (2020). https://doi.org/10.1007/s10009-020-00562-3
35. Celebi, B.T., Kaymakci, O.T.: Verifying the accuracy of interlocking tables for railway signalling systems using abstract state machines. J. Mod. Transp. **24**(4), 277–283 (2016). https://doi.org/10.1007/s40534-016-0119-1
36. Chiappini, A., et al.: Formalization and validation of a subset of the European train control system. In: Proceedings of the 32nd ACM/IEEE International Conference on Software Engineering (ICSE 2010), vol. 2, pp. 109–118. ACM (2010). https://doi.org/10.1145/1810295.1810312
37. Ciancia, V., Belmonte, G., Latella, D., Massink, M.: A hands-on introduction to spatial model checking using VoxLogicA. In: Laarman, A., Sokolova, A. (eds.) SPIN 2021. LNCS, vol. 12864, pp. 22–41. Springer, Cham (2021). https://doi.org/10.1007/978-3-030-84629-9_2
38. Clark, G., et al.: The Möbius modeling tool. In: Proceedings of the 9th International Workshop on Petri Nets and Performance Models (PNPM 2001), pp. 241–250. IEEE (2001). https://doi.org/10.1109/PNPM.2001.953373
39. Clarke, E.M., Henzinger, T.A., Veith, H., Bloem, R. (eds.): Handbook of Model Checking. Springer, Heidelberg (2018). https://doi.org/10.1007/978-3-319-10575-8
40. Comptier, M., Déharbe, D., Perez, J.M., Mussat, L., Thibaut, P., Sabatier, D.: Safety analysis of a CBTC system: a rigorous approach with Event-B. In: Fantechi, A., Lecomte, T., Romanovsky, A.B. (eds.) RSSRail 2017. LNCS, vol. 10598, pp. 148–159. Springer, Cham (2017). https://doi.org/10.1007/978-3-319-68499-4_10
41. Comptier, M., Leuschel, M., Mejia, L.-F., Perez, J.M., Mutz, M.: Property-based modelling and validation of a CBTC zone controller in Event-B. In: Collart-Dutilleul, S., Lecomte, T., Romanovsky, A. (eds.) RSSRail 2019. LNCS, vol. 11495, pp. 202–212. Springer, Cham (2019). https://doi.org/10.1007/978-3-030-18744-6_13
42. Cunha, A., Macedo, N.: Validating the hybrid ERTMS/ETCS level 3 concept with Electrum. Int. J. Softw. Tools Technol. Transf. **22**(3), 281–296 (2020). https://doi.org/10.1007/s10009-019-00540-4
43. Dabney, J.B., Harman, T.L.: Mastering Simulink. Pearson, London (2003)
44. DaSilva, C., Dehbonei, B., Mejia, F.: Formal specification in the development of industrial applications: subway speed control system. In: Diaz, M., Groz, R. (eds.) Proceedings of the IFIP TC6/WG6.1 5th International Conference on Formal Description Techniques for Distributed Systems and Communication Protocols (FORTE 1992). IFIP Transactions, vol. C-10, pp. 199–213. North-Holland (1992)
45. David, A., Jensen, P.G., Larsen, K.G., Mikučionis, M., Taankvist, J.H.: UPPAAL STRATEGO. In: Baier, C., Tinelli, C. (eds.) TACAS 2015. LNCS, vol. 9035, pp. 206–211. Springer, Heidelberg (2015). https://doi.org/10.1007/978-3-662-46681-0_16
46. David, A., Larsen, K.G., Legay, A., Mikučionis, M., Poulsen, D.B.: UPPAAL SMC tutorial. Int. J. Softw. Tools Technol. Transf. **17**(4), 397–415 (2015). https://doi.org/10.1007/s10009-014-0361-y

47. Dghaym, D., Dalvandi, M., Poppleton, M., Snook, C.: Formalising the hybrid ERTMS level 3 specification in iUML-B and Event-B. Int. J. Softw. Tools Technol. Transf. **22**(3), 297–313 (2020). https://doi.org/10.1007/s10009-019-00548-w
48. Dollé, D., Essamé, D., Falampin, J.: B dans le transport ferroviaire: l'expérience de Siemens transportation systems. Tech. Sci. Inf. **22**(1), 11–32 (2003). https://doi.org/10.3166/tsi.22.11-32
49. Dongol, B., et al.: On formal methods thinking in computer science education. Form. Asp. Comput. (2024)
50. Essamé, D., Dollé, D.: B in large-scale projects: the Canarsie line CBTC experience. In: Julliand, J., Kouchnarenko, O. (eds.) B 2007. LNCS, vol. 4355, pp. 252–254. Springer, Heidelberg (2006). https://doi.org/10.1007/11955757_21
51. European Committee for Electrotechnical Standardization: CENELEC EN 50128—Railway applications – Communication, signalling and processing systems – Software for railway control and protection systems (2011). https://standards.globalspec.com/std/1678027/cenelec-en-50128
52. Ferrari, A., ter Beek, M.H.: Formal methods in railways: a systematic mapping study. ACM Comput. Surv. **55**(4), 69:1–69:37 (2023). https://doi.org/10.1145/3520480
53. Ferrari, A., et al.: Survey on formal methods and tools in railways: the ASTRail approach. In: Collart-Dutilleul, S., Lecomte, T., Romanovsky, A. (eds.) Reliability, Safety, and Security of Railway Systems. Modelling, Analysis, Verification, and Certification. RSSRail 2019. LNCS, vol. 11495, pp. 226–241. Springer, Cham (2019). https://doi.org/10.1007/978-3-030-18744-6_15
54. Ferrari, A., Grasso, D., Magnani, G., Fantechi, A., Tempestini, M.: The Metrô Rio case study. Sci. Comput. Program. **78**(7), 828–842 (2013). https://doi.org/10.1016/j.scico.2012.04.003
55. Ferrari, A., Mazzanti, F., Basile, D., ter Beek, M.H.: Systematic evaluation and usability analysis of formal methods tools for railway signaling system design. IEEE Trans. Softw. Eng. **48**(11), 4675–4691 (2022). https://doi.org/10.1109/TSE.2021.3124677
56. Ferrari, A., Mazzanti, F., Basile, D., ter Beek, M.H., Fantechi, A.: Comparing formal tools for system design: a judgment study. In: Proceedings of the 42nd ACM/IEEE International Conference on Software Engineering (ICSE 2020), pp. 62–74. ACM (2020). https://doi.org/10.1145/3377811.3380373
57. Fukuda, M., Hirao, Y., Ogino, T.: VDM specification of an interlocking system and a simulator for its validation. IFAC Proc. **33**(9), 187–192 (2000). https://doi.org/10.1016/S1474-6670(17)38144-2. Proceedings of the 9th IFAC Symposium on Control in Transportation Systems (CTS 2000)
58. Furness, N., van Houten, H., Arenas, L., Bartholomeus, M.: ERTMS level 3: the game-changer. IRSE News **232**, 2–9 (2017). https://www.irse.nl/resources/170314-ERTMS-L3-The-gamechanger-from-IRSE-News-Issue-232.pdf
59. Fürst, A., Hoang, T.S., Basin, D.A., Sato, N., Miyazaki, K.: Large-scale system development using abstract data types and refinement. Sci. Comput. Program. **131**, 59–75 (2016). https://doi.org/10.1016/j.scico.2016.04.010
60. Garavel, H., ter Beek, M.H., van de Pol, J.: The 2020 expert survey on formal methods. In: ter Beek, M.H., Ničković, D. (eds.) FMICS 2020. LNCS, vol. 12327, pp. 3–69. Springer, Cham (2020). https://doi.org/10.1007/978-3-030-58298-2_1
61. Guiho, G., Hennebert, C.: SACEM software validation. In: Proceedings of the 12th International Conference on Software Engineering (ICSE 1990), pp. 186–191. IEEE (1990)

62. Hamid, B., Pérez, J.: Supporting pattern-based dependability engineering via model-driven development: approach, tool-support and empirical validation. J. Syst. Softw. **122**, 239–273 (2016). https://doi.org/10.1016/j.jss.2016.09.027

63. Hansen, D., et al.: Validation and real-life demonstration of ETCS hybrid level 3 principles using a formal B model. Int. J. Softw. Tools Technol. Transf. **22**(3), 315–332 (2020). https://doi.org/10.1007/s10009-020-00551-6

64. Hierons, R.M., et al.: Using formal specifications to support testing. ACM Comput. Surv. **41**(2), 9:1–9:76 (2009). https://doi.org/10.1145/1459352.1459354

65. Idani, A., Ledru, Y., Ait Wakrime, A., Ben Ayed, R., Collart-Dutilleul, S.: Incremental development of a safety critical system combining formal methods and DSMLs. In: Larsen, K.G., Willemse, T. (eds.) FMICS 2019. LNCS, vol. 11687, pp. 93–109. Springer, Cham (2019). https://doi.org/10.1007/978-3-030-27008-7_6

66. Jaeger, M., Jensen, P.G., Larsen, K.G., Legay, A., Sedwards, S., Taankvist, J.H.: Teaching Stratego to play ball: optimal synthesis for continuous space MDPs. In: Chen, Y.-F., Cheng, C.-H., Esparza, J. (eds.) ATVA 2019. LNCS, vol. 11781, pp. 81–97. Springer, Cham (2019). https://doi.org/10.1007/978-3-030-31784-3_5

67. James, P., Moller, F., Nga, N.H., Roggenbach, M., Schneider, S.A., Treharne, H.: Techniques for modelling and verifying railway interlockings. Int. J. Softw. Tools Technol. Transf. **16**(6), 685–711 (2014). https://doi.org/10.1007/s10009-014-0304-7

68. Jifeng, H.: From CSP to hybrid systems. In: Roscoe, A.W. (ed.) A Classical Mind: Essays in Honour of C. A. R. Hoare. Prentice Hall International Series in Computer Science, pp. 171–189. Prentice Hall (1994)

69. Jin, Y., Xie, G., Chen, P., Hei, X., Ji, W., Zhao, J.: High-speed train emergency brake modeling and online identification of time-varying parameters. Math. Probl. Eng. **2020** (2020). https://doi.org/10.1155/2020/3872852

70. Khan, S.A., Zafar, N.A.: Towards the formalization of railway interlocking system using Z-notations. In: Proceedings of the 2nd International Conference on Computer, Control and Communication (IC4 2009), pp. 1–6. IEEE (2009). https://doi.org/10.1109/IC4.2009.4909202

71. Kitchenham, B.: Procedures for performing systematic reviews. Technical report TR/SE-0401, Keele University (2004)

72. Kitchenham, B., Linkman, S., Law, D.: DESMET: a methodology for evaluating software engineering methods and tools. Comput. Control. Eng. J. **8**(3), 120–126 (1997). https://doi.org/10.1049/cce:19970304

73. Kramer, J.: Is abstraction the key to computing? Commun. ACM **50**(4), 36–42 (2007). https://doi.org/10.1145/1232743.1232745

74. Lano, K.: The B Language and Method: a Guide to Practical Formal Development. FACIT. Springer, London (1996). https://doi.org/10.1007/978-1-4471-1494-9

75. Legay, A., Lukina, A., Traonouez, L.M., Yang, J., Smolka, S.A., Grosu, R.: Statistical model checking. In: Steffen, B., Woeginger, G. (eds.) Computing and Software Science. LNCS, vol. 10000, pp. 478–504. Springer, Cham (2019). https://doi.org/10.1007/978-3-319-91908-9_23

76. Leuschel, M., Falampin, J., Fritz, F., Plagge, D.: Automated property verification for large scale B models with ProB. Form. Asp. Comput. **23**(6), 683–709 (2011). https://doi.org/10.1007/s00165-010-0172-1

77. Mammar, A., Frappier, M., Tueno Fotso, S.J., Laleau, R.: A formal refinement-based analysis of the hybrid ERTMS/ETCS level 3 standard. Int. J. Softw. Tools Technol. Transf. **22**(3), 333–347 (2020). https://doi.org/10.1007/s10009-019-00543-1

78. Marais, J., Beugin, J., Berbineau, M.: A survey of GNSS-based research and developments for the European railway signaling. IEEE Trans. Intell. Transp. Syst. **18**(10), 2602–2618 (2017). https://doi.org/10.1109/TITS.2017.2658179
79. Mazzanti, F., Ferrari, A., Spagnolo, G.O.: Towards formal methods diversity in railways: an experience report with seven frameworks. Int. J. Softw. Tools Technol. Transf. **20**(3), 263–288 (2018). https://doi.org/10.1007/s10009-018-0488-3
80. Newborn, M.: Automated Theorem Proving. Springer, Germany (2001). https://doi.org/10.1007/978-1-4613-0089-2
81. Petersen, K., Vakkalanka, S., Kuzniarz, L.: Guidelines for conducting systematic mapping studies in software engineering: an update. Inf. Softw. Technol. **64**, 1–18 (2015). https://doi.org/10.1016/j.infsof.2015.03.007
82. Reichl, K., Fischer, T., Tummeltshammer, P.: Using formal methods for verification and validation in railway. In: Aichernig, B.K.K., Furia, C.A.A. (eds.) TAP 2016. LNCS, vol. 9762, pp. 3–13. Springer, Cham (2016). https://doi.org/10.1007/978-3-319-41135-4_1
83. Robinson, J.A., Voronkov, A. (eds.): Handbook of Automated Reasoning. Elsevier, Amsterdam (2001)
84. SAE International: Architecture Analysis & Design Language (AADL) (2022). https://doi.org/10.4271/AS5506D
85. Scupin, R.: The KJ method: a technique for analyzing data derived from Japanese ethnology. Hum. Organ. **56**(2), 233–237 (1997). https://doi.org/10.17730/humo.56.2.x335923511444655
86. Seisenberger, M., et al.: Safe and secure future AI-driven railway technologies: challenges for formal methods in railway. In: Margaria, T., Steffen, B. (eds.) ISoLA 2022. LNCS, vol. 13704, pp. 246–268. Springer, Cham (2022). https://doi.org/10.1007/978-3-031-19762-8_20
87. Snook, C.F., Hoang, T.S., Dghaym, D., Fathabadi, A.S., Butler, M.J.: Domain-specific scenarios for refinement-based methods. J. Syst. Archit. **112** (2021). https://doi.org/10.1016/j.sysarc.2020.101833
88. Tueno Fotso, S.J., Frappier, M., Laleau, R., Mammar, A.: Modeling the hybrid ERTMS/ETCS level 3 standard using a formal requirements engineering approach. Int. J. Softw. Tools Technol. Transf. **22**(3), 349–363 (2020). https://doi.org/10.1007/s10009-019-00542-2
89. Wang, S., Zhan, N., Zou, L.: An improved HHL prover: an interactive theorem prover for hybrid systems. In: Butler, M., Conchon, S., Zaïdi, F. (eds.) ICFEM 2015. LNCS, vol. 9407, pp. 382–399. Springer, Cham (2015). https://doi.org/10.1007/978-3-319-25423-4_25
90. Wang, Y., Chen, L., Kirkwood, D., Fu, P., Lv, J., Roberts, C.: Hybrid online model-based testing for communication-based train control systems. IEEE Intell. Transp. Syst. Mag. **10**(3), 35–47 (2018). https://doi.org/10.1109/MITS.2018.2842230
91. Wu, D., Schnieder, E.: Scenario-based system design with colored Petri nets: an application to train control systems. Softw. Syst. Model. **17**(1), 295–317 (2018). https://doi.org/10.1007/s10270-016-0517-1
92. Zhan, B., et al.: Compositional verification of interacting systems using event monads. In: Andronick, J., de Moura, L. (eds.) Proceedings of the 13th International Conference on Interactive Theorem Proving (ITP 2022). LIPIcs, vol. 237, pp. 33:1–33:21. Schloss Dagstuhl - Leibniz-Zentrum für Informatik (2022). https://doi.org/10.4230/LIPIcs.ITP.2022.33

Research Papers

Formal Modeling and Analysis of Apache Kafka in Alloy 6

Saloni Sinha[✉] and Eunsuk Kang

School of Computer Science, Carnegie Mellon University, Pittsburgh, PA, USA
{salonisi,eunsukk}@andrew.cmu.edu

Abstract. Apache Kafka is a distributed, fault-tolerant and highly available open-source technology that utilizes a publish-subscribe communication model to stream large volumes of data. It is widely being used in various domains such as finance, entertainment, online education, and e-commerce for real-time data processing and analytics. This paper demonstrates an application of Alloy 6—the latest version of Alloy with built-in temporal logic operators—to formal modeling and analysis of a complex distributed system like Kafka. The architecture and key operations of Kakfa are modeled, and its various properties, including fault-tolerance, data availability, service availability, consistency, and recoverability, are analyzed using the Alloy Analyzer. The result of the analysis provides insights into how Kafka maintains the properties that it claims to have, and the circumstances under which these properties may be violated.

1 Introduction

Apache Kafka is a popular distributed messaging platform that enables real-time communication using a publish-subscribe model [4]. It is widely being used in various domains such as finance, entertainment, online education, and e-commerce for real-time data processing and analytics. It is well-known for its excellent performance, low latency, fault tolerance, and high throughput.

A typical distributed system involves multiple entities that act independently but also need to synchronize together to achieve a set of system-level properties. Given the complex architecture and behavior of distributed systems such as Kafka, it is important to rigorously verify whether the system behavior does in fact satisfy the properties it was designed to exhibit. Formal modeling is one such tool that can aid architects of such a system in specifying the proposed behavior of various entities in a design, and verify properties against a specification. Formal verification can also expose the conditions that may occur in the real-world under which the system could fail to satisfy a desired property. These findings can further guide design decisions and mitigation strategies to employ if and when such conditions do arise.

Several studies [9,17,20,21,25,26] have been conducted to specify and verify properties of distributed systems using tools like PAT [22], TLA+ [13], and Alloy [11]. In this study, we have chosen Alloy 6 [1] (originally based on Electrum [7], which has been integrated into the latest release of the Alloy Analyzer) as the formal modelling tool to demonstrate its ability to flexibly specify Kafka's architecture, behavior and key

© The Author(s), under exclusive license to Springer Nature Switzerland AG 2024
S. Bonfanti et al. (Eds.): ABZ 2024, LNCS 14759, pp. 25–42, 2024.
https://doi.org/10.1007/978-3-031-63790-2_2

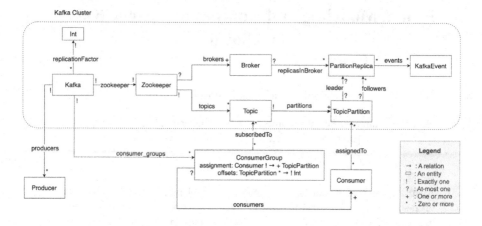

Fig. 1. Conceptual Model of Kafka

properties, and verify the model against those properties. To the best of our knowledge, our work is the first that makes use of Alloy to model Kafka, and is one of the largest Alloy models to have been developed (around 1400 lines of code). In addition, our study demonstrates the utility of temporal logic available in Alloy 6, in the context of a complex distributed system.

In this paper, we first introduce the basic concepts in the Kafka architecture (Sect. 2) and demonstrate how its key entities and relationships among them can be modeled using Alloy 6 (Sect. 3). We then describe a model that captures various types of actions in Kafka, including message consumption, message production, server failure, and server recovery (Sect. 4). We describe temporal logic specifications of important Kafka properties, including fault tolerance, data availability, consistency, service availability, recoverability, and sequential message consumption (Sect. 5). We discuss the results of an automated analysis of these properties using Alloy 6, including counterexamples that demonstrate conditions under which Kafka may fail to satisfy some of these properties. Finally, we close with a discussion of the related work (Sect. 6) and challenges faced during our modeling experience (Sect. 7).

2 Preliminaries

Kafka Overview. The high-level view of the Kafka architecture, presented as an object model, is shown in Fig. 1. Each box in this diagram represents a Kafka entity while an edge between any two of them establishes a relation between them. The symbols – '*', '+', '!', '?'– on either side of a relation show the multiplicity relationship between the two objects, as described in the legend of Fig. 1. Developing this conceptual model of the system first helped us form an abstract mental model of the components and aided in the subsequent Alloy model development.

In the Kafka world, a *topic* is the main data storage unit and the highest data organization level, further divided into one or more *partitions*. Each partition is associated with a list of messages called Kafka *events*, which are stored in the order of event arrival time. *Producers* and *consumers* are client applications that publish and consume events to and from partitions, respectively. A Kafka *cluster* consists of a ZooKeeper instance and multiple servers called Kafka *brokers*, which can store events belonging to one or more partitions. ZooKeeper is responsible for keeping track of the cluster meta-data, such as topics, partitions, servers, etc. Kafka offers high fault tolerance and data availability as its key quality attributes, which it achieves by storing multiple replicas of every partition (and therefore every event) on brokers. In case a broker fails, data remains available in live brokers [3,16,25].

Alloy 6. The Alloy Analyzer 6, the latest release of the tool, is an extension of Alloy 5 that includes support for stateful variables and specifications in linear temporal logic (LTL) [19]. These innovations were initially proposed in Electrum [7], which has been integrated into the official release of the Alloy Analyzer. In the previous versions, Alloy provided no built-in concept of states, requiring the user to use modeling idioms to explicitly encode states into a model [11]. In Alloy 6, however, the concept of mutable state variables is now built into the language, along with support for temporal operators, which greatly aids in specifying how the state of the system evolves over time. An instance of the model, previously represented as a set of tuples in relations, is now represented as a trace (i.e., a sequence of states over time). Beside the original SAT-based bounded analysis, Alloy 6 also provides an ability to perform unbounded model checking over a finite-state model by translation to the nuXmv tool [8].

Similar to Alloy 5, objects in Alloy 6 can be defined using signatures. Relations from an object to another can be defined using fields inside a signature (the domain) associated to another signature (the range). Keywords such as *one*, *lone*, *set* and *some* can be used to define the multiplicity of relations that translate to the symbols '!', '?', '*' and '+', respectively, in the object model shown earlier [2]. To express the multiplicity of at-most-one on the domain side, the *disj* keyword can be used to put a constraint such that no two values in the range are mapped by more than one value in the domain.

In Alloy 6, actions can be modeled using first-order logic expressions that relate the pre-state (say, s) to the post-state (s') by using the prime (') operator. Alloy 6 offers the standard temporal operators such as *always*, *eventually*, *after*, *until* and *releases*, which can be used to specify the system's temporal behavior and properties. In addition, Alloy 6 offers past-based temporal operators such as *historically*, *before*, *once*, *since*, and *triggered*. In our experience, past-based operators make Alloy 6 more expressive in specifying properties where an event or state configuration at some point in the trace can only happen if another event or state has already been seen in the past.

3   Architecture Specification in Alloy

In this section, we describe the specification of the Kafka architecture in Alloy 6[1]. We have divided this discussion in four parts to incrementally build the reader's understanding of Kafka and the corresponding Alloy model.

---

[1] All signatures present at: https://github.com/cmu-soda/kafka-alloy/blob/main/signatures.als.

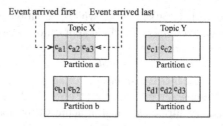

Fig. 2. Topics and their partitions

(i) Data Organization. Atomic data elements in the Kafka world are called events, and are organized in topics and partitions. Figure 2 shows a visual representation of the data organization.

- Kafka Event: A message in the Kafka world is called an event. From now onward, an event refers to a single message that is published and stored in a Kafka instance.
- Topic: A Kafka topic is the highest organization level of events. There can be multiple uniquely identifiable topics in a cluster.
- Topic Partition: Data in every topic is further divided into multiple partitions. Each partition stores a list of events, ordered by time of arrival. However, no such ordering exists between any two partitions.

The snippet in Fig. 3 shows how the concepts of *Topic* and *TopicPartition* can be defined using *signatures* in Alloy. The relation *partitions* inside the *Topic* signature on line 6 establishes a relationship between *Topic* and *TopicPartition* such that at least one partition exists in a topic, but also that a partition is not associated with multiple topics. Line 23 adds a constraint that every partition must be associated with a topic, using a *signature fact* in *TopicPartition*. Although Kafka events are logically associated with a partition, they are stored in partition replicas, which we will discuss later in the section along with the relations *leader* and *followers* (declared in *TopicPartition* on lines 16 and 18, respectively).

(ii) Kafka Cluster. As we briefly mentioned earlier, a Kafka cluster contains multiple brokers, and a single instance of ZooKeeper service to manage the cluster.

- Brokers: A Kafka cluster consists of multiple servers that are called brokers. Brokers are responsible for storing events belonging to each partition [3,16].
- ZooKeeper: Apache ZooKeeper is a service that Kafka utilizes to store metadata about the cluster such as information about topics and brokers that are part of the cluster, and replicas' location in the cluster [12]. One may wonder how Kafka maintains fault tolerance given that there is a single ZooKeeper instance that manages the cluster. ZooKeeper is in fact a fault tolerant service that has a clustered setup of its own [5,16]. However, we will not be modeling ZooKeeper's internal behavior, and keep our focus limited to Kafka to make the modeling task tractable.

The Alloy model in Fig. 4 shows Kafka with one ZooKeeper instance. ZooKeeper is responsible for maintaining cluster information such as brokers present, and the topics

```
1   /* Signature: Topic is the entity that stores streamed data
2    points in its partitions */
3   sig Topic {
4     -- A topic should have at least one partition
5     -- No two topics can share the same partition
6     partitions: disj some TopicPartition
7   } {
8     -- Each Topic should be associated with a cluster
9     Topic = ZooKeeper.topics
10  }
11  /* Signature: Represents a partition of a topic which stores
12   * published events in a sequential manner */
13  sig TopicPartition {
14    -- At-most one Leader that cannot be shared
15    -- by any other partition
16    var leader: disj lone PartitionReplica,
17    -- No two TopicPartitions should share a FollowerReplica
18    var followers: disj set PartitionReplica,
19  } {
20    -- Signature fact: A replica can't have both leader and follower role
21    disj[leader, followers]
22    -- TopicPartitions must always be associated with Topics
23    TopicPartition = Topic.partitions
24  }
```

Fig. 3. Alloy signatures capturing topics and topic partitions

```
1   /* Kafka instance representing the state of the Cluster
2    * This model considers a single Kafka cluste */
3   one sig Kafka {
4     -- Fix the number of replicas that should be present
5     -- for each partition
6     replicationFactor: one Int,
7     -- One unshared zookeeper to manage cluster metadata
8     zookeeper: disj one ZooKeeper,
9     -- Consumer groups should not be shared across multiple clusters
10    consumer_groups: disj set ConsumerGroup,
11    -- Producers should not be shared across multiple clusters
12    producers: disj set Producer
13  }
14  /* Zookeeper is responsible for managing metadata about the cluster */
15  sig ZooKeeper {
16    -- Cluster must contain at least one broker
17    -- Broker not shared with another cluster
18    var brokers: disj some Broker,
19    -- Cluster can contain 0 or more topics
20    -- A topic cannot belong to two clusters (zookeepers)
21    topics: disj set Topic
22  } {
23    -- Zookeeper only associated with Kafka
24    ZooKeeper = Kafka.zookeeper
25  }
26  /* A Broker is a single server in a cluster of servers which store
27   * replicas of Topic partitions */
28  sig Broker {
29    -- No two brokers can have the same replica instance
30    var replicasInBroker: disj set PartitionReplica
31  }
```

Fig. 4. Alloy signature representing Kafka cluster components

belonging to the cluster (lines 18 and 21). The in-line comments in the model provide detailed explanations of relations. We will describe the utility of the relations *replicationFactor*, *consumer_groups*, *producers*, and *replicasInBroker* later in the section.

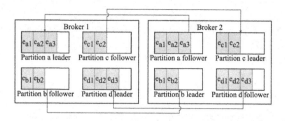

Fig. 5. Replica storage across 2 brokers. Arrows represent followers syncing with corresponding leaders.

```
1   /* A partition replica is associated with a TopicPartition
2    * Replicas store KafkaEvent instances */
3   sig PartitionReplica {
4     -- Ordered sequence of KafkaEvents
5     var events: seq KafkaEvent,
6   } {
7     -- Every event must be unique
8     !events.hasDups[]
9     -- replicas cannot be shared between two partitions
10    -- E.g. A leader of one partition cannot be follower of another.
11    all p : TopicPartition |
12      disj[p.(leader + followers),
13        (TopicPartition - p).(leader + followers)]
14  }
15  /* KafkaEvent represents a message */
16  sig KafkaEvent {} {
17    -- An event cannot belong to two partitions
18    all p : TopicPartition |
19      disj[p.(leader+followers).events.elems,
20        (TopicPartition - p).(leader+followers).events.elems]
21  }
```

Fig. 6. Alloy signatures for partition replication

(iii) Data Replication and Storage. Kafka achieves high fault tolerance and data availability by exploiting data redundancy as the main tactic. As shown in Fig. 5, partitions in Kafka are replicated across multiple brokers in the cluster to ensure data availability in the event of a broker failure [3, 16, 25].

Partition Replica: A replica of each partition is maintained in the Kafka cluster in order to maintain data backups in case of broker failure. The number of replicas is decided by a configurable parameter called *replication factor* defined at the time of cluster setup. No two replicas of a partition can reside on the same broker in the cluster. Thus, the number of brokers must at least be equal to the replication factor.

- Leader: Each partition has a single leader replica that maintains the set of events stored by the partition and is also responsible for servicing clients.
- Follower: Each partition can have zero or more follower replicas that stay up-to-date with the leader of the partition to maintain a backup copy of all events.

In Fig. 6, KafkaEvent instances are stored as a sequence inside *PartitionReplica* instances using the built-in *seq* keyword (line 5). A replica can be associated with a *TopicPartition* through the relations *leader* and *followers* present inside *TopicPartition* signature mentioned in Fig. 3, lines 16 and 18. Additional constraints such as event uniqueness and replica exclusivity have been specified as part of the signature fact (lines 7–13, Fig. 6). Since *KafkaEvent* is logically associated with a partition, its signature fact constrains an event to belong to only one *TopicPartition* (lines 18–21, Fig. 6). Relational joins are useful in indirectly correlating *TopicPartition* and *KafkaEvent* using relations *leaders* and *followers* mentioned in Fig. 3, and the relation *events*.

(iv) Kafka Clients. Kafka has two types of clients – producers and consumers – that produce and consume messages to and from a partition, respectively. One or more consumers are organized in consumer groups whereas producers operate independently. Producers can publish events to any partition in the cluster, while consumer groups subscribe to topics and consumers belonging to a group are assigned to a specific topic partition. The signatures relevant to Kafka clients are shown in Fig. 7. No two consumers belonging to the same group can be assigned the same partition. Although individual consumers as well as consumer groups can subscribe to topics, we have only considered topic subscriptions by consumer groups to keep the model simple. A consumer can consume events in the sequence stored in a partition by maintaining the index from which it should read the assigned partition. These indices are called *offsets* (line 23) that *ConsumerGroup* instances must keep track of. Producers on the other hand are fairly simple in the sense that they can produce events to any partition, which then get appended to the ordered event log of the partition replicas [3, 16].

4   Behavior Specification

4.1   Actions

Having defined the static structure of the system, our model must allow the mutable relations to evolve over time through actions. An action in Alloy can be specified as a predicate over pre- and post-states. In Alloy 6, only signatures and relations associated with the *var* keyword can be modified during a state transition while everything else will remain static. An action predicate consists of three parts: (i) preconditions that must be satisfied in the pre-state before an action can occur, (ii) conditions that must be satisfied in the post-state, and (iii) frame conditions that constrain unchanged state variables. Although these can be encapsulated in a single predicate, we have found that separating these into separate predicates helps improve the readability of the model.

In our model, we have specified four actions[2] that correspond to the basic functionalities that Kafka offers through its API. The model assumes that each of the specified actions is atomic. The specified actions are described below.

○ **readEvent[k: Kafka, c_multiple : Consumer, e: KafkaEvent, p : TopicPartition]**: One or more consumers (c_multiple) read an event (e) from a partition (p). As a result, the offset corresponding to this partition stored in consumers' respective consumer groups, must be incremented.

---

[2] All actions can be found at: https://github.com/cmu-soda/kafka-alloy/blob/main/actions.als.

```
1   /* Producer publishes KafkaEvents to a Partition */
2   sig Producer {} {
3       -- Producer always associated with a cluster
4       Producer = Kafka.producers
5   }
6   /* A Consumer client application */
7   abstract sig Consumer {
8       -- A consumer can be assigned to multiple partitions
9       -- Multiple consumers can be assigned to a partition
10      assignedTo: set TopicPartition
11  }
12  /* A ConsumerGroup represents a group of Consumer instances
13   * It subscribes to certain topics and maintains
14   * Consumer -> TopicPartition assignment
15   * and TopicPartition -> Int offset data */
16  sig ConsumerGroup {
17      -- No two groups can have the same consumer
18      consumers: disj some Consumer,
19      -- A Consumer Group subscribes to a set of Topics
20      -- Many consumer groups can subscribe to the same Topic
21      subscribedTo: set Topic,
22      -- Maintain the index of the TopicPartition that it last read
23      var offsets: TopicPartition -> {i : Int | i >= 0},
24      -- Consumers are assigned to partitions
25      assignments: Consumer -> TopicPartition
26  } {
27      ...
28  }
```

Fig. 7. Kafka clients in Alloy

○ **pushEvent[k : Kafka, prod : Producer, e: KafkaEvent, p : TopicPartition]**: A producer (prod) publishes an event (e) to a partition (p). As a result, the new event should be appended to the last index of event list saved in the leader replica of the partition. Follower partition replicas should stay up-to-date with the leader and store this new event in their logs. Specification of this action is shown in Fig. 8.

○ **brokerCrash[k: Kafka, b : Broker]**: A broker (b) present in the Kafka cluster (k) fails. As a result, the broker is removed from the cluster. In case the failed broker contained leader replica(s) of certain partitions, a new leader for the said partitions are elected from one of its live followers. In case of follower replica loss, the followers are simply de-linked from the system and no additional action is required. This action does not allow a broker to crash if it contains the sole live replica of a partition.

○ **brokerRecover[k: Kafka, b : Broker]**: A previously failed broker (b) or a new broker (b) joins the cluster (k). All partitions that have number of replicas lesser than the configured replication factor are replicated and stored on the new server. Each of these replicas is given the follower role for their respective partitions.

4.2 Temporal Behavior

The overall behavior of a system is defined as the set of traces that can be generated by executing the system. In Alloy, this behavior can be defined as a predicate by specifying (i) the initial condition and (ii) the set of actions that can be executed to evolve the system to the next state from any given pre-state along the trace. Here, temporal operators can be used to model action execution at each state along the trace. In addition, any additional constraints can also be defined as part of the behavior. We have defined

```
1   pred pushEvent[k : Kafka, prod : Producer, e: KafkaEvent,
2     p : TopicPartition] {
3     // Pre conditions
4       canProducerPushEvent[k, prod, e, p]
5     // Post conditions
6       -- add KafkaEvent e to the leader PartitionReplica of p
7       p.leader.events' = p.leader.events.add[e]
8       -- Follower replicas should sync up
9       sync[p.leader, p.followers]
10    // Frame conditions
11      pushEventFrame[p]
12  }
13  pred canProducerPushEvent[k : Kafka, prod : Producer,
14    e: KafkaEvent, p : TopicPartition] {
15    -- Partition p should belong to cluster
16    p in k.zookeeper.topics.partitions
17    -- Producer prod should be confugured in the cluster
18    prod in k.producers
19    -- KafkaEvent e should not exist anywhere in the cluster pre-state
20    e not in k.zookeeper.topics.partitions.leader.events.elems
21    -- Event not already belonging to a internal/external PartitionReplica
22    no events.e
23  }
24  pred sync[leader_replica, follower_replicas: PartitionReplica] {
25    all f : follower_replicas | f.events' = leader_replica.events'
26  }
27  pred pushEventFrame[p : TopicPartition] {
28    -- Events in other partitions should stay the same
29    all r : PartitionReplica - p.(leader + followers) | r.events' = r.events
30    -- Preserve unaffected state variables
31    pushEventUnaffectedVariablesFrame
32  }
33  pred pushEventUnaffectedVariablesFrame {
34    offsets' = offsets
35    brokers' = brokers
36    leader' = leader
37    followers' = followers
38    replicasInBroker' = replicasInBroker
39  }
```

Fig. 8. *pushEvent* action modelled in Alloy 6

two behaviors over which we will be checking satisfaction of properties[3]. In the Alloy specification of both behaviors shown in Fig. 9, *InvariantsStrict* defines the initial state of every trace. We will explain the predicates that are present in *InvariantsStrict* in the next section.

- ○ **kafkaSimpleBehavior[repFactor: Int]**: Given a valid initial state, at every step, this behavior involves executing any of the four actions defined in the previous section in one step (*doSomething*), or stuttering (*doNothing*). This behavior allows brokers to crash continuously without any constraint imposed on broker recovery.
- ○ **kafkaFaultTolerantBehavior[repFactor: Int]**: This behavior does everything that *kafkaSimpleBehavior* does. However, it imposes a constraint so that it does not allow two broker crashes to occur in sequence if a recovery has not occurred between the two crashes (lines 24–25, Fig. 9).

---

[3] Behaviors as Alloy predicates: https://github.com/cmu-soda/kafka-alloy/blob/main/kafka_main.als.

```
1    /**
2     * Initial state of the cluster
3     * @repFactor: configure the replication factor of the cluster
4     */
5    pred Init[repFactor: Int] {
6      Kafka.replicationFactor = repFactor
7      InvariantsStrict[Kafka]
8    }
9    pred kafkaSimpleBehavior[repFactor : Int] {
10     -- Initial state --
11     Init[repFactor]
12     -- Transition --
13     always ( -- Execute some action or stay idle
14       doSomething or doNothing
15     )
16   }
17   pred kafkaFaultTolerantBehavior[repFactor : Int] {
18     -- Initial state --
19     Init[repFactor]
20     -- Transition --
21     always (
22       (doSomething or doNothing) -- Execute some action or stay idle
23       -- Can't allow brokers to keep crashing without a recovery in between
24       and (executeBrokerCrash implies after((not executeBrokerCrash)
25       until executeBrokerRecover))
26     )
27   }
```

Fig. 9. Behaviors of a Kafka cluster model

5   Property Specification and Analysis

5.1   Properties

As explained in earlier sections, a Kafka cluster is configured with a parameter called replication factor, which defines the number of replicas each partition should have [3]. This also implies that the cluster is always expected to have the specified number of replicas for each partition at every point in time. However, this criteria may be violated if and when a broker goes down, after which, Kafka will try to achieve the same replication factor again when new broker joins the cluster [16]. Below are some the Kafka properties that Kafka tries to achieve. These properties have been translated in Alloy either in the form of predicates specifying state invariants[4], or in the form of assertions[5] specifying a temporal relationship between actions. These have also been explained later in the paper.

State Invariants

Fault Tolerance. Partition replication is the main tactic that Kafka utilizes to provide its clients with high fault tolerance and data availability. The system is fault tolerant at a state where it contains event backups, as specified in the invariant *topicPartition-MustHaveBackups*. Kafka replicates new events and manages partition replicas in the following ways:

---

[4] Invariants as Alloy predicates: https://github.com/cmu-soda/kafka-alloy/blob/main/invariants. als.

[5] All assertions defined here: https://github.com/cmu-soda/kafka-alloy/blob/main/kafka_main. als.

o Kafka ensures that each partition is associated with multiple identical replicas stored in different brokers at any given point in time.
o Every time an event is published to a partition, the leader replica receives it first, while the followers store that event by communicating with the leader. This has been specified in action *pushEvent*.
o When a broker goes down, some partitions will lose their leaders, and some will lose their followers. If a partition loses its leader, a new leader is elected from the set of surviving followers. If a partition loses one of its followers, the partition de-links it and continues to operate with the surviving leader and follower replicas, if any. It is worth noting that this is acceptable because a partition that lost its follower could not have lost its leader at the same time. This is because Kafka makes sure that replicas of the same partition do not exist in the same broker. This system transition has been specified in the action *brokerCrash* earlier discussed.

Data Availability. Kafka ensures that all events of topics belonging to the cluster are present at all times. This property has been specified in the invariant *someTopicPartitionReplicaPresentInCluster*.

Service Availability. Clients reading from or writing to a partition are always served by the leader replica of the partition. Therefore Kafka must ensure that a leader replica is always alive for each partition in the cluster to make the service available. This has been specified in the invariant *topicPartitionMustHaveOneLeader*.

Consistency. Each partition's follower replicas should contain the same order of events present in the partition's leader replica. This has been specified in the invariant *followersMustBeInSyncWithLeader*.

Invariant Specification. Based on Kafka's architecture and properties discussed earlier, Kafka is expected to maintain the following set of invariants in addition to others that are mentioned in the model. These invariants have been specified using Alloy:

1. *topicPartitionMustSatisfyReplicationFactor*[k : *Kafka*]: Each partition should have total replicas equal to the configured replication factor.
2. *topicPartitionMustHaveOneLeader*[k : *Kafka*]: Each partition should have exactly one leader replica.
3. *allTopicReplicasInBrokers*[k : *Kafka*]: All alive partition replicas of topics belonging to the cluster should be present in brokers of the cluster.
4. *someTopicPartitionReplicaPresentInCluster*[k : *Kafka*]: One or more partition replicas of each partition belonging to the cluster must be present in the cluster at all times.
5. *followersMustBeInSyncWithLeader*[k : *Kafka*]: For each partition, all events stored in the leader replica must also be present in follower replicas, in the same order.
6. *topicPartitionMustHaveBackups*[k : *Kafka*]: Each partition should have more than one replica.

Kafka is expected to satisfy the above invariants at all times. However, in case a broker crashes, the invariant *topicPartitionMustSatisfyReplicationFactor* may not hold. Therefore, two groups of invariants have been defined with varying levels of strictness.

○ *InvariantsStrict[k : Kafka]*: This invariant includes all invariants defined above.

○ *InvariantsAfterCrash[k : Kafka]*: This invariant is a slightly relaxed version that includes all but invariant #1 to accommodate for broker failures. Note that *InvariantsAfterCrash* still includes invariant #6, which means some backup replica(s) need to be present for each partition. For example, when a broker crashes in a cluster with *replicationFactor* = 3, *InvariantsStrict* will not hold but *InvariantsAfterCrash* will continue to hold as at least 2 replicas of each partition will still exist after the broker crashes.

Action-Based Properties

Recoverability. When Kafka notices that a broker has joined after a crash, Kafka creates new follower replicas for the partitions requiring replication by syncing up the partitions' leader replicas. It's interesting to note that only followers are created because Kafka needs to ensure that only one leader is present for each partition [16]. This behavior has been specified in action *brokerRecover*. The property of Recoverability has been specified in the assertions *BrokerRecoverAfterCrashPreservesInvariantsStrict* and *FaultTolerantKafkaEventuallyRecoversAfterCrash*.

Sequential Event Consumption Within a Partition. Events within a topic partition can only be consumed in the chronological order that they were published in [3]. This has been specified in the assertion *SequentialityWithinPartition*.

5.2   Verification

We describe a verification step to check whether the invariants and properties that we earlier defined indeed hold in all possible traces allowed within the system behavior. In Alloy, this can be done by defining assertions as LTL expressions and running a *check* command as follows:

```
1   check <assertion-name> for <scope> but <trace-len> steps
```

The *check* command enumerates all possible traces and checks if the assertion is invalidated in any one of them. <scope> defines the maximum number of elements that can exist in any signature set, and <trace-len> defines the maximum time steps that Alloy will check. In case there is a violation of the assertion within the specified scope and trace length, the analyzer returns a counterexample trace that shows this violation.

The code below is a specification of one such assertion we checked. The assertion states that if a system exhibits *kafkaSimpleBehavior* with *replication factor* of 3, then *InvariantStrict* must hold throughout every possible trace (of length up to 10).

```
1   assert InvariantsStrictAlwaysSatisfiesWithSimpleKafka {
2       -- Counterexample is expected for this assertion
3       kafkaSimpleBehavior[3] implies always(InvariantsStrict[Kafka])
4   }
5   check InvariantsStrictAlwaysSatisfiesWithSimpleKafka for 4 but 10 steps
```

Using the above approach, we checked[6] satisfaction of properties earlier defined against behaviors *kafkaSimpleBehavior* and *kafkaFaultTolerantBehavior*. To this end,

---

[6] Assertions were checked on an Apple MacBook Pro machine, with M2 Chip and 8 GB RAM.

```
1   assert BrokerRecoverAfterCrashPreservesInvariantsStrict {
2     kafkaFaultTolerantBehavior[3] implies always (
3       -- After broker failure, InvariantsAfterCrash satisfies until recovery
4       (executeBrokerCrash implies after(InvariantsAfterCrash[Kafka]
5           until executeBrokerRecover))
6       -- Strict invariants start to satisfy once a broker recovers
7       and (executeBrokerRecover implies after(InvariantsStrict[Kafka]))
8     )
9   }
10  check BrokerRecoverAfterCrashPreservesInvariantsStrict for 3
```

Fig. 10. BrokerRecoverAfterCrashPreservesInvariantsStrict specification

the following assertions were specified[7], checked, and their results tabulated in Table 1. We also note that for our analysis, we used the SAT-based backend, not the one based on nuXmv, as in our experience, we found that the former tends to be more efficient at finding counterexamples than the latter.

1. Invariants Strict Always Satisfies With Simple Kafka: *InvariantStrict* always satisfies when Kafka exhibits *kafkaSimpleBehavior*.
2. Invariants Strict Always Satisfies With Fault Tolerant Kafka: *InvariantStrict* always satisfies when Kafka exhibits *kafkaFaultTolerantBehavior*.
3. Simple Kafka Preserves Invariants After Crash: *InvariantAfterCrash* always satisfies when Kafka exhibits *kafkaFaultTolerantBehavior*.
4. Fault Tolerant Kafka With Three Replicas Preserves Invariants After Crash: *InvariantsAfterCrash* always satisfies with *kafkaFaultTolerantBehavior* with *replicationFactor=3*.
5. Fault Tolerant Kafka With Two Replicas Preserves Invariants After Crash: *InvariantsAfterCrash* always satisfies when Kafka exhibits *kafkaFaultTolerantBehavior* with *replicationFactor=2*.
6. Broker Recover After Crash Preserves Invariants Strict: When Kafka exhibits *kafka FaultTolerantBehavior* with *replicationFactor=3* and a broker fails, *InvariantsAfter Crash* holds until the broker is restored, after which *InvariantStrict* is satisfied again. This is an example of an action-based property, shown in Fig. 10.
7. Never Broker Crash Preserves Strict Invariants: Kafka preserves *InvariantStrict* if a broker never crashes when Kafka exhibits either *kafkaSimpleBehavior* or *kafkaFaultTolerantBehavior* with *replicationFactor=2*.
8. Fault Tolerant Kafka Eventually Recovers After Crash: If Kafka exhibits *kafkaFaultTolerantBehavior* with *replicationFactor=3*, a broker eventually recovers after a crash and no other broker crashes again before the broker does recover.
9. Event Can Only Be Read After Being Pushed: If Kafka exhibits either *kafkaFaultTolerantBehavior* or *kafkaSimpleBehavior*, an event can only be read after it has been pushed/published.
10. Sequentiality Within Partition: A consumer can only consume events from a partition in the order that they were published in.
11. Sequentiality Between Two Partitions: A consumer can only consume events belonging to different partitions in the order that they were published in.

---

[7] All assertions found here: https://github.com/cmu-soda/kafka-alloy/blob/main/kafka_main.als.

Table 1. Results of assertion checking *Assertion, [a]Scope/Trace length, [b]Counterexample found, [c]CNF Generation time (ms), [d]Solving time (ms), [e]Total analysis time (ms)*

A* #	Small Scope					Larger Scope				
	S/TL^a	CE^b	$CNFT^c$	ST^d	TAT^e	S/TL^a	CE^b	$CNFT^c$	ST^d	TAT^e
1	4/10	Yes	604	146	750	5/10	Yes	8004	260	8264
2	4/10	Yes	7919	1509	9428	5/10	Yes	146943	3013	149956
3	3/10	Yes	542	93	635	4/10	Yes	3072	246	3318
4	3/10	No	57519	18325	75844	4/10	No	928091	1868237	2796328
5	4/10	Yes	24759	854	25613	5/10	Yes	356573	692	357265
6	3/10	No	15829	145	15974	4/9	No	604674	428819	1033493
7	3/10	No	139380	7738	147118	4/6	No	5790138	5816899	11607037
8	4/10	No	39830	372	40202	5/9	No	68395	381	68776
9	3/10	No	103479	25209	128688	4/9	No	3387925	5073704	8461629
10	3/10	No	172644	22521	195165	4/9	No	1089454	2640708	3730162
11	4/10	Yes	110647	12711	123358	5/10	Yes	286566	46677	333243

5.3   Discussion of Verification Results

As can be seen from the results, a counterexample has been encountered while verifying assertion #1. Since *InvariantStrict* contains the invariant *topicPartitionMustSatisfyReplicationFactor* and Kafka does not guarantee that replication factor *must* be maintained at all times, a counterexample is expected here. Along similar lines, assertion #2 also generates a counterexample, as *kafkaFaultTolerantBehavior* does not guarantee satisfaction of *replicationFactor* even though it prevents two crashes without recovery in between. Assertion #3 does not hold because *kafkaSimpleBehavior[3]* allows brokers to crash continuously, which can lead to less than 2 replicas being present.

As described earlier, *InvariantsAfterCrash* is more relaxed than *InvariantsStrict* as it does not require *replicationFactor* number of replicas to be present, but does require at least 2 replicas of each partition to be present in the system at any given time. This is the reason why assertion #4 does not lead to a counterexample, which shows that *kafkaFaultTolerantBehavior* with *replicationFactor=3* is able to satisfy *InvariantsAfterCrash* at all points in all possible traces allowed. A counterexample on assertion #5 shows that even with *kafkaFaultTolerantBehavior*, setting *replicationFactor=2* is not sufficient for satisfaction of *InvariantsAfterCrash*, since failure of one broker can result in less than 2 replicas being present[8].

With the above results, we can conclude that Kafka maintains **data availability** and **service availability** when the system is designed such that no two brokers can consecutively fail without a recovery in between, since *kafkaFaultTolerantBehavior* satisfies the invariant *topicPartitionMustHaveOneLeader* at all times. In addition, configuring *replicationFactor=3* ensures data redundancy at all times (which satisfies the property of **fault tolerance**). Since both *InvariantsStrict* and *InvariantsAfterCrash* contain

---

[8] Assertion #5 counterexample in Alloy model visualizer: https://github.com/cmu-soda/kafka-alloy/blob/main/counterexample.pdf.

the invariant *followersMustBeInSyncWithLeader*, *kafkaFaultTolerantBehavior* also preserves **consistency** between leaders and followers. Results of assertion #6 and #8 show no counterexamples, which supports Kafka's **recoverability** property with *kafkaFaultTolerantBehavior*.

No counterexamples on assertion #10 suggests **sequential event consumption property within a given partition**, which implies that a consumer can consume events belonging to a given partition only in the order they were published in. A similar assertion was made in assertion #11 but for different partitions, which led to a counterexample. This shows that a consumer can consume events belonging to different partitions in an order that is different than the one they were published in. This is expected as Kafka doesn't guarantee any consumption order for events in different partitions. The above discussion demonstrates the power of Alloy in helping an engineer understand the behaviors and configurations under which the system operates as expected and those where the system might fail.

As stated in Sect. 4, we have assumed each individual action to be atomic. However, in the real-world, it is possible that failures or other interfering events may occur anytime in the middle of an action. Therefore, modeling actions with higher granularity would provide greater insight and confidence in Kafka's satisfaction of properties when action steps are interleaved with each other.

We also note that our initial analysis of these assertions was bounded (up to the specified scope and default trace length of 10). Thus, it is possible that even if the analyzer does not return any counterexample, one may exist in a larger scope. However, during our analysis process, we experimented with larger scopes to increase our confidence in the conclusions drawn from the analysis. As shown in Table 1, a larger scope leads to an increase in the size of the generated CNF, which, in turn, tends to result in an increased amount of analysis time.

6 Related Work

Closest to our work is the one by Xu et al. [25], where they used the PAT modeling tool [22] to specify and analyze Kafka's behavior in communicating sequential processes (CSP) [10]. This work however does not discuss satisfaction of properties under different replication factors and broker recovery patterns, and does not verify the possibility of out-of-order event consumption between two partitions.

Alloy has been used to model and analyze distributed systems and protocols. Zave used Alloy to analyze a model of the Chord distributed hashing protocol, demonstrating that the invariants suggested by the creators of the protocol did not hold [26]. The work by Rouland et al. [21] models three common types of communication models used in distributed systems – Message Passing, Remote Procedure Calls, and Distributed Shared Memory – using Alloy 5, verifying their functional requirements. Pai et al. utilized Alloy to model the OAuth 2.0 authentication protocol, finding a known security vulnerability that is present in OAuth 2.0 [18]. In comparison to these works, our goal was to use newly added features in Alloy 6 (mutable state variables and temporal operators) to demonstrate its capability to model and analyze a complex technology being used in the industry.

McCaffrey's article discusses the difficulty of gaining confidence in distributed systems due to asynchronous components and partial failure, and how Amazon Web Services utilized TLA+ [13] as the formal modeling tool to verify their protocols [15], discovering several bugs in S3, DynamoDB, their internal distributed lock manager [17]. Chevrou et al. also leveraged TLA+ to model and verify peer-to-peer, multicast and convergecast protocols [9]. As far as we are aware, TLA+ has not been used to model Kafka, although it would be an interesting study to compare the resulting model to ours along different dimensions (such as expressiveness and analysis performance) [14].

7   Conclusion and Discussion

Alloy was useful in verifying many of the key properties of Kafka and giving an insight into the kinds of behavior that ensures that a Kafka cluster maintains all invariants that it is expected to. It also highlights the conditions under which Kafka may fail to satisfy some of the properties, e.g., Kafka fails to maintain data backups if there is no broker recovery mechanism or if a broker crashes in a cluster with replication factor of 2.

A major strength of Alloy is its model visualizer and evaluator, which helps in identifying undesirable states and further inform design decisions. Alloy 6 renders separate object models for pre-state and post-state, which acts as a visual representation of a state transition. In our model, only relations are tagged with *var* keywords, which constraints the objects to remain static while relations change over time. This greatly simplified the process of specifying actions, considering that Kafka's architecture and behavior is quite complex. However, defining frame conditions with mutable relations can be tricky as one needs to model how the domain, range and relation between entities might evolve. Alloy operators of domain and range exclusion ($<:$ and $:>$) specially come in handy for this purpose. We found the use of past-based LTL operators to be very expressive in specifying assertions related to sequential and parallel event consumption.

On the downside, we found it quite challenging to identify and debug our Alloy model. Understanding the factors that led to a counterexample can be challenging in Alloy as it does not highlight the specific part of the system actions or constraints that led to a violation. Similarly, in the case where an Alloy model contains inconsistent predicates, the built-in *unsatisfable core* feature [23] is recommended as a way to identify contradictory logical statements; while this feature is sometimes useful, it often requires the user to further diagnose the inconsistency, which we found to be a time-consuming task. Due to the above two reasons, it can be difficult to isolate the specific design decision(s) that make a system deviate from its specification. Further research to facilitate this process (possibly leveraging techniques such as fault localization [24] or model repair [6]) would be a valuable addition.

Our work could also be extended to perform unbounded model checking using the nuXmv tool, to find any counterexamples that the SAT-based analysis might have missed. Such an analysis would increase confidence that the system as modeled satisfies its desirable properties.

Acknowledgements. This work was supported in part by a CMU Master of Software Engineering (MSE) Graduate Research Fellowship and the U.S. NSF award CCF-2144860.

Competing Interests. The author(s) has no competing interests to declare that are relevant to the content of this manuscript.

References

1. Alloy 6 homepage. https://alloytools.org/alloy6.html. Accessed 12 Mar 2023
2. Alloy 6 lexical issues. https://alloytools.org/spec.html. Accessed 04 Oct 2024
3. Apache kafka documentation. https://kafka.apache.org/documentation/#introduction. Accessed 26 Feb 2024
4. Apache kafka homepage. https://kafka.apache.org/. Accessed 12 Mar 2023
5. Zookeeper, administrator's guide. https://zookeeper.apache.org/doc/r3.4.10/zookeeperAdmin.pdf. Accessed 12 Mar 2023
6. Brida, S.G., et al.: BeAFix: an automated repair tool for faulty alloy models. In: 36th IEEE/ACM International Conference on Automated Software Engineering (ASE), pp. 1213–1217. IEEE (2021)
7. Brunel, J., Chemouil, D., Cunha, A., Macedo, N.: The electrum analyzer: model checking relational first-order temporal specifications. In: 33rd ACM/IEEE International Conference on Automated Software Engineering (ASE), pp. 884–887 (2018)
8. Cavada, R., et al.: The NUXMV symbolic model checker. In: Biere, A., Bloem, R. (eds.) CAV 2014. LNCS, vol. 8559, pp. 334–342. Springer, Cham (2014). https://doi.org/10.1007/978-3-319-08867-9_22
9. Chevrou, F., Hurault, A., Quéinnec, P.: A modular framework for verifying versatile distributed systems. J. Log. Algebraic Methods Program. **108**, 24–46 (2019). https://doi.org/10.1016/j.jlamp.2019.05.008
10. Hoare, C.A.R.: Communicating Sequential Processes. Prentice-Hall, Saddle River (1985)
11. Jackson, D.: Software Abstractions - Logic, Language, and Analysis. MIT Press, Cambridge (2006)
12. Kumar, M., Singh, C.: Building Data Streaming Applications with Apache Kafka. Packt Publishing, Birmingham (2017)
13. Lamport, L.: Specifying Systems, The TLA+ Language and Tools for Hardware and Software Engineers. Addison-Wesley, Boston (2002)
14. Macedo, N., Cunha, A.: Alloy meets TLA+: an exploratory study. CoRR **abs/1603.03599** (2016). http://arxiv.org/abs/1603.03599
15. McCaffrey, C.: The verification of a distributed system: a practitioner's guide to increasing confidence in system correctness. Queue **13**(9), 150–160 (2015). https://doi.org/10.1145/2857274.2889274
16. Narkhede, N., Shapira, G., Palino, T.: Kafka: The Definitive Guide, 1st edn. O'Reilly Media Inc., Sebastopol (2017)
17. Newcombe, C., Rath, T., Zhang, F., Munteanu, B., Brooker, M., Deardeuff, M.: How amazon web services uses formal methods. Commun. ACM **58**(4), 66–73 (2015). https://doi.org/10.1145/2699417
18. Pai, S., Sharma, Y., Selvaraj, S.K., Singh, S.: Formal verification of OAuth 2.0 using alloy framework, June 2011. https://doi.org/10.1109/CSNT.2011.141
19. Pnueli, A.: The temporal logic of programs. In: 18th Annual Symposium on Foundations of Computer Science, pp. 46–57 (1977). https://doi.org/10.1109/SFCS.1977.32
20. Power, D., Slaymaker, M., Simpson, A.: Conformance checking of dynamic access control policies. In: Qin, S., Qiu, Z. (eds.) ICFEM 2011. LNCS, vol. 6991, pp. 227–242. Springer, Heidelberg (2011). https://doi.org/10.1007/978-3-642-24559-6_17

21. Rouland, Q., Hamid, B., Jaskolka, J.: Formal specification and verification of reusable communication models for distributed systems architecture. Futur. Gener. Comput. Syst. **108**, 178–197 (2020). https://doi.org/10.1016/j.future.2020.02.033
22. Sun, J., Liu, Y., Dong, J.S., Pang, J.: PAT: towards flexible verification under fairness. In: 21st International Conference on Computer Aided Verification (CAV), pp. 709–714 (2009)
23. Torlak, E., Chang, F.S., Jackson, D.: Finding minimal unsatisfiable cores of declarative specifications. In: 15th International Symposium on Formal Methods (FM), pp. 326–341 (2008)
24. Wang, K., Sullivan, A., Marinov, D., Khurshid, S.: Fault localization for declarative models in alloy. In: 31st IEEE International Symposium on Software Reliability Engineering (ISSRE), pp. 391–402. IEEE (2020)
25. Xu, J., Yin, J., Zhu, H., Xiao, L.: Modeling and verifying producer-consumer communication in Kafka using CSP. In: 7th Conference on the Engineering of Computer Based Systems. ECBS 2021, Association for Computing Machinery, New York, NY, USA (2021). https://doi.org/10.1145/3459960.3459961
26. Zave, P.: Using lightweight modeling to understand chord. Comput. Commun. Rev. **42**(2), 49–57 (2012)

Event-B Development of Modelling Human Intervention Request in Self-driving Vehicle Systems

Fahad Alotaibi[1,2](✉) [ID], Thai Son Hoang[2] [ID], Asieh Salehi Fathabadi[2] [ID], and Michael Butler[2] [ID]

[1] College of Applied Computer Sciences (CACS), King Saud University, Riyadh 11543, Saudi Arabia
[2] School of Electronics and Computer Science (ECS), University of Southampton, Southampton SO17 1BJ, UK
{f.a.alotaibi,t.s.hoang,a.salehi-fathabadi,m.j.butler}@soton.ac.uk

Abstract. In the design of autonomous systems, seamless integration with human operators is crucial, particularly when humans are considered as a fail-safe for intervening in hazardous situations. This study presents an Event-B intervention timing pattern designed to include human drivers' responses when they act as fallback mechanisms in Self-Driving Vehicle (SDV) systems. The proposed pattern outlines specific timings for driver interventions following alerts from SDVs, offering a clear set of expectations and conditions for human drivers during these critical takeover instances. The usability of this pattern is demonstrated through a case study, highlighting its importance for situations that require interventions. Ultimately, it sheds light on the operational aspects of SDVs, ensuring a safe and orderly transition from automated to manual control.

Keywords: SDV · Driver Interventions · Event-B · Timing Patterns

1 Introduction

Autonomy has advanced the modern way of cooperation between humans and machines. With the rapid development of advanced tools and techniques, the interactions between humans and autonomous machines are becoming increasingly complex [20]. Several classification approaches for defining autonomy have been developed in different domains [19]. The International Society of Automotive Engineers (SAE) [17] classified the autonomy in Self-Driving Vehicles (SDVs) into six levels for performing the Dynamic Driving Task (DDT). Beside fully manual (Level 0), automation levels 1 to 3 (semi-automation) involve a human driver within the DDTs, while automation levels 4 and 5 (high-automation systems) do not engage with a human driver in DDTs [7]. Similarly, Unmanned Aerial Systems (UAS), also known as drones, is organised into four levels, where the inspector (human) is responsible for supervising a system at most levels [16].

The engagement between humans and machines is widely known as the Human-In-The-Loop System (HITLS) [10]. The HITLS can add advanced qualifications to the autonomous system model to make it the top safety pick. According to the Insurance Institute for Highway Safety (IIHS) [12], the SDVs can become '*the safety pick*' when it is integrated with technology to prevent crashes. One of these integrated systems is an HITLS that aims to prevent collisions by creating a digital collaboration space between drivers and machines [4].

Although the SDVs can be built on the HITLS architecture, the behaviour of drivers might have caused fatal accidents. When investigating an Uber self-driving crash, the National Transportation Safety Board (NTSB) [8] found the accident was caused by the internal components of an SDV when the autopilot module failed to detect the later victim. The SDV was implemented to give a human driver control of the vehicle in unmanaged areas; however, the driver was distracted and did not react at the appropriate time.

Automotive companies, such as Tesla and Comma.ai, have used notification mechanisms to ensure the responsiveness of human drivers. For instance, the autopilot software of Comma.ai, known as OpenPilot [9], gives a driver 4 s to react when the intervention request is sent. However, if the human driver ignores intervention, the OpenPilot will gradually reduce the speed of the vehicle after 6 s until the car is totally stopped.

Modelling intervention requests is crucial, especially when human drivers play a key role in potential interventions. The need arises to develop methods that thoroughly investigate the requirements and assumptions linked to human responses. Understanding the intricacies of cognitive processes and decision-making mechanisms during interventions is vital for ensuring the safety of a system and the collaboration between humans and autonomous systems.

Therefore, this article presents the modelling methodology of time in Event-B [1] using *patterns*. The intervention timing pattern is introduced to formally model the timing properties when the automated machines may ask humans to take control of a system. Our pattern is a specialisation of the *trigger-response* pattern, in which trigger and response are both events (i.e., guarded actions) combining with a the *deadline* pattern [18].

The main advantage of the Event-B model is its support for a stepwise modelling approach by refinements. The second strength of an Event-B model is supported by the toolset Rodin [2], which involves both theorem proving and model checking (ProB) [14]. These advantages of Event-B, make it an appropriate method for formal modelling of complex systems.

The rest of the paper is structured as follows. Section 2 provides background on the Event-B formal modelling language and the introduction to our case study. Section 3 introduces the intervention timing pattern for modelling driver responses. Section 4 illustrates the approach using the case study. Section 5 discusses the advantages and results of using the intervention timing pattern. Section 6 presents related work and Sect. 7 concludes our article.

2   Background

In this section, we first review some background information on Event-B (Sect. 2.1) before giving the introduction to our case study (Sect. 2.2).

2.1   Event-B

Event-B [1] is a formal method commonly used for system analysis and modelling. Event-B is similar to other formal methods, as it uses concise mathematical language to address the inaccuracy and vagueness of requirements specification. The safety properties treated as invariants are verified, which aims to remove any inconsistency in the verified model.

A formal model in Event-B [1] includes two parts: *contexts* and *machines*. Contexts involve the static parts of a model and provide axiomatic characteristics. A context contains the definition of the carrier sets, constants and axioms that constrain the constants and carrier sets. Machines are the dynamic parts of the model. An Event-B machine involves variables v, invariants I(v) that constrain the variables, and events. An event is *'an atomic transition'* that changes the states of the system. The transition state of an event is constrained through the guards and the actions. For instance, for an event e with parameters t, the guard of the event can be written as G(t,v), and the action of the event can be represented as $v := E(t, v)$. An event e can only be enabled when its guard $G(t, v)$ holds for some parameter t and its affects on variable v is specified by the action E(t,v).

$$e == any \ t \ where \ G(t,v) \ then \ v := E(t,v) \ end$$

One of the principal advantages of Event-B is its utilisation of patterns to address complex modelling challenges. The Event-B pattern serves as a generic structure that can be applied to various aspects of modelling the dynamic behaviours of a system. Furthermore, the machine inclusion plug-in [11] facilitates the transformation of a pattern into a concrete example, thereby easing the application of these generic structures across numerous use cases. Machine inclusion in Event-B introduces two principles: 1) machine inclusion (includes clause), and 2) event synchronisation (synchronises clause). For instance, inclusion allows for modularising and combining models. A machine m0 could be included in a new machine m1 as follows:

$$machine \ m1 \ includes \ m0 \ as \ inclusionName$$

(The keyword as allows the inclusion of multiple copies of the same machine with appropriate prefixing). This inclusion means that event e1 of m1 may synchronise with event e0 of m0 specified as follows:

$$event \ e1 \ synchronises \ inclusionName.e0 \ end$$

Synchronisation means the guards of e1 and e0 are conjoined and their actions are executed simultaneously [11].

2.2   The ALC Case Study

The case study examined in this article focuses on the Automated Lane Centring (ALC). The primary function of the ALC system is to maintain the SDV in the centre of its desired/target lane, with the human driver responsible for performing lane change manoeuvres [3, p. 3]. Furthermore, it is crucial to acknowledge that the ALC system does not replace the need for a human driver. Even though it assists with lane centring, the human driver is expected to stay alert and prepared to assume manual control when necessary.

Given the unpredictability of human drivers, there is a possibility that warnings and intervention signals may be disregarded. A study from the Crash Warning Interface Metrics program (CWIM) [13] suggests that after receiving an auditory alert, a driver may take roughly 700 milliseconds to override the system and steer manually. Other research indicates a more extended period, with drivers taking around 10 s to refocus and attend to the road [15]. Automotive companies such as Tesla and OpenPilot have thus incorporated notification systems to keep human drivers alert. For instance, OpenPilot [9] gives drivers a 4-second window to react to an intervention prompt. If ignored, OpenPilot emits an auditory warning, and after 6 s, it decelerates the vehicle until the SDV comes to a complete stop.

For example, Fig. 1 depicts a scenario involving an SDV and the need for driver intervention. Subfigure 1a demonstrates the vehicle accurately positioned within its target lane. However, a noticeable shift towards the right lane line occurs in Subfigure 1b, necessitating corrective input from the driver. Despite this assistance, Subfigure 1c continues the SDV's trajectory towards the right. The situation escalates in Subfigure 1d, where the SDV is precariously close to exiting its lane, underscoring the urgency for immediate driver intervention to prevent a potential hazard.

Furthermore, it is critical to expeditiously elucidate how the SDV system signals a human driver to assume manual control of the vehicle. Figure 2 provides a vital illustration of this integral sequence within the operations of SDVs, with a particular emphasis on the transition from autonomous operation to manual intervention. Upon detection of a scenario necessitating human involvement, the SDV system promptly issues an intervention notification to the driver, concurrently initiating a countdown sequence. In the event of a delayed response from the driver, the system activates an auditory alarm, serving as an additional prompt, and institutes a supplementary waiting period. In the continued absence of driver responsiveness, the system proactively transitions to a mitigation strategy mode, implementing a series of safety measures, including vehicular deceleration. Subsequent to this intervention, the SDV system retains control for a predefined duration, ensuring the maintenance of vehicular stability.

In this article, particular attention is given to the scenarios where human drivers might not respond aptly to the ALC's intervention alerts. The objective is to examine the sequence of a driver's actions when the ALC system prompts manual intervention, as follows:

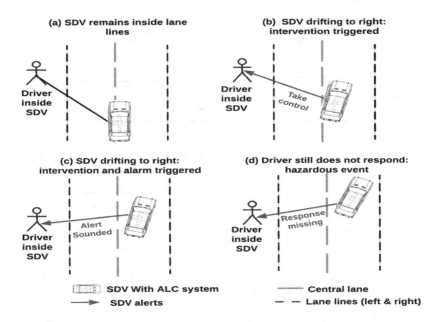

Fig. 1. From stability to hazard: tracing lane-assistance in ALC

1. The ALC system issues a request for intervention and initiates a pre-specified time (countdown) for the driver's response.
2. If the driver does not respond within the specified time, the ALC system triggers an auditory alert to attract the driver's attention.
3. From the moment of the auditory alert, the driver is given a further specific time window in which to react.
4. If the driver still does not react within the specified time, the ALC system proactively reduces the SDV 's speed.

3   Intervention Timing Pattern

The intervention timing pattern investigates how a human operator might respond when the automated machine asks for intervention. Our pattern not only models the reaction of a human operator but introduces new requirements and assumptions that need to be considered to make the SDV system safe.

This pattern explains our modelling choice and offers a broad context for understanding key properties such as *time progression, the clock (timer), human reaction time* and *alert time*. The primary concept involves using guarded events with time constraints; thus these guarded events can be triggered only when the system reaches a specific time.

The time progression is also designed as *an event*; therefore, there is no need to modify the underlying language of Event-B. The variable *time* is defined as a natural number, which allows time constraints, such as *alert time*, to be expressed as constants or as relationships between different times. Moreover,

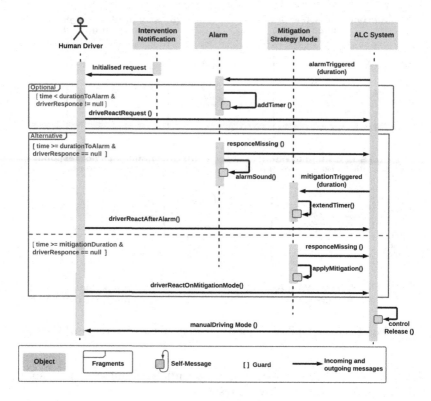

Fig. 2. Human driver intervention sequence in ALC system

time observations can be represented by other events determining future states (events) of a system.

3.1 Defining the Pattern

The intervention pattern is explained through an example Event-B model. This model can be reused in order to add different time considerations. As shown in the below, the intervention pattern has six variables:

```
machine m0
variables
redFlag  //denotes a system enters a hazardous event
time  //indicates any time of a system
requestTime  //time when automated system issues a request to intervene
alarmFlag  //sounding an alarm
alarmTime  //time waiting for a response before the alarm is sounding
reactionTime  //time when a human operator may react
invariants
@inv1: time ∈ ℕ₁        @inv2: requestTime ∈ ℕ    @inv3: alarmTime ∈ ℕ
@inv4: redFlag ∈ BOOL   @inv5: alarm ∈ BOOL       @inv6: reactionTime ∈ ℕ
....
```

– time: This represents the current time of a system. The incrementation of this value implies the time progression.

- requestTime: This indicates any time in the future when a system may issue a request to intervene.
- reactionTime: This indicates any time in the future when a driver may respond to a request to intervene.
- alarmTime: This denotes a future time when a driver does not react to a request to intervene, and the auditory notification is immediately sounded.
- redFlag: This is a boolean flag that indicates a system issuing a request to intervene.
- alarmFlag: This is also a boolean flag that explains the status of the sound alert.

The three categories focus on various aspects of timing. The first category involves establishing an intervention timer within hazardous events that require intervention. An example can be found in the request event, which indicates the entrance of a hazardous event when a system waits for a response before an alarm is raised. This event is triggered when the machine prompts a request for intervention. Consequently, the intervention timer is configured within this event as follows:

```
event request
any
/* Maximum time of a system waiting for a response before raises an alert*/
duration
when
/*Any time is given for waiting for a human's response*/
@grd1: duration ∈ ℕ₁
/*No intervention request and alarm is OFF*/
@grd2: redFlag = FALSE ∧ alarmFlag = FALSE
then
/*Specify a time of waiting for a driver before the alarm sounds*/
@act1: alarmTime := time + duration
/*Update the time of issuing a request to intervene*/
@act2: requestTime := time
/*Update a flag of issuing a request to intervene*/
@act3: redFlag := TRUE
/*No reaction from human yet*/
@act4: reactionTime := 0
end
```

After the creation of the intervention timer in the request event, the timeline for the intervention pattern is as outlined in Fig. 3. It includes the first requirement (R1), which must be considered to allow the human operator to respond when the automation issues a request to intervene. The initialisation of time for a request to intervene (requestTime) is defined according to the current time of a system (time). In order to give a driver a chance to respond, the parameter duration indicates the waiting time of a system before the alarm is sounded. Therefore, the alert time (alarmTime) can be defined as the end of the waiting time.

First Requirement (R1): When an intervention request is issued, the automated machine should give the human operator a limited time to react (duration).

The second category of the intervention timer is time progression, as shown in Fig. 4. In this modelling technique, the current time can be changed with an observation of the tick event as follows:

```
event tick where
/*Work only if a system issued a request to intervene*/
@flag_intervene: redFlag = TRUE
/*System time doesn't reach an alert time yet*/
@no_alarm: redFlag = TRUE ∧ alarmFlag = FALSE ⇒ time ≤ alarmTime
/*System time arrives on alert time, so the alarm must be operating*/
@alarmOn: (time = alarmTime ∧ redFlag = TRUE) ⇒ alarmFlag = TRUE
then
/* Increment timer */
@act1: time := time + 1
end
```

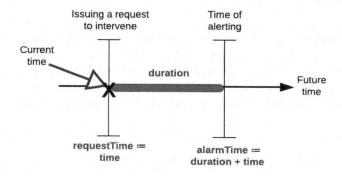

Fig. 3. Creation of intervention timer

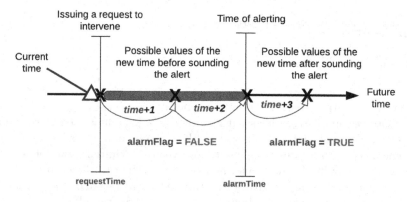

Fig. 4. Time progression in intervention timer

The tick schedules the time progression associated with the alarm property. For instance, the guard alarmOn captures a critical specification when the current time is already at the alert time; therefore, the auditory notification must be sounded before computing the new value of time. To model the alarm property, the second requirement (R2) is introduced, signifying that the autonomous system will send an auditory notification if the human response is still pending.

Second Requirement (R2): If the human operator fails to react within the duration time, the automated machine should immediately trigger an alarm (auditory notification)

This aspect is modelled in the notify event as follows:

```
event notify where
/*System issues a request to intervene, while an alarm is not sounding */
@grd1: alarmFlag = FALSE ∧ redFlag = TRUE
/*System time equal to or has moved beyond alert time*/
@timeAlarm: time ≥ alarmTime
then
/*Update value of alarm*/
@act1: alarmFlag := TRUE
end
```

The third category of the intervention timer models human interventions that occur either before or after the auditory notification sounds. To capture these two potential forms of human reaction, the intervene event is outlined with various time intervals. The first variant of this event, addressing human reactions prior to the auditory notification, is modelled as follows:

```
event intervene when
@grd1: redFlag = TRUE
/*Possible values of system time when a human may react*/
@grd2: time < alarmTime
then
/*Update a driver reaction time*/
@receivedReaction: reactionTime := time
@updateflag: redFlag := FALSE
end
```

The guards within the first variant of the intervene event play a crucial role in encapsulating the third requirement (R3), which highlights the potential for a human response prior to the activation of the auditory alarm. The grd2 guard in this initial form of the intervene event sets a confined timeframe, allowing for human reaction before the system's current time aligns with the alert time. Under these specified conditions, Fig. 5 demonstrates the narrow window of opportunity available for a human to respond before triggering the auditory notification.

Third Requirement (R3): A human operator might respond before sounding an auditory notification.

Similarly, the second form of the intervene event outlines several conditions that allow a human to react after the auditory notification has sounded, which is modelled as follows:

```
event intervene when
@grd1: redFlag = TRUE
/*System has already raised an alarm*/
@grd2: time ≥ alarmTime
then
/*Update a driver reaction time*/
@receivedReaction: reactionTime := time
/*Update values of flag*/
@updateflag: redFlag := FALSE
end
```

The adjustment in the grd2 guard contributes to capturing the fourth requirement (R4) that indicates the possibility of receiving a human response after the alarm sounds. Specifically, it implies that the system's current time has already

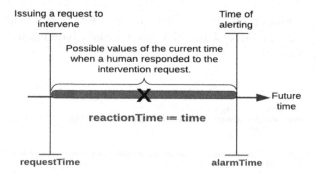

Fig. 5. Human's response window time before alert notification

surpassed the alert time. Given these conditions, Fig. 6 illustrates the possible window of time in which a human may react after the auditory notification is triggered.

Fourth Requirement (R4): A human operator might respond after sounding an auditory notification.

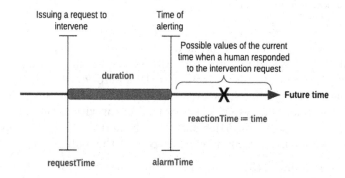

Fig. 6. Human's response window time after alert notification

Since the intervention timer is executed only when a request to intervene is issued, the invariants between the automated machine and a human are simple, and we have only to satisfy the following three invariants.

@alarm_state: alarmFlag = TRUE ⇒ redFlag = TRUE

@waiting_response: redFlag = TRUE ∧ alarmFlag = FALSE ⇒ requestTime ≤ time ∧ time ≤ alarmTime

@alerting: alarmFlag = TRUE ∧ redFlag = TRUE ⇒ time ≥ alarmTime

The invariant alarm_state indicates that the alarm signal can only be sent if there is still a need for human intervention. Additionally, the invariant waiting_response underscores that a system allocates a specific duration for the human to respond if an intervention request is dispatched (i.e., redFlag = TRUE). Specifically, the current time of the system (time) can go beyond the moment of issuing the intervention request (requestTime) up to the alert time (alarmTime). This duration is thus represented as requestTime $\leq$ duration $\leq$ alarmTime, where the system time equals the time of issuing the intervention request. On the other hand, the invariant alerting denotes that an auditory notification is only activated (i.e., alarmFlag = TRUE) if the system's current time exceeds this defined duration.

In this modelling strategy, three assumptions (As) are incorporated into the formal model:

- **A1:** A human operator might respond immediately or after the auditory notification is activated.
- **A2:** The waiting time, or duration, is not strictly defined, for example 3 s. Instead, it is treated as a parameter representing any positive number.
- **A3:** The automated machine is assumed to be in a safe state during the entire process of alerting and receiving responses from the human operator.

4   Application to ALC Case Study

This section describes the application of the intervention timing pattern to the ALC case study. Considering that this pattern primarily addresses moments when the system initiates intervention prompts, we have partitioned our application into two distinct Event-B machines[1]. The first machine covers the driving scenarios in which the ALC system is likely to issue intervention requests during the actuation task. Following that, the second machine employs Event-B refinement to show the implementation of the intervention timing pattern in response to a potential intervention request arising from the abstract model. The majority of proof obligations in this application are verified either automatically using Rodin provers or with the assistance of additional external prover plugins, such as Satisfiability Modulo Theories (SMT) for theory solving. Detailed discussions of the Event-B model are presented in their subsequent sections.

4.1   Abstract Machine: (*ALC Actuation Task*)

The abstract machine presents a scenario where intervention might be needed in the operation of the ALC system. A problematic situation can occur if the ALC system autonomously modifies the steering angle and vehicle speed, leading to the SDV drifting from the target lane. This potential issue is elaborated upon and visually represented in Fig. 1.

In the static part of the model, the potential positions of an SDV are represented by the abstract set POSITION, which denotes the various positions to which an SDV may travel. Since a lane could be considered part of these positions, we define the constant Lane as a subset of set POSITION in the following manner:

---

[1] An Event-B model is publicly available as a Rodin archive at: .

@typeof−Lane: Lane ⊆ POSITION

To model the movement of an SDV, we introduce an abstract constant MOVE, which activates a specific speed and steering angle to achieve a new position, enabling the SDV to transition across multiple locations.

@typeof−move: MOVE ∈ POSITION × SPEED × STEERING_ANGLE → $\mathbb{P}_1$ (POSITION)

Note that for a position pos, a speed spd, and a steering angle agl, MOVE(pos ↦ spd ↦ agl) gives the set of positions that the vehicle might move into.

In the dynamic part of the model, the physical position of the SDV is modelled as a variable ALC_POSITION, accompanied by a safety invariant ALC_POSITION ∈ Lane, signifying that the SDV must always reside within the Lane. Furthermore, the initial position of the SDV is represented as a constant init_position, which stipulates that the SDV's starting position must be within the Lane, denoted as init_position ∈ Lane. The modelling of the actuation task for an ALC system involves five events. The first event, ALC_actuation, abstractly captures the determination of the steering and speed settings for an SDV as follows:

```
event ALC_actuation any speed steering
where
/*Definition of steering and speed*/
@grd1: speed ∈ SPEED
@grd2: steering ∈ STEERING_ANGLE
/*No intervention request*/
@grd3: redFlag = FALSE
then
/*Specify steering and speed for ALC system*/
@act1: ALC_SPEED := speed
@act2: ALC_STEERING := steering
end
```

The second event, accept_move, presumes that the SDV can transition to a new position as described below:

```
event accept_move where
/*A new position leads to a position inside Lane*/
@grd1: MOVE(ALC_POSITION ↦ ALC_SPEED ↦ ALC_STEERING ) ⊆ Lane
/*No intervention request*/
@grd2: redFlag = FALSE
then
/*Moved into a new position inside the target lane */
@act1: ALC_POSITION :∈ MOVE(ALC_POSITION ↦ ALC_SPEED ↦ ALC_STEERING)
end
```

The third event, required_intervention, initiates an intervention request when the speed and steering are set to move the SDV to a position outside the lane, as detailed below:

```
event required_intervention where
/*A new position leads to a position outside Lane*/
@grd1: MOVE(ALC_POSITION ↦ ALC_SPEED ↦ ALC_STEERING ) ⊄ Lane
@grd2: redFlag = FALSE
then
/*Initiates an intervention request*/
@act1: redFlag := TRUE
end
```

The fourth event, mitigate_move, presumes that the ALC system is capable of implementing a mitigation strategy when the proposed speed and steering risk moving the SDV out of the lane. This is achieved by instituting an adjusted or mitigated steering and speed as detailed below:

```
event mitigate_move any mitigated_sp mitigated_steer
where
@grd1: mitigated_sp ∈ SPEED ∧ mitigated_steer ∈ STEERING_ANGLE
/*Intervention request was sent*/
@grd2: redFlag = TRUE
/*Specification on the ALC mitigation mode*/
@grd3: MOVE(ALC_POSITION ↦ mitigated_sp ↦ mitigated_steer) ⊆ Lane
then
/*Moved into a new position inside the lane*/
@act1: ALC_POSITION :∈ MOVE(ALC_POSITION ↦ mitigated_sp ↦ mitigated_steer)
end
```

The final event, human_intervene, simulates the human response to the intervention request as follows:

```
event human_intervene any manual_sp manual_steer
where
@grd1: manual_sp ∈ SPEED ∧ manual_steer ∈ STEERING_ANGLE
@grd2: redFlag = TRUE
/*Assumption that the human responses correctly*/
@grd3: MOVE(ALC_POSITION ↦ manual_sp ↦ manual_steer) ⊆ Lane
then
/*Moved into a new position inside the target lane */
@act1: ALC_POSITION :∈ MOVE(ALC_POSITION ↦ manual_sp ↦ manual_steer)
@act2: redFlag := FALSE
end
```

4.2   Refined Machine: (*Intervention Timing Pattern*)

The refined model is specifically developed to incorporate the intervention timing pattern within its structure. This model utilises the concept of machine inclusion in Event-B to extend and build upon the foundational concepts presented in Sect. 3.1. The main benefit of this approach lies in its ability to instantiate the intervention timing pattern on two separate occasions within the model:

1. The first instantiation models the time-sensitive aspects leading up to the point at which an auditory notification is issued to the driver.

   ```
   machine m1 refines m0 sees c0
   /*First instantiation is included as beforeAlarm*/
   includes interventionTimingPattern.m0 as beforeAlarm
   ```

2. The second instantiation of the intervention timing pattern is activated following the auditory notification. At this stage, the SDV engages its mitigation mode, which is a response mechanism to correct or manage the situation that requires the intervention.

   ```
   machine m1 refines m0 sees c0
   /*Second instantiation is included as afterAlarm*/
   includes interventionTimingPattern.m0 as afterAlarm
   ```

These applications of the intervention timing pattern will be summarised in the following steps.

1) Pre-Notification Temporal Modelling and Establishing Intervention Timing Before Auditory Alerts: The implementation of the intervention timing pattern in the refined machine incorporates intervention events. The temporal elements involved are synchronised with the request event, which is integrated into the abstract required_intervention event. Consequently, the model initialises the timing aspects at the moment when the ALC system requires intervention.

```
/*Timing aspects modelled in the request event are included in the required intervention event*/
event required_intervention extends required_intervention synchronises beforeAlarm.request end
```

The tick event, which is associated with the initiation of an intervention request, is incorporated as follows:

```
/*The time progression associated when ALC issues a request to intervene*/
event tick synchronises beforeAlarm.tick end
```

When the time progression reaches the alert moment and the driver has not reacted, an auditory notification is issued. This is facilitated by the synchronised notify event within the alarm event, detailed as follows:

```
/*Auditory notification is issued if driver does not react*/
event alarm synchronises beforeAlarm.notify end
```

However, the driver may react during the time progression before the auditory notification is sent. This response is captured by the synchronised intervene event, which aligns with the abstract human_intervene event, as outlined below:

```
/*Driver may intervene before auditory notification*/
event human_intervene extends human_intervene synchronises beforeAlarm.intervene end
```

2) Post-Notification Mitigation Strategy and ALC Response Mechanisms Following Auditory Alerts: The implementation of the intervention timing pattern also addresses the timing properties subsequent to the activation of the auditory notification. Thus, the synchronised request event is integrated within the event that presumes the auditory notification has been issued, as described below.

```
/*Reinitialise the intervention timer after alarm sounded*/
event alarm synchronises afterAlarm.request end
```

The tick event is also synchronised with the progression of time that corresponds to the moment when the alarm sounds, as outlined below:

```
/*Schedule time progression with the alarm is sounded*/
event tick synchronises afterAlarm.tick end
```

To capture the essential timing property that allows a driver to respond after the auditory notification has been issued, the abstract human_intervene event is extended to the human_react_after_alarm event. This expansion includes the synchronised intervene event, as illustrated below:

```
/*Driver may intervene after auditory notification*/
event human_react_after_alarm extends human_intervene synchronises afterAlarm.intervene end
```

However, if a driver fails to respond, the mitigation strategy of the ALC system may be initiated. In this instance, the synchronised notify event is incorporated as follows:

```
/*Mitigated movement applied if a driver fails to respond*/
event mitigate_move extends mitigate_move synchronises afterAlarm.notify end
```

5   Discussion

The intervention timing pattern is a critical component in the development of SDV systems, especially when considering the human driver as a fallback option during hazardous driving events. It outlines a structured method for specifying the timing properties needed to model the windows of opportunity for a driver's intervention response. This pattern finds applicability in autonomous or semi-autonomous systems where a human operator has an oversight role and is expected to take more active control in some hazardous situations, such as veering outside lanes. In these systems, a failsafe mode is available, for instance, to decelerate, in case the operator does not respond in a timely manner.

The analysis employs a two-step instantiation process to precisely chart the timing of a driver's potential responses to the ALC system's prompts. This modelling strategy differentiates between scenarios in which a driver might respond before the urgency of auditory notification is perceived, and situations where the driver's reaction occurs after acknowledging the notification. This approach facilitates a thorough examination of the range of a driver's possible reaction times in relation to the auditory signals from the ALC system.

The benefits of utilising the intervention timing pattern in SDV systems are multifaceted:

- **Requirement and Assumption Identification:** The intervention timing pattern serves as a structured framework that identifies specific requirements and assumptions related to the driver's engagement in the SDV's autonomous operations. By explicitly defining these parameters, it assists in shaping a comprehensive understanding of the role and expectations of human intervention, ensuring that both system developers and stakeholders have a clear blueprint to refer to.
- **Addressing Modelling Challenges:** One of the complex aspects of modelling SDV systems lies in accounting for the uncertain nature of a driver's response during autonomous operations. The intervention timing pattern plays a crucial role in overcoming this issue. It establishes a methodical framework that integrates the possibility of human responses into the system's functional procedures, ensuring that these variables are included in the system design even if they are not directly detectable. Therefore, it ensures that the model remains robust and reflective of real-world scenarios where driver reactions may not always be apparent.
- **Driver Inclusion Beyond Fallback:** Traditionally, the role of a driver in an SDV system is often relegated to that of a mere fallback option-intervening only when the system fails or is unsure of the next course of action. However, the intervention timing pattern encourages developers to transcend this limited view. It prompts the consideration of the driver an active participant, capable of varying responses across different scenarios. This, in turn, aids in crafting a more robust and realistic model of fallback mechanisms within the SDV system.

In summary, the intervention timing pattern not only accentuates the intricacies of human intervention in automated systems but also propels a forward-thinking approach to SDV system development. This pattern is instrumental in acknowledging the range of possible human reactions, guiding the creation of systems that excel technically while also being attuned to human behaviour and needs. Such an approach promotes a seamless integration of humans and machines, aiming for a balanced and cooperative relationship.

6   Related Work

Cansell et al. [6] developed a pattern to model the timing and order of events within systems, using time-stamped actions and reactions to simulate real-time processes. Their model uses a clock (timer) to track current time and events set to trigger at future times. The system advances time and activates events accordingly. However, this model does not handle interruptions during event sequences.

Butler and Falampin [5] proposed a refinement strategy of timing properties that introduces a clock variable representing the current time and an operation that progresses the clock. Therefore, time constraints are added to the clock to handle interruptions during event sequences where the clock cannot move beyond the specific point at which the deadline is violated.

Based on this methodology, many studies, such as [18,21], have been carried out to extend Event-B with timing properties. Sarshogh and Butler [18] propose a trigger response pattern to develop Event-B models with several timing properties such as deadline, delay and expiry. Their approach assigns timestamps for trigger and response events and employs a tick event to prevent the global clock from moving to a point where time constraints between the trigger and response events would be violated. Zhu et al. [21] extended the work of [5,18] to provide formally the semantics and syntax between the trigger and response events.

In autonomous systems, our pattern targets how humans react when automated machines trigger intervention. We specify an intervention timeline based on the human reaction time and the alert time. The deadline can be seen as the time when a driver may react, while the alert time combines the delay and expiry based on the received human's response. Therefore, we specify the criteria for triggering intervention based on these timelines. Nonetheless, the time-sensitive characteristics associated with the autonomous functions continue to be a significant issue. For instance, the timing aspects related to observing the driving environment and determining the target path are not fully investigated.

7   Conclusion and Future Work

This paper introduced the intervention timing pattern for managing the timing of interventions in SDV systems, conceptualised within the Event-B framework. The focus was on defining the time-sensitive parameters that handle when and how human drivers should take over control in critical situations. The intervention timing pattern specifies the essential temporal constraints when human drivers must intervene. Various driver responses were identified and their implications for system functionality were analysed. The actuation task of the ALC system served as a case study, validating the adaptability of the timing pattern to accommodate different driver behaviours. Future research is set to explore additional temporal dimensions in SDV systems, especially those timing properties critical to autonomous operations such as environmental perception and the determination of driving decisions.

Competing Interests. The author(s) has no competing interests to declare that are relevant to the content of this manuscript.

References

1. Abrial, J.R.: Modeling in Event-B: System and Software Engineering. Cambridge University Press, Cambridge (2010)
2. Abrial, J.R., Butler, M., Hallerstede, S., Hoang, T.S., Mehta, F., Voisin, L.: Rodin: an open toolset for modelling and reasoning in Event-B. Int. J. Softw. Tools Technol. Transfer **12**(6), 447–466 (2010)
3. Becker, C., Yount, L., Rozen-Levy, S., Brewer, J., et al.: Functional safety assessment of an automated lane centering system. Technical report, United States. Department of Transportation. National Highway Traffic Safety ...(2018)
4. Blanco, M., et al.: Human factors evaluation of level 2 and level 3 automated driving concepts. Technical report, National Highway Traffic Safety Admin (2014)
5. Butler, M., Falampin, J.: An approach to modelling and refining timing properties in B. In: Refinement of Critical Systems (RCS) (2002)
6. Cansell, D., Méry, D., Rehm, J.: Time constraint patterns for Event B development. In: Julliand, J., Kouchnarenko, O. (eds.) B 2007. LNCS, vol. 4355, pp. 140–154. Springer, Heidelberg (2006). https://doi.org/10.1007/11955757_13
7. Christensen, A., et al.: Key considerations in the development of driving automation systems. In: 24th Enhanced Safety Vehicles Conference. Gothenburg, Sweden (2015)
8. Claybrook, J., Kildare, S.: Autonomous vehicles: no driver... no regulation? Science **361**(6397), 36–37 (2018)
9. Comma.ai: Openpilot: an open source driver assistance system (2022). https://github.com/commaai/openpilot/
10. Fridman, L.: Human-centered autonomous vehicle systems: principles of effective shared autonomy. arXiv preprint arXiv:1810.01835 (2018)
11. Hoang, T.S., Dghaym, D., Snook, C., Butler, M.: A composition mechanism for refinement-based methods. In: 2017 22nd International Conference on Engineering of Complex Computer Systems (ICECCS), pp. 100–109. IEEE (2017)
12. HSRC: Top Safety Picks by HSRC (Highway safety research & communications). https://www.iihs.org/iihs/ratings/TSP-List. Accessed 22 June 2022
13. Lerner, N., Jenness, J., Robinson, E., Brown, T., Baldwin, C., Llaneras, R.E., et al.: Crash warning interface metrics. Technical report, United States. National Highway Traffic Safety Administration (2011)

14. Leuschel, M., Butler, M.: ProB: an automated analysis toolset for the B Method. Int. J. Softw. Tools Technol. Transfer **10**(2), 185–203 (2008)
15. Merat, N., Jamson, A.H., Lai, F.C., Daly, M., Carsten, O.M.: Transition to manual: driver behaviour when resuming control from a highly automated vehicle. Transport. Res. F: Traffic Psychol. Behav. **27**, 274–282 (2014)
16. Radovic, M.: Tech talk: Untangling the 5 levels of drone autonomy. https://droneii.com/project/drone-autonomy-levels. Accessed 25 Nov 2022
17. SAE: Taxonomy and definitions for terms related to on-road motor vehicle automated driving systems. SAE Standard J **3016**, 1–16 (2014)
18. Sarshogh, M.R., Butler, M.: Specification and refinement of discrete timing properties in Event-B. Electron. Commun. EASST **36** (2011)
19. Vagia, M., Rødseth, Ø.J.: A taxonomy for autonomous vehicles for different transportation modes. In: Journal of Physics: Conference Series. IOP Publishing (2019)
20. Xu, W.: From automation to autonomy and autonomous vehicles: challenges and opportunities for human-computer interaction. Interactions **28**(1), 48–53 (2020)
21. Zhu, C., Butler, M., Cirstea, C.: Formalizing hierarchical scheduling for refinement of real-time systems. Sci. Comput. Program. **189**, 102390 (2020)

Alloy Goes Fuzzy

Pedro Silva[1,3](✉) , Alcino Cunha[1,3] , Nuno Macedo[2,3] ,
and José N. Oliveira[1,3]

[1] Universidade do Minho, Braga, Portugal
`{alcino,jno}@di.uminho.pt`
[2] Universidade do Porto, Porto, Portugal
`nmacedo@fe.up.pt`
[3] INESC TEC, Porto, Portugal
`pedro.d.silva@inesctec.pt`

Abstract. Humans are good at understanding subjective or vague statements which, however, are hard to express in classical logic. Fuzzy logic is an evolution of classical logic that can cope with vague terms by handling *degrees of truth* and not just the crisp values true and false.

Logic is the formal basis of computing, enabling the formal design of systems supported by tools such as model checkers and theorem provers.This paper shows how a model checker such as Alloy can evolve to handle both classical and fuzzy logic, enabling the specification of high-level quantitative relational models in the fuzzy domain.

In particular, the paper showcases how QAlloy-F (a conservative, general-purpose quantitative extension to standard Alloy) can be used to tackle fuzzy problems, namely in the context of validating the design of fuzzy controllers. The evaluation of QAlloy-F against examples taken from various classes of fuzzy case studies shows the approach to be feasible.

Keywords: Fuzzy relations · Formal methods · Model checking · Alloy

1 Introduction

Expressing subjective statements based on personal experience is something that comes naturally to people. Humans hear remarks such as "the weather is cold today" and have no problem making sense of the meaning. However, when communicating with machines, conveying such phrases becomes challenging, as machines are used to dealing with precise information only. After all, from the previous statement alone one is just unable to determine what the exact outside temperature is. In fact, that very same phrase may be said under drastically different values of the temperature, depending on who is saying it, their background, where they are located and the climate that they are used to.

Zadeh [39] establishes a means to express such statements through *fuzzy set theory* (more commonly referred to as *fuzzy logic*), arising as a generalization of classical set theory. Rather than making use of Boolean values, one

S. Bonfanti et al. (Eds.): ABZ 2024, LNCS 14759, pp. 61–79, 2024.
https://doi.org/10.1007/978-3-031-63790-2_4

reasons over real numbers which, within the unit interval, describe *degrees of truth*. Since Zadeh's pioneering work there has been a lot of interest in fuzzy logic and fuzzy systems, both from the theoretical and practical sides, see e.g. [9,17,28,38]. Moreover, tools such as MATLAB®'s Fuzzy Logic Toolbox™ [14] and FuzzyLite [27] provide means of designing fuzzy controllers, exploring different inputs, experimenting with different values of the inputs and seeing the resulting behaviour.

However, as far as the authors are aware, there are no tools that provide high-level modelling and verification techniques readily available for structural modelling within the fuzzy domain. Existing work either acts at a low-level of abstraction [3,36,37], or is concerned with checking the behaviour of fuzzy systems [23,26,31,35]. We argue that, precisely due to the uncertain nature of fuzzy systems, high-level tools that can be used by domain experts are essential, whereby alternative designs can be explored in the early stages of development.

Alloy [13] excels in such structural modelling when standard logic is used, and a recent extension by this team, QAlloy [30], allows reasoning about quantitative models. The main contribution of this paper is to showcase how a variant of QAlloy can be used to tackle fuzzy problems through fuzzy relational reasoning, thus enabling one to specify high-level quantitative relational models in the fuzzy domain. We denote this variant as QAlloy-F, and consider it orthogonal to the originally proposed QAlloy-I for the integer domain.

The rest of the paper is structured as follows: Sect. 2 provides some background on fuzzy logic. Section 3 presents QAlloy-F by example, followed by its formal presentation in Sect. 4. Section 5 shows its application to the design of fuzzy controllers and Sect. 6 evaluates the tool. Lastly, Sect. 7 presents related work and Sect. 8 wraps up the paper.

2 Background

Standard predicate calculus deals with either true or false statements. It is common to represent the truth values *false* by 0 and *true* by 1 subject to logic operators, making a Boolean algebra. For instance, given $p, q \in \{0, 1\}$ the multiplication $p \cdot q$ expresses logic *conjunction*, $p \wedge q$. Similarly, $p \vee q = p + q - p \cdot q$ defines logic *disjunction*, $\neg p = 1 - p$ logic *negation*, and so on.

The use above of simple arithmetic operations over $\{0, 1\}$ to express Boolean operators is suggestive of a possible generalization: what if one uses the *whole interval* $[0, 1]$ of real numbers and not just its boundaries $\{0, 1\}$? The closer some $p \in [0, 1]$ would be to 1 (resp. 0), the "more true" (resp. "more false") it would be. The arithmetic operator definitions could stay the same and one would deal with *degrees of truth* rather than discrete truth or falsehood, obtaining a more expressive and flexible logical framework. Such is the motivation and formal basis of *fuzzy logic* [39].

Fuzzy Logic. As hinted above, in fuzzy logic the standard logic connectives $x \wedge y$ and $x \vee y$ become real number functions of type $[0, 1] \times [0, 1] \rightarrow [0, 1]$. Instead of $x \wedge y$, the notation $t(x, y)$ is used in fuzzy logic, t being named the *triangular norm* (or *t-norm*, for short). Dually, disjunction is expressed by $s(x, y)$, the so-called *triangular conorm* (abbrev. *t-conorm*). To make formulæ more readable we adopt the infix notations $x \sqcap y$ for $t(x, y)$ and $x \sqcup y$ for $s(x, y)$. Triangular (co)norms may vary in fuzzy logic. Table 1 gives a few standard definitions, the so-called *algebraic product* being the instance that opened this section. In general, the t-norm is a binary operation that must enjoy the properties of commutativity, associativity, monotonicity and respect the boundary condition $x \sqcap 1 = x$ for any $x \in [0, 1]$. The dual t-conorm must abide to the same properties, its boundary condition being $0 \sqcup x = x$, for all $x \in [0, 1]$. The algebraic product, Gödelian and Łukasiewicz t-norms of Table 1 are the most popular.

Table 1. Triangular norms and conorms

t-norm	$x \sqcap y$	t-conorm	$x \sqcup y$
Gödelian minimum	$\min(x, y)$	Gödelian maximum	$\max(x, y)$
Łukasiewicz intersection	$\max(0, x + y - 1)$	Łukasiewicz union	$\min(x + y, 1)$
Algebraic product	$x \cdot y$	Algebraic sum	$x + y - x \cdot y$
Drastic product	$\begin{cases} x & \text{if } y = 1 \\ y & \text{if } x = 1 \\ 0 & \text{otherwise} \end{cases}$	Drastic sum	$\begin{cases} x & \text{if } y = 0 \\ y & \text{if } x = 0 \\ 1 & \text{otherwise} \end{cases}$
Einstein product	$\frac{x \cdot y}{1 + (1-x) \cdot (1-y)}$	Einstein sum	$\frac{x+y}{1+x \cdot y}$

Fuzzy Relation Algebra. A *fuzzy set* A over the universe $\mathcal{U}$ is defined by its characteristic function $\mu_A : \mathcal{U} \to [0, 1]$ mapping all elements of the universe to their respective degree of truth (or membership). This function μ_A is usually named the *membership function* of A. We follow [29] and abbreviate $\mu_A(x)$ to $A(x)$. Wherever, for every $x \in \mathcal{U}$, $A(x) = 0$ or $A(x) = 1$, A is said to be a *crisp set*, representing a classical set. Analogously, a *fuzzy (binary) relation* [38] $R : X \to Y$ between two crisp sets X and Y is characterized by the membership function $\mu_R : X \times Y \to [0, 1]$, specifying the degree of membership of each pair (x, y) in R. Again, we abbreviate $\mu_R(x, y)$ by $R(x, y)$. Binary relations can be seen as sets whose elements are pairs, and all operations on sets can be applied to binary relations. Moreover, the concept can be generalized to relations of higher arity.

The standard operations on sets and relations can "go fuzzy" as follows:

- The *complement* of a fuzzy set A is the fuzzy set $\overline{A}$ defined by the membership function $\overline{A}(x) = 1 - A(x)$, for every $x \in \mathcal{U}$.
- Two fuzzy sets A and B may be combined through *intersection* $(A \cap B)(x) = A(x) \sqcap B(x)$ or *union* $(A \cup B)(x) = A(x) \sqcup B(x)$.
- The *Cartesian product* of two fuzzy sets A and B follows the definition of the t-norm, i.e., $(A \times B)(x, y) = A(x) \sqcap B(y)$ for $x, y \in \mathcal{U}$.
- A fuzzy set A is *contained* in another fuzzy set B, written $A \subseteq B$, whenever $A(x) \leq B(x)$ for every $x \in \mathcal{U}$.
- Every fuzzy relation $R : X \to Y$ has a *converse* relation $R^\circ : Y \to X$, which is such that $R^\circ(y, x) = R(x, y)$, for all $x, y \in \mathcal{U}$.

– Two fuzzy relations $R : X \to Y$ and $S : Y \to Z$ can be *composed* to create the relation $R \cdot S : X \to Z$ such that $(R \cdot S)(x, z) = (\bigsqcup y : R(x, y) \sqcap S(y, z))$.

A fuzzy operator that arises from the notion of crispness is the α-*cut*. The α-cut of a fuzzy set A is the crisp set $A^\alpha = \{a \in \mathcal{U} \mid A(a) \geq \alpha\}$.

3   QAlloy-F by Example

Let us start with a simple, classical fuzzy problem — Sanchez's approach to performing medical diagnosis [29].

$$Patient \xrightarrow{Q} Symptom \xrightarrow{R} Disease$$
$$T \supseteq Q \cdot R$$

Given a fuzzy relation $Q : Patient \to Symptom$ that encodes the symptoms exhibited by a set of patients, and a fuzzy relation $T : Patient \to Disease$ that determines how experts diagnosed those patients, in [29] the authors propose to synthesize the medical knowledge as a fuzzy relation $R : Symptom \to Disease$ such that $Q \cdot R \subseteq T$. This relation could then be applied to other patients, with the disease(s) that display the highest degree selected as diagnoses. This is expected to be an iterative process in which experts validating the candidate R relations could be easily supported by QAlloy-F.

Lines 1–7 of Fig. 1 show how these relations could be encoded in QAlloy-F. The structure is introduced through the declaration of *signatures* and *fields* relating them. Signature **Patient** represents patients. The particular symptoms and diseases present in the collected data are declared as specializations of their parent signatures **Symptom** and **Disease**, respectively, which are marked as **abstract** to avoid atoms outside those specializations.

Regular fields in Alloy relate each atom of the parent signature with atoms of other signatures, according to some multiplicity. In QAlloy-F, however, these can be annotated with keyword **fuzzy**, denoting that the membership of a tuple in such relations is no longer Boolean but rather a value between 0 and 1. In the example, we have a fuzzy field relating each patient with **some** symptoms, and another relating each symptom with a **set** of diseases.

The (fuzzy) diagnosis of a patient is simply encoded as **Q.R**, where **.** denotes relational composition, which by default has a Gödelian min-max semantics (recall Table 1): for a patient **p**, a disease **d** and a symptom **s**, select the minimum between the degree **p** exhibits **s** and the degree **s** is related with **d**; then the degree between **p** and **d** is the maximum among all available symptoms.

Table 2. Example of a medical diagnosis relation R

R	Viral Fever	Typhoid	Stomach problem	Malaria	Chest problem
Temperature	0.4	0.3	0.1	0.7	0.1
Cough	0.4	0.2	0.2	0.7	0.2
Stomach pain	0.1	0.2	0.8	0	0.2
Chest pain	0.1	0.1	0.2	0.1	0.8
Headache	0.3	0.6	0.2	0.2	0

```
1  sig Patient {
2    fuzzy Q : some Symptom }
3  abstract sig Symptom {
4    fuzzy R : set Disease }
5  one sig Temp, Cough, StmPn, ChtPn, Hdche extends Symptom {}
6  abstract sig Disease {}
7  one sig ViralFv, Typhoid, StmPrb, Malaria, ChtPrb extends Disease {}
8
9  fun diagnosis : Patient → Disease {
10   { p:Patient, d:Disease | d in max[p.Q.R] } }
11
12 fun expert_R : Symptom → Disease {
13   (0.4**Temp + 0.4**Cough + 0.1**StmPn + 0.1**ChtPn + 0.3**Hdche) → ViralFv +
14   (0.7**Temp + 0.2**Hdche + 0.7**Cough + 0.1**ChtPn) → Malaria +
15   (0.3**Temp + 0.2**Cough + 0.1**ChtPn + 0.6**Hdche + 0.2**StmPn) → Typhoid +
16   (0.1**Temp + 0.2**Cough + 0.8**StmPn + 0.2**ChtPn + 0.2**Hdche) → StmPrb +
17   (0.1**Temp + 0.2**StmPn + 0.8**ChtPn + 0.2**Cough) → ChtPrb }
18
19 run two_diagnosis {
20   R = expert_R and
21   some p:Patient |
22     Malaria + ChtPrb in p.diagnosis } for 1 Patient
23
24 run same_diagnosis {
25   R = expert_R and
26   some p1,p2:Patient |
27     p1.diagnosis = p2.diagnosis and no p1.Q & p2.Q } for 2 Patient
28
29 check maxChestPain {
30   R = expert_R implies all p:Patient |
31     ChtPn in max[p.Q] implies ChtPrb in p.diagnosis }
```

Fig. 1. Encoding of the fuzzy medical diagnosis in QAlloy-F

The final diagnosis is obtained by selecting the disease(s) with maximum degree through auxiliary function **diagnosis** (ll. 9–10). It constructs by comprehension a crisp relation between each patient and the diseases diagnosed with maximum degree (function **max** returns a crisp relation with the tuples with maximum degree). Finally, we need to encode the relation R determined by the experts. As an example, consider the relation R of Table 2, which is taken from reference [9]. To keep the model flexible and allow for the exploration of alternative solutions, we encode it as a function **expert_R** (ll. 12–17). In QAlloy-F, concrete fuzzy relations are created with scalar multiplication ******. Here, we create fuzzy sets of symptoms and assign them to diseases through Cartesian product →. Symptoms with degree 0 are simply absent from the resulting relation.

Given this model, we can make use of QAlloy-F's model finding capabilities to validate the provided R. Instances can be generated with **run** commands accompanied by further restrictions. For instance, suppose we want to see scenarios where the provided R leads to two diseases being diagnosed for the same patient. The command in ll. 19–22 asks for instances where R is exactly the expert data and there is some patient diagnosed with malaria and chest prob-

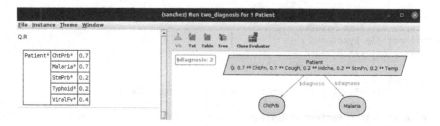

Fig. 2. Instance visualization for model in Fig. 1

lems. Q is left unrestricted so that all possible symptom valuations are explored by the finder. For now we focus on scenarios with a single patient, so we restrict the command's scope, which determines how many atoms each signature may contain. Running the command results in the instance shown in Fig. 2, after some theme customization to enhance readability. Interestingly, the patient is mostly showing signs of chest pain and coughing, which lead to 2 diagnosed diseases. The evaluator (left-hand side) can be used to further inspect the instance, whereby it will show that a patient with those symptoms is most likely afflicted by chest problems and malaria, the diseases of maximum degree 0.7. Alternative witnesses to this scenario can also be enumerated from the visualizer.

As another example, consider the command in ll. 24–27, which asks for scenarios where two patients have the same diagnosis but disjoint symptoms (notice the increased scope on patients). The command is valid, and experts would need to validate the scenarios and act accordingly.

Besides encoding scenarios as **run** commands, we can also rely on **check** commands to check whether bottom-line properties hold. For instance, the command in ll. 29–31 checks whether having chest pain among the most relevant symptoms implies chest problems among the diagnosis. QAlloy-F searches for all possible symptoms for patients and finds no counter-example, meaning that the property is always true for the provided R. Experts can encode several of these properties to be automatically checked for alternative R values. Note that we do not have to completely fix R with the expert knowledge. Say we want to check whether the property still holds for alternative relationships between chest pain and stomach problems. We could just constrain R to a subset of expert_R by writing R − ChtPn→StmPrb = expert_R − ChtPn→StmPrb, leaving the degree to which chest pain is related to stomach problems free. QAlloy-F will show that the property no longer holds by assigning it a large degree in R.

4   The QAlloy-F Analyzer

Language. The full syntax of the QAlloy-F language is presented in Fig. 3, with changes relative to standard Alloy underlined. Compared to QAlloy-I [30] for the integer domain, the **int** keyword was replaced with **fuzzy** to declare quantitative relations over the unit interval of real numbers. Much like in the integer domain,

```
spec     ::= module qualName [ [ name,⁺ ] ] import* paragraph*
import   ::= open qualName [ [ qualName,⁺ ] ] [ as name ]
paragraph ::= sigDecl | factDecl | funDecl | predDecl | asrtDecl | chckCmd
sigDecl  ::= [ fuzzy ] [ abstract ] [ mult ] sig name,⁺
                     [ sigExt ] { fuzzyDecl,* } [ block ]
sigExt   ::= extends qualName | in qualName [ + qualName ]*
mult     ::= lone | some | one
decl     ::= [ disj ] name,⁺ : [ disj ] expr
fuzzyDecl ::= [ fuzzy ] decl
factDecl ::= fact [ name ] block
asrtDecl ::= assert [ name ] block
funDecl  ::= fun name [ [ decl,* ] ] : expr { expr }
predDecl ::= pred name [ [ decl,* ] ] block
expr     ::= const | qualName | @name | this | unOp expr | expr binOp expr
           | expr arrowOp expr | expr [ ! | not ] compareOp expr
           | expr ( => | implies ) expr else expr | quant decl,⁺ blockOrBar
           | expr [ expr,* ] | ( expr ) | block | { decl,⁺ blockOrBar }
const    ::= none | univ | iden
unOp     ::= ! | not | no | mult | set | ~ | * | ^ | #
           | drop | real ** | real–cut
binOp    ::= || | or | && | and | <=> | iff | => | implies
           | & | + | − | ++ | <: | :> | .
           | add | sub | mul | div | rem
arrowOp  ::= [ mult | set ] → [ mult | set ]
compareOp ::= in | = | != | < | ≤ | > | ≥
letDecl  ::= name = expr
block    ::= { expr* }
blockOrBar ::= block | | expr
quant    ::= all | no | mult
chckCmd  ::= check qualName [ scope ]
scope    ::= for integer [ but typescope,⁺ ] | for typescope,⁺
typescope ::= [ exactly ] integer qualName
qualName ::= [ this/ ] ( name/ )* name
```

Fig. 3. Concrete syntax of the QAlloy-F language

numeric values (which are now real numbers belonging to $[0, 1]$) can no longer be stand-alone expressions, but must be associated with the *scalar multiplication* operator (**), relying on Alloy's rich type system to perform simple dimensional analysis. **drop** can be used to transform fuzzy relations into Boolean ones, taking every non-zero value to 1. A new operator that arises from the fuzzy domain is the α–**cut** introduced in Sect. 2, with $\alpha \in [0, 1]$. Although in the integer domain we provided two variants of the join operator that were deemed relevant, there are simply too many variants available for the fuzzy domain. Thus, we have opted to let the user select the desired t-norm (and respective t-conorm), from which the semantics of the join operator is derived.

Similarly to QAlloy-I, the formal semantics of QAlloy-F expressions is determined by a *quantity function* that is defined inductively over relational expressions, as Fig. 4 shows for a fragment of the language. Let $\mathcal{A}$ be the universe of atoms, determined from the scope of the command at hand, and s be a *binding*, i.e., a function that for every free relation r and tuple t with appropriate arity returns its quantity $q = s(r,t)$. The quantity function of a relational expression Γ under the binding s is given by $[\![\Gamma]\!]_s$. A tuple t belongs to Γ under the binding s iff $[\![\Gamma]\!]_s(t) \neq 0$. Signatures and fields are declared as in QAlloy-I. The semantics of fuzzy relational operations are defined as presented in Sect. 2, varying according to the t-norm ($\sqcap$) and t-conorm ($\sqcup$) considered. Arithmetic operators are still supported but truncated in the range [0,1], and the scalar multiplication ($**$) now takes a real number $\alpha \in [0,1]$ instead of an integer. The semantics of QAlloy-F formulas is identical to QAlloy-I, for which the reader is redirected to [30]. It is worth noting that QAlloy-F is retro-compatible, so a model with no fuzzy relations/expressions is equivalent to a standard Alloy model.

Backend. QAlloy extends Kodkod [34] to support generic *numeric structures* to manage the numeric matrices. This was extended to handle real numbers and represent fuzzy relations, with the matrix operations being further generalized to depend on the definition of t-norms, adding support for those in Table 1. With the quantitative Kodkod problem encoded through fuzzy matrices combined through linear algebra operations, QAlloy-F makes use of SMT solvers to automatically solve the resulting formulas. This SMT problem uses *real function symbols* instead of integer ones, and takes into consideration the definition of the selected t-norm/t-conorm pair. Moreover, the SMT solvers perform verification of these problems according to the *Theory of Reals*, namely over the logic fragment QF_NRA (*Quantifier-free real arithmetic*) [4].

Alloy Analyzer. The QAlloy-F Analyzer[1] is responsible for parsing the model, encoding it into a quantitative Kodkod problem and then for interpreting back the results obtained and presenting them to the user. It has therefore been adapted in a similar way to QAlloy-I. A key difference is that in this context, the Analyzer provides to the user the various t-norms supported by selecting T-norm in the Options in the menu bar. Alternatively it can be set through a special annotation in the model, making it self-contained.

After obtaining a solution, the user may further interact with it through the Analyzer features such as the *Visualizer* and *Evaluator*, which were adapted to present the fuzzy information to the user (see Fig. 2) and allow the evaluation of fuzzy expressions, respectively.

5   Validating Fuzzy Inference Systems with QAlloy-F

Fuzzy controllers are one of the main applications of fuzzy logic and, in some scenarios, they have shown to be almost as effective as precise mathematical models, being cheaper to develop and implement [28].

---

[1] QAlloy-F is publicly available at https://github.com/pf7/QAlloy-F/.

$$[\![r]\!]_s(t) = s(r,t)$$

$$[\![x]\!]_s((a)) = s(x,(a))$$

$$[\![\texttt{univ}]\!]_s((a)) = 1$$

$$[\![\texttt{none}]\!]_s((a)) = 0$$

$$[\![\texttt{iden}]\!]_s((a,b)) = \begin{cases} 1 \text{ if } a = b \\ 0 \text{ otherwise} \end{cases}$$

$$[\![\Gamma + \Delta]\!]_s(t) = [\![\Gamma]\!]_s(t) \sqcup [\![\Delta]\!]_s(t)$$

$$[\![\Gamma \,\&\, \Delta]\!]_s(t) = [\![\Gamma]\!]_s(t) \sqcap [\![\Delta]\!]_s(t)$$

$$[\![\Gamma - \Delta]\!]_s(t) = \begin{cases} 0 & \text{if } [\![\Gamma]\!]_s(t) = 0 \\ [\![\Gamma]\!]_s(t) - \min([\![\Gamma]\!]_s(t), [\![\Delta]\!]_s(t)) & \text{otherwise} \end{cases}$$

$$[\![\texttt{add}[\Gamma,\Delta]]\!]_s(t) = min([\![\Gamma]\!]_s(t) + [\![\Delta]\!]_s(t), 1)$$

$$[\![\texttt{sub}[\Gamma,\Delta]]\!]_s(t) = max([\![\Gamma]\!]_s(t) - [\![\Delta]\!]_s(t), 0)$$

$$[\![\texttt{mul}[\Gamma,\Delta]]\!]_s(t) = [\![\Gamma]\!]_s(t) \times [\![\Delta]\!]_s(t)$$

$$[\![\texttt{div}[\Gamma,\Delta]]\!]_s(t) = min([\![\Gamma]\!]_s(t) \,/\, [\![\Delta]\!]_s(t), 1)$$

$$[\![\texttt{rem}[\Gamma,\Delta]]\!]_s(t) = [\![\Gamma]\!]_s(t) \,\%\, [\![\Delta]\!]_s(t)$$

$$[\![\alpha \mathbin{**} \Gamma]\!]_s(t) = \alpha [\![\Gamma]\!]_s(t)$$

$$[\![\Gamma . \Delta]\!]_s((a_1,...,a_{n-1},b_2,...,b_m)) = \bigsqcup_{c \in \mathcal{A}} ((([\![\Gamma]\!]_s((a_1,...,a_{n-1},c)) \sqcap [\![\Delta]\!]_s((c,b_2,...,b_m)))))$$

$$[\![\Gamma \rightarrow \Delta]\!]_s((a_1,...,a_n,b_1,...,b_m)) = [\![\Gamma]\!]_s((a_1,...,a_n)) \sqcap [\![\Delta]\!]_s((b_1,...,b_m))$$

$$[\![\sim\!\Gamma]\!]_s((a,b)) = [\![\Gamma]\!]_s((b,a))$$

$$[\![\mathord{\hat{}}\Gamma]\!]_s((a,b)) = \bigsqcup([\![\Gamma]\!]_s((a,b)), [\![\Gamma . \Gamma]\!]_s((a,b)), [\![\Gamma . \Gamma . \Gamma]\!]_s((a,b)),...)$$

$$[\![\{x_1 : \Gamma_1,...,x_n : \Gamma_n \mid \phi\}]\!]_s((a_1,...,a_n)) = \begin{cases} [\![\Gamma_1]\!]_s((a_1)) \times ... \times [\![\Gamma_n]\!]_s((a_n)) & \text{if } s' \models \phi \\ 0 & \text{otherwise} \end{cases}$$

where $s' = s \oplus (x_1,(a_1)) \mapsto [\![\Gamma_1]\!]_s((a_1)) \oplus ... \oplus (x_n,(a_n)) \mapsto [\![\Gamma_n]\!]_s((a_n))$

$$[\![\texttt{drop}\ \Gamma]\!]_s(t) = \begin{cases} 0 \text{ if } [\![\Gamma]\!]_s(t) = 0 \\ 1 \text{ otherwise} \end{cases}$$

$$[\![\alpha\texttt{-cut}\ \Gamma]\!]_s(t) = \begin{cases} 1 \text{ if } [\![\Gamma]\!]_s(t) \geq \alpha \\ 0 \text{ otherwise} \end{cases}$$

$$[\![\#\Gamma]\!]_s(t) = \begin{cases} min(\sum_{t' \in \lceil\Gamma\rceil} [\![\Gamma]\!]_s(t'), 1) & \text{if } t \in \lceil\Gamma\rceil \\ 0 & \text{otherwise} \end{cases}$$

Fig. 4. Semantics QAlloy-F relational expressions ($\mathcal{A}$ is the declared universe, n and m the arity of Γ and Δ, respectively)

Such controllers use *Fuzzy Inference Systems* (FIS) for their decision making, a process depicted in Fig. 5. The most popular FIS types are the *Mamdani* [24] and *Takagi-Sugeno-Kang* (Sugeno in short) [32], the former being better suited for humane usage, while the latter is computationally more efficient [28]. This section describes how Mamdani-type FISs can be encoded and validated in QAlloy-F; a Sugeno-type FIS is used in the evaluation in Sect. 6.

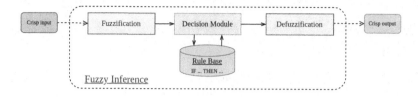

Fig. 5. Fuzzy inference process

5.1 Developing a FIS for an Automatic Heater

This section describes the development of a fuzzy controller for an automatic heater, using standard tools such as MATLAB®'s Fuzzy Logic Toolbox™.

The controller is expected to react to the temperature and the relative humidity of the environment — input variables $T \in [-20, 50]$ (°C) and $H \in [0, 1]$ (%), respectively — and in turn adjust the power level of the heater — output variable $P \in [0, 1]$, ranging from turned off (0) to providing its maximum heat (1). These crisp values can be described through vague terms in the fuzzy realm, known as *linguistic variables*, each represented by a fuzzy set — here, cold, warm and hot for temperature, dry, normal and wet for humidity, and low, mid and high for heater power. This enables reasoning over statements such as "The heater is currently emitting heat at a low power".

At the core of FISs are the so-called *fuzzy rules*. The process starts by *fuzzifying* the crisp values into fuzzy ones through the definition of membership functions. For instance, Fig. 6 shows variables T, H and P fuzzified in MATLAB® according to trapezoid, triangular, z- and s-shapes, following the defined linguistic variables. These decisions, which affect the performance of the fuzzy system [1], are commonly made by domain experts or inferred from big data.

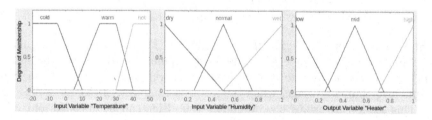

Fig. 6. Variables for the automatic heater designed in MATLAB®

The behaviour of the controller is mainly determined by the *rule base* and is also designed with expert insight. An example of a rule is the following, stating that the system must react to cold temperatures and wet air by raising the power to high levels. A rule may depend on multiple antecedents, combined through fuzzy connectives (here, ⊓).

$$\text{IF } T \text{ is } cold \text{ AND } H \text{ is } wet \text{ THEN } P \text{ is } high \qquad \text{(R1)}$$

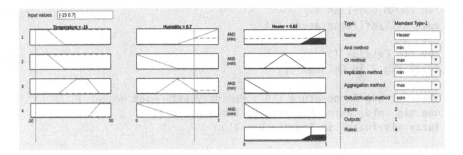

Fig. 7. Rules for the automatic heater designed in MATLAB®

The rule inference process is configured to determine the strength of each rule when triggered. This includes selecting operations for calculating the *antecedent* of each rule, an *implication* method to combine the antecedent strength with the output membership function, and an *aggregation* method to combine the output membership function of each rule into a single fuzzy set. Lastly the *defuzzification* step selects a crisp value from the calculated output fuzzy set. This process is shown in Fig. 7 for a system with 4 rules, the first being rule R1.

At this point, the user can select concrete inputs and check the resulting output ($-15°C$ and 70% in Fig. 7). The highly configurable nature of FISs should be clear by now. Note that the parameters of each step affect its behaviour and also its performance [2, 15, 16]. This motivates the need for tools such as QAlloy-F to complement existing tools for FIS design, by helping the designer validate the fuzzy system and continuously refine it through a back-and-forth between said tools and QAlloy-F, until a satisfactory fuzzy controller is achieved.

5.2 Encoding FISs in QAlloy-F

A possible encoding in QAlloy-F of the FIS just described is shown in Fig. 8. The configuration of a FIS developed in MATLAB® is stored in a .fis file. We have implemented a prototype, also provided in the QAlloy-F repository, to automatically translate them into such a QAlloy-F model.

QAlloy-F supports Boolean and fuzzy relations only, so it is not possible to directly specify real-numbered crisp values such as e.g. temperatures. We assume that such a range is normalized to the unit interval and T modelled as a fuzzy set, declared with respect to its type **Celsius** (ll. 4–5). Omitted for space-economy, variables H and P are declared analogously as fuzzy sets on **Percentage** and **Power**. The linguistic variables are also defined as signatures, and those for temperature are shown in ll. 7–8. Fuzzy subset signatures **fuzzyT** (l. 9), **fuzzyH** and **fuzzyP** are declared to represent the fuzzified variables. We encoded in a utility module **mf** some function shapes. For instance, by opening **mf** over linguistic variable **Temperature** and crisp value **T** (l. 2), function **trapezoid** returns the corresponding fuzzy input variable according to that shape, as imposed in fact **fuzzification** (ll. 11–16). Note that these shape ranges act on the $[0, 1]$

```
1 /*# TNORM Godelian #*/
2 open util/mf[Temperature, T]
3 ...
4 one sig Celsius {}
5 fuzzy sig T in Celsius {}
6
7 abstract sig Temperature { R : Humidity set → set Heater }
8 one sig cold, warm, hot extends Temperature {}
9 fuzzy sig fuzzyT in Temperature {}
10 ...
11 fact fuzzification {
12   fuzzyT =
13     linz[0.214**cold, 0.429**cold] +
14     trapezoid[0.357**warm, 0.571**warm, 0.714**warm, 0.857**warm] +
15     lins[0.714**hot, 0.857**hot]
16   ...}
17
18 fun ruleBase : Temperature → Humidity → Heater {
19   cold → wet → high +
20   cold → dry → mid +
21   warm → normal → low +
22   hot → dry → low }
23
24 fun aggregated : Heater { fuzzyH.(fuzzyT.R) }
25
26 fact defuzzification {
27   aggregated :> max[aggregated] ≤ fuzzyP :> max[aggregated]
28   no max[aggregated] implies P = 0.5 ** Power }
```

Fig. 8. Excerpt of an automatic heater based on Mamdani FIS in QAlloy-F

normalized crisp values rather than on the temperature interval $[-20, 50]$. Our translation from .fis configurations automatically performs this normalization.

Rules relate linguistic variables and are naturally represented as a Boolean ternary relation, as declared in l. 7. Function ruleBase (ll. 18–22) encodes the provided rule base, with the first entry denoting rule R1. In the decision process we consider only a subset of methods supported in MATLAB® to keep the model succinct and maintainable. In particular, we assume the antecedent and aggregation methods use the selected t-norm (set as a special annotation in l. 1). Thus, by composing the rule base with the fuzzy input variables simultaneously calculates the antecedent with ⊓, and aggregates all rules with ⊔. This is shown in function aggregated (l. 24), which returns a fuzzy set on Heater linguistic variables. The implication and defuzzification steps are encoded together in a fact given in ll. 26–28. Currently, we only support the maximum defuzzification method by selecting the maximum linguistic variable from aggregated. Then, given minimum as the implication method, the fuzzy value of P is forced to take at least said aggregated value. When no rule is triggered, the heater will default to work at mid-power (l. 28), a convention followed by MATLAB®.

5.3   FIS Validation and Verification

Given the translation above, one can write commands to simulate the FIS or check for properties. But rather than running the FIS for concrete inputs, we can ask for underspecified scenarios. For instance, the following command asks for instances where the temperature is high but the heater running on low. QAlloy-F quickly answers with an instance with very low level of humidity.

```
run highTemperature {
  ruleBase = R and P < 0.1**Power and T > 0.8**Celsius }
```

We can also test for red flags in our model, for instance: is it ever possible to have the heater run on high power with moderate/hot temperature? QAlloy-F will answer that there is no such instance.

```
check highPower {
  ruleBase = R and T > 0.5**Celsius implies P ≤ 0.5**Power }
```

Perhaps more interestingly, the user can relax the constraints to explore different designs. For instance, expert-information like membership function ranges or the rule base can be partially specified and left for QAlloy-F to explore. Let us say that we want to extend the rule base, and wish to check whether this may break the property above. We can state that R is larger than the provided ruleBase as follows:

```
check highPowerExtends {
  ruleBase in R and T > 0.5**Celsius implies P ≤ 0.5**Power }
```

QAlloy-F now reports a counter-example: if rule warm $\rightarrow$ dry $\rightarrow$ mid is added, a low level of humidity will turn the power up.

Given that scenario, we may wish to search for rules where even with low humidity, the power stays low. The following command can be used, which will suggest to use warm $\rightarrow$ dry $\rightarrow$ low instead.

```
run lowHumidityExtends {
  ruleBase in R and T = 0.5**Celsius and no H and P < 0.5**Power }
```

6   Evaluation

We explored the applicability of QAlloy-F to other fuzzy scenarios, leading to the following example models that are also used for performance evaluation:

– **Diagnosis.** The medical diagnosis example presented in Sect. 3, with the commands presented in Fig. 1.

- `Intuitionistic`. Some authors [9] have argued that the diagnosis problem addressed in Sect. 3 is better encoded in an *intuitionistic* setting, where each set A has a membership function μ_A and a *non-membership* function ν_A, related by a score function [7]. QAlloy-F is sufficiently flexible to address this encoding, including intuitionistic composition, which applies regular max-min composition to μ_A but min-max composition to ν_A. We check commands similar to the non-intuitionistic version, but, perhaps unsurprising, `maxChestPain` is now invalid: even if chest pain has maximum membership degree, when the non-membership degree outweighs it, it is unlikely that the patient is affected by chest problems.

- `Portrait`. Boolean equivalence relations can be used to partition the universe at hand. Similarly, a fuzzy equivalence relation can be transformed into a Boolean one by performing $\alpha-$**cut**s over it, with different α values yielding different clusters. This approach has been applied to determine groups of portraits based on visual similarities [33]. We model fuzzy equivalence relations in QAlloy-F, and use these to determine clusters according to desirable characteristics (**run** `threeToTwo`); as well to check that increasing the $\alpha-$**cut** results in finer-grained clusters (**check** `invProportionality`).

- `Mamdani`. The automatic heater Mamdani FIS model described in Sect. 5, with an $\sqcap$-based rule base, with the commands presented in Sect. 5.3.

- `Sugeno`. A classical FIS example[2] for determining the tip in regards to the service quality and food taste. We model it as a Sugeno FIS, and in contrast to `Mamdani`, we take a $\sqcup$-based rule base, which is not only modelled through a Boolean relation `R`, but also with a fuzzy relation `W` for the antecedent step and a fuzzy relation `Y` to model its linear/constant rule output functions, both of which are used to model the defuzzification weighted average method in the end. We use QAlloy-F to evaluate different scenarios (e.g. **run** `findGenerousTip`) or to evaluate the strength of known rules (e.g. **check** `cheapTip`) for example.

Our evaluation of QAlloy-F then aimed to answer the following questions:

RQ1 Is the analysis of QAlloy-F models feasible?
RQ2 What is the impact of choosing different t-norms?
RQ3 What is the impact of choosing different SMT solvers?

To answer these questions we measured the execution time of various commands for the examples described above, for every SMT solver currently integrated in QAlloy-F — Z3 [25] (v4.8.18), MathSAT [8] (v5.6.6), CVC4 [5] (v1.8) and Yices [11] (v2.6.4) — and for the algebraic product, Gödelian, and Łukasiewicz t-norms. All tests were run in a commodity octa-core 3.2 GHz AMD Ryzen™7 5800H with 16 GB of RAM; and QAlloy-F running with 8192 MB maximum memory and 8192k of maximum stack size, with a timeout of 10 mins. The models, the benchmark script and the full results are available in the QAlloy-F repository. Table 3 presents an excerpt of the results.

---

[2] https://www.mathworks.com/help/fuzzy/fuzzy-inference-process.html.

Concerning **RQ1**, our analysis procedures seem to be feasible even for more complex models such as `Mamdani` and `Sugeno`, with all commands solved in a few seconds for some solver and t-norm. Interestingly, there is no clear evidence that satisfiable problems perform better than unsatisfiable ones. Regarding **RQ2**, it is interesting to see that the outcome of some commands actually changes depending on the selected t-norm. In particular, the `maxChestPain` discussed in Sect. 3 is only valid under the default Gödelian. In terms of performance there is no t-norm clearly outperforming the others, and it often depends on the selected SMT solver. Nonetheless, the algebraic product seems to be the t-norm that most often leads to timeouts in all solvers. As for **RQ3**, there is also no clear SMT solver outperforming the others, but Z3 and MathSAT seem to be overall the most consistent when it comes to arriving at a result in usable times.

Table 3. Evaluation results (in ms), entry omitted if all TO, best times in bold, entries associated with "unknown" responses are crossed out

Model	Cmd	Scope	T-norm	Result	Z3	MSAT	CVC4	Yices
Diagnosis	same_diagnosis	2	Gödelian	SAT	5703	**641**	12162	TO
			Łukasiewicz	SAT	627	**160**	2697	TO
	maxChestPain	4	Gödelian	UNSAT	19765	**1097**	20170	TO
			Łukasiewicz	SAT	4463	**164**	3802	313710
			Product	SAT	**109**	TO	TO	264
Intuitionistic	same_diagnosis	2	Gödelian	SAT	16402	**11255**	20569	293413
			Łukasiewicz	SAT	17276	**198**	2448	258994
	maxChestPain	1	Gödelian	SAT	479	**423**	1503	14455
			Łukasiewicz	SAT	15306	**97**	611	8742
Portrait	threeToTwo	4	**Gödelian**	SAT	718	485	3905	**314**
			Łukasiewicz	SAT	679	488	3923	**325**
			Product	SAT	672	490	3930	**316**
	invProportionality	6	Gödelian	UNSAT	1313	**182**	61969	201
			Łukasiewicz	UNSAT	2321	**150**	2047	701
			Product	UNSAT	302	158	5302	**143**
Mamdani	highPower	NA	Gödelian	UNSAT	263	**104**	353	121
			Łukasiewicz	UNSAT	603	**61**	173	2894
			Product	UNSAT	**41**	TO	228	194
	highPowerExtends	NA	Gödelian	SAT	272	**137**	726	2877
			Łukasiewicz	SAT	5375	**43**	280	2042
			Product	SAT	TO	TO	**243**	1189
Sugeno	findGenerousTip	3	Gödelian	SAT	2771	**2202**	TO	55676
			Łukasiewicz	SAT	**430**	453	TO	TO
			Product	UNK	~~54214~~	~~290755~~	TO	TO
	cheapTip	4	Gödelian	UNSAT	**7025**	7551	TO	25303
			Łukasiewicz	UNSAT	**1863**	2009	TO	TO
			Product	UNSAT	**52852**	~~342107~~	TO	TO

7   Related Work

Previous work has relied on SMT solvers to verify formulas in fuzzy logics. Reference [3] describes how SMT solvers can be used to automatically prove formulas of infinitely-valued logics. Reference [37] generalizes this approach to more logics, in particular, continuous t-norm-based logics. Reference [36] further extends [37] to support modal fuzzy logic. The QAlloy backend interprets the fuzzy relational operators as a linear algebra over fuzzy matrices and converts them into SMT formulæ according to the selected t-norm, similarly to these approaches. (They are also considered within fragments of the theory of reals.) But unlike QAlloy, these techniques do not provide a specification language to encode fuzzy models. FLOPER [6] instead relies on fuzzy logic programming to derive all valid models of a formula. It is implemented in Prolog and supports truth degrees defined as a complete bounded lattice $\mathcal{L}$. The authors of [40] describe ongoing work to verify fuzzy logic models, introducing an approach based on symbolic execution, whose prototype also makes use of an SMT solver.

Considerable work has been done on model checking fuzzy systems, including checking branching-time temporal logics over fuzzy Kripke structures [12,23,26, 31], branching-time [20,21] and linear-time [18,19,22] temporal logics over possibilistic Kripke structures (which extend fuzzy logic by considering both a possibility and necessity degree). In [10,35] a modified version of the CMurφ model checker is proposed for the verification of fuzzy control systems, which relies on external C/C++ functions from the controller. QAlloy is currently focused on the validation of the structural part of fuzzy systems, but extending QAlloy to the temporal capabilities of Alloy 6 is planned future work, as described below.

8   Conclusions and Future Work

By the very nature of the underlying logic, fuzzy systems are challenging to design and validate. This paper proposes QAlloy-F, a specification language for fuzzy relational models, backed by automatic analysis procedures for validation and verification in the tradition of Alloy. We show that the language is sufficiently rich to encode fuzzy inference systems, and our evaluation shows the analysis procedures to be performant for models of this complexity.

There are still open issues with quantitative relational model finding that we plan to address. We expect to unify QAlloy-F and QAlloy-I to allow reasoning about integer-valued models with uncertainty. We also intend to integrate the temporal capabilities of Alloy 6 into QAlloy. The techniques implemented in standard Alloy for solution iteration are not effective in generating varied quantitative solutions, so symmetry breaking must be addressed in this context.

Acknowledgements. The work by J.N. Oliveira is financed by National Funds through the FCT - Fundação para a Ciência e a Tecnologia, I.P. (Portuguese Foundation for Science and Technology) within the project IBEX, with reference PTDC/CCI-COM/4280/2021. The work by P. Silva, subject to the PhD studentship grant with reference 2023.01186.BD, is financed by National Funds through the Portuguese funding agency, FCT - Fundação para a Ciência e a Tecnologia, within project LA/P/0063/2020. DOI 10.54499/LA/P/0063/2020.

Competing Interests. The author(s) has no competing interests to declare that are relevant to the content of this manuscript.

References

1. Adil, O., Ali, A., Sumait, B.: Comparison between the effects of different types of membership functions on fuzzy logic controller performance. Int. J. Emerging Eng. Res. Technol. **3**, 76–83 (2015)
2. Ahmad, K., Mesiarova, A.: Choosing t-norms and t-conorms for fuzzy controllers, vol. 2, pp. 641–646 (2007). https://doi.org/10.1109/FSKD.2007.216
3. Ansótegui, C., Bofill, M., Manyà, F., Villaret, M.: Building automated theorem provers for infinitely-valued logics with satisfiability modulo theory solvers. In: 2012 IEEE 42nd International Symposium on Multiple-Valued Logic, pp. 25–30 (2012). https://doi.org/10.1109/ISMVL.2012.63
4. Barrett, C., Fontaine, P., Tinelli, C.: The Satisfiability Modulo Theories Library (SMT-LIB) (2016). http://www.SMT-LIB.org
5. Barrett, C., et al.: CVC4. In: Gopalakrishnan, G., Qadeer, S. (eds.) CAV 2011. LNCS, vol. 6806, pp. 171–177. Springer, Heidelberg (2011). https://doi.org/10.1007/978-3-642-22110-1_14
6. Bofill, M., Moreno, G., Vázquez Pérez-Íñigo, C., Villaret, M.: Automatic proving of fuzzy formulae with fuzzy logic programming and SMT. In: Proceedings of XIII Spanish Conference on Programming and Languages, PROLE 2013 (2014). https://doi.org/10.14279/tuj.eceasst.64.991.974
7. Chen, T.: A comparative analysis of score functions for multiple criteria decision making in intuitionistic fuzzy settings. Inf. Sci. **181**(17), 3652–3676 (2011). https://doi.org/10.1016/J.INS.2011.04.030
8. Cimatti, A., Griggio, A., Schaafsma, B.J., Sebastiani, R.: The MathSAT5 SMT solver. In: Piterman, N., Smolka, S.A. (eds.) TACAS 2013. LNCS, vol. 7795, pp. 93–107. Springer, Heidelberg (2013). https://doi.org/10.1007/978-3-642-36742-7_7
9. De, S.K., Biswas, R., Roy, A.R.: An application of intuitionistic fuzzy sets in medical diagnosis. Fuzzy Sets Syst. **117**(2), 209–213 (2001)
10. Della Penna, G., Intrigila, B., Magazzeni, D.: Evaluating fuzzy controller robustness using model checking. In: Di Gesù, V., Pal, S.K., Petrosino, A. (eds.) WILF 2009. LNCS, pp. 303–311. Springer, Heidelberg (2009). https://doi.org/10.1007/978-3-642-02282-1_38
11. Dutertre, B.: Yices 2.2. In: Biere, A., Bloem, R. (eds.) CAV 2014. LNCS, vol. 8559, pp. 737–744. Springer, Cham (2014). https://doi.org/10.1007/978-3-319-08867-9_49
12. Ebrahimi, M., Sotudeh, G., Movaghar, A.: Symbolic checking of fuzzy CTL on fuzzy program graph. Acta Informatica **56** (2019).https://doi.org/10.1007/s00236-018-0311-3
13. Jackson, D.: Alloy: a language and tool for exploring software designs. Commun. ACM **62**(9), 66–76 (2019). https://doi.org/10.1145/3338843
14. Jang, J., Gulley.: Matlab: fuzzy logic toolbox user's guide. the math-works, inc., natick, 19-127 (1997)

15. Kiszka, J.B., Kochańska, M.E., Sliwińska, D.S.: The influence of some fuzzy implication operators on the accuracy of a fuzzy model-part i. Fuzzy Sets Syst. **15**(2), 111–128 (1985).https://doi.org/10.1016/0165-0114(85)90041-7, https://www.sciencedirect.com/science/article/pii/0165011485900417

16. Kiszka, J.B., Kochańska, M.E., Sliwińska, D.S.: The influence of some fuzzy implication operators on the accuracy of a fuzzy model-part ii. Fuzzy Sets Syst. **15**(3), 223–240 (1985).https://doi.org/10.1016/0165-0114(85)90016-8, https://www.sciencedirect.com/science/article/pii/0165011485900168

17. Kumar, S., Gangwal, C.: A study of fuzzy relation and its application in medical diagnosis. Asian Res. J. Math. 6–11 (2021).https://doi.org/10.9734/arjom/2021/v17i430289

18. Li, Y.: Quantitative model checking of linear-time properties based on generalized possibility measures. Fuzzy Sets Syst. **320**, 17–39 (2017)

19. Li, Y., Li, L.: Model checking of linear-time properties based on possibility measure. IEEE Trans. Fuzzy Syst. **21**(5), 842–854 (2013)

20. Li, Y., Li, Y., Ma, Z.: Computation tree logic model checking based on possibility measures. Fuzzy Sets Syst. **262**, 44–59 (2015)

21. Li, Y., Ma, Z.: Quantitative computation tree logic model checking based on generalized possibility measures. IEEE Trans. Fuzzy Syst. **23**(6), 2034–2047 (2015)

22. Li, Y., Wei, J.: Possibilistic fuzzy linear temporal logic and its model checking. IEEE Trans. Fuzzy Syst. **29**(7), 1899–1913 (2021). https://doi.org/10.1109/TFUZZ.2020.2988848

23. Ma, Z., Li, Z., Li, W., Gao, Y., Li, X.: Model checking fuzzy computation tree logic based on fuzzy decision processes with cost. Entropy **24**(9) (2022). https://doi.org/10.3390/e24091183, https://www.mdpi.com/1099-4300/24/9/1183

24. Mamdani, E., Assilian, S.: An experiment in linguistic synthesis with a fuzzy logic controller. Int. J. Man-Mach. Stud. **7**(1), 1–13 (1975). https://doi.org/10.1016/S0020-7373(75)80002-2, https://www.sciencedirect.com/science/article/pii/S0020737375800022

25. de Moura, L., Bjørner, N.: Z3: an efficient SMT solver. In: Ramakrishnan, C.R., Rehof, J. (eds.) TACAS 2008. LNCS, vol. 4963, pp. 337–340. Springer, Heidelberg (2008). https://doi.org/10.1007/978-3-540-78800-3_24

26. Pan, H., Li, Y., Cao, Y., Ma, Z.: Model checking fuzzy computation tree logic. Fuzzy Sets and Systems **262**, 60–77 (2015).https://doi.org/10.1016/j.fss.2014.07.008, https://www.sciencedirect.com/science/article/pii/S0165011414003157. theme: Logic and Computer Science

27. Rada-Vilela, J.: The fuzzylite libraries for fuzzy logic control (2018). https://fuzzylite.com/

28. Reznik, L.: Fuzzy controllers handbook: how to design them, how they work. Elsevier (1997)

29. Sanchez, E.: Solutions in composite fuzzy relation equations: application to medical diagnosis in brouwerian logic. In: Dubois, D., Prade, H., Yager, R.R. (eds.) Readings in Fuzzy Sets for Intelligent Systems, pp. 159–165. Morgan Kaufmann (1993). https://doi.org/10.1016/B978-1-4832-1450-4.50017-1, https://www.sciencedirect.com/science/article/pii/B9781483214504500171

30. Silva, P., Oliveira, J.N., Macedo, N., Cunha, A.: Quantitative relational modelling with QAlloy. In: Proceedings of the 30th ACM Joint European Software Engineering Conference and Symposium on the Foundations of Software Engineering, pp. 885–896. ESEC/FSE 2022, Association for Computing Machinery, New York, NY, USA (2022). https://doi.org/10.1145/3540250.3549154

31. Sotudeh, G., Movaghar, A.: Abstraction and approximation in fuzzy temporal logics and models. Formal Aspects Comput. **27**(2), 309–334 (2015)
32. Takagi, T., Sugeno, M.: Fuzzy identification of systems and its applications to modeling and control. IEEE Trans. Syst. Man, Cybern. **SMC-15**(1), 116–132 (1985). https://doi.org/10.1109/TSMC.1985.6313399
33. Tamura, S., Higuchi, S., Tanaka, K.: Pattern classification based on fuzzy relations. IEEE Trans. Syst. Man, Cybern. **SMC-1**(1), 61–66 (1971). https://doi.org/10.1109/TSMC.1971.5408605
34. Torlak, E., Jackson, D.: Kodkod: a relational model finder. In: Grumberg, O., Huth, M. (eds.) TACAS 2007. LNCS, pp. 632–647. Springer, Heidelberg (2007). https://doi.org/10.1007/978-3-540-71209-1_49
35. Tronci, E., et al.: A model checking technique for the verification of fuzzy control systems. In: International Conference on Computational Intelligence for Modelling, Control and Automation and International Conference on Intelligent Agents, Web Technologies and Internet Commerce (CIMCA-IAWTIC 2006), vol. 1, pp. 536–542 (2005). https://doi.org/10.1109/CIMCA.2005.1631319
36. Vidal, A.: MNiBLoS: a SMT-based solver for continuous t-norm based logics and some of their modal expansions. Inf. Sci. **372**, 709–730 (2016). https://doi.org/10.1016/j.ins.2016.08.072, https://www.sciencedirect.com/science/article/pii/S0020025516306491
37. Vidal, A., Bou, F., Godo, L.: An SMT-based solver for continuous t-norm based logics. In: Hüllermeier, E., Link, S., Fober, T., Seeger, B. (eds.) SUM 2012. LNCS, vol. 7520, pp. 633–640. Springer, Heidelberg (2012). https://doi.org/10.1007/978-3-642-33362-0_53
38. Winter, M.: Goguen Categories–A Categorical Approach to L-Fuzzy Relations. Trends in Logic, vol. 25. Springer, Dordrecht (2007)
39. Zadeh, L.: Fuzzy sets. Inf. Control **8**(3), 338–353 (1965). https://doi.org/10.1016/S0019-9958(65)90241-X, https://www.sciencedirect.com/science/article/pii/S001999586590241X
40. Zhao, S., Li, Z., Chen, Z., Wang, J.: Symbolic verification of fuzzy logic models, pp. 1787–1789 (2023). https://doi.org/10.1109/ASE56229.2023.00087

Transpilation of Petri-nets into B
Shallow and Deep Embeddings

Akram Idani[(⊠)] [ID]

Univ. Grenoble Alpes, CNRS, LIG, 38000 Grenoble, France
`akram.idani@univ-grenoble-alpes.fr`

Abstract. Petri-nets and their variants (Place/Transition nets, High-Level Petri Nets, etc.) are widely used in the development of safety critical-systems. Their success is related to three major aspects: a formal semantics, a graphical syntax and the availability of verification tools. In our previous work we presented a new vision for the semantic definition of Petri-nets applying a Formal Model-Driven Engineering (FMDE) built on the B method. The approach is powered by **Meeduse**, a language workbench that we developed in order to formally instrument executable Domain-Specific Languages (xDSLs) by applying a deep embedding technique and the B method. However, because of the abstract nature of the underlying formal models, our deep embedding is suitable for the validation and verification activities at the design stage but not sufficient to generate code for target platforms. This paper advances our previous work with a shallow embedding technique taking benefit of the B method tools in order to safely synthesize executable Petri-net controllers that can be embedded in target platforms.

Keywords: B Method · Petri-nets · Verification · Formal MDE

1 Introduction

Several research works [22,25,26] have been devoted to method integration, especially the integration of semi-formal methods (*e.g.* UML, BPMN) and formal methods (*e.g.* B, Z, Maude). Their main motivation is to circumvent the shortcomings of the former thanks to the contributions of the latter. In the literature the underlying mappings between formalisms are called embeddings [10,36] and they are built on two kinds of approaches: "shallow embedding" and "deep embedding". In the first approach a direct translation from a source model into a target model is done, while in the second approach the mapping leads to structures that represent data types.

In our previous work [19] we applied deep embedding and the B method [1] to formally define the semantics of executable Domain Specific Languages (DSLs) in a Model-Driven Engineering (MDE) architecture. The work led to the development of **Meeduse** [17,31], the only existing language workbench today that applies theorem proving to deal with the correctness of DSLs. The tool defines the semantic domain of a DSL using B data structures and invariants. In [16,18],

S. Bonfanti et al. (Eds.): ABZ 2024, LNCS 14759, pp. 80–98, 2024.
https://doi.org/10.1007/978-3-031-63790-2_5

we revisited the work of C. Attiogbé [4] by applying Meeduse to the Petri-net DSL and showed its usefulness in comparison with existing DSL-based approaches [14,24,30,35]. We refer the reader to [16,18] for a critical review of these works. The analysis showed that failures or unsafe behaviours may originate from several artifacts:

- The meta-model and its underlying modeling operations, because often execution semantics apply the modeling operations to update the input model.
- The model itself, because incorrect behaviours may not be exhibited from models, especially when the DSL builder applies internal choices that are not conformant to the standard semantics.
- The implementation of the execution semantics that may be distant or not conformant to the reference specification.
- The execution engine of the meta-language. For example, EMF/OCL based engines wrongly support non-determinism.

In addition to the use of the formal B method in order to reason about the correctness of Petri-nets, the advantage of our approach is its genericity. In fact, the translation of the Petri-net meta-model into B and the specification of its execution semantics are done once and for all; since in a deep embedding approach the resulting artifacts do not depend on particular models but are built on semantic concerns. Unfortunately this technique is not suitable for synthesizing an executable Petri-net controller that can be embedded in a target platform (*e.g.* C, ADA, etc.). A transpilation technique is required in order to extract an implementation from a given Petri-net model. Nonetheless, code generation approaches may be error-prone without a good support for verification especially as Petri-nets are intended to be used for the design of safety-critical systems. The question is therefore: how to establish the conformity of the Petri-net model and its underlying execution semantics with the resulting implementation of the embedded controller? This paper addresses this challenge and advances our previous work with a formally defined transpilation approach. We propose a shallow embedding technique built on PNML (the Petri-Net Markup Language) [15] and the B method tools: PROB [28] (an animator and model-checker) and AtelierB [3] (a theorem prover with code generation facilities).

Section 2 summarizes our approach and discusses its various artifacts. In Sect. 3 we show how the deep embedding approach of Meeduse is applied to PNML. Section 4 gives the principles of our transpilation approach, which complements the deep embedding with a shallow embedding technique. Section 5 gives evidence about the correctness of the transpilation outputs. In Sect. 6 we compare our work to the state of the art. Finally, Sect. 7 presents the conclusions and the perspectives of this work.

2   Overall Approach

The approach of this paper is summarized in Fig. 1. It first extends our previous work [16] by providing support for PNML, the international ISO/IEC 15909 standard for Petri-nets [15,32], and by introducing code generation facilities.

PNML is an XML language whose well-established meta-model is made available by the Petri-net community. It is recommmended that for interoperability tools either build on this meta-model (*e.g.* The ePNK [34]) or provide import/export mechanisms (*e.g.* TINA [6] or Roméo [29]). In our work we define the semantic domain of PNML by translating its meta-model (MM_{PNML}) into an equivalent formal B specification (B_{PNML}) and we propose a correct-by-design technique for code generation. Our objective is two-fold: (1) apply tools of the B method in order to formally reason about the correctness of Petri-net models, and (2) safely synthesize executable controllers that can be embedded in target platforms using programming languages.

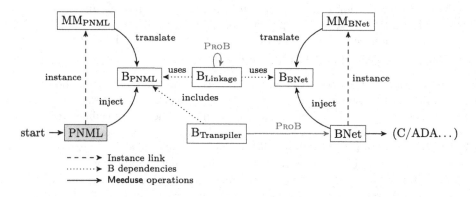

Fig. 1. Overall approach of MeeNET

The deep embedding approach favors the execution of Petri-nets at the modeling stage, which is suitable for the validation and verification activities but it is not sufficient if we would like to go towards target platforms because of the abstract nature of the underlying formal models. One way to reach this objective is to apply B refinements and incrementally produce an implementation from the abstract specifications. However, this means that every Petri-net model would have its own refinements, which is not convenient because refining the specifications is a complex and time consuming task. The proposed solution is to apply a shallow embedding built on a novel transpilation technique ($B_{Transpiler}$) that extracts concrete B specifications (called BNet) from PNML files. The concrete character of BNet models allows AtelierB to automatically produce correct implementations in languages such as C or ADA.

The advantages of our technique are: first the transpilation is itself written in B and executed by PROB, which allows us to verify its well-definedness rules while executing it; and second BNet is defined as a DSL with its own semantics, which is useful to prove the correctness of the transpilation outputs. In order to guarantee that the proposed shallow embedding preserves the semantics of the source Petri-net model we build an additional formal specification ($B_{Linkage}$) in which we define the invariants that establish a correct relationship between the semantic domain of BNet (called B_{BNet}) and that of PNML (B_{PNML}).

Note that the approach presented in this paper can be applied to other kinds of DSLs. Currently it covers the Place/Transition class of PNML (PT-nets) and High-Level Petri Nets (HLPN). For the sake of simplicity and for space reasons, we focus in the remainder on the PT-nets class.

3   Deep Embedding: A Quick Overview

We apply our deep embedding approach and Meeduse to instrument PNML in a new tool that we call MeeNET (Meeduse for Petri-nets). Figure 2 is a screen-shot of the tool while running a PNML file of the bounded-buffer producer/consumer synchronisation [8].

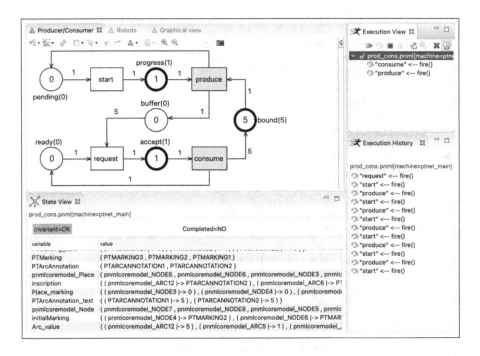

Fig. 2. Running a PNML file in MeeNET

The top-left side shows the graphical representation of the PT-Net model where two processes share a common buffer: the producer (whose states are pending and progress) and the consumer (whose states are ready and accept). In this model, sequence (*start*; *produce*)∗ increases the number of tokens in place buffer until a fixed bound is reached; and sequence (*request*; *consume*)∗ decreases this number by five. In the initial marking only places pending, ready and bound gather tokens (respectively one, one and ten tokens).

The other views of Fig. 2 are provided by Meeduse for interactive animation and debugging: (1) the execution view from which the user can select and run possible instances of the B operation for transition firing, (2) the execution history view allowing an omniscient debugging, which is useful to go backward in time, and (3) the state view giving the various valuations of the B variables in the current state. The tool also informs the user whether the invariant is preserved or not. These features are built on PROB [28], an animator and model-checker of the B method. In addition to the animation of Petri-nets, MeeNET benefits from numerous model-checking strategies such as heuristic-based and breadth/depth search, reachability analysis with LTL formulas, predicate decomposition, etc. Our deep embedding builds on a formal specification defining the semantic domain of PNML (B_{PNML}). Figures 3 and 4 give an excerpt of this specification.

```
/* Class Variables */
    core_Node, core_Arc, core_Transition, core_Place,
    /* Core Meta-Model */
    Place, Arc, PTMarking, PTArcAnnotation
    /* PT-nets Meta-Model */
```

$$/* \text{ Class inheritence } */$$
$$core\_Transition \subseteq core\_Node \land$$
$$core\_Place \subseteq core\_Node \land$$
$$Place \subseteq core\_Place \land$$
$$Arc \subseteq core\_Arc \land$$
$$core\_Transition \cap core\_Place = \emptyset$$

$$/* \text{ Associations } */$$
$$source \in core\_Arc \rightarrow core\_Node \land$$
$$target \in core\_Arc \rightarrow core\_Node \land$$
$$initialMarking \in Place \rightarrowtail PTMarking \land$$
$$inscription \in Arc \rightarrowtail PTArcAnnotation \land$$

$$/* \text{ Attributes } */$$
$$core\_Node\_id \in core\_Node \rightarrowtail STRING \land$$
$$core\_Arc\_id \in core\_Arc \rightarrowtail STRING \land$$
$$PTMarking\_text \in PTMarking \rightarrow \mathbb{N} \land$$
$$PTArcAnnotation\_text \in PTArcAnnotation \rightarrow \mathbb{N}^+ \land$$
$$Place\_marking \in Place \rightarrow \mathbb{N} \land Arc\_value \in Arc \rightarrow \mathbb{N}^+$$

Fig. 3. PT-nets static semantics

Note that the PNML meta-model identifies concepts that are common to the various classes of Petri-nets in a so-called PNML Core model, and then specific concepts of a given class are defined as specializations of PNML Core. The static semantics part is generated automatically and the dynamic semantics part is written by hand once and for all. Variables *core_ Node*, *core_ Arc*, *core_ Transition* and *core_ Place* are issued from PNML Core and variables *Place*, *Arc*, *PTMarking* and *PTArcAnnotation* are specific to the PT-nets class. The other parts of this formal specification translate the inheritance between classes by means of set inclusion, and apply specializations of relational functions to represent the associations and attributes.

```
/* Definitions */
inputs(tt) == {pp, aa | pp ∈ Place ∧ aa ∈ Arc ∧ source(aa) = pp ∧ target(aa) = tt
                        ∧ Arc_value(aa) ≤ Place_marking(pp)} ;
outputs(tt) == {pp, aa | pp ∈ Place ∧ aa ∈ Arc ∧ target(aa) = pp ∧ source(aa) = tt
                        ∧ Place_marking(pp) + Arc_value(aa) ≤ MAXINT} ;
consume(tt) == {pp, nn | pp ∈ dom(inputs(tt))
                        ∧ nn = Place_marking(pp) - Arc_value(inputs(tt)(pp))} ;
produce(tt) == {pp, nn | pp ∈ dom(outputs(tt))
                        ∧ nn = Place_marking(pp) + Arc_value(outputs(tt)(pp))}
```

```
/* Firing PT-net transitions */
tr ← fire ≙
    ANY tt WHERE tt ∈ core_Transition
        ∧ card(inputs(tt)) = card(target⁻¹[{tt}])
        ∧ card(outputs(tt)) = card(source⁻¹[{tt}])
    THEN
        Place_marking := Place_marking ◁− consume(tt) ;
        Place_marking := Place_marking ◁− produce(tt) ;
        tr := core_Node_id(tt)
    END
END
```

Fig. 4. PT-nets execution semantics

The execution semantics of PT-nets is defined with operation $tr \leftarrow$ **fire**. This operation sequentially overrides variable *Place_ marking* in order to consume and produce tokens respectively in the input and the output places of transition tt. The strength of Meeduse is its ability to inject a DSL's instance (in this case a PNML file instance of MM_{PNML}) as B data in the formal specification of its semantic domain. In Fig. 5 we provide the valuations issued from transition request and places buffer, accept and ready. This technique allows one to animate the B specification and jointly execute the model as shown in Fig. 2.

```
core_Node := {n1,n2,n3,n4} || core_Transition := {n4} || core_Place := {n1,n2,n3} ||
core_Arc := {r1,r2,r3} || Place := {n1,n2,n3} || Arc := {r1,r2,r3} ||
source := {(r1 ↦ n1),(r2 ↦ n2),(r3 ↦ n4)} ||
target := {(r1 ↦ n4),(r2 ↦ n4),(r3 ↦ n3)} ||
core_Node_id := {(n1 ↦ "buffer"),(n2 ↦ "ready"),(n3 ↦ "accept"),(n4 ↦ "request")} ||
core_Arc_id := {(r1 ↦ "a6"),(r2 ↦ "a7"),(r3 ↦ "a8")} ||
PTMarking := {pm1} || PTMarking_text := {(pm1 ↦ 1)} ||
PTArcAnnotation := {pa1} || PTArcAnnotation_text := {(pa1 ↦ 5)} ||
initialMarking := {(n2 ↦ pm1)} || inscription := {(r1 ↦ pa1)} ||
```

Fig. 5. B values injected by Meeduse from an input PNML file.

This deep embedding approach is well-mastered today with the support of Meeduse. Its application to PNML opens a broad spectrum of possibilities to our formal MDE approach, because it shows by practice how the embedding of a formal method and XML-based standards, already approved by experts of other communities, can be done and instrumented in a user-friendly language workbench. This is especially useful when the standard holds execution features. Indeed, several communities have developed XML-based standards to structure domain concepts and improve the interoperability of the growing number of computer applications that use these domain concepts. We can refer for example to RailML for railway systems, SCXML for D. Harel's state-charts, XACML for access control, etc. All these are approved DSLs with execution features that can be formally instrumented as presented in this paper for PNML.

4   Shallow Embedding

The Meeduse approach is generic and allows one to build and run a proven executable DSL, which is commonly seen as a high-level language that is expected to behave as the final application should run. However, often the target system is either encoded via a classical development process or by applying code generation techniques. In both cases, there is a need to guarantee the conformity between the target implementation and the models built at a higher-level.

Our proposal is to define a textual PT-net DSL (that we call BNet) whose concrete syntax is that of the B language, but whose semantics is a projection of the semantic domain of PT-nets. On the one hand, using the B language for the concrete syntax makes possible the application of AtelierB to generate a correct implementation; and on the other hand, the conformance of the BNet semantics to the standard definition of PT-nets makes the transformation from PNML to BNet quite straightforward. In fact, mapping the abstract syntax of PNML into the abstract syntax of the B language would be much harder because these are two different technological spaces, and also because the target B model applies a limited subset of the B language that can be isolated in a full-fledged DSL.

4.1   Concrete Syntax

Before discussing the semantics of BNet − which is left to Sect. 5 − we present in Fig. 6 our shallow embedding of the producer/consumer PT-net in a concrete formal B specification. The figure focuses on transition request and places ready, buffer and accept. This BNet model is a low-level B specification since it features concrete variables, substitution IF... THEN... END and a sequencing of simple assignments (represented with ';'). In addition to the application of the PROB model-checker in order to verify its properties (e.g. deadlock-free, etc.), this specification can be refined automatically by AtelierB into an implementation and can be further translated into any AtelierB target language (e.g. C or ADA). Regarding the execution semantics, it is ensured by the various operations of the specification. For example, when triggered, operation request verifies both the consumption and the production conditions and then updates the variable values by increasing or decreasing them.

In this specification the PT-net places are represented with natural numbers and their initial marking is set in clause INITIALISATION. The transitions are defined with B operations and the input/output arcs are embedded in the body of these operations together with their values.

```
MACHINE producer_consumer
DEFINITIONS
/* Consumption Guards */
    ready_request == ready ≥ 1
    ; buffer_request == buffer ≥ 5
/* Production Guards */
    ; request_accept == accept + 1 ≤ MAXINT
/* Actions */
    ; a6 == buffer := buffer − 5
    ; a7 == ready := ready − 1
    ; a8 == accept := accept + 1      [; ...]
CONCRETE_VARIABLES
    ready, buffer, accept [, ...]
INVARIANT
    ready ∈ NAT ∧ accept ∈ NAT ∧ buffer ∈ NAT [∧ ...]
INITIALISATION
    ready := 1 ; buffer := 0 ; accept := 0 [; ...]
OPERATIONS
request =
    IF /* Enabledness properties */
        ready_request ∧ buffer_request ∧ request_accept
    THEN /* Update actions */
        a6 ; a7 ; a8
    END      [...]
END
```

Fig. 6. Producer/Consumer PT-net written in BNet Concrete syntax.

4.2 Transpilation

To generate BNet models from PNML files, we propose a transpilation technique that is built on B and the external libraries of PROB for strings manipulation and I/O operations. Figure 7 is the B machine that defines the transpilation of the PT-net arcs into B definitions.

In this formal model we apply the *printf* predicate for the outputs. Note that this predicate is always true and that PROB prints its argument values when all of them have been fully computed. There are two main arguments: ~w for printing a value and ~n for a newline. The global idea of our transpiler is to first specify the well-definedness conditions and the iterations under which the transpilation is to be done, and then intertwit the *printf* predicate to ensure the various outputs. For example, the transpilation of PNML arcs is not defined for arcs that link two transitions $((target \vartriangleright core\_ Transition) \cap (source \vartriangleright core\_ Transition) = \emptyset)$ or two places $((target \vartriangleright Place) \cap (source \vartriangleright Place) = \emptyset)$. This well-definedness

```
MACHINE genBnetDefinitions INCLUDES B_PNML
DEFINITIONS
    ArcTarget(aa) == core_Node_id(target(aa)) ;
    ArcSource(aa) == core_Node_id(source(aa)) ;
VARIABLES definitions
INVARIANT definitions ∈ BOOL
INITIALISATION
definitions := bool(
  (target ▷ core_Transition) ∩ (source ▷ core_Transition) = ∅ ∧
  (target ▷ Place) ∩ (source ▷ Place) = ∅ ∧
  printf("~w~n",["DEFINITIONS"]) ∧
  ∀ aa.(aa ∈ Arc ⇒
    (aa ∈ dom(target ▷ core_Transition)
      ∧ printf("    ~w_~w == ~w >= ",[ArcSource(aa),ArcTarget(aa),ArcSource(aa)])
      ∧ printf("~w;~n",[Arc_value(aa)] )
      ∧ printf("    ~w == ~w := ~w - ",[core_Arc_id(aa),ArcSource(aa),ArcSource(aa)])
      ∧ printf("~w;~n",[Arc_value(aa)]) )
    ∨
    (aa ∈ dom(source ▷ core_Transition)
      ∧ printf("    ~w_~w == ~w + ",[ArcSource(aa),ArcTarget(aa),ArcTarget(aa)])
      ∧ printf("~w",[Arc_value(aa)])
      ∧ printf(" <= ~w;~n",["MAXINT"])
      ∧ printf("    ~w == ~w := ~w + ",[core_Arc_id(aa),ArcTarget(aa),ArcTarget(aa)])
      ∧ printf("~w;~n",[Arc_value(aa)]) )
  )
)
```

Fig. 7. Transpilation of PNML arcs into B definitions.

rule refers to the correctness of the input PNML file. If this condition is not respected, variable *definitions* gets value FALSE, which allows us to debug the transpilation and locate the errors. The use of the universal quantifier ($\forall$) applies iterations (similarly to a for loop in a programming language) for every arc *aa* such that $aa \in Arc$ and goes towards two directions depending on whether it is an incoming arc ($aa \in$ **dom** (*target* ▷ *core_ Transition*)) or an outgoing one ($aa \in$ **dom** (*source* ▷ *core_ Transition*)) with regards to the PT-net transitions. By animating the initialization of this B machine, PROB verifies that the well-definedness rules are correct and generates the transpilation outputs.

To our knowledge, PROB, and model-checkers in general, were not used before for the verification as well as the execution of model-to-text transformations. The proposed approach is more global than the particular case of PT-nets and shows how to confer to a formal method a central role all along the process of code generation. We have applied the same principles for the generation of the other clauses (invariants, operations, etc.). The global idea is that every target clause has a dedicated B machine with the corresponding well-definedness rules and outputs, and then the transpilation is done by asking PROB to sequentially initialize all these machines including the valued specification of the input PNML file (B_PNML). For example, the execution by PROB of B_Transpiler after including the valuations of Fig. 5, produces the model of Fig. 6.

4.3   Experiments

We have applied our technique to several PNML files from the Model-Checking Contest benchmark [2][1]. Table 1 gives the sizes of the underlying PT-nets and the transpilation results by means of execution time (in seconds) and the number of lines of the generated BNet models. These experiments have been performed on a computer equipped with a 3 GHz Intel Core i7 processor and 16 Gb of RAM.

These executions would be obviously slower than a hard-coded transpiler that applies a programming language. However, we believe that the obtained results remain reasonable, even for the large size PT-net, because the execution process includes the verification of the well-definedness rules. In fact, we do not dissociate the verification and the generation processes because our objective is to provide a transpilation approach that combines both aspects. Furthermore, in our view these results are also acceptable because, once validated, the formal specification of the transpiler can be seen as a reference model from which the implementation of the final code generator program can be done.

Table 1. Experiments.

Model	PT-Net Size			Transpilation time (s)	BNet nb of lines
	Places	Transitions	Arcs		
Producer/Consumer	6	4	12	0,15	101
Robot Manipulation	15	11	34	0,20	258
Satellite Memory	13	10	40	0,21	271
Smart Home (small)	38	113	321	2,65	2086
Smart Home (large)	741	809	1844	99,02	14463

5   Semantics and Correctness

The well-definedness rules used during the transpilation deal only with the constructs of the input file for which the transpilation is feasible. They do not guarantee that the output BNet model is correct since the transpilation is a model-to-text transformation. We need to define the semantics of the output constructs in order to be able to check their correctness.

5.1   PNML Semantics

In general, regardless of the concrete syntax used to represent PT-nets, whether it is XML-based such as in the case of PNML, or built on other representations (*e.g.* the one used by the TINA tool [6]), the semantic domain of a PT-net is a 5-tuple (P, T, A, ν, μ) where:

---

[1] Robot manip: https://mcc.lip6.fr/2024/pdf/RobotManipulation-form.pdf
Satellite memory: https://mcc.lip6.fr/2024/pdf/SatelliteMemory-form.pdf
Smart Home: https://mcc.lip6.fr/2024/pdf/SmartHome-form.pdf.

- P and T are finite sets of places and transitions,
- A a finite set of arcs composed of:
  - $A_c \subseteq (P \times T)$, denotes the input arcs,
  - $A_p \subseteq (T \times P)$, denotes the output arcs,
- $\nu \in P \to \mathbb{N}$, is a total function that denotes the initial marking of P,
- $\mu \in A \to \mathbb{N}^+$ is a weighting function.

Any correct PT-net based DSL is a projection of the above definitions. For example, the latters can be mapped to the PNML semantics as:

$$
\begin{aligned}
&P \rightsquigarrow Place \\
&T \rightsquigarrow core\_Transition \\
&A_c \rightsquigarrow Place \triangleleft source^{-1}; target \triangleright core\_Transition \\
&A_p \rightsquigarrow (Place \triangleleft target^{-1} ; source \triangleright core\_Transition)^{-1} \\
&\nu \rightsquigarrow (initialMarking ; PTMarking\_text) \cup (Place - \mathbf{dom}(initialMarking)) \times \{0\} \\
&\mu \rightsquigarrow (inscription ; PTArcAnnotation\_text) \cup (Arc - \mathbf{dom}(inscription)) \times \{1\}
\end{aligned}
$$

The projection of P and T is direct, and that of A, ν and μ relies on simple computation actions that provide the correctness of a PNML model with respect to the semantic domain on PT-nets. The projection of A means that in the PNML file an arc can only link a place (from set *Place*) and a transition (from set *core_Transition*). The projection of ν ensures a correct initial marking. As relation *initialMarking* is a partial function, then if a place is linked to a *PTMarking* via relation *initialMarking*, its value is computed with (*initialMarking*; *PTMarking_text*), otherwise it is set by default at 0 ((*Place* − **dom** (*initialMarking*)) × {0}). The same principle is applied to function μ, but the default value is 1 if the arc does not have an inscription.

5.2 BNet Semantics

In order to have a semantic reasoning for BNet, we define its abstract syntax using an Xtext [7] grammar (Fig. 8) where the various constructs are not those of the B method, but those commonly used in the Petri-nets jargon.

In this grammar, the PT-net transitions are defined by rule Transition and with two references: grds+=[Guard] and acts+=[Action]. The guards represent the enabledness properties of the transition and the actions represent the effect of the transition on its input and output places. Guards and actions are declared in clause 'DEFINITIONS' and are respectively specialised by rules Consumption/Production and Consume/Produce. A consumption guard verifies that the source place has a sufficient number of tokens (*e.g. buffer* ≥ 5) and a production guard verifies that the accumulation of tokens in the target place is possible and would not lead to an overflow (*e.g. accept* $+ 1 \leq$ MAXINT). A guard (respectively an action) has a fixed number of tokens (attribute token) and refers to a given place via reference pGrd=[Place] (respectively pAct=[Place]). The advantage of Xtext is that it generates a full infrastructure, including an ANTLR parser API with a type-checker and auto-completion facilities. Furthermore, the tool extracts from the grammar an equivalent meta-model (*i.e.* MM$_{\text{BNet}}$

```
BNetModel: 'MACHINE' name=ID
           'DEFINITIONS' defs+=(Guard | Action)*
           'CONCRETE_VARIABLES' (plcs+=Place)*
           'INVARIANT' (invs+=PlaceTyping)*
           'INITIALISATION' (inits+=InitialMarking)*
           'OPERATIONS' (ops+=Transition)*
           'END' ;
Guard: Consumption | Production ;
Consumption: name=ID '==' pGrd=[Place] '>=' token=INT (';')? ;
Production: name=ID '==' pGrd=[Place] '+' token=INT '<=' 'MAXINT' (';')? ;
Action: Consume | Produce ;
Consume: name=ID '==' pAct=[Place] ':=' pAct=[Place] '-' token=INT (';')? ;
Produce: name=ID '==' pAct=[Place] ':=' pAct=[Place] '+' token=INT (';')? ;
Place: name=ID (',')? ;
PlaceTyping: refP=[Place] ':' 'NAT' ('&')? ;
InitialMarking: initP=[Place] ':=' token=INT (';')? ;
Transition: name=ID '=' 'IF' (grds+=[Guard] ('&')?)*
                        'THEN' (acts+=[Action] (';')?)*
                        'END' (';')? ;
```

Fig. 8. Xtext grammar of BNet DSL.

in Fig. 1), which defines its static semantics. This feature is useful because as soon as a meta-model exists, Meeduse can be applied to generate the formal specification (*i.e.* B_{BNet}) and instrument the DSL in a formal framework. Figure 9 gives the typing invariant generated by Meeduse from the BNet grammar.

VARIABLES

  Place, Transition, Guard, Action,
  [...]

INVARIANT

/* Grammar rules */
  Consumption $\subseteq$ *Guard* $\land$
  Production $\subseteq$ *Guard* $\land$
  Consume $\subseteq$ *Action* $\land$
  Produce $\subseteq$ *Action* $\land$
  Consumption $\cap$ *Production* $= \emptyset$ $\land$
  Produce $\cap$ *Consume* $= \emptyset$
  [...]

/* Attributes and Relations */
  initP $\in$ *InitialMarking* $\to$ *Place* $\land$
  pGrd $\in$ *Guard* $\to$ *Place* $\land$
  grds $\in$ *Transition* $\leftrightarrow$ *Guard* $\land$
  pAct $\in$ *Action* $\to$ *Place* $\land$
  acts $\in$ *Transition* $\leftrightarrow$ *Action* $\land$
  Place_name $\in$ *Place* $\rightarrowtail$ *STRING* $\land$
  InitialMarking_token $\in$ *InitialMarking* $\to$ $\mathbb{N}$ $\land$
  Transition_name $\in$ *Transition* $\rightarrowtail$ *STRING* $\land$
  Guard_name $\in$ *Guard* $\rightarrowtail$ *STRING* $\land$
  Guard_token $\in$ *Guard* $\to$ $\mathbb{N}^+$ $\land$
  Action_name $\in$ *Action* $\rightarrowtail$ *STRING* $\land$
  Action_token $\in$ *Action* $\to$ $\mathbb{N}^+$ $\land$

Fig. 9. Semantic domain of BNet.

Attribute *name* is translated into a total injection ($\rightarrowtail$) since Xtext identifies objects with their names (name=ID); single valued and mandatory attributes (*e.g.* token=INT) give rise to total functions ($\to$); and finally, multi-valued attributes (*e.g.* grds+=[Guard]*) lead to simple relations ($\leftrightarrow$). Having this formal specification, we define the semantic domain of BNet as:

$$
\begin{array}{l}
P' \rightsquigarrow Place \\
T' \rightsquigarrow Transition \\
A'_c \rightsquigarrow (grds \triangleright Consumption \; ; pGrd)^{-1} \\
A'_p \rightsquigarrow (grds \triangleright Production \; ; pGrd) \\
\nu' \rightsquigarrow initP^{-1}; \; InitialMarking\_token \\
\mu' \rightsquigarrow ((pGrd \otimes grds^{-1})^{-1}; \; Guard\_token)
\end{array}
$$

As for PNML, Meeduse extracts B data from a BNet instance and injects them in the formal specification of the grammar. Figure 10 gives the initialization clause of the valued B specification issued from the BNet model of Fig. 6.

INITIALISATION
$Place := \{pl1,pl2,pl3\}$ || $Transition := \{tr1\}$ ||
$Place\_name := \{(pl1 \mapsto$ "buffer"$),(pl2 \mapsto$ "ready"$),(pl3 \mapsto$ "accept"$)\}$ ||
$Transition\_name := \{(tr1 \mapsto$ "request"$)\}$ ||
$Action := \{ac1,ac2,ac3\}$ || $Consume := \{ac3\}$ || $Produce := \{ac1,ac2\}$ ||
$Guard := \{gu1,gu2,gu3\}$ || $Consumption := \{gu1,gu2\}$ ||
$Production := \{gu3\}$ ||
$Action\_name := \{(ac1 \mapsto$ "a6"$),(ac2 \mapsto$ "a7"$),(ac3 \mapsto$ "a8"$)\}$ ||
$Guard\_name :=$
    $\{(gu1 \mapsto$ "buffer_request"$),(gu2 \mapsto$ "ready_request"$),$
    $(gu3 \mapsto$ "request_accept"$)\}$ ||
$Guard\_token := \{(gu1 \mapsto 5),(gu2 \mapsto 1),(gu3 \mapsto 1)\}$ ||
$Action\_token := \{(ac1 \mapsto 5),(ac2 \mapsto 1),(ac3 \mapsto 1)\}$ ||
$InitialMarking := \{in1,in2,in3\}$ ||
$InitialMarking\_token := \{(in1 \mapsto 0),(in2 \mapsto 1),(in3 \mapsto 0)\}$ ||
$acts := \{(tr1 \mapsto ac1),(tr1 \mapsto ac2),(tr1 \mapsto ac3)\}$ ||
$grds := \{(tr1 \mapsto gu1),(tr1 \mapsto gu2),(tr1 \mapsto gu3)\}$ ||
$pGrd := \{(gu1 \mapsto pl1),(gu2 \mapsto pl2),(gu3 \mapsto pl3)\}$ ||
$initP := \{(in1 \mapsto pl1),(in2 \mapsto pl2),(in3 \mapsto pl3)\}$ ||
$pAct := \{(ac1 \mapsto pl1),(ac2 \mapsto pl2),(ac3 \mapsto pl3)\}$ ||

Fig. 10. Valued B specification generated by Meeduse from a BNet model

5.3   Correctness

The correctness of BNet models that are generated from PNML files is verified with a set of invariants defining the equivalence between the semantic domains of PNML and BNet. This is done in an additional B machine, called $B_{Linkage}$ (Fig. 11) that includes machines B_{BNet} and B_{PNML}. In this machine, the semantic domains of PNML and BNet are defined as presented in the previous sub-sections by means of PT-net tuples: (P, T, A, ν, μ) and (P', T', A', ν', μ').

We introduce a mapping function $\mathcal{M}$ that maps the concepts of BNet to those of PNML using their respective identifiers. In PNML, places and transitions are identified using attribute id that is defined in a super-class named Node. This attribute is represented in B_{PNML} with relation $core\_Node\_id$. In

---

MACHINE B_{Linkage} **INCLUDES** $pnml.B_{\text{PNML}}$, $bnet.B_{\text{BNet}}$
DEFINITIONS
    [...] /* Definitions of $(P,\ T,\ A,\ \nu,\ \mu)$
    and $(P',\ T',\ A',\ \nu',\ \mu')$ */
    $\mathcal{M}_P == (bnet.Place\_name\ ;\ pnml.core\_Node\_id^{-1})$;
    $\mathcal{M}_T == (bnet.Transition\_name\ ;\ pnml.core\_Node\_id^{-1})$
    $\mathcal{M}_I(p,t) == (pnml.source \otimes pnml.target)^{-1}(\mathcal{M}_P(p) \mapsto \mathcal{M}_T(t))$;
    $\mathcal{M}_O(t,p) == (pnml.source \otimes pnml.target)^{-1}(\mathcal{M}_T(t) \mapsto \mathcal{M}_P(p))$
INVARIANT
    inv1: $pnml.core\_Node\_id[P] = bnet.Place\_name[P'] \wedge$
    inv2: $pnml.core\_Node\_id[T] = bnet.Transition\_name[T'] \wedge$
    inv3: $A'_c = \{p,\ t \mid p \in P' \wedge t \in T' \wedge (\mathcal{M}_P(p) \mapsto \mathcal{M}_T(t)) \in A_c\}$
    inv4: $A'_p = \{t,\ p \mid t \in T' \wedge p \in P' \wedge (\mathcal{M}_T(t) \mapsto \mathcal{M}_P(p)) \in A_p\}$
    inv5: $\nu' = \{p,\ v \mid p \in P' \wedge v \in \mathbb{N} \wedge (\mathcal{M}_P(p) \mapsto v) \in \nu\}$
    inv6: $\mu' = \{p,\ t,\ v \mid p \in P' \wedge t \in T' \wedge v \in \mathbb{N}^+$
                    $\wedge (((p \mapsto t) \in A'_c \wedge (\mathcal{M}_I(p,t) \mapsto v) \in \mu)$
                    $\vee ((t \mapsto p) \in A'_p \wedge (\mathcal{M}_O(t,p) \mapsto v) \in \mu))\}$

Fig. 11. Machine B_{Linkage}

BNet, places and transitions are identified by their names. Hence the composition $(bnet.Place\_name;\ pnml.core\_Node\_id^{-1})$ produces couples of places having the same identifiers. The same principle is applied to transitions. Relation $\mathcal{M}_P$ maps the BNet places to the PNML places and relation $\mathcal{M}_T$ maps the BNet transitions to the PNML transitions. For example, based on the valued B specifications of Figs. 5 and 10, relations $\mathcal{M}_P$ and $\mathcal{M}_T$ are as follows:

$$\mathcal{M}_P = \{(pl1 \mapsto n1), (pl2 \mapsto n2), (pl3 \mapsto n3)\}, \mathcal{M}_T = \{(tr1 \mapsto n4)\}$$

Regarding arcs, they do not have an explicit representation in BNet contrary to PNML where a class `Arc` is defined. We map them based on the involved places and transitions. $\mathcal{M}_I\ (p,\ t)$ takes a place p and a transition t from BNet and gives the corresponding input arc in PNML if it exists. $\mathcal{M}_O\ (t,p)$ follows the same principle but for output arcs. For example, $\mathcal{M}_I\ (pl1,\ tr1) = r1$, $\mathcal{M}_I\ (pl2,tr1) = r2$, $\mathcal{M}_O\ (tr1,\ pl3) = r3$.

In B_{Linkage}, the first two invariants (**inv1** and **inv2**) ensure that the identifiers are the same in both models, meaning that the transpilation did not miss any place and any transition and also did not create additional ones − since the identifiers are unique in both models. The four other invariants (**inv3–6**) guarantee the semantic correctness of BNet with respect to PNML. In the underlying equalities we compute the expected values, using set definitions and the mapping function $\mathcal{M}$, and then we compare them with those issued from BNet. Figure 12 gives the invariant analysis view of PROB exhibiting the left and right sides of each equality. The figure shows that all the equalities are preserved for the illustrative example of Figs. 5 and 10.

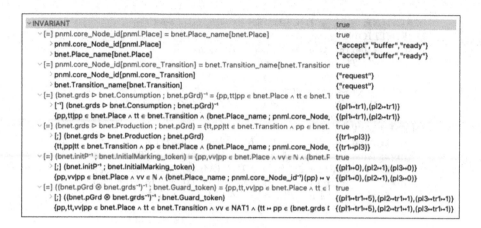

Fig. 12. Evaluation console of PROB.

We used PROB with machine $B_{Linkage}$ to verify the correctness of BNet models that are generated from the PNML files of the MCC benchmark. The PROB results are presented in Table 2.

Table 2. PROB results after checking $B_{Linkage}$.

PT-net Model	Verification time (ms)	Invariants
Producer/Consumer	131	OK
Robot Manipulation	136	OK
Satellite Memory	135	OK
Smart Home (small)	275	OK
Smart Home (large)	12568	OK

On the one hand all the extracted BNet models successfully passed the six invariants; and on the other hand the execution times of PROB during this step were acceptable. These results show that a shallow embedding approach applying a formal method for both transpilation and verification is realistic and can be explored further.

6   Related Works

Several research works have been devoted to the embedding of B specifications within Petri-nets. In [23] the authors present a mapping method of low level Petri-nets to abstract B machines and to Event B specifications. We refer also to the works of C. Attiogbé [4], that we revisited to define the execution semantics of PNML. Other kinds of Petri-nets were addressed, for example in [9], a non-hierarchical CP-net with numerical data-structures is translated into B. Meeduse itself (as illustrated in [17]) includes a translator from CP-nets to B in order to provide a readable graphical front-end for the specification of a DSL's execution semantics. This strong state of the art shows that the extraction of B specifications from Petri-nets is beneficial. However, these works (including our previous work) did not show how to synthesize a correct low level implementation of a Petri-net based controller that can be embedded in a target system. Existing works refer to B refinements as a way to produce an implementation; nonetheless, this was never shown in practice.

In our experiments we took several realistic case studies provided by the Petri-net community (Robot manipulation, Satellite memory, Smart home small and large). By applying B refinements such as advocated by existing works, every case study would lead to its own refinement, which would take several days. By applying our transpilation approach, few milliseconds were sufficient, which is in our opinion a major contribution since we do not lose sight of verification and we ensure the correctness of the resulting artifacts. Other contributions are worthreviewing. First, contrary to our approach, existing works do not favour the animation of the input Petri-net model. They propose a translation approach and then they often "get lost" in the formal process. Second, technically we execute PNML (the Petri-net standard) itself, while existing works have their own internal representation requiring additional import/export mechanisms, if one would like to make them interoperable.

To our knowledge, the execution of transpilers and/or Model-to-Text transformations was never done using formal tools (*i.e.* animators and model-checkers). They are mostly hard-coded and often verified by testing. In this paper, we execute the transpiler by animating its specification and we ensure its verification by means of B invariants that represent the semantic equivalence between the input and output source codes. Nonetheless, the idea behind the transpiler is inspired by the work of M. Leuschel about the usage of ProB for document generation [27]. The general ideas of this paper can be seen as a way to rethink Text-to-Text transformations through formal methods and tools. We could have investigated another approach: to apply a Model-to-Model transformation built on meta-models and proven B operations, and then serialize the resulting instance of the BNet meta-model in order to obtain the B textual file. In [20], we used Meeduse to address Model-to-Model transformations; the underlying application won the award of best verification at the transformation tool contest (TTC'19). This paper complements our works with a new vision for code generation techniques covering specification, verification and execution.

7   Conclusion

This paper introduced the B method within the Petri-net field thanks to MeeNET, an MDE tool where both deep and shallow embeddings are investigated. The debugging, the transpilation and the semantic verification are fully automated and supported by Meeduse and PROB. The only manual task is the design of the Petri-net instance in any convenient modeler built on PNML or able to export a PNML file. MeeNET also contributes to existing works interested by the integration of MDE and Petri-nets. Indeed, there exist a plethora of approaches [5,11,12] that extract Petri-nets from modeling languages (UML, BPMN, etc.) in order to ensure verification. Many of them apply model-driven tools (*e.g.* EMF [33], Acceleo [13], ATL [21], etc.) with the aim to generate a Petri-net representation that can be checked by external tools. MeeNET provides a unifying framework because it is itself built on an MDE architecture that can interoperate with the aforementioned tools and because it embeds PROB, it therefore includes the required verification features. Furthermore, the concrete character of BNet models makes possible the use of AtelierB in order to safely generate a Petri-net based controller that can be used in the target platform.

Beyond the particular case of PT-nets, as discussed all along this paper, the principles of our approach can be applied to other DSLs with execution features. An executable DSL allows one to simulate the behaviour of a system at a high level, using domain specific notations; but the implementation of the final system is either hand-coded or generated using transpilation or code generation techniques. In this paper we showed that a formal method and a model-checker can be central and can replace a programming language to execute transpilers.

Competing Interests. The author(s) has no competing interests to declare that are relevant to the content of this manuscript.

References

1. Abrial, J.R.: The B-Book: Assigning Programs to Meanings. Cambridge University Press, New York (1996)
2. Amparore, E., et al.: Presentation of the 9th edition of the model checking contest. In: Beyer, D., Huisman, M., Kordon, F., Steffen, B. (eds.) TACAS 2019. LNCS, vol. 11429, pp. 50–68. Springer, Cham (2019). https://doi.org/10.1007/978-3-030-17502-3_4
3. AtelierB. http://www.atelierb.eu/en/. Accessed 27 May 2021
4. Attiogbé, C.: Semantic embedding of Petri nets into Event-B. In: Integration of Model-based Formal Methods Tools, Dusseldorf, Germany (2009)
5. Bendraou, R., Combemale, B., Crégut, X., Gervais, M.P.: Definition of an eXecutable SPEM 2.0. In: 14th Asia-Pacific Software Engineering Conference (APSEC), Nagoya, Japan, pp. 390–397. IEEE CS Press (2007)
6. Berthomieu, B., Ribet, P.O., Vernadat, F.: The tool TINA - construction of abstract state spaces for Petri nets and time Petri nets. Int. J. Prod. Res. **42**(14), 2741–2756 (2004). https://doi.org/10.1080/00207540412331312688
7. Bettini, L.: Implementing Domain-Specific Languages with Xtext and Xtend, 2nd edn. Packt Publishing (2016)
8. Bobbio, A.: System modelling with Petri nets. In: Colombo, A.G., de Bustamante, A.S. (eds.) Systems Reliability Assessment, pp. 103–143. Springer, Netherlands, Dordrecht (1990). https://doi.org/10.1007/978-94-009-0649-5_6
9. Bon, P., Collart-Dutilleul, S.: From a solution model to a B model for verification of safety properties. J. Univers. Comput. Sci. **19**(1), 2–24 (2013)

10. Boulton, R.J., Gordon, A., Gordon, M.J.C., Harrison, J., Herbert, J., Tassel, J.V.: Experience with embedding hardware description languages in HOL. In: Proceedings of the IFIP TC10/WG 10.2 International Conference on Theorem Provers in Circuit Design: Theory, Practice and Experience, pp. 129–156. North-Holland Publishing Co., NLD (1992)
11. Distefano, S., Scarpa, M., Puliafito, A.: From UML to Petri nets: the PCM-based methodology. IEEE Trans. Softw. Eng. **37**(1), 65–79 (2011). https://doi.org/10.1109/TSE.2010.10
12. Dumas, M., García-Bañuelos, L.: Process mining reloaded: event structures as a unified representation of process models and event logs. In: Devillers, R., Valmari, A. (eds.) PETRI NETS 2015. LNCS, vol. 9115, pp. 33–48. Springer, Cham (2015). https://doi.org/10.1007/978-3-319-19488-2_2
13. Eclipse: Acceleo (2012). http://www.eclipse.org/acceleo/
14. Hartmann, T., Sadilek, D.A.: Undoing operational steps of domain-specific modeling languages. In: Proceedings of the 8th OOPSLA Workshop on Domain-Specific Modeling (DSM 2008) - University of Alabama at Birmingham (2008)
15. Hillah, L.M., Kordon, F., Petrucci, L., Trèves, N.: PNML framework: an extendable reference implementation of the Petri net markup language. In: Lilius, J., Penczek, W. (eds.) PETRI NETS 2010. LNCS, vol. 6128, pp. 318–327. Springer, Heidelberg (2010). https://doi.org/10.1007/978-3-642-13675-7_20
16. Idani, A.: Dependability of model-driven executable DSLs. In: Muccini, H., et al. (eds.) ECSA 2020. CCIS, vol. 1269, pp. 358–373. Springer, Cham (2020). https://doi.org/10.1007/978-3-030-59155-7_27
17. Idani, A.: Meeduse: a tool to build and run proved DSLs. In: Dongol, B., Troubitsyna, E. (eds.) IFM 2020. LNCS, vol. 12546, pp. 349–367. Springer, Cham (2020). https://doi.org/10.1007/978-3-030-63461-2_19
18. Idani, A.: Formal model-driven executable DSLs: application to Petri-nets. Int. NASA J. Innov. Syst. Softw. Eng. (ISSE) **18**(4), 543–566 (2022). https://doi.org/10.1007/s11334-021-00408-4
19. Idani, A., Ledru, Y., Vega, G.: Alliance of model driven engineering with a proof-based formal approach. Int. NASA J. Innov. Syst. Softw. Eng. (ISSE) **16**(3) (2020)
20. Idani, A., Vega, G., Leuschel, M.: Applying formal reasoning to model transformation: the Meeduse solution. In: Proceedings of the 12th Transformation Tool Contest, co-located with STAF 2019, Software Technologies: Applications and Foundations. CEUR Workshop Proceedings, vol. 2550, pp. 33–44 (2019)
21. Jouault, F., Allilaire, F., Bézivin, J., Kurtev, I., Valduriez, P.: ATL: A QVT-like transformation language. In: Companion to the 21st ACM SIGPLAN Symposium on Object-oriented Programming Systems, Languages, and Applications, OOPSLA 2006, pp. 719–720. ACM, New York (2006)
22. Kim, S.-K., David, C.: Formalizing the UML class diagram using object-Z. In: France, R., Rumpe, B. (eds.) UML 1999. LNCS, vol. 1723, pp. 83–98. Springer, Heidelberg (1999). https://doi.org/10.1007/3-540-46852-8_7
23. Korecko, S., Sobota, B.: Petri-nets to B-language transformation in software development. Acta Polytechnica Hungarica **11**, 187–206 (2014)
24. Langer, P., Mayerhofer, T., Kappel, G.: Semantic model differencing utilizing behavioral semantics specifications. In: Dingel, J., Schulte, W., Ramos, I., Abrahão, S., Insfran, E. (eds.) MODELS 2014. LNCS, vol. 8767, pp. 116–132. Springer, Cham (2014). https://doi.org/10.1007/978-3-319-11653-2_8
25. Lano, K., Clark, D., Androutsopoulos, K.: UML to B: formal verification of object-oriented models. In: Boiten, E.A., Derrick, J., Smith, G. (eds.) IFM 2004. LNCS,

vol. 2999, pp. 187–206. Springer, Heidelberg (2004). https://doi.org/10.1007/978-3-540-24756-2_11

26. Lausdahl, K., Lintrup, H.K.A., Larsen, P.G.: Connecting UML and VDM++ with open tool support. In: Cavalcanti, A., Dams, D.R. (eds.) FM 2009. LNCS, vol. 5850, pp. 563–578. Springer, Heidelberg (2009). https://doi.org/10.1007/978-3-642-05089-3_36

27. Leuschel, M.: Formal model-based constraint solving and document generation. In: Ribeiro, L., Lecomte, T. (eds.) SBMF 2016. LNCS, vol. 10090, pp. 3–20. Springer, Cham (2016). https://doi.org/10.1007/978-3-319-49815-7_1

28. Leuschel, M., Butler, M.: ProB: an automated analysis toolset for the B method. Softw. Tools Technol. Transfer (STTT) **10**(2), 185–203 (2008)

29. Lime, D., Roux, O.H., Seidner, C., Traonouez, L.-M.: Romeo: a parametric model-checker for Petri nets with stopwatches. In: Kowalewski, S., Philippou, A. (eds.) TACAS 2009. LNCS, vol. 5505, pp. 54–57. Springer, Heidelberg (2009). https://doi.org/10.1007/978-3-642-00768-2_6

30. Mayerhofer, T., Langer, P., Wimmer, M., Kappel, G.: xMOF: executable DSMLs based on fUML. In: Erwig, M., Paige, R.F., Van Wyk, E. (eds.) SLE 2013. LNCS, vol. 8225, pp. 56–75. Springer, Cham (2013). https://doi.org/10.1007/978-3-319-02654-1_4

31. Meeduse. https://vasco.imag.fr/tools/meeduse/. Accessed 19 Feb 2024

32. PNML. http://www.pnml.org. Accessed 27 May 2021

33. Steinberg, D., Budinsky, F., Paternostro, M., Merks, E.: EMF: Eclipse Modeling Framework, 2nd edn. Addison-Wesley (2008)

34. The ePNK. http://www2.compute.dtu.dk/~ekki/projects/ePNK/index.shtml. Accessed 15 Dec 2020

35. Wachsmuth, G.: Modelling the operational semantics of domain-specific modelling languages. In: Lämmel, R., Visser, J., Saraiva, J. (eds.) GTTSE 2007. LNCS, vol. 5235, pp. 506–520. Springer, Heidelberg (2008). https://doi.org/10.1007/978-3-540-88643-3_16

36. Wildmoser, M., Nipkow, T.: Certifying machine code safety: shallow versus deep embedding. In: Slind, K., Bunker, A., Gopalakrishnan, G. (eds.) TPHOLs 2004. LNCS, vol. 3223, pp. 305–320. Springer, Heidelberg (2004). https://doi.org/10.1007/978-3-540-30142-4_22

A Lean Reflective Abstract State Machine Definition

Egon Börger[ID] and Vincenzo Gervasi[(✉)][ID]

Department of Computer Science, University of Pisa, Pisa, Italy
`vincenzo.gervasi@unipi.it`

Abstract. We propose a definition of a class of reflective Abstract State Machines (ASMs) that extends the class of Parallel Guarded Assignments (PGAs), a subclass of single-agent sequential ASMs, and can serve as ground model for refinements of reflectivity in concrete programming languages.

Keywords: Reflection · Abstract State Machine · Parallel Guarded Assignment (PGA)

1 Introduction

In [5] the authors propose an axiomatisation of the intuitive concept of self-modifying (also called adaptive or reflective) sequential algorithms (RSAs) and the definition of a set of reflective sequential Abstract State Machines (ASMs). They show that the resulting two sets of algorithms respectively ASMs are computationally equivalent. This work builds upon [4] where an axiomatization of a subset of 'sequential algorithms' (in the intuitive meaning of the term) has been proposed and shown to be computationally equivalent to a set of ASMs that are misleadingly called 'sequential ASMs'; we call them Parallel Guarded Assignments (PGAs) to avoid the misunderstanding of this subclass of sequential ASMs as the class of all 'sequential ASMs' (to which in our understanding also reflective PGAs belong, among others, see the epistemological discussion in [1, Sect. 8.2]). The program executed by a PGA is (by definition, see below) a state-independent read-only description of the updates the machine performs in its execution steps; these updates include no update of the program description (and also no update of the signature), because the program does not belong to any dynamic part of the machine state.

To make a PGA reflective, besides including a representation of its program into its states one must also determine the possible updates of the signature and rules in that representation. This is done in [5] following the linguistic reflection approach (for numerous references see op.cit.) using a tree representation of programs. In particular a function *raise* is used which turns terms that are viewed as values into interpretable (read: executable) terms and an inverse function *drop* that turns terms into values. Using these two functions the computation of

© The Author(s), under exclusive license to Springer Nature Switzerland AG 2024
S. Bonfanti et al. (Eds.): ABZ 2024, LNCS 14759, pp. 99–104, 2024.
https://doi.org/10.1007/978-3-031-63790-2_6

updates of rules and signature can be specified in a detailed way, supported by a rather sophisticated tree algebra background to handle bulk tree data structures, resulting in a rather involved axiomatization of reflectivity and a corresponding definition of sequential reflective ASMs.

In this paper we propose an approach that abstracts from most of the tree manipulation details and permits a lean definition of reflective ASMs. It is inspired by the way CoreASM [3] handles the dynamic program feature and simplifies the definition of a ground model for reflective PGAs that can be instantiated to reflective programs in well-known imperative, logical, and functional programming languages. In Sect. 2 we shortly review the definition of PGAs and formulate the basic intuitive idea how to extend them by a lean concept of reflectivity. In Sect. 3 we define the class ReflectPGA of reflective PGAs. In Sect. 4 we point to three instantiations of these abstract pseudo-code programs in some well-known imperative, logical, and functional programming languages.

We assume the reader to have some basic knowledge of ASMs (see Def.14 in [1, p.32], for example).

2   Intuitive Meaning of Reflectivity

PGAs are ASMs that can be inductively defined from assignment rules (also called instructions) $f(t_1, \ldots, t_n) := t$ using guarded rules **if** *cond* **then** M and parallel rules M **par** N. The functions that appear in a PGA constitute its signature. The interest in PGAs stems from the fact that they compute a large class of sequential algorithms (in the intuitive meaning of the notion), as shown by the following theorem proved in [4]. The theorem is based upon three intuitive *Sequential Postulates* that are satisfied by a large class of algorithms: to perform computations in sequential steps that are described by a fixed transition function *step* (Sequential Step Postulate), to work on abstract states (Tarski structures with some dynamic functions) (Abstract State Postulate), and to have a computational behaviour that is determined by a finite number of variable-free terms that depend only on the algorithm and not on its runs (Bounded Exploration Postulate).

Theorem 1 (PGA Theorem [4]). *Every algorithm that satisfies the Sequential Postulates can be simulated by a PGA with the same states, the same initial states and the same step function.*

To extend PGAs (and more generally algorithms) into reflective machines (respectively algorithms) implies to add to their 'object-level' view—as description of instructions that are read and interpreted in runs as actions to execute on the computational data—a 'meta-level' view where the instructions are seen as run-time-modifiable data and thus are part of the evolving states of the machine (or algorithm). In [5] the above mentioned linguistic reflection approach is used to characterize reflective sequential algorithms (in the intuitive meaning of the notion) by an axiomatization on top of the (appropriately changed) Sequential Postulates. This includes a rather complex description in particular of two functions *raise* and *drop* mentioned above. We want to preserve the simplicity and generality of PGAs as well as their natural intuitive character by defining a reflectivity concept that turns PGAs into reflective machines. In other words we define a ground model for reflectivity in concrete programming languages. To achieve this two features have to be provided:

- **incorporate programs into the states they manipulate** in such a way that the programs can be modified by themselves,
- **define a general form of program manipulating instructions** that can easily be refined to concrete reflectivity instances.

To incorporate a program into its states it suffices to introduce the program as dynamic, i.e. as value (in every state S) of a dynamic say 0-ary abstract function pgm^S so that a) the step function gets parameterized to $step_{pgm^S}$ (object-level view), and b) a step of pgm^S in states S may generate updates $(pgm, rule)$ whose execution modifies pgm^S to a value $rule = pgm^{S'}$ (meta-level view), the value that will be executed by $step_{pgm^{S'}}(S')$ in the successor state S' (if there is one).

The form of instructions for program manipulation depends on the structure of the considered programs. For example, in the functional language LISP every expression can be part of a program and therefore subject to updates of expressions. In an imperative language, say programs of the Random Access Machine with reflection, the numerically encoded (read: Gödelized) constituents of instructions are stored in number registers that are subject to updates by the current program. In the logic programming language Prolog instructions are logical clauses that can be inserted and deleted by the current program.

The constituting elements of PGA programs are of three kinds: the above mentioned ASM rules (read: instructions), expressions (also called formulae used as guards of conditional rules), and terms (that occur in guards). All of them are candidates for a general form of updates of program elements that can be refined to update schemes for programs of concrete programming languages. Technically this is supported by adding update instructions (also called partial updates) to assignment instructions so that the location pgm can be updated by a set of simultaneous updates of pgm constituents.

Last but not least some mechanism is needed to handle a dynamic signature in cases where a program update introduces new functions, maybe together with some initialization. For this it comes natural to extend PGAs by the ASM **import** construct.

3 Definition of Reflective PGAs

Syntactically we extend PGAs by two more inductive clauses: a) for the **import** construct (to be used to express updates of the signature Σ), and b) for program update instructions (to express program changes by simultaneous updates of possibly multiple program constituents). Their semantics is the usual one (see [1]). In the following definition, for simplicity of exposition but without loss of generality we make some common notational abuse by treating a PGA sometimes as one rule and sometimes as a set of rules (that are executed simultaneously, in parallel) and by using Σ for both a 0-ary function symbol but also for its interpretation as signature.

Definition 1 (Reflective PGA). *We call an ASM M a reflective PGA if it extends a PGA by the following two features:*

- **Signature:** *The signature of M contains a 0-ary dynamic function pgm and a 0-ary dynamic signature function Σ. The initial program (in every initial state S of M) is $pgm^S = M$. In every state S of a run the executed step is a step of the current program pgm^S; it computes the successor state $S' = step_{pgm^S}(S)$ (if there is one).*
- **Rules:** *Besides its PGA rules, M uses program update instructions and the* **import** *construct (added to the inductive definition of PGA rules).*

In a successor state S' of S the program $pgm^{S'}$ that is executed in state S' can be different from pgm^S due to updates of pgm^S as part of the $step_{pgm^S}(S)$. As explained in the preceding section, the structure of PGA rules suggests various forms of pgm update instructions. We specify one simple replacement scheme that is easily refined to express partial updates to change, insert, or delete rules, expressions, terms, etc. This simple definition of pgm update instructions abstracts from the complex technical details in [5] that are involved in the definition of pgm updates if programs (whether represented by texts or by parse trees) are treated as terms to which the basic term evaluation procedure is applied. For separation of concerns our abstraction pushes the aggregation of partial pgm updates to the background in a refinable way; e.g. in CoreASM it can be implemented by a language plugin.

Rule Replacement. We want to express by a generic rule that a particular occurrence of a PGA *rule* in a given PGA *program* should be replaced by some PGA *rule'*, say by an update instruction of the following form:

$$\text{REPLACERULE } rule_i \textbf{ by } rule' \textbf{ in } program$$

with the effect to generate a partial update

$$(program, (rule_i, rule', program), replaceRule)$$

To make this technically precise it suffices to label all occurrences of the to-be-replaced *rule* in the *program*, say by $rule_1, \ldots, rule_n$. In practice, macro names—a language construct that is commonly used to group semantically significant parts of a program—can be used as labels in most cases.

Rule deletion and insertion are simple instances of rule replacement; insertion of a *rule* makes sense only in case *rule* becomes a **par** companion of some rule occurrence in the given *program*.

$$\text{DELETERULE } rule_i \textbf{ from } program = $$
$$\quad \text{REPLACERULE } rule_i \textbf{ by } \textbf{ skip } \textbf{ in } program$$

INSERTRULE $rule'$ **at** $rule_i$ **into** $program$ =
    REPLACERULE $rule_i$ **by** **par** $(rule_i, rule')$ **in** $program$

The same scheme can be applied to formula (also called expressions and used as guards) and term update instructions:

- REPLACEFORMULA $cond_i$ **by** $cond'$ **in** $program$ is defined to generate the partial update triple $(program, (cond_i, cond', program), replaceFormula)$.
- REPLACETERM t_i **by** t' **in** $program$ is defined to generate the partial update triple $(program, (t_i, t', program), replaceTerm)$.

Here, again, the issue of identifying formulas and terms to be replaced can be tackled through explicit labeling, or by providing background functions for navigating the constituent elements of a program.

In conclusion we can define as universal Program Update Instructions of reflective PGAs the REPLACERULE with its instances INSERTRULE, DELETERULE and the corresponding formula/term update instructions REPLACEFORMULA, and REPLACETERM.

4 Instantiations of Reflective PGAs

We shortly relate reflective PGAs by appropriate ASM refinements to reflectivity in some well-known programming languages. For detailed ASM models of the involved language interpreters see [1, Ch.4].

As characteristic example for a logic programming language consider PROLOG. Reflectivity is present via adding or deleting clauses to or from the current program, a list of logic clauses that is denoted as db (data base). This is a simple data refinement of the pgm and the INSERTRULE and DELETERULE in reflective PGAs. No partial updates are needed because in each step a PROLOG program can perform only one—a regular—update of db. The **import** rule is used to introduce new predicates P to form db clauses; technically this refinement consists in a declaration of P as *Dynamic*.

A similar but slighty more involved refinement does work for reflection in imperative languages. Consider as example Random Access Machine (RAM) programs. Here an encoded form (a Gödelization) of the instructions of the current program is allocated to a part pgm of memory whose locations can be changed in a run like any other memory location. So the REPLACERULEs are refined in accordance with the structure of instructions to replace or add entire instructions or only some of their parameters. Every **import** of a new element is refined by a *heap* extension.

In a functional language like LISP there is no separately defined pgm memory; every syntactically correct list expression exp represents a program the LISP interpreter can execute (by evaluating it), but as list expression exp can also be updated (e.g. by evaluating **setcar** and **setcdr** terms applied to the list). Expressions are atoms or constructs made up by two functions *head* and *tail* which permit to define any desired data structures. Since list expressions can be modified only using *head* and/or *tail*, these two functions represent a global reflective *pgm*. The updates of *pgm* in reflective PGAs are refined by the meta-level operations on list expressions *exp*, those that update (or inspect) the *head* and/or the *tail* of *exp* in state S, resulting in a successor state S' with a new *exp'* that can be executed in the next step.

5   Concluding Remarks

The two definitions of reflective sequential ASMs (in [5] and here) describe an equivalent ASM-step behaviour (the traditional updates and an update of *pgm*) so that the two notions are computationally equivalent. We see the definition in [5] as a possible ASM refinement of the 'simpler' definition described above; the latter is more abstract than the former but at the same time can serve as specification of an implementation, e.g. by a CoreASM plugin [2].

It may be worth to investigate what happens if one applies the reflectivity extension of PGAs (or the reflectivity axioms in [5]) to concurrent programs or to ASMs with unbounded choice or parallelism.

Competing Interests. The author(s) has no competing interests to declare that are relevant to the content of this manuscript.

References

1. Börger, E., Gervasi, V.: Structures of Computing. A Guide to Practice-Oriented Theory. Springer, Cham (2024). https://doi.org/10.1007/978-3-031-54358-6
2. The CoreASM Project (2005). http://www.coreasm.org. https://github.com/CoreASM/coreasm.core/wiki/Documentation
3. Farahbod, R., Gervasi, V., Glässer, U.: CoreASM: an extensible ASM execution engine. Fundamenta Informaticae XXI **77**(1-2), 71–103 (2007). http://dl.acm.org/citation.cfm?id=1365972.1365976
4. Gurevich, Y.: Sequential abstract state machines capture sequential algorithms. ACM Trans. Comput. Logic **1**(1), 77–111 (2000)
5. Schewe, K.D., Ferrarotti, F.: Behavioural theory of reflective algorithms I: reflective sequential algorithms. Sci. Comput. Program. **223** (2022)

Loose Observation in Event-B

Stefan Hallerstede[(✉)]

Aarhus University, Aarhus, Denmark
sha@ece.au.dk

Abstract. Refinement of Event-B machines is based on changing internal variables to obtain different data representations. One approach is expressed only in terms of internal variables. In the extreme case it permits refining a machine by another by choosing the gluing invariant "true". The other one is based on relating external variables that can be refined functionally, so that properties expressed in terms of external variables are preserved. In practice, the first approach is used and gluing invariants are suitably chosen to achieve a meaningful relationship between refined machines. The second approach is based on the idea of observing a machine in terms of its external variables. It is more complicated, restrictive and not commonly used.

In this paper we propose a different approach to observing Event-B machines that is more constraining than the first approach but less complicated and restrictive than the second approach. We extend Event-B refinement by permitting introducing new events and eliminating old events. The concept of observation is made more flexible by permitting non-observation of certain states as well as observing sets of values related to a states. Although this complicates relating observed fixed points and traces of machines, the proof obligations remain uncomplicated.

1 Introduction

Event-B [1] refinement permits to relate machines by simulations called glueing invariants. Typically, it is used to show that specifications have specific implementations the details of which are introduced step by step. This approach permits to master complex details by addressing a smaller number of simpler details at each step. It can also be applied if one is not interested in implementing but in alternative specification. To maintain the abstraction provided by the specification one also shows that the specification refines the alternative specification, so that the two are equivalent. This equivalence is judged in terms of observable behaviour that only considers properties of "interesting" states.

The behaviour of formal models is usually defined in terms of certain elements of it that are considered observable, for instance, certain variables, functions, procedures, or channels. In Event-B *external variables* are used in this way: the states S of a machine M are observed by means of a projection f to an *external set* E,

$$f \in S \to E \ .$$

If M is refined by a machine N with states T, projection g and external set F, the abstract states S is linked to the concrete states T by a relation r and the set E to the set F by a total function h,

© The Author(s), under exclusive license to Springer Nature Switzerland AG 2024
S. Bonfanti et al. (Eds.): ABZ 2024, LNCS 14759, pp. 105–122, 2024.
https://doi.org/10.1007/978-3-031-63790-2_7

$$S \xrightarrow{\ f\ } E$$
$$r \uparrow \qquad \uparrow h$$
$$T \xrightarrow[\ g\ ]{} F$$

Formally this diagram corresponds to the set inclusion

$$r^{-1} \,;\, g \subseteq f \,;\, h^{-1} \,, \tag{1}$$

stating that modulo the projections f and g the relation r describes a total function h on the external sets. Letting f and g equal id, the inclusion (1) simply becomes $r \subseteq h$ making r a function.

The approach just outlined is limiting in two ways. Firstly, the projections onto external variables fix some variables that take on a special role in a machine; secondly, the refinement between external variables must be functional. In this paper we consider a less strict approach to observation, roughly, allowing f, g and h to be relations. The resulting loose observations permit to choose which states to observe, that is, not every state is necessarily projected, and the relationship between different observations does not need to be functional. It matches well with the Event-B method, including observation into the properties to be specified. In addition, the associated proof obligations are simple and in line with the existing proof obligations.

To prove refinement of machine M by machine N and the reverse we require forward and backward simulation. Although backward simulation is discussed in [1], it is not included in the refinement method. Whereas the Event-B approach permits introducing new events, it does not permit removing them. We use forward and backward simulation extended in this way and discuss related state reachability and trace semantics mapped to external sets as described above. The Rodin tool supports a very specific view of refinement described in detail in [1,14]. This view is not sufficient for our present purposes, thus all formalisations and proofs have been carried out in Isabelle/HOL [16]. We use Event-B notation in the presentation of the material but deviate from the syntax in [1] because it does not support the more general approach taken in this paper, in particular, mixing forward and backward simulation. We introduce the necessary notation keeping as close as possible to the known Event-B notation.

2   Event-B

This section discusses briefly proof obligations and behavioural semantics of Event-B machines. We note down lemmas without proof that are relevant for dealing with loose observation in the ensuing section.

2.1   Some Mathematical Notation

We make use of some set-theoretical notation used in Event-B and notation for sequences borrowed from the Z notation [20]. In addition to commonly used symbols of set theory, Event-B makes use of some less common ones: The relational image $r[s]$ of a set s under a relation r is defined by $\{y \mid \exists x \cdot x \mapsto y \in r\}$. Domain restriction $s \lhd r$ of a relation r by a set s is defined by $\{x \mapsto y \mid x \in s \land x \mapsto y \in r\}$, range restriction by $r \rhd s$ by $(s \lhd r^{-1})^{-1}$. Relational composition $r_1 ; r_2$ is defined by means of composition $r_1 \circ r_1$. The set theory is typed, so that the complement $\bar{s}$ of a set s yields all x of the corresponding type that are not in s. In the same way all concepts are polymorphic and do not refer to a universe of all values. The set of sequence values composed of elements from a set s is denoted by $\text{seq}(s)$, the empty sequence by $\langle \rangle$, and the sequence consisting of n elements x_1 to x_n in that order by $\langle x_1, \dots, x_n \rangle$. Sequence concatenation of two sequences t_1 and t_2 is denoted by $t_1 \frown t_2$.

2.2   Machines and Events

An Event-B machine M consists of an initialisation mi that describes possible initial states of the machine, and a collection of events $ev_1, \dots, ev_n$ that describes possible state transitions of the machine. If S is the set of all states of machine M, then $mi \subseteq S$ and $ev_k \subseteq S \times S$ for all $k \in 1 .. n$.

The definitions in this section conflate collections of events $ev_1, \dots, ev_n$ into one event $ev = ev_1 \cup \dots \cup ev_n$. Separating into events $ev_1, \dots, ev_n$ in the definitions is not difficult using the laws

$$(x \cup y) ; z = (x ; z) \cup (y ; z) , \qquad x ; (y \cup z) = (x ; y) \cup (x ; z) ,$$
$$x \cup y \subseteq z \Leftrightarrow x \subseteq z \land y \subseteq z , \qquad x \subseteq y \land z \subseteq x \Rightarrow z \subseteq y .$$

Making use of transitivity makes the definitions stronger, so that the separated versions are not equivalent to the stated definitions. This may affect completeness in some situations but not soundness with respect to behavioural semantics as discussed below.

2.3   Consistency Proof Obligations

Let mi be the initialisation and ev the events of a machine M. Set i is called an *invariant* of M if $mi \subseteq i$ and $ev[i] \subseteq i$. It is called a *reverse invariant* if $ev^{-1}[i] \subseteq i$. It is called *bidirectional* if it is an invariant and a reverse invariant.

2.4   Simulation Proof Obligations

Let mia be the initialisation and eva the events of a machine M, and mic the initialisation and evc events of a machine N. Using machines M and N we define two simulations that permit addition of new events and removal of old events. A *guide* g and a *measure* w are used to steer an abstract machine into states where a simulation can be continued. This can be imagined like a while-loop of the shape

> while $\bar{g}$ do
>   perform abstract event that corresponds to concrete stuttering
>   decreasing the measure w
> end
> assertion g holds
> abstract event can simulate concrete event

If the guide g is $\overline{\varnothing}$, the definition of forward simulation corresponds to that of "plain" Event-B. Note, that g occurs in conditions (FW2) and (BW2) below. This permits to record the "result" of a series of abstract stuttering steps when the simulation is continued. We state the abstract invariants i and concrete invariants j to clarify their use as assumptions and because they have to satisfy different conditions in forward and backward simulation.

Definition 1 (Forward Simulation). M *forward simulates* N, $M \approx N$, *if*

$$mic \cap j \subseteq r^{-1}[mia] \tag{FW1}$$

$$(g \lhd i \lhd r^{-1} \rhd j) \; ; \; evc \subseteq (eva \cup \mathrm{id}) \; ; \; r^{-1} \tag{FW2}$$

$$\overline{g} \lhd i \lhd r^{-1} \rhd j \subseteq eva \; ; \; r^{-1} \tag{FW3}$$

$$\overline{g} \lhd i \lhd eva \subseteq w^{-1} \tag{FW4}$$

for some invariants i of M, j of N, a gluing invariant r, a guide g, and a well-founded relation w.   □

Definition 2 (Backward Simulation). M *backward simulates* N, $M \approx N$, *if*

$$i \cap r[mic \cap j] \subseteq mia \tag{BW1}$$

$$evc \; ; \; (j \lhd r \rhd i \rhd g) \subseteq r \; ; \; (eva \cup \mathrm{id}) \tag{BW2}$$

$$j \lhd r \rhd i \rhd \overline{g} \subseteq r \; ; \; eva \tag{BW3}$$

$$eva \rhd i \rhd \overline{g} \subseteq w \tag{BW4}$$

$$j \subseteq r^{-1}[i] \tag{BW5}$$

for a reverse invariant i of M, a bidirectional invariant j of N, a gluing invariant r, a guide g, and w a well-founded relation.   □

For either simulation we refer to M as the *abstract* and to N as the *concrete* machine. If M simulates N forward or backward, we write $M \sim N$. Furthermore, we write $M \approx N$ if $M \sim N$ and $N \sim M$. Invariants are accumulated by successive simulations. This is a key to structuring refinement proofs along a series of simulations in Event-B. The extended simulations stated above feature this property. Of course, it is trivially satisfied by backward simulation because of (BW5).

Lemma 1. *If M and N satisfy* (FW1) – (FW4) *or* (BW5), , i *and j are invariants and r, g and w as above, then $j \cap r^{-1}[i]$ is an invariant of N.*   □

In proofs i and j fulfil the role of typing invariants that constrain the states of abstract and concrete machines, and r describes the simulation between the machines.

2.5   Behaviour

Let mi be the initialisation and ev the events of a machine M. We define the states reachable by M by the image of mi under the reflexive transitive closure ev^* of ev,

$$\mathcal{R}(M) = ev^*[mi] \; .$$

Simulation permits to relate the reachable states of abstract and concrete machine by inclusion.

Lemma 2. *Let r be a gluing invariant from N to M. Then $\mathcal{R}(N) \subseteq r^{-1}[\mathcal{R}(M)]$ for either simulation.*   □

Using the invariance properties of i and j we can extend Lemma 2.

Lemma 3. *Let r be a gluing invariant from N to M, i and j as in Definition 1 resp. 2. Then $\mathcal{R}(N) \subseteq (i \lhd r^{-1} \rhd j)[\mathcal{R}(M)]$ for either simulation.*   □

An alternative way to characterise the behaviour of a machine uses state traces that record state transitions described by its operations step by step. The traces of machine a M are the smallest set $\mathcal{T}(M)$ satisfying (TR1)–(TR4).

$$\langle\rangle \in \mathcal{T}(M) \tag{TR1}$$

$$x \in mi \;\Rightarrow\; \langle x \rangle \in \mathcal{T}(M) \tag{TR2}$$

$$t^\frown\langle x \rangle \in \mathcal{T}(M) \wedge x \mapsto y \in ev \;\Rightarrow\; t^\frown\langle x\rangle^\frown\langle y\rangle \in \mathcal{T}(M) \tag{TR3}$$

$$t^\frown\langle x \rangle \in \mathcal{T}(M) \;\Rightarrow\; t^\frown\langle x\rangle^\frown\langle x\rangle \in \mathcal{T}(M) \tag{TR4}$$

The empty trace $\langle\rangle$ is included in the set $\mathcal{T}(M)$ so that $\mathcal{T}(M)$ is non-empty and down-closed: $t^\frown\langle x \rangle \in \mathcal{T}(M)$ implies $t \in \mathcal{T}(M)$ for all t. The first element of a non-empty trace is an initial states, and any trace can be extended either by appending a successor state specified by an event, replicating the last state, that is, by stuttering.

The last state of a state trace is a reachable state. This establishes a simple relationship between state traces and reachable states of M.

Lemma 4. $\mathcal{R}(M) = \{x \mid \exists t \cdot t^\frown\langle x \rangle \in \mathcal{T}(M)\}$.   □

In order to lift an invariant i to a relation on traces we define the relation $\mathcal{I}$ such that $t \mapsto i \in \mathcal{I}$ if $\forall k \cdot 0 \leq k \wedge k < \#t \Rightarrow t(k) \in i$. Similarly, we lift a gluing invariant r to a relation on traces by defining the relation $\mathcal{G}_r$, where $u \mapsto t \in \mathcal{G}_r$ if

$$\#t = \#u \wedge (\forall k \cdot 0 \leq k \wedge k < \#t \Rightarrow t(k) \mapsto u(k) \in r) \ .$$

For $n \geq 0$, let $x \circledast n$ be the sequence $\langle x, \ldots, x \rangle$ repeating x exactly n times. Define the *finite stuttering closure* to be the smallest set that satisfies (CL1) and (CL2).

$$\langle\rangle \mapsto \langle\rangle \in \mathcal{C} \tag{CL1}$$

$$u \mapsto t \in \mathcal{C} \wedge n \geq 1 \;\Rightarrow\; (x \circledast n)^\frown u \mapsto (x \circledast 1)^\frown t \in \mathcal{C} \tag{CL2}$$

The finite stuttering closure $\mathcal{C}$ is a reflexive transitive relation: $\mathrm{id} \subseteq \mathcal{C}$ and $\mathcal{C} \,;\, \mathcal{C} \subseteq \mathcal{C}$. If $u \mapsto t \in \mathcal{C}$, we can say that u corresponds to trace t with stuttering added, or that t corresponds to trace u with stuttering removed. We require both views.

Below we list some properties of the stuttering closure that we need in Sect. 3. The finite stuttering closure of the traces of a machine does not add any new traces. This is the consequence of (TR4) in the definition of $\mathcal{T}$.

Lemma 5. $\mathcal{C}^{-1}[\mathcal{T}(M)] \subseteq \mathcal{T}(M)$.   □

If finite stuttering is added to a lifted invariant, this results in a corresponding lifted invariant that includes the stuttering.

Lemma 6. $\mathcal{C} \, ; \mathcal{I} \subseteq \mathcal{I}$. $\square$

If machine N refines machine M, then any trace of N with possibly some finite stuttering removed can be mapped by the lifted gluing invariant to a trace of M. Without removal of events stuttering could be ignored in this relationship.

Lemma 7. *Let r be a gluing invariant from N to M. Then $\mathcal{T}(N) \subseteq (\mathcal{C} \circ \mathcal{G}_r)[\mathcal{T}(M)]$ for either simulation.* $\square$

We reformulate this statement in a form that we need later on.

Lemma 8. *Let r be a gluing invariant from N to M. Then, for all traces $t \in \mathcal{T}(N)$ there are traces $u \in \mathcal{C}^{-1}[\{t\}]$ and $s \in \mathcal{T}(M)$ such that $s \mapsto u \in \mathcal{G}_r$ for either simulation.* $\square$

2.6   Event and Invariant Notation

We summarise briefly the Event-B notation used in this paper. We list the variables of a machine informally interspersed with explanations of their purpose. Events are stated in the form

$$\text{any } x \text{ where } c(x, v) \text{ then } v :| \; p(x, v, v') \text{ end} \; ,$$

denoting the relation $\{v \mapsto v' \mid \exists x \cdot c(x, v) \wedge p(x, v, v')\}$, where v and v' are the variables of the machine and x variables bound locally to the event. The predicate $c(x, v)$ is called the *guard* of the event and $v :| \; p(x, v, v')$ its *action*. Events must be *feasible*, that is, $c(x, v) \Rightarrow \exists v' \cdot p(x, v, v')$. Actions can also be written $v :\in e(x, v)$ for $v :| \; v' \in e(x, v)$, and $v := e(x, v)$ for $v :| \; v' = e(x, v)$. The notation for events without bound variables x is when $c(v)$ then $v :| \; p(v, v')$ end, without guards it is begin $v :| \; p(v, v')$ end. The initialisation of machine is denoted by initialisation. Invariants are preceded by the keyword invariant, by invariant(bid) if the invariant is bidirectional, and by invariant(sim) if it is a gluing invariant.

3   Loose Observation

There are many ways to observe the behaviour of a machine. One can observe possible final states of a sequence of event occurrences as least or greatest fixed point [17], relationally or mapped to predicate transformers; a projection of the states according to a set of external variables [3]; the order of occurrence events as event traces in terms of the names of the events with or without parameters [8, 10, 18]; the latter possibly extended with failures and divergences or infinite traces [19]. Each kind of observation provides a basis for a semantics of a machine with a collection of proof obligations tailored to suit that semantics [13]. In the presentation below we focus on least relational fixed points, that is the *reachable states*, and finite state traces for which the collection of proof obligations discussed in Subsect. 2.4 is sufficient.

Instead of observing the states directly or projections thereof, we map reachable states to sets of observations. This permits "looseness" in observation. We may ignore some states, observe other states faithfully and yet others imprecisely. This is related to the intent of retrenchment [6] but it avoids the non-monotonicity in the reasoning.

3.1 Observation

Let mi be the initialisation and ev the events of a machine M with states S, and let E be an external set. An *observation* m is a relation from S to E,

$$m \in S \leftrightarrow E \ .$$

What is being observed and how is considered part of the specification captured by a machine. A state x is not observed if $m[\{x\}] = \varnothing$, it is observed loosely if $m[\{x\}]$ contains more than one element. Relation m corresponds to an additional event of a machine that takes states to observed values. One could also say, states are probed and measurements of interest recorded in an appropriate form. We consider observation not as given directly in terms of declared variables but as a concept explicitly specified.

Reachable States. Instead of observing the reachable states of M directly, we observe the image of $\mathcal{R}(M)$ under m, as expressed by the set $m[\mathcal{R}(M)]$.

State Traces. A state trace is a sequence of states. The corresponding observation is a sequence of matching observations (c.f. interval analysis [9]). In order to deal with non-observed states we consider a totalised variant $\widehat{m}$ of observation m, where

$$\widehat{m} \;=\; \overline{\mathrm{dom}(m)} \times \{\varnothing\} \cup \{x \mapsto y \mid y \neq \varnothing \land y \subseteq m[\{x\}]\} \ .$$

Using the totalised observation $\widehat{m}$ we define *trace observation* $\mathcal{O}_m$ that maps a trace t to a possibly observed value v,

$$t \mapsto v \in \mathcal{O}_m \;\Leftrightarrow\; \#v = \#t \ \land \ (\forall k \cdot 0 \le k \land k < \#t \ \Rightarrow \ v(k) \in \widehat{m}[t(k)]) \ .$$

We note, that any observation that we can make for some trace t can be extended to any trace in the finite stuttering closure of t.

Lemma 9. *If $u \in \mathcal{C}^{-1}[\{t\}]$ and $t \mapsto v \in \mathcal{O}_m$, then there is a $w \in \mathcal{C}^{-1}[\{v\}]$ such that $u \mapsto w \in \mathcal{O}_m$.* $\qquad\square$

3.2 Machine Refinement

We consider refinement with respect to reachable states followed by that of state traces.

Reachable States. Refinement in the presence of observation is based on the following simple fact: if the reachable states of N and M are related by a relation h, then we only need to have $h \, ; n \subseteq m$, for the relationship to carry over to the observations.

Lemma 10. *If $\mathcal{R}(N) \subseteq h[\mathcal{R}(M)]$ and $h \, ; n \subseteq m$, then $n[\mathcal{R}(N)] \subseteq m[\mathcal{R}(M)]$.* $\qquad\square$

Using the concepts of Sect. 2.4 we say observation m *simulates* observation n if

$$(i \lhd r^{-1} \rhd j) \, ; n \subseteq m \ . \tag{OR1}$$

Condition (OR1) can be attached to forward or backward simulation in order to achieve the effect described by Lemma 10, as stated in Theorem 1.

Theorem 1. *If $M \sim N$ and* (OR1) *holds with invariants and gluing invariant as stated in Definitions 1 and 2, then $n[\mathcal{R}(N)] \subseteq m[\mathcal{R}(M)]$.*

Proof.

$$n[\mathcal{R}(N)]$$
$$\subseteq n[(i \lhd r^{-1} \rhd j)[\mathcal{R}(M)]] \qquad \{ \text{ Lemma 3 } \}$$
$$\subseteq ((i \lhd r^{-1} \rhd j) \,;\, n)[\mathcal{R}(M)] \qquad \{ \text{ set theory } \}$$
$$\subseteq m[\mathcal{R}(M)] \qquad\qquad \{(OR1)\} \qquad\qquad \square$$

State Traces. Compared to the approach to reachable states we also need to take care of states that have no observation. This is achieved by condition (OR2) that ensure that for each abstract observation there is a corresponding concrete observation.

$$(i \lhd r^{-1} \rhd j)[\mathrm{dom}(m)] \subseteq \mathrm{dom}(n) \qquad\qquad\qquad (OR2)$$

Inclusion of this condition yields the result corresponding to Theorem 1 for trace semantics.

Theorem 2. *If $M \sim N$ and* (OR1) *and* (OR2) *hold with invariants and gluing invariant as stated in Definitions 1 and 2, then $\mathcal{O}_n[\mathcal{T}(N)] \subseteq (\mathcal{C} \circ \mathcal{O}_m)[\mathcal{T}(M)]$.*

Proof. Let $v \in \mathcal{O}_n[\mathcal{T}(N)]$. Then, there is a $t \in \mathcal{T}(N)$ such that $t \mapsto v \in \mathcal{O}_n$. Hence by Lemma 8, there are traces $u \in \mathcal{C}^{-1}[\{t\}]$ and $s \in \mathcal{T}(M)$ such that $s \mapsto u \in \mathcal{G}_r$. We have $s \mapsto i \in \mathcal{I}$ for the invariant i of M because $s \in \mathcal{T}(M)$. Also, $u \mapsto j \in \mathcal{I}$ for the invariant j of N because $t \mapsto u \in \mathcal{C}^{-1}$ and $t \in \mathcal{T}(N)$ by Lemmas 5 and 6. Hence, $s \mapsto u \in \mathcal{G}_{j \lhd r \rhd i}$ conjoining j and i at each index. From $u \in \mathcal{C}^{-1}[\{t\}]$ and $t \mapsto v \in \mathcal{O}_n$ it follows by Lemma 9 that there is a $w \in \mathcal{C}^{-1}[\{v\}]$ such that $u \mapsto w \in \mathcal{O}_n$. We have $\#w = \#s$ because $s \mapsto u \in \mathcal{G}_r$ and $u \mapsto w \in \mathcal{O}_n$. Furthermore, proceeding index by index we have $\forall k \cdot 0 \leq k \wedge k < \#s \Rightarrow w(k) \in \widehat{m}[s(k)]$; for indices k where $m[u(k)] \neq \varnothing$ using (OR1), and for $m[u(k)] = \varnothing$ using (OR2). Thus, $s \mapsto w \in \mathcal{O}_m$ and finally, $v \in (\mathcal{C} \circ \mathcal{O}_m)[\mathcal{T}(M)]$, since $w \mapsto v \in \mathcal{C}$. $\qquad\square$

The closure $\mathcal{C}$ appearing in Theorem 2 is transitive which implies that machine refinement with respect to traces is transitive.

Theorem 3. *If $M_1 \sim M_2$ and $M_2 \sim M_3$ with observations m_1, m_2 and m_3 then $\mathcal{O}_{m_1}[\mathcal{T}(M_1)] \subseteq (\mathcal{C} \circ \mathcal{O}_{m_3})[\mathcal{T}(M_3)]$.* $\qquad\square$

3.3   Observation Replacement

Observations m and n in a refinement can be replaced by new observations p and q that map states to different external sets. Dealing with (OR1) this can be achieved by means of two relations a and b as described in Theorem 4. We use the full gluing invariant $i \lhd r^{-1} \rhd j$ in this and the following subsection to make it easier to match the statements to those of Subsect. 2.4.

Theorem 4. *If* $(i \lhd r^{-1} \rhd j) ; n \subseteq m$ *and*

$$q ; b \subseteq n , \quad m \subseteq p ; a^{-1} , \quad \mathrm{id} \subseteq b ; a^{-1} , \text{ and } \quad a^{-1} ; a \subseteq \mathrm{id},$$

then $(i \lhd r^{-1} \rhd j) ; q \subseteq p.$

Proof. We have

$$\begin{aligned}
&(i \lhd r^{-1} \rhd j) ; n \subseteq m \\
\Rightarrow \ &(i \lhd r^{-1} \rhd j) ; (q ; b) \subseteq (p ; a^{-1}) &&\{ q ; b \subseteq n \text{ and } m \subseteq p ; a^{-1} \} \\
\Rightarrow \ &(i \lhd r^{-1} \rhd j) ; (q ; b) ; a \subseteq (p ; a^{-1}) ; a &&\{ \text{";" left monotonous } \} \\
\Rightarrow \ &(i \lhd r^{-1} \rhd j) ; q ; (b ; a) \subseteq p ; (a^{-1} ; a) &&\{ \text{";" associative } \} \\
\Rightarrow \ &(i \lhd r^{-1} \rhd j) ; q \subseteq p &&\{ \mathrm{id} \subseteq b ; a^{-1} \text{ and } a^{-1} ; a \subseteq \mathrm{id} \} \ \square
\end{aligned}$$

Alternatively, and simpler, this can be done by means of a partial surjection a as stated by Corollary 1. It is just a special case of Theorem 4 with $b = a^{-1}$.

Corollary 1. *If* $(i \lhd r^{-1} \rhd j) ; n \subseteq m$ *and*

$$q ; a^{-1} \subseteq n , \quad m \subseteq p ; a^{-1} , \text{ and } a \text{ is a partial surjection,}$$

then $(i \lhd r^{-1} \rhd j) ; q \subseteq p.$ □

The preservation of condition (OR2) requires that the domains of the observations are related suitably as expressed by Theorem 5.

Theorem 5. *If* $(i \lhd r^{-1} \rhd j)[\mathrm{dom}(m)] \subseteq \mathrm{dom}(n)$ *and*

$$\mathrm{dom}(n) \subseteq \mathrm{dom}(q) \quad \text{and} \quad \mathrm{dom}(p) \subseteq \mathrm{dom}(m) ,$$

then $(i \lhd r^{-1} \rhd j)[\mathrm{dom}(p)] \subseteq \mathrm{dom}(q).$ □

3.4 Observation Refinement

If a concrete observation n can be decomposed into an observation q and an "adapter" c such that $n \subseteq q ; c$, then, instead of n the "finer" observation q can be used to prove (OR1). Theorem 6 describes the introduction of the refined observation q, and Theorem 8 the refinement of refined observations.

Theorem 6. *If* $(i \lhd r^{-1} \rhd j) ; q ; c \subseteq m$ *and* $n \subseteq q ; c,$
then $(i \lhd r^{-1} \rhd j) ; n \subseteq m.$ □

The condition (OR2) for introducing and refining refined observations is handled by Theorems 7 and 9. The conditions in both theorems can be simplified if c is required to be total. Then c can be dropped from the premises, for the price of the one addition, that c be total.

Theorem 7. *If* $(i \lhd r^{-1} \rhd j)[\mathrm{dom}(m)] \subseteq \mathrm{dom}(q\ ;\ c)$ *and* $\mathrm{dom}(q\ ;\ c) \subseteq \mathrm{dom}(n)$, *then* $(i \lhd r^{-1} \rhd j)[\mathrm{dom}(m)] \subseteq \mathrm{dom}(n)$. □

Refinement of refined observations is straightforward. It is just necessary to remember the "adapter" in the conclusion.

Theorem 8. *If* $(i \lhd r^{-1} \rhd j)\ ;\ q \subseteq p$, *then* $(i \lhd r^{-1} \rhd j)\ ;\ q\ ;\ c \subseteq p\ ;\ c$. □

The refinement conditions for (OR2) becomes as simple as the one in Theorem 8 if c is required to be total which only would have to be proved once. We have not considered this in the more general theorems here as the modification is trivial.

Theorem 9. *If* $(i \lhd r^{-1} \rhd j)[\mathrm{dom}(p)] \subseteq \mathrm{dom}(q)$ *and* $\mathrm{ran}(q) \subseteq \mathrm{dom}(c)$, *then* $(i \lhd r^{-1} \rhd j)[\mathrm{dom}(p\ ;\ c)] \subseteq \mathrm{dom}(q\ ;\ c)$. □

The statement and refinement of observations is largely orthogonal to machine refinement. So, most of the time one can think of one or the other. Occasionally, properties of the invariants are needed to prove results about observations. But the different kinds of proofs are not strongly intertwined. This has the practical advantage that one can construct more complex proofs without considering all constraints at all times.

3.5 Observation Notation

Because an observation is just a relation with some variables o where it is recorded, we declare the variable together with a corresponding event that assigns to it,

$$\text{observe } o \text{ event } = \textit{event assigning to variables } o \ .$$

4 Context-Free Languages

As an example of using the approach to observation described in the preceding section we present a development of a machine that generates the language for a given context-free language, showing the equivalence of derivations following different rules. We begin by introducing the concepts required for the formalisation. The actual development is presented in Sect. 5. For detailed information about context-free languages and the related theoretical concepts see, e.g., [15]. Here, we focus on the modelling and discussion of observation in terms of reachable states. For the machines that we present the observations made from the relevant reachable states describe just the words that can be derived in the grammar, that is, the language generated. Symbols SYM used in the derivation are split into terminal TRM and non-terminal symbols NNT, formally, $SYM = TRM \cup NNT$ where $TRM \cap NNT = \varnothing$.

A production is a pair $h \mapsto b$ where $h \in NNT$ and $b \in \mathrm{seq}(SYM)$. We use the two functions *head* and *body* to access the components of a production, where $head(h \mapsto b) = h$ and $body(h \mapsto b) = b$. Let PRD denote the set of all productions.

A (context-free) grammar g is a quadruple $t \mapsto n \mapsto s \mapsto P$ where $t \in TRM$, $n \in NNT$, $s \in NNT$, $P \subseteq PRD$ such that the start symbol is the head of one production $\exists p \cdot p \in P \land head(p) = s$ and the start symbol does not occur in the body of any production $\forall p \cdot s \notin \text{ran}(body(p))$. Similarly to productions we define accessor functions for the different components. These are the terminal symbols trm of a grammar, $trm(t \mapsto n \mapsto s \mapsto P) = t$, the non-terminal symbols nnt of the grammar $nnt(t \mapsto n \mapsto s \mapsto P) = n$, the start symbol of the grammar $sts(t \mapsto n \mapsto s \mapsto P) = s$, and the productions of the grammar $prd(t \mapsto n \mapsto s \mapsto P) = P$.

The set of sentences $SENT(g)$ of grammar g is defined by $\{w \mid \text{ran}(w) \subseteq trm(g)\}$. A derivation step $v \mapsto w \in \sigma(g \mapsto s)$ in grammar g with derivation rule s is defined by $\exists a, h, b, c \cdot h \mapsto b \in prd(g) \wedge v = a^\frown \langle h \rangle^\frown c \wedge a \mapsto c \in s \wedge w = a^\frown b^\frown c$. using derivation steps, we define a derivation of w in n steps $n \mapsto d \in \Delta(g \mapsto s \mapsto w)$ by

$$\#d = n + 1 \wedge d(0) = sts(g) \wedge d(n) = w \wedge$$
$$(\forall k \cdot 0 \leq k \wedge k < n \Rightarrow d(n+1) \in \sigma(g \mapsto s \mapsto d(n))) \ .$$

There are three different derivation rules ao, rm and lm. Arbitrary derivations (ao) place no restrictions on the choice of the non-terminal to be replaced in a derivation step, so $a \mapsto c \in ao \Leftrightarrow \top$. A right-most derivation (rm) replaces the right-most non-terminal, $a \mapsto c \in rm \Leftrightarrow \text{ran}c \subseteq TRM$. Finally, in left-most derivation (lm) the left-most non-terminal is replaced, $a \mapsto c \in lm \Leftrightarrow \text{ran}a \subseteq TRM$.

In the following section we prove the equivalence of two specifications describing arbitrary and right-most derivations. The equivalence of the derivations is a well-known result that can be found in [15]. Concerning the equivalence with respect to generated languages some extra work is required. We use simulation proofs to establish this equivalence, mapping suitable states to the words generated. We only treat the equivalence of ao and rm. The equivalence with lm follows from the corresponding theorem in [15] but we have not carried this out as this would not provide any new insights.

5   Equivalence of Derivations

We assume that grammar g is given in some context and that the machines are parametric in the derivation rule s. This permits to instantiate the machines with specific rules ao and rm to establish the overall equivalence. The simulation proofs establish the equivalence between "direct" derivations and "trace" derivations. The "trace" derivations can be reordered to transform derivations following different rules into each other. The equivalence of the "direct" derivations follows by "self-simulation" with rule ao and rm. The proofs have been carried out in Isabelle/HOL [16] instead of Rodin [2] because Rodin imposes some restrictions that would make the development impossible. The proofs require a more general framework than is offered by Rodin including different forms of simulations and parameterised self-simulations, specifically, proving the same machine to be a refinement of itself, parameterised in two different ways.

We consider the machines and refinement steps as part of a proof of the equivalence. They are named **A**, **B**, ... The series of refinements should not be read as a sequence of development steps, but as steps that make a complex proof easier to handle.

5.1   Machine A(s)

The initial machine **A** has a single variable w of type $\text{seq}(SYM)$ that is a sentential form (consisting of any sequence of symbols) or a sentence (consisting of a sequence of terminal symbols). Any derivation starts from the start symbol $sts(g)$ of grammar g.

$$\text{initialisation} = \text{begin } w := sts(g) \text{ end}$$

Given a current sentential form w a derivation step may occur using derivation rule s.

$$\text{event } step = \text{begin } w :\in \sigma(g \mapsto s \mapsto w) \text{ end}$$

If w is a sentence, it can observed. Note that for grammars that cannot derive sentences, nothing can ever be observed. Their language is empty.

$$\text{observe } \omega \text{ event} = \text{when } w \in SENT(g) \text{ then } \omega := w \text{ end}$$

5.2 Machine B(s)

The first refinement **B** simply records the derivation that leads to w (in the abstract machine). It uses a variable $d \in \text{seq}(\text{seq}(SYM))$ to record the derivation and a variable n to count the number of steps. Variables c and x are only introduced to simplify some of the formulas in the machine and the invariants (see invariant $B2$). In summary, variables n, c and x are redundant but improve readability.

The initialisation of machine **B** puts sets up the derivation d with start symbol from where sentences may be derived and sets all other variables consistently with d.

$$\text{initialisation} = \text{begin } d, n, c, x := \langle\langle sts(g)\rangle\rangle, 0, \langle\rangle, \langle sts(g)\rangle \text{ end}$$

A step in the derivation is chosen according to the derivation rule and appended to d.

$$\text{event } step = \text{any } w \text{ where } w \in \sigma(g \mapsto s \mapsto x) \text{ then}$$
$$d, n, c, x := d^\frown\langle w\rangle, n + 1, d, w$$
$$\text{end}$$

If the last element x of d is a sentence then x is observed in that state.

$$\text{observe } \omega \text{ event} = \text{when } x \in SENT(g) \text{ then } \omega := x \text{ end}$$

The proof is supported by the following invariant. To use it in a subsequent refinement proof, we also show that it is bidirectional.

$$\text{invariant(bid)} \quad @B1 \quad \#d = n + 1$$
$$@B2 \quad d = c^\frown\langle x\rangle$$
$$@B3 \quad n \mapsto d \in \Delta(g \mapsto s \mapsto x)$$

Using ($B1$) and ($B2$) we can show that $d(n) = x$, and from ($B3$) it follows that $sts(g) \mapsto x \in \sigma(g \mapsto s)^n$. The latter property permits to prove properties about derivations in terms of relational iterates. Finally, the gluing invariant is straightforward. It just singles out the last element of the derivation d.

$$\text{invariant(sim)} \quad @B4 \quad w = x$$

Both refinement directions are by forward simulation.

Lemma 11. $\mathbf{A}(s) \approx \mathbf{B}(s)$ *and* $\mathbf{B}(s) \approx \mathbf{A}(s)$.   □

The simplicity of the observation refinement in either direction reflects that of the gluing invariant.

Lemma 12. $w = x \wedge x \in SENT(g) \wedge \omega = x \Rightarrow w \in SENT(g) \wedge \omega = w$.   □

Lemma 13. $w = x \wedge w \in SENT(g) \wedge \omega = w \Rightarrow x \in SENT(g) \wedge \omega = x$.   □

5.3 Machine C(s)

The second refinement chooses some sentential form u that can be derived in N steps and then constructs a derivation leading to that sentential form. This is an intermediate step towards choosing the entire derivation to be followed during initialisation. Variables d, n, c, and x are the same as in machine **B**. Variables $N \in \mathbb{N}$ and $u \in \text{seq}(SYM)$ as just described are introduced new.

Initially, N and u are chosen non-deterministically, so that machine **C** can produce any possible derivation. Note, that u does not need to be a sentence.

$$
\begin{aligned}
&\text{initialisation} = \text{begin} \\
&\quad d, n, c, x := \langle\langle sts(g)\rangle\rangle, 0, \langle\rangle, \langle sts(g)\rangle \\
&\quad N, u :| \; sts(g) \mapsto u' \in \sigma(g \mapsto s)^{N'} \\
&\text{end}
\end{aligned}
$$

Derivation steps in machine **C** are chosen to lead towards u. The initialisation of u guarantees that it is possible in N steps, so that at any point in time $N - n$ remain towards u.

$$
\begin{aligned}
&\text{event } step = \text{any } w \text{ where} \\
&\quad w \in \sigma(g \mapsto s \mapsto x) \wedge n < N \wedge x \mapsto u \in \sigma(g \mapsto s)^{N-n} \\
&\text{then} \\
&\quad d, n, c, x := d^\frown\langle w\rangle, n + 1, d, w \\
&\text{end}
\end{aligned}
$$

The observation is unchanged from machine **B** while progress in the derivation towards u is recorded by the bidirectional invariant for machine **C**.

$$
\begin{aligned}
&\text{invariant(bid) } @C1 \;\; n \mapsto d \in \Delta(g \mapsto s \mapsto x) \\
&\qquad\qquad\quad @C2 \;\; x \mapsto u \in \sigma(g \mapsto s)^{N-n}
\end{aligned}
$$

The gluing invariant is just the equality between identically named abstract and concrete variables. The proof that machine **B** refines **C** requires a backward simulation because **C** makes an initial choice that lies in the future when machine **B** is initialised.

Lemma 14. $\mathbf{B}(s) \approx \mathbf{C}(s)$ *and* $\mathbf{C}(s) \approx \mathbf{B}(s)$.   □

5.4   Machine D(s)

The third refinement chooses the entire derivation D of some w initially and then uses the counter n to record the current location in that derivation. Variable n is the same as in machine **C**, and variable $D \in \text{seq}(\text{seq}(SYM))$ is new.

The machine is initialised to the derivation it has to follow.

$$\begin{aligned} \text{initialisation} &= \text{begin} \\ &D :|\ \exists m, w \cdot m \mapsto D' \in \Delta(g \mapsto s \mapsto w) \\ &n := 0 \\ &\text{end} \end{aligned}$$

While the end of that derivation has not been reached n, the current position in the derivation, is increased.

$$\text{event } step = \text{when } n + 1 < \#D \text{ then } n := n + 1 \text{ end}$$

Finally, $D(n)$ is observed if it is a sentence.

$$\text{observe } \omega \text{ event} = \text{when } D(n) \in SENT(g) \text{ then } \omega := D(n) \text{ end}$$

The bidirectional invariant of machine **D** states that D is a derivation of its last element and that any prefix of D until the current location is a derivation of $D(n)$.

$$\begin{aligned} \text{invariant(bid)} \ @D1 \ \ &D \neq \langle\rangle \wedge n < \#D \\ @D2 \ \ &\#D - 1 \mapsto D \in \Delta(g \mapsto s \mapsto D(\#D - 1)) \\ @D3 \ \ &\#n \mapsto 0 .. n \lhd D \in \Delta(g \mapsto s \mapsto D(n)) \end{aligned}$$

The gluing invariant states that derivation d is a prefix of derivation D that finally derives u.

$$\text{invariant(sim)} \ @D5 \ \ \#D = N + 1 \wedge d = 0 .. n \lhd D \wedge D(N) = u$$

Again, forward and backward simulation are needed for the refinement proofs.

Lemma 15. $\mathbf{C}(s) \approx \mathbf{D}(s)$ *and* $\mathbf{D}(s) \approx \mathbf{C}(s)$.   □

Using the gluing invariant both proofs of observation refinement are straightforward.

Lemma 16. $\ldots \wedge d(n) = x \wedge d = 0 .. n \lhd D \wedge D(n) \in SENT(g) \wedge \omega = D(n) \Rightarrow x \in SENT(g) \wedge \omega = x$.   □

Lemma 17. $\ldots \wedge d(n) = x \wedge d = 0 .. n \lhd D \wedge x \in SENT(g) \wedge \omega = x \Rightarrow D(n) \in SENT(g) \wedge \omega = D(n)$.   □

5.5   Machine E(s)

The fourth refinement (machine **E**) limits the considered derivations H to those that derive sentences, that is, the last element of H is a sentence. Machine **E** introduces the new variables $H \in \text{seq}(\text{seq}(SYM))$ and $m \in \mathbb{N}$.

The preceding machines **A** to **D** have feasible initialisations, that is, for each of those machines it can be proved that there is an initial state. For machine **E** this is not true. If a grammar does not have sentences, the initialisation of **E** is impossible. (The trace semantics of this machine would only contain the empty trace.) Derivations that do not lead to a sentence do not continue beyond the start symbol.

initialisation $=$ any D, k, w where
$\quad k \mapsto D \in \Delta(g \mapsto s \mapsto w) \wedge (\#D > 1 \Leftrightarrow D(\#D - 1) \in SENT(g))$
then
$\quad H, m := D, 0$
end

Derivation steps of machine **E** are similar to those of the preceding machines.

event $step =$ when $m + 1 < \#H$ then $m := m + 1$ end

Observations now are expressed in terms of the location in the derivation. There is no need to check whether at the considered index $H(\#H - 1)$ is a sentence.

observe w event $=$ when $m > 0 \wedge m = \#H - 1$ then $w := H(m)$ end

The (bidirenctional) invariant of machine **E** contains some case distinctions that permit to identify states occuring in machine **D**. For instance, after initialisation a derivation in machine **D** has length 1.

invariant(bid) @E1 $H \neq \langle\rangle \wedge m < \#H$
$\qquad$ @E2 $\#H - 1 \mapsto H \in \Delta(g \mapsto s \mapsto H(\#H - 1))$
$\qquad$ @E3 $\#m \mapsto 0 .. m \lhd H \in \Delta(g \mapsto s \mapsto H(m))$
$\qquad$ @E4 $\#H > 1 \Leftrightarrow H(\#H - 1) \in SENT(g)$
$\qquad$ @E5 $\#H \leq 1 \Leftrightarrow H = \langle\langle sts(g)\rangle\rangle \wedge m = 0$

The gluing invariant contains some boilerplate around the property $D = H \wedge m = n$ in E8 in order to deal with the possibly infeasible initialisation of machine **E**.

invariant(sim) @E6 $m \leq n$
$\qquad$ @E7 $\#H > 1 \Rightarrow D = H \wedge m = n$
$\qquad$ @E8 $\#H > 1 \Leftrightarrow D(\#D - 1) \in SENT(g)$

To prove that machine **E** refines machine **D**, transitions from machine **D** are removed.

Lemma 18. $\mathbf{D}(s) \approx \mathbf{E}(s)$. $\qquad\qquad$ □

Therefore the proof of Lemma 18 requires the additional guide

$$D(\#D - 1) \in SENT(g) \vee n + 1 \geq \#D$$

and the measure $D = D' \wedge m \leq \#D \wedge m' \leq D' \wedge \#D - m < \#D' - m'$. The associated observation refinement is easy to show.

Lemma 19. $(\#H > 1 \Leftrightarrow H(\#H - 1) \in SENT(g)) \wedge (\#H > 1 \Rightarrow D = H \wedge m = n) \wedge m > 0 \wedge m = \#H - 1 \wedge w = H(m) \Rightarrow D(n) \in SENT(g) \wedge w = D(n)$. □

The opposite refinement requires backward simulation once more.

Lemma 20. $\mathbf{E}(s) \approx \mathbf{D}(s)$.   □

The corresponding observation refinement uses the property that a sentence can only be the last element of a derivation. It cannot occur in the middle.

Lemma 21. $D3 \wedge E8 \wedge E9 \wedge D(n) \in SENT(g) \wedge \omega = D(n) \Rightarrow m > 0 \wedge m = \#H - 1 \wedge \omega = H(m)$.

Proof. $D(n) \in SENT(g)$ and $D4$ imply $n = \#D - 1$ because the derivation cannot be continued with non-terminal symbols. Hence, $D(\#D - 1) \in SENT(g)$ and by $E9$ it follows $\#H > 1$. Using $E8$, we have $D = H$ and $m = n$. Finally, $m = n = \#D - 1 = \#H - 1 > 0$ and $\omega = D(n) = H(n) = H(m)$.   □

5.6 Machines $\mathbf{E}(ao)$ and $\mathbf{E}(rm)$

Using machine $\mathbf{E}$ we can prove that $\mathbf{E}(ao) \approx \mathbf{E}(rm)$. The proof of this statement requires "self-simulation" of a machine with different parameters. Let machine $\mathbf{EA}$ be $\mathbf{E}(ao)$ with H renamed to P and machine $\mathbf{ER}$ be $\mathbf{E}(rm)$ with H renamed to Q, and similarly for their invariants, we specify the gluing invariant

$$\text{invariant(sim)} \ @F1 \ \ \#P = \#Q \wedge P(\#P - 1) = Q(\#Q - 1)$$

The proof of the two simulations is based on the idea of reordering derivations of one kind to achieve another. Such a proof can be found in [15], for instance.

Lemma 22. $\mathbf{EA} \approx \mathbf{ER}$ *and* $\mathbf{ER} \approx \mathbf{EA}$.   □

In summary, we have proved the equivalence of the two machines $\mathbf{A}(ao)$ and $\mathbf{A}(rm)$,

$$\mathbf{A}(ao) \approx \mathbf{B}(ao) \approx \mathbf{C}(ao) \approx \mathbf{D}(ao) \approx \mathbf{E}(ao)$$
$$\approx \mathbf{E}(rm) \approx \mathbf{D}(rm) \approx \mathbf{C}(rm) \approx \mathbf{B}(rm) \approx \mathbf{A}(rm) \ .$$

6 Discussion

We have presented a more flexible approach to observing behaviour of Event-B machines and shown how it may be applied by means of a development showing the equivalence of machines that describe context-free languages. The proofs dealing with observable sentences are usually straightforward and do not interfere with the simulation proofs. The possibility of not observing every state permits to focus more on the purpose of the overall model. The approach could also be useful to deal with approximations necessary to deal with continuous behaviour as in hybrid Event-B [4] or based on differential dynamic logic [7,12] where discrete implementations cannot fulfill continuous specifications exactly [5,11].

More generally, the presented model consisting of several machines considers a series of machines just a possible way to split a complex proof into smaller parts. The first machine of that model captures the essence of the derivation of sentences of context-free languages. One could also just start with some reasonable machine, giving no special significance to what is stated first. In this view, the Event-B method is notation combined with a method of reasoning, comparable to first-order logic that comes in different flavours. Taking this perspective, we liberally use forward and backward simulation to relate any two machines, specify which state and part thereof is observable, and permit to limit initialisations. The latter permits us to ignore grammars in initialisation that cannot derive any sentences.

Removing the focus from detailed observation permits to treat Event-B as a proof method and not a development method for software and systems. We believe that is provides a good foundation to explore different proof methods driven by the different purposes a model and an associated proof might have.

Competing Interests. The author(s) has no competing interests to declare that are relevant to the content of this manuscript.

References

1. Abrial, J.R.: Modeling in Event-B: System and Software Engineering. Cambridge University Press, Cambridge (2010)
2. Abrial, J.R., Butler, M., Hallerstede, S., Hoang, T.S., Mehta, F., Voisin, L.: Rodin: an open toolset for modelling and reasoning in Event-b. Int. J. Softw. Tools Technol. Transfer **12**(6), 447–466 (2010). https://doi.org/10.1007/s10009-010-0145-y
3. Back, R.J.R., von Wright, J.: Trace refinement of action systems. In: Jonsson, B., Parrow, J. (eds.) CONCUR 1994. LNCS, vol. 836, pp. 367–384. Springer, Heidelberg (1994). https://doi.org/10.1007/978-3-540-48654-1_28
4. Banach, R.: Core hybrid event-b iii: Fundamentals of a reasoning framework. Sci. Comput. Program. **231** (2024). https://doi.org/10.1016/j.scico.2023.103002, https://www.sciencedirect.com/science/article/pii/S0167642323000849
5. Bertrane, J., et al.: Static analysis and verification of aerospace software by abstract interpretation. Found. Trends® in Program. Lang. **2**(2-3), 71–190 (2015). https://doi.org/10.1561/2500000002
6. Banach, R.: UseCase-wise development: retrenchment for Event-B. In: Börger, E., Butler, M., Bowen, J.P., Boca, P. (eds.) ABZ 2008. LNCS, vol. 5238, pp. 167–180. Springer, Heidelberg (2008). https://doi.org/10.1007/978-3-540-87603-8_14
7. Dupont, G., Aït-Ameur, Y., Pantel, M., Singh, N.K.: Proof-based approach to hybrid systems development: dynamic logic and Event-B. In: Butler, M., Raschke, A., Hoang, T.S., Reichl, K. (eds.) ABZ 2018. LNCS, vol. 10817, pp. 155–170. Springer, Cham (2018). https://doi.org/10.1007/978-3-319-91271-4_11
8. Butler, M.J.: Stepwise refinement of communicating systems. Sci. Comput. Program. **27**(2), 139–173 (1996)
9. Cousot, P.: Principles of Abstract Interpretation. MIT Press, Cambridge (2021)
10. Derrick, J., Boiten, E.: More relational concurrent refinement: traces and partial relations. Electron. Notes Theoret. Comput. Sci. **214**, 255–276 (2008). https://doi.org/10.1016/j.entcs.2008.06.012
11. Rutenkolk, K.: Extending modelchecking with ProB to floating-point numbers and hybrid systems. In: Glässer, U., Creissac Campos, J., Méry, D., Palanque, P. (eds.) ABZ 2023. LNCS, vol. 14010, pp. 366–370. Springer, Cham (2023). https://doi.org/10.1007/978-3-031-33163-3_27

12. Platzer, A.: Refinements of hybrid dynamical systems logic. In: Glässer, U., Creissac Campos, J., Méry, D., Palanque, P. (eds.) ABZ 2023. LNCS, vol. 14010, pp. 3–14. Springer, Cham (2023). https://doi.org/10.1007/978-3-031-33163-3_1

13. Hallerstede, S.: On the purpose of Event-B proof obligations. Formal Aspects Comput. **23**(1), 133–150 (2011). https://doi.org/10.1007/s00165-009-0138-3

14. Hoang, T.S.: An introduction to the event-b modelling method. In: Romanovsky, A., Thomas, M. (eds.) Industrial Deployment of System Engineering Methods. Appendix A. Springer, Cham (2013). https://doi.org/10.1007/978-3-642-33170-1

15. Hopcroft, J.E., Motwani, R., Ullman, J.D.: Introduction to Automata Theory, Languages, and Computation, 2nd edn. Addison-Wesley, Boston (2003)

16. Nipkow, Tobias, Wenzel, Markus, Paulson, Lawrence C.. (eds.): 5. the rules of the game. In: Isabelle/HOL. LNCS, vol. 2283, pp. 67–104. Springer, Heidelberg (2002). https://doi.org/10.1007/3-540-45949-9_5

17. Roever, W., Engelhardt, K.: Data refinement: model-oriented proof methods and their comparison. Cambridge Tracts in Theoretical Computer Science, vol. 47, Cambridge University Press, Cambridge (1998)

18. Schneider, S., Treharne, H., Wehrheim, H.: Bounded retransmission in event-B‖CSP: a case study. Electron. Notes Theoret. Comput. Sci. **280**, 69–80 (2011). https://doi.org/10.1016/j.entcs.2011.11.019

19. Schneider, S.A., Treharne, H., Wehrheim, H.: A CSP Account of Event-B Refinement. In: Refine@FM (2011)

20. Spivey, J.M.: The Z Notation: A Reference Manual. Prentice Hall International Series in Computer Science, 2nd edn. (1992)

Modal Extensions of the Logic
of Abstract State Machines

Flavio Ferrarotti[1]([⊠])[ID] and Klaus-Dieter Schewe[2][ID]

[1] Software Competence Centre Hagenberg, Hagenberg, Austria
`flavio.ferrarotti@scch.at`
[2] Linz, Austria
`kd.schewe@liwest.at`

Abstract. Based on the logic of non-deterministic Abstract State Machines (ASMs) we define a modal extension $\mathcal{ML}_{\text{ASM}}$ by first introducing multi-step predicates and then adding quantification over the number of steps. We show that liveness conditions such as invariance, conditional and unconditional progress, and persistence on all or some runs of an ASM can be expressed in this logic. We show the existence of a complete fragment of $\mathcal{ML}_{\text{ASM}}$, which still contains the interesting liveness conditions, and demonstrate the usefulness of this complete fragment by an example concerning mutual exclusion.

Keywords: Abstract State Machines · temporal logic · liveness conditions · completeness · verification · mutual exclusion

1 Introduction

Abstract State Machines (ASMs), originally introduced by Gurevich [12], are a well-known state-based rigorous method emphasising states as Tarski structures and state transitions exploiting unbounded parallelism and choice (see Börger's monograph [5]). Extensions comprise concurrent ASMs emphasising concurrent runs[1], which are not restricted to interleaving [4], and reflective ASMs, which provide means to also update the defining rule in every state transition [22].

Like other rigorous methods such as Event-B [1] and TLA$^+$ [16] ASMs are associated with a logic that is tailored to reason about desirable conditions on states and state transitions. The first ASM logic developed by Stärk and

---

[1] Throughout this paper we use the ASM terminology of *runs*, i.e. sequences of states defined by a machine. In other state-based methods as well as in the literature on temporal logics the term *trace* is used. These notions can be used interchangeably.

The research of Flavio Ferrarotti has been funded by the Federal Ministry for Climate Action, Environment, Energy, Mobility, Innovation and Technology (BMK), the Federal Ministry for Digital and Economic Affairs (BMDW), and the State of Upper Austria in the frame of the COMET Module Dependable Production Environments with Software Security (DEPS) within the COMET - Competence Centers for Excellent Technologies Programme managed by Austrian Research Promotion Agency FFG.

S. Bonfanti et al. (Eds.): ABZ 2024, LNCS 14759, pp. 123–140, 2024.
https://doi.org/10.1007/978-3-031-63790-2_8

Nanchen was defined as a definitional extension of first-order logic [25], but due to problems of handling consistency was restricted to deterministic machines (see the discussion in [5, p. 326ff]). Most important in this logic are predicates $\mathrm{upd}_{r,f}(\bar{x}, y)$ with the informal meaning that applying the ASM rule r yields an update such that $f(\bar{x}) = y$ with an n-tuple $\bar{x}$ holds in the successor state, where n is the arity of the function symbol f, and $[r]\varphi$ with the informal meaning that after applying the rule r the condition φ holds in the successor state. Note that formulae in this logic are interpreted over states of an ASM, even though the formulae can express properties of finite prefixes of runs of fixed bounded length. This reflects the fact that a state S of a deterministic ASM M together with the rule r of M uniquely determines the run of M starting in S.

The open problem of generalisation to non-deterministic machines was closed by Ferrarotti et al., who defined a logic for ASMs as a fragment of second-order logic, which is complete with respect to Henkin semantics [11]. The key idea is to separate the building of an update set X in a state from the effects of applying X and thus building a successor state. Thus, $\mathrm{upd}_{r,f}(\bar{x}, y)$ is generalised by a predicate $\mathrm{upd}_r(X)$ with the informal meaning that the rule r yields the update set X, and then $[r]\varphi$ is replaced by $[X]\varphi$ with the meaning that applying the update set X leads to a successor state satisfying φ. The full ASM logic is based on meta-finite structures and captures synchronisation operators for unbounded parallelism, therefore also dealing with update multisets, which requires the use of so-called ϱ-terms as well as predicates $\mathrm{upm}_r(\ddot{X})$ with the informal meaning that an application of rule r yields an update multiset $\ddot{X}$ [10]. However, this logic of non-deterministic ASMs preserves the fact that formulae are interpreted over states of an ASM, as a state S determines the runs starting in S.

It was further shown that concurrent ASMs can be simulated by non-deterministic ASMs, so the logic of ASMs can also be used to reason about concurrent systems, provided that the one-step predicate $\mathrm{upd}_r(X)$ is generalised to an n-step predicate $\mathrm{upd}_r^n(X)$ [11]. This can further be used to extend the logic to a logic for reflective ASMs by introducing variables for rules, i.e. in the logic of reflective ASMs predicates $\mathrm{upd}^n(r, X)$ are used, where r is interpreted by the rule stored in the given state [23].

Besides conditions on states and state transitions (including multi-step transition for some bounded number of steps as in concurrent and reflective systems) general liveness conditions that are defined over complete runs of a machine are of further interest. In the context of Event-B Abrial and Hoang studied several such conditions known as invariance, existence, progress and persistence conditions, and discovered sound derivation rules [14]. For this they exploited variant terms for convergence and divergence as well as modal operators $\square$ and $\lozenge$ (referring to all or some states in a run) adopted from Pnueli's Linear-Time Temporal Logic (LTL) [20]. However, while LTL is a temporal extension of propositional logic, in Abrial's and Hoang's work the LTL operators—to be precise, the operators of the UNTIL-fragment of LTL[2]—are added to the logic of Event-B [24]. This

---

[2] As state transitions, i.e. events, are intrinsic part of Event-B, the NEXT-operator is de facto already captured by the logic of Event-B, so the restriction to the UNTIL-fragment is no loss of generality.

work was taken further by Ferrarotti et al., who discovered a complete fragment of this integrated logic LTL(EB) [9] with slightly generalised derivation rules.

In this paper we investigate the analogous problem for the logic of ASMs. However, as a definitional extension for multi-step state transitions has already been defined, we simply make the number of steps first-class objects, i.e. we use predicates $\mathrm{upd}_r^*(n, X)$ (same as $\mathrm{upd}_r^n(X)$ above) with the difference that now quantification over n will be enabled. The informal meaning remains the same, i.e. n iterated applications of the rule r yield the combined update set X. For the moment we ignore reflection, i.e. r will remain an extra-logical variable as in the logic of ASMs. The first contribution of this paper will be the formal definition of this logic, which we denote as $\mathcal{ML}_{\mathrm{ASM}}$. Naturally, this logic is very powerful, and we most likely lose completeness. It should also be noted that also formulae of $\mathcal{ML}_{\mathrm{ASM}}$ are interpreted over states of an ASM and not over runs, although the formulae can express properties of runs. This is possible, because ASM states determine the runs starting in them.

We will show how to express temporal formulae $\Box\varphi$ and $\Diamond\varphi$ as well as UNTIL-formulae $\varphi\mathcal{U}\psi$ in $\mathcal{ML}_{\mathrm{ASM}}$. Then the liveness conditions mentioned above can also be expressed in $\mathcal{ML}_{\mathrm{ASM}}$. As the logic of ASMs deals with non-deterministic machines, we can further distinguish formulae that are to hold in all runs from those that hold in just one run. For the latter ones we introduce additional modal operators $\Box^1$, $\Diamond^1$ and $\mathcal{U}^1$, which can be freely combined with the other operators. In this way we enable quantification over runs as well as defining teams of runs without leaving the frame of a second-order logic with Henkin semantics. This marks a fundamental difference to propositional logics such as LTL, CTL and the like, which must be interpreted over runs. States in such runs are unrelated, so it does not make sense to interpret a temporal LTL formula in a state, whereas in $\mathcal{ML}_{\mathrm{ASM}}$ this makes perfectly sense.

Then the second contribution of the paper will be the definition of a fragment of $\mathcal{ML}_{\mathrm{ASM}}$ analogous to the $\Box$LTL fragment of LTL(EB) investigated in [9]. Selected liveness conditions such as invariance, existence, progress and persistence can be expressed in this fragment. Furthermore, different to the work in [9], where liveness conditions must hold in all runs of an Event-B machine, the fragment of $\mathcal{ML}_{\mathrm{ASM}}$ will permit quantification over runs. It is very likely that the fragment defined this way will remain complete provided that certain variant terms are defined in an ASM, which can always be achieved by correct refinements. The completeness should be achievable by a generalisation of derivation rules for the selected liveness conditions of interest. A full proof of a completeness theorem will be made available soon in a technical report.

Finally, we apply our logic to the well known problem of mutual exclusion in concurrent systems. Though usually in the literature these runs are confined to a semantics based on interleaving (see e.g. [14,19]), we will investigate the problem using more general concurrent ASM runs [4], and we will exploit that concurrent ASMs can be simulated by non-deterministic ASMs, so the logic $\mathcal{ML}_{\mathrm{ASM}}$ becomes applicable for this problem.

Previous and Related Work. Pnueli's Linear-Time Temporal Logic (LTL) [20] is generally considered as a pioneering contribution to the verification of liveness properties of sequential systems. LTL is a modal extension of propositional logic, so formulae involving operators NEXT and UNTIL as well as derived operators $\square$ (ALWAYS) and $\lozenge$ (EVENTUALLY) are interpreted over runs, i.e. sequences of propositional theories. In many applications it suffices to consider only the UNTIL-fragment of LTL, which was exploited in the work of Manna and Pnueli on the verification of invariance and liveness conditions [17]. Computation Tree Logic (CTL) [6] overcomes the restriction to single runs, but only its extension CTL* also covers all conditions that are expressible in LTL.

In LTL, CTL and CTL* it is impossible to adequately express conditions that refer to relations between runs. More recently, the notion of hyperproperties was introduced to overcome this limitation [7]. This has led to several extensions such as HyperLTL, HyperCTL, HyperCTL* emphasising variables for runs and quantification over them [8] as well as TeamLTL and TeamCTL emphasing team semantics, i.e. the interpretation of formulae over arbitrary sets of runs [13]. A deeper investigation of TeamLTL was conducted in [15]. In security verification a common problem is concerned with the preservation of secrets from agents with insufficient access rights. As shown in Biskup's monograph on secure information systems this problem can be formalised by non-interference of runs of a concurrent system [2]. The ability to solve this problem using HyperLTL was celebrated as breakthrough, while im $\mathcal{ML}_{\mathrm{ASM}}$ the problem becomes a simple transition invariant.

In the context of rigorous specifications using state-based methods such as ASMs [5], Event-B [1] or TLA$^+$ [16] the fact that these temporal logics are confined to states as propositional theories, i.e. arbitrary sets of propositions, has to be considered as a restriction that needs to be overcome, which can be done by replacing propositions by formulae in the logics associated with these methods such as the logics of deterministic and non-deterministic ASMs [11], the logic of Event-B [24] or the logic of TLA$^+$ [18]. While on one side a NEXT operator can be dispensed with, this leads to very powerful logics such as $\mathcal{ML}_{\mathrm{ASM}}$ without perspective to preserve completeness. On the other hand $\mathcal{ML}_{\mathrm{ASM}}$ is defined as an extension of the logic of ASM, and as such all formulae are interpreted over states rather than runs, which is fundamentally different from propositional temporal logics..

Abrial and Hoang started work on derivation rules that would support mechanical proofs of the most interesting liveness conditions mentioned above [14], and indeed, Rivière et al. integrated these derivation rules into the EB4EB framework extending RODIN [21]. This was recently extended and slightly modified by Ferrarotti et al., who defined a complete fragment of the logic of LTL(EB), in which all these conditions and derivation rules can be expressed.

Organisation of the Paper. In Sect. 2 we first recall the basic definitions of the logic of Abstract State Machines from [11], then introduce syntax and semantics of the modal extensions, which define the logic $\mathcal{ML}_{\mathrm{ASM}}$. We show that the common operators of logics such as LTL or CTL* can be expressed as shortcuts in this logic, which includes quantification over runs and the definition of teams. Section 3 is dedicated to the formalisation of liveness conditions such as invariance, conditional and unconditional progress, and persistence, which also come in different versions depending, whether all or only one run is considered. We use the form of these liveness constraints to define a fragment of $\mathcal{ML}_{\text{ASM}}$, for which we present a sound and complete system of derivation rules analogous to the one used in [9] for Event-B. In Sect. 4 we apply our logic to a verification problem concerning mutual exclusion [19]. We conclude with a brief summary in Sect. 5. Throughout the paper due to space limitations proofs are omitted. They will be included in a forthcoming extended version, which will be made available soon as technical report.

2   The Modal ASM Logic $\mathcal{ML}_{\text{ASM}}$

We consider a simplified version of the logic $\mathcal{L}$ of non-deterministic ASMs as defined in [10], which we extend to a logic capturing multiple steps of an ASM with rule r. Then we show that with quantification over the the number of steps we can express the common temporal operators used in LTL or CTL*.

2.1   The Logic of ASMs

We disregard meta-finiteness, ϱ-terms for synchronisation and update multisets. We just consider a single uniform signature Σ of an ASM, so terms are defined in the usual way. In order to define formulae inductively we extend the set of first-order variables with a countable set of second-order (relation) variables of arity r for each $r \geq 1$.

(i) If s and t are terms, then $s = t$ is a formula.
(ii) If $t_1, \ldots, t_r$ are terms and X is a second-order variable of arity r, then $X(t_1, \ldots, t_r)$ is a formula.
(iii) If r is a rule and X is a second-order variable of arity 3, then $\text{upd}_r(X)$ is a formula.
(iv) If φ and ψ are formulae and x is a first-order variable, then $\neg\varphi$, $\varphi \vee \psi$ and $\forall x(\varphi)$ are formulae.
(v) If φ is a formula and X is a second-order variable, then $\forall X(\varphi)$ is a formula.
(vi) If φ is a formula and X is a second-order variable of arity 3, then $[X]\varphi$ is a formula.

Conjunction and existential quantification are defined as usual as shortcuts. The second-order variables of arity 3 are used to capture update sets. Note that closed first-order formulae in $\mathcal{L}$ define conditions on states and are therefore called *state formulae*.

The semantics of the logic is defined by Henkin structures. A *Henkin pre-structure* S is a state of signature Σ with base set B extended with a new universe D_n of n-ary relations for each $n \geq 1$, where $D_n \subseteq \mathcal{P}(B^n)$. Furthermore, in order to represent update sets, the logic $\mathcal{L}$ uses constants c_f for all dynamic function symbols $f \in \mathcal{F}_{\text{dyn}}$. By abuse of notation we also assume special values in the base sets B, which we also denote as c_f. The interpretation of the logical constant c_f in any state S is then always the special value $c_f \in B$, i.e. $c_f^S = c_f$.

Variable assignments ζ into a Henkin prestructure S are defined as usual: $\zeta(x) \in B$ for each first-order variable x, and $\zeta(X) \in D_n$ for each second-order variable X of arity n. Then the interpretation of a term in a Henkin prestructure S with a variable assignment ζ is defined as usual.

We extend this interpretation to formulae. For a variable assignment ζ and an arbitrary rule r, which may contain free variables, we use $\Delta(r, S, \zeta)$ as notation for the set of update sets produced by the rule r in the state S with ζ providing values for the free variables. Then for a second-order variable X of arity 3 we abuse the notation by writing $val_{S,\zeta}(X) \in \Delta(r, S, \zeta)$ meaning that there is a set $U \in \Delta(r, S, \zeta)$ such that $(f, a_0, a_1) \in U$ iff $(c_f, a_0, a_1) \in val_{S,\zeta}(X)$. For a formula φ its truth value on S under ζ is denoted as $[\![\varphi]\!]_{S,\zeta}$. For formulae $upd_r(X)$ and $[X]\varphi$ these are defined as follows—for the other formulae the definition is standard.

- If φ is of the form $upd_r(X)$, then

$$[\![\varphi]\!]_{S,\zeta} = \begin{cases} true & \text{if } val_{S,\zeta}(X) \in \Delta(r, S, \zeta) \\ false & \text{otherwise} \end{cases}.$$

- If φ is of the form $([X]\psi)$, then

$$[\![\varphi]\!]_{S,\zeta} = \begin{cases} false & \text{if } \zeta(X) \text{ represents an update set } U \\ & \quad \text{such that } U \text{ is consistent and } [\![\psi]\!]_{S+U,\zeta} = false \\ true & \text{otherwise} \end{cases}.$$

The universes D_n of the Henkin prestructures should not be arbitrary collections of n-ary relations. Thus, it is reasonable to restrict our attention to some collections of n-ary relations that we can define, i.e. we restrict our attention to Henkin structures.

A *Henkin structure* is a Henkin prestructure S that is closed under definability, i.e. for every formula φ, variable assignment ζ and arity $n \geq 1$, we have that $\{\bar{a} \in A^n \mid [\![\varphi]\!]_{S,\zeta[a_1 \mapsto x_1, \ldots, a_n \mapsto x_n]} = true\} \in D_n$.

The main result in [10] states that the logic for ASMs defined here is complete with respect to Henkin semantics.

2.2 Multi-step Extension and $\mathcal{ML}_{\text{ASM}}$

In order to extend the logic in a way such that conditions over ASM runs can be expressed we first define an extension of the predicate $upd_r(X)$ from a single step to multiple steps. As for the logic of reflective ASMs [23] we introduce a new predicate $upd_r^*(n, X)$ with the informal meaning that n iterated steps of the ASM yield the update set X.

Clearly, we have $\mathrm{upd}_r^*(1, X) \leftrightarrow \mathrm{upd}_r(X)$ and $\mathrm{upd}_r^*(0, X) \leftrightarrow X = \emptyset$. For arbitrary values of n we exploit the definition of $\mathrm{upd}_r(X)$ for sequence rules as originally defined in [10]. For this we need the definition of consistent update sets in the logic:

$$\mathrm{conUSet}(X) \equiv \bigwedge_{f \in \mathcal{F}_{dyn}} \forall xyz \Big(\big(X(c_f, x, y) \wedge X(c_f, x, z) \big) \rightarrow y = z \Big)$$

for the set $\mathcal{F}_{dyn}$ of constants representing the dynamic function symbols in Σ. Then we can use $\mathrm{con}_r(X)$ to express that X represents one of the possible update sets generated by a rule r and that X is consistent:

$$\mathrm{con}_r(X) \equiv \mathrm{upd}_r(X) \wedge \mathrm{conUSet}(X).$$

Then we further define

$$\mathrm{upd}_r^*(n+1, X) \leftrightarrow \big(\mathrm{upd}_r(X) \wedge \neg \mathrm{conUSet}(X) \big) \vee$$
$$\big(\exists Y_1 Y_2 (\mathrm{upd}_r(Y_1) \wedge \mathrm{conUSet}(Y_1) \wedge [Y_1]\mathrm{upd}_r^*(n, Y_2) \wedge$$
$$\bigwedge_{f \in \mathcal{F}_{dyn}} \forall xy (X(c_f, x, y) \leftrightarrow ((Y_1(c_f, x, y) \wedge \forall z(\neg Y_2(c_f, x, z))) \vee Y_2(c_f, x, y)))))$$

A formula $\mathrm{upd}_r^*(x, X)$ always yields *false*, if the variable x is interpreted by a value that is not a non-negative integer.

With this definitional extension and the fact that universal and existential quantification over x (for x appearing in $\mathrm{upd}_r^*(x, X)$) are already included in our definition above we obtain the logic $\mathcal{ML}_{\mathrm{ASM}}$.

2.3   Temporal Operators in $\mathcal{ML}_{\mathrm{ASM}}$

Liveness conditions can be expressed by temporal logics formulae that are interpreted over complete runs of an ASM M. We will show now that the common operators of temporal logics can be expressed as shortcuts in the logic $\mathcal{ML}_{\mathrm{ASM}}$.

We say that M satisfies the formula $\Box \varphi$ (with $\varphi \in \mathcal{ML}_{\mathrm{ASM}}$)—denoted as "$\varphi$ always holds in all runs"—iff for all runs $S_0, S_1, \ldots$ of M we have $S_i \models \varphi$ for all $i \geq 0$. We write $M \models \Box \varphi$ for this. Then we see that $\Box \varphi$ is merely a shortcut for the $\mathcal{ML}_{\mathrm{ASM}}$ formula

$$\forall n \forall X (\mathrm{upd}_r^*(n, X) \rightarrow [X]\varphi).$$

Analogously we say that M satisfies the formula $\Diamond \varphi$ (with $\varphi \in \mathcal{ML}_{\mathrm{ASM}}$)—denoted as "$\varphi$ eventually holds in all runs"—iff for all runs $S_0, S_1, \ldots$ of M we have $S_i \models \varphi$ for some $i \geq 0$. We write $M \models \Diamond \varphi$ for this. We can see that $\Diamond \varphi$ is also a shortcut of an $\mathcal{ML}_{\mathrm{ASM}}$ formula, which in this case is slightly more complex. First note that every update set X that results from $n > 0$ steps of a machine M in some state S can be written as sequential composition of a consistent update set X_1 yielded from $m < n$ steps in S and an update set X_2

yielded from $n - m$ steps in the m'th successor state of S resulting from applying X_1 to S. Sequential composition of update sets can be expressed by the $\mathcal{ML}_{\text{ASM}}$ formula

$$\bigwedge_{f \in \mathcal{F}_{\text{dyn}}} \forall yz\big(X(c_f, y, z) \leftrightarrow X_2(c_f, y, z) \vee (X_1(c_f, y, z) \wedge \forall x \, \neg X_2(c_f, y, x))\big),$$

for which we use the notation $\text{comp}(X_1, X_2, X)$. Then $\Diamond \varphi$ is a shortcut for the following $\mathcal{ML}_{\text{ASM}}$ formula

$$\exists n \forall X \Big((\text{upd}_r^{c*}(n, X) \wedge \text{conUSet}(X) \wedge [X]\neg\varphi) \to \exists m.\big(m < n \wedge \exists X_1 X_2$$

$$(\text{upd}_r^*(m, X_1) \wedge [X_1]\text{upd}_r^*(n - m, X_2) \wedge \text{comp}(X_1, X_2, X) \wedge [X_1]\varphi)\big) \Big),$$

where we use $\text{upd}_r^{c*}(X)$ as a shortcut for the formula

$$\text{upd}_r^*(n, X) \vee \exists n'(n' < n \wedge \text{upd}_r^*(n', X) \wedge \forall Y([X]\text{upd}_r(Y) \to \neg\text{conUSet}(Y))),$$

which allows us to capture also finite runs.

We can also express UNTIL-formulae in $\mathcal{ML}_{\text{ASM}}$. M satisfies the formula $\varphi \mathcal{U} \psi$ (with $\varphi, \psi \in \mathcal{ML}_{\text{ASM}}$)—denoted as "$\varphi$ holds until ψ in all runs"—iff for all runs $S_0, S_1, \ldots$ of M there exists some $i \geq 0$ with $S_i \models \psi$ and $S_j \models \varphi$ for all $j < i$. We write $M \models \varphi \mathcal{U} \psi$ for this. We can see that $\varphi \mathcal{U} \psi$ is the $\mathcal{ML}_{\text{ASM}}$ formula

$$\forall m \forall X \big(\text{upd}_r^*(m, X) \wedge [X](\neg\varphi \vee \psi) \to \exists n_2 \exists Y \big(n_2 \leq m \wedge$$
$$\text{upd}_r^*(n_2, Y) \wedge [Y]\psi \wedge \forall n_1 \forall X_1 X_2(n_1 < n_2 \wedge \text{upd}_r^*(n_1, X_1) \wedge$$
$$[X_1]\text{upd}_r^*(n_2 - n_1, X_2) \wedge \text{comp}(X_1, X_2, Y) \to [X_1]\varphi)\big)\big).$$

We can further introduce formulae referring to at least one run of an ASM M. We say that M satisfies the formula $\square^1 \varphi$ (with $\varphi \in \mathcal{ML}_{\text{ASM}}$)—denoted as "$\varphi$ always holds in some run"—iff there exists a run $S_0, S_1, \ldots$ of M with $S_i \models \varphi$ for all $i \geq 0$. We write $M \models \square^1 \varphi$ for this. In this case $\square^1 \varphi$ is a shortcut for the $\mathcal{ML}_{\text{ASM}}$ formula

$$\forall n \exists X \Big(\text{upd}_r^{c*}(n, X) \wedge \text{conUSet}(X) \wedge [X]\varphi \wedge \forall m.\big(m < n \to \forall X_1 X_2.$$

$$(\text{upd}_r^*(m, X_1) \wedge [X_1]\text{upd}_r^*(n - m, X_2) \wedge \text{comp}(X_1, X_2, X)) \to [X_1]\varphi\big) \Big).$$

We also see that $\neg\square^1\neg\varphi$ is equivalent to $\Diamond\varphi$, as it should be.

We say that M satisfies the formula $\Diamond^1 \varphi$ (with $\varphi \in \mathcal{ML}_{\text{ASM}}$)—denoted as "$\varphi$ eventually holds in some run"—iff there exists a run $S_0, S_1, \ldots$ of M with $S_i \models \varphi$ for some $i \geq 0$. We write $M \models \Diamond^1 \varphi$ for this. We can see that $\Diamond^1 \varphi$ is a shortcut for the $\mathcal{ML}_{\text{ASM}}$ formula

$$\exists n \exists X (\text{upd}_r^*(n, X) \wedge [X]\varphi)$$

and $\neg\lozenge^1\neg\varphi$ is equivalent to $\square\varphi$.

Finally, the analogous formula in $\mathcal{ML}_{\text{ASM}}$ expressing that "φ holds until ψ in some run" can be written as

$$\exists n \exists X \big(\text{upd}_r^*(n, X) \wedge [X]\psi \wedge \forall m \forall X_1 X_2 (m < n \wedge \text{upd}_r^*(m, X_1) \wedge$$
$$[X_1]\text{upd}_r^*(n - m, X_2) \wedge \text{comp}(X_1, X_2, Y) \to [X_1]\varphi) \big).$$

We write $M \models \varphi \mathcal{U}^1 \psi$ for this expressing that there exists a run $S_0, S_1, \ldots$ of M and some $i \geq 0$ with $S_i \models \psi$ and $S_j \models \varphi$ for all $j < i$.

All modal operators $\square$, $\lozenge$, $\mathcal{U}$, $\square^1$, $\lozenge^1$ and $\mathcal{U}^1$ can be freely combined in $\mathcal{ML}_{\text{ASM}}$.

3 A Fragment of $\mathcal{ML}_{\text{ASM}}$ Capturing Liveness Conditions

We now introduce a fragment of $\mathcal{ML}_{\text{ASM}}$ that is defined by some combinations of the temporal operators introduced in the last section and captures some relevant liveness conditions. We consider the same liveness conditions as in [9] with the difference that we now also consider conditions that only hold in one run. The main result of this section is a sound and complete set of derivation rules for the fragment.

3.1 Auxiliary Predicates and Variants

In order to obtain sound derivation rules for selected temporal formulae extending the sound and complete derivation rules for the logic $\mathcal{L}$ (see [10,11]) we first introduce several auxiliary predicates, which are inspired by the work in [9] and extended to our purpose here.

We say that for an ASM M a state formula φ_2 is *always* (or *sometimes*) *next* to a state formula φ iff the first (or second, respectively) of the following formulae holds for all states S:

$$\text{next}(\varphi_1, \varphi_2) \equiv \varphi_1 \to \exists X(\text{upd}_r(X) \wedge \forall X(\text{upd}_r(X) \wedge \text{conUSet}(X) \to [X]\varphi_2))$$
$$\text{next}^1(\varphi_1, \varphi_2) \equiv \varphi_1 \to \exists X(\text{upd}_r(X) \wedge \text{conUSet}(X) \wedge [X]\varphi_2).$$

With these formulae we can express that for states S satisfying φ_1 there always exists a successor state, and all or at least one successor state satisfies φ_2.

It will also be necessary to distinguish infinite and finite runs. The formula

$$\text{dlf}(\varphi) \equiv \varphi \to \exists X(\text{upd}_r(X) \wedge \text{conUSet}(X))$$

for a state formula φ expresses that states satisfying φ always have successor states, i.e. no run can terminate in such a state.

One reason for the completeness result in [9] is that the selected formulae in the fragment of interest all express conditions, where certain conditions cannot hold forever. This suggests the use of proof arguments based on variants, i.e.

terms that are decremented, which for non-negative integers (or any other well-founded set) cannot be done forever. Therefore, we introduce slightly generalised variant terms, which will become useful for proofs of $\mathcal{ML}_{\text{ASM}}^{\text{live}}$ formulae.

We distinguish between c-variants and d-variants, which allow us to derive convergence and divergence, respectively, in all or one run with respect to a state formula φ. We say that an ASM is *convergent* in φ iff in all/one run(s) $S_0, S_1, \ldots$ there is no ℓ such that $S_k \models \varphi$ holds for all $k \geq \ell$. Convergence is denoted as $M \models \text{conv}(\varphi)$ or $M \models \text{conv}^1(\varphi)$, respectively. We say that an ASM is *divergent* in φ iff in all/one infinite run(s) $S_0, S_1, \ldots$ there exists some ℓ such that $S_k \models \varphi$ holds for all $k \geq \ell$. Divergence is denoted as $M \models \text{div}(\varphi)$ or $M \models \text{div}^1(\varphi)$, respectively. In the following formulae we use a predicate PosInt, where $\text{PosInt}(x)$ expresses that x is a positive integer.

– A closed term t is an *all-run c-variant* for a state formula φ iff the formula

$$\text{var}_c(t, \varphi) \equiv \varphi \to \text{PosInt}(t) \wedge \exists X(\text{upd}_r(X) \wedge \text{conUSet}(X)) \wedge$$
$$\forall X(\text{upd}_r(X) \wedge \text{conUSet}(X) \to \forall v(t = v \to [X](t < v)))$$

holds in all states S of M.
– A closed term t is a *one-run c-variant* for a state formula φ iff the formula

$$\text{var}_c^1(t, \varphi) \equiv \varphi \to \text{PosInt}(t) \wedge \exists X(\text{upd}_r(X) \wedge \text{conUSet}(X) \wedge$$
$$\forall v(t = v \to [X](t < v)))$$

holds in all states S of M.
– A closed term t is an *all-run d-variant* for a state formula φ iff the formula

$$\text{var}_d(t, \varphi) \equiv \big(\neg\varphi \to \text{PosInt}(t) \wedge \forall X(\text{upd}_r(X) \wedge \text{conUSet}(X) \to$$
$$\forall v(t = v \to [X](t < v)))\big)$$
$$\wedge\big(\varphi \to \forall X(\text{upd}_r(X) \wedge \text{conUSet}(X) \to \forall v(t = v \to [X](t \leq v))))$$

holds in all states S of M.
– A closed term t is a *one-run d-variant* for a state formula φ iff the formula

$$\text{var}_d^1(t, \varphi) \equiv \big((\neg\varphi \wedge \exists X(\text{upd}_r(X) \wedge \text{conUSet}(X))) \to$$
$$(\text{PosInt}(t) \wedge \exists X(\text{upd}_r(X) \wedge \text{conUSet}(X) \wedge \forall v(t = v \to [X](t < v)))))$$
$$\wedge\big((\varphi \wedge \exists X(\text{upd}_r(X) \wedge \text{conUSet}(X))) \to$$
$$\exists X(\text{upd}_r(X) \wedge \text{conUSet}(X) \wedge \forall v(t = v \to [X](t \leq v))))$$

holds in all states S of M.

Proposition 1. *The derivation rules*

CONV: $\quad \dfrac{var_c(t, \varphi)}{conv(\varphi)}$ $\qquad$ DIV: $\quad \dfrac{var_d(t, \varphi)}{div(\varphi)}$

CONV^1: $\quad \dfrac{var_c^1(t, \varphi)}{conv^1(\varphi)}$ $\qquad$ DIV^1: $\quad \dfrac{var_d^1(t, \varphi)}{div^1(\varphi)}$

are sound for the derivation of convergence and divergence conditions.

The proof is straightforward[3]. For the completeness of these rules together with the system $\mathfrak{R}$ of derivation rules for the logic of ASMs [10] we need to show that the appropriate variant terms always exists. This is at least the case for "sufficiently refined" ASMs in the sense of the following proposition.

Proposition 2. *Let M be an ASM satisfying $conv(\varphi)$ (or $conv^1(\varphi)$, $div(\varphi)$, $div^1(\varphi)$, respectively). Then there exists a correct refinement M' of M and a closed term t defined over the signature of M', such that t is an all-run c-variant (or one-run c-variant, all-run d-variant, one-run d-variant, respectively) for φ.*

The proof is quite analogous to the proofs of Lemmata 3 and 4 in the extended version of [9]. Proposition 2 shows the existence of a sound and complete set of derivation rules for convergence and divergence conditions for sufficiently refined ASMs. The derivation rules comprise all derivation rules of the logic of ASMs plus the rules from Proposition 1.

3.2 Definable Teams of Runs

It is sometimes necessary to only consider a subset of the set of runs of an ASM, in particular, when a desired condition trivially holds in some subset of the set of all runs. Sets of runs are called *teams* in team semantics for temporal logics such as in TeamLTL and its derivatives [13]. For ASMs runs are defined by the rule of a machine and different runs for the same initial state result from choices. Thus, in principle it is always possible to refine an ASM M in such a way that the runs of the refined machine M' are just a subset of the runs of M, i.e. we can define teams by correct refinement. We will build teams into temporal formulae of the logic $\mathcal{ML}_{\mathrm{ASM}}$ as defined above.

We write $M \models \Box(\varphi)\colon \psi$, if in all runs $S_0, S_1, \ldots$ of M satisfying φ we have $S_i \models \psi$ for all i, and we write $M \models \Diamond(\varphi)\colon \psi$, if in all runs $S_0, S_1, \ldots$ of M satisfying φ we have $S_i \models \psi$ for some i. Furthermore, we write $M \models \Box^1(\varphi)\colon \psi$, if there exists a run $S_0, S_1, \ldots$ of M satisfying φ such that $S_i \models \psi$ holds for all i, and we write $M \models \Diamond^1(\varphi)\colon \psi$, if there exists a run $S_0, S_1, \ldots$ of M satisfying φ with $S_i \models \psi$ for some i.

The investigation, which of these formulae can be represented in $\mathcal{ML}_{\mathrm{ASM}}$ in general is beyond the scope of this article. Note that $\Diamond(\varphi)\colon \psi$ is equivalent to $\neg\Box^1(\varphi)\colon \neg\psi$, and $\Diamond^1(\varphi)\colon \psi$ is equivalent to $\neg\Box(\varphi)\colon \neg\psi$. For our purposes here we consider formulae $\Box(\varphi)\colon \psi$ and $\Box^1(\varphi)\colon \psi$, in which φ is a divergence formula $div(\chi)$.

In order to express $\Box(div(\varphi))\colon \psi$ in $\mathcal{ML}_{\mathrm{ASM}}$ we have to adapt the defining formula for $\Box\psi$ in such a way that $[X]\psi$ is required to hold only in those states S that appear in a run satisfying $div(\varphi)$. This gives rise to the following defining $\mathcal{ML}_{\mathrm{ASM}}$ formula

$$\forall n \forall X \big(\mathrm{upd}_r^*(n, X) \wedge \mathrm{conUSet}(X) \wedge$$
$$\exists m \exists Y ([X]\mathrm{upd}_r^*(m, Y) \wedge \mathrm{conUSet}(Y) \wedge [Y]\Box^1\varphi) \rightarrow [X]\psi).$$

---

[3] For analogous proofs in the context of Event-B consider Lemmata 1 and 2 in the long version of [9].

In the same way we obtain a defining formula for $\Box^1(\mathrm{div}(\varphi))$: ψ by adaptation of the defining formula for $\Box^1\psi$ by adding the requirement that a run, in which all states satisfy ψ, also satisfies $\mathrm{div}(\varphi)$. This gives rise to the following defining $\mathcal{ML}_{\mathrm{ASM}}$ formula

$$\forall n \exists X \Big(\mathrm{upd}_r^{c*}(n, X) \wedge \mathrm{conUSet}(X) \wedge [X]\psi \wedge \forall m.\big(m < n \to \forall X_1 X_2.$$

$$(\mathrm{upd}_r^*(m, X_1) \wedge [X_1]\mathrm{upd}_r^*(n - m, X_2) \wedge \mathrm{comp}(X_1, X_2, X)) \to [X_1]\psi)$$

$$\wedge \exists m \exists Y ([X]\mathrm{upd}_r^*(m, Y) \wedge \mathrm{conUSet}(Y) \wedge [Y]\Box^1\varphi) \Big).$$

3.3 Selected Liveness Conditions

The following conditions on runs are of particular interest.

Invariance. An *invariance condition* is given by an $\mathcal{ML}_{\mathrm{ASM}}$ formula $\Box\varphi$ for some state formula $\varphi \in \mathcal{L}$. Such a condition is satisfied by an ASM M iff all states S in all runs of M satisfy φ. In addition, a *one-run invariance condition* is given by an $\mathcal{ML}_{\mathrm{ASM}}$ formula $\Box^1\varphi$, which is satisfied by M iff there exists a run such that φ holds in all satates of this run.

Existence. An *existence condition* (also called *unconditional progress condition*) is given by an $\mathcal{ML}_{\mathrm{ASM}}$ formula $\Box\Diamond\varphi$ for some state formula $\varphi \in \mathcal{L}$. Such a condition is satisfied by an ASM M iff in every infinite run of M there is an infinite subsequence of states satisfying φ, and every finite run of M terminates in a state satisfying φ. We also consider *one-run existence conditions*[4] $\Box^1\Diamond\varphi$ with some state formula $\varphi \in \mathcal{L}$. Such a condition is satisfied by M iff there exists an infinite run with an infinite subsequence of states satisfying φ or there exists a finite run terminating in a state satisfying φ. Note that existence and convergence conditions are the same.

Progress. A *(conditional) progress condition* is given by an $\mathcal{ML}_{\mathrm{ASM}}$ formula $\Box(\varphi \to \Diamond\psi)$ for some state formulae $\varphi, \psi \in \mathcal{L}$. Such a condition is satisfied by an ASM M iff in every run of M each state S_i satisfying φ is followed by a state S_j $(j \geq i)$ satisfying ψ. A progress condition with $\varphi = \mathbf{true}$ degenerates to an existence condition. Same as for existence conditions we consider *one-run progress conditions*[5] $\Box^1(\varphi \to \Diamond\psi)$ with some state formula φ. Such a condition is satisfied by M iff there exists a run, in which each state S_i satisfying φ is followed by a state S_j $(j \geq i)$ satisfying ψ.

Persistence. A *persistence condition* is given by an $\mathcal{ML}_{\mathrm{ASM}}$ formula $\Diamond\Box\varphi$ for some state formula $\varphi \in \mathcal{L}$. Such a condition is satisfied by an ASM M iff every infinite run of M ends with an infinite sequence of states satisfying φ, i.e. for some k we have $S_i \models \varphi$ for all $i \geq k$, and every finite run of M terminates

---

[4] Note that $\Box\Diamond^1\varphi$ expresses the same as $\Box^1\Diamond\varphi$, whereas $\Box^1\Diamond^1\varphi$ merely expresses the same as $\Diamond^1\varphi$. We will therefore disregard such formulae.

[5] We disregard formulae $\Box^1(\varphi \to \Diamond\psi)$, which express the same as $\Box^1(\varphi \to \Diamond\psi)$, as well as $\Box^1(\varphi \to \Diamond^1\psi)$, which do not express any interesting liveness condition.

in a state satisfying φ. We also add *one-run persistence conditions*[6] $\Diamond^1\Box\varphi$, which are satisfied by an ASM M iff there exists an infinite run of M ending with an infinite sequence of states satisfying φ or a finite run terminating in a state satisfying φ. Note that persistence and divergence conditions are the same on infinite runs.

It therefore makes sense to define a fragment of $\mathcal{ML}_{\mathrm{ASM}}$ as the closure of the ASM logic $\mathcal{L}$ under constructors, which basically have the form of the formulae above. We denote this fragment as $\mathcal{ML}_{\mathrm{ASM}}^{\mathrm{live}}$. The set of well-formed formulae of $\mathcal{ML}_{\mathrm{ASM}}^{\mathrm{live}}$ is inductively defined by the following rules:

- If $\varphi \in \mathcal{L}$, then φ is a well-formed formula of $\mathcal{ML}_{\mathrm{ASM}}^{\mathrm{live}}$;
- For $\varphi \in \mathcal{ML}_{\mathrm{ASM}}^{\mathrm{live}}$ the formulae $\Box\varphi$, $\Box^1\varphi$, $\Box\Diamond\varphi$, $\Box^1\Diamond\varphi$, $\Diamond\Box\varphi$ and $\Diamond^1\Box\varphi$ are well-formed formulae of $\mathcal{ML}_{\mathrm{ASM}}^{\mathrm{live}}$;
- For state formulae $\varphi, \chi \in \mathcal{ML}_{\mathrm{ASM}}$ and $\psi \in \mathcal{ML}_{\mathrm{ASM}}^{\mathrm{live}}$ the formulae $\Box(\varphi \to \Diamond\psi)$, $\Box^1(\varphi \to \Diamond\psi)$, $\Box(\mathrm{div}(\chi)){:}\,\psi$, and $\Box^1(\mathrm{div}(\chi)){:}\,\psi$ are well-formed formulae of $\mathcal{ML}_{\mathrm{ASM}}^{\mathrm{live}}$.

3.4   Derivation Rules

We are now able to prove the soundness of a set of derivation rules for $\mathcal{ML}_{\mathrm{ASM}}^{\mathrm{live}}$

Proposition 3. *For state formulae* $\varphi, \psi \in \mathcal{ML}_{ASM}$ *the derivation rules*

$$INV\colon \frac{\varphi \quad next(\varphi,\varphi)}{\Box\varphi} \qquad\qquad INV^1\colon \frac{\varphi \quad next^1(\varphi,\varphi)}{\Box^1\varphi}$$

$$LIVE\colon \frac{conv(\neg\varphi)}{\Box\Diamond\varphi} \qquad\qquad LIVE^1\colon \frac{conv^1(\neg\varphi)}{\Box^1\Diamond\varphi}$$

$$PERS\colon \frac{div(\varphi) \quad dlf(\neg\varphi)}{\Diamond\Box\varphi} \qquad PERS^1\colon \frac{div^1(\varphi) \quad dlf(\neg\varphi)}{\Diamond^1\Box\varphi}$$

are sound for the derivation of invariance, existence and persistence formulae in $\mathcal{ML}_{ASM}^{live}$.

The proofs are extensions of the proofs of Lemmata 6, 7 and 9 in the extended version of [9].

Proposition 4. *For state formulae* $\varphi, \psi, \chi \in \mathcal{ML}_{ASM}$ *and* $\alpha \equiv div(\neg\chi)$, $\beta \equiv next(\chi \wedge \neg\psi, \chi \vee \psi)$, $\beta^1 \equiv next(\chi \wedge \neg\psi, \chi \vee \psi)$ *and* $\gamma \equiv \varphi \wedge \neg\psi \to \chi$ *the following derivation rules*

$$PROG_0\colon \frac{\Box(div(\neg\psi)){:}\,\alpha \quad \Box(div(\neg\psi)){:}\,\beta \quad \Box(div(\neg\psi)){:}\,\gamma}{\Box(\varphi \to \Diamond\psi)}$$

$$PROG_1\colon \frac{conv(\neg\psi)}{\Box(\varphi \to \Diamond\psi)} \qquad\qquad PROG_2\colon \frac{\Box\neg\varphi}{\Box(\varphi \to \Diamond\psi)}$$

$$PROG_0^1\colon \frac{\Box(div(\neg\varphi \wedge \neg\psi)){:}\,\alpha \quad \Box(div(\neg\varphi \wedge \neg\psi)){:}\,\beta^1 \quad \Box(div(\neg\varphi \wedge \neg\psi)){:}\,\gamma}{\Box^1(\varphi \to \Diamond\psi)}$$

---

[6] Formulae $\Diamond\Box^1\varphi$ and $\Diamond^1\Box^1\varphi$ express the same as $\Diamond^1\Box\varphi$ and are therefore disregarded.

$$\mathrm{PROG}_1^1: \frac{div(\neg\chi) \quad next(\chi \wedge \neg\psi, \chi \vee \psi) \quad \Box^1(\varphi \wedge \neg\psi \to \chi)}{\Box^1(\varphi \to \Diamond\psi)}$$

$$\mathrm{PROG}_2^1: \frac{conv^1(\neg\psi)}{\Box^1(\varphi \to \Diamond\psi)} \qquad\qquad \mathrm{PROG}_3^1: \frac{\Box^1\neg\varphi}{\Box^1(\varphi \to \Diamond\psi)}$$

are sound for the derivation of progress formulae in $\mathcal{ML}_{ASM}^{live}$.

The proof is an extension of the proof of Lemma 8 in the extended version of [9]. Note that the restriction to teams of runs satisfying $div(\neg\psi)$ or $div(\neg\varphi \wedge \neg\psi)$ in PROG_0 and PROG_0^1 is possible, because for other runs there is an infinite subsequence of states all satisfying ψ, which immediately entails the conclusion of the rules.

Further note that subformulae in these derivation rules are restricted to state formulae, whereas in the definition of the fragment $\mathcal{ML}_{ASM}^{live}$ foresees deeply nested temporal constructors. We therefore need additional derivation rules as in [9, Lemma 10].

Proposition 5. *The following derivation rules are sound for the derivation of formulae in* $\mathcal{ML}_{ASM}^{live}$:

$$\Box: \frac{\Box\varphi}{\Box\Box\varphi} \qquad\qquad \Diamond\Box_1: \frac{\Diamond\Box\varphi}{\Diamond\Box\Box\varphi}$$

$$\Box\Diamond_1: \frac{\Diamond\Box\varphi}{\Box\Diamond\Box\varphi} \qquad\qquad \Diamond\Box_2: \frac{\Box(\varphi_1 \to \Diamond\varphi_2)}{\Diamond\Box\Box(\varphi_1 \to \Diamond\varphi_2)}$$

$$\Box\Diamond_2: \frac{\Box(\varphi_1 \to \Diamond\varphi_2)}{\Box\Diamond\Box(\varphi_1 \to \Diamond\varphi_2)} \qquad\qquad \Diamond\Box_3: \frac{\Diamond\Box\varphi}{\Diamond\Box\Diamond\Box\varphi}$$

$$\Box^1: \frac{\Box^1\varphi}{\Box^1\Box\varphi} \qquad\qquad \Diamond^1\Box_1: \frac{\Diamond^1\Box\varphi}{\Diamond^1\Box\Box\varphi}$$

$$\Box^1\Diamond_1: \frac{\Diamond^1\Box\varphi}{\Box^1\Diamond\Box\varphi} \qquad\qquad \Diamond^1\Box_2: \frac{\Box^1(\varphi_1 \to \Diamond\varphi_2)}{\Diamond^1\Box\Box(\varphi_1 \to \Diamond\varphi_2)}$$

$$\Box^1\Diamond_2: \frac{\Box^1(\varphi_1 \to \Diamond\varphi_2)}{\Box^1\Diamond\Box(\varphi_1 \to \Diamond\varphi_2)} \qquad\qquad \Diamond^1\Box_3: \frac{\Diamond^1\Box\varphi}{\Diamond^1\Box\Diamond\Box\varphi}$$

We are confident that taking all our derivation rules together we can also show completeness, i.e. $M \models \varphi$ entails $M \vdash_{\mathfrak{R}} \varphi$ for sufficiently refined ASMs M. For the proof an extension of the proof of Theorem 11 in the extended version of [9] should be no problem, but we still need to check the details, in particular the use of defined teams allows us to eliminate the restriction to tail-homogeneity.

4   Example: Mutual Exclusion for Two Processes

Same as in [14] we consider Peterson's mutual exclusion algorithm for two processes [19] as a simple example for the application of liveness conditions. For the general case with any number of processes Börger presented a rigorous solution based on Lamport's bakery algorithm using concurrent ASMs in [5].

A mutual exclusion protocol aims to guarantee that it never happens that two processes are simultaneously in the "critical code section". In addition, it must also guarantee that every process that attempts to enter the critical section will eventually enter it. These two properties are known as, respectively, *mutual exclusion* and (conditional) *progress*.

We assume a concurrent ASM with two processes (agents) P_1 and P_2. Following the presentation in [3] of Peterson's mutex algorithm, each time P_1 needs to access the critical section, it must use the following protocol:

```
AccessProtocolP₁ =
PAR
    IF state(P₁) = try
    THEN PAR   flag(P₁) := 1
               state(P₁) := getStick
         ENDPAR
    ENDIF
    IF state(P₁) = getStick
    THEN PAR   IF ¬stickHolder = P₁ THEN stickHolder := P₁ ENDIF
               state(P₁) := waitToWin
         ENDPAR
    ENDIF
    IF state(P₁) = waitToWin
    THEN IF flag(P₂) = 0 ∨ stickHolder = P₂
         THEN state(P₁) := critical
         ELSE skip
         ENDIF
    ENDIF
ENDPAR
```

The corresponding AccessProtocolP$_2$ is obtained by simply replacing every occurrence of P_1 by P_2 and vice versa in AccessProtocolP$_1$. In every initial state, neither processes wants to enter the critical section, i.e., $flag(P_1) = flag(P_2) = 0$, and furthermore $stickHolder \in \{P_1, P_2\}$ and $state(P_1) = state(P_2) = idle$. The natural assumption here is that neither process can remain forever in the critical code section. Moreover, each process P_i sets $state(P_i) = idle$ and $flag(P_i) = 0$ upon exiting it.

Note that it is *not* checked in [14] whether a process has the stick or not (called turn there) before assigning it. This is the case because in event-B, only one event is fired in each step, resulting in interleaving runs (traces in event-B terminology). Here we do not assume an interleaving semantics, using the more general notion of concurrent (ASM) runs as defined in [4]. Therefore, we need this guard to avoid clashes.

As shown in [11] (see Sect. 7), a concurrent ASM can always be mimicked by a non-deterministic ASM, in the sense that the set of all possible runs of both machines will coincide. Therefore, we assume the rule r used in the formulae below is actually the rule of the non-deterministic ASM that mimics the concurrent ASM described earlier, with two processes P_1 and P_2 that use, respectively, the rules ACCESSPROTOCOLP$_1$ and ACCESSPROTOCOLP$_2$ to access the critical section. Thus $\mathcal{ML}_{\text{ASM}}$ can be used to express the required properties.

Mutual exclusion can be expressed by the following invariant formula, which is easy to prove using the derivation rule INV from Proposition 3.

$$\Box\big(\neg(state(P_1) = critical) \lor \neg(state(P_2) = critical)\big)$$

Progress for process P_1 can be expressed using the following formulae.

$$\text{ProgP}_1 \equiv \Box\big(flag(P_1) = 1 \land state(P_1) = waitToWin \rightarrow \Diamond state(P_1) = critical\big)$$

Likewise we can express progress for P_2. Notice that it is also the case that the formula $\Box(flag(P_1) = 1 \rightarrow \Diamond state(P_1) = waitToWin)$ is valid, which implies together with ProgP_1 the validity of

$$\Box\big(flag(P_1) = 1 \rightarrow \Diamond state(P_1) = critical\big).$$

In order to show that the progress sentence for P_1 is valid, we can use the rule PROG$_0$, where $\chi \equiv (flag(P_2) = 0 \lor stickHolder = P_2) \land state(P_1) = waitToWin$. This requires to show that the following are valid formulae, which due to space restriction we leave as an exercise for the reader:

(i) $\Box(\text{div}(\neg state(P_1) = critical))$:
$$\text{div}(\neg((flag(P_2) = 0 \lor stickHolder = P_2) \land state(P_1) = waitToWin))$$

(ii) $\Box(\text{div}(\neg state(P_1) = critical))$:
$$\text{next}((flag(P_2) = 0 \lor stickHolder = P_2) \land state(P_1) = waitToWin \land$$
$$\neg state(P_1) = critical,$$
$$((flag(P_2) = 0 \lor stickHolder = P_2) \land state(P_1) = waitToWin) \lor$$
$$state(P_1) = critical)$$

(iii) $\Box(\text{div}(\neg state(P_1) = critical))$:
$$flag(P_1) = 1 \land state(P_1) = waitToWin \land \neg state(P_1) = critical \rightarrow$$
$$(flag(P_2) = 0 \lor stickHolder = P_2) \land state(P_1) =$$
$$waitToWin)$$

5   Concluding Remarks

In this paper we continued the research in [9] in the context of Abstract State Machines. We defined a full temporal extension $\mathcal{ML}_{\text{ASM}}$ of the logic of ASMs from [11] capturing ALWAYS-, EVENTUAL- and UNTIL-formulae as well as quantification over runs and definable teams, i.e. definable subsets of the set of runs. However, the runs only occur implicitly in the logic, so it remains a second-order logic with Henkin semantics. We discovered a fragment of $\mathcal{ML}_{\text{ASM}}$, in which liveness conditions for invariance, existence, progress and persistence (as introduced in [14] for Event-B) can be expressed and proven. We demostrated the applicability of the logic and its derivation rules on an example relevant for concurrent systems, concerning mutual exclusion for access of two different processes to critical code sections. Full proofs including a completeness theorem for the fragment will appear in a forthcoming extended version.

Competing Interests. The author(s) has no competing interests to declare that are relevant to the content of this manuscript.

References

1. Abrial, J.R.: Modeling in Event-B - System and Software Engineering. Cambridge University Press, Cambridge (2010). https://doi.org/10.1017/CBO9781139195881
2. Biskup, J.: Security in Computing Systems - Challenges, Approaches and Solutions. Springer, Heidelberg (2009). https://doi.org/10.1007/978-3-540-78442-5
3. Börger, E.: Modeling distributed algorithms by abstract state machines compared to petri nets. In: Butler, M., Schewe, K.-D., Mashkoor, A., Biro, M. (eds.) ABZ 2016. LNCS, vol. 9675, pp. 3–34. Springer, Cham (2016). https://doi.org/10.1007/978-3-319-33600-8_1
4. Börger, E., Schewe, K.D.: Concurrent abstract state machines. Acta Inform. **53**(5), 469–492 (2016)
5. Börger, E., Stärk, R.: Abstract State Machines. Springer, Heidelberg (2003). https://doi.org/10.1007/978-3-642-18216-7
6. Clarke, E.M., Emerson, E.A.: Design and synthesis of synchronization skeletons using branching-time temporal logic. In: Kozen, D. (ed.) Logics of Programs. Lecture Notes in Computer Science, vol. 131, pp. 52–71. Springer, Heidelberg (1982). https://doi.org/10.1007/bfb0025774
7. Clarkson, M.R., Finkbeiner, B., Koleini, M., Micinski, K.K., Rabe, M.N., Sánchez, C.: Temporal logics for hyperproperties. In: Abadi, M., Kremer, S. (eds.) POST 2014. LNCS, vol. 8414, pp. 265–284. Springer, Heidelberg (2014). https://doi.org/10.1007/978-3-642-54792-8_15
8. Clarkson, M.R., Schneider, F.B.: Hyperproperties. J. Comput. Secur. **18**(6), 1157–1210 (2010). https://doi.org/10.3233/JCS-2009-0393
9. Ferrarotti, F., Rivière, P., Schewe, K.D., Singh, N.K., Aït Ameur, Y.: A complete fragment of LTL(EB). In: Meyer, A., Ortiz, M. (eds.) FoIKS 2024. LNCS, vol. 14589, pp. 237–255. Springer, Cham (2024). https://doi.org/10.1007/978-3-031-56940-1_13. An extended version is available at http://arxiv.org/abs/2401.16838
10. Ferrarotti, F., Schewe, K.D., Tec, L., Wang, Q.: A complete logic for database abstract state machines. Log. J. IGPL **25**(5), 700–740 (2017). https://doi.org/10.1093/JIGPAL/JZX021
11. Ferrarotti, F., Schewe, K.D., Tec, L., Wang, Q.: A unifying logic for non-deterministic, parallel and concurrent abstract state machines. Ann. Math. Artif. Intell. **83**(3–4), 321–349 (2018). https://doi.org/10.1007/s10472-017-9569-3
12. Gurevich, Y.: Evolving algebras 1993: Lipari guide. In: Specification and Validation Methods, pp. 9–36. Oxford University Press (1995)
13. Gutsfeld, J.O., Meier, A., Ohrem, C., Virtema, J.: Temporal team semantics revisited. In: Baier, C., Fisman, D. (eds.) 37th Annual ACM/IEEE Symposium on Logic in Computer Science (LICS 2022), pp. 44:1–44:13 (2022). https://doi.org/10.1145/3531130.3533360

14. Hoang, T.S., Abrial, J.-R.: Reasoning about liveness properties in event-B. In: Qin, S., Qiu, Z. (eds.) ICFEM 2011. LNCS, vol. 6991, pp. 456–471. Springer, Heidelberg (2011). https://doi.org/10.1007/978-3-642-24559-6_31

15. Kontinen, J., Sandström, M.: On the expressive power of TeamLTL and first-order team logic over hyperproperties. In: Silva, A., Wassermann, R., de Queiroz, R. (eds.) WoLLIC 2021. LNCS, vol. 13038, pp. 302–318. Springer, Cham (2021). https://doi.org/10.1007/978-3-030-88853-4_19

16. Lamport, L.: Specifying Systems – The TLA⁺ Language and Tools for Hardware and Software Engineers. Addison-Wesley (2002)

17. Manna, Z., Pnueli, A.: Adequate proof principles for invariance and liveness properties of concurrent programs. Sci. Comput. Program. **4**(3), 257–289 (1984). https://doi.org/10.1016/0167-6423(84)90003-0

18. Merz, S.: On the logic of TLA⁺. Comput. Artif. Intell. **22**(3–4), 351–379 (2003)

19. Peterson, G.L.: Myths about the mutual exclusion problem. Inf. Process. Lett. **12**(3), 115–116 (1981). https://doi.org/10.1016/0020-0190(81)90106-X

20. Pnueli, A.: The temporal logic of programs. In: 18th Annual Symposium on Foundations of Computer Science (FoCS 1977), pp. 46–57. IEEE Computer Society (1977). https://doi.org/10.1109/SFCS.1977.32

21. Rivière, P., Singh, N.K., Aït Ameur, Y., Dupont, G.: Formalising liveness properties in Event-B with the reflexive EB4EB framework. In: Rozier, K.Y., Chaudhuri, S. (eds.) NFM 2023. LNCS, vol. 13903, pp. 312–331. Springer, Cham (2023). https://doi.org/10.1007/978-3-031-33170-1_19

22. Schewe, K.D., Ferrarotti, F.: Behavioural theory of reflective algorithms I: reflective sequential algorithms. Sci. Comput. Program. **223**, 102864 (2022). https://doi.org/10.1016/J.SCICO.2022.102864

23. Schewe, K.D., Ferrarotti, F., González, S.: A logic for reflective ASMs. Sci. Comput. Program. **210**, 102691 (2021). https://doi.org/10.1016/J.SCICO.2021.102691

24. Schmalz, M.: Formalizing the logic of event-B. Ph.D. thesis, ETH Zürich (2012)

25. Stärk, R.F., Nanchen, S.: A logic for abstract state machines. J. Univ. Comput. Sci. **7**(11), 980–1005 (2001)

An Analysis of the Impact of Field-Value Instance Navigation in Alloy's Model Finding

César Cornejo[1,3]($\boxtimes$), María Marta Novaira[1], Sonia Permigiani[1],
Nazareno Aguirre[1,3], Marcelo Frias[2], Simón Gutiérrez Brida[1,3],
and Germán Regis[1,3]

[1] University of Río Cuarto, Río Cuarto, Argentina
`ccornejo@dc.exa.unrc.edu.ar`
[2] University of Texas at El Paso, El Paso, USA
[3] National Council for Scientific and Technical Research (CONICET),
Buenos Aires, Argentina

Abstract. The use of SAT-based model finding for specification analysis is a crucial characteristic of Alloy, and a main reason of its success as a language for software specification. When a property of a specification is analyzed and deemed satisfiable, the user usually explores instances of the corresponding satisfiability, in order to understand the analysis outcome. The order in which instances are obtained during exploration can impact the efficiency and effectiveness with which specification analysis is carried out. This has been observed by various researchers, and different instance exploration strategies have been proposed, besides the standard SAT-solver driven strategy implemented with the Alloy Analyzer.

In this paper, we concentrate on a strategy recently proposed in the literature, that we refer to as "field-value" driven, and has been implemented in the tool HawkEye. The tool allows the user to interactively guide instance exploration, by enforcing constraints requiring fields to contain (resp., do not contain) specific values. We design an experiment involving faulty Alloy specifications featuring combinations of over constraints and under constraints, and perform a user study to analyze the impact of this instance exploration strategy, in comparison with the standard SAT-solver driven exploration. The study focuses on HawkEye's facility of interactive instance querying and how it may favor users, in its current realization, during Alloy model analysis and debugging. We perform an assessment of the evaluation, and summarize some of the reasons that may diminish the impact of field-value exploration in model finding.

1 Introduction

Formal methods are known to have a great potential to reduce bugs in software, and in general to improve the quality of software [15]. By helping developers to build abstract formal models of software, its design and domain constraints, formal specification allows for mathematical reasoning on these models, leading to early identification of various issues, including problem misconceptions,

© The Author(s), under exclusive license to Springer Nature Switzerland AG 2024
S. Bonfanti et al. (Eds.): ABZ 2024, LNCS 14759, pp. 141–159, 2024.
https://doi.org/10.1007/978-3-031-63790-2_9

non-trivial contradictions, and the invalidity of expected software properties [8]. While formal methods traditionally employ (semi automated) deductive reasoning on formal specifications, the use of fully automated specification analysis, as realized with model checkers [7] and model finders [18, 36], has significantly improved the practical applicability of formal methods. In this context, the Alloy formal specification language [18], and its automated specification analysis tool Alloy Analyzer, have received increasing attention by the formal methods and software engineering communities [2–5, 10, 13, 14, 23, 28, 35]. Besides the simplicity and expressiveness of the Alloy language, a main reason for the language's success is indeed the possibility of automatically analyzing specifications. Alloy Analyzer implements a bounded-exhaustive instance finding technique, that given an Alloy formula α and a bound n, is able to report satisfying instances of α bounded by n, or otherwise inform that α is unsatisfiable within bound n [18]. Alloy Analyzer resorts to SAT solving to implement instance finding, and when a formula is found satisfiable, it is able to sequentially explore *all* satisfying instances (up to isomorphism) within bound n [18, 21]. Alloy exploits instance finding in two ways: to check *assertions* (checking that no violating instances exist within a bound n), and to query the satisfiability of *predicates* (used to model software operations or specific software properties, among other uses).

When a property of a specification is analyzed and deemed satisfiable, e.g., when an assertion is found to be invalid, or a predicate is confirmed to be consistent with the assumptions in the specification, the user usually explores instances of the corresponding satisfiability, as a way of understanding the analysis outcome. Such exploration of instances is a powerful mechanism that users employ to either confirm their expectations (obtained instances are what the developers expected), or help in the debugging process (e.g., when the satisfying instances are counterexamples of an intended property). During the instance exploration process, the order in which instances are provided to the user can impact the efficiency and effectiveness with which specification analysis is carried out: as satisfying instances can grow combinatorially, users typically explore a few before deciding to confirm a specification behaves as expected, or decide on what to modify when the outcome is incorrect. This has been observed by various researchers, and different instance exploration strategies have been proposed, including size-sorted instances [22], instances that favor minimality [31], and instances that feature further differences with respect to previously reported ones [29]. Alloy's standard instance finding strategy, implemented in the Alloy Analyzer, is driven by the underlying SAT solver, and thus is relatively unguided.

The importance of instance exploration, and the relevance of satisfying instance orderings, call for novel ways of reporting satisfying instances in Alloy, a topic that receives significant interest. A newly proposed mechanism to produce Alloy satisfying instances is the one put forward by A. Sullivan with her HawkEye tool [33]. HawkEye allows developers to interactively guide instance exploration. We call this instance exploration "field-value" driven, since the developer guides the exploration by enforcing constraints requiring fields to contain, or alternatively do not contain, specific values. This paper concentrates on HawkEye's instance exploration, and studies the impact of this interactive strategy in Alloy specification analysis and debugging. We design an experiment involving faulty Alloy specifications featuring combinations of over constraints and under constraints, and perform a user study to analyze the impact of this instance exploration strategy, in comparison with the standard SAT-solver driven exploration. The evaluation is based on various quantitative metrics, that aim at assessing whether field-value driven exploration provides a significant improvement in the debugging process or not. We also perform an assessment of the evaluation, and summarize some of the reasons that may diminish the impact of field-value exploration in model finding.

2   Preliminaries

In this section we briefly present Alloy and its main specification analysis approach, including instance exploration. We also present HawkEye, the instance exploration strategy that is the subject of our study.

2.1   Alloy

Alloy is a formal specification language, that proposes to capture software properties using a logical language with a relational flavor [17,18]. Alloy puts a strong emphasis in automated analysis [21], and is accompanied by an efficient fully automated mechanism for bounded analysis of specification properties, that resorts to SAT solving to query for the bounded satisfiability or bounded validity of Alloy formulas [19]. Alloy features simple yet powerful syntax and semantics for specifications, or *models*, as they are typically called in the Alloy context. The usual way in which an Alloy specification is written starts by defining the model's data domains using *signatures*. Signatures describe data domains, and may include *fields*, which define relations between signatures. Signatures can also be extended by other signatures (akin to class extensions), meaning simply that the set of elements in the extending signature is a subset of the elements of the extended one. A signature can also be declared *abstract*, indicating that its corresponding elements are solely those of its extending signatures. As an example, consider a *secure laboratory* specification shown in Fig. 1 (this is an adaptation of a specification from [34]). The domain of *rooms* is defined by a corresponding signature Room. In the model a distinguished *secure room* is defined as secure_lab, a singleton (one) extension of *rooms*. Similarly, the laboratory's *administrative staff* and *researchers* are defined as extensions of the Person signature. The Person signature indicates that every person owns a set of *keys*. Signature Key captures the *keys* of the laboratory, and features fields to indicate which *person* is authorized to use a key, and which *room* a key opens.

Relations and constraints on model elements are specified by using *facts*, *predicates* and *functions*. These specifications are written in Alloy's relational logic, a first-order logic extended with relational operators, such as union (+), intersection (&), join (.), and most importantly, transitive closure (^). Alloy formulas use standard logical connectives (and, or, not, etc.), quantifiers (all, some, no, the latter corresponding to "there is no"), relational inclusion (in) and equality (=). Facts are formulas assumed to hold in the model. For instance, the laboratory specification indicates that every key that opens the secure lab, necessarily authorizes a researcher (each key authorizes a single person). Predicates are parameterized formulas, that can be used to state properties, and capture operations, among other things. For instance, CanEnter relates persons with rooms, specifying that a person p can enter a room r only if there exists a key that authorizes p, and opens room r. In order to state *intended* properties of the model, i.e., formulas that are expected to hold, Alloy allows developers to specify *assertions*. As an example, assertion OnlyResearchersInSecureLab states that any person that can enter the secure laboratory room must be a researcher.

Both predicates and assertions can be automatically analyzed, by searching for satisfying instances, in the case of predicates, and for counterexamples (witnessing property violations), in the case of assertions. Analyses are defined via *commands*: runs for predicates, and checks for assertions. The search exhaustively explores all possible instances bounded by a *scope*, the maximum number of elements to consider for each domain (associated with signatures). Scopes can be set as part of the command and can be different for each signature. As an example, the command:

```
run CanEnter for 3 Room, 5 Person, 5 Key
```

queries for instances containing up to three rooms, five people and five keys, that satisfy predicate CanEnter (as well as the model's facts). Alloy's bounded-exhaustive search for model instances is implemented by resorting to SAT solving, i.e., by translating Alloy analyses into propositional formulas in such a way that every satisfying valuation of the resulting formula corresponds to an instance of the predicate (resp., a counterexample of the assertion), within the corresponding scope. Alloy Analyzer, the tool implementing this technique, allows one to use a number of different off-the-shelf SAT solvers to analyze Alloy specification predicates and assertions.

Alloy has been recently extended to support linear-time temporal logic, among other features [6, 24]. Since the instance exploration strategy that is the subject of this study is implemented only for "standard" Alloy, we do not consider here these newer characteristics of Alloy.

2.2 Alloy's Instance Exploration

When a command is executed using Alloy Analyzer and the corresponding formula is deemed satisfiable, the tool allows the developer to explore the satisfying instances of the formula. Instances can be sequentially inspected, one at a time, in a bounded-exhaustive fashion (all satisfying instances can be generated, up to isomorphism [20], using a mechanism known as *incremental solving* [16]). As satisfying instances correspond to satisfying valuations of the boolean formula that resulted from the translation from Alloy to propositional logic, and these are obtained by the execution of a SAT solver, the order in which satisfying

```
sig Room { }
one sig secure_lab extends Room { }

abstract sig Person {
    owns: set Key
}

sig Admin extends Person { }
sig Researcher extends Person { }

sig Key {
    authorizes: one Person,
    opens: one Room
}

fact {
    all k: Key | secure_lab = k.opens implies
                    k.authorizes in Researcher
}

pred CanEnter[p: Person, r:Room] {
    some k: Key | k.authorizes = p and r = k.opens
}
run CanEnter

assert OnlyResearchersInSecureLab {
    all p : Person | CanEnter[p, secure_lab] implies p in Researcher
}
check OnlyResearchersInSecureLab
```

Fig. 1. A simple Alloy model describing a secure laboratory.

instances are retrieved and presented to the developer depends on the underlying SAT solver. Thus, the developer has no direct control on the order in which these instances are obtained. This instance exploration order is of course important for model analysis. In particular, if a specification is weaker than intended, then the specification will lead to unwanted instances; how fast these are identified greatly depends on the order in which instances are retrieved. If, on the other hand, a specification is stronger than intended (but still satisfiable), then the developer will probably explore many specification instances until realizing that some expected "scenarios" are not being generated. This process can be labor-intensive, as the number of satisfying instances of Alloy formulas tends to grow combinatorially as the scope is increased. Specifications that are weaker than intended feature the so-called *underspecification* problem, i.e., not enough constraints are imposed and thus unwanted scenarios arise as a consequence. On the other hand, specifications that are stronger than intended have *overspecification* problems: the effect of stronger-than-intended assumptions is that some desired behaviors will be disallowed. Generally, underspecification problems are easier to identify via instance exploration than overspecification cases. The latter, as mentioned earlier, would in principle require one to explore all satisfying instances in order to acknowledge that there are missing scenarios.

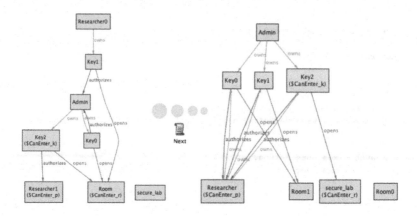

Fig. 2. Two satisfying instances of predicate `CanEnter`.

As an example of the impact of the instance visualization ordering provided by Alloy Analyzer, consider Fig. 2. The figure shows the first instance generated for the `CanEnter` predicate (with default scope 3), and the first instance of this predicate where, contrary to the expectations of the developer, an administrative staff member has access to the secure lab (meaning that the administrative person owns a key that opens the secure lab). This first unwanted instance is the 657th obtained instance, meaning that, by exploring instances of `CanEnter`, the developer would realize of this unwanted behavior after observing 656 previous instances. Moreover, assertion `OnlyResearchersInSecureLab` has no counterexamples in this model, so the analysis of this other assertion does not help us in identifying the defects present in this specification. Let us remark that the issue here, that leads to the unwanted scenarios, is associated with the fact that key ownership and authorization are different concepts, captured by different fields (`owns` and `authorizes`, respectively). The unwanted behaviors arise because no constraint enforces that a person may only own keys that authorize himself/herself, thus allowing admin staff to access the secure lab in some scenarios.

2.3   HawkEye

As explained above, the order in which instances are obtained during exploration can impact the efficiency and effectiveness with which specification analysis is carried out. Thus, having more control on how these instances can be visited or generated has the potential of significantly increasing the efficiency and effectiveness with which an Alloy model is analyzed. Precisely this hypothesis is what led to the development of HawkEye [33]. HawkEye is a technique put forward by A. Sullivan and implemented over the Alloy Analyzer that allows the developer to have more control on instance exploration, by interactively guiding the exploration, through the enforcement of constraints requiring to keep (resp., change) previously obtained values for signatures and relations. Therefore, we call this

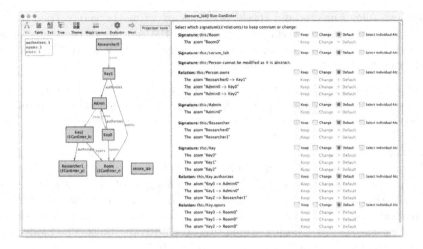

Fig. 3. HawkEye visualization interface.

strategy for instance exploration *field-value* guided. As depicted in Fig. 3, Hawk-Eye allows the user to manually instruct *how* to generate the next satisfying instance. It offers three possible actions on signature atoms, fields, and field tuples: one can *keep* an element of the current instance (enforcing it to be maintained as is in the next instance), *change* an element, causing it to be different from its current value in the next instance, or leave it unconstrained (the default) for the next instance.

HawkEye implements its instance exploration strategy by a more sophisticated use of incremental solving: it encodes the user-provided constraints as additional propositional clauses, that are conjoined with the formula being analyzed, in order to generate the "next" satisfying instance [33]. This is rather efficient, as incremental solving allows one to incorporate these extra clauses without having to restart the solving process [16]. The mechanism has been shown to allow for a faster convergence to violating scenarios in underspecification contexts, and to more quickly converge to unsatisfiability outcomes in over specification cases [33].

3   The Experiment

The instance exploration strategy proposed with HawkEye has been assessed using some case studies, and studying expressiveness possibilities, as well as convergence to identifying underconstraint and overconstraint issues in the considered case studies [33]. Our objective in this paper is to complement previous evaluations with a controlled user study, in which we analyze the impact of HawkEye's instance exploration, compared to standard Alloy, in debugging various Alloy specifications. Our study comprises two similar experiments with undergraduate students who have had some instruction on Alloy specification, using both Alloy Analyzer and HawkEye. These experiments were carried out in two consecutive years (we will refer to these as the *editions* of the study), and assessed the performance of the students in debugging four faulty Alloy models taken from the literature. The four models are:

- *Java Inheritance* (J.Inh): the model was taken from [34] and describes how class inheritance behaves in the Java programming language. This model contains an under constraint issue. Both editions of the experiment used exactly the same version of this faulty model.
- *Linked List* (L.List): the specification was taken from [34] and captures a formal specification of singly linked lists, with some associated properties such as sortedness. There were some slight changes to this model across the two editions of the experiment: the first edition used a faulty model with two bugs (an underconstraint bug and an overconstraint bug), while the version used for the second experiment had two overconstraint bugs. The model and one of the bugs were adapted from a case study in [33].
- *Secure Lab* (S.Lab): this model describes a security protocol of a laboratory with a secure room, which is meant to be accessed only by researchers (we used a variant of this model for illustration purposes in the preliminaries section). The specification is adapted from one originally introduced in [34]. The version used in the first edition contained an overconstraint bug, while the version for the second edition was improved, crafting an underconstraint bug instead.
- *Graph*: this specification was taken from [26], and captures graphs and some of their properties: undirectedness, transitivity and strong connectivity. The model used for the first edition of the experiment had an over constraint bug. The model was simplified for the second edition, and had no bugs.

In all cases, the specifications were complemented with corresponding detailed narratives, explaining what each specification was intended to express. Each student participating in the study received these specifications and their narratives. Students were also informed that the specifications may be correct or incorrect; in case a specification was considered correct, they had to simply explicitly state it and leave the specification as is; if a specification was considered incorrect, they had to debug it, and provide a modified specification with the identified issues fixed. No time limit was imposed, but the experiment was designed with an expected duration of two hours (this is also the reason why the experiment is limited to four faulty specifications). Time was not taken into account as a metric during the evaluation.

In both editions of the experiment, students were split into two groups: one of the groups was assigned the standard Alloy Analyzer, the other group was assigned HawkEye. The work of each student in each group was individual. The first edition of the experiment was carried out several months after students had instruction on Alloy in the context of an undergraduate course. For this reason, before the experiment, students received a brief summary of Alloy's syntax and semantics, as well as a brief demo on the use of Alloy Analyzer and HawkEye; students in HawkEye's group were also presented with the specific characteristics of HawkEye's instance exploration, and its mechanism to enforce constraints for "next instance" generation. The second edition of the experiment was performed in the context of the undergraduate course featuring Alloy; HawkEye was included in the course as an additional tool for specification analysis, and thus the students did not need any notation summary or tool demo prior to the experiment.

When the students finished their corresponding assignments, they were asked to fill in a questionnaire. Questions in the questionnaire asked about problems found in the specifications, opinions on the user-friendliness of the corresponding tool, issues that may have emerged during the assignments, and their overall opinions on the tools, the specification language, and possible suggestions to improve modeling and analysis in the Alloy context.

The interaction of the students with the corresponding tools during specification debugging was measured along the following general metrics:

- *Number of instances* explored during the analysis/debugging of each model.
- *Number of edits* made to the specification in order to fix it. Some standard "interaction" edits such as adding a `run show` command were not taken into account.

For the students that received HawkEye, we also measured the *number of guided instances* visited during instance exploration. Moreover, when guided instance exploration was used, we also assessed the complexity of the added constraints, measured in terms of the number of constraints used, their type (change or keep), and their granularity (whole field vs. specific field values, for instance). A total of 30 students participated in the experiment, 10 students in the first edition, and 20 students in the second edition. In both editions the participating students were split into two groups of the same size, and assigned a tool to each group.

3.1   Recording Student Interactions

Students were informed that their interactions with the corresponding tools was going to be logged, and assessed anonymously. It is worth mentioning that the participation in the experiment was optional, and thus all participating students voluntarily did so. The logging of user actions was realized via implementations of interaction logging into the Alloy Analyzer and HawkEye. The logging was completely transparent to the users, and generated logging data in a folder, that the corresponding student submitted when the assignment concluded. All relevant actions and events were logged: edits to a model and the corresponding modified lines; syntactic checks on models; command executions and their corresponding outcomes; instance exploration activity, including the visualized instances, their number, etc.; and of course the specific restrictions in the interactive instance generation for the case of HawkEye. All this information and the faulty models are available in [1].

4   Evaluation

We now present the results of the experiment, and an evaluation of the information collected from the interaction of the participating students with the tools. Our first part of the analysis performs a higher level comparison of the two tools, based on the metrics described in the previous section. The second part concentrates more deeply on the specific usage of HawkEye, tries to examine how the users exploited the instance constraints provided by HawkEye, and how this feature facilitated specification debugging.

4.1   Higher Level Comparison of the Tools

Let us first summarize the general results, in terms of bugs found and models fixed, corresponding to the two analyzed tools. Table 1 provides this information. Each row corresponds to a bug in a specific model, indicated by its abbreviation, and provides information about the model the bug corresponds to (using v1 and v2 for distinguishing the models used in the two editions of the experiment), and the type of bug ('O' for overconstraint, 'U' for underconstraint, and 'correct' for the non-buggy model). In each row we indicate how many participants found the corresponding bug (identified the correct bug location), and how many of these were able to correctly fix the specification (notice then that the "model fixed" column value is always smaller or equal to the corresponding "Bug Found" column value), separated in the two tool groups. Regarding incorrect bug identification, we had only a few cases: one student (HawkEye group) reported a bug in Graph v1, but did not correctly locate the bug in the model; two students (both from the HawkEye group) reported bugs in Graph v2, which is a correct model; and finally a student (Alloy group) reported a bug in Java Inheritance v2, without correctly locating it. The bugs in models on Java Inheritance and Linked List were the ones in which participants showed a better performance. The only overconstraint bug in this group is LinkedList v2 bug 2, which is identifiable by a provided assert. The remaining overconstraint bugs in Linked List, Secure Lab and Graph showed a significantly worse overall performance. In general, in terms of these high level metrics, HawkEye did not provide a clear advantage in debugging, over Alloy Analyzer. Overconstraint bugs seem more difficult to spot via instance exploration than underconstraint bugs (with the exception of Linked List v2 bug 2, as mentioned above), as expected.

Let us further analyze the corresponding interactions with the tools. Table 2 shows the total numbers of edits that participants made to the models during debugging, and the instances explored during analysis (for HawkEye users, the table also reports the number of constraints set during instance exploration, i.e., the overall use of guided instance exploration). Overall, participants using Alloy Analyzer explored more instances than those using HawkEye. However, we did not observe a correlation between the use of constraints in HawkEye with exploring fewer instances (it is worth noting that the numbers in the table are total numbers, but only 8 out of 15 students in this group used constraints). Notice that some cells in Table 2 have two reported numbers (one of them within parentheses). These

Table 1. Summary of bugs found and models fixed with the analyzed tools

Model	Alloy		HawkEye	
	Bug found	Model fixed	Bug found	Model fixed
Graph v1 bug (O)	0	0	0	0
J.Inh v1 bug (U)	5	4	5	4
L.List v1 bug 1 (U)	5	4	4	2
L.List v1 bug 2 (O)	3	2	1	1
S.Lab v1 bug (O)	4	4	2	1
Graph v2 correct	–	–	–	–
J.Inh v2 bug (U)	7	5	8	3
L.List v2 bug 1 (O)	1	1	2	1
L.List v2 bug 2 (O)	5	4	7	5
S.Lab v2 bug (U)	4	2	6	1
Total underconst. (U)	21	15	23	10
Total overconst. (O)	13	11	12	8

Table 2. User Interactions, in terms of editions to models and instances explored during analysis.

Model	Alloy		HawkEye		
	Explored instances	Edits	Explored instances	Constraints	Edits
Graph v1	40	0	54	2	0
J.Inh v1	71	11	109 (169)	17	25 (96)
L.List v1	95 (257)	15	126	8	25
S.Lab v1	188	17	79	1	9
Graph v2	372	27	432	0	37
J.Inh v2	366	79	285	12	108
L.List v2	1890	92	530	44	113
S.Lab v2	341	41	88	0	24
Total	3363	282	1703	84	341

are depicted to highlight some outliers in the analysis. In the Java Inheritance v1 model, a HawkEye user interpreted a "check" command as a "run" command, and since the student expected instances which were not obtained (the assertion had no counterexamples), many subsequent edits were performed on the model after having repaired it. Value 25 in this case corresponds to the edits until the model was fixed, whereas 96 is the total number of edits (including the unnecessary edits after the model was first fixed). Similarly, in Linked List v1, an Alloy user bounded exhaustively checked *all* instances of the "sorted" predicate, a behavior that is uncommon compared with the usual. We report between parentheses the total number of explored instances, including this unusual case.

Table 3. Average user interactions, in terms of editions to models and instances explored during analysis.

Model	Alloy		HawkEye	
	Explored instances	Edits	Explored instances	Edits
Graph v1	8.0	0.0	10.8	0.0
J.Inh v1	14.2	2.2	22.0	5.0
L.List v1	19.0	3.0	25.2	5.0
S.Lab v1	37.6	3.4	15.8	1.8
Graph v2	37.2	2.7	43.2	3.7
J.Inh v2	36.6	7.9	20.8	9.9
L.List v2	189.0	9.2	53.0	11.3
S.Lab v2	34.1	4.1	8.8	2.4
Total	224.2	18.8	113.5	22.7

We also analyzed in more depth the impact of HawkEye constraints in model edits and repairs. Overall, in eight opportunities users performed a model edit immediately after querying for an instance under a manually specified HawkEye constraint. In terms of model fixing, in one case, a model was repaired immediately after querying for an instance under a manually specified constraint. To better understand the "per user" interaction with the corresponding tools, Table 3 reports the average number of edits and instances explored, for each of the case studies, and the analyzed tools. Again, in general Alloy Analyzer users explored more instances (roughly twice as many compared to HawkEye users) and performed slightly fewer model edits during debugging (about 17% fewer edits, compared with HawkEye users).

4.2   Detailed Analysis of HawkEye Usage

We now turn our attention to a more detailed analysis of how HawkEye's instance exploration is used/exploited. First, it is worth remarking that the instance exploration facility of HawkEye may be mimicked by standard Alloy users by manually writing specific "specializations" of existing predicates or introducing additional facts (these specializations would enforce the constraints that a Hawk-Eye user would set during instance exploration). However, none of the Alloy users exhibited this behavior. Although it is difficult to understand why users did not do this kind of modification, we conjecture that users do not do so because of the associated cost of writing additional predicates or facts. On the other hand, HawkEye users, who had this facility "built-in", made use of it, indicating that it is indeed a facility that users find useful (8 out of 15 participants used HawkEye constraints in at least one model).

Regarding the specific constraints used during instance exploration with HawkEye, Table 4 summarizes the observations. In the table, Atom refers to constraints that enforce changes in specific atoms, whereas All refers to the coarser

Table 4. Types of constraints used in HawkEye's instance explorations

Model	Signatures		Relations		Keep	Change
	Atom	All	Atom	All		
Graph v1	0	1	1	1	1	2
J.Inh v1	10	9	11	6	32	4
L.List v1	1	10	0	13	15	9
S.Lab v1	3	4	4	1	11	1
Graph v2	0	0	0	0	0	0
J.Inh v2	7	6	10	2	25	0
L.List v2	0	40	12	57	100	21
S.Lab v2	0	0	0	0	0	0
Total	21	70	38	80	184	37

granularity constraint that enforces a change (or a keep) on the whole signature or field. Overall, there were more "keep" constraints than "change" constraints, and users favored coarser granularity in the constraints (whole signatures/fields, over specific elements or tuples in these).

Let us now focus on how the use of HawkEye constraints evolved as the experiments progressed. Figure 4 shows the number of explored instances, with and without the use of constraints, as users progressed from one model to the next, during the experiment. Regarding which models the participants chose to work on, 14 participants started with Java Inheritance and the rest chose Graph; 13 participants chose Linked List as the second model, while one student worked on each of the other models as their second model; the third model was Secure Lab for 11 participants, 2 worked on Linked List, and 2 on Graph; and finally 11 students worked on Graph as their last model and the rest on Secure Lab. As the Figure shows, the use of constraints decreased as time progressed (and so did the proportion of constrained instances vs unconstrained ones). More precisely, for the first model, 4.52% of the instance explorations corresponded to "constrained" ones (25 out of 553); for the second model, the percentage was 8.04% (51 out of 583 instance explorations); for the third model, this percentage decreased to 1.24% (3 out of 239), and finally for the last model the percentage was 0.35% (1 out of 282 explorations).

It is worth turning our attention back to the Secure Lab (v1 and v2) case study, where, as we have seen earlier in this section, instance exploration by Alloy users was significantly greater than the number of instance explorations by HawkEye users. It is worth noting however that almost no guiding constraints were used for this case study by HawkEye users (only one participant set exactly one constraint for instance exploration). This leads us to believe that, for this case study, HawkEye participants used the tool mostly in the style of Alloy Analyzer, i.e., without guided instance exploration. On the other hand, LinkedList v2 is a case study in which HawkEye seemed to have provided more benefits:

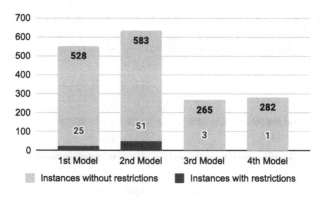

Fig. 4. Use of constraints vs standard instance exploration, by HawkEye users, as the experiment progressed from model to model.

significantly fewer instances explored compared to Alloy users, which correlates in this case with an important use of constraints.

4.3 Discussion

Overall, our experiment does not indicate that field-value guided instance exploration significantly improves model analysis and debugging. Guided instance exploration received attention by the HawkEye users in our experiments, i.e., users actually exercised this functionality. But the use of guided instance exploration was not maintained as the experiment progressed, and had no significant impact in debugging and fixing, as far as the metrics considered allowed us to assess.

We believe that guided instance exploration is worthwhile, but the results may be affected by issues that have to do with the current tool support, i.e., the current implementation, and lack of clarity of the results of the analyses when guided constraints are employed. More precisely, during our questionnaire after the experiment, users valued positively the constraint editor, and said that it allowed them to more easily converge to specific instances they were interested in observing. However, they also reported some limitations. Concretely, two users mentioned that HawkEye does not save previous constraints, and sets everything back to default after querying for a "next" instance. Also, when subsequent constraints are set, users reported that it is not clear whether newly produced instances also satisfy the first constraints set or not, making it more difficult to interpret the results. There is no clear way of knowing which constraints one has accumulated during a use session of instance exploration with HawkEye. In other words, having a clearer picture of the accumulated constraints and their potential contradictions, is useful information that is currently not present during HawkEye's exploration sessions.

We asked users to rank the tool usability and clarity from extremely easy (1) to extremely difficult (10). HawkEye had an average of 5.2 (standard deviation

1.55) vs. the 5 (standard deviation 1.63) average of Alloy Analyzer, showing in general terms a relatively similar usage effort across the tools. It must also be mentioned that, in the first edition of our experiment, all participants had some previous experience with Alloy Analyzer, but none with HawkEye specifically. Thus, it seems reasonable to assume that users were more accustomed to Alloy instance exploration concepts, compared to the more novel exploration offered by HawkEye. Our second edition corrected this issue, but except for LinkedList v2, the use of constraints was, in general terms, maintained. An extended study, with further participants and different levels of expertise, and perhaps with more models with different characteristics, is definitely a must to generalize the results of our experiment, and try to find a correlation between the use of constraints and specification characteristics. In our opinion, based on the observations of the participants and our own experience with HawkEye, the explicit information of the accumulated constraints is crucial. Moreover, it seems relatively natural to think of constraints during instance exploration as a query *refinement* process, that may be more inherently tree-like, rather than linear, as in standard Alloy's instance exploration.

5 Related Work

The order in which satisfying instances of a formula are reported by a model finder is generally agreed to have an important impact in model analysis and debugging. Thus, different instance exploration approaches have been proposed. Aluminum [31] favors *minimality*, i.e., it attempts to first generate the smallest instances that satisfy a particular Alloy formula. REACH [22] follows a related policy, by generating instances in ascending order by size. Bordeaux [29] exploits partial max satisfiability [12] to generate pairs of satisfying and non-satisfying instances, that are as similar as possible, thus helping to understand what is being captured by a formula. N. Macedo et al. [25] also proposed using partial max satisfiability to visit satisfying instances with minimal or maximal differences with respect to previously generated satisfying instances. In this same line, Amalgam [30] complements instance finding with explanations of why (or why not) specific components are part (or are not part) of a satisfying instance. More recently, Ringert and Sullivan [32] also studied how instances are presented to the user, concentrating on the relevant parts of instances, in relation to the property being analyzed. They proposed a notion of *abstract instance*, which summarizes the important aspects in the satisfaction (or, more precisely, in the violation) of a property, and abstracts away the irrelevant aspects that are common to many instances. HawkEye [33], the subject of our study, is the only instance exploration strategy that allows for an interactive exploration of instances, by allowing users to essentially build some specialized queries for subsequent instances during instance exploration. Other works such as [11,27] involve users studies. The former examines how users interact cognitively with model-finder output, and explores how those tools can be enhanced to assist them more effectively. The latter explores how both non-novice and novice users employ the Alloy Analyzer to detect bugs and create models based on natural language specifications.

The impact of different strategies for Alloy instance exploration has been studied in the past [9], including comparisons with various techniques such as Aluminum and Amalgam. These studies are prior to the development of HawkEye, and thus our work complements them. We focused specifically in the facility of interactive instance querying, as implemented in HawkEye, and how it may favor developers, in its current realization, during Alloy model analysis and debugging.

6   Conclusion

The exploration of satisfying instances of a specification component, e.g., counterexamples of intended properties or sample instances of predicates of a specification, is known to be a very powerful mechanism that users employ to validate as well as to debug specifications. How these instances are explored, or more precisely the order in which these are reported to developers, is very important, and can improve the effectiveness and efficiency of specification analysis. This is confirmed by the various different instance exploration strategies that have been proposed for the Alloy language [22,29,31,33].

In this paper, we have studied HawkEye [33], one of these strategies, the first, as far as we are aware of, that allows for an *interactive* mechanism to explore instances. HawkEye provides a mechanism that allows the user to enforce constraints on subsequent instances, during specification instance exploration. We proposed a user study, with the aim of assessing the impact of this dynamic instance exploration strategy in specification debugging and analysis. Our experiment involved voluntary students, with certain experience with Alloy and HawkEye, who undertook the task of debugging a number of faulty Alloy specifications, some using Alloy Analyzer, some using HawkEye. Our results indicate that the interactive instance exploration offered by HawkEye, while attractive and found useful by users, has no substantial impact in model debugging and repairability. We remark however that our study is limited both in the number of participating users, and their expertise level (in total, the study only involved 30 novice users). Finally, our observations also suggest that further development and refinement of HawkEye's underlying concepts and implementation are needed to match the maturity level of traditional Alloy instance exploration, including a better handling of constraint relationships during exploration sessions.

Acknowledgements. We would like to thank the anonymous reviewers of this paper for their detailed feedback. This work is supported by Argentina's ANPCyT through grants PICT 2019-3134, 2019-2050, 2020-2896, and 2021-0601; by an Amazon Research Award; and by EU's Marie Sklodowska-Curie grant No. 101008233 (MISSION).

Competing Interests. The author(s) has no competing interests to declare that are relevant to the content of this manuscript.

References

1. Replication package. https://sites.google.com/view/field-value-evaluation
2. Abad, P., et al.: Improving test generation under rich contracts by tight bounds and incremental SAT solving. In: Sixth IEEE International Conference on Software Testing, Verification and Validation, ICST 2013, Luxembourg, Luxembourg, 18–22 March 2013, pp. 21–30. IEEE Computer Society (2013)
3. Alhanahnah, M., Stevens, C., Bagheri, H.: Scalable analysis of interaction threats in IoT systems. In: Khurshid, S., Pasareanu, C.S. (eds.) ISSTA 2020: 29th ACM SIGSOFT International Symposium on Software Testing and Analysis, Virtual Event, USA, 18–22 July 2020, pp. 272–285. ACM (2020)
4. Bagheri, H., Kang, E., Malek, S., Jackson, D.: A formal approach for detection of security flaws in the android permission system. Formal Aspects Comput. **30**(5), 525–544 (2018)
5. Bagheri, H., Sadeghi, A., Behrouz, R.J., Malek, S.: Practical, formal synthesis and automatic enforcement of security policies for android. In: 46th Annual IEEE/IFIP International Conference on Dependable Systems and Networks, DSN 2016, Toulouse, France, 28 June–1 July 2016, pp. 514–525. IEEE Computer Society (2016)
6. Brunel, J., Chemouil, D., Cunha, A., Macedo, N.: The electrum analyzer: model checking relational first-order temporal specifications. In: Huchard, M., Kästner, C., Fraser, G. (eds.) Proceedings of the 33rd ACM/IEEE International Conference on Automated Software Engineering, ASE 2018, Montpellier, France, 3–7 September 2018, pp. 884–887. ACM (2018)
7. Clarke, E.M., Grumberg, O., Kroening, D., Peled, D.A., Veith, H.: Model Checking, 2nd edn. MIT Press, Cambridge (2018)
8. Clarke, E.M., Wing, J.M.: Formal methods: state of the art and future directions. ACM Comput. Surv. **28**(4), 626–643 (1996)
9. Danas, N., Nelson, T., Harrison, L., Krishnamurthi, S., Dougherty, D.J.: User studies of principled model finder output. In: Cimatti, A., Sirjani, M. (eds.) SEFM 2017. LNCS, vol. 10469, pp. 168–184. Springer, Cham (2017). https://doi.org/10.1007/978-3-319-66197-1_11
10. Dennis, G., Chang, F.S.-H., Jackson, D.: Modular verification of code with SAT. In: Pollock, L.L., Pezzè, M. (eds.) Proceedings of the ACM/SIGSOFT International Symposium on Software Testing and Analysis, ISSTA 2006, Portland, Maine, USA, 17–20 July 2006, pp. 109–120. ACM (2006)
11. Dyer, T., Nelson, T., Fisler, K., Krishnamurthi, S.: Applying cognitive principles to model-finding output: the positive value of negative information. Proc. ACM Program. Lang. **6**(OOPSLA1), 1–29 (2022)
12. Fu, Z., Malik, S.: On solving the partial MAX-SAT problem. In: Biere, A., Gomes, C.P. (eds.) SAT 2006. LNCS, vol. 4121, pp. 252–265. Springer, Heidelberg (2006). https://doi.org/10.1007/11814948_25
13. Galeotti, J.P., Rosner, N., Pombo, C.G.L., Frias, M.F.: TACO: efficient sat-based bounded verification using symmetry breaking and tight bounds. IEEE Trans. Softw. Eng. **39**(9), 1283–1307 (2013)
14. Galeotti, J.P., Rosner, N., Pombo, C.L., Frias, M.F.: Analysis of invariants for efficient bounded verification. In: Tonella, P., Orso, A. (edis.) Proceedings of the Nineteenth International Symposium on Software Testing and Analysis, ISSTA 2010, Trento, Italy, 12–16 July 2010, pp. 25–36. ACM (2010)

15. Ghezzi, C., Jazayeri, M., Mandrioli, D.: Fundamentals of Software Engineering, 2nd edn. Prentice Hall (2003)
16. Hooker, J.N.: Solving the incremental satisfiability problem. J. Log. Program. **15**(1&2), 177–186 (1993)
17. Jackson, D.: Alloy: a lightweight object modelling notation. ACM Trans. Softw. Eng. Methodol. **11**(2), 256–290 (2002)
18. Jackson, D.: Software Abstractions - Logic, Language, and Analysis. MIT Press, Cambridge (2006)
19. Jackson, D.: Alloy: a language and tool for exploring software designs. Commun. ACM **62**(9), 66–76 (2019)
20. Jackson, D., Jha, S., Damon, C.: Isomorph-free model enumeration: a new method for checking relational specifications. ACM Trans. Program. Lang. Syst. **20**(2), 302–343 (1998)
21. Jackson, D., Schechter, I., Shlyakhter, I.: Alcoa: the alloy constraint analyzer. In: Ghezzi, C., Jazayeri, M., Wolf, A.L. (eds.) Proceedings of the 22nd International Conference on on Software Engineering, ICSE 2000, Limerick Ireland, 4–11 June 2000, pp. 730–733. ACM (2000)
22. Jovanovic, A., Sullivan, A.: REACH: refining alloy scenarios by size (tools and artifact track). In: IEEE 33rd International Symposium on Software Reliability Engineering, ISSRE 2022, Charlotte, NC, USA, 31 October–3 November 2022, pp. 229–238. IEEE (2022)
23. Khalek, S.A., Yang, G., Zhang, L., Marinov, D., Khurshid, S.: TestEra: a tool for testing java programs using alloy specifications. In: Alexander, P., Pasareanu, C.S., Hosking, J.G. (eds.) 26th IEEE/ACM International Conference on Automated Software Engineering (ASE 2011), Lawrence, KS, USA, 6–10 November 2011, pp. 608–611. IEEE Computer Society (2011)
24. Macedo, N., Brunel, J., Chemouil, D., Cunha, A., Kuperberg, D.: Lightweight specification and analysis of dynamic systems with rich configurations. In: Zimmermann, T., Cleland-Huang, J., Su, Z. (eds.) Proceedings of the 24th ACM SIGSOFT International Symposium on Foundations of Software Engineering, FSE 2016, Seattle, WA, USA, 13–18 November 2016, pp. 373–383. ACM (2016)
25. Macedo, N., Cunha, A., Guimarães, T.: Exploring scenario exploration. In: Egyed, A., Schaefer, I. (eds.) FASE 2015. LNCS, vol. 9033, pp. 301–315. Springer, Heidelberg (2015). https://doi.org/10.1007/978-3-662-46675-9_20
26. Macedo, N., et al.: Experiences on teaching alloy with an automated assessment platform. Sci. Comput. Program. **211**, 102690 (2021)
27. Mansoor, N., Bagheri, H., Kang, E., Sharif, B.: An empirical study assessing software modeling in alloy. In: 11th IEEE/ACM International Conference on Formal Methods in Software Engineering, FormaliSE 2023, Melbourne, Australia, 14–15 May 2023, pp. 44–54. IEEE (2023)
28. Mirzaei, N., Garcia, J., Bagheri, H., Sadeghi, A., Malek, S.: Reducing combinatorics in GUI testing of android applications. In: Dillon, L.K., Visser, W., Williams, L.A. (eds.) Proceedings of the 38th International Conference on Software Engineering, ICSE 2016, Austin, TX, USA, 14–22 May 2016, pp. 559–570. ACM (2016)
29. Montaghami, V., Rayside, D.: Bordeaux: a tool for thinking outside the box. In: Huisman, M., Rubin, J. (eds.) FASE 2017. LNCS, vol. 10202, pp. 22–39. Springer, Heidelberg (2017). https://doi.org/10.1007/978-3-662-54494-5_2
30. Nelson, T., Danas, N., Dougherty, D.J., Krishnamurthi, S.: The power of "why" and "why not": enriching scenario exploration with provenance. In: Bodden, E., Schäfer, W., van Deursen, A., Zisman, A. (eds.) Proceedings of the 2017 11th Joint

Meeting on Foundations of Software Engineering, ESEC/FSE 2017, Paderborn, Germany, 4–8 September 2017, pp. 106–116. ACM (2017)

31. Nelson, T., Saghafi, S., Dougherty, D.J., Fisler, K., Krishnamurthi, S.: Aluminum: principled scenario exploration through minimality. In: Notkin, D., Cheng, B.H.C., Pohl, K. (eds.) 35th International Conference on Software Engineering, ICSE 2013, San Francisco, CA, USA, 18–26 May 2013, pp. 232–241. IEEE Computer Society (2013)

32. Ringert, J.O., Sullivan, A.: Abstract alloy instances. In: Chechik, M., Katoen, J.P., Leucker, M. (eds.) FM 2023. LNCS, vol. 14000, pp. 364–382. Springer, Cham (2023). https://doi.org/10.1007/978-3-031-27481-7_21

33. Sullivan, A.: Hawkeye: user-guided enumeration of scenarios. In: Jin, Z., et al. (eds.) 32nd IEEE International Symposium on Software Reliability Engineering, ISSRE 2021, Wuhan, China, 25–28 October 2021, pp. 569–578. IEEE (2021)

34. Wang, K., Sullivan, A., Khurshid, S.: Automated model repair for alloy. In: Huchard, M., Kästner, C., Fraser, G. (eds.) Proceedings of the 33rd ACM/IEEE International Conference on Automated Software Engineering, ASE 2018, Montpellier, France, 3–7 September 2018, pp. 577–588. ACM (2018)

35. Zave, P.: Reasoning about identifier spaces: how to make chord correct. IEEE Trans. Softw. Eng. 43(12), 1144–1156 (2017)

36. Zhang, H., Zhang, J.: MACE4 and SEM: a comparison of finite model generators. In: Bonacina, M.P., Stickel, M.E. (eds.) Automated Reasoning and Mathematics. LNCS (LNAI), vol. 7788, pp. 101–130. Springer, Heidelberg (2013). https://doi.org/10.1007/978-3-642-36675-8_5

From Concept to Code: Unveiling a Tool for Translating Abstract State Machines into Java Code

Andrea Bombarda$^{(\boxtimes)}$ (ID), Silvia Bonfanti (ID), and Angelo Gargantini (ID)

Dipartimento di Ingegneria Gestionale, dell'Informazione e della Produzione,
Università degli Studi di Bergamo, Bergamo, Italy
{andrea.bombarda,silvia.bonfanti,angelo.gargantini}@unibg.it

Abstract. Formal methods play a crucial role in modeling and quality assurance, but to be deployed on real systems, formal specifications need to be translated into implementation. Manually converting formal models into code poses challenges such as increased costs, limitations in specification reuse, and the potential for introducing errors. To overcome these limitations, Model-Driven Engineering (MDE) approaches enable developers to generate software code automatically. This paper proposes the `Asmeta2Java` tool for the automatic translation of formal `Asmeta` specifications into executable Java code. The designers start at an abstract level and perform refinement steps and verification activities. At the end, they automatically generates the code by applying the model-to-code transformation. Moreover, a process to validate and evaluate the transformation is presented.

1 Introduction

Formal methods are frequently employed to abstractly model the requirements of a system. These formal requirement models can undergo various quality assurance processes, including dynamic analysis such as simulation or animation, and static analysis like property verification. Nevertheless, establishing a clear connection between the ultimate implementation and its abstract specification can be challenging, as the implementation may incorporate platform-specific details, be expressed in a programming language, and operate on specific hardware. Engaging in the manual conversion of formal models into code not only raises expenses but also restricts the potential for reusing a formal specification. This approach is susceptible to errors, even if validation and verification activities have been performed at the model-level, as faults may be introduced during the code-writing process, and it can act as a hindrance to the broader acceptance of formal methods. Assisting designers during this critical final phase of the development process would be highly beneficial.

Abstract State Machines (ASMs) [10, 16] are a formal method proposing a rigorous software and systems development process, starting from the modeling to the model

The work of Andrea Bombarda is supported by PNRR - ANTHEM (AdvaNced Technologies for Human-centrEd Medicine) - Grant PNC0000003 – CUP: B53C22006700001 - Spoke 1 - Pilot 1.4.

S. Bonfanti et al. (Eds.): ABZ 2024, LNCS 14759, pp. 160–178, 2024.
https://doi.org/10.1007/978-3-031-63790-2_10

simulation and animation, from the model validation to its verification, and, finally, to the transformation of informal requirements into implementation. The `Asmeta` framework [2] supports the user during the complete process and allows him/her to work by refinement: all the details of the system under analysis are captured by a sequence of refined models with decreasing levels of abstraction and, during the process, validation and verification (V&V) activities are executed. At the end of this iterative process, the final step consists in translating the formal specification into the actual implementation, e.g., in Java. Classically, this activity is performed manually but, as mentioned above, having a way to automatize it is advisable (e.g., in the case in which the specification error is discovered while running the implementation, and having a way to automatically regenerate the code after a fix in the specification can facilitate developers' work). However, translating ASM specifications into a classical programming language such as Java, is challenging as ASMs support complex constructs (e.g., parallelism of rules, non-determinism, abstract domains, etc.) that have to be correctly mapped to general-purpose constructs in the chosen programming language.

In this paper, we present our approach for automatically translating `Asmeta` specifications into Java code. This approach is supported by the `Asmeta2Java` tool. As our previous effort [9] addressed the translation from `Asmeta` to C++, `Asmeta2Java` automatically maps `Asmeta` functions, rules, and domains into Java functions, methods, variables, and objects. The presented approach is a typical application of the model-driven engineering (MDE) paradigm [17] where, starting from the model of the system (the `Asmeta` specification), the executable source code embeddable into the final system is obtained. For this reason, the rigorous quality and the correctness of the whole automatic process have to be assured. Thus, we have spent considerable effort not only in defining suitable transformations but also in building a framework for the validation of such transformations. Indeed, we have assured the correctness by checking whether the generated code was compilable and did not contain any syntactic errors, and by statically analyzing the source code.

The remainder of this paper is structured as follows. In Sect. 2, we introduce the basics of ASMs and of the `Asmeta` framework. The generation of Java code is explained in Sect. 3, where we explain the principles guiding our translation, the process we follow, and we show how `Asmeta` constructs and concepts are translated into Java. Section 4 shows our proposal for the validation of the transformation of `Asmeta` specification into Java code. Finally, Sect. 5, Sect. 6, and Sect. 7, respectively, present related work, discuss future work, and conclude the paper.

2   The ASMETA Framework

In this section, we introduce Abstract State Machines (ASMs) and the `Asmeta` framework [2], which embeds the `Asmeta2Java` tool presented in this paper. The `Asmeta` framework comprises various tools designed to assist developers in different stages of the software life-cycle: design, development, and operation (see Fig. 1). The *design* phase involves conducting activities such as modeling, validation, and verification, starting from the system requirements. Once the requirements are formalized and verified, they can be enhanced by incorporating additional details into the existing model

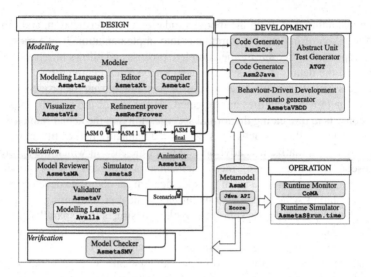

Fig. 1. The ASM development process powered by the `Asmeta` framework

in a chain of refinements. Subsequently, *development* and *operation* can proceed independently. The former entails generating code from models, while the latter facilitates runtime simulation and monitoring activities. In this paper, we will focus on the *development* phase, and, in particular, we introduce the `Asmeta2Java` tool.

The `Asmeta` framework supports Abstract State Machines (ASMs), a precise state-based formal method that transforms abstract *states* through the use of *transition rules*. Each state comprises algebraic structures, representing domains of objects with functions and predicates defined on them. Specifically, an `Asmeta` specification can be seen as an executable pseudo-code, as the well-known example shown in Listing 1. This specification models the behavior of a simple coffee vending machine. It can dispense three different types of products, namely coffee, tea, and milk, and requires the user to insert one or a half coin. If a half coin is inserted, the machine can dispense milk, if it is still available. Otherwise, if the user inserts a coin, the machine randomly chooses tea or coffee, if they are available. As in the case of the example of the coffee vending machine, an `Asmeta` specification comprises four different sections:

– The signature section contains the declaration of the *domains* and *functions*. The StandardLibrary provides predefined domains (such as Integers, Boolean, String, and so on), but customized and static/dynamic ones can be declared by the user (e.g., the CoinType, Product, QuantityDomain and CoinDomain in Listing 1). Functions are classified into three categories: static, derived, and dynamic. More specifically, dynamic functions are further classified in: controlled, monitored, out, and shared. Controlled functions (as the coins and available ones in Listing 1) are read in the current state and updated in the next one by the machine, while monitored functions (as insertedCoin in Listing 1) are updated by the environment and read by the machine. Finally, out functions are written by the machine and sent as output to the

```
 1  asm coffeeVendingMachine                          rule r_serveProduct($p in Product) = par        18
 2  import StandardLibrary                               available($p) := available($p) − 1            19
 3                                                       coins := coins + 1                            20
 4  signature:                                         endpar                                          21
 5  enum domain CoinType = {HALF, ONE}                                                                 22
 6  enum domain Product = {COFFEE, TEA, MILK}          main rule r_Main = if(coins < 25) then          23
 7  domain QuantityDomain subsetof Integer                if(insertedCoin = HALF) then                 24
 8  domain CoinDomain subsetof Integer                      if(available(MILK) > 0) then               25
 9                                                            r_serveProduct[MILK] endif               26
10  controlled coins: CoinDomain                       else choose $p in Product with $p != MILK and   27
11  controlled available: Product −> QuantityDomain         available($p) > 0 do r_serveProduct[$p]
12  monitored insertedCoin: CoinType                                                                   28
13                                                     endif endif                                     28
14  definitions:                                                                                       29
15  domain QuantityDomain = {0 : 10}                   default init s0:                                30
16  domain CoinDomain = {0 : 25}                         function coins = 0                            31
                                                         function available($p in Product) = 10        32
```

Listing 1. Example of an `Asmeta` specification for the Coffee Vending Machine

environment, and shared functions are written and read both by the machine and the environment.

- The definitions section contains the specification of *static/derived functions*, *domains*, and *transition rules*. Various transition rules can be employed based on the system's behavior. For instance, the update rule assigns a specific value to a function, while guarded updates (if-then and switch-case) execute actions conditionally. Simultaneous updates (par) allow for parallel execution, while sequential execution is allowed by the seq construct. For example, Listing 1 utilizes the par rule to concurrently perform two updates in the r_serveProduct rule. Asmeta supports the non-determinism by means of the choose rule (such as at line 27 in Listing 1). With this rule, a random element, possibly satisfying a defined condition, is picked out from a certain domain (the Product domain, in our case).
- The main rule is the entry point of each computation step. When the main rule is executed, the other rules are called depending on the implemented behavior.
- The default init section initializes the value of the dynamic functions (e.g., in Listing 1, the coins function is initialized to 0 in the initial state).

After having modeled the requirements, the developers can validate the Asmeta specification by using the simulator AsmetaS [4] or animate it with AsmetaA [7]. Additionally, scenario-based validation is supported by the validator AsmetaV [11]. Besides validation, system properties can be verified with the model checker AsmetaSMV [3]. When executable source code is needed, e.g., to be embedded in other software systems, it can be automatically obtained starting from Asmeta specifications. In the case C++ code is needed, the tool Asm2C++ [8] can be used.

3 Generation of Java Code

In this section, we describe the process of Java code generation from Asmeta specifications. First, we present the principles we have considered when implementing the Asmeta2Java tool and the design process. Then, we describe how Asmeta concepts are mapped into Java ones.

3.1 Principles for the Translation

First, we discuss some principles we wanted to follow when defining the translation and implementing it. We came up with the following general principles.

1. *Quality* of the produced code: we want that the Java code produced from `Asmeta` specifications is not only correct, but it must have some code qualities, like readability, which normally are not sought in generated code. The reason these qualities are sometimes neglected is that the generated code is generally not meant to be read or understood. In our opinion, instead, we believe that also generated code must be understandable and easy to inspect.
2. *Traceability* refers to the possibility of easily mapping Java constructs in the generated code with specification elements. For example, we will try not to change the names of entities (like rules, functions, and so on). This facilitates understanding how `Asmeta` behavior is translated into Java.
3. *Minimality* consists in avoiding adding useless code. We have observed in the past that generated code often contains some boilerplate code that is always present, regardless of the specification that is translated. We tried to put in the generated code only what is necessary and leave out what is useless.
4. *Extendability* of the generated code: we assume that the programmer may want to extend the generated code, by adding some details (for instance, data structures) that do not have the abstractness necessary to be considered in the formal specifications. For example, we rarely use the `final` keyword, so the programmers can extend the code without limitations. We recognize that allowing the user to extend the generated code may lead to changing or interfering with the actual behavior of the system. However, considering the higher expressiveness of high-level programming languages and the complexity of actual systems, extending the code is sometimes needed.

Other qualities, like efficiency, were not considered as important as those presented above. During the definition of the translation, we relied on these principles: when multiple alternatives to translate the same concept were available, we chose the one maximizing them. However, sometimes the principles are in contrast. For example, what should be done with variables declared but never used? Should they be added to Java code or not? If one favors traceability, they must be added; if one favors minimality instead, they can be safely skipped.

3.2 Design of the Process for Implementing the Transformations

Different approaches could be applied to implement the transformation process from `Asmeta` specification to Java code. We have analyzed both the Model to Text (M2T) and Model to Model + Model to Text (M2M + M2T) [13] approaches. We noted that only the meta-model of the source model (`Asmeta`) is available, while the target meta-model, i.e., Java, is not. For this reason, and to avoid the intermediate steps required by the M2M + M2T approach to translate the original specification into executable Java code, we have selected the M2T approach.

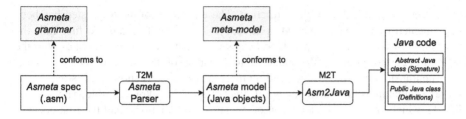

Fig. 2. Transformation process: from Asmeta specification to Java code

The approach is presented in Fig. 2. Given an Asmeta specification conforming to the Asmeta grammar, by applying the Text to Model (T2M) transformation by means of the Asmeta parser, it is possible to quickly get the Asmeta model (in terms of Java objects) conforming to the Asmeta meta-model. Given the Asmeta model, the Asmeta2Java tool employs a M2T transformation to automatically generate the Java code.

Asm2Java. The translation performed by the Asmeta2Java tool is implemented in the Xtend programming language, a flexible and expressive dialect of Java that is integrated into the Xtext[1] framework. It is based on the Eclipse modeling framework (EMF) and provides code generation facilities like a meta-model (Ecore) to describe the models, a set of Java classes for the components of the model, a set of adapter classes that enable viewing and command-based editing of the model, a basic editor, and the integrated development environment (IDE).

When translating an Asmeta specification with the name asmName, the Asmeta2Java tool generates two classes in a single file (asmName.java): an abstract class (asmNameSig) which mainly contains the signature of the Asmeta specification, and a public Java class (in asmName) which contains the rule definitions and extends the class asmNameSig.

3.3 Translation of Asmeta into Java

In this section, we describe how an Asmeta specification is translated into Java. First, we need to introduce the differences between the state evolution in the two approaches, as many design decisions have been taken to address these differences and obtain the same behavior between the formal model and its code implementation.

ASM State Evolution in Java. One of the main differences between ASM and Java is the execution of a machine in ASM or of a program in Java. In ASM, the execution consists of a sequence of steps where each step executes the main rule and builds the update set, which is applied in order to obtain the next state. On the other hand, in Java, the execution corresponds to a sequence of instructions executed step by step, and

---

[1] http://www.eclipse.org/Xtext/.

the values are updated at each instruction. The emulation of an ASM step has been implemented by using the method `updateASM()` in Java. This method first calls the translation of the main rule, which computes the update set. Then, it applies with the method `fireUpdateSet()` the update set to the values of the locations in the new state.

The translation of the coffee vending machine example is shown in Listing 2. The `Asmeta` signature is translated into the abstract class `coffeeVendingMachineSig` (see line 1), which contains the definition of domains and functions, and the rule declaration. Then, the rules are implemented as Java methods in the `coffeeVendingMachine` class (see line 52), which extends the abstract class `coffeeVendingMachineSig`, and overrides the previously defined abstract methods. In addition, this class implements the methods performing the application of the update set (`fireUpdateSet()` at line 94), and the execution of the simulation step (`updateASM()` at line 99). As shown in the code, `updateASM()` calls the translation of the main rule as the first instruction (`r_Main()` at line 76). The execution of the `coffeeVendingMachine` can be performed by instantiating an object of that class and repeatedly calling (e.g., in a loop) the `updateASM()` method.

In the following, we explain in detail how the different `Asmeta` structures and concepts are translated in Java. Note that only a subset of the `Asmeta` language is supported, at the moment, by `Asmeta2Java`. If an `Asmeta` specification contains some unsupported constructs, domains, or terms, the translation fails. For example, the following are unsupported domains: Complex, Agent, and rule domains. We are working on extending `Asmeta2Java` to fully support all `Asmeta` constructs, domains, and terms.

Functions. To translate functions, we introduce four inner classes: `Fun0Ctrl` and `Fun0` for 0-ary functions (respectively controlled or not) and `FunNCtrl` and `FunN` for n-ary functions (respectively controlled or not), shown in Listing 3. These classes have a method `set` that sets the value to be taken by the function in the next step for the controlled one or in the current state for the monitored ones. They have a method `get` that returns the value of the function in the current state.

Each `Asmeta` function is translated into an object of these classes, by using the mapping shown in Table 1. This specific way to translate `Asmeta` functions in Java has been chosen to implement the same state-evolution process in both approaches, namely in `Asmeta` and Java (see Sect. 3.4 for additional details).

Domains. The translation of `Asmeta` domains into Java datatypes or classes is reported in Table 2. `Asmeta` domains are implemented using Java datatypes when there is a straightforward mapping, e.g., for primitive types or collections. In the case of an abstract domain, its translation is a regular class with the constructor that takes only the name of the abstract element. In `elems`, the class D keeps track of all the elements belonging to the abstract domain.

Also in the case of concrete domains (defined as subset of other domains), the translation in Java requires to declare, for each of them, a new class. Note that, in `Asmeta` elements of a concrete domain $D1$ subset of another domain $D2$ can be interchangeable with elements of the parent domain $D2$, and vice versa, while in Java this is not

```
1   abstract class coffeeVendingMachineSig {
2     // Enumerative domains
3     static enum CoinType {HALF,ONE}
4     static enum Product {COFFEE,TEA,MILK}
5
6     // Concrete domain
7     static class QuantityDomain {
8       static List<Integer> elems = new
              ArrayList <>();
9       Integer value;
10
11      static QuantityDomain valueOf(Integer val
              ) {
12        QuantityDomain n = new QuantityDomain();
13        n.value = val;
14        return n;
15      }
16
17      static QuantityDomain valueOf(
              QuantityDomain val) { return val; }
18
19      @Override public boolean equals(Object
              obj) {
20        if (!(obj instanceof QuantityDomain))
21          return false;
22        return value.equals(((QuantityDomain)
              obj).value);
23      }
24
25      @Override public int hashCode() {
26        return value.hashCode(); }
27    }
28    // Concrete domain
29    static class CoinDomain { ... }
30    CoinDomain_elem CoinDomain_elem = new
            CoinDomain();
31
32    // Classes for controlled functions
33    class Fun0Ctrl<C> {...}
34    static class FunNCtrl<D, C> {...}
35
36    // Classes for monitored functions
37    class Fun0<C> {...}
38    class FunN<D, C> {...}
39
40    // Controlled functions
41    Fun0Ctrl<CoinDomain> coins = new Fun0Ctrl
            <>();
42    FunNCtrl<Product, QuantityDomain>
            available = new FunNCtrl<>();
43
44    // Monitored functions
45    Fun0<CoinType> insertedCoin = new Fun0<>()
              ;
46
47    // RULE DEFINITION
48    abstract void r_serveProduct(Product _p);
49    abstract void r_Main();
50  }
51  public class coffeeVendingMachine extends
            coffeeVendingMachineSig {
52    coffeeVendingMachine() {
```

```
51    // Static domain initialization
52    QuantityDomain.elems = Collections.
            unmodifiableList(Arrays.asList(0, 1,
            ..., 10));
53    ...
54
55    // Function initialization
56    CoinDomain_elem.value = 0;
57    coins.oldValue = coins.newValue =
            CoinDomain_elem;
58    for (Product _p:Product.values()) {
59      QuantityDomain a = new QuantityDomain();
60      a.value = 10;
61      available.oldValues.put(_p, a);
62      available.newValues.put(_p, a);
63    }
64  }
65
66  // Translation of ASM rules into Java
67  @Override
68  void r_serveProduct(Product _p) { { //par
69    QuantityDomain qD = new QuantityDomain()
              ;
70    qD.value = available.get(_p).value - 1;
71    available.set(_p, qD);
72    ... } //endpar
73  }
74
75  @Override
76  void r_Main() {
77    if ((coins.get().value < 25)) {
78      if ((insertedCoin.get() == CoinType.HALF
              )) {
79        if ((available.get(Product.MILK).value
              > 0))
80          r_serveProduct(Product.MILK);
81      } else {
82        List<Product> point0 = new ArrayList<
              Product>();
83        for (Product _p : Product.values())
84          if ((_p != Product.MILK) && (available
              .get(_p).value > 0))
85            point0.add(_p);
86        int rndm = ThreadLocalRandom.current().
              nextInt(0, point0.size());
87        Product _p = point0.get(rndm);
88        if (point0.size() > 0) r_serveProduct(
              _p);
89      }
90    }
91  }
92
93  // Update set applying
94  void fireUpdateSet() {
95    coins.oldValue = coins.newValue;
96    available.oldValues = available.newValues
              ;
97  }
98
99  void updateASM() {
100   r_Main();
101   fireUpdateSet();
102 }
103 }
```

Listing 2. Translation of the Coffee Vending Machine Asmeta specification to Java

possible, since D1 and D2 are unrelated types in Java. We could not use the inheritance in Java, because several Java types we use (like Integer) are final. Thus, the D1 class includes, for each object, the corresponding value in the parent domain D2 and some utility method that allows the conversion from D1 and D2, such as valueOf, and the comparison between objects in D1 with those in D2, like equals and hashCode. Additionally, a list of all the "primitive" values is kept and is static. Finally, in the case of the ProductDomains (i.e., domains defined over the Cartesian product of more

```
class FunOCtrl<C> {                          class FunO<C> {
  C oldValue;                                  C value;
  C newValue;
  void set(C d) { newValue = d; }              void set(C d) {value = d; }
  C get() {return oldValue;}                    C get() { return value; }
}                                            }
class FunNCtrl<D, C> {                        class FunN<D, C> {
  Map<D, C> oldValues = new HashMap             Map<D, C> values = new HashMap
    <>();                                        <>();
  Map<D, C> newValues = new HashMap
    <>();
                                               void set(D d, C c) {
  void set(D d, C c) {                           values.put(d, c);
    newValues.put(d, c); }                     }
  C get(D d) {                                 C get(D d) {
    return oldValues.get(d); }                   return values.get(d);
}                                              }
                                             }
```

(a) Classes for controlled functions   (b) Classes for monitored functions

Listing 3. Java classes for controlled and monitored functions

Table 1. Function - translation from Asmeta to Java. F: function name, D: function domain, C: function codomain, $\tau(C)$: codomain translation, $\tau(D)$: domain translation

Asmeta	Translation in Java
static $F: C$	static $\tau(C)$ F;
static $F: D\text{->} C$	static $\tau(C)$ $F(\tau(D))$;
derived $F: C$	$\tau(C)$ $F()$;
derived $F: D\text{->} C$	$\tau(C)$ $F(\tau(D))$;
dynamic monitored $F: C$	FunO<$\tau(C)$> F;
dynamic monitored $F: D\text{->} C$	FunN<$\tau(D)$, $\tau(C)$> F;
dynamic controlled $F: C$	FunOCtrl<$\tau(C)$> F;
dynamic controlled $F: D\text{->} C$	FunNCtrl<$\tau(D)$, $\tau(C)$> F;
dynamic out $F:C$	FunO<$\tau(C)$> F;
dynamic out $F: D\text{->} C$	FunN<$\tau(D)$, $\tau(C)$> F;

domains) they are translated in Java as Pairs, Triplets, and so on. We import these types from the Apache Commons library.

Terms. Table 3 reports the mapping between Asmeta terms and Java constructs. Some mapping is straightforward, such as for the ConditionalTerm and CaseTerm, which can be easily transformed into conditional operations in Java. However, Asmeta implements different types of terms, but some of them are not available in classical programming languages like Java. This is the case of ForAllTerm, ExistsTerm, and LetTerm, which do not have a direct correspondence in Java. To solve this limitation, we adopt the java.util.function.Function<A,B> interface, which allows one to define a function that takes an object of type A and returns an object of type B. To execute the function, we call the apply method.

Table 2. Domain definition - translation from `Asmeta` to Java

Asmeta	Translation in Java
Natural	`Integer`
Integer	`Integer`
Real	`Double`
String	`String`
Char	`char`
Boolean	`Boolean`
Powerset	`HashSet`
Bag	`HashBag`
Sequence	`ArrayList`
Map	`HashMap`
enum	`enum`
abstract domain D	```public class D {``` ```static List<D> elems = new ArrayList<>();``` ```D (String name){...}``` ```...``` ```}```
[dynamic] domain $D1$ subsetof $D2$ $D1$: name of the concrete domain $D2$: type-domain which identifies the structure of the elements of $D1$	```[static] class D1 {``` ```static List<τ(D2)> elems = new ArrayList<>();``` ```τ(D2) value;``` ```D1(τ(D2)) { ... }``` ```static D1 valueOf(τ(D2) val) {...}``` ```static D1 valueOf(D1 val) {...}``` ```public boolean equals(Object obj) {...}``` ```public int hashCode() {...}``` ```}``` $D1$: name of the concrete domain $τ(D2)$: translation of type-domain $D2$

$Prod(D1, D2)$
 $Prod(D1, D2, D3)$
 ...
 $Prod(D1, D2, ..., D10)$
 $D1, D2, D3..., D10$: domains over which the cartesian product is defined
	`Pair<D1, D2>`
	 `Triplet<D1, D2, D3>`
	 ...
	 `Decade<D1, D2, ..., D10>`
	 $D1, D2, D3,..., D10$: domains over which the cartesian product is defined

[dynamic] domain $D1$ subsetof t_D domain $D1 = \{5,9,12\}$ $D1$: name of the concrete domain t_D: type-domain which identifies the structure of the elements of $D1$ $\{5,9,12\}$: domain elements	```[static] class D1 { .. }``` ```List<τ(t_D)> D1_elems =``` ```Collections.unmodifiableList(``` ```Arrays.asList(5,9,12);``` $D1$: name of the concrete domain $τ(t_D)$: translation of type-domain t_D $\{5,9,12\}$: domain elements

Transition Rules. Transition rules are translated into class methods, where every rule is implemented using the Java libraries and basic constructs. The translation is linear most of the time. For example, the conditional rule is translated with the if-else construct in Java, as shown in Table 4, where terms and rules are also translated accordingly. A particular translation has been adopted for the update rule, which may be critical in the presence of parallelism (see Sect. 3.4).

3.4 Mapping `Asmeta` **Parallelism and Non-determinism in Java**

ASMs have two semantic concepts that do not have a direct implementation in Java. The first one is the parallel execution of all rules, while the other problem is non-determinism. How these two issues have been addressed by our approach is explained below.

Table 3. Terms - translation from `Asmeta` to Java

Term	Asmeta	Translation in Java

Conditional Term	`if` *cond* `then`
	    t_{then}
	`[else`
	    t_{else}`]`
	`endif`
	
	cond: term (Boolean condition)
	t_{then}, t_{else}: terms
		`if` $\tau(cond)$ `{`
		    $\tau(t_{then})$`;`
		`[} else {`
		    $\tau(t_{else})$`;]`
		`}`
		
		$\tau(cond)$: conditional term translation
		$\tau(t_{then})$, $\tau(t_{else})$: terms translation

Case Term	`switch` *t*
	    `case` t_1 `:` s_1
	    ...
	    `case` t_k `:` s_k
	    `[otherwise`
	    s_{k+1}`]`
	`endswitch`
	
	t_1,...t_k: terms
	s_1, ..., s_k, s_{k+1}: terms
		`if (`$\tau(t)$`==`$\tau(t_1)$`) {`
		    $\tau(s_1)$`;`
		    ...
		`} else if (`$\tau(t)$`==`$\tau(t_k)$`) {`
		    $\tau(s_k)$`;`
		`} [else {`
		    $\tau(s_{k+1})$`));`
		`}]`
		
		$\tau(t)$, $\tau(t_1)$, ..., $\tau(t_k)$: terms translation
		$\tau(s_1)$, ..., $\tau(s_k)$, $\tau(s_{k+1})$: terms translation

Tuple Term	(t_1, t_2)
	...
	$(t_1,...t_{10})$
	
	t_1,...t_{10}: terms
		`Pair.with(`$\tau(t_1)$`, `$\tau(t_2)$`)`
		...
		`Decade.with(`$\tau(t_1)$`,...`$\tau(t_{10})$`)`
		
		$\tau(t_1)$, ..., $\tau(t_{10})$: terms translation

ForAll Term	`forall` v_1 `in` D_1, ..., v_k `in` D_k
	`with` $G_{v_1,...,v_k}$
	
	v_1,...v_k: variables
	D_1,...D_k: domains where v_i take values
	$G_{v_1,...,v_k}$: term (condition over v_1,...v_k)
		`new Function<Void, Boolean>() {`
		    `@Override`
		    `public Boolean apply(Void input) {`
		        `for(`$\tau(D_1)$ $\tau(v_1)$`: `$\tau(D_1)$`.elems) {`
		            ...
		            `for(`$\tau(D_k)$ $\tau(v_k)$`: `$\tau(D_k)$`.elems) {`
		                `if(!`$\tau(G_{v_1,...,v_k})$`) {`
		                    `return false;`
		            `}}...}`
		        `return true;`
		`}}.apply(null);`
		
		$\tau(v_1)$,..., $\tau(v_1)$: variables translation
		$\tau(D_1)$, ..., $\tau(D_k)$: domains translation
		$\tau(G_{v_1,...,v_k})$: term translation

Exist Term	`exist` v_1 `in` D_1, ..., v_k `in` D_k
	`with` $G_{v_1,...,v_k}$
	
	v_1,...v_k: variables
	D_1,...D_k: domains where v_i take value
	$G_{v_1,...,v_k}$: term (condition over v_1,...v_k)
		`new Function<Void, Boolean>() {`
		    `@Override`
		    `public Boolean apply(Void input) {`
		        `for(`$\tau(D_1)$ $\tau(v_1)$`: `$\tau(D_1)$`.elems) {`
		            ...
		            `for(`$\tau(D_k)$ $\tau(v_k)$`: `$\tau(D_k)$`.elems) {`
		                `if(`$\tau(G_{v_1,...,v_k})$`) {`
		                    `return true;`
		            `}}...}`
		        `return false;`
		`}}.apply(null);`
		
		$\tau(v_1)$,..., $\tau(v_1)$: variables translation
		$\tau(D_1)$, ..., $\tau(D_k)$: domains translation
		$\tau(G_{v_1,...,v_k})$: term translation

Let Term	`let (`v_1`=`t_1, ..., v_k`=`t_k`) in` $t_{v_1,...,v_k}$
	`endlet`
	
	v_1,...v_k: variables
	t_1, ..., t_k: terms
	$t_{v_1,...,v_k}$: term with free occurrences of v_1,...,v_k
		`new Function<Void, `$\tau(D)$`>() {`
		    `@Override`
		    `public `$\tau(D)$` apply(Void input) {`
		        $\tau(D_1)$ $\tau(v_1)$ `= `$\tau(t_1)$`;`
		        ...
		        $\tau(D_k)$ $\tau(v_k)$ `= `$\tau(t_k)$`;`
		        `return `$\tau(t_{v_1,...,v_k})$`;`
		`}.apply(null);`
		
		$\tau(D)$: transl. of the domain where $t_{v_1,...,v_k}$ takes value
		$\tau(D_1)$, ..., $\tau(D_k)$: transl. of the domains of v_i
		$\tau(v_1)$, ..., $\tau(v_k)$: variables translation
		$\tau(t_1)$, ..., $\tau(t_k)$: terms translation
		$\tau(t_{v_1,...,v_k})$: terms translation

Size Of Enumerable Term	`|cSet|` or `|cBag|` or `|cMap|` or `|cList|`	`cSet.size()` or `cBag.size()` or `cMap.size()` or `cList.size()`

Table 4. Rules - translation from `Asmeta` to Java

Rule	Asmeta	Translation in Java
Definition	rule r_1 $(x_1$ in D_1, ..., x_k in D_k) =	`void` r_1 $(\tau(D_1)$ $x_1,\ldots,\tau(D_k)$ $x_k)$ `{...}`
	$r1$: rule name	r: method name
	$x_1,...,x_k$: parameters of the rule	$\tau(D_1)$, ..., $\tau(D_k)$: translation of domains
	$D_1,...,D_k$:domains where parameters take value	x_1, ..., x_k: parameters of the method
Update	$l := t$	$\tau(l)$`.set(`$\tau(t)$`.get());`
	l: location term or variable	$\tau(l)$: translation of location term or variable
	t: generic term	$\tau(t)$: term translation

Conditional	if *cond* then
	  R_{then}
	  [else
	  R_{else}]
	endif
		`if (`$\tau(cond)$`){`
		  $\tau(R_{then})$`;`
		`[}else {`
		  $\tau(R_{else})$`;]`
		`}`

	cond: term representing a boolean condition	$\tau(cond)$: conditional term translation
	R_{then}, R_{else}: transition rules	$\tau(R_{then})$, $\tau(R_{else})$: rules translation

Parallelism. Parallelism is a fundamental point of ASMs because the operations performed in the same transition step are done in parallel. Since we did not want to introduce multithreading (which may result in unforeseen behavior and complicate the translation), we decided to use standard Java. We have implemented a parallel-like execution by creating, when necessary, a copy of the current state and using that in a sequentially executed thread, following the approach proposed by others, including J. Schmid [22]. ASMs run in discrete steps, where each step consists of four operations: acquire inputs, perform the main rule, update the state, and release the outputs. The machine state (represented by controlled functions) is modified only during the execution of the main rule. To simulate parallel execution, the controlled part of the state is duplicated: the present state (i.e., oldValue) and the future state (i.e., newValue). Modifications made to controlled functions will affect only the future state, while status readings will refer to the current state. The modification made to controlled functions will take place only when the execution of the main rule is finished, which means in the `fireUpdateSet()` function. This approach guarantees the proper evolution of the machine state, even though it is not true parallelism. The code reported in Listing 4 shows a simple example of parallelism, swapping the values of variables x and y. If we translated this example in Java as a simple sequence x=y; y=x;, the result would have not been the same as in ASM: both variables x and y would contain the value of y. For this reason, as presented in Sect. 3.3, we represented the controlled functions by using classes and embedding into them both the present state and the future one. In this way, we translate each assignment in Java following this rule: we set the next state by using the `set` method, and we access to the current state of controlled functions by using the `get` method. After the execution of the rules in the current state (the `mainRule()` method in Java), we assign all the values of the next state to the current state with the `fireUpdateSet()` method. The new current state is used in the next step of execution. We do not consider the case of inconsistent updates (a function assumes two different values in the same state) because the methodologies applied during the analysis of the ASMETA model guarantee that inconsistent updates will not occur as the model should be checked priorly its translation with the `AsmetaMA` tool (see [2] for further information).

controlled x: Integer
controlled y: Integer
...
rule r_parallel =
  par
    x := y
    y := x
  endpar
	```void r_parallel() { //par```
	``` x.set(y.get());```
	``` y.set(x.get());```
	```} //endpar```
	```void fireUpdateSet() {```
	``` x.oldValue = x.newValue;```
	``` y.oldValue = y.newValue;```
	```}```

(a) `Asmeta`   (b) Java code

Listing 4. Parallelism - translation in Java

Note that for the example given above, a simple translation like `temp=x; x=y; y=temp;` which uses a temporary variable will also suffice, and this is the approach proposed by other research works, such as Dalvandi et al. [14]. However, in an `Asmeta` specification, we cannot lose the current value of controlled functions that may be used in other rules.

Non-determinism. Non-determinism in `Asmeta` is implemented by the ChooseRule, which allows for picking a random element out of a domain (i.e., the set of terms of the same nature). This random choice is performed by generating a random number, which corresponds to the index of the element, to be picked inside the domain. When translating `Asmeta` specifications into Java code, we keep track of all objects created in a domain through a list. Therefore, we implement non-determinism in Java by generating a random integer index in the range between 0 and the number of terms belonging to the domain of interest. An example is shown in the coffee vending machine translation (see Listing 1 at line 27), where a drink is randomly chosen from the available products list by excluding the milk. In the generated source code shown in Listing 2, a list of selectable drinks is populated (those belonging to the `Product` domain except milk) at line 83, then a random index is generated at line 86 and, finally, an element is taken from the list of selectable products (see line 87).

4   Validation of the Transformation

We have devised a process to validate the transformations presented so far, depicted in Fig. 3. The process is iterative; initially, we have modified several times the transformation code in order to improve its quality (A). Then, we have applied the transformation to several `Asmeta` specifications, and we have analyzed the correctness[2] and quality of produced code (B). Both the results obtained from steps (A) and (B) have been used to improve the quality and correctness of the code used for the transformation of `Asmeta` specification to Java code. In the following, we explain in detail steps (A) and (B).

---

[2] With *correctness* we indicate both syntactical correctness and behavioral conformance of the produced code w.r.t. the `Asmeta` specification.

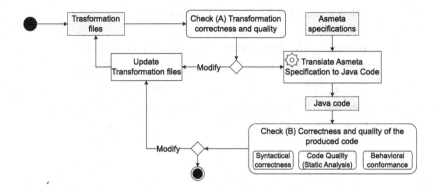

Fig. 3. Quality assurance process followed during the `Asmeta2Java` development

(A) Transformation Correctness and Quality. First, we check that the transformation programs written in `Xtend` do not contain errors and satisfy the quality attributes themselves, and they can successfully be compiled into their corresponding Java code. Second, we check that the code of the transformations in Java does not contain errors and passes the quality checks the designer desires to establish. In our case, to check the quality of the Java source code, we used the SonarLint tool[3]. SonarLint is a static analyzer and is capable of detecting possible bugs, code smells, and vulnerabilities. It contains around 5000 rules that check the quality of the code in terms of reliability, maintainability, readability, and security. With an iterative process, such as that represented in Fig. 3, we have improved our transformation code and fixed all the 57 warnings signaled by SonarLint (see Table 5).

The checks carried out in (A) refer to the quality of the programs performing the transformations. Although they play a very important role, there is no guarantee that a *good* transformation code according to our criteria (A) will produce a *good* code, since the produced code may contain errors or other issues. For this reason, we have decided to check the correctness and quality of the code *produced* by the transformation (B). An error or some low-quality warning of the produced code must not prompt the modification of the generated code itself; instead, it requires a modification of the transformation code that caused the insertion of that error or the low-quality code.

(B) Correctness and Quality of the Produced Code. We can distinguish three main activities we can perform to check the generated code:

(B.1) Syntactical correctness: checks that the generated code compiles.
(B.2) Code quality: applies quality checks to the produced code.
(B.3) Behavioral conformance: aims to check whether the `Asmeta` specification and the Java code implement the same behavior.

While for (B.1) a Java compiler suffices, for (B.2) we have used SonarLint as in (A). When we initially checked the generated code, we found 1,809 warnings (see Table 5).

---

[3] https://www.sonarsource.com/products/sonarlint/.

Table 5. Quality warnings on transformation and generated code

Warning Severity		A - Transformation code		B - Generated code	
		Before	After	Before	After
Critical ⊙		4	0	106	22
Medium ⬢		31	0	51	51
Low ⊙		22	0	1652	456
Total		57	0	1809	560

Thus, we have modified the transformation code to fix most of them and reduced the warnings on the generated code to 560. On the one hand, this analysis has allowed us to better implement the principles that have guided our implementation and are described in Sect. 3.1. For example, we have removed many useless imports that were always added but used only in particular situations (such as those of the classes used for the tuples or structured domains). However, on the other hand, given the principles we have described in Sect. 3.1, we were not able to remove all warnings. For example, to maintain traceability, we decided to keep the classes with the same name as the ASM, and, when these start with a lowercase character, the corresponding classes start with a lowercase character too, leading to warnings signaled by Sonarlint. Similarly, the same warnings are signaled by Sonarlint for the name of the fields in the classes: whenever the functions were declared with a leading uppercase character, we decided to keep the same initial character for the fields as well. A last example concerns the name of the rules. In Asmeta rules are required to start with r_, and, to guarantee traceability in the Java code, the rules are translated into methods having the same name. However, the Java guidelines suggest not to have an underscore in the method's name.

In this paper, we skip the activities to perform behavioral conformance analysis (B.3), which will be presented as future work (see Sect. 6). To guarantee the maximization of the results obtained in (B), the Asmeta specifications used as input for the validation process must cover most of the constructs available in Asmeta. To do this, we have measured, by using Eclemma[4], the coverage of the Asmeta constructs when translating all the Asmeta specifications available in our considered examples. The result obtained is that 89% of the Asmeta constructs handled by Asmeta2Java are covered by our experiments.

5 Related Work

Automatic code generation from formal specifications is available as a part of tool support for several formal methods, e.g., MATLAB/Simulink[5] provides this feature as a commercial off-the-shelf solution. However, other free tools are available for other formal methods. For B users [1], executable C, C++, Java, and Ada code can be generated

---

[4] https://www.eclemma.org/.
[5] https://www.mathworks.com/products/simulink.html.

from formal specifications by the Atelier B platform[6], which is free in its Community Edition. Additionally, for the Event-B formal method, the EventB2Java tool integrated into the Rodin platform allows developers to generate executable code [12]. The generation of Java code is also provided by other non-formal approaches. For example, executable Java code can be generated starting from UML class and sequence diagrams [18], or state-charts [20]. However, the advantages of these approaches are limited only to the reuse of (non-formal) models, but no guarantee on safety properties or system behavior is given.

For what concerns Abstract State Machines, the Asmeta framework already provides the Asm2C++ translator [9] which, starting from Asmeta specifications, produces executable C++ code, possibly also providing the source code for its integration with Arduino. The approach presented in [9] is very similar to that we present in this paper. However, if developers work with Java code, Asmeta2Java, as presented in this paper, is preferable since no manual intervention is needed to integrate the source code produced by the Asmeta environment while deploying the final system. Another preliminary work that translates CASM specification to C code is presented in [19,21]. In these works, the authors present an optimized compiler for ASM specifications that could be easily retargeted to different programming languages and hardware target domains (but currently only C/C++ code is supported). They present a compilation scheme and an implementation of a runtime system supporting inconsistent updates checking and efficient execution of ASMs. Another approach supported by a tool called JASMine, is presented in [15]. The design goal of JASMine is to allow interaction between ASM and Java, rather than full integration. The goal of their work is not the translation, but rather to access Java objects and classes from inside an ASM specification. The approach presented in this last work differs from that we propose, especially for what concerns the handling of updates. In Asmeta2Java, we build the next update set for each function and we apply it when the step is executed, by keeping two copies of the ASM state in Java. In JASMine, instead, the authors collect all the *deferred* updates and apply them after checking their consistency.

6   Future Work

According to the best practices of MDE, the implementation of a system should be obtained from its model through a systematic model-to-code transformation, as we have presented in this paper. Furthermore, following the same approach, unit tests should be obtained automatically from abstract tests. With Asmeta, users can validate their specifications by means of Avalla scenarios, which can be considered abstract tests that may be concretized to obtain executable unit tests. Thus, as previously done for C++ [6], we plan to enhance the Asmeta2Java tool by adding an automatic translation of Avalla scenarios into jUnit test cases. Specifically targeting the behavior of the system, these test cases can also be used to verify the *semantical* correctness of the code produced by Asmeta2Java (see Sect. 4).

When it comes to embedding the modeled specification in the final executable, possibly having a GUI, two different approaches may be used. On the one hand, the formal

---

[6] https://www.atelierb.eu/en/.

specification can be executed by embedding the `Asmeta` simulator in the final artifact, as shown in [5]. On the other hand, as we have presented in this paper, the executable source code can be generated from the formal specification and, then, directly used in the final executable. In this last case, having a way to visualize the behavior of the obtained source code is advisable. Thus, we plan to introduce a procedure for the automatic generation of a UI, allowing the user to interact with the generated Java code in a simplified way.

7   Conclusion

In this paper, we have presented the translation of formal models into Java code to automatically obtain the system implementation. This process follows the MDE paradigm: the source code is obtained from `Asmeta` specifications by applying a set of M2T transformations. Furthermore, we have presented the principles guiding our approach and introduced activities for the validation of the transformation to guarantee the correctness of the process. The Java code generation process starts from the ASM specification, and using `Asmeta2Java`, the Java code of the model is automatically generated. We have shown how a simple case study of a coffee vending machine is translated, and then, for each `Asmeta` construct, we have displayed the translation we have adopted. We have dealt with two characteristics of ASM models, namely the parallelism and the non-determinism, that are non-trivial in Java, and we have found the solution to maintaining in the Java code the same ASM behavior. The application of the activities presented in this paper guarantees that, starting from a validated and verified `Asmeta` specification, users can automatically generate a code implementation compliant with the validated and verified behavior. As future work, we are working on further extending the functionalities offered by the `Asmeta2Java` tool, and allowing him to generate jUnit test cases, which can be useful both to validate the translation process and to perform regression testing when manual intervention on the Java code is needed.

Competing Interests. The author(s) has no competing interests to declare that are relevant to the content of this manuscript.

References

1. Abrial, J.-R.: The B-Book: Assigning Programs to Meanings. Cambridge University Press, Cambridge (2005)
2. Arcaini, P., Bombarda, A., Bonfanti, S., Gargantini, A., Riccobene, E., Scandurra, P.: The ASMETA approach to safety assurance of software systems. In: Raschke, A., Riccobene, E., Schewe, K.-D. (eds.) Logic, Computation and Rigorous Methods. LNCS, vol. 12750, pp. 215–238. Springer, Cham (2021). https://doi.org/10.1007/978-3-030-76020-5_13
3. Arcaini, P., Gargantini, A., Riccobene, E.: AsmetaSMV: a way to link high-level ASM models to low-level NuSMV specifications. In: Frappier, M., Glässer, U., Khurshid, S., Laleau, R., Reeves, S. (eds.) ABZ 2010. LNCS, vol. 5977, pp. 61–74. Springer, Heidelberg (2010). https://doi.org/10.1007/978-3-642-11811-1_6
4. Arcaini, P., Gargantini, A., Riccobene, E., Scandurra, P.: A model-driven process for engineering a toolset for a formal method. Softw. Practice Exp. **41**, 155–166 (2011)

5. Bombarda, A., Bonfanti, S., Gargantini, A.: *formal* MVC: a pattern for the integration of ASM specifications in UI development. In: Glässer, U., Creissac Campos, J., Méry, D., Palanque, P. (eds.) ABZ 2023. LNCS, vol. 14010, pp. 340–357. Springer, Cham (2023). https://doi.org/10.1007/978-3-031-33163-3_25

6. Bonfanti, S., Gargantini, A., Mashkoor, A.: Generation of C++ unit tests from abstract state machines specifications. In: IEEE Computer Society (ed.) 2018 IEEE International Conference on Software Testing, Verification and Validation Workshops (ICSTW), pp. 185–193, April 2018

7. Bonfanti, S., Gargantini, A., Mashkoor, A.: AsmetaA: animator for abstract state machines. In: Butler, M., Raschke, A., Hoang, T.S., Reichl, K. (eds.) ABZ 2018. LNCS, vol. 10817, pp. 369–373. Springer, Cham (2018). https://doi.org/10.1007/978-3-319-91271-4_25

8. Bonfanti, S., Gargantini, A., Mashkoor, A.: Validation of transformation from abstract state machine models to C++ code. In: Medina-Bulo, I., Merayo, M.G., Hierons, R. (eds.) ICTSS 2018. LNCS, vol. 11146, pp. 17–32. Springer, Cham (2018). https://doi.org/10.1007/978-3-319-99927-2_2

9. Bonfanti, S., Gargantini, A., Mashkoor, A.: Design and validation of a C++ code generator from Abstract State Machines specifications. J. Softw. Evol. Process **32**(2), e2205 (2019)

10. Börger, E., Stark, R.F.: Abstract State Machines: A Method for High-Level System Design and Analysis. Springer, New York (2003)

11. Carioni, A., Gargantini, A., Riccobene, E., Scandurra, P.: A scenario-based validation language for ASMs. In: Börger, E., Butler, M., Bowen, J.P., Boca, P. (eds.) ABZ 2008. LNCS, vol. 5238, pp. 71–84. Springer, Heidelberg (2008). https://doi.org/10.1007/978-3-540-87603-8_7

12. Cataño, N., Rivera, V.: EventB2Java: a code generator for event-B. In: Rayadurgam, S., Tkachuk, O. (eds.) NFM 2016. LNCS, vol. 9690, pp. 166–171. Springer, Cham (2016). https://doi.org/10.1007/978-3-319-40648-0_13

13. Czarnecki, K., Helsen, S.: Feature-based survey of model transformation approaches. IBM Syst. J. **45**(3), 621–645 (2006)

14. Dalvandi, M., Butler, M., Rezazadeh, A., Salehi Fathabadi, A.: Verifiable code generation from scheduled event-B models. In: Butler, M., Raschke, A., Hoang, T.S., Reichl, K. (eds.) ABZ 2018. LNCS, vol. 10817, pp. 234–248. Springer, Cham (2018). https://doi.org/10.1007/978-3-319-91271-4_16

15. Gervasi, V., Farahbod, R.: JASMine: accessing Java code from CoreASM. In: Abrial, J.-R., Glässer, U. (eds.) Rigorous Methods for Software Construction and Analysis. LNCS, vol. 5115, pp. 170–186. Springer, Heidelberg (2009). https://doi.org/10.1007/978-3-642-11447-2_11

16. Gurevich, Y.: Evolving Algebras 1993: Lipari Guide, pp. 9–36. Oxford University Press, Inc., Oxford (1995)

17. Hutchinson, J., Rouncefield, M., Whittle, J.: Model-driven engineering practices in industry. In: Proceedings of the 33rd International Conference on Software Engineering, ICSE 2011. ACM, May 2011

18. Kluisritrakul, P., Limpiyakorn, Y.: Generation of Java code from UML sequence and class diagrams. In: Information Science and Applications (ICISA) 2016. LNEE, vol. 376, pp. 1117–1125. Springer, Singapore (2016). https://doi.org/10.1007/978-981-10-0557-2_106

19. Lezuo, R., Paulweber, P., Krall, A.: CASM: optimized compilation of abstract state machines. ACM SIGPLAN Not. **49**(5), 13–22 (2014)

20. Niaz, I.A., Tanaka, J.: Code generation from UML statecharts. In: Proceedings of the Seventh IASTED International Conference on Software Engineering and Applications, pp. 315–321, December 2003

21. Paulweber, P., Zdun, U.: A model-based transformation approach to reuse and retarget CASM specifications. In: Butler, M., Schewe, K.-D., Mashkoor, A., Biro, M. (eds.) ABZ 2016. LNCS, vol. 9675, pp. 250–255. Springer, Cham (2016). https://doi.org/10.1007/978-3-319-33600-8_17
22. Schmid, J.: Compiling abstract state machines to C++. J. Univ. Comput. Sci. 7(11), 1068–1087 (2001)

Short Research Papers

An Event-B Formal Model for Access Control and Resource Management of Serverless Apps

Mehmet Said Nur Yagmahan$^{(\boxtimes)}$ ⓘ, Abdolbaghi Rezazadeh ⓘ,
and Michael Butler ⓘ

School of Electronics and Computer Science (ECS), University of Southampton,
Southampton SO17 1BJ, UK
{msny1y17,m.j.butler}@soton.ac.uk, ra3@ecs.soton.ac.uk

Abstract. Cloud computing technologies help developers build scalable distributed apps. Serverless architecture, or Function as a Service (FaaS), which separates app businesses into multiple functions, is one of the cloud-native architectures that has gained popularity. Those functions can be developed and deployed independently without provisioning infrastructure.

Despite the considerable advantages and increasing popularity of cloud-native apps, developers face many challenges when building their cloud-native applications. To ensure the robustness and security of cloud-native apps and protect crucial resources, the design and implementation of functions and associated access control systems play a pivotal role.

In this paper, we have employed formal methods and tools to develop a set of patterns to help cloud-native application developers to design robust serverless apps. We have used Event-B and its associated toolset, Rodin, to construct these formal patterns and demonstrated how these patterns can be used in practical case studies.

Keywords: Serverless · FaaS · AWS · Access Control · Authorisation · Formal Modelling · Event-B · Formal Methods

1 Introduction

Cloud computing not only facilitates data and resource sharing but also serves as a platform for creating new types of distributed cloud-native apps. Cloud-native apps adopt innovative architectural models, such as serverless architecture, which offers to divide an app's business logic into functions that act as a glue between cloud platform resources and services to meet system requirements.

Access control manage resource and function usage, with variations across cloud platforms. Our focus is on AWS, a top provider in cloud systems [12].

The first author is supported by the Turkish National Education Ministry in the U.K. Butler is supported by the HD-Sec project, part of the Digital Security by Design (DSbD) Programme delivered by UKRI to support the DSbD ecosystem.

Defects in system design, especially in access control, can lead to catastrophic issues or losses. A report by Synergy Research Group [10] highlights that 65% of cloud incidents result from customer misconfigurations. This paper introduces a formal approach to modelling serverless apps and their access control on AWS. By employing the robustness and verification power of formal methods, we aim to provide modelling patterns to guide developers in accurately modelling serverless systems and access control, enhancing system security and reliability.

2 Background

In this section, we first provide an overview of Serverless systems, particularly in the AWS cloud environment. And then, we briefly introduce Event-B.

2.1 Serverless Architecture

Serverless architecture is "an event-driven cloud execution model" [7] that breaks down app logic into small, independent functions [8].

In this architecture, authentication via Cognito and IAM (Identity and Access Management) roles provides varying access levels to AWS resources for app users [13]. Users interact with API Gateway endpoints, each mapping to a serverless app functionality. Endpoint execution depends on user roles. After execution, the endpoint triggers the related lambda function to fulfil requests. Function execution may involve input from other AWS services, requiring appropriate permissions granted via IAM roles.

IAM manages AWS authorization, using IAM identities for authentication and IAM policies for resource authorization. IAM policies categorize into identity-based (granting access to IAM identities) and resource-based (attached directly to resources). For example, a lambda function triggered by an API Gateway endpoint requires permission granted by the function's resource-based policy.

AWS policies comprise statements granting or restricting permissions for actions on resources. IAM roles whose permission is defined by IAM policies enable app users or functions to access AWS resources. "Principal" in resource-based policy's statement shows actors who can access the corresponding resource [3].

When a request for a resource is made, AWS evaluates authorization by pulling related policy statements. Requests are denied by default. If an allow statement exists without a deny statement, the request is permitted. A deny statement overrides allow statements, resulting in request rejection.

2.2 Event-B

Event-B [1] is a formal modelling language based on set theory and predicate logic, developed by Abrial. The key features of the Event-B language are abstraction and refinement, which help to manage system complexity [5]. Although refinement is a common feature in formal methods, the step-wise refinement mechanism in Event-B [1] is a particular feature. To verify the model's correctness and the consistency between refinement steps, mathematical proofs are used [1].

An Event-B model consists of two components: *context* and *machine*. The former represents the static part of the model, while the latter includes the dynamic components of the model. Contexts provide axiomatic properties of the model, whereas machines provide behavioural properties of the model [6].

Rodin, an Eclipse-based open-source toolset, supports Event-B modelling, refinement, and mathematical proof [2]. There is a considerable set of extensions on the Rodin platform to assist in modelling in Event-B.

3   Modelling Request Handling and Authorization

In this section, we develop a generic pattern for request handling (RHP) and then we introduce authorization mechanisms through subsequent refinements.

3.1   Request Handling Pattern

Functionalities of cloud-native apps rely on individual or sequenced requests. To model these applications, modeling request execution is a key aspect.

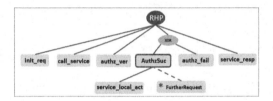

Fig. 1. A Graphical Representation for Request Handling Pattern

The tree-like diagram in Fig. 1 represents the Request Handling Pattern (RHP), detailing request execution stages. Inspired by Fathabadi's work [11] on Event Refinement Structure (ERS), we use a similar notation for hierarchical request handling. It is worth noting that in our application, different levels in the diagram represent successive requests rather than step-wise refinements. Leaves in the RHP diagram represent different request handling stages, mapped to Event-B events. Like ERS, nodes are considered from left to right. "XOR" connectors indicate a decision point based on *authz_ver* outcome, leading to either *service_local_act* or *service_fail*, resulting in *service_resp* from the cloud system. To handle complex scenarios where fulfilling the initial request can lead to several subsequent requests, the RHP pattern can be applied iteratively, as shown by 'FurtherRequest' (star-marked leaf).

In the model, we define *REQUEST*, *STATUS*, and *EFFECT* sets. *STATUS* includes potential request execution stages (*Initiated, Called, Succeeded, Failed*). *EFFECT* includes potential authorization outcomes (*Allow, Deny*).

The variable *req_status* tracks current existing requests' status (*inv0_3*), while the *req_authz* variable represents requests' authorization outcome.

@inv0_3 : req_status ∈ request→STATUS
@inv0_4 : req_authz ∈ request ↦ EFFECT

Figure 2 shows the Event-B representation of the RHP pattern, in which events map to the leaves in the tree diagram in Fig. 1. Before a request is made, only *init_req* is enabled. The *init_req* represents the initiation of a new request (*new_req*) by adding it to the *request* variable (*@act0_1* in the *init_req* event) and setting its status as *Initiated* (*@act0_2*), which enables the *call_service* event.

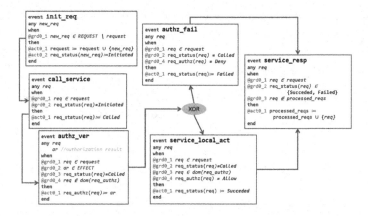

Fig. 2. Request Handling Pattern in Event-B

Event-B's abstraction and refinement help us handle authorization complexity. First, we focus on the outcome of an authorization process, which is either to accept or reject. *authz_ver* in Fig. 2 models the authorization mechanism at a high level. This event assigns the request authorization outcome non-deterministically using the *ar* parameter. The value of *ar* determines which event is enabled in the next stage (*grd0_2*). See the whole model at [14].

3.2 A Unifying Generic Approach for RHP

On a cloud platform, each service is a resource, with each access requiring a request. We introduce *RESOURCE* to systematically represent resource hierarchy. Following this, we categorise *RESOURCE*, the abstract concept, into distinct sub-types (*axm1_1*), like functions or data tables.

@axm1_1 : partition(RESOURCE, Cognito, Function, Data, IAM, EndPoint...)

@inv1_1 : req_res ∈ request → RESOURCE
@inv1_2 : req_act ∈ request → ACTION

Moreover, *inv1_1* and *inv1_2* define the requested resource and action in the request context.

We can apply the same concept to various entities via subtyping. Using *req_res* in *inv1_1* indicates a request for any type of resource. This also helps us to abstract events as well. By specifying the abstract variable, an abstract event can be refined into a into a more concrete event.

3.3 Refinements for Modelling Authorization Mechanism

To successfully fulfil a request, the requester must have appropriate permissions to access the requested resource. We used Event-B abstraction and stepwise refinement to handle the complexity of AWS authorization mechanisms.

Permissions are defined by statements whose structure is shown in Fig. 3A. Each statement allows/denies (*inv2_5*) to perform a set of actions (*inv2_4*) on a set of resources (*inv2_3*). In resource-based permissions (*inv2_2*), a set of *actor* entities who are authorised to access the resource is specified (*inv2_6*).

@inv2_1 statement ⊆ STATEMENT	
@inv2_2 ext_statement ⊆ statement	@inv2_5 sta_ef ∈ statement → EFFECT
@inv2_3 sta_res ∈ statement↔RESOURCE	@inv2_6 sta_pr ∈ ext_statement ↔
@inv2_4 sta_act ∈ statement↔ACTION	(Endpoint ∪ Function ∪ CogUser)
A) The Structure of a Permission Statement	

| @inv2_10 actor_permission ∈ actor ↔ (statement\ext_statement) |
| @inv2_12 resource_permission ∈ access_managable_resource ↔ ext_statement |
| B) Abstraction for Permission Statement Relations |

| @inv3_comp1a **actor_permission** =(actor_role;role_policy;id_policy_statement) |
| @inv3_comp2a **resource_permission** =(res_access_policy;res_policy_statement) |
| C) Refinement for Permission Statement Relations |

Fig. 3. Event-B Invariants authorization Mechanism

The core idea of this abstraction is to link actors/requesters directly to their corresponding permission statements, bypassing IAM roles and policies for simplicity, as shown in Fig. 3B. We used the *actor* variable to represent all AWS entities that can perform actions based on their associated permission statements (*inv2_10*), while *access_managable_resouce* is a subset of resources that incorporates features allowing which actors can access them.

Introducing concrete variables of the access control paves the way for refining authorisation rules. Figure 4 illustrates the authorisation mechanism. A request context consists of the requester (*requester*), the requested action (*req_act*), and the requested resource (*req_res*). Moreover, a *request* will only be allowed if the pairs of *action-resource* in the *request* context are covered by those in the corresponding permission statements. Permissions can be actor-based or resource-based, represented by *actor_permission* and *resource_permission*, respectively

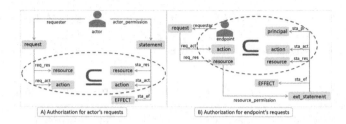

Fig. 4. Authorization of a request

@inv2_14 ∀r·r∈request ∧ req_authz(r)=Allow ∧ requester(r)∈ actor ⇒ (∃s·s∈statement ∧ requester(r)↦s ∈ actor_permission∧ req_res(r) ∈sta_res ∧ s↦req_act(r) ∈sta_act ∧ sta_ef(s)= Allow)	@inv2_15 ∀r·r∈request ∧ req_authz(r)=Allow∧ requester(r)∈ Endpoint ⇒ (∃s·s∈statement ∧ req_res(r)↦s∈ resource_permission ∧ s↦req_res(r) ∈sta_res ∧ s↦req_act(r) ∈sta_act ∧ s↦requester(r)∈sta_pr ∧ sta_ef(s)= Allow)

Fig. 5. Event-B Encoding of the Request Authorization

(Fig. 4A and B). Conditions illustrated in Fig. 4A and 4B are encoded in $inv2\_14$ and $inv2\_15$ in Fig. 5.

After introducing necessary variables and invariants, we refine the authorization mechanism ($authz\_ver$) to make it deterministic. The process distinguishes between actor and endpoint requesters and checks for the presence of corresponding permission. For example, Fig. 6A shows guards that capture the case that the requester is an actor having an *allow* value in the statement. Guard $grd2\_1$ ensures that the requester is an actor, while $grd2\_3$ states that pm includes all the requester's statements that are related to the requested action on the requested resource. Moreover, $grd2\_4$ ensures that there is at least one statement in the pm that grants permission, whereas $grd2\_5$ makes sure there is no deny statement for the requested action in pm.

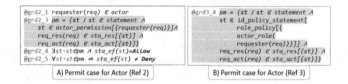

Fig. 6. Guards for Deterministic Authorizer Events

In further refinement, IAM roles and policies are introduced. The core idea is to replace the *actor_permission* and *resource_permission* relations with more concrete versions that encompass IAM roles and IAM policies, as defined in $inv3\_comp1a$ and $inv3\_comp2a$ in Fig. 3A. In more detail, *actor_permission* is replaced with an actor role that is linked with policies that have a set of statements ($inv3\_comp1a$), while *resource_permission* is replaced with a resource-based policy (res_access_policy) that has a set of statements ($inv3\_comp2a$).

Figure 6B shows the refinement of abstract guards in authorization mechanism events. For example, *grd3_4* replaces abstract *grd2_3*, specifying that *pm* includes all statements of policies of the requester actor's role related to the requested action on the requested resource. See the whole model at [14]

4   Modelling a Specific Serverless App's Scenario

In this section, our focus is on demonstrating the applicability of our proposed patterns. We chose a scenario from a serverless project management app to apply our patterns. This scenario represents updating the status of a project.

4.1   Modelling "Update Project Status" Scenario

The implementation of the scenario involves the orchestration of multiple AWS services. This scenario starts with a client app's initiating a request to the API Gateway endpoint. The API Gateway in turn initiates a subsequent request for a lambda function execution. The function execution results in yet another request to DB management to update the 'Project' table. Figure 7 demonstrates how this scenario can be modelled by applying the RHP pattern to the initial and subsequent chain of requests.

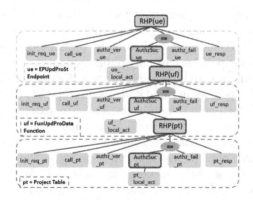

Fig. 7. Use of the RHP pattern to Model a Scenario

In Fig. 7, *RHP(ue)* indicates the request targeting the 'EPUpdProSt' endpoint by an app user, while *RHP(uf)* represents the request sent to the 'FunUpdProData' function by the 'EPUpdProSt' endpoint. Moreover, *RHP(pt)* shows the request by sending the function to update the 'Project' table. This diagram demonstrates that the RHP pattern, as detailed in Fig. 1, is capable of being recursively applied to encompass an entire serverless app's functionality.

As previously discussed, the authorization mechanism in serverless applications is encapsulated at a high level in the *authz_ver_...* events of the RHP

Table 1. Proof Control Statistics

Element Name	Total	Auto	Interactive
machine01_RHP	18	18	0
machine02_LSR	94	58	36
machine03_LSR_Auth_perm	106	77	29
machine04_LSR_Auth_Role_pol	74	51	23
"Update Project Status" Model	295	207	88

patterns. These events undergo further refinement, detailed in Sects. 3.3. Due to space limitations, the complete Event-B representation of the entire scenario is not included here, but it can be accessed from [14].

Finally, Table 1 shows the proof obligations (POs) statistics in the Event-B model of the "update project status" scenario. POs are formal conditions ensuring model correctness and consistency, categorised across different modelling stages, reflecting the model's evolution and refinement. For discharging POs, SMT solver and Atelier B prover are used.

5   Related Work

Since 2011, Amazon has implemented formal methods, which assist Amazon engineers in resolving challenging design problems [9]. The Amazon security team developed ZELKOVA [4], a tool based on formal techniques for customers to check whether their policies have any public access.

There is also some research focusing on using formal reasoning to find conflicts in authorization policies in cloud systems. In [15], IAM policies are modelled to find conflicts between policy statements, while [16] extends the work to cover conflicts in policy statements from multi-cloud environments.

Both [15] and [16] focus on conflicts in policy statements, whereas ZELKOVA [4] checks only the openness of a policy in the AWS environment. However, our work focuses on modelling serverless apps' functionalities built on an AWS environment and corresponding access control configurations. The aim is to help developers design their serverless systems rigorously.

6   Conclusion and Future Work

Serverless systems, characterized by their highly distributed and complex nature, necessitate rigorous formal design to ensure robustness. Formal modeling clarifies system and environment understanding, aiding in complexity management through the strategic use of abstraction.

We identified some key features of AWS-based serverless apps, such as request handling and access control and developed a number of generic patterns to formally represent these aspects. In devising these patterns, we used a number of techniques, such as generalization, sub-typing, and a hierarchical strategy to represent authorization, and resource management in the AWS platform. Our efforts in identifying and modelling these patterns resulted in a number of useful patterns such as RHP that we used to model a real-world scenario to demonstrate applicability of our patterns.

Furthermore, we plan to extend our study to include threat modelling scenarios in our models. This will allow us to identify potential security vulnerabilities systematically and address them by integrating appropriate controls into the model. Another direction could be the automation of pattern instantiation.

Competing Interests. The author(s) has no competing interests to declare that are relevant to the content of this manuscript.

References

1. Abrial, J.R.: Modeling in Event-B: System and Software Engineering. Cambridge University Press, Cambridge (2010). https://doi.org/10.1017/CBO9781139195881
2. Abrial, J.-R., Butler, M., Hallerstede, S., Voisin, L.: A roadmap for the Rodin toolset. In: Börger, E., Butler, M., Bowen, J.P., Boca, P. (eds.) ABZ 2008. LNCS, vol. 5238, p. 347. Springer, Heidelberg (2008). https://doi.org/10.1007/978-3-540-87603-8_35
3. Amazon Web Services Inc.: AWS services that work with IAM (2022). https://docs.aws.amazon.com/IAM/latest/UserGuide/reference_aws-services-that-work-with-iam.html
4. Backes, J., et al.: Semantic-based automated reasoning for AWS access policies using SMT. In: Proceedings of the 18th Conference on Formal Methods in Computer-Aided Design, FMCAD 2018. IEEE (2018). https://doi.org/10.23919/FMCAD.2018.8602994
5. Butler, M.: Mastering system analysis and design through abstraction and refinement. Eng. Dependable Softw. Syst. (2013). https://doi.org/10.3233/978-1-61499-207-3-49
6. Butler, M., Fathabadi, A.S., Silva, R.: Event-B and Rodin. In: Industrial Use of Formal Methods: Formal Verification. Wiley-ISTE (2012). https://doi.org/10.1002/9781118561829.ch7
7. Kanso, A., Youssef, A.: Serverless: beyond the cloud. In: Proceedings of the 2nd International Workshop on Serverless Computing (2017). https://doi.org/10.1145/3154847.3154854
8. McGrath, G., Brenner, P.R.: Serverless computing: design, implementation, and performance. In: 2017 IEEE 37th International Conference on Distributed Computing Systems Workshops (ICDCSW). IEEE (2017). https://doi.org/10.1109/ICDCSW.2017.36
9. Newcombe, C., Rath, T., Zhang, F., Munteanu, B., Brooker, M., Deardeuff, M.: How Amazon web services uses formal methods. Commun. ACM (2015). https://doi.org/10.1145/2699417
10. Palo Alto Networks: Unit 42 cloud threat report (2020)
11. Salehi Fathabadi, A., Butler, M., Rezazadeh, A.: Language and tool support for event refinement structures in Event-B. Formal Aspects Comput. https://doi.org/10.1007/s00165-014-0311-1

12. Synergy Research Group: Huge cloud market still growing at 34% per year; Amazon, Microsoft & Google now account for 65% of the total, April 2022. https://tinyurl.com/yhy7hdwy
13. Windley, P.: Simplify fine-grained authorization with Amazon verified permissions and Amazon Cognito (2023). https://aws.amazon.com/blogs/security/simplify-fine-grained-authorization-with-amazon-verified-permissionsand-amazon-cognito/
14. Yagmahan, M.S.N., Rezazadeh, A., Butler, M.: RHP (request handling pattern) and authorization mechanism in Event-B, June 2024. https://doi.org/10.5258/SOTON/D3041
15. Zahoor, E., Asma, Z., Perrin, O.: A formal approach for the verification of AWS IAM access control policies. In: De Paoli, F., Schulte, S., Broch Johnsen, E. (eds.) ESOCC 2017. LNCS, vol. 10465, pp. 59–74. Springer, Cham (2017). https://doi.org/10.1007/978-3-319-67262-5_5
16. Zahoor, E., Ikram, A., Akhtar, S., Perrin, O.: Authorization policies specification and consistency management within multi-cloud environments. In: Gruschka, N. (ed.) NordSec 2018. LNCS, vol. 11252, pp. 272–288. Springer, Cham (2018). https://doi.org/10.1007/978-3-030-03638-6_17

Property Ownership Formal Modelling Using Event-B and iUML-B

Manar Altamimi[1,2](✉) [iD], Nawfal Al Hashimy[2] [iD], Asieh Salehi Fathabadi[2] [iD], and Gary Wills[2] [iD]

[1] College of Computer Science and Information, Information System Department, Princess Nourah Bint Abdulrahman University, Riyadh, Kingdom of Saudi Arabia
[2] School of Electronics and Computer Science, University of Southampton, Southampton, UK
{mmma2c18,Nawfal,A.Salehi-Fathabadi,gbw}@soton.ac.uk

Abstract. This paper introduces a novel approach to formal modelling and verification of ownership, addressing safety concerns in property transfer processes. The Event-B formal method, graphically represented using iUML-B notation, is used to establish a robust framework for modeling and verifying ownership systems. The verified Event-B model refines and enhances user requirements at the design stage before system implementation. The research focuses on property ownership within the legal framework of the Kingdom of Saudi Arabia, specifically property sales. The research uncovers that, despite conscientious efforts to scrutinise user requirements, the formal model development exposes limitations and inadequacies in the initial specifications. The verification process introduces essential requirements to mitigate potential fraudulent activities, enhancing the security and dependability of ownership claims.

Keywords: ownership · safety · formal methods · Event-B · iUML-B

1 Introduction and Motivation

Proof of ownership is sensitive and valuable information in land registration systems. Land registration systems are complex and comprise numerous interconnected entities [11,16]. The presence of this complexity resulted in a dearth of availability of pertinent property information and a failure to prove ownership. Roughly 70% of the global population lacks access to cost-effective mechanisms for safeguarding their ownership [8]. The procedure of transfer ownership has been developed based on a framework that was conducted by our earlier study [3]. The procedure presents challenges in three primary forms: a potential sale of ownership to multiple owners, an inconsistency of property ownership, and a risk of fraudulent activities, such as identity theft.

Problem Statement: *The oversight of neglecting critical safety considerations within ownership transfer processes leaves the process vulnerable to fraudulent activities that pose typical challenges within the realm of safety-critical cyber-physical systems.*

© The Author(s), under exclusive license to Springer Nature Switzerland AG 2024
S. Bonfanti et al. (Eds.): ABZ 2024, LNCS 14759, pp. 191–200, 2024.
https://doi.org/10.1007/978-3-031-63790-2_12

This paper addresses the challenges arising from the complexity of the legal process in transferring ownership by constructing the Event-B formal model [1]. The model accurately represents the component architecture involved in the process of transferring property ownership, including interactions with stakeholders and other system components. The research question guiding this investigation is: *How can challenges in land registration systems, including double sales, falsification susceptibility, and the risk of fraudulent activities, be effectively addressed?*

The initial step in the process is identifying the approach to construct the model in Sect. 3. This involves a description of user needs in Sect. 3, identifying the strategy to construct the model, and modelling the process in Sect. 4. Lastly, we verify the model against the challenges in Sect. 5.

2   Related Work

Multiple scholarly inquiries have examined how technology can be used to tackle the difficulties related to property ownership in land registration systems [4,10,15]. The work in [15] asserts that the implementation of a distributed title database in a land registry would offer a theoretically secure and distributed solution to tackle issues. The work in [4] asserts that the primary purpose of electronic records in land registry, facilitated by a digital signature, is to allow users to transfer property ownership online, eliminating the requirement for physical presence. The work in [10] shows that the integration of blockchain technology into property ownership enhanced security and immutability. Nevertheless, these approaches fail to take into account the process associated with improving property ownership.

To enhance the process, [6] has opted iUML-B to address concerns related to safety-critical cyber-physical systems within railway control systems. In [7], have been employed formal methods to enhance safety and security standards in autonomous missions to overcome challenges associated with system specification. While these approaches offer solutions for system specification difficulties, their use cases are often limited to railway or autonomous driving scenarios. This paper, on the other hand, utilises the Event-B formal model to integrate safety requirements into the transfer ownership process, effectively mitigating challenges and tackling the complexity of an industrial system.

3   Overview of Modelling Approach

The approach used to simulate the transfer of property ownership involves four distinct stages. The initial stage includes understanding the specifications of ownership and determining the refinement strategy, followed by the construction of the model. Refinement strategy and modeling are iterative processes until an appropriate refinement strategy is achieved. The model is verified using model checking and proof of obligation to ensure compliance with the requirements specification and the consistency of the model. The approach depicted in Fig. 1

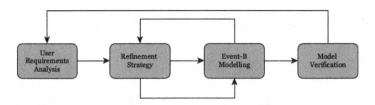

Fig. 1. Model development approach.

demonstrates the sequential delivery of each stage. However, it is important to note that this strategy is implemented iteratively. The iterative process plays a crucial role in enhancing our comprehension of ownership by facilitating the selection of an optimal refinement strategy for constructing the model. We give a concise description of the first stage in this Section and describe the following stages in Sect. 4 and Sect. 5.

The process of transferring ownership in Saudi Arabia involves four steps: ownership declaration, claiming ownership, the process of transferring ownership, and conveyance. The first step involves identifying the user as a purchaser, owner, or seller. The owner must **claim** their ownership title, which can be transferred to the purchaser through legal means. The process of transferring ownership involves specifying the seller as a seller or allowing the seller to **sell** the property. The purchaser can **request** multiple properties at once, and the seller can accept or withdraw the transaction. The **conveyance** step involves verifying the proof of purchase and ensuring the original and timestamped property information is original to the source. In Fig. 2, we give a concise description of the process using an activity diagram.

However, the scenarios have not shown control requirements to avoid double sales, inconsistency in property information, and fraud. Double sales involve consecutive sales by the same seller to different purchasers, requiring stricter control measures to prevent multiple buyers. Inconsistency in information arises from inefficiencies in recording property information and incomplete records. Owners should claim ownership before registering a property and organise it to reflect changes in ownership. Fraud concerns the intentional misuse of assets, such as stealing identities, and requires verification of user identities. Considering the challenges in the process, Event-B modelling contributes to enhancing the process and exposes limitations and inadequacies in the initial specifications.

4 Event-B Model and Refinement Strategy

The refinement strategy is correct-construction [5,6], achieved using Event-B modeling. The modelling is graphically presented in six refinements using iUML-B. The strategy constructs the model gradually, and every refinement addresses one aspect of the process[1].

---

[1] The complete model can be accessed at: https://shorturl.at/cfqxS.

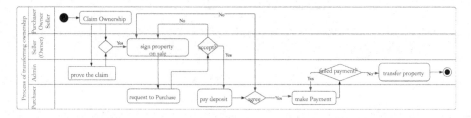

Fig. 2. Activity diagram: the process of transferring ownership

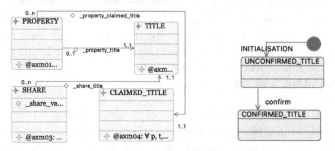

(a) Class diagram: main components   (b) State machine: title states

Fig. 3. iUML-B Diagrams: Abstract level

Background knowledge: Event-B [1,9] is a formal method for system development that consists of two types of component: a context and a machine. Contexts represent static data, while machines represent dynamic data. Contexts include carrier sets, constants and axioms (constrain the carrier sets and constants). A machine can access the static part of the model, including s, invariants (constraining variables) and events. An event defines a transition activity with pre-conditions (guards), and actions which modify variables. Event-B is supported by Rodin toolset [2], for modeling, verification. Model verification ensures model correctness and refinement consistency; validation ensures the construction of the right model using model checking. iUML-B [12–14] is a diagrammatic modelling notation that provides state machines and class diagrams to represent the Event-B model. It generates Event-B elements automatically and visually presents the model.

Abstract Model:Property The ownership model involves property and title, with each property linked to a title listing all owners' shares, as shown in Fig. 3a. The title has two states indicating the status of ownership claims. When owners claim ownership, the status of ownership is confirmed or remains claimed; otherwise, ownership remains unconfirmed or unclaimed, see Fig. 3b. These details have not been shown in the analysis. However, they were achieved through the iterative development of modeling.

Forward composition: $p \; ; q$
$$\forall p,q \cdot p \in S \leftrightarrow T \wedge q \in T \leftrightarrow U \Rightarrow p \,;q = \{x \mapsto y \; (\exists z \cdot x \mapsto z \in p \wedge z \mapsto y \in q)\}$$

Range restriction: $r \triangleright T \ r \triangleright T = \{x \mapsto y : x \mapsto y \in r \wedge y \in T\}$

Inverse: $r \sim \ r \sim \ = \{y \rightarrow x : x \rightarrow y \in r\}$

Four sets or classes are specified in the context, as shown in Fig. 3a. The relationships show the association between sets, and the cardinality indicates the type of association. Every PROPERTY is associated with one TITLE. The TITLE lists owners' shares SHARE. The CLAIMED_TITLE is a record where owners claim their ownership. These specifications are specified as axioms: @axm01: _equivalent_to = _property_claimed_title^{-1}; _property_title, this ensures that the title and claimed title are associated with the same property.

The title's states are modelled in the machine, Fig. 3b. The state moves to claimed or confirmed when all owners claim ownership using the event confirm. The state of the title is safely controlled, specified as an invariant:

@inv01: partition(TITLE, UNCONFIRMED_TITLE, CONFIRMED_TITLE)

First Refinement: Property Control The abstract context is extended, and a new set, ADMIN, is introduced, Fig. 4a. The model considers admin to be the entity responsible for maintaining property information. admin can addTitle and addShares, as well as confirm ownership when the user claims their property.

In the refining machine, the admin users added the TITLE(@inv03) using event addTitle. The same admin added the SHARE(@inv02) using event addShare.

@inv02: is_added $\in$ SHARE $\rightarrowtail$ ADMIN

@inv03: title_adm $\in$ TITLE $\rightarrowtail$ ADMIN

Further constraints (@inv04 and @inv05) are introduced to control the property:

@inv04: $\forall t \cdot \ t \in$ CONFIRMED_TITLE $\Rightarrow t \in$ dom(title_adm)

@inv05: $\forall s \cdot \ s \in$ dom(share_title) $\Rightarrow s \in$ dom(is_added) $\wedge$

_share_title(s) $\in$ dom((title_adm; is_added^{-1})$\triangleright\{s\}$) .

Accordingly, the confirm, addTitle, and addShare events are not satisfied with the new invariants. Therefore, guards are added to ensure that only the admin can confirm the property and to make the current refinement consistent. event addShare: @grd01: share $\in$ dom(is_added)

event confirm: @grd01:title $\in$ dom(title_adm)

Second refinement: Ownership This refinement entails modelling ownership and its association with owners. This ensures consistency of property information with owners that reflects changes over time. Ownership represents the proportion of ownership that each owner possesses. An owner could claim ownership of their property by providing proof of their claimed title. After confirming ownership, the title becomes attainable for sale. This refinement describes the procedure for proof of ownership, as mentioned in the previous analysis, before conducting any conveyance transaction. The context is extended in Fig. 5. New sets are introduced: a USER associate it with SHARE, specified as the axiom: @axm04: _unconfirmed_ownership= _share_title^{-1}; _share_user

Only owners can claim ownership if and only if they have a copy of the claim title that is equivalent to the title:

@axm05:$\forall t, ct, p \cdot \ p \in$ PROPERTY $\wedge t \in$ ran(_share_title) $\wedge ct \in$ CLAIMED_TITLE

$\wedge p \mapsto t \in$_property_title $\wedge ct \in$ dom(_equivalent_to) $\wedge$ _equivalent_to(ct) = t

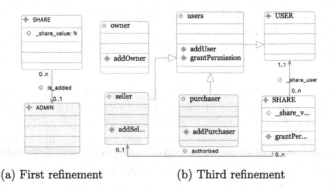

(a) First refinement   (b) Third refinement

Fig. 4. Class diagrams: yellow: new classes, white: abstract classes (Color figure online)

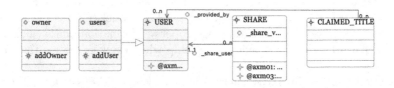

Fig. 5. Second refinement: part of iUML-B class diagrams

$\Rightarrow$ _provided_by[{ct}] = ran(ran(_share_title $\rhd$ {t}) $\lhd$ _unconfirmed_ownership)

The machine is refined to support the specification in this context. The ownership structure consists of three components: share_title, share_user, and ownership. We define users according to USER type to represent system users. share_title is the number of shares. share_user is an association of users with shares. ownership is an association title with users. One type of user role, the owner, is introduced at this level: ran(ownership). An archive of ownership inv06 should be kept as part of the requirements, specified as an invariant:

@inv06: archiveOwnership $\in$ share_title $\leftrightarrow$ users

inv07 is an archive information is a timestamp of transfer ownership:

@inv07: archiveDate $\in$ archiveOwnership $\rightarrow$ DATE

We model this by initially assigning all shares to the model's user and then updating to the transfer date.

Third refinement: User Type The context remains unchanged while the machine is refined to introduce new variables, purchaser and seller to represent the roles of users at different states in the model Fig. 4b. Although the user can play all roles, they cannot simultaneously be the seller and purchaser in the same transaction. When an owner intends to sell the property, they must grant permission grantPermission either to themselves or someone else:

@inv08: authorised $\in$ SHARE $\leftrightarrow$ seller

purchaser and seller can be added by using events addPurchaser and addSeller, respectively. We explicitly define the purchaser and seller as types of users to maintain the consistency of the model.

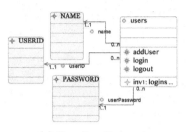

(a) Fourth refinement

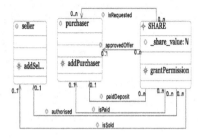

(b) Fifth refinement.

Fig. 6. Part of iUML-B Diagrams: class diagrams

Fourth refinement: User Identity This refinement focuses on preventing fraudulent activity by enforcing a security policy. Each user is given NAME, USERID, PASSWORD, see Fig. 6a. A safety property is added to the model to verify the user's identity. This can be modelled using the variable logins and adding two events: login and logout. The logins variable is a subset of user. When the user logs in, they should declare their userid and password. logout is basically removing the user from logins set.

Fifth refinement: Ownership Process This refinement involves the modelling of the property acquisition process while preventing double sales in the process, Fig. 6b shows the static part, while 7 shows the transition part. The process commences when the state of title is CONFIRMED_TITLE. CONFIRMED_TITLE can only exist in four states. The initial state is NOT_FOR_SALE once the title is confirmed by ADMIN using event confirm. Each transition is carried out by multiple users, each fulfilling their assigned roles. For example, a seller engages in the activities of sell and acceptedOffers. Given that a confirmed title cannot be associated with several states throughout the purchasing process, it is crucial to specifically define the user's role and their connection to ownership. This will ensure that distinct users are identified for different states. For instance, multiple purchasers can make requests to acquire a property (@inv09), but only one request is accepted (@inv10):

@inv09: isRequested $\in$ SHARE $\leftrightarrow$ purchaser

@inv10: approvedOffer $\in$ SHARE $\nrightarrow$ purchaser

Safety invariants are included to assure the safety process, some of them are:

@inv11: dom(isRequested) $\subseteq$ dom(isSold)

@inv12: approvedOffer $\subseteq$ isRequested

@inv11 and @inv12 ensure that any title that is requested should be on sale and only an approved offer is being requested, respectively.

5   Model Verification

This section summarises theorem proving and model checking effort of the presented Event-B model of the ownership supported by the Rodin toolsets.

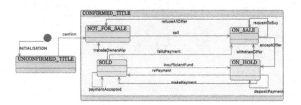

Fig. 7. Fifth refinement: iUML-B state machine

Theorem Proving. The Event-B theorem proving technique uses invariant preservation (e/v/INV) Proof Obligation (PO) and guard strengthening (e/g/GRD) PO to ensure concrete guards are stronger than abstract ones. A model of six machines yielded 233 POs, with 86% of cases automatically proven using the Rodin prover. However, there are some POs, mostly generated to prove invariant preservation, that are not discharged automatically and require interactive (manually) proving. The majority of POs occur in the last refinement, with 65 POs manually proved. An example of invariant preservation manually proved is isSold ∈ SHARE → seller when executing sell. This invariant is discharged when we ensure that the share of ownership is not on sale by adding a guard to the event. The invariant prevents the resale a share that is already on sale.

ProB Model Checking. ProB in Event-B is an effective tool for assessing probabilistic behaviours in system models. It helps capture and evaluate uncertainties within the model, allowing for exploration of potential system states and behaviors. This tool captures both deterministic and stochastic aspects, fostering a more realistic representation of complex systems during the construction phase. For example, (...grantPermission, sell, requestToBuy...) are sequences of events that demonstrate the scenario to address double sales for the same seller and property by ensuring that the seller cannot resell the ownership multiple times:

    at time i: sell and requestToBuy are not active.
    at time $i + 1$: grantPermission and requestToBuy are not active.
    at time $i + 2$: grantPermission and sell are not active.

6 Conclusion and Future Work

The paper addresses the research question of how effectively tackling challenges at different refinement levels, focusing on property ownership inconsistency, reducing fraudulent activities, and double sales. It uses formal methods to understand the legal complexity of transferring ownership, reveal inadequate system specifications, and introduce missing requirements to mitigate potential fraudulent activities. These requirements improve coherence and clarify user scenarios, ultimately enhancing the land registration systems.

The formal modelling and verification approach for ownership can be expanded to identify, analyse, and mitigate security risks in systems. Further research could generalise the model to cover jointly owned assets like luxury jewellery and harvesters, enhancing its potential for enhancing system security.

Competing Interests. The author(s) has no competing interests to declare that are relevant to the content of this manuscript.

References

1. Abrial, J.R.: Modeling in Event-B: System and Software Engineering. Cambridge University Press, Cambridge (2010)
2. Abrial, J.R., Butler, M., Hallerstede, S., Hoang, T.S., Mehta, F., Voisin, L.: Rodin: an open toolset for modelling and reasoning in Event-B. Int. J. Softw. Tools Technol. Transf. **12**(6), 447–466 (2010)
3. Altamimi, M., Al Hashimy, N., Wills, G.: Expert review of the land registration framework in the kingdom of Saudi Arabia. Int. J. ICT Res. Africa Middle East (IJICTRAME) **11**(1), 1–18 (2022)
4. Brennan, G.: Defining title registration. In: Brennan, G. (ed.) The Impact of eConveyancing on Title Registration, pp. 115–151. Springer, Cham (2015). https://doi.org/10.1007/978-3-319-10341-9_4
5. Dghaym, D., Hoang, T.S., Turnock, S.R., Butler, M., Downes, J., Pritchard, B.: An STPA-based formal composition framework for trustworthy autonomous maritime systems. Saf. Sci. **136**, 105139 (2021)
6. Dghaym, D., Poppleton, M., Snook, C.: Diagram-led formal modelling using iUML-B for hybrid ERTMS level 3. In: Butler, M., Raschke, A., Hoang, T.S., Reichl, K. (eds.) ABZ 2018. LNCS, vol. 10817, pp. 338–352. Springer, Cham (2018). https://doi.org/10.1007/978-3-319-91271-4_23
7. Dghaym, D., Turnock, S.R., Butler, M.J., Downes, J., Hoang, S., Pritchard, B.: Developing a framework for trustworthy autonomous maritime systems. In: Proceedings of the International Seminar on Safety and Security of Autonomous Vessels (ISSAV) and European STAMP Workshop and Conference (ESWC) 2019 (2020). https://api.semanticscholar.org/CorpusID:209056678
8. World Bank Group: Enhancing public sector performance: Malaysia's experience with transforming land administration. World Bank (2017)
9. Hoang, T.S.: An introduction to the Event-B modelling method. Ind. Deployment Syst. Eng. Methods 211–236 (2013)
10. Peck, M.E.: Blockchain world - do you need a blockchain? This chart will tell you if the technology can solve your problem. IEEE Spectr. **54**(10), 38–60 (2017). https://doi.org/10.1109/MSPEC.2017.8048838
11. Rizal Batubara, F., Ubacht, J., Janssen, M.: Unraveling transparency and accountability in blockchain. In: ACM International Conference Proceeding Series. 20th Annual International Conference on Digital Government Research (dg.o 2019), pp. 204–213 (2019).https://doi.org/10.1145/3325112.3325262
12. Said, M.Y., Butler, M., Snook, C.: A method of refinement in UML-B. Softw. Syst. Model. **14**(4), 1557–1580 (2015)
13. Snook, C.: iUML-B state machines new features and usage examples. In: Proceedings of the 5th Rodin User and Developer Workshop. University of Southampton (2014). https://eprints.soton.ac.uk/365301/

14. Snook, C., Butler, M.: UML-B: formal modeling and design aided by UML. ACM Trans. Softw. Eng. Methodol. (TOSEM) **15**(1), 92–122 (2006)
15. Szabo, N.: Secure property titles with owner authority. Nakamoto Inst. 1–5 (1998). https://nakamotoinstitute.org/secure-property-titles/
16. Zevenbergen, J.: A systems approach to land registration and cadastre. Nordic J. Surv. Real Estate Res. **1** (2004)

A Modeling and Verification Framework for Ethereum Smart Contracts

Simone Valentini⬛, Chiara Braghin⁽✉⁾⬛, and Elvinia Riccobene⬛

Computer Science Department, Università degli Studi di Milano,
via Celoria 18, Milan, Italy
{simone.valentini,chiara.braghin,elvinia.riccobene}@unimi.it

Abstract. Blockchain has shown to be a versatile technology with applications ranging from financial services and supply chain management to healthcare, identity verification, etc. Thanks to the usage of smart contracts, blockchain can streamline and automate complex processes, eliminating the need for intermediaries and reducing administrative overhead. Smart contracts often handle valuable assets and execute critical functions, making them attractive targets for attackers. Thus, secure and reliable smart contracts are necessary.

The long-term research we present aims to face the problem of safety and security assurance of smart contracts at design time. We are investigating the usage of the Abstract State Machine (ASM) formal method for the specification, validation, and verification of Ethereum smart contracts. We provide (*i*) a set of ASM libraries that simplify smart contracts modeling, (*ii*) models of malicious contracts to be used to check the robustness of a contract against some given attacks, (*iii*) patterns of properties to be checked to guarantee the operational correctness of the contract and its adherence to certain predefined properties.

Keywords: Blockchain · Ethereum · Smart contract verification · Abstract State Machine

1 Introduction

As blockchain-based smart contracts gain mainstream adoption, the demand for reliable and secure smart contract design and development becomes increasingly vital. Smart contracts are programs that govern high-value financial assets, but they carry a substantial risk due to their public availability, immutability, and the ability for anyone to execute them. For example, the infamous DAO hack drained $70 million worth of Ether from a vulnerable smart contract that was not properly verified [2]. Costly vulnerabilities and exploits can seriously hinder trust and acceptance in the blockchain ecosystem. Formal verification may contribute

This work was partially supported by project SERICS (PE00000014) under the MUR National Recovery and Resilience Plan funded by the European Union - NextGenerationEU.

to the overall maturity and spread of blockchain technology by providing a robust methodology for ensuring the correctness of smart contracts.

The field of formal verification for smart contracts has made notable progress but still faces challenges. Existing tools have several limitations: bytecode-based tools cannot reason about contracts at design time, some tools use complex notations requiring a strong mathematical base that discourages many designers or engineers, others target only a limited number of vulnerabilities [11,12].

Our work aims to explore the potential of using Abstract State Machines (ASMs) [6,7] for specification and verification of Ethereum smart contracts written in Solidity. To this aim, we formalized the Ethereum Virtual Machine (EVM) and key language primitives to enable functional correctness proofs [8]. Currently, we can verify intra-contract properties and model inter-contract interactions to check the robustness of a contract against some given attacks. Our long-term vision is to build a practical verification framework using ASMs as the foundational formalism. Specific goals include:

1. Modeling the full semantics of Ethereum smart contracts;
2. Developing automatic mappings between Solidity source code and ASM models;
3. Identifying common smart contract patterns and functionalities across different blockchain platforms to define a domain-specific language in order to enhance the consistency and reliability of verification results;
4. Implementing a graphical interface to help correct-by-design smart contract development.

The rest of the paper is organized as follows: in Sect. 2 we provide a background description of Ethereum smart contracts, and we briefly presents the ASM-based modeling of the Ethereum virtual machine, and of smart contracts. In Sect. 3 we discuss how to exploit validation and verification techniques supported by ASMETA to detect smart contracts vulnerabilities. In Sect. 4 we compare our results with existing approaches. Section 5 concludes the paper and outlines future research directions.

2   Smart Contract Modeling with ASM

The first and one of the most popular platforms implementing smart contracts is Ethereum [9,13]. Ethereum's structure is similar to Bitcoin, with the introduction of two main additional components: (*i*) the ability to embody some data into a transaction, and (*ii*) a stack-based virtual machine named *Ethereum Virtual Machine* (EVM) that allows code execution as a reaction to a transaction. In Ethereum, there are two types of accounts: *externally owned accounts* and *smart contract accounts*. They both have common attributes, such as an ether (ETH) balance or an identifying address, but contract accounts also provide a reference to some code stored within the blockchain, allowing them to respond to a transaction with a code execution that depends on the transaction data received. The EVM can then be considered as a distributed state machine with

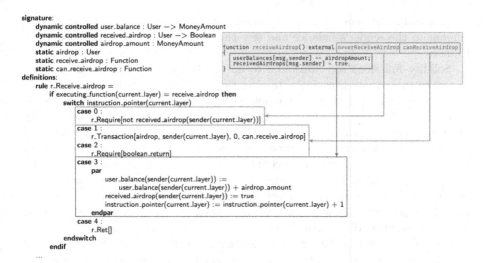

Fig. 1. An example of smart contract translation to ASMETA model.

a global state encompassing account balances, storage, and code that is updated when transactions are executed, rather than just a distributed ledger.

Smart contracts are written in Solidity, a high-level programming language, and then compiled into low-level bytecode. In [8], we showed how to use Abstract State Machines to model the EVM and smart contracts through the ASMETA framework [3] to exploit its powerful toolset. We presented some ASMETA libraries that, like the Ethereum Virtual Machine, provide rules and functions to model the Ethereum accounts with their specific attributes, and some primitives to model smart contract execution and their possible interactions. In particular, the library defines a stack structure that models the Ethereum execution stack and two rules to move along the stack, called **r_Transaction** and **r_Ret**. The rule **r_Transaction** models a transaction execution by increasing the stack size and storing within the stack layer all the relevant information on the transaction and the new execution environment, e.g., the executing contract and the instruction pointer; the rule also increases the value of caller's instruction pointer. The second one stops the execution by decreasing the stack structure and resuming the last execution.

In Fig. 1, we highlight the rationale for the translation of a Solidity smart contract into **AsmetaL**, the textual ASMETA's notation, presented in detail in [8]. The Solidity code on the right is the main function **receiveAirdrop()** of the Airdrop contract, which distributes liquidity to the accounts asking for it. The function first checks that two conditions are satisfied: (*i*) that the claiming account has not already received liquidity (i.e., the **neverReceivedAirdrop** modifier checks that **receivedAirdrops** value is false); and (*ii*) that the claimer is an eligible account (i.e., the **canReceiveAirdrop** modifier returns true, meaning that the claimer is a regular user, or a smart contract that can receive the

Airdrop). If both conditions are satisfied, then the contract adds the airdrop amount to the sender's balance and sets the sender's `receivedAirdrops` value to true.

Solidity functions are translated to an ASMETA rule that mainly consists of a `case` rule, which is essential to refer to the Solidity instructions within the function, and allows the instruction pointer to jump to a specific instruction when needed. The left part of Fig. 1 shows the transition rule corresponding to the function `receiveAirdrop()`. The modifiers checking the two initial conditions are translated into two `r_Require` rules that stop the function execution in case the condition is false. In particular, since the second condition, in order to check the eligibility of the claiming smart contract, makes a function call to the `canReceiveAirdrop` function implemented by the contract, it calls the `r_Transaction` rule that stops the execution of the current function and proceeds with the execution of the called function. More specifically, a new frame to the stack is added, with the `instruction_pointer` set to 0, and a new value for the `executing_function` and `executing_contract` fields. The `r_Ret[]` rule models the end of function execution by removing the frame on top of the stack structure and turning back to the previous layer. Please, notice that the Airdrop smart contract is vulnerable to a reentrancy attack since the `receivedAirdrops` value is updated only after the `canReceiveAirdrop` modifier is executed: a malicious user can make the `canReceiveAirdrop` function to call the `receiveAirdrop()` function multiple times, allowing the attacker to earn the airdrop amount more than once.

3   Smart Contract Verification with ASM

Smart contracts are often susceptible to various vulnerabilities that can lead to security breaches, financial losses, and other undesirable consequences. Design-time error detection would allow developers to catch and rectify issues before the smart contract is deployed on the blockchain, enhancing the overall security, reliability, and trustworthiness of smart contracts.

For the verification of smart contracts at design time, we used the ASMETA tool-set, which allows different forms of model analysis. In particular, model verification is possible by verifying properties expressed in temporal logic: the model checking `AsmetaSMV` maps `AsmetaL` models to the model checker `NuSMV`: the tool will check if the property holds during all possible model executions. In particular, we can verify both intra-contract properties and vulnerabilities exploitable by malicious users through inter-contract interactions.

An example of intra-contract properties is a logical error inside a contract definition. For instance, consider the Airdrop contract described in the previous section, and suppose that the contract contains a logical error in a function `destroy` that invokes the Solidity library function `selfdestruct` without checking the sender, i.e., allowing any account to terminate the contract, remove the bytecode from the Ethereum blockchain, and send the contract funds to a specified address. The `destroy` function can be modeled by the rule in Fig. 2.

```
rule r_Destroy =
    if executing_function(current_layer) = destroy then
        switch instruction_pointer(current_layer)
            case 0 :
                par
                    selfdestroy(executing_contract) := true
                    instruction_pointer = instruction_pointer + 1
                endpar
            case 1 :
                r_Ret[]
        endswitch
    endif
```

```
function destroy(address apocalypse) public {
    selfdestruct(payable(apocalypse));
}
```

Fig. 2. The AsmetaL rule (on the left) of the Solidity function destroy (on the right).

The vulnerability can be detected through the AsmetaSMV tool by using the following CTL specification, asserting that, if the executing contract is airdrop, the executing function is autodestroy and the instruction pointer is 0, then the transaction sender (i.e., sender(current_layer)) that invoked the method has to be the contract owner:

```
CTLSPEC ag((executing_contract=airdrop and executing_function=autodestroy and instruction_pointer=0)
        implies (owner(airdrop)=sender(current_layer)))
```

Other more complex vulnerabilities involve the interaction among contracts. In Sect. 2, we mentioned how the Airdrop contract is vulnerable to the reentrancy attack. This attack involves a malicious contract that interrupts the normal flow of the canReceiveAirdrop modifier and executes some loop calls to the receiveAirdrop() function. The receiveAirdrop()'s body instructions updating the user's balance (e.g., user_balance attribute) and recording that the user has received the airdrop are triggered after the exit of each reentrancy call, when the neverReceiveAirdrop modifier is still true. Once the attacker model has been imported into the model of the main contract and the two models are executed in parallel (so to build a multi-agents ASM with an agent running the Airdrop contract and an attacker agent running the malicious one), it is possible to state some CTL formulas on the two interacting contracts. E.g., we can check if the user_balance attribute exceeds the airdrop_amount value through the following property, detecting the reentrancy attack.

```
CTLSPEC ag((forall $u in User with user_balance($u) <= airdrop_amount))
```

Given the heterogeneous nature of the possible types of vulnerabilities (e.g., unchecked external codes, gas limit and out-of gas issues, timestamp dependencies reentrancy attacks, unintended exposure of sensitive data, or errors in the flow logic), starting from the taxonomy of vulnerabilities causes in [4], we have started to build a catalog (available at[1]) of:

– *patterns of properties* to guarantee the operational correctness of the contract and its adherence to certain predefined intra-contract properties;

---

[1] https://github.com/smart-contract-verification/ethereum-via-asm.

– *models of malicious contracts* to check the robustness of a contract against those vulnerabilities that allow malicious contracts to manipulate the behavior of the vulnerable contract (i.e., due to unsafe inter-contract interaction).

4   Related Work

Several approaches and tools have been developed to formally verify smart contracts, particularly those written in languages like Solidity. However, challenges and research areas still require further development and improvement. For example, the languages and tools used for formal verification may not fully capture the specific features and behaviors of smart contracts. In addition, while formal verification tools can prove simple properties and catch common vulnerabilities, proving complex properties or verifying more sophisticated aspects of a smart contract's behavior remains challenging. Scalability is also a relevant issue, formal verification can be computationally expensive and time-consuming, especially for complex smart contracts or large codebases. In addition, smart contracts often interact with external systems, such as oracles and other smart contracts. Formal verification tools often struggle to model and verify the behavior of such external dependencies. At the moment, our approach also has some of these limitations, however with our approach, we are able to effectively handle external interactions.

Among the most relevant approaches, Certora [1] is a formal verification tool specifically designed for Ethereum smart contracts. It supports the verification of correctness properties and functional specifications. Other relevant works are remarkable for their usage of symbolic execution, like Oyente [10], which performs a symbolic execution analysis on Ethereum smart contracts. Instead, other works are focused on automatic translation from smart contract code, in particular, F* language [5] is a functional language that allows performing some verification; however, this method has a limited application since it does not support the translation of the full Solidity language.

5   Conclusion

In this paper, we presented the first results of ongoing long-term research that investigates the usage of the Abstract State Machine formal method for the specification and verification of Ethereum smart contracts. We developed libraries within the ASMETA framework that allow specifying Solidity contracts in ASMs, simulating their behavior, and formally verifying key properties. As demonstrated through examples, this enables detecting at design-time various vulnerabilities, such as access control issues, or reentrancy attacks. The long-term vision is to build an integrated environment that supports correct-by-design smart contract development, by providing automatic mappings between Solidity and ASMs, a GUI for ASM modeling, and seamless access to the verification back-end. There are also opportunities for extending this approach to other blockchain platforms beyond Ethereum. Overall, formal methods like ASMs can potentially increase the reliability and security of smart contracts, which is essential for their widespread adoption across domains. Further research is needed in this direction.

Competing Interests. The author(s) has no competing interests to declare that are relevant to the content of this manuscript.

References

1. Certora Technology White Paper. https://docs.certora.com/en/latest/docs/whitepaper/index.html. Accessed 20 Feb 2024
2. Alchemy, N.: A short history of smart contract hacks on Ethereum: A.k.a. why you need a smart contract security audit (2019)
3. Arcaini, P., Gargantini, A., Riccobene, E., Scandurra, P.: A model-driven process for engineering a toolset for a formal method. Softw.: Pract. Exp. **41**(2), 155–166 (2011). https://doi.org/10.1002/spe.1019
4. Atzei, N., Bartoletti, M., Cimoli, T.: A survey of attacks on ethereum smart contracts (SoK). In: Maffei, M., Ryan, M. (eds.) POST 2017. LNCS, vol. 10204, pp. 164–186. Springer, Heidelberg (2017). https://doi.org/10.1007/978-3-662-54455-6_8
5. Bhargavan, K., et al.: Formal verification of smart contracts: short paper. In: Proceedings of the 2016 ACM workshop on Programming Languages and Analysis for Security, pp. 91–96 (2016)
6. Börger, E., Raschke, A.: Modeling Companion for Software Practitioners. Springer, Heidelberg (2018). https://doi.org/10.1007/978-3-662-56641-1
7. Börger, E., Stärk, R.: Abstract State Machines: A Method for High-Level System Design and Analysis. Springer, Heidelberg (2003). https://doi.org/10.1007/978-3-642-18216-7
8. Braghin, C., Riccobene, E., Valentini, S.: State-based modeling and verification of smart contracts. In: 39th ACM/SIGAPP Symposium on Applied Computing (2024, accepted)
9. Foundation, E.: Ethereum (2017)
10. Luu, L., Chu, D.H., Olickel, H., Saxena, P., Hobor, A.: Making smart contracts smarter. In: Proceedings of the 2016 ACM SIGSAC Conference on Computer and Communications Security, pp. 254–269 (2016)
11. Madl, G., Bathen, L., Flores, G., Jadav, D.: Formal verification of smart contracts using interface automata. In: IEEE International Conference on Blockchain, pp. 556–563 (2019)
12. Mavridou, A., Laszka, A.: Designing secure ethereum smart contracts: a finite state machine based approach. In: Meiklejohn, S., Sako, K. (eds.) FC 2018. LNCS, vol. 10957, pp. 523–540. Springer, Heidelberg (2018). https://doi.org/10.1007/978-3-662-58387-6_28
13. Wood, G., et al.: Ethereum: a secure decentralised generalised transaction ledger. Ethereum Proj. Yellow Pap. **151**(2014), 1–32 (2014)

Semantics Formalisation – From Event-B Contexts to Theories

Thai Son Hoang[1]([⊠]) [iD], Laurent Voisin[2] [iD], Karla Vanessa Morris Wright[3] [iD], Colin Snook[1] [iD], and Michael Butler[1] [iD]

[1] ECS, University of Southampton, Southampton SO17 1BJ, UK
{t.s.hoang,cfs,m.j.butler}@soton.ac.uk
[2] Systerel, 1115 rue René Descartes, 13100 Aix-en-Provence, France
laurent.voisin@systerel.fr
[3] Sandia National Laboratories, 7011 East Avenue, Livermore, CA 94550, USA
knmorri@sandia.gov

Abstract. The Event-B modelling language has been used to formalise the semantics of other modelling languages such as Time Mobility (TiMo) or State Chart XML (SCXML). Typically, the syntactical elements of the languages are captured as Event-B contexts while the semantical elements are formalised in Event-B machines. An alternative for capturing a modelling language's semantics is to use the Theory plug-in to build datatypes capturing the syntactical elements of the language and operators to represent the various semantical aspects of the language. This paper draws on our experience on the statemanchines (part of SCXML) to compare the two approaches in terms of modelling efforts.

Keywords: Statecharts · SCXML · Event-B · Theory plugin · Semantics formalisation

1 Introduction

Previously, Event-B [1] has been used to formalise the semantics of modelling languages such as Time Mobility (TiMo) [4] or State Chart XML (SCXML) [9]. Essentially, the semantics of the languages are captured as discrete transition systems represented by the Event-B models. An advantage of this approach is that the generic properties of the semantics can be captured as invariants of the Event-B models while the syntactical constraints are expressed as the axioms, to ensure the correctness of the semantics. Recent work on the Theory plug-in for Rodin [6] enabled the formalisation of the Event-B method within the EB4EB framework [7].

Our motivation for this paper is to explore the use of the Theory plugin for capturing the semantics of other modelling languages. In particular, we want to compare the pros and cons of the two modelling styles, using Event-B models and the Theory plugin. We will use the SCXML as the example of the language to be modelled, in particular, focusing on the untriggered state machine fragment.

S. Bonfanti et al. (Eds.): ABZ 2024, LNCS 14759, pp. 208–214, 2024.
https://doi.org/10.1007/978-3-031-63790-2_14

In this short paper, we focus on the modelling efforts to capture the semantics of SCXML. More in-depth comparison including the proving efforts will be our future work.

The structure of the paper is as follows. Section 2 gives some background information about Event-B, the Theory plugin, and the formalisation of SCXML semantics using Event-B standard constructs, i.e., contexts and machines. Section 3 gives some comparison in formalising of the SCXML semantics using the Theory plugin and using Event-B standard constructs. Section 4 gives a summary of the paper.

2 Background

In this section, we briefly review the Event-B modelling method, the Theory plugin, and the formalisation of SCXML using Event-B models.

Event-B is a formal modelling method for system development [1]. An Event-B model contains two types of components: *contexts* and *machines*. Contexts represent the static part of an Event-B model and can contain carrier sets (types), constants and axioms constraining them. Machines capture the dynamic part of an Event-B model as transition systems where the states are represented by variables and the transitions are expressed as guarded events. An important feature of a machine is invariants which are safety properties that must be satisfied in all reachable states. Proof obligations are generated to ensure that the invariants are indeed established and maintained by the Event-B machines. To cope with system complexity, contexts can be extended by further contexts (adding more carrier sets, constants, or axioms), and machines can be refined. Consistent refinement in Event-B guarantees that safety properties (e.g., invariants) are maintained through the refinement process.

The Theory plugin for Rodin [3] enables developers to define new polymorphic data types and operators upon those data types. These additional modelling concepts (datatypes and operators) might be defined axiomatically or directly (including inductive definitions). Not only restricted to the modelling capability, the Theory plugin also offers developers the opportunity of extending the reasoning capacity by writing automatic/interactive inference rules or rewrite rules.

A formalisation of SCXML in Event-B is presented in [9]. SCXML [2] describes UML-style statemachines with run-to-completion semantics. SCXML diagrams provide a compact representation for modelling hierarchy, concurrency and communication in systems design. In [9], we develop a formalisation of the semantics of SCXML by separately modelling statemachines (untriggered statecharts) and the run-to-completion semantics (triggered mechanism), and combine them together using the inclusion mechanism [5].

Our formalisation of Statemachines using Event-B contexts and machines [9], relies on the mathematical definition of irreflexive transitive closure (in context closure) and of a tree-shape structure (in context tree). The syntactical elements of statemachines are captured in three separate contexts (each one extending the other in order) named tree_structure, regions, and transformations. Machine active_states essentially specifies the semantics of the statemachines, captured as the set of active states. This can be seen on the left-hand side of Fig. 1.

3   Formalisation Using Contexts/Machines vs Theories

In this section, we present an attempt to formalise the semantics of statemachines using theories, in comparison with the contexts/machines as in [9]. Figure 1 show our strategy for developing a semantics of statecharts using theories. Here inter represents the intersection.

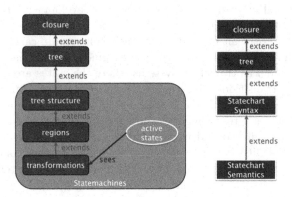

Fig. 1. Formalisation of statemachines: contexts/machines vs theories

3.1   Formalisation of Closure

In [9], the (irreflexive) transitive closure is formalised as a constant with an axiom defining its value. Various theorems capturing the properties of closure are derived from the axiom. Here STATE is a carrier set defining the set of states in the statemachines.

```
constants closure
axioms
  @def−closure: closure = (λ r · r ∈ STATE ↔ STATE | inter({p | r ⊆ p ∧ p;p ⊆ p}))
  theorem @typeof−closure: closure ∈ (STATE ↔ STATE) → (STATE ↔ STATE)
  theorem @closure_strengthen: ∀ r · r ⊆ closure(r)
  theorem @closure_transitivity: ∀ r · closure(r) ;closure(r) ⊆ closure(r)
  theorem @closure_minimal: ∀ r · (∀ p · r⊆p ∧ p;p⊆p ⇒ closure(r)⊆p)
```

Using the Theory plug-in, closure is defined as an operator in a theory for type parameter S. This operator is polymorphic with respect to this type parameter and hence can be utilised in different contexts (compared with the constant defined in the context for a specific STATE set).

```
THEORY
  closure
TYPE PARAMETERS
  S
OPERATORS
  •closure  :  closure  EXPRESSION  PREFIX
  direct definition
    closure≜ (λ r · r ∈ S ↔ S | inter({p | r ⊆ p ∧ p;p ⊆ p}))
THEOREMS
  typeof-closure      :   closure ∈ (S ↔ S) → (S ↔ S)
  closure_strengthen  :   ∀r · r ∈ S ↔ S ⇒ r ⊆ closure(r)
  closure_transitivity :  ∀r · r ∈ S ↔ S ⇒ closure(r);closure(r) ⊆ closure(r)
  closure_minimal     :   ∀r · r ∈ S ↔ S ⇒ (∀p · p ∈ S ↔ S ∧ r ⊆ p ∧ p;p ⊆ p ⇒ closure(r) ⊆ p)
```

3.2 Formalisation of Tree

Using contexts, the definition of trees is given as a constant Tree with its value defined using set comprehension and utilising transitive closure. In this definition, Sts represents the set of nodes in a tree, rt represents the root of the tree, prn is the parent relationship of the tree, and cl is the same previously defined closure operator.

axioms @def−Tree: Tree = {Sts ↦ rt ↦ prn |
    Sts ⊆ STATE ∧ rt ∈ Sts ∧ prn ∈ Sts \ {rt} → Sts ∧ (∀ n · n ∈ Sts \ {rt} ⇒ rt ∈ cl(prn)[{n}])}

Following the EB4EB framework [7], we formalise tree as a datatype with a well-definedness operator. The datatype is polymorphic with a type parameter NODE and operator TreeWD stating similar conditions in the axiom @def−Tree.

```
THEORY
  Tree
IMPORTS THEORY PROJECTS
  [Closure]
  THEORIES
    closure
TYPE PARAMETERS
  NODE
DATATYPES
  TREE(NODE)  ≜
    ▶ Cons_TREE(States:P(NODE), Root:NODE, Parent:P(NODE × NODE))
OPERATORS
  •TreeWD  :  TreeWD(tr : TREE(NODE))  PREDICATE  PREFIX
  direct definition
    TreeWD(tr : TREE(NODE)) ≜ Root(tr) ∈ States(tr) ∧
    Parent(tr) ∈ States(tr) \ {Root(tr)} → States(tr)
    ∧ (∀ n · n ∈ States(tr) \ {Root(tr)} ⇒ Root(tr) ∈ closure(Parent(tr))[{n}])
```

3.3 Formalisation of the Statechart Syntactical Elements

The syntactical elements of the statecharts are captured in three contexts to introduce the different aspects gradually: (1) tree-shape structure (2) parallel regions, and (3) transformations (an abstraction of transitions between states, including enabling, entering, and exiting states for each transformation). We will not present the details of the formalisation here, but refer the readers to [9]. Using the Theory plugin, we define the STATECHART datatype as in Fig. 2. Notice that we decide to define the STATECHART datatype all at once rather than gradually introducing its aspects. Datatypes in the Theory plugin are closed and hence

```
▽ DATATYPES ⊛
    ▽ ⊙ ⊙  STATECHART    //
        ▽ Type Arguments ⊛
            ○ ⊛  STATE ▼
            ○ ⊛  TRANSFORMATION ▼
        ▽ Constructors ⊛
            ☑ ⊙ ⊙  Cons_STATECHART    //
                ▽ Destructors ⊛
                    ⊛ ⊙  Tree     Type: TREE(STATE)    //
                    ⊛ ⊙  Regions     Type: P(P(STATE))    //
                    ⊛ ⊙  Transformation     Type: P(TRANSFORMATION)    //
                    ⊛ ⊙  Enabling     Type: P(TRANSFORMATION × P(STATE))
                    ⊛ ⊙  Exiting     Type: P(TRANSFORMATION × P(STATE))
                    ⊛ ⊙  Entering     Type: P(TRANSFORMATION × P(STATE))
```

Fig. 2. Statechart datatype

cannot be extended. An example is the use of the Tree datatype for part of the STATECHART datatype resulting in a "nesting" effect. This results in operators of the form shown to define the well-definedness for Regions of a statechart. In order to get to the states of a statechart st, one needs to use States(Tree(st)) due to this nesting effect.

```
•RegionsWD  :  RegionsWD(st : STATECHART(STATE, TRANSFORMATION))  PREDICATE  PREFIX
direct definition
    RegionsWD(st : STATECHART(STATE, TRANSFORMATION)) ≙ Regions(st) ⊆ P(States(Tree(st)))
    ∧ (∀r1, r2 · r1 ∈ Regions(st) ∧ r2 ∈ Regions(st) ∧ r1 ≠ r2 ⟹ r1 ∩ r2 = ∅)
    ∧ union(Regions(st)) = States(Tree(st)) \ {Root(Tree(st))}
    ∧ (∀ r · r ∈ Regions(st) ⟹ (∃p · p ∈ States(Tree(st)) ∧ Parent(Tree(st))[r] = {p}))
```

3.4   Formalisation of the Statechart Semantical Elements

In [9], the semantical elements of the statecharts are captured in a machine with a variable representing the active states of the statechart. Invariants capture properties, such as there is always an active state and if a child state is active then its parent state must be active.

Using the Theory plugin, we define a datatype ACTIVE_STATECHART for this purpose (we omit some details due to space reasons). This datatype wraps the STATECHART datatype together with the active states. The well-definedness operator ActiveStatechartWD captures the properties that we want to impose on the statechart semantics.

```
DATATYPES
    ACTIVE_STATECHART(STATE, TRANSFORMATION)  ≙
        ▶ Cons_ACTIVE_STATECHART(Statechart:STATECHART(STATE, TRANSFORMATION), Active:P(STATE))
OPERATORS
    •ActiveStatechartWD  :  ActiveStatechartWD(a_sc : ACTIVE_STATECHART(STATE, TRANSFORMATION))  PREDICATE  PREFIX
    direct definition
        ActiveStatechartWD(a_sc : ACTIVE_STATECHART(STATE, TRANSFORMATION)) ≙ Active(a_sc) ⊆ States(Tree(Statechart(a_sc)))
        ∧ Active(a_sc) ≠ ∅
        ∧ (∀ s · s ∈ Active(a_sc) \ {Root(Tree(Statechart(a_sc)))} ⟹ Parent(Tree(Statechart(a_sc)))(s) ∈ Active(a_sc))
```

The semantics of the statechart is captured as the following direct definition of the transform operator.

```
Cons_ACTIVE_STATECHART(Statechart(a_sc),
    (Active(a_sc) \ Exiting(Statechart(a_sc))(tr)) ∪ Entering(Statechart(a_sc))(tr))
```

Given a well-defined active statechart a_sc and a transformation tr of that state-chart, i.e., tr ∈ Transformations(Statechart(a_sc)), the transform operator construct a new active statechart by updating the active states of the statechart by removing tr's exiting states and then adding the entering states of tr.

Consistency of the statechart semantics can now be expressed as the following theorem (to be proved).

thm1   :   ∀a_sc, tr · a_sc ∈ ACTIVE_STATECHART(STATE, TRANSFORMATION) ∧
                ActiveStatechartWD(a_sc) ∧ tr ∈ Transformation(Statechart(a_sc)) ⟹
                ActiveStatechartWD(transform(a_sc, tr))

The theorem says that any transformation of an active statechart preserves the well-definedness of the active statechart. The proof of this theorem using the Theory plugin will be our future work.

4 Summary

This short paper provides some insights comparing the two modelling styles for formalising semantics of modelling languages: using Event-B contexts/machines (Approach 1) vs using the Theory plugin's theories (Approach 2). Using Approach 1, essentially the model corresponds to a single statemachine, whereas with Approach 2, statemachines are modelled as a datatype. Context extension is a natural way to develop the statemachine's syntactical elements gradually in Approach 1, however, attempts to do this using theory extensions with Approach 2 results in nested datatypes which are cumbersome to use (see Sect. 3). An alternative is to use type class extension for theories [8]. In both approaches, the syntactical constraints on the models can be represented. In Approach 1, these are captured as axioms in the context constraining the syntactical elements. Using Approach 2, the well-formedness conditions are encoded as well-definedness predicate operators. Semantical properties are also captured in both approaches: as machine invariants in Approach 1, and as theory theorems in Approach 2. In the future, reasoning about refinement using Approach 1 requires duplication of the models (representing the abstract and the concrete statemachines). On the other hand, the explicit representation of statemachines as objects from a datatype in Approach 2 allows us to write theorems in first-order logic about these well-defined objects. We expect that using Theory will help with stating and reasoning about refinement relationships. While we use the example of statemachines to compare Approaches 1 and 2, these comparisons are applicable to formalisation of other type of models, e.g., UML-B statemachines, SCXML statecharts, etc.

Competing Interests. The author(s) has no competing interests to declare that are relevant to the content of this manuscript.

References

1. Abrial, J.R.: Modeling in Event-B: System and Software Engineering. Cambridge University Press, Cambridge (2010)
2. Barnett, J.: Introduction to SCXML. In: Dahl, D.A. (ed.) Multimodal Interaction with W3C Standards, pp. 81–107. Springer, Cham (2017). https://doi.org/10.1007/978-3-319-42816-1_5
3. Butler, M., Maamria, I.: Practical theory extension in Event-B. In: Liu, Z., Woodcock, J., Zhu, H. (eds.) Theories of Programming and Formal Methods. LNCS, vol. 8051, pp. 67–81. Springer, Heidelberg (2013). https://doi.org/10.1007/978-3-642-39698-4_5
4. Ciobanu, G., Hoang, T.S., Stefanescu, A.: From TiMo to Event-B: event-driven timed mobility. In: 2014 19th International Conference on Engineering of Complex Computer Systems, Tianjin, China, 4–7 August 2014, pp. 1–10. IEEE Computer Society (2014). https://doi.org/10.1109/ICECCS.2014.10
5. Hoang, T.S., Dghaym, D., Snook, C.F., Butler, M.J.: A composition mechanism for refinement-based methods. In: 22nd International Conference on Engineering of Complex Computer Systems, ICECCS 2017, Fukuoka, Japan, 5–8 November 2017, pp. 100–109. IEEE Computer Society (2017). https://doi.org/10.1109/ICECCS.2017.27
6. Hoang, T.S., Voisin, L., Salehi, A., Butler, M.J., Wilkinson, T., Beauger, N.: Theory plug-in for Rodin 3.x. CoRR abs/1701.08625 (2017). http://arxiv.org/abs/1701.08625
7. Riviere, P., Singh, N.K., Ameur, Y.A., Dupont, G.: Formalising liveness properties in Event-B with the reflexive EB4EB framework. In: Rozier, K.Y., Chaudhuri, S. (eds.) NFM 2023. LNCS, vol. 13903, pp. 312–331. Springer, Cham (2023). https://doi.org/10.1007/978-3-031-33170-1_19
8. Snook, J., Butler, M., Hoang, T.S.: Developing a new language to construct algebraic hierarchies for Event-B. In: Feng, X., Müller-Olm, M., Yang, Z. (eds.) SETTA 2018. LNCS, vol. 10998, pp. 135–141. Springer, Cham (2018). https://doi.org/10.1007/978-3-319-99933-3_9
9. Morris Wright, K.V., Hoang, T.S., Snook, C.F., Butler, M.J.: Formal language semantics for triggered enable statecharts with a run-to-completion scheduling. In: Ábrahám, E., Dubslaff, C., Tarifa, S.L.T. (eds.) ICTAC 2023. LNCS, vol. 14446, pp. 178–195. Springer, Cham (2023). https://doi.org/10.1007/978-3-031-47963-2_12

Using Symbolic Execution to Transform Turbo Abstract State Machines into Basic Abstract State Machines

Giuseppe Del Castillo$^{(\boxtimes)}$ (ID)

Munich, Germany
`giuseppedelcastillo@acm.org`

Abstract. This paper introduces a transformation method that uses symbolic execution to eliminate sequential composition (`seq`) rules from turbo ASM rules by translating them into equivalent rules without `seq`. Under some circumstances `iterate` rules can also be eliminated. The material presented here is work in progress. A prototype implementation of the transformation is publicly available.

1 Introduction

Abstract State Machines (ASM) [4] are a well-established, rigorous state-based method for system design and analysis. An important extension to Gurevich's initial definition [9] is the "turbo ASM" introduced by Börger and Schmid [3], with rules for sequential composition, iteration and parameterized submachines. It provides a very expressive structuring mechanism, but the implications of its semantics, with non-observable intermediate steps and hidden states, are not straightforward, especially in combination with **par** rules of basic ASM (see [7]).

Therefore, in some situations, it may be desirable to transform a turbo ASM into a basic sequential ASM as defined in [9], for example if one wants to translate an ASM into the language of a model checker (as done in [1,5], among others). In such a language, models are typically specified in terms of the relation between current and next state in a sequence of states. This fits well with the computation model of basic ASM, but not with turbo ASM. In fact, none of the model checking interfaces that we are aware of supports turbo ASM.

In this paper, a method that uses symbolic execution to transform a subset of turbo ASM into basic ASM is introduced. Symbolic execution is a rather old technique that dates back to the 1970s [10,14] and has started seeing renewed interest with the advent of SMT solvers, which have increased its practical applicability (see [2] for a recent overview). Related works using symbolic execution of ASM for other purposes than the present paper include [11] (for translation validation of compiler-generated code), [13] (for verification of properties of ASM models with theorem provers using a calculus based on symbolic execution) and [12] (for estimation of worst-case execution time using a timed variant of ASM).[1]

---

[1] Some previous works such as [8] already used symbolic execution techniques in ad hoc manner, but did not address the systematic symbolic execution of ASM rules. A special application of symbolic execution of control state ASM is described in [6].

© The Author(s), under exclusive license to Springer Nature Switzerland AG 2024
S. Bonfanti et al. (Eds.): ABZ 2024, LNCS 14759, pp. 215–222, 2024.
https://doi.org/10.1007/978-3-031-63790-2_15

A Note on ASM Language. For space reasons, we omit a summary of the ASM language (besides the overview of rules in Table 1) and refer to [4]. The ASM language used here diverges from [4] in that it is (i) typed[2] and (ii) the minimal subset of ASM strictly necessary to illustrate our method. The limitations are: only static, controlled and monitored functions; no variables nor variable-binding constructs, only ground terms; no logic formulas, but terms of *Boolean* type instead; only six kinds of rules: skip, update, conditional, seq, par, iterate.

The semantics (evaluation) of a term t or rule R in state S is a value $x = \{\!\{t\}\!\}_S$ or update set $U = \{\!\{R\}\!\}_S$, respectively.[3] The notation $U_1 \oplus U_2$ stands for:

$$U_1 \oplus U_2 = U_2 \cup \{(l, x) \in U_1 \mid \text{there is no } x' \text{ with } (l, x') \in U_2\}$$

Table 1. Evaluation of rules

$\{\!\{t_i\}\!\}_S = x_i$ for $i \in \{1, \ldots, n\}$	
$\{\!\{f(t_1, \ldots, t_n) := t\}\!\}_S = \{((f, (x_1, \ldots, x_n)), \{\!\{t\}\!\}_S)\}$	$\{\!\{\text{skip}\}\!\}_S = \emptyset$
$\{\!\{G\}\!\}_S = \textbf{true}$	$\{\!\{G\}\!\}_S = \textbf{false}$
$\{\!\{\text{if } G \text{ then } R_1 \text{ else } R_2\}\!\}_S = \{\!\{R_1\}\!\}_S$	$\{\!\{\text{if } G \text{ then } R_1 \text{ else } R_2\}\!\}_S = \{\!\{R_2\}\!\}_S$
$\{\!\{R_1\}\!\}_S = U_1$ $\{\!\{R_2\}\!\}_S = U_2$	$\{\!\{R_1\}\!\}_S = U_1$ U_1 is inconsistent
$\{\!\{R_1 \text{ par } R_2\}\!\}_S = U_1 \cup U_2$	$\{\!\{R_1 \text{ seq } R_2\}\!\}_S = U_1$
$\{\!\{R_1\}\!\}_S = U_1$ U_1 is consistent $\{\!\{R_2\}\!\}_{S+U_1} = U_2$	
$\{\!\{R_1 \text{ seq } R_2\}\!\}_S = U_1 \oplus U_2$	
$\{\!\{R\}\!\}_S = \emptyset$	$\{\!\{R\}\!\}_S \neq \emptyset$
$\{\!\{\text{iterate } R\}\!\}_S = \emptyset$	$\{\!\{\text{iterate } R\}\!\}_S = \{\!\{R \text{ seq } (\text{iterate } R)\}\!\}_S$

2   Symbolic Execution Framework

Uninterpreted Locations and Functions. The starting point for symbolic execution is an incompletely defined ASM state S where the value of some or all locations $(f, \overline{x})$ of one or more non-static function names f is *unknown*, also

---

[2] Strong typing is necessary for an effective use of SMT solvers to support symbolic execution. A type system which does not use *undef* to model partial functions, such the one described in [15], while being a significant departure from the standard ASM definition, may further facilitate the use of SMT solvers.

[3] The unusual $\{\!\{\cdot\}\!\}$ is used because $[\![\cdot]\!]$ will be used later to denote symbolic evaluation.

written "$f_S(\overline{x})$ is unknown".[4] We call such locations *uninterpreted locations*. If all possible locations $(f, \overline{x})$ of a function name f are uninterpreted in S, we say that f is uninterpreted in S. A location $(f, \overline{x})$ that is uninterpreted in S becomes interpreted in a sequel state $S' = S + U$ if there is an update of $(f, \overline{x})$ in U.

Symbolic States. The ASM states are replaced by *symbolic states*, where the (symbolic) values of locations are *partially evaluated terms*, see definition below, rather than regular values. Starting from an incompletely defined state S, an initial symbolic state $\mathsf{S} = symstate(S)$ mapping each (interpreted or uninterpreted) location of S to a symbolic value is defined as follows:

$$\mathsf{f}_\mathsf{S}(x_1, \ldots, x_n) = \begin{cases} \langle \text{val } y \rangle & \text{if } \mathsf{f}_S(x_1, \ldots, x_n) = y \\ \langle \text{initial } (f, (x_1, \ldots, x_n)) \rangle & \text{if } \mathsf{f}_S(x_1, \ldots, x_n) \text{ is unknown.} \end{cases}$$

Partially Evaluated Terms. Partially evaluated terms ("pe-terms") are similar to terms, but the base case of their inductive definition includes the *val* and *initial* symbolic values introduced above, in addition to nullary functions:

$$t ::= f(t_1, \ldots, t_n) \mid \langle \text{val } x \rangle \mid \langle \text{initial } (f, \overline{x}) \rangle$$

The *symbolic evaluation* $[\![t]\!]_{\mathsf{S},\mathsf{C}}$ of a pe-term t in a symbolic state S under path conditions C is defined in Table 2. The operator $\mathsf{simplify\_formula}[\,\mathsf{C}, \varphi\,]$ used in the evaluation of Boolean terms (i.e. formulas) reduces, if possible, a formula φ to $\langle \text{val } \mathbf{true} \rangle$ or $\langle \text{val } \mathbf{false} \rangle$ in view of the path conditions C:

$$\mathsf{simplify\_formula}[\,\mathsf{C}, \varphi\,] = \begin{cases} \langle \text{val } \mathbf{true} \rangle & \text{if it can be proved that } \bigwedge_{\psi \in \mathsf{C}} \psi \Rightarrow \varphi \\ \langle \text{val } \mathbf{false} \rangle & \text{if it can be proved that } \bigwedge_{\psi \in \mathsf{C}} \psi \Rightarrow \neg\varphi \\ \varphi & \text{otherwise} \end{cases}$$

How $\mathsf{simplify\_formula}$ tries to prove the formulas is a matter of implementation (our prototype uses a combination of: directly checking $\varphi \in \mathsf{C}$, $\neg\varphi \in \mathsf{C}$, applying Boolean rewrite rules, invoking SMT solver if the previous measures fail).

For some t and S, $[\![t]\!]_{\mathsf{S},\mathsf{C}}$ is undefined. In particular, it fails for $t = f(t_1, \ldots, t_n)$ if f is not static and not all t_i can be fully evaluated to a $\langle \text{val } x_i \rangle$ in S.

---

[4] We deliberately use the term "unknown" instead of "undefined" to avoid any confusion with the *undef* value normally used to model partial functions, which is an element of the ASM superuniverse. A location $(f, \overline{x})$ with $f(\overline{x}) = undef$ is not uninterpreted: its value is known and equals *undef*. The question may arise how the two can be distinguished. For the purpose of transforming turbo ASM into basic ASM, which is the focus of this paper, this is not necessary, as all non-static functions must be uninterpreted (see Sect. 3). For other uses of symbolic execution, a tool may need to provide some syntax to distinguish between *undef* und "unknown value".

Table 2. Symbolic evaluation of pe-terms

$[\![\langle \text{val } x\rangle]\!]_{\mathsf{S},\mathsf{C}} = \langle \text{val } x\rangle$ $[\![\langle \text{initial } (f,\overline{x})\rangle]\!]_{\mathsf{S},\mathsf{C}} = \langle \text{initial } (f,\overline{x})\rangle$

$[\![t_i]\!]_{\mathsf{S},\mathsf{C}} = \langle \text{val } x_i\rangle$ for all $i \in \{1,\ldots,n\}$

$[\![f(t_1,\ldots,t_n)]\!]_{\mathsf{S},\mathsf{C}} = f_{\mathsf{S}}(x_1,\ldots,x_n)$

$f : T_1,\ldots,T_n \to T \quad T \neq Boolean \quad f$ is static

$[\![t_i]\!]_{\mathsf{S},\mathsf{C}} = t_i'$ for $i = 1,\ldots,n \qquad t_i' \neq \langle \text{val } x_i\rangle$ for some $i \in \{1,\ldots,n\}$

$[\![f(t_1,\ldots,t_n)]\!]_{\mathsf{S},\mathsf{C}} = f(t_1',\ldots,t_n')$

$f : T_1,\ldots,T_n \to Boolean \qquad f$ is static

$[\![t_i]\!]_{\mathsf{S},\mathsf{C}} = t_i'$ for $i = 1,\ldots,n \quad t_i' \neq \langle \text{val } x_i\rangle$ for some $i \in \{1,\ldots,n\}$

$[\![f(t_1,\ldots,t_n)]\!]_{\mathsf{S},\mathsf{C}} = \mathsf{simplify\_formula}[\,\mathsf{C}, f(t_1',\ldots,t_n')\,]$

$[\![t_i]\!]_{\mathsf{S},\mathsf{C}} \neq \langle \text{val } x_i\rangle$ for some $i \in \{1,\ldots,n\} \qquad f$ is not static

$[\![f(t_1,\ldots,t_n)]\!]_{\mathsf{S},\mathsf{C}}$ is not defined

This is to make sure that locations are identified unambiguously, i.e. to avoid *aliasing*.[5]

When the symbolic evaluation of a pe-term t succeeds, its result $t' = [\![t]\!]_{\mathsf{S},\mathsf{C}}$, seen as a tree, has: (i) application terms $f(\overline{t})$, where f is a static function name, as inner nodes; (ii) symbolic values of the form $\langle \text{val } x\rangle$ or $\langle \text{initial } (f,\overline{x})\rangle$ as leaves. This implies that the value of the pe-term t' is not state-dependent.

Symbolic Update Sets. A *symbolic update set* U is a finite set of *symbolic updates* of the form $((f,\overline{x}),t)$, where $(f,\overline{x})$ is the location to be updated and t is a pe-term to be stored therein. Transitions between symbolic states are defined accordingly.[6] The sequel symbolic state $\mathsf{S}' = \mathsf{S} + \mathsf{U}$ obtained by applying U to symbolic state S is such that, for each controlled function name f:

---

[5] For example, consider an ASM with controlled function names f (unary) and i, j (nullary), uninterpreted in a state S. If the symbolic evaluation of $f(i)$ and $f(j)$ were not undefined, it would produce $f(\langle \text{initial } i\rangle)$ and $f(\langle \text{initial } j\rangle)$, i.e. two pe-terms that do not unambiguously identify a location (they may or may not refer to the same location depending on whether $i = j$ holds in S, which cannot be determined). In order to avoid this issue, the symbolic evaluation of such terms is not defined, i.e. fails. This is the main limitation of the symbolic execution approach presented in this paper. There are various ways to address this issue, but working out a good solution in detail requires further work.

[6] With respect to consistency, we adopt a stronger definition than for regular update sets: a symbolic update set U is *consistent* if it does not contain two symbolic updates of the same location l. For a discussion of why this is a reasonable choice, see [13].

$$f_{S+U}(\overline{x}) = \begin{cases} t & \text{if } ((f, \overline{x}), t) \in U \\ f_S(\overline{x}) & \text{otherwise.} \end{cases}$$

Partially Evaluated Rules. Partially evaluated rules ("pe-rules") are similar to rules, with an additional $\langle \text{upd } U \rangle$ rule encapsulating a symbolic update set U (normally obtained from a subrule that can be fully evaluated):

$R ::= \dots$ (all previously defined rules, see Sect. 1 and Table 1)

   | $\langle \text{upd } U \rangle$ (update set rule)

The *symbolic evaluation* $[\![R]\!]_{S,C}$ of a pe-rule R under path conditions C in a symbolic state S is defined in Table 3. For any R, $[\![R]\!]_{S,C}$ is either an update set rule $\langle \text{upd } U \rangle$ or a conditional rule.

Reconversion to ASM Rule. A pe-rule generated according to Table 3 can be converted back to an ASM rule without $\langle \text{upd} \dots \rangle$, $\langle \text{val} \dots \rangle$, $\langle \text{initial} \dots \rangle$ using the to-rule operator. This operator replaces any $\langle \text{val } x \rangle$ with a static term that evaluates to x (e.g. a constant), any $\langle \text{initial } (f, \overline{x}) \rangle$ with a corresponding application term and any $\langle \text{upd } U \rangle$ with a **par** block of update rules.

3 Transforming Turbo ASM into Basic ASM

Using the symbolic pe-rule evaluation $[\![\cdot]\!]$ defined in Table 3, a turbo ASM rule R with **seq** and/or **iterate** subrules (but no submachine calls) can be transformed into an equivalent basic ASM rule R' with no **seq** nor **iterate** as follows[7]:

$$R' = \text{to-rule}[\, [\![\text{to-pe-rule}[R]]\!]_{symstate(S_0^-), \emptyset} \,]$$

where S_0 is the initial state of the original ASM and S_0^- is a state in which the static function names have the same interpretation as in S_0 and all non-static (i.e. controlled and monitored) function names are uninterpreted.[8]

The transformation is not limited to the symbolic execution of a fixed number n of sequential steps, but keeps rewriting the turbo ASM pe-rule until all **seq** and **iterate** are eliminated. However, it can fail. In particular, it fails if the symbolic evaluation of a pe-term or pe-rule is not defined due to potential aliasing (see Tables 2 and 3 and footnote 5). In the presence of **iterate**, it can also fail due to non-termination, either because the original **iterate** itself does not terminate or because simplify_formula is unable to fully evaluate the termination conditions. Finally, it may fail due to the stronger consistency condition (see footnote 6).

Tool and Repository. A prototype implementation is publicly available at

    https://github.com/constructum/asm-symbolic-execution

This repository also comprises additional material, including an extended version of this paper with examples and more detailed explanations.

---

[7] The to-pe-rule operator represents the (trivial) conversion of a rule to a pe-rule.

[8] This is necessary because the transformed rule R' must produce the same update set as R in any state of an ASM run. Therefore, it must not depend on the interpretation of any non-static function name.

Table 3. Symbolic evaluation of pe-rules

$[\![\mathbf{skip}]\!]_{\mathsf{S},\mathsf{C}} = \langle \text{upd } \emptyset \rangle$ $\qquad\qquad$ $[\![\langle \text{upd } \mathsf{U} \rangle]\!]_{\mathsf{S},\mathsf{C}} = \langle \text{upd } \mathsf{U} \rangle$

$[\![t_i]\!]_{\mathsf{S},\mathsf{C}} = \langle \text{val } x_i \rangle$ for all $i \in \{1, \ldots, n\}$

$[\![f(t_1, \ldots, t_n) := t]\!]_{\mathsf{S},\mathsf{C}} = \langle \text{upd } \{((f, (x_1, \ldots, x_n)), [\![t]\!]_{\mathsf{S},\mathsf{C}})\} \rangle$

$[\![t_i]\!]_{\mathsf{S},\mathsf{C}} \neq \langle \text{val } x_i \rangle$ for some $i \in \{1, \ldots, n\}$

$[\![f(t_1, \ldots, t_n) := t]\!]_{\mathsf{S},\mathsf{C}}$ is not defined

---

$[\![G]\!]_{\mathsf{S},\mathsf{C}} = \langle \text{val } \mathbf{true} \rangle$ or $[\![R_1]\!]_{\mathsf{S},\mathsf{C}} = [\![R_2]\!]_{\mathsf{S},\mathsf{C}}$ $\quad$ $[\![G]\!]_{\mathsf{S},\mathsf{C}} = \langle \text{val } \mathbf{false} \rangle$

$[\![\mathbf{if}\ G\ \mathbf{then}\ R_1\ \mathbf{else}\ R_2]\!]_{\mathsf{S},\mathsf{C}} = [\![R_1]\!]_{\mathsf{S},\mathsf{C}}$ $\quad$ $[\![\mathbf{if}\ G\ \mathbf{then}\ R_1\ \mathbf{else}\ R_2]\!]_{\mathsf{S},\mathsf{C}} = [\![R_2]\!]_{\mathsf{S},\mathsf{C}}$

$[\![G]\!]_{\mathsf{S},\mathsf{C}} = G'$ $\quad$ $G' \notin \{\langle \text{val } \mathbf{true} \rangle, \langle \text{val } \mathbf{false} \rangle\}$ $\quad$ $[\![R_1]\!]_{\mathsf{S},\mathsf{C}} \neq [\![R_2]\!]_{\mathsf{S},\mathsf{C}}$

$[\![\mathbf{if}\ G\ \mathbf{then}\ R_1\ \mathbf{else}\ R_2]\!]_{\mathsf{S},\mathsf{C}} = \mathbf{if}\ G'\ \mathbf{then}\ [\![R_1]\!]_{\mathsf{S},\mathsf{C}\cup\{G'\}}\ \mathbf{else}\ [\![R_2]\!]_{\mathsf{S},\mathsf{C}\cup\{\neg G'\}}$

$[\![R_1]\!]_{\mathsf{S},\mathsf{C}} = \langle \text{upd } \mathsf{U}_1 \rangle$ $\quad$ $[\![R_2]\!]_{\mathsf{S},\mathsf{C}} = \langle \text{upd } \mathsf{U}_2 \rangle$

$[\![R_1\ \mathbf{par}\ R_2]\!]_{\mathsf{S},\mathsf{C}} = \langle \text{upd } (\mathsf{U}_1 \cup \mathsf{U}_2) \rangle$

$[\![R_1]\!]_{\mathsf{S},\mathsf{C}} = \langle \text{upd } \mathsf{U}_1 \rangle$ $\quad$ $[\![R_2]\!]_{\mathsf{S},\mathsf{C}} = \mathbf{if}\ G_2\ \mathbf{then}\ R_{21}\ \mathbf{else}\ R_{22}$

$[\![R_1\ \mathbf{par}\ R_2]\!]_{\mathsf{S},\mathsf{C}} = [\![\mathbf{if}\ G_2\ \mathbf{then}\ (\langle \text{upd } \mathsf{U}_1 \rangle\ \mathbf{par}\ R_{21})\ \mathbf{else}\ (\langle \text{upd } \mathsf{U}_1 \rangle\ \mathbf{par}\ R_{22})]\!]_{\mathsf{S},\mathsf{C}}$

$[\![R_1]\!]_{\mathsf{S},\mathsf{C}} = \mathbf{if}\ G_1\ \mathbf{then}\ R_{11}\ \mathbf{else}\ R_{12}$ $\quad$ $(R_2$ is any rule$)$

$[\![R_1\ \mathbf{par}\ R_2]\!]_{\mathsf{S},\mathsf{C}} = [\![\mathbf{if}\ G_1\ \mathbf{then}\ (R_{11}\ \mathbf{par}\ R_2)\ \mathbf{else}\ (R_{12}\ \mathbf{par}\ R_2)]\!]_{\mathsf{S},\mathsf{C}}$

$[\![R_1]\!]_{\mathsf{S},\mathsf{C}} = \langle \text{upd } \mathsf{U}_1 \rangle$ $\quad$ U_1 is inconsistent

$[\![R_1\ \mathbf{seq}\ R_2]\!]_{\mathsf{S},\mathsf{C}} = \langle \text{upd } \mathsf{U}_1 \rangle$

$[\![R_1]\!]_{\mathsf{S},\mathsf{C}} = \langle \text{upd } \mathsf{U}_1 \rangle$ $\quad$ U_1 is consistent $\quad$ $[\![R_2]\!]_{\mathsf{S}+\mathsf{U}_1,\mathsf{C}} = \langle \text{upd } \mathsf{U}_2 \rangle$

$[\![R_1\ \mathbf{seq}\ R_2]\!]_{\mathsf{S},\mathsf{C}} = \langle \text{upd } (\mathsf{U}_1 \oplus \mathsf{U}_2) \rangle$

$[\![R_1]\!]_{\mathsf{S},\mathsf{C}} = \langle \text{upd } \mathsf{U}_1 \rangle$ $\quad$ $[\![R_2]\!]_{\mathsf{S}+\mathsf{U}_1,\mathsf{C}} = \mathbf{if}\ G_2\ \mathbf{then}\ R_{21}\ \mathbf{else}\ R_{22}$

$[\![R_1\ \mathbf{seq}\ R_2]\!]_{\mathsf{S},\mathsf{C}} = [\![\mathbf{if}\ G_2\ \mathbf{then}\ (\langle \text{upd } \mathsf{U}_1 \rangle\ \mathbf{seq}\ R_{21})\ \mathbf{else}\ (\langle \text{upd } \mathsf{U}_1 \rangle\ \mathbf{seq}\ R_{22})]\!]_{\mathsf{S},\mathsf{C}}$

$[\![R_1]\!]_{\mathsf{S},\mathsf{C}} = \mathbf{if}\ G_1\ \mathbf{then}\ R_{11}\ \mathbf{else}\ R_{12}$ $\quad$ $(R_2$ is any rule$)$

$[\![R_1\ \mathbf{seq}\ R_2]\!]_{\mathsf{S},\mathsf{C}} = [\![\mathbf{if}\ G_1\ \mathbf{then}\ (R_{11}\ \mathbf{seq}\ R_2)\ \mathbf{else}\ (R_{12}\ \mathbf{seq}\ R_2)]\!]_{\mathsf{S},\mathsf{C}}$

$[\![R]\!]_{\mathsf{S},\mathsf{C}} = \langle \text{upd } \emptyset \rangle$ $\qquad\qquad$ $[\![R]\!]_{\mathsf{S},\mathsf{C}} \neq \langle \text{upd } \emptyset \rangle$

$[\![\mathbf{iterate}\ R]\!]_{\mathsf{S},\mathsf{C}} = \langle \text{upd } \emptyset \rangle$ $\qquad$ $[\![\mathbf{iterate}\ R]\!]_{\mathsf{S},\mathsf{C}} = [\![R\ \mathbf{seq}\ (\mathbf{iterate}\ R)]\!]_{\mathsf{S},\mathsf{C}}$

4   Further Work

This is work in progress. Further work may include: extending the method to a larger subset of ASM (including submachines, aliasing); using the method to add turbo ASM support to model checking interfaces; formalising the constructions more precisely and proving their correctness; practical applications.

Acknowledgments. Thanks to Egon Börger for various discussions and interactions which renewed my interest in ASM, to Sylvain Lelait for his helpful comments on a preliminary version of this paper and to the anonymous reviewers for their insightful remarks and good suggestions, which I tried to address as much as possible.

Competing Interests. The author(s) has no competing interests to declare that are relevant to the content of this manuscript.

References

1. Arcaini, P., Gargantini, A., Riccobene, E.: AsmetaSMV: a way to link high-level ASM models to low-level NuSMV specifications. In: Frappier, M., Glässer, U., Khurshid, S., Laleau, R., Reeves, S. (eds.) ABZ 2010. LNCS, vol. 5977, pp. 61–74. Springer, Heidelberg (2010). https://doi.org/10.1007/978-3-642-11811-1_6
2. Baldoni, R., Coppa, E., Cono D'Elia, D., Demetrescu, C., Finocchi, I.: A survey of symbolic execution techniques. ACM Comput. Surv. **51**(3) (2018). https://doi.org/10.1145/3182657
3. Börger, E., Schmid, J.: Composition and submachine concepts for sequential ASMs. In: Clote, P.G., Schwichtenberg, H. (eds.) CSL 2000. LNCS, vol. 1862, pp. 41–60. Springer, Heidelberg (2000). https://doi.org/10.1007/3-540-44622-2_3
4. Börger, E., Stärk, R.: Abstract State Machines. Springer, Heidelberg (2003). https://doi.org/10.1007/978-3-642-18216-7
5. Del Castillo, G., Winter, K.: Model checking support for the ASM high-level language. In: Graf, S., Schwartzbach, M. (eds.) TACAS 2000. LNCS, vol. 1785, pp. 331–346. Springer, Heidelberg (2000). https://doi.org/10.1007/3-540-46419-0_23
6. Dorfmeister, D., Ferrarotti, F., Fischer, B., Haslinger, E., Ramler, R., Zimmermann, M.: An approach for safe and secure software protection supported by symbolic execution. In: Kotsis, G., et al. (eds.) DEXA 2023. CCIS, vol. 1872, pp. 67–78. Springer, Cham (2023). https://doi.org/10.1007/978-3-031-39689-2_7
7. Fruja, N.G., Stärk, R.F.: The hidden computation steps of turbo abstract state machines. In: Börger, E., Gargantini, A., Riccobene, E. (eds.) ASM 2003. LNCS, vol. 2589, pp. 244–262. Springer, Heidelberg (2003). https://doi.org/10.1007/3-540-36498-6_14
8. Glesner, S., Goos, G., Zimmermann, W.: Verifix: Konstruktion und Architektur verifizierender Übersetzer (Verifix: Construction and architecture of verifying compilers). it - Inf. Technol. **46**(5), 265–276 (2004). https://doi.org/10.1524/itit.46.5.265.44799
9. Gurevich, Y.: Evolving algebras 1993: Lipari guide. In: Specification and Validation Methods, pp. 9–36. Oxford University Press (1995)
10. King, J.C.: Symbolic execution and program testing. Commun. ACM **19**(7), 385–394 (1976). https://doi.org/10.1145/360248.360252

11. Lezuo, R.: Scalable translation validation. Ph.D. thesis, Vienna University of Technology (2014). https://www.complang.tuwien.ac.at/tbfg
12. Paun, V.A., Monsuez, B., Baufreton, P.: Integration of symbolic execution into a formal abstract state machines based language. In: IFAC-PapersOnLine **50**(1), 11251–11256 (2017). https://doi.org/10.1016/j.ifacol.2017.08.1610, 20th IFAC World Congress
13. Schellhorn, G., Ernst, G., Pfähler, J., Bodenmüller, S., Reif, W.: Symbolic execution for a clash-free subset of ASMs. Sci. Comput. Program. **158**, 21–40 (2018). https://doi.org/10.1016/j.scico.2017.08.014
14. Topor, R.W.: Interactive program verification using virtual programs. Ph.D. thesis, University of Edinburgh (1975). https://era.ed.ac.uk/handle/1842/6610
15. Zimmermann, W., Weißbach, M.: A framework for modeling the semantics of synchronous and asynchronous procedures with abstract state machines. In: Raschke, A., Riccobene, E., Schewe, K.-D. (eds.) Logic, Computation and Rigorous Methods. LNCS, vol. 12750, pp. 326–352. Springer, Cham (2021). https://doi.org/10.1007/978-3-030-76020-5_18

Multi-model Animation with JeB

Jean-Pierre Jacquot[(✉)] [iD]

LORIA, Université de Lorraine, CNRS, 54506 Vandoeuvre lès Nancy, France
jean-pierre.jacquot@loria.fr

Abstract. A challenge posed by model-based formal methods such as
Event-B is the validation of the models. This has been recognized and
some tools have been created to provide modelers with means to animate models and to explore their behaviour through graphical display.
These tools are quite effective on standalone models but lack the ability to connect the model to other external models. CPS systems fall
under this category, as well as systems built of components interacting
through a communication network. In the context of Jeb, an animation
tool for Event-B models based on JavaScript, we explore the possibility
of connecting models through Websockets. The paper presents a simple
protocol to connect simulations. Using an example inspired by the Lung
Ventilator case study, it shows how the implementation expands JeB
functionality without modifying its core.

Keywords: Event-B · Validation · Simulation · Multi-Model
Animation

1 Introduction

Formal methods are mostly focused on producing correct software through the
development of mathematically consistent models. With incremental methods
such as Event-B [2], the development goes through a chain of refinements, i.e.,
a sequence of more and more complex models, whose consistency is guaranteed.
Nowadays, powerful tools are provided to support this verification process. A
difficulty for practitioners is to validate the models, i.e., to assess they are an
acceptable representation of reality or of the intended software [8,9]. Several
strategies have been developed to validate models; among them, animation, i.e.,
the actual execution of the model, is crucial in involving all kinds of stakeholders
of the development [5]. In the context of Event-B, fully automated tools such
as ProB [6], Brama or AnimB are available. One of the limits of these tools is
the degree of non-determinism which can lead to combinatorial explosion. We
proposed to complement those tools with JeB [13], a simulation environment
based on JavaScript which can be used at any stage of the refinement chain.
The foundational idea of JeB is that simulations result from the collaboration
of the user and the tool: the later generates JavaScript code which enforces the
operational semantics of the model while the former provides the snipets of code
which resolve the non-deterministic elements.

The usefulness of JeB has been demonstrated on several case-studies ([4] for instance). However, it became soon apparent that many systems are composed of several parts that can, and should, be modeled independently. For instance, in the landing gear case-study, the system can be viewed as two interacting models: one for the controling software, one for the sensors and actuators hardware. While initial software models can be simulated as stand-alone, more refined models needs to interact with models of the hardware. Projects such as Discont [1] have studied this issue; [11,12] propose solutions at the modeling level. Some experimental implementations using RODIN and ProB have been proposed [10]; they have shown that multi-model simulations can be achieved within RODIN. Their current status is unclear.

In this study, we propose a pragmatic approach, using existing tools and the capability of safely adding code in a JeB simulation, to animate a system composed of independent models. Using the Websocket technology, we discuss the animation of a (very simplified) Ventilator system [3] consisting of two distinct Event-B models: the GUI and the Controler. We present the protocol implemented as a Websocket server to connect the executable models and the generic JavaScript code to add to the JeB-generated programs.

2   Event-B and JeB

The Event-B method [2] targets the design of complex (reactive) systems. It allows the gradual refinement of a high level specification of the system toward an implementable model through a sequence of *refinement* steps. Each refinement adds new elements into the model such as data refinement, behaviour refinement, or invariant reinforcement.

An Event-B model consists of three parts:

- a set of constants called *Context*,
- a *State* which consists of variables and invariants, and
- a set of *Events* which make the state evolve when triggered.

The correction of the model is guaranteed through the generation of proof-obligations which, when discharged, ensure that events can only evolve an invariant-verifying state into another invariant-verifying state. The specification of the values associated to constants, variables, and invariants is written in a language coding set-theory and first-order logic. Events can be seen as guarded transitions, where guards are predicates on the state and on the values of event parameters. Refinement is a relation between models; it is defined by a set of proof-obligations which ensure that the refined model maintain the invariant and can be abstracted into the abstract model. The RODIN platform implements editors for the language, generators of proof-obligations, proof assistants to help discharge the obligations, and an API to connect plug-ins.

The operational semantics of Event-B is intuitive: once an initial state has been set-up, check which events have their guards true, pick one, execute it, and loop. The difficulties are of a technical nature: choosing a value for a event parameter which checks a guard or choosing a value defined only through properties. The following is an event from the Controler model.

Event PCVParamChangeAction ⟨ordinary⟩ ≙
refines SetPCVParams
  any
    RRVn
    IERn
  where
    RRValuen: $RRVn \in 4..50$
    IEration: $IERn \in 10..40$
    newParams: $ParamChanging = 1$
    state: $PCVcycleState = GoToInhalePCV$
  then
    RRValue: $RRValue := RRVn$
    IER: $IEratioDen := IERn$
    changeParam: $ParamChanged := 1$
  end

The event *PCVParamChangeAction* takes two parameters: *RRVn* and *IERn*.

This event can be triggered when the values *RRVn* and *IERn* have appropriate values, and when the ventilator is at the beginning of an inhale cycle and new settings are to be registered.

When executed, the variables in the Ventilator's state are assigned new values.

JeB [13] is an environment dedicated to the execution of Event-B models. It consists of three elements: a RODIN plugin which transforms the Event-B model into a JavaScript program and generates HTML pages to control and display the simulation, a set library implementing the Event-B operators, the set and logic operators, and a runtime implementing the evaluation loop of the operational semantics. All features of Event-B are covered by JeB; they are either translated as calls to functions in the library or as function skeletons to be completed by the user. During the transformation process, JeB builds separate files which contain the elements that can, or must, be safely specified by users: `jeb_user.js` which contains customization shared by all refinements, and `<machine>_users.js` for the custom code specific to a particular machine. The most notable customizable elements are the `get_<param>` which are generated for getting the values of each event parameters. The native strategy is to generate values for parameters until the guard is true or a user-defined limit has been reached. For instance, JeB generates the following (left) for the *PCVParamChangeAction* event parameter *RRVn*, or even the following for a parameter just typed as INTEGER (right).

```
// Auto-generated function: argument generator
var get_RRVn = function( eventId ) {
    if (eventId == $evt.e18) {
        return $B.UpTo($B('4'), $B('50')).anyMember();
    }
};
```

```
/*
var get_nPatient = function( eventId ) {
    if (eventId == $evt.e2) {
        // @TODO
    }
};
*/
```

The expression after the **return** on the left side is the translation of the B expression :∈ 4..5, i.e., any element of the integer interval [4, 50]. By providing other implementations for the `get_<param>` function, it is possible to drive the simulation by following predefined scenarios. This feature will also be used heavily in the multi-model simulation protocol.

3 The Ventilator Models

In the Ventilator case study description, the GUI and the Controler are described as two separate communicating components. While there are theoretical ways to decompose/recompose models in Event-B, it is still a complex process, not well supported by RODIN. Instead, we chose another strategy: to model each component independently and make them communicate during the simulation. We must stress that our choice was motivated by the desire to build an animation involving two different models. We are neither recommending or disparaging this strategy for a real modeling of the case study.

The Controler model is a straightforward description of the state machine on Fig. 4 in [3]. It was built with three refinements (4 machines): Cycle0 gives the high-level view of the ventilator state, Cycle1 refines the PCV mode by modeling the PCV cycle, Cycle2 refines the PSV mode, Cycle3 introduces the communication with the GUI. Communication here are limited to the setting of new parameters for the PCV and PSV modes, with a small acknowledgement protocol. Cycle3 has 20 events with 4 specialized in the communication with the GUI component.

The GUI component is a simple panel which allows for the modification of 5 parameters (ITS, ETS, RRV, IEratio, ApneaLag) and the declaration of a new patient. We can imagine 2 buttons per parameter (one step up, one step down), a button for a new patient, and a "send new parameters" button. The model has 13 events: 12 modeling the "buttons" and one to received the acknowledgement that the Controler has modified the parameters.

The serial communication hinted at Fig. 1.1 of [3] is not explicitly modeled. The communication protocol that we propose is an implicit implementation.

4 Interaction Implementation

This section presents the technical details of the multi-model communication. First, we present the principles of the protocol; next, we discuss the implementation within JeB.

4.1 Protocol

The protocol is based on a server which accepts five kinds of messages:

initSimulation can be sent by any communicating model; it initialises the internal state of the server,

register is sent by models to register the variables they will export. There must be one message per exported variable. Variable names are mapped to the address of the registering model,

request is sent by a model requesting a value from another model. After maping the variable requested with the address of the requesting model, the request is forwarded to the model managing the variable,

value is received when a model answers a request. It is forwarded to the requesting model,

update is received when an exported variable has been modified. The server broadcasts this message to all connected models.

The protocol is voluntarily simple at this stage of the research. It implements an asynchronous communication strategy. To work, it requires that the names of the variables which can be requested are all different. For models in Event-B, this is consistent with the constraint on managing different name spaces for the recomposition of models to be correct. At this stage of the study, it is not optimised to take care of multiple requests on the same variable, or managing delays when values of variables are not yet available.

On the model side, the simulations must be able to respond to the **request**, **value**, and **update** messages. The communication occurs only for parameters of events, i.e. when event guards are checked.

– When a model needs an external value, it sends a **request** message and sets up the waiting valuation map. The simulation continues.
– When a model receives a **value** message, it check that the variable is waiting for a valuation, assigned it to the parameters, and trigger the simulation loop.
– When the model receives an **update** message, it resets the variable valuation state.
– When a model receives a **request** message, it returns a **value** message with the actual value of the variable.

At this stage of the work, the protocol is not protected against errors such as requesting a non existing variable, or detecting when a model has stopped. This will need further refinements.

4.2   JavaScript Implementation

The server is implemented as a `Node.js` server, using the WebSocket library. Its state consists of two maps and a list:

– `var whereTo = new Map();` is the map associating variables with the models which manage them,
– `var requestedBy = new Map();` is the map associating requested variables with the stacks of models which requested them, and
– `var connectedSockets = [];` is the list of connected models used to broadcast update messages.

The protocol code is about 80 lines of straightforward WebSocket code.

```
jebSocket.on('connection',
    (ws) => {
    ws.on('message', (JSonRequest) => {
     const message = JSON.parse(JSonRequest);

     if (message.type == "value") {
     // forward the value
        let v = message.variable;
```

```
while (requestedBy.get(message.variable).length != 0) {
  let mSock = requestedBy.get(message.variable).pop();
  mSock.send(JSON.stringify(
    {type:"value",
     variable : v,
     value: message.value} ));
  }
}
[ ... ]
```

On the models side, the implementation has two parts: the setup of the communication and the management of the request/value messages. The setup phase consists in: (1) creating and opening a WebSocket on the server, (2) sending a `initSimulation` message, and (3) registering the variables which can be requested. JeB provides the skeleton for the `jeb.animator.init` function which is used to initialized the graphical display of the simulation. This is the natural place for the protocol setup.

```
jeb.animator.init = function() {
  $anim.canvas.width = 1000;
  $anim.canvas.height = 50;
  $anim.canvas.style.display = '';

  initComm();
  registerVariables(vars);
}
```

The function template is generated by JeB. The calls to the initialization functions are simply added in. The argument **vars** is a list of the variables which can be requested from this model.

The request/value protocol is asynchronous, which makes it trickier to implement than the initialisation protocol. It has four steps:

request: when an external variable is requested, we first check if it has already received a value. If not, a **request** message is sent and the variable becomes a key in the map recording the current requests (called `waitingFor`).

value: when a **value** message is received, the (variable, value) pair is inserted in the `waitingFor` map. A new simulation cycle is then triggered by re-evaluating the guards of all events.

consumption: the aynchronous nature of the communication implies that an event requesting several parameters will not receive them simultaneously. So, clearing the `waitingFor` map must not be done when a value is read, but when the value has been actually used by executing the event, which can only occur when all its guards have been validated.

update: when an **update** message is received, the `waitingFor` map is reset for the variable affected by the update.

The JavaScript implementation of the first two steps are shown below. The get_RRVn function is for the RRVn argument of the PCVParamChangeAction of the controler model; the requested value, RRValue, is a variable of the GUI model.

```
// Auto-generated function: argument generator
var get_RRVn = function( eventId ) {
    if (eventId == $evt.e18) {
        return getExternalValue("RRValue");
    }
};

var getExternalValue = function(v) {
    if (waitingFor.has(v)) {
        return waitingFor.get(v);
    } else {
        socket.send(JSON.stringify(
            { type: "request",
              variable: v
            }));
waitingFor.set(v,"");
return "";
    }
}
```

```
socket.onmessage = function(event) {
    var msg = JSON.parse(event.data);
    if (msg.type == "value") {
        let v = msg.variable;
        if (waitingFor.has(v)) {
            if (msg.value === undefined) {
                // model not yet started -- clean
                waitingFor.delete(v);
            } else {
                let value = eval(msg.value).toString();
                waitingFor.set(v,value);
            }
        }
    }
    jeb.scheduler.testAllGuards();
}

            [...]
```

Since the empty string is not a valid Event-B value, it is used as an indication that the value is not yet defined. The `jeb.scheduler.testAllGuards` function is part tof the JeB runtime; it invokes the evaluation of all the guards of the events.

The third step is actually implemented through an extension of the JeB runtime by adding a new property and a new method to the `jeb.Event` internal structure and by changing the scheduler so that the new extensions are used.

```
jeb.lang.Event.prototype.postAction =
    function () {}


jeb.lang.Event.prototype.doPostAction =function() {
    var self = this;
    if (this.postAction != null) {
this.postAction();
    }
}
```

```
jeb.scheduler.execute = function( event ) {
    jeb.scenario.save( 'parameter' );
    event.doActions();
    event.doPostAction();
    jeb.scenario.save( 'variable', event.label );
    jeb.animator.draw();
    jeb.scheduler.checkInvariants();
};
```

As JavaScript is a prototype-based and not a class-based language, all the modifications above are written in the `jeb_user` file: nothing is changed in the core JeB files.

The new version of the scheduler is a copy of the one provided in the JeB core file where the line `event.doPostAction();` has been added.

To clear the `waitingFor` map, we just need to add declarations of the *postActions* in the `jeb_user` file such as:

```
$evt.e18.postAction = function() {
    cleanExternalParams(["RRVn", "IERn"]);
}
```

The update step is implemented by using the same technique. When an event modifies an exported variable, a *postAction* is introduced to broadcast the modification (left hand side). The models interested in the exported variable then reset it (right hand side).

```
function broadcastUpdated(vs) {          socket.onmessage = function(event) {
  for (v of vs) {                          var msg = JSON.parse(event.data);
socket.send(JSON.stringify(              [...]
  {type:"update",                           if (msg.type == "update") {
    variable: v                               let v = msg.variable;
  }));                                        if (waitingFor.has(v)) {
  }                                           waitingFor.delete(v);
}                                           jeb.scheduler.testAllGuards();
// from GUI model                           }
$evt.e10.postAction = function(){         }
  broadcastUpdated(["ApneaLag", "newParams"]);    [...]
}
```

4.3   Animation of the Ventilator Model

Figure 1 presents a screen shot of the animation. The simulation of the GUI is running in Safari (left hand side), the simulation of the Controler is running in Chrome (right hand side), and the Node.js server is running in the bottom window. Preliminary tests have shown that the protocol is working. The multi-model simulations have allowed us to detect several mistakes in each of the models.

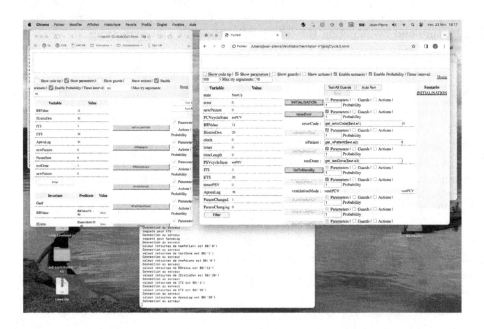

Fig. 1. Multi-model animation

5   Results, Future Work, and Conclusion

So far, the experiment with the protocol has been successful. It has shown us that:

- the protocol is clean and simple; it works on, admittedly, small-case examples,
- the implementation has been done without touching any of the JeB core files. This implies that the generic code for multi-model animation can be distributed simply as a set of JavaScript files to include into the appropriate jeb_user files.

Of course, many issues are still open and require further research. A first issue concerns the protocol itself: can it scale up? how to improve its robustness? can its correctness be asserted?

The case study is composed of two homogeneous discrete models. We need to assess the protocol on hybrid systems where at least one sub-model is continuous. We could model the respiratory cycle of the patient through the evolution of the sensors readings and valves positions.

A second issue concerns the overall correctness of the multi-model simulation. For stand-alone simulations, we have defined a notion of *fidelity* which ensures that execution of the simulation can be trusted [7]. We need to check whether this notion can be applied to multi-model simulations or if it needs to be extended.

Competing Interests. The author(s) has no competing interests to declare that are relevant to the content of this manuscript.

References

1. Le project DISCONT. http://www.agence-nationale-recherche.fr/Projet-ANR-17-CE25-0005. http://discont.loria.fr
2. Abrial, J.R.: Modeling in Event-B - System and Software Engineering. Cambridge University Press, Cambridge (2010)
3. Bonfanti, S., Gargantini, A.: Mechanical lung ventilator. In: Proceedings of ABZ24
4. Jacquot, J.P.: Premières leçons sur la spécification d'un train d'atterrissage en B Événementiel. Revue des Sciences et Technologies de l'Information - Série TSI: Technique et Science Informatiques **34**(5), 549–573 (2016). https://inria.hal.science/hal-01262077
5. Jacquot, J.P., Mashkoor, A.: The role of validation in refinement-based formal software development. In: Models: Concept, Theory, Logic, Reasoning, and Semantics. College Publications (2018). https://inria.hal.science/hal-01788768
6. Leuschel, M., Butler, M.J.: ProB: an automated analysis toolset for the B method. STTT **10**(2), 185–203 (2008)
7. Mashkoor, A., Yang, F., Jacquot, J.: Refinement-based validation of Event-B specifications. Softw. Syst. Model. **16**(3), 789–808 (2017). https://doi.org/10.1007/s10270-016-0514-4
8. Rushby, J.: Formal methods and the certification of critical systems. TR SRI-CSL-93-7, Computer Science Laboratory, SRI International (1993). http://www.csl.sri.com/papers/csl-93-7/
9. Rushby, J.M.: Enhancing the utility of formal methods. ACM Comput. Surv. **28**(4es), 123 (1996). https://doi.org/10.1145/242224.242382
10. Savicks, V., Butler, M., Colley, J.: Co-simulation environment for Rodin: landing gear case study. In: Boniol, F., Wiels, V., Ait Ameur, Y., Schewe, K.-D. (eds.) ABZ 2014. CCIS, vol. 433, pp. 148–153. Springer, Cham (2014). https://doi.org/10.1007/978-3-319-07512-9_11

11. Su, W., Abrial, J.R., Zhu, H.: Formalizing hybrid systems with Event-B and the RODIN platform. Sci. Comput. Program. **94**, 164–202 (2014)
12. Vu, F., Leuschel, M., Mashkoor, A.: Validation of formal models by timed probabilistic simulation. In: Raschke, A., Méry, D. (eds.) ABZ 2021. LNCS, vol. 12709, pp. 81–96. Springer, Cham (2021). https://doi.org/10.1007/978-3-030-77543-8_6
13. Yang, F.: Un environnement de simulation pour la validation de spécifications B événementiel. Ph.D. thesis (2013). http://www.theses.fr/2013LORR0158, université de Lorraine 2013

Meta-programming Event-B

Advancing Tool Support and Language Extensions

Julius Armbrüster and Philipp Körner[✉][iD]

Faculty of Mathematics and Natural Science, Department of Computer Science,
Heinrich Heine University Düsseldorf, 40225 Düsseldorf, Germany
{julius.armbruester,p.koerner}@hhu.de

Abstract. Transforming models based on their textual representation
is a cumbersome task. This is particularly the case for Event-B, where
the predominant representation is a set of XML files. As a consequence,
tool support is lacking, even for minor refactoring operations.

The contribution of this paper extends the *lisb* library with a front
and backend based on Event-B. The aim is to bring benefits, that have
been demonstrated for classical B, such as an easily transformable data
representation of formal specifications as well as creation of custom DSLs
and tooling, to Event-B.

We see great benefits of such a meta-programming approach for formal specifications and advocate that similar mechanisms will be sensi-
ble extensions to the expressiveness of formal methods. Ultimately, our
work facilitates language extensions (e.g., re-introducing if-then-else constructs to Event-B which generate multiple events or a proper macro system to avoid code duplication) and tool support (e.g., refactoring tools
or automatic refinement).

Keywords: B-Method · Event-B · Meta-Programming

1 Introduction

The benefits of DSLs in formal methods is well-known and many tools have been
brought forth in particular for B and Event-B [10,11,24]. The *lisb* library[1] [12]
embeds the classical B language in a general-purpose programming language.
In contrast to similar embeddings [14,17], this means that not only expressions
and predicates can be solved; but instead an intermediate representation (IR) of
the underlying B machine is generated that is still susceptible to programmatic
transformations (e.g., to implement custom DSLs or data refinement tools [12]).

In this article, we present our work to bring this meta-programming approach to Event-B by extending *lisb* to support Event-B. This approach caters
to programmers who will (i) prefer a data representation in a programming language to generated specifications from data; (ii) obtain easier way to modify
their specification (e.g., DSLs, shared sub-expressions or refactoring); (iii) prefer

---

[1] https://www.github.com/pkoerner/lisb.

© The Author(s), under exclusive license to Springer Nature Switzerland AG 2024
S. Bonfanti et al. (Eds.): ABZ 2024, LNCS 14759, pp. 233–240, 2024.
https://doi.org/10.1007/978-3-031-63790-2_17

a text-based format over the default structural editors Rodin offers; (iv) gain the ability to quickly prototype tools for Event-B.

The rest of the paper is structured as follows: We give an overview of B and Event-B as well as the *lisb* library in Sect. 2. Next, we describe extensions made for Event-B to *lisb* in Sect. 3. Related work will be presented in Sect. 4. We discuss our contribution in context of possible future developments in Sect. 5.

2   Background

In this section, we first give an overview of B and Event-B. Details can be found in a survey on their industrial usage [5] as well as a comparison of the formalisms [15]. We also outline the architecture of and our additions to *lisb*.

2.1   B and Event-B

Both B [1] (or "classical B") and Event-B [2] are state-based formal methods. They share a *correct-by-construction* workflow. Starting from an abstract, mathematical description based on set theory, the model is iteratively refined by adding implementation details. Each refinement step is linked with the previous via *proof obligations*. Assisted by automatic provers, one can prove that the overall behaviour of the system is preserved. Once a low-level subset of B is reached, one can apply code generators (e.g., [18]) to obtain executable code.

Main Differences Between B and Event-B. The mathematical sublanguage used for predicates and expressions is almost identical in both formalisms. However, there are some discrepancies:

- *Operators*: Some operators are present in only one formalism (e.g., FIN (the set of finite subsets) in classical B, or `partition(S, x, y, ...)` (S is a disjoint union of x, y, ...) and `finite(S)` (a set S is finite) in Event-B). Others differ slightly (e.g., minus - and multiplication * are polymorphic w.r.t. numbers and sets in B, while two operators each are used in Event-B).
- *Guarded Substitutions*: Classical B offers different substitutions (SELECT, PRE, IF, CASE, ...) that can be nested arbitrarily. Event-B only offers flat events that allow only guards and assignments.
- *Machine Structure*: B specifications can be structured as a set of machines with a variety of clauses for inclusion and reference (USES, INCLUDES, SEES, EXTENDS, ...). Event-B separates the static components (as *contexts*) from the dynamic parts (as *machines*). Then, machines may refine a single other machine at most, but can reference multiple contexts.

Rodin [3] is the de facto IDE for Event-B that we target with *lisb* (though AtelierB [8] supports Event-B as well). Its two built-in editors allow manipulation of the structure (e.g., adding nodes for guards, operations or invariants) due to the underlying file format (details will be discussed in Sect. 3.3). As the workflow of these structural editors can be inconvenient, proper text-based editor were developed as plug-ins [4,9].

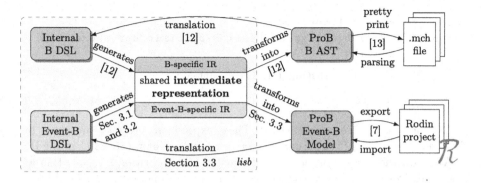

Fig. 1. Simplified Overview of the *lisb* Architecture

2.2 *lisb*

The *lisb* library [12] embeds the B language in Clojure, a functional Lisp running on the JVM. This allows to make use of (i) Lisp's powerful macro systems (for DSLs) and (ii) PROB's Java API [13] and its powerful toolchain (including PROB's B parser, pretty printer, type and model checker, etc.).

The *lisb* library itself consists of three components: (i) An internal DSL which is intended to be read and written by humans and which can be freely extended by user DSLs. (ii) An intermediate representation (IR) which is readable but appropriate for programmatic transformations (e.g., data refinement, refactoring or translation). (iii) A tool backend that is the translation target for the IR. For classical B, PROB [16] was used to output the corresponding .mch file(s).

Figure 1 depicts this architecture. We extend the upper half, i.e., an internal DSL for B, an intermediate representation and the integration of PROB's AST as a backend. The article's contributions can be found in the lower half, by adding an internal DSL for Event-B, extending the IR for Event-B and integrating a generation of Rodin projects. These are discussed in Sect. 3 below.

3 Embedding Event-B in *lisb*

In this section, we outline three categories of extensions made to the *lisb* library. First, language components that are part of both classical B and Event-B (with the same semantics); Second, additions made to the IR which are specific to Event-B; Third, how an Event-B (Rodin) project is obtained from the IR, and how an Event-B project is transformed back to *lisb*'s internal Event-B DSL.

3.1 Shared Sub-Language

Large parts of B and Event-B are very similar, e.g., logical predicates or number and set operators. In these instances, the exact same IR can be generated.

Note that the IR is not concerned with syntactic differences: E.g., the Cartesian product of S and T can be written as S * T (classical B), as S ** T (Event-B

```
(defmacro eventb [body]
  `(b (let [... bindings of Event-B-specific operators ...]
      ~body)))
```

Listing 1.1. The eventb-Macro

ASCII) or $S \times T$ (Event-B Unicode). These expressions are all represented by the same data literal {:tag :cartesian-product, :sets (:S :T)} in the IR.

We show the concept of the internal Event-B DSL in Listing 1.1. Note that an eventb expression in *lisb* introduces Event-B-specific operators in a local binding. Everything else is evaluated in the *context* of classical B expressions. The internal DSL inherits almost the entire sub-language of predicates and expressions from B, generates exactly the same data (IR) for the shared language, and is also arbitrarily to extendable. This also allows shadowing B-specific operators, e.g., one could disallow B's FIN operator and throw an exception instead.

3.2 Event-B-Specific Extensions

Below, we give examples for language elements that are specific to Event-B.

Operators. The partition(S, T1, ... Tn) predicate, which holds true iff the set S is equal to the disjoint union of an arbitrary number of other sets $T_1, \ldots, T_n$, is particular to Event-B. There are two possibilities how to add this to *lisb*:

A *DSL-based* approach maps an operator to a B expression, i.e., partition is re-written to $S = \bigcup_{i=1}^{n} T_i \wedge T_1 \cap T_2 = \varnothing \wedge \ldots \wedge T_{n-1} \cap T_n = \varnothing$. This means that an export to or import from Rodin will always generate this bloated formula.

Instead, we opted for an *IR-based* approach that adds a partition node to the IR. This node is handled by the Event-B backend (emitting the idiomatic predicate) but is rejected by the classical B backend. If needed in classical B, one can add the re-writing rule above as an IR-to-IR transformation.

Machine Structure. Specifications in Event-B are split into contexts and machines. While we can re-use the IR of some existing structures (e.g., machines as sets of clauses), most structuring elements specific to Event-B require additions to the IR. Examples are contexts or the additional variant clause in machines. Even the structure of events differ too much, as they may include witnesses, may be marked as convergent, etc.

3.3 Interacting with Rodin Projects

A more accurate image than Fig. 1 for our Event-B extension is given in Fig. 2. In the following, we will discuss the details of how a Rodin project is obtained from the intermediate representation in *lisb* and vice versa.

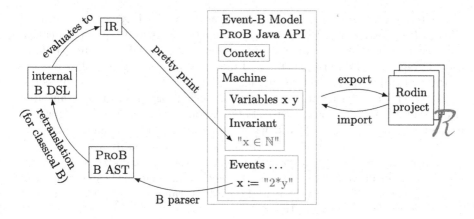

Fig. 2. Transformations Between IR and Rodin Projects

Generation of a Rodin Project. In the Rodin XML files, predicates (for guards, invariants, theorems, etc.) and expressions (for substitutions) are stored as pretty-printed strings. Thus, one step in the translation from the IR to Rodin projects is a pretty printer for such predicates and expressions. For the rest of the structure of the file, we make use of the PROB Java API [13]:

As part of a DSL for Algorithm Descriptions [7], a Java representation of Event-B models was created. E.g., in this Java representation one can construct guards, actions or parameters from pretty-printed strings and re-combine them into an Event object. Step by step, the model is then made up of multiple machine and context objects. This representation can then be exported to .bum and .buc files as well as the .project file containing the Rodin project description.

Reading a Rodin Project. To obtain the IR from a given project, we use the same Java representation for Event-B models. We generate the code for the internal Event-B DSL that evaluates to the IR. The structure of this code aligns with the structure of the model; e.g., machines consisting of invariants, variants, variables and events, and events in turns consist of guards, actions, etc.

PROB's parser suite offers an extension of its classical B parser that is also able to parse Event-B-specific operators. We make use of this parser to obtain an AST. The existing re-translation from B yields the internal DSL for classical B for all operators that are present in B and Event-B. As no B-specific terms can be read from an Event-B project, the obtained DSL must be valid Event-B. The re-translation is extended to also support all Event-B-specific operators.

4 Related Work

Embedding specification languages in general-purpose programming languages is not a novel approach. A first prototype of *lisb* only embedded the predicate and expression sub-language of classical B with the aim of generating constraints from external data sources [21]. This is comparable with αRby, an embedding of Alloy in Ruby [17]. Yet, αRby focuses on mixed execution of both specification and programming language, allowing interaction with partial solutions. No data-oriented representation of the generated model seems to be accessible.

PlusCal [14] is an imperative language in which arbitrary TLA$^+$ expressions can be inserted, catering to programmers. Such programs can be translated to pure TLA$^+$ for verification with TLC. A similar approach is an algorithm description language [7] by Clark, which provides a similar language but with Event-B expressions. A version of such DSLs is also shipped by *lisb*.

Another approach to programmatic transformations is to make use of a meta-model, i.e., a formal model that represents another model in the hosted formalism as data. Most notable for Event-B is the EB4EB framework [19] which extends the core formalism via a meta-theory.

5 Discussion

In this paper, we showed how we integrated the Event-B notation in *lisb*, which allows easy construction of DSLs and tools for the formalism. Further, the library can be used to implement translations *between* formalisms: As a proof of concept, we implemented an IR-to-IR transformation that translates (only) the B-specific IR to constructs that are shared or specific to Event-B — resulting in a tool that translates B machines to Rodin projects[2]. While a large portion of B is covered, some kinds of substitutions and ways to include machines are still missing. If extended by further formalisms (with a similar mathematical core), one could obtain a universal translation tool.

We think our approach ultimately combines several ideas stemming from different formal methods sub-communities:

- Rozier et al. [20] presented their vision of a yet to be named model checking framework[3]. The goal is to translate all specification languages to a common IR so that a singular tool implementing advanced algorithms suffices.
- By adding frontends (and translating only specifics), it is easy to *integrate* multiple formalism. This is in line with combined formalisms such as Circus [23] or CSP∥B [22].
- Meta-approaches for specification languages allow easier implementation of DSLs, generation of specifications and advanced transformations tools.
- Better and easier integration of formal methods in general-purpose programming languages will allow non-expert to interact with and integrate formal models into their work. It can also make it more accessible for students [6].

We do not argue that *lisb* will be the ultimate answer. Instead, we hope to see that in the long run, specification languages will evolve and adopt similar, powerful mechanisms for meta-development.

---

[2] https://github.com/jarmbrue/b2eventb.
[3] https://www.aere.iastate.edu/modelchecker/.

Competing Interests. The author(s) has no competing interests to declare that are relevant to the content of this manuscript.

References

1. Abrial, J.R.: The B-Book: Assigning Programs to Meanings. Cambridge University Press, Cambridge (1996)
2. Abrial, J.R.: Modeling in Event-B: System and Software Engineering. Cambridge University Press, Cambridge (2010)
3. Abrial, J.-R., Butler, M., Hallerstede, S., Voisin, L.: An open extensible tool environment for event-B. In: Liu, Z., He, J. (eds.) ICFEM 2006. LNCS, vol. 4260, pp. 588–605. Springer, Heidelberg (2006). https://doi.org/10.1007/11901433_32
4. Bendisposto, J., Fritz, F., Jastram, M., Leuschel, M., Weigelt, I.: Developing Camille, a text editor for Rodin. Softw. Pract. Exp. **41**, 189–198 (2011)
5. Butler, M., et al.: The first twenty-five years of industrial use of the B-method. In: ter Beek, M.H., Ničković, D. (eds.) FMICS 2020. LNCS, vol. 12327, pp. 189–209. Springer, Cham (2020). https://doi.org/10.1007/978-3-030-58298-2_8
6. Cerone, A., et al.: Rooting formal methods within higher education curricula for computer science and software engineering — a white paper —. In: Cerone, A., Roggenbach, M. (eds.) FMFun 2019. CCIS, vol. 1301, pp. 1–26. Springer, Cham (2021). https://doi.org/10.1007/978-3-030-71374-4_1
7. Clark, J., Bendisposto, J., Hallerstede, S., Hansen, D., Leuschel, M.: Generating Event-B specifications from algorithm descriptions. In: Butler, M., Schewe, K.-D., Mashkoor, A., Biro, M. (eds.) ABZ 2016. LNCS, vol. 9675, pp. 183–197. Springer, Cham (2016). https://doi.org/10.1007/978-3-319-33600-8_11
8. ClearSy: Atelier B, User and Reference Manuals. Aix-en-Provence, France (2016). http://www.atelierb.eu/
9. Hoang, T.S., Snook, C., Dghaym, D., Salehi Fathabadi, A., Butler, M.: The CamilleX framework for the Rodin platform. In: Raschke, A., Méry, D. (eds.) ABZ 2021. LNCS, vol. 12709, pp. 124–129. Springer, Cham (2021). https://doi.org/10.1007/978-3-030-77543-8_11
10. Idani, A.: Meeduse: a tool to build and run proved DSLs. In: Dongol, B., Troubitsyna, E. (eds.) IFM 2020. LNCS, vol. 12546, pp. 349–367. Springer, Cham (2020). https://doi.org/10.1007/978-3-030-63461-2_19
11. Iliasov, A., Lopatkin, I., Romanovsky, A.: The SafeCap platform for modelling railway safety and capacity. In: Bitsch, F., Guiochet, J., Kaâniche, M. (eds.) SAFECOMP 2013. LNCS, vol. 8153, pp. 130–137. Springer, Heidelberg (2013). https://doi.org/10.1007/978-3-642-40793-2_12
12. Körner, P., Mager, F.: An embedding of B in Clojure. In: Companion Proceedings MODELS (International Conference on Model Driven Engineering Languages and Systems: Companion Proceedings), pp. 598–606. ACM (2022)
13. Körner, P., Bendisposto, J., Dunkelau, J., Krings, S., Leuschel, M.: Integrating formal specifications into applications: the ProB Java API. Form. Methods Syst. Des. **57**, 160–187 (2020)
14. Lamport, L.: The PlusCal algorithm language. In: Leucker, M., Morgan, C. (eds.) ICTAC 2009. LNCS, vol. 5684, pp. 36–60. Springer, Heidelberg (2009). https://doi.org/10.1007/978-3-642-03466-4_2

15. Leuschel, M.: Spot the difference: a detailed comparison between B and Event-B. In: Raschke, A., Riccobene, E., Schewe, K.-D. (eds.) Logic, Computation and Rigorous Methods. LNCS, vol. 12750, pp. 147–172. Springer, Cham (2021). https://doi.org/10.1007/978-3-030-76020-5_9

16. Leuschel, M., Butler, M.: ProB: an automated analysis toolset for the B method. Softw. Tools Technol. Transf. **10**(2), 185–203 (2008)

17. Milicevic, A., Efrati, I., Jackson, D.: αRby—an embedding of alloy in ruby. In: Ait Ameur, Y., Schewe, K.D. (eds.) Abstract State Machines, Alloy, B, TLA, VDM, and Z. ABZ 2014. LNCS, vol. 8477, pp. 56–71. Springer, Berlin, Heidelberg (2014). https://doi.org/10.1007/978-3-662-43652-3_5

18. Rivera, V., Cataño, N., Wahls, T., Rueda, C.: Code generation for Event-B. Softw. Tools Technol. Transf. **19**(1), 31–52 (2017)

19. Rivière, P., Singh, N.K., Aït-Ameur, Y., Dupont, G.: Standalone Event-B models analysis relying on the EB4EB meta-theory. In: Glässer, U., Creissac Campos, J., Méry, D., Palanque, P. (eds.) ABZ 2023. LNCS, vol. 14010, pp. 193–211. Springer, Cham (2023). https://doi.org/10.1007/978-3-031-33163-3_15

20. Rozier, K.Y., Shankar, N., Tinelli, C., Vardi, M.: Developing an open-source, state-of-the-art symbolic model-checking framework for the model-checking research community. In: Proceedings FMCAD (Tutorial at the Conference on Formal Methods in Computer-Aided Design), p. 1 (2023)

21. Schneider, D.: Constraint modelling and data validation using formal specification languages. Ph.D. thesis, Universitäts- und Landesbibliothek der Heinrich-Heine-Universität Düsseldorf (2017)

22. Schneider, S., Treharne, H.: CSP theorems for communicating B machines. Form. Aspects Comput. **17**(4), 390–422 (2005)

23. Woodcock, J., Cavalcanti, A.: The semantics of *Circus*. In: Bert, D., Bowen, J.P., Henson, M.C., Robinson, K. (eds.) ZB 2002. LNCS, vol. 2272, pp. 184–203. Springer, Heidelberg (2002). https://doi.org/10.1007/3-540-45648-1_10

24. Yar, A., Idani, A., Collart-Dutilleul, S.: Merging railway standard notations in a formal DSL-based framework. In: Muccini, H., et al. (eds.) ECSA 2020. CCIS, vol. 1269, pp. 411–419. Springer, Cham (2020). https://doi.org/10.1007/978-3-030-59155-7_30

Event-B as DSL in Isabelle and HOL
Experiences from a Prototype

Benoît Ballenghien⬤ and Burkhart Wolff[(⊠)]⬤

Université Paris-Saclay, LMF, Gif-sur-Yvette, France
{benoit.ballenghien,burkhart.wolff}@universite-paris-saclay.fr

Abstract. The proof assistant Isabelle/HOL is made available inside a flexible system framework allowing for logically safe extensions, which comprise both theories as well as implementations for code-generation, documentation, and specific support for a variety of formal methods.

Following the techniques in [9] and the theoretical groundwork in [4], we show the major milestones for the implementation of a B-Tool and the resulting refinement method inside the Isabelle/HOL platform. The prototype HOL-B provides IDE support, documentation support, a theory for the *Z-Mathematical Toolkit* underlying the B-Method, and a generated denotational semantics for a B MACHINE specification implemented as a specification construct in Isabelle/HOL.

Extended by more automated proof machinery geared to refinements, HOL-B can serve as a more portable, flexible and extensible tool for Event-B that may profit from the large Isabelle/HOL libraries providing Algebra and Analysis theories.

Keywords: Event-B · DSLs · Formal Methods · Isabelle/HOL · Refinement

1 Introduction

A recurring question in formal methods research groups is:

What is actually a domain specific language (DSL) ?

The second author of this paper proposed a particular answer to this question, that led to a number of infrastructure developments in the Isabelle/HOL [7] platform. The infrastructure exploits the fact that the Isabelle/HOL proof assistant is made available inside a flexible system framework allowing logically safe extensions, which comprise both theories as well as implementations for an IDE, documentation, specific support for a variety of formal methods and code-generation.

Boiling down [9] and its more theoretical groundwork in [4] to just one sentence, this can be read like this:

A DSL is a function from a DSL syntax to a conservative theory transformation,

S. Bonfanti et al. (Eds.): ABZ 2024, LNCS 14759, pp. 241–247, 2024.
https://doi.org/10.1007/978-3-031-63790-2_18

so, a bit more formally, a function of type $DSL_{syntax} \Rightarrow theory \Rightarrow theory$, where we still have to clarify what *conservative* means.

The objective of this paper is to make this idea still more precise and to construct along this line a prototype for Event-B [1–3,5,8] inside the Isabelle/HOL platform. The result, Isabelle/HOL-B, offers a library for basic Event-B concepts (the *Z-Mathematical Toolkit* underlying the B Method), syntax and IDE support for editing, and the generation of a denotational semantics for Event-B [9] machines, which can be used for refinement proofs. However, sophisticated support for the latter, i.e. Event-B specific automated proof support, is out of the scope of this paper. (The latter is, in our view, the true research question.)

We will proceed as follows: after the introduction of HOL and a strict minimum of the Isabelle platform API in SML, we will describe the *Z-Mathematical Toolkit*, and finally the parser, type-checker, and encoder parts of the DSL function. The resulting Isabelle/HOL-B[1] will be demonstrated with an example.

2   Background

2.1   Isabelle, HOL and the Conservative Method

Isabelle is a platform for proof assistants in various logics, where Higher-Order Logic (HOL) is the one which is most commonly used. It has a fairly small kernel in the tradition of LCF provers, which certifies all derivations on formulas. Formulas and logical rules are represented in typed terms of the polymorphic λ-calculus. Induction and closure rules can be derived within the system. Modeling in HOL has strong similarities with programming in a functional programming language.

The core of the logic HOL can be based on a very small set of seven axioms introducing the equality, the type *bool*, the logical connectives, and a type *ind* which must have an infinite carrier set. HOL comes by construction with a typed set theory; α *set*'s are characteristic functions of type $\alpha \Rightarrow bool$ with $\{\}$ as notation for $\lambda x.$ *False* and *UNIV* as $\lambda x.$ *True*.

Extensions of this core are built exclusively by two syntactically restricted axiom schemes:

- the *constant definitions* which state the equality of a fresh constant symbol to a closed λ-term (not containing this symbol)
- the *type definitions* which state an isomorphism between a fresh type constructor symbol to a closed λ-term denotating a nonempty set.

The first can be seen as the introduction of an abbreviation for a known concept; the latter as an introduction as constraint of a subset of some type constructed over *bool* and *ind*. It is not difficult to see that these definitional axioms will preserve logical consistency of the HOL core.

---

[1] ... available at https://gitlab.lisn.upsaclay.fr/burkhart.wolff/hol-csp2.0/-/tree/master/Event-B.

The HOL library provides a rich number of mathematical concepts like carte-sian products, number theories, inductive sets and datatypes. For the latter constructions, Isabelle/HOL provides specific support in form of DSL's for these *specification constructs*, that compile them into definitional axioms and derive the proof rules from them usually automatically. This includes recursive function definitions as well as record notations built over cartesian products.

2.2   A Gentle Introduction into Isabelle Programming

The final result of our programming exercise is shown in Fig. 1: A theory command deeply integrated in the Isabelle IDE allowing continuous parsing and type-checking, navigation into the resulting implicit definitions as well as the underlying background theory adding the set theory operators (that B actually inherited from the "Z-Mathematical Toolkit"). Here, *navigation* means that the IDE treats the MACHINE as a hypertext allowing to link to a corresponding (implicit) declaration by mouse click. In the following, we will describe the techniques to construct the DSL function and its integration into Isabelle which results in this behaviour.

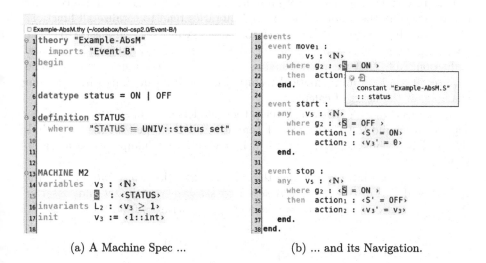

(a) A Machine Spec ...   (b) ... and its Navigation.

Fig. 1. A B-Machine Specification in Isabelle/HOL-B

First, there are commands giving access to the underlying SML toplevel; by:

ML ‹... *some ML code* ... ›

we get a programming IDE that gives access to the interfaces of the Isabelle system. In particular, the concrete datatype **term** provides a syntactic model of λ-terms (consisting of free/bound variables, abstraction, application), with the usual operations (substitution, reduction etc.). Terms are annotated by explicit type information, which we have to compute before terms can be certified and used by more complex operations like "generate a definition" or "generate a record to represent the MACHINE state". The concrete datatype **theory** captures the signature of a theory (with type constructor declarations, constant symbol declaration, and syntax configurations) as well as a set of axioms and derived theorems. Both were captured in the concrete datatype **thm** which captures the traditional triple $\Gamma \vdash_{Th} \varphi$ (from local assumptions Γ within the theory Th the formula φ has been derived).

3   The Z Mathematical Toolkit

In this section, we will discuss the background theory of Z, B and Event-B which was developed in the 80 s at the University of Oxford and which led, at least in the Z case, to a standardized *Mathematical Toolkit*. HOL and B have closely related, but different foundations: HOL is based on functions, while Z/B are based on sets. The former has the advantage that typed-lambda calculi have higher-order term normal-forms which are decidable, while the latter permits a more traditional mathematical presentation. These foundational choices have consequences in the modeling style: HOL libraries tend to totalize all functions ($1/0$ is usually defined by 0 in many HOL systems) while Z/B emphasize to model partiality explicitly, even at the cost of additional complexity in substitution and deduction. Note that we are not saying here that the HOL approach is unsound - we recall the long mathematical tradition to totalize functions which lies, for example, at the heart of calculus.

Given that most Z/B users develop their models in a typed way anyway, we suggest to rebuild the Mathematical Toolkit inside the typed set theory of HOL rather than axiomatic set theory, which is viable, but hampers the access to HOL libraries.

As a start, we have to redefine the set operators (i. e. *constants* in HOL) $\emptyset$, $A \times B$, and $\mathbb{P}\, A$ of type $'\alpha\ set$, $'\alpha\ set \Rightarrow '\beta\ set \Rightarrow ('\alpha \times '\beta)\ set$ and $'\alpha\ set \Rightarrow '\alpha\ set\ set$, respectively. On top we define the set operators from the book:

> **definition** *rel*:: ⟨[$'a\ set$, $'b\ set$] $\Rightarrow$ ($'a \Leftrightarrow 'b$) set⟩ (**infix** ⟨↔⟩ *100*)
> **where** ⟨$A \leftrightarrow B \equiv \mathbb{P}\ (A \times B)$⟩
> **definition** *pfun* :: ⟨[$'a\ set$, $'b\ set$] $\Rightarrow$ ($'a \Leftrightarrow 'b$) set⟩   (⟨- ⇸ -⟩ *[54,53] 53*)
> **where** ⟨$S \rightarrowtail R \equiv \{f \in S \leftrightarrow R.\ \forall x\ y_1\ y_2.\ (x, y_1){\in}f \wedge (x, y_2){\in}f \longrightarrow y_1 = y_2\}$⟩
> **definition** *pinj*::⟨[$'a\ set$,$'b\ set$] $\Rightarrow$ ($'a \Leftrightarrow 'b$) set⟩   (⟨- ⤔ -⟩ *[54,53] 53*)
> **where** ⟨$S{\rightarrowtail} R \equiv \{s \in S \leftrightarrow R.\ \forall x_1\ x_2\ y.\ (x_1,y){\in}s \wedge (x_2,y){\in}s \longrightarrow x_1 = x_2\}$⟩
> **definition** *dom-restr* :: ⟨[$'a\ set$, $'a \Leftrightarrow 'b$] $\Rightarrow$ ($'a \Leftrightarrow 'b$)⟩ (⟨- ◁ -⟩ *[71,70] 70*)
> **where** ⟨$S \lhd R \equiv \{(x, y).\ (x, y) \in R \wedge x \in S\}$⟩
> **definition** *dom-substr* ::⟨[$'a\ set$, $'a \Leftrightarrow 'b$] $\Rightarrow 'a \Leftrightarrow 'b$⟩   (⟨- ⩤ -⟩ *[71,70] 70*)
> **where** ⟨$S \lhd\!\!\!- R \equiv \{(x, y).\ (x, y) \in R \wedge x \notin S\}$⟩ ... etc. etc.

From this definitional basis, we derive the laws from the mathematical toolkit, which is usually an easy exercise. Here are a few examples:

$$dom \ (S \lhd R) = S \cap dom \ R \qquad S \lhd R \rhd T = S \lhd (R \rhd T)$$
$$dom \ (Q \ \mathbin{\raise1pt\hbox{$\scriptstyle\circ$}}\ R) = (Q^{-1})\langle\!\langle dom \ R\rangle\!\rangle \qquad p \in s \lhd r \Longrightarrow p \in r$$
$$dom \ (dom \ g \lhd f) \cap dom \ g = \emptyset \qquad f \in A \leftrightarrow B \Longrightarrow s \in \mathbf{P} \ A \Longrightarrow s \lhd f \in A \leftrightarrow B$$

Some definitions are a bit more delicate: since functions in B are relations, the application needs to be distinguished from the built-in application in HOL. These two definitions describe the conversions between functional and function-as-relation applications:

$$\langle Lambda \ A \ f \equiv \{(x, y). \ x \in A \land y = f \ x\}\rangle$$
$$\langle R \cdot x \quad \equiv SOME \ y. \ (x, y) \in R\rangle$$

which results in the beta-reduction rule: $a \in A \Longrightarrow (Lambda \ A \ f) \cdot a = f \ a$.

While the derivation of most rules from the definitions is straightforward, there are some cases which actually required some more serious proof work: the definitions of the various closure operators (reflexive/transitive ...) in the Z Mathematical Toolkit take partiality into account; the resulting induction rules therefore need different justifications than their HOL counterparts.

4 The Event-B Encoder

4.1 Getting Started: Parsing and Toplevel-Integration

Isabelle's API provides a common infrastucture to construct parsers; a type synonym 'a parser which are functions that map a stream of input tokens to a parsed value and rest-stream, i.e. a function of type *token list* → *'a * token list*. Parsing combinators [6] allow this kind of functions to be combined; notably by the sequential composition $P \ -\!- \ P'$ of parsers, the alternative $P \ || \ P'$ and the mapping of a function f into the result of a parsing $P >> f$. The toplevel function of the MACHINE parser reads as follows:

$$val \ parse\text{-}machine\text{-}spec = ($$
$$\qquad Parse.binding$$
$$\qquad -\!- \ \textbf{keyword} \ \langle variables\rangle \qquad -\!- \ (Scan.repeat1 \ parse\text{-}var\text{-}decl)$$
$$\qquad -\!- \ \textbf{keyword} \ \langle invariants\rangle \qquad -\!- \ (Scan.repeat1 \ parse\text{-}invariant)$$
$$\qquad -\!- \ \textbf{keyword} \ \langle init\rangle \qquad -\!- \ (Scan.repeat1 \ parse\text{-}init)$$
$$\qquad -\!- \ \textbf{keyword} \ \langle events\rangle \qquad -\!- \ (Scan.repeat1 \ parse\text{-}transition)$$
$$\qquad -\!- \ \textbf{keyword} \ \langle end.\rangle$$
$$)$$

which allows for the toplevel composition of the DSL function by:

$$command \ \textbf{command-keyword} \ \langle MACHINE\rangle$$
$$\qquad Machine \ Specification$$
$$\qquad (parse\text{-}machine\text{-}spec >> context\text{-}check >> (Toplevel.theory \ o \ semantics))$$

and its binding to the keyword *MACHINE* and thus its integration into the Isabelle document model.

4.2   Getting Started: Semantics

We have to clarify some leftovers from the previous section. First, the function *context-check* has to be constructed: it has type *absy0* → *theory* → *absy*, i. e. it converts a raw abstract syntax into a function that produces a richer syntax where all sub-expressions are type-checked in the given theory context of the MACHINE specification. Isabelle annotates the content in the IDE with coloring and navigation information during this process.

Second, the *semantics* which is a function that takes the *theory* → *absy* function as input, executes it, and produces a theory extension *theory* → *theory* that is lifted via the Isabelle combinator *Toplevel.theory* into a global transition of the Isabelle system state. This completes the construction of the aforementioned DSL function as well as its integration into the Isabelle system level. Note that the pure functional API enables parallel execution inside the Isabelle kernel.

The *semantics* function generates type and constant definitions, notably:

- a record definition modeling the entire machine *state*; this constructs also the definition of the "variables" of the spec as selectors in that state,
- a constant definition that comprises all variable constraints,
- a constant definition is generated for the initial state,
- a predicate of *state* ⇒ *bool* for the invariant and a constant *STATES* comprising the set of states satisfying the invariant,
- for each event declaration L_i, there is a constant definition of the form L_i-*trans* ≡ $\lambda\sigma$ e σ'. ∃ $a_1...a_n$. *guard* σ e $a_1...a_n$ ∧ *action* σ e σ' $a_1...a_n$
- there is a constant definition for *TRANS* that composes the global transition relation as union of the L_i-*trans*itions.

For example, the *start* event in Fig. 1 is converted into the definition: *start-trans* ≡ $\lambda\sigma$ *event* σ'. ∃ v_5. v_5 ∈ $\mathbf{N}$ ∧ S σ = *OFF* ∧ S σ' = *ON* ∧ v_3 σ' = 0.

5   Conclusion

In this paper, we demonstrated how a perhaps little known technique to construct DSL's can be used to build tool support for the B method inside the Isabelle platform. The resulting prototype offers a typed version of the mathematical toolkit underlying B and Event-B, based on definitional principles and derived rules, and continuous parsing and type-checking. Its integration into the Isabelle document model also permits seamless navigation into models and libraries as well as document generation. The specification constructs were translated into a family of definitions capturing the denotational semantics representing the states, events and transitions of a Machine specification. While quite powerful, our prototype is fairly small: about 450 lines for the encoder and about 3000 lines of definitions and proofs for the mathematical toolkit.

The potential benefit of our approach for the ABZ community is to profit from the developments in the generic Isabelle platform wrt. libraries, powerful prover technologies, and user interface technologies rather than investing effort into own tools.

Future work will have to address specialized proof automation for the refinement of B machines. Another line of extension is to adapt the powerful generic code-generators of Isabelle to the idiom of the mathematical toolkit and to generate code and animations of B specifications.

Competing Interests. The author(s) has no competing interests to declare that are relevant to the content of this manuscript.

References

1. Abrial, J.: The B-Book - Assigning Programs to Meanings. Cambridge University Press, Cambridge (1996). https://doi.org/10.1017/CBO9780511624162
2. Abrial, J.R.: Modeling in Event-B: System and Software Engineering. Cambridge University Press, Cambridge (2010)
3. Abrial, J., Butler, M.J., Hallerstede, S., Hoang, T.S., Mehta, F., Voisin, L.: Rodin: an open toolset for modelling and reasoning in Event-B. Int. J. Softw. Tools Technol. Transf. **12**(6), 447–466 (2010). https://doi.org/10.1007/S10009-010-0145-Y
4. Brucker, A.D., Tuong, F., Wolff, B.: Model transformation as conservative theory-transformation. J. Object Technol. **19**(3), 3:1–16 (2020) https://doi.org/10.5381/JOT.2020.19.3.A3
5. Cansell, D., Méry, D.: Foundations of the B method. Comput. Artif. Intell. **22**(3-4), 221–256 (2003). http://www.cai.sk/ojs/index.php/cai/article/view/456
6. Hutton, G.: Higher-order functions for parsing. J. Funct. Program. **2**(3), 323–343 (1992). https://doi.org/10.1017/S0956796800000411
7. Nipkow, T., Wenzel, M., Paulson, L.C. (eds.): Isabelle/HOL—A Proof Assistant for Higher-Order Logic. LNCS, vol. 2283. Springer, Heidelberg (2002). https://doi.org/10.1007/3-540-45949-9
8. Robinson, K.A.: Introduction to the B method, pp. 3–37. Springer, London (1999). https://doi.org/10.1007/978-1-4471-0585-5_1
9. Wenzel, M., Wolff, B.: Building formal method tools in the Isabelle/Isar framework. In: Schneider, K., Brandt, J. (eds.) TPHOLs 2007. LNCS, vol. 4732, pp. 352–367. Springer, Heidelberg (2007). https://doi.org/10.1007/978-3-540-74591-4_26

ThoR: An Alloy5-Like DSL for Interactive Theorem Proving in Coq

Bodo Igler[(✉)] [iD] and Andreas Mayer

RheinMain University of Applied Sciences, Wiesbaden, Germany
{bodo.igler,andreas.mayer}@hs-rm.de
http://www.hs-rm.de

Abstract. The steep learning curve associated with interactive theorem proving poses a significant entry barrier for the learner. While the Alloy specification language [1] has simplified the introduction to and application of formal methods, transitioning to interactive theorem proving, such as with Coq [2], remains daunting due to the inherent complexity of formal reasoning and the sophisticated tooling required.

We introduce ThoR, an extension for the Coq proof assistant that incorporates an Alloy5-like domain-specific language: Specifications, propositions and proofs are formulated in an Alloy5-like syntax. This reduces tool and language complexity, and makes interactive theorem proving more accessible. The implementation is based on Coq's syntax extension capabilities and the mathematical components library (mathcomp) [4].

This paper reports on work in progress. It contributes an approach for the embedding of Alloy into Coq based on a set-theoretic interpretation, a proof calculus for Alloy with soundness by construction, a prototypical implementation and its validation via a simple token ring example.

Keywords: Alloy · Interactive Theorem Proving · Coq

1 Introduction

The work described in this paper is a first step towards a proof assistant based on the specification language Alloy [1]. "Lightweight formal methods" like the application of the Alloy Analyzer facilitate a gentle introduction to formal methods [7]. It is, from our experience with formal methods in education, at least one order of magnitude harder to become proficient in applying a proof assistant. This is partly due to the higher complexity of writing formalized proofs. However, a substantial part of the complexity stems from the tools and tool languages themselves. At least from the learner's perspective, the abstraction level of state of the art proof assistants like e.g. Coq [2], Isabelle [3] and Lean [5] is at the same level as assembler language.

We postulate that the transition from the Alloy Analyzer to a proof assistant can be made significantly easier by reducing tool and language complexity, thus enabling the learner to focus on the actual formal reasoning. We therefore suggest

© The Author(s), under exclusive license to Springer Nature Switzerland AG 2024
S. Bonfanti et al. (Eds.): ABZ 2024, LNCS 14759, pp. 248–254, 2024.
https://doi.org/10.1007/978-3-031-63790-2_19

the application of an Alloy-like language as "high-level logical language" not only for the formulation of specifications, but also for the development of formal proofs. This is further facilitated by the fact that Alloy has been used in a wide variety of applications and, in particular from a learner's perspective, easily digestible Alloy specifications abound [1].

We further postulate that the Alloy language can serve as the basis for a fully-practical interactive theorem prover with corresponding calculus. We are in the process of developing the Coq-based library ThoR[1] which provides both an Alloy-like language for the specification of software abstractions and a proof calculus within the syntactical and conceptual frame of Alloy. We plan to use and evaluate this tool in future introductory courses on formal methods. The current ThoR version is based on Alloy 5.

Section 2 outlines our approach and sketches the basic elements of ThoR. Section 3 gives a brief overview on related work and alternative approaches. Section 4 describes the current limitations of ThoR and concludes the paper.

2   Approach

Our approach consists in (1) embedding Alloy as a domain-specific language into Gallina (Coq's logical specification language), (2) mapping it to the set theoretical concepts modelled in the mathcomp library [4] and (3) enriching it with lemmata and proof tactics to facilitate "Alloy-style reasoning".

The basic objective of (1) and (2) consists in transforming the Alloy syntax to Gallina, i.e. to a type-theoretical formulation equivalent to the semantics of the Alloy specification language, cf. Appendix C in [7].[2] The embedding utilizes the Coq language features *module* and *notation scope* in order to extend (and not change) Coq. It is based on the syntax extension facilities of Coq with a LL1 parser at their core. These facilities pose some restrictions on how faithfully the embedding can be carried out. The resulting formal language ThoR has the expressiveness of first-order logic plus quantification over relations and therefore leads to an undecidable language.

The basic objective of (3) is to provide inference and conversion rules based on (1) and (2) which facilitate the development of proofs in the Alloy-like language ThoR. In particular, the formulation of propositions, proof states, proof obligations and tactics have to be meaningful to the Alloy user.

The remainder of this section utilizes a simple token ring example[3] to illustrate the basic ideas and the application of ThoR.

---

[1] **Theory of Relational Operators.**

[2] [14] shows that this is generally feasible: The theoretical foundation of Gallina, the Calculus of Inductive Constructions, can be encoded in Zermelo-Frænkel set theory, and vice versa. For our purposes, finite sets of arbitrary size and relations (tuple sets) of arbitrary arity form the basic building blocks. These are encoded in mathcomp as predicates resp. dependent types based on these predicates.

[3] Some network nodes form a ring. Each node passes on received tokens. This example captures – despite its simplicity – several typical ingredients of an Alloy 5 specification, in particular: static structure plus dynamic aspects. The latter are modelled via a **Time** signature.

2.1   Embedding

This subsection gives an outline of the above-mentioned embedding (1) and mapping to mathcomp (2). We follow the sketch of the "kernel semantics" of Alloy in appendix C in [7].

Declarations. An Alloy specification is based on a collection of declarations of relations, the Alloy *signatures* and *signature fields*, e.g.:

```
sig Time, Token {}
sig Node {succ: one Node, tokens: Token -> Time}
```

This is interpreted in set theory as follows: `Time`, `Token`, `Node` declare relation symbols, `succ` a binary relation symbol and `tokens` a ternary relation symbol with the multiplicity constraint $\forall_{n:Node}\exists!_{n':Node}(n, n') \in succ$.

In ThoR unary relation symbols are modelled as variables of type `sig`, n-ary relations with type constraints as variables of type `{rel ⊂ ...}`.

```
Variables Time Node Token: sig.
Variable  succ: {rel ⊂ Node --> Node | set -- one}.
Variable  tokens: {rel ⊂ Node --> Token --> Time}.
```

ThoR relations are based on the concepts tuple and finite set (of arbitrary size) in mathcomp. (`U` is an arbitrary, finite type representing the universe.)

```
Notation "n .-ary" := ({set (n.-tuple U)}) ...
```

`sig` ist just a synonym for `1.-ary`. The type for relations with constraints is basically modelled as a family of Σ-types (dependent pair types) $R_P :=$ $\sum_{r:n.-ary} P$ `r` indexed by the discriminating predicate `P:n.-ary -> bool`, e.g. `P r := r ⊂ q` for relations `r, q` of same arity. This is an important prerequisite for the general and type-safe definition of relational operators.

Formulas and Expressions. The interpretation of ThoR via mathcomp is denoted by $(\!|.|\!)$ and closely mimics the set-theoretic interpretation of Alloy according to Appendix C in [7].[4] Some details (e.g. type casts in mathcomp) have been omitted for the sake of brevity in the following examples:

$$(\!|r \cdot q|\!) := \begin{cases} \text{[set u:(n+m).-tuple thorUniv | [exists x,} \\ \quad \text{(rcons\_tuple (take n u) x) \textbackslash in } (\!|r|\!) \text{ \&\&} \\ \quad \text{(cons\_tuple x (drop n u)) \textbackslash in } (\!|q|\!) \text{]]} \\ \text{arity of } (\!|r|\!) = n+1, \text{ arity of } (\!|q|\!) = m+1, n+m > 0 \end{cases}$$

$$(\!|\text{[all x: e | p]}|\!) := \text{[forall x, x⊂ } (\!|e|\!) \text{ \&\& one x ==> } (\!|p|\!)\text{]}$$

The syntax for formulas and expressions in Alloy and ThoR is to a great deal identical. Some symbols and notations, however, have to be adapted in ThoR in order to prevent ambiguities, e.g. "`r.q`" → "`r·q`", "`r = q`" → "`r == q`", "`r in q`" → "`r ⊂ q`", "`all x: e | p`" → "`[all x: e | p]`".

---

[4] The Alloy semantics interprets operations on relation symbols as the according set operations and the constant symbols as corresponding tuple sets. Propositional and predicate logic is interpreted as usual for untyped predicate logic.

Definitions. Alloy models comprise the declaration of relation symbols (see above) and named definitions: (signature) facts, predicates, functions and assertions. ThoR uses `Conjecture` for Alloy facts, `Definition` for the definition of Alloy predicates and functions, and `Lemma` for Alloy assertions (s. Section 2.2 for examples). The Alloy module concept is modelled as a combination of `Module` for namespace separation and `Section` for parametrization. The following example supplements the preceding declarations with the facts on the behaviour of the nodes in the token ring:

```
From ThoR Require Import ordering.
Definition first := Ordering.first Time.
Definition last  := Ordering.last Time.
Definition next  := Ordering.next Time.

Conjecture ring : [all n:Node | Node ⊂ n·^succ].
Conjecture init : one tokens·first.

Definition stutter (t t': 1.-ary) := tokens·t' == tokens·t.
Definition send (t t' n: 1.-ary) :=
  let n' := n·succ in let others := Node - n - n' in
  n'·tokens·t' == n·tokens·t + n'·tokens·t &&
  n·tokens·t' == none && others·tokens·t' == others·tokens·t.
Conjecture traces: [all t:Time-last | let t':=t·next in
  (stutter t t') || [some n:Node | send t t' n]].
```

2.2 Calculus

The ThoR calculus is based on lemmata for algebraic rules for the manipulation of terms that contain set and relational operators (in particular the dot-join and transitive closure), and on lemmata and proof tactics for inference rules (including natural deduction in the language of ThoR and the treatment of Alloy idioms). This approach ensures the soundness of the calculus. These are two examples for inference rules:

∀-introduction in ThoR has to take the additional constraint **one a** into account:

$$\forall \text{ intro} \frac{(\text{n,nat}),(\text{A,n.-ary}),(\text{P,n.-pred})\in \Gamma}{\Gamma :: (\text{a,n.-ary}) \vdash \text{a} \subset \text{A \&\& one a ==> P a}}{\Gamma \vdash [\text{all a:A | P}]}$$

The inference rule ◯-induction is part of the ThoR-module `ordering` and applicable to signatures (`1.-ary`) that are equipped with an ordering `next`:

$$◯\text{-induction} \frac{(\text{T,sig}),(\text{P: 1.-pred})\in \Gamma \qquad \Gamma \vdash P \text{ first} \qquad \Gamma \vdash [\text{all t:T-last | P t ==> P (t·next)}]}{\Gamma \vdash [\text{all t: T | P t}]}$$

The following, abbreviated example demonstrates the application of the proof tactic `next_induction` (○-induction rule). It is based on the preceding ThoR code snippets:

```
Lemma stutter_one_token (t:1.-ary): let t':=t·next in
  t ⊂ Time-last -> one tokens·t -> stutter t t'-> one tokens·t'.
Proof. ... Qed.

Lemma step_one_token (t n:1.-ary): let t':=t·next in
  t ⊂ Time-last -> one t -> n ⊂ Node -> one n ->
  one tokens·t -> send t t' n-> one tokens·t'.
Proof. ... Qed.

Lemma TokenConservation: [all t:Time | one tokens·t].
Proof.
  next_induction. (* yields base case and induction step *)
  apply init. (* base case: identical to fact init *)
  ... (* induction step: distinguish cases stutter and step *) ...
  apply stutter_one_token. ...
  apply step_one_token. ...
Qed.
```

3   Alternative Approaches

Alloy has been transformed to several formal languages for proof assistants, c.f. [6,8,10,12,13]. All these approaches treat Alloy as an external DSL that is translated to the logical language of a theorem prover. In addition, [12,13] ensure that the translation result is conceptually similar to the original Alloy specification. This is complemented by a set of Alloy-specific lemmata. Thus, theorem proving with these approaches is based on a structure that resembles the original Alloy structure. [10] goes one step further and adds a pretty-printer that displays proof obligations in an Alloy-like syntax.

Accordingly, the user experience that results from [10] is closest to our approach. [12] is, like ThoR, based on Coq. However, the approach treats Gallina as a target (not host) language and theorem proving is not based on an Alloy-like syntax.

Software abstractions can of course also be directly modelled in Coq. Consider e.g. a straight-forward, naive specification of the token ring example in Gallina. The basic declarations can be easily rendered similar in structure to the declaration of signatures and signature fields in ThoR:

```
Variables Time Node Token : Type.
Variable  tokens : Time -> Node -> list Token.
Variable  next : Time -> option Time.
Variable  succ : Node -> Node.
```

However, the remaining specification is burdened with several low-level details and intricate formulations (e.g. finiteness of the types `Time` and `Node` via enumerability, set equality via list permutation, ring topology property via a distance modulo ring size function that is compatible with succ). This about triples the number of lines of code for the specification. The proofs get cluttered with the additional details, too. Initial experience from this and further examples indicates that ThoR helps better focus on the basics of proof mechanization and on the abstraction being explored.

Alternatively, existing Coq libraries for sets and relations (e.g. mathcomp) and/or for network topologies (e.g. PADEC[5]) could be applied. The resulting formalization is similar to ThoR w.r.t. level of abstraction and complexity. However, this requires familiarization with the libraries and usually in addition a good understanding of Coq beyond the basic concepts of proof mechanization.

4   Conclusion

We have presented the current status of ThoR, a Coq-extension that facilitates the formulation of specifications for software abstractions and the interactive development of proofs in an Alloy5-like language. Validation via a simple example (token ring) demonstrates the feasibility of the approach. ThoR is work in progress and currently has some limitations, mainly:

Coq possesses a "one-pass" processing nature and certain basic-level syntax which is difficult to change via the syntax-extension facilities of the Coq parser. As ThoR takes the form of an internal DSL embedded in Coq, ThoR therefore differs from Alloy in certain respects. Signatures and signature fields have to be declared before their first use. Signature field names cannot be overloaded. Signature inheritance has to be formulated as a separate constraint. Disjointness and redundancy are not flagged during the formulation of formulas. Some notations (e.g. dotjoin operator symbol, bracketing of quantification) differ slightly. While there exist workarounds (e.g. detection of disjointness and redundancy via proof automation), a clean solution requires changes to Coq's parsing and elaboration process (as opposed to merely extending parsing rules).

ThoR is currently based on the Alloy 5 language. Incorporating the Alloy 6 features mutability and temporal logic into ThoR requires in particular the selection of a suitable deduction system for temporal logic (cf. e.g. the component for LTL in [11] and the discussion in [9]).

Acknowledgments. We would like to thank the anonymous reviewers for valuable feedback on this paper.

Disclosure of Interests. The authors have no competing interests to declare that are relevant to the content of this article.

---

[5] http://www-verimag.imag.fr/~altisen/PADEC/padec.html.

References

1. Alloy. https://alloytools.org/applications.html
2. The Coq Proof Assistant. https://coq.inria.fr/
3. Isabelle. https://isabelle.in.tum.de/
4. Mathematical Components. https://math-comp.github.io/
5. Programming Language and Theorem Prover - Lean. https://lean-lang.org/
6. Arkoudas, K., Khurshid, S., Marinov, D., Rinard, M.: Integrating model checking and theorem proving for relational reasoning. In: Berghammer, R., Möller, B., Struth, G. (eds.) RelMiCS 2003. LNCS, vol. 3051, pp. 21–33. Springer, Heidelberg (2004). https://doi.org/10.1007/978-3-540-24771-5_3
7. Jackson, D.: Software Abstractions: Logic, Language, and Analysis. The MIT Press, Cambridge, Massachusetts London, England, revised edn (2016)
8. Macedo, N., Cunha, A.: Automatic Unbounded Verification of Alloy Specifications with Prover9, September 2012. http://arxiv.org/abs/1209.5773, arXiv:1209.5773 [cs]
9. Marchignoli, D.: Natural Deduction Systems for Temporal Logics. Disseration, Dipartimento di Informatica, Università di Pisa (2002)
10. Moscato, M.M., Pombo, C.G.L., Frias, M.F.: Dynamite: a tool for the verification of alloy models based on PVS. ACM Trans. Softw. Eng. Methodol. **23**(2), 1–37 (2014). https://doi.org/10.1145/2544136, https://dl.acm.org/doi/10.1145/2544136
11. Renz, B., et al.: LWB Logic Workbench. https://esb-dev.github.io/lwb
12. Souaf, S., Loulergue, F.: A first step in the translation of alloy to Coq. In: Ait-Ameur, Y., Qin, S. (eds.) ICFEM 2019. LNCS, vol. 11852, pp. 455–469. Springer, Cham (2019). https://doi.org/10.1007/978-3-030-32409-4_28
13. Ulbrich, M., Geilmann, U., El Ghazi, A.A., Taghdiri, M.: A proof assistant for alloy specifications. In: Flanagan, C., König, B. (eds.) TACAS 2012. LNCS, vol. 7214, pp. 422–436. Springer, Heidelberg (2012). https://doi.org/10.1007/978-3-642-28756-5_29
14. Werner, B.: Sets in types, types in sets. In: Abadi, M., Ito, T. (eds.) TACS 1997. LNCS, vol. 1281, pp. 530–546. Springer, Heidelberg (1997). https://doi.org/10.1007/BFb0014566

Verifying HyperLTL Properties in Event-B

Jean-Paul Bodeveix[1]([✉])[iD], Thomas Carle[1][iD], Elie Fares[1,4][iD],
Mamoun Filali[2][iD], and Thai Son Hoang[3][iD]

[1] Univ. Toulouse 3 – IRIT, Toulouse, France
bodeveix@irit.fr
[2] IRIT – CNRS, Toulouse, France
[3] University of Southampton, Southampton, UK
[4] Higher Colleges of Technology, Ras Al Khaimah, United Arab Emirates

Abstract. The study presented in this paper is motivated by the verification of properties related to hardware architectures, namely timing anomalies that qualify a counter-intuitive timing behaviour. They are avoided by a monotonicity property which is an Hyper-LTL property. We present how to prove some classes of Hyper-LTL properties with Event-B.

1 Introduction

The study presented in this paper is motivated by the verification of properties related to hardware architectures, especially multicore platforms. We are concerned about timing anomalies that qualify a counter-intuitive timing behaviour: a locally faster execution leads to an increase in the execution time of the whole program [7]. Monotonicity is a property that ensures such timing anomalies do not occur. The monotonicity property does not belong to the usual safety and liveness classes because it relates to two distinct execution traces. Such kind of properties have already been identified and coined as hyperproperties [2]. Here, we investigate the notion of hyperproperties and evaluate their verification methods [6] for our Event-B context[1]. The verification of hyperproperties has mainly been studied in the context of model-checking. Here, our models are parameterized and will be formalized and reasoned about with the help of proof assistants. For this purpose, in Sect. 3, we reuse a proof-based framework [3] on top of the Rodin Event-B framework.

2 Hyperproperties

Definitions. Hyperproperties introduce universal and existential trace quantifiers as in the general purpose TLA+ [5] language or in the specialized language HyperLTL [1] extending linear temporal logic with trace quantifiers:

$$\varphi ::= \exists \pi \cdot \varphi \mid \forall \pi \cdot \varphi \mid \psi \qquad \psi ::= a_\pi \mid \psi \vee \psi \mid \neg \psi \mid \mathbf{X}\,\psi \mid \psi\;\mathbf{U}\,\psi$$

---

[1] Hyperproperties have been mainly applied to the security domain.

S. Bonfanti et al. (Eds.): ABZ 2024, LNCS 14759, pp. 255–261, 2024.
https://doi.org/10.1007/978-3-031-63790-2_20

where $\mathbf{\forall}\pi$ and $\mathbf{\exists}\pi$ are universal and exisitential quantification over some trace π, a_π is atomic proposition interpreted on a trace π, $\mathbf{X}$ and $\mathbf{U}$ are LTL next and until temporal operators. Other logical and temporal operators can be defined as syntactical sugar accordingly.

HyperLTL Semantics. Let P be a set of propositions, $\mathcal{T} \subseteq \mathbb{N} \to 2^P$ a set of traces, Π a set of path identifiers and $T \in \Pi \nrightarrow \mathcal{T}$. The judgment $T \models_i \varphi$ (φ is satisfied by the assignments T at time i) is defined as:

$$
\begin{aligned}
&T \models_i a_\pi && \text{if } a \in T[\pi][i] \\
&T \models_i \neg\psi && \text{if } T \not\models_i \psi \\
&T \models_i \psi_1 \vee \psi_2 && \text{if } T \models_i \psi_1 \text{ or } T \models_i \psi_2 \\
&T \models_i \mathbf{X}\,\psi && \text{if } T \models_{i+1} \psi \\
&T \models_i \psi_1 \mathbf{U} \psi_2 && \text{if } \exists j \geq i \text{ s.t. } T \models_j \psi_2 \text{ and } \forall i \leq k < j,\ T \models_k \psi_1 \\
&T \models_i \mathbf{\exists}\pi \cdot \varphi && \text{if } \exists t \in \mathcal{T} \text{ s.t. } \pi \mapsto t, T \models_i \varphi \\
&T \models_i \mathbf{\forall}\pi \cdot \varphi && \text{if } \forall t \in \mathcal{T} : \pi \mapsto t, T \models_i \varphi
\end{aligned}
$$

where $\pi \mapsto t, T$ denote the same function as T, except π is mapped to t. An important point to note is that time advances synchronously in every considered trace.

Examples of Hyperproperties. Hyperproperties have mainly been introduced for security. We illustrate the use of HyperLTL through the expression of two security properties. They use a predicate P encoding the behavior of the considered system.

- *Observational determinism* is a 2-safety property. It states that two traces agree at any time on their observable outputs if they agree at any time on their observable inputs:

$$
\mathbf{\forall}\pi_1 \cdot \mathbf{\forall}\pi_2 \cdot P(\pi_1) \wedge P(\pi_2) \wedge \Box(inp_{\pi_1} \Leftrightarrow inp_{\pi_2}) \Rightarrow \Box(out_{\pi_1} \Leftrightarrow out_{\pi_2})
$$

- *Generalized non-interference*: It states that observing public information reveals no private information: one can find a trace π that agrees with π_1 on its public inputs and with the private part of any other trace π_2, thus not revealing π_1 private information.

$$
\begin{aligned}
&\mathbf{\forall}\pi_1 \cdot \mathbf{\forall}\pi_2 \cdot P(\pi_1) \wedge P(\pi_2) \implies \\
&\quad \mathbf{\exists}\pi \cdot P(\pi) \wedge \Box(pub_\pi \Leftrightarrow pub_{\pi_1} \wedge priv_\pi \Leftrightarrow priv_{\pi_2})
\end{aligned}
$$

Example 1 (Secret Transfer). Consider a system where *Alice* wants to send a secret bit h to *Bob* by "spliting" h into two bits t_1 and t_2 such that $h = t_1\,XOR\,t_2$ and transfer t_1 and t_2 separately using different channel to *Bob*. Upon receiving both t_1 and t_2, *Bob* reconstructs the received bit $r = t_1\,XOR\,t_2$ accordingly. Assuming that any intruder can only have access to either t_1 or t_2 but not both, the protocol ensures that the value of the secret h is not revealed.

- *Observational determinism.* if two traces have the same input h, they have the same output r: $\forall \pi_1, \pi_2 \cdot h_{\pi_1} = h_{\pi_2} \Rightarrow r_{\pi_1} = r_{\pi_2}$.
- *Generalized non-interference.* For every two traces π_1 and π_2, there exists trace π such that $h_\pi = h_{\pi_1}$ and $t_{1\pi} = t_{1\pi_2}$, i.e., leaking information about t_1 alone does not reveal the secret h.

An Event-B model of *split* and *merge* can be seen below. Note that variable *time* is used to ensure event ordering. At time 0, `split` splits the Boolean h into t_1 and t_2. Afterwards, `merge` computes the result r.

```
event split
any c1 c2
where
        @grd1: time = 0          event merge
        @split: c1 XOR c2 = h    when
then                                 @grd1: time ≥ 1
        @act1: time = 1          then
        @act2: t1 = c1               @act1: r = t1 XOR t2
        @act3: t2 = c2               @act2: time = time + 1
end                              end
```

3   Verification in Rodin/Event-B

Verifying HyperLTL properties needs comparing several executions and thus, in the context of Event-B, several copies of the same machine using copies of state variables. This comes to build composed machines, a feature present in the CamilleX [4] plugin. We thus present this plugin and how it can be used to produce proof obligations ensuring some HyperLTL properties.

The CamilleX plugin is a Rodin plugin which brings several syntactic extensions to Event-B among which are machine inclusion and event synchronization.

- machine inclusion: the command **includes** M as $m_1 \ldots m_k$ inserts k copies of M variables and invariants to the current machine, variables of each copy being prefixed by the corresponding alias m_k.
- event synchronization: the command **synchronises** $m_i \cdot e$ called from an event ev where m_i is machine inclusion prefix and e an event of the included machine adds e parameters and guards to ev after prefixing these parameters and the variables referenced by the guards by m_i.

The CamilleX plugin has some limitations we have bypassed through some extensions. The first one concerns the set of copied parameters, guards and invariants. The second one concerns the copy of proofs.

Parameters, Guards and Invariants. The original CamilleX plugin only copies information from the directly included machine. We have modified this behavior as follows: (1) the machine inclusion command copies invariants of (indirectly) refined machines that do not use hidden machine variables. (2) the event synchronization command copies event parameters and guards of the whole chain of event extensions.

It has to be noted that copied invariants are not guaranteed to be preserved both in the original and the modified CamilleX plugins. Their preservation proof in the included machine may depend on the invariants established in the whole chain of refinements. We only copy invariants referring visible variables.

Proofs. We have added to the CamilleX plugin the generation of proofs of the invariants copied from included machines. Consider a machine M as the one given in the next section. The preservation of invariant I by the event ev leads to a proof obligation named ev/I/INV. Consider a machine M1 including two copies of M prefixed m1 and m2 and thus two invariants named m1.I and m2.I. The introduction of the event ev in M1 leads to the generation of two proof obligations named ev/m1.I/INV and ev/m2.I/INV. Their proofs have in fact already been done in machine M up to the renaming of variables V and of M and parameters P of the event ev of M. The copied proofs may be incorrect because they use invariants visible by M and not copied in M1. They are thus replayed.

4   Verification of Hyperproperties with CamilleX

We now use the (extended) CamilleX plugin to build machines in charge of producing proof obligations matching the assertion of the fact that a machine satisfies some HyperLTL properties. The class of properties supported by this methodology should have the shape $M \models \forall^+ \exists^? \Box P$ (any non negative number of universal quantifiers followed by at most one existential quantifier).

Consider the machine M having a set of variables V together with invariants I and an indexed family of events ev_i:

```
machine M   variables V  invariants I
   event evi  when Gi then Ai end
end
```

The universal prefix is obtained through composition: we create the synchronous product of several copies of the machine M to be checked. The optional existential quantifier is managed by refinement, where the machine corresponding to the existential quantification is refined by the synchronous product of several copies of machine M. In order to make the schema simpler, we separate $\forall^+$ and $\forall^+ \exists$ managements.

4.1 $M \models \forall^+ \Box P$ Verification

In order to check the $\forall^+ \Box P$ property over our given machine M, we build a check machine containing two or more independent copies of M state variables together with their invariants. The box property P is added as an invariant over the product state space. To simulate the universal quantifications over the behaviors, a free product of machine events is build: the behavior of the product machine is obtained by independently choosing at each step an event in each machine.

```
machine check includes M as m1 m2
  // two copies of M state variables and invariants
  invariants P(m1_V,m2_V) // property to be proved as invariant
  events // synchronous product (one step in each copy)
    event ev_ij synchronises m1·evi synchronises m2·evj end
end
```

Additional invariants might be required for the proof of the HyperLTL property.

Example 2 (Linear Pipeline). To illustrate the verification of a $\forall\forall$ property, we consider a strongly simplified specification of a linear pipeline and its monotony property. A processor cycle processes a stream of instructions through a sequence of stages. The `pos` variable maps instructions to their stage. Instructions may skip some stages. This feature is described by the `jumps` state variable. It must be seen as an input fixed during machine initialization and left unchanged during execution. A cycle moves instructions to the right while performing jumps as required.

```
machine mRISC sees cGEN // defines State as ℕ₁
  variables pos jumps
  invariants
    @pos pos ∈ 1..LEN ↣ State
    @jumps jumps ∈ 1..LEN → ℙ(State) // skipped states (hits),
    @pos_jumps ∀i·i ∈ 1..LEN ⇒ pos(i) ∉ jumps(i)
  events ...
    event cycle any P where
      @P_ty P ∈ 1..LEN ↣ State
      @P_gt ∀i·i ∈ 1..LEN ⇒ pos(i) < P(i)
      @H_to_P ∀i·i∈1..LEN ⇒ pos(i)+1..P(i)−1 ⊆ jumps(i)
      @at_P ∀i·i∈1..LEN ⇒ P(i) ∉ jumps(i)
    then @npos pos := P end
  end
```

The property to be checked is that if a behavior makes fewer jumps, all the instructions are less advanced in the pipe.

```
machine check sees cGEN includes mRISC as m1 m2
  invariants
    @jumps ∀i·i∈1..LEN ⇒ m1_jumps(i) ⊆ m2_jumps(i)
    @isLate ∀i· i∈1..LEN ⇒ m1_pos(i) ≤ m2_pos(i)
  events
    event INITIALISATION ... end
    event product synchronises m1·cycle synchronises m2·cycle end
  end
```

4.2 $M \models \forall^+\exists\Box P$ Verification

In order to check that M satisfies the hyperproperty $\forall\pi^+\exists\pi'\Box P(V_\pi^+, V_{\pi'})$, we first introduce a **check** machine which represents the product composition of the

$\forall+$ portion (similar to the previous section) and prove that this machine refines the original machine M so that the property P is satisfied at any instant. To find the matching abstract trace, we must provide an event-to-event mapping. The **refines** clause allows specifying such a mapping.

```
machine check refines M includes M as m1 m2
  invariants   P(V+, V) // state-only body of hyper property
  events
    event ev_ij  refines ev_k // selected to get P
    synchronises m1·ev_i // Syncrhonise with the ev_i of m1
    synchronises m2·ev_j // Syncrhonise with the ev_j of m2
    end
end
```

Discharging the proof obligations of the machine **check** guarantees the correctness of the HyperLTL property as refinement proof obligations the existence of an abstract trace linked to the concrete trace through the provided gluing invariant. However, a failure in these proof attempts is inconclusive.

Example 3 (Secret Transfer non-interference). Consider Example 1 and focus on the generalised non-interference property, which can be formalized as $\forall \pi_1 \forall \pi_2 \exists \pi. h_\pi = h_{\pi_1} \wedge t_{1\pi} = t_{1\pi_2}$. We construct a composition machine for π_1 and π_2 and state that it is a refinement of M with the appropriate gluing invariants.

```
machine check refines M includes M as m1 m2
  @glue−h h = m1_h    @glue−t1 t1 = m2_t1
  events
    event m1_split_m2_split  refines split
    synchronises m1· split synchronises m2· split
    with
      @c1 c1 = m2_c1    @c2 c2 = m1_h XOR m2_c1
    end

    event m1_merge_m2_merge refines merge
    synchronises m1·merge synchronises m2·merge end
    ...
end
```

The refinement proof relies on the notion of "witnesses" in Event-B when the hidden bit is split. The witness for $c1$ (which will eventually be the value for $t1$) is chosen the same as $m2\_c1$ (so that the observed bit $t1$ will be the same for π_2 and π). The witness for (hidden) $c2$ is then chosen to ensure that $c1\ XOR\ c2 = m1\_h$ (since the hidden input h is the same for π_1 and π). In general, to prove refinement, it can be necessary to add invariants or revise the abstract model by event splitting.

5   Conclusion

This paper has presented a way to verify HyperLTL properties in the Event-B framework thanks to the use of the CamilleX plugin for building products of Event-B machines. As we have said, our example is strongly simplified. We envision to enrich this work first with respect the instrumentation of the verification of HyperLTL properties and with respect to our initial case study.

Competing Interests. The author(s) has no competing interests to declare that are relevant to the content of this manuscript.

References

1. Clarkson, M.R., Finkbeiner, B., Koleini, M., Micinski, K.K., Rabe, M.N., Sánchez, C.: Temporal logics for hyperproperties. CoRR **abs/1401.4492** (2014). http://arxiv.org/abs/1401.4492
2. Clarkson, M.R., Schneider, F.B.: Hyperproperties. J. Comput. Secur. **18**(6), 1157–1210 (2010). https://doi.org/10.3233/JCS-2009-0393
3. Hoang, T.S., Snook, C., Dghaym, D., Fathabadi, A.S., Butler, M.: The CamilleX framework for the Rodin platform. In: ABZ 2021- 8th International Conference on Rigorous State Based Methods: ABZ 2021 (07/06/21–11/06/21), pp. 124–129, June 2021. https://eprints.soton.ac.uk/448174/
4. Hoang, T.S., Snook, C., Dghaym, D., Fathabadi, A.S., Butler, M.: Building an extensible textual framework for the rodin platform. In: Masci, P., Bernardeschi, C., Graziani, P., Koddenbrock, M., Palmieri, M. (eds.) Software Engineering and Formal Methods. SEFM 2022 Collocated Workshops. SEFM 2022. LNCS, vol. 13765, pp. 132–147. Springer, Cham (2023). https://doi.org/10.1007/978-3-031-26236-4_11
5. Lamport, L.: Specifying Systems: The TLA+ Language and Tools for Hardware and Software Engineers. Addison-Wesley Longman Publishing Co., Inc., USA (2002)
6. Lamport, L., Schneider, F.B.: Verifying hyperproperties with TLA. In: 34th IEEE Computer Security Foundations Symposium, CSF 2021, Dubrovnik, Croatia, 21–25 June 2021, pp. 1–16. IEEE (2021). https://doi.org/10.1109/CSF51468.2021.00012
7. Reineke, J., et al.: A definition and classification of timing anomalies. In: Mueller, F. (ed.) 6th International Workshop on Worst-Case Execution Time (WCET) Analysis, 4 July 2006, Dresden, Germany. OASIcs, vol. 4. Internationales Begegnungs- und Forschungszentrum fuer Informatik (IBFI), Schloss Dagstuhl, Germany (2006). http://drops.dagstuhl.de/opus/volltexte/2006/671

Small Step Incremental Verification of Compilers

Wolf Zimmermann, Thomas Kühn$^{(\boxtimes)}$, Edward Sabinus, and Mandy Weißbach

Institut für Informatik, Martin-Luther-Universität Halle-Wittenberg, 06120
Halle(Saale), Germany
{wolf.zimmermann,thomas.kuehn,edward.sabinus,
mandy.weissbach}@informatik.uni-halle.de

Abstract. Previously, we introduced the idea of agile compiler development, i.e., starting from an initial compiler for the most simple program of a language and extending it in small versions, each introducing a new language concept. Following this idea, in this paper, we propose an approach for incrementally verifying the dynamic semantics specified with abstract state machines (ASMs), such that definitions of previous versions must not be altered in subsequent versions. As a result, the compiler can be verified incrementally without revising the proofs of previous versions. As our first step, in this paper, we formalize and verify the memory mapping of the initial versions with ASMs and discuss their extensibility for the next increments. We plan to demonstrate this approach through the agile implementation and verification of a Sather-K compiler generating MIPS assembly language.

Keywords: Abstract State Machines · Compiler Verification ·
Incremental Development · Dynamic Semantics

1 Introduction

In practice, compilers are developed iteratively [1]. Development starts with an initial version of the compiler for a sub-language which is continuously expanded to include new language concepts until the full language is supported. In theory, a compiler is verified once it is completed, while in practice most compilers continue to grow including new language concepts. Therefore, after each release, the new compiler version must be fully verified again. To remedy this, we proposed the idea of agile compiler development [16], i.e., starting from an initial compiler for the most simple program of a language and extending it in small increments. While the *Initial Version* establishes the whole compiler architecture, each increment $\Delta_{version}$ only adds definitions for a single language concept, e.g., a new statement or operation, without altering previous definitions: $\textbf{Compiler}_{1.0} = (\dots (\textit{Initial Version} + \Delta_{0.1}) + \cdots) + \Delta_{0.n}$. Following this idea, in this paper, we propose an approach for the incremental verification of compilers, such that each new compiler version can be verified incrementally without revising proofs of previous versions.

© The Author(s), under exclusive license to Springer Nature Switzerland AG 2024
S. Bonfanti et al. (Eds.): ABZ 2024, LNCS 14759, pp. 262–269, 2024.
https://doi.org/10.1007/978-3-031-63790-2_21

```
1 class Main is          1 main: SKIP
2    main is end         2       RETURN
3 end -- Main            3 prog: CALL main
```

List. 1: Sather-K program and abstract representation for the *Initial Version*.

Our hypothesis is: **Given** the dynamic semantics of the source language, intermediate languages, and machine languages are incrementally defined in the same increments, whereas definitions of previous versions are **not** revised by following versions. **Then** each compiler version can be verified incrementally without revising proofs of previous versions.

To illustrate our approach, in Sect. 3, we formalize the dynamic semantics of the *Initial Version* of Sather-K [6] and the target assembly language, i.e., MIPS [9], with *Abstract State Machines* (ASMs) [3]. Based on this formalization, we are able to verify the memory mapping of the *Initial Version*. Moreover, in Sect. 4, we discuss how the *Initial Version* can be extended to include *local variables* ($\Delta_{0.1}$) without altering the *Initial Version*. In conclusion, we found that the key property of our formalization is its extensibility, i.e., a formalization that permits the addition of new definitions without affecting existing proofs.

Although we can only propose our approach in this paper, we plan to demonstrate the viability of agile compiler development and the incremental compiler verification by constructing and verifying a compiler from Sather-K to the MIPS assembly language. Sather-K is an object-oriented language with a 35-page language specification [5] featuring many *modern* language concepts, e.g., streams/iterators, subtype inheritance and include inheritance (analogous to module imports). Likewise, the MIPS assembly language is a small yet well documented machine language. Thus far, we have developed the *Initial Version* of the Sather-K compiler accepting the smallest possible program, cf. Listing 1, and we have planned over 200 small step increments.

While we concede that preplanning all increments might be infeasible in general, the careful consideration of the language specification enables incremental compiler development and verification.

2   Background on (Incremental) Compiler Verification

Schellhorn and Ahrendt [14] showcased an approach that systematically investigates the verification of ASMs following an incremental construction process. Starting from an initial ASM capturing the dynamic semantics of Prolog, they refined this ASM in six consecutive steps towards representing the semantics of the Warren Abstract Machine. Similar to our approach, they proved the correctness of each refinement step with invariants upon a one-to-one simulation employing the *Karlsruhe Interactive Verifier*. While they followed a similar approach, they did not attempt applying it to verify the dynamic semantics of a programming language. The *ProCos* approach [8] applies proven algebraic identities during compilation. While they assume that all language concepts are orthogonal, we maintain that concepts, such as, exception handling and explicit return statements, influence the semantics of procedure calls. They applied their approach only to Dijkstra's small guarded command language. In contrast, the *Verifix* project developed approaches to verify realistic compilers [7]. They developed and verified the correctness of the specification and generation/implementation of each compilation phase. In detail, they verified the correctness of the complete back-end employing ASMs. However, they did not construct a fully verified compiler. This was done later by Xavier Leroy with *CompCert* [10]. He constructed a realistic compiler for a sub-language of C producing PowerPC assembly code and proved its correctness completely with the interactive theorem prover *Coq*. Subsequent extensions added new language concepts [2] and optimizations [11,12]. Notably though, these extensions required them to adapt and revise the previous *Coq* theorems and proofs. Similar to *Verifix*, Xavier Leroy's notion of correctness requires that only programs without undefined behavior and violations of resource constraints should be considered correct and thus be compiled. Last but not least, Schmid, Stärk, and Börger proved the correctness of a realistic compiler from *Java* to the *Java Byte Code* [15] running on the *Java Virtual Machine*. Like *Verifix* or *CompCert*, they proved the correctness of each compilation phase. However, they followed an incremental compiler development approach with coarse-grained increments. For each increment, new language concepts were introduced and proven correct. While the static and dynamic semantics was completely specified with ASMs, all proofs were done manually. Fortunately, however, due to their formalization with ASMs most of the theorems and proofs could be reused when proving the next increment. In conclusion, while many approaches have verified realistic compilers, none have considered employing small step compiler construction to construct verified compilers. While all of the above approaches define the language's dynamic semantics, only the ASMs, employed in [7,14,15], have demonstrated their suitability for incremental compiler construction, as they permit the addition of definitions without requiring to revise previous definitions and proofs.

3   Formalization and Verification of the Initial Version

As proposed in [4], we follow the three steps to verify the correctness of the memory mapping of the *Initial Version*. Henceforth, we employ ASMs of the form $ASM \triangleq (\Sigma, I, R)$ with a partial order-sorted signature Σ, a Σ-algebra I (as the *initial state*), and a set of guarded rules R based on [17]. We consider ASMs that execute all applicable rules in parallel, as this permits later addition of new language concepts. We refer the reader to [17] for a more detailed introduction.

Step 1: Dynamic Semantics of the Initial Version. The dynamic semantics of the initial version—$ASM_1 \triangleq (\Sigma_1, I_1, R_1)$—are outlined in Fig. 1. It is limited to the language concepts required to cover the simple main program (cf. Listing 1), i.e., the program PROG, procedures PROC, procedure calls CALL, procedure returns RETURN, and no-operations SKIP. These are all subsorts of NODE, a node of the abstract syntax tree. We employ occurrences

Sorts:

NODE, PROG ⊑ NODE, PROC ⊑ NODE, CALL ⊑ NODE, RETURN ⊑ NODE, NAT, OCC, LOC, ENV, FRM

Static functions:

occ:PROG × OCC →?NODE $first$:PROG → NODE $first$:PROG × PROC → NODE

$next$:PROG × OCC →?OCC $proc$:PROG × OCC →?PROC $qual$:PROG × OCC →?OCC

$push$:ENV × FRM → ENV pop:ENV →?ENV top:ENV →?FRM

$frame$:OCC × OCC × LOC → FRM $length$:ENV → NAT

Dynamic functions: $prog$: PROG env: ENV val: OCC →?LOC ip: OCC

Transition Rules:

if ct **is CALL then**	**if** ct **is RETURN then**	**if** ct **is SKIP then**
$env := push(env, procframe)$	$env := pop(env)$	$ip := next(prog, ip)$
$ip := first(prog, calledproc)$	$ip := getReturn(top(env))$	

$\quad$ **where** $\quad ct \triangleq occ(prog, ip)$ $\qquad calledproc \triangleq proc(prog, ip)$

$\qquad\qquad\qquad obj \triangleq val(qual(prog, ip))$ $\quad procframe \triangleq frame(calledproc, next(prog, ip), obj)$

Initial State:

$\qquad ip := first(prog)$ $\qquad val(m) := null$ $\qquad env := push(createEnv, initframe)$

$\qquad$ **where** $occ(prog,m)$ is main method $\qquad initframe \triangleq frame(first(prog), nil, null)$

Fig. 1. Sketch of ASM_1 for the dynamic semantics of the *Initial Version*.

OCC, introduced in [13], to select specific nodes with the occ function. Henceforth, nil will denote an undefined occurrence. Likewise, the function $first$ yields the first instruction (as occurrence) of a program or procedure. The function $next$ determines the next instruction (as occurrence) to be executed and $proc$ the procedure an instruction belongs to, whereas $qual$ refers to the qualifier (i.e., self) of the procedure being called. The environment ENV represents a stack of frames FRM and provides the usual functions. A frame is created with $frame$ providing the corresponding procedure, the instruction to return to (as occurrence), and the reference to *self* (as location). For brevity, we have omitted the corresponding functions $getProc$, $getReturn$, and $getSelf$, respectively. A state of ASM_1 consists of the $prog$ being executed, the stack of frames env, the current value of the qualifiers of the procedure calls val, and finally the instruction pointer ip referring to the currently executed instruction (as occurrence). Given the simple program (Listing 1), the dynamic semantics of Sather-K starts by initializing the MAIN class and then calling the main method. As this is a static call, the reference self is set to null within the procedure call. After returning from main, the program terminates. In correspondence with this, ASM_1 is initialized by pushing the initial frame $initframe$ on an empty stack $createEnv$. Note, that the qualifier, i.e., self, is set to the location $null$. The semantics of the transition rules simply perform the CALL and RETURN operations, as well as the SKIP no-operation.

Step 2: Dynamic Semantics for the Initial Version Using Concepts of the Target Machine. As our target is a MIPS processor, $ASM_2 \triangleq (\Sigma_2, I_2, R_2)$ (cf. Fig. 2) operates directly on the machine's memory by means of the dynamic function mem assigning values VALUE to ADDR, whereas both are 32-Bit words. Of particular importance here is our mapping of the stack of frames to memory. We use a frame pointer fp and a stack pointer sp as dynamic functions. Figure 3a

Additional sorts: $OCC \sqsubseteq VALUE$, $ADDR \sqsubseteq VALUE$, $BOOL$
Additional static functions: $size : PROC \to NAT$ $isShared : PROC \to BOOL$
Dynamic functions: $prog : PROG$ $mem : ADDR \to VALUE$ $fp : ADDR$ $sp : ADDR$ $ip : OCC$
Transition Rules:

if ct **is CALL** $\wedge$ $(sp - framesize > min)$ **then**   **if** ct **is RETURN then**   **if** ct **is SKIP then**
$\quad mem(fp - framesize) := sp$ $\quad sp := fp + framesize$ $\quad ip := next(prog, ip)$
$\quad mem(fp - framesize + 4) := next(prog, ip)$ $\quad fp := mem(fp)$
$\quad fp := fp - framesize$ $\quad ip := mem(fp + 4)$
$\quad sp := sp - framesize$ **if** ct **is CALL** $\wedge$ $(sp - framesize > min)$ $\wedge$
$\quad ip := first(proc(prog, ip))$ $\quad isShared(proc(prog, ip))$ **then**
$\quad$**where** $framesize \triangleq size(proc(prog, ip))$ $\quad mem(fp - framesize + 8) := 0$

Initial State: $ip := first(prog)$ $fp := base$ $sp := base - 4$
$\quad mem(base) := bos$ $mem(base + 4) := nil$ $mem(base + 8) := 0$
$\quad$**where** $base \triangleq bos - size(prog)$

Fig. 2. Sketch of ASM_2 for the dynamic semantics of the *Initial Version* using concepts of the target machine.

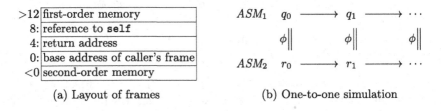

>12	first-order memory
8:	reference to **self**
4:	return address
0:	base address of caller's frame
<0	second-order memory

(a) Layout of frames   (b) One-to-one simulation

Fig. 3. Memory layout of frames in ASM_2 (a) and one-to-one simulation (b).

shows the general layout of each frame. Note, that both the first and second-order memory is not used in the *Initial Version*. Moreover, in MIPS addresses are signed integers and the stack grows downwards. Each frame contains the frame pointer of the caller, the return address, and a reference to self, as well as second-order memory for storing, for instance, spill code. The static function *size* determines the size (in Bytes) of the frame. In this version $size(m)$ is 12 for any **main** method m, however, in later versions each frame size depends on the called procedure. Note that the program *prog* and the instruction pointer *ip* remain unchanged.

The transition rules in Fig. 2 of ASM_2 operate directly on the memory by manipulating fp and sp, such that CALL and RETURN reflect the behavior of pushing onto and popping off the stack, respectively. Notably, two rules handle procedure calls. The first rule checks, if enough memory is available on the stack. Here, *min* denotes the smallest available address. The second rule sets **self** to 0, when a static procedure (or shared procedure in Sather-K) is called. In a later version, an additional rule would be added to set **self** when calling a non-static procedure (object method). In contrast to the initial state of ASM_1, ASM_2 writes the initial frame (*initframe*) directly to memory, starting from the *base* address, whereas the bottom of the stack (*bos*) denotes the address of the initial frame.

Step 3: Proving that ASM_2 one-to-one Simulates ASM_1. Finally, the states of ASM_2 must be mapped to the states of ASM_1, so that their runs

$$\phi \triangleq Inv_1 \wedge Inv_2 \wedge Inv_3 \wedge Inv_4$$
$$Inv_1 \triangleq \forall i : \mathsf{NAT} \bullet i < length(env) \Rightarrow getReturn(top(pop^i(env))) = mem(mem^i(fp) + 4)$$
$$Inv_2 \triangleq \forall i : \mathsf{NAT} \bullet i < length(env) \Rightarrow addr(getSelf(top(pop^i(env))) = mem(mem^i(fp) + 8)$$
$$Inv_3 \triangleq \forall i : \mathsf{NAT} \bullet i < length(env) - 1 \Rightarrow mem^i(fp) + size(getProc(top(pop^i(env)))) < mem^{i+1}(fp)$$
$$Inv_4 \triangleq sp < fp \wedge \exists i : \mathsf{NAT} \bullet mem^i(fp) = bos$$
$$\mathbf{where}\ op^i(p) \triangleq \underbrace{op(\dots(op(p)))}_{i-times}\ \text{for operations}\ op : \mathsf{T} \to \mathsf{T}$$

Fig. 4. Invariants between ASM_1 and ASM_2.

Additional Sorts: LOCALDECL $\sqsubseteq$ NODE, IDENT, VALUE
Additional static functions:

$identifier$:PROG $\times$ OCC $\to$?IDENT $bind$:FRAME $\times$ IDENT $\times$ LOC $\to$ ENV

$getBinding$:FRAME $\times$ IDENT $\to$?LOC

Additional dynamic functions: $alloc$: LOC $\to$?VALUE
Additional transition Rules:

if ct **is** LOCALDECL **then**
  choose l : LOC $\bullet$ $alloc(l) = \bot$ **from**
    $env := push(pop(env), bind(top(env), name, l))$
    $alloc(l) := 0$
    $ip := next(prog, ip)$

if ct **is** RETURN **then**
  forall id : IDENT$\bullet$
    $getBinding(top(env), id) \neq \bot$ **do**
    $alloc(getBinding(top(env), id)) := \bot$
    where $name \triangleq identifier(prog, ip)$

Fig. 5. Increment $\Delta_{0.1}$ adding local variables to the *Initial Version*.

---

are a one-to-one simulation, illustrated in Fig. 3b, upto violation of memory limitations. For instance, if ASM_2 ends in a stack overflow exhausting all memory, ASM_1 would continue regardless. The relation ϕ, depicted in Fig. 4, relates the states of ASM_1 and ASM_2, i.e., it uses sorts and functions of both ASMs. In detail, ϕ is defined as the conjunction of four propositional formula. The first two ensure that both the return address of each caller and `self` are stored at relative address four and eight, respectively. In contrast, Inv_3 ensures that two frames do not overlap in memory. Last but not least, Inv_4 specifies that the stack pointer refers to a free address and that the chain of base addresses (relative address 0) will eventually reach the bottom of the stack bos.

For a formal proof we join the two ASMs, whereas the joined ASM is defined as: $ASM_1 \oplus ASM_2 \triangleq (\Sigma_1 \cup \Sigma_2, I_1 \oplus I_2, R_1 \cup R_2)$. Here $I_1 \oplus I_2 \triangleq \{q \in \mathsf{Alg}(\Sigma)\ |\ q|_{\Sigma_1} \in I_1 \wedge q|_{\Sigma_2} \in I_2\}$ denotes the joined initial states. The ASMs are *joinable*, because the joined initial state is non-empty $I_1 \oplus I_2 \neq \emptyset$. The simulation relation ϕ can now be treated as invariant of the joined ASM. The proof then boils down to first proving the consistency of $ASM_1 \oplus ASM_2$ and then showing that the invariant $q_0 \models \phi$ holds in the initial state $q_0 \in I_1 \oplus I_2$ and $q' \models \phi$ holds for all reachable successor states q' of q with $q \models \phi$. The proofs have been omitted, due to the lack of space.

4 Discussion of Incremental Compiler Verification

To illustrate the extensibility of the dynamic semantics and incremental verification, we add *local variables* as the first increment in $\Delta_{0.1}$. As ASMs permit extending both the state space, i.e., introducing static and dynamic functions, and the initial state, as well as adding new transition rules. Figure 5
shows the additions to ASM_1 needed to introduce *local variables*. Local declarations LOCALDECL non-deterministically selects a currently unallocated location LOC (denoted as $alloc(l) = \bot$), adds the corresponding binding *bind* to the
current frame $(top(env))$, allocates the location assigning the default value 0,
and advances the instruction pointer *ip*. Upon returning from a method call
RETURN, all locations of bindings $(getBinding)$ of the current frame $(top(env))$
are selected and deallocated (set to $\bot$). However, we need to add new equations
to the static functions *getProc*, *getReturn*, and *getSelf* to unravel all bindings,
e.g.,$getProc(bind(f, n, l)) = getProc(f)$. Similarly, ASM_2 is expanded to store
local variables in first-order memory. For brevity, we have omitted the corresponding additional definitions. In fact, all previous definitions of ASM_1 and
ASM_2 do not need to be revised. Notably though, we have to specify a new
invariant Inv_5 between both extensions. This invariant ensures that all allocated
locations, when mapped to memory, do not coincide with addresses where a
frame pointer, a return address or a reference to `self` is stored.

   To prove the memory mapping of this increment, first the extended ASMs
must be joined, i.e. $ASM_1' \oplus ASM_2'$. Then the consistency of the joined ASM
must be checked, and finally every reachable state q of the joined ASM must
$q \models \phi \wedge Inv_5$. While the consistency of the joined ASM must still be verified
wrt. all reachable states, existing proofs $q \models \phi$ must still hold for all reachable
states q. Thus, it is sufficient, to only proof that $q \models Inv_5$ holds for every
reachable state q of the joined ASM. This, in turn, drastically reduces the effort
to verify a compiler as previous proofs are maintained. Granted, this requires
meticulous planning of each increment wrt. the language specification, such that
no revision of previously introduced definitions is needed. However, whenever
existing proofs fail, the last increment was the cause.

5 Conclusions

In this paper, we have shown the first steps in verifying the memory mapping
of the initial version of our Sather-K compiler and discussed its extensibility to
subsequent versions. In detail, we argued that formalizing the dynamic semantics
and memory mapping by means of ASMs permits their subsequent extension.
While we concede that this approach requires effort to plan the increments, we
maintain that the benefits of small step incremental compiler verification are
well worth it. As we have just started this research project, we see several major
challenges ahead, e.g., extensible incremental verification of the static semantics. Moreover, we will create and verify further refinements of ASM_2 towards
the targeted machine language. Furthermore, we aim to create tool support for
checking an ASM's consistency proving whether invariants hold.

Acknowledgements. We would like to thank the three anonymous reviewers for their valuable feedback.

Competing Interests. The author(s) has no competing interests to declare that are relevant to the content of this manuscript.

References

1. Basil, V.R., Turner, A.J.: Iterative enhancement: a practical technique for software development. IEEE Trans. Softw. Eng. **SE-1**(4), 390–396 (1975)
2. Boldo, S., Jourdan, J.-H., Leroy, X., Melquiond, G.: Verified compilation of floating-point computations. J. Autom. Reason. **54**, 135–163 (2015)
3. Börger, E.: Abstract state machines: a unifying view of models of computation and of system design frameworks. Ann. Pure Appl. Log. **133**(1–3), 149–171 (2005)
4. Glesner, S., Goos, G., Zimmermann, W.: Verifix: Konstruktion und Architektur verifizierender Übersetzer (Verifix: Construction and architecture of verifying compilers). IT-Inf. Technol. **46**(5), 265–276 (2004)
5. Goos, G.: Sather-k. Technical report, Universität Karlsruhe, Fakultät für Informatik, 1996. Revised Report with Heinz Schmidt
6. Goos, G.: Sather-K - the language. Software-Concepts Tools **18**(3), 91–109 (1997)
7. Goos, G., Zimmermann, W.: Verification of compilers. Correct System Design: Recent Insights and Advances, p. 201 (1999)
8. Hoare, C.A.R., Jifeng, H., Sampaio, A.: Normal form approach to compiler design. Acta Informatica **30**, 701–739 (1993)
9. Kane, G., Heinrich, J.: MIPS RISC Architectures. Prentice-Hall, Inc., Hoboken (1992)
10. Leroy, X.: Formal verification of a realistic compiler. Commun. ACM **52**(7), 107–115 (2009)
11. Monniaux, D., Six, C.: Formally verified loop-invariant code motion and assorted optimizations. ACM Trans. Embed. Comput. Syst. **22**(1), 1–27 (2022)
12. Mullen, E., Zuniga, D., Tatlock, Z., Grossman, D.: Verified peephole optimizations for compcert. In: Proceedings of the 37th Conference on Programming Language Design and Implementation, pp. 448–461. ACM (2016)
13. Poetzsch-Heffter, A.: Developing efficient interpreters based on formal language specifications. In: Fritzson, P.A. (ed.) CC 1994. LNCS, vol. 786, pp. 233–247. Springer, Heidelberg (1994). https://doi.org/10.1007/3-540-57877-3_16
14. Schellhorn, G., Ahrendt, W.: Reasoning about abstract state machines: the WAM case study. J. Univers. Comput. Sci. **3**(4), 377–413 (1997)
15. Stärk, R.F., Schmid, J., Borger, E.: Java and the Java Virtual Machine: Definition, Verification, Validation. Springer, Berlin, Heidelberg (2012). https://doi.org/10.1007/978-3-642-59495-3
16. Zimmermann, W., Kühn, T., Weißbach, M.: Developing efficient interpreters based on formal language specifications. In: 22. Kolloquium Programmiersprachen und Grundlagen der Programmierung, pp. 176–183. RWTH Aachen University (2023)
17. Zimmermann, W., Weißbach, M.: A framework for modeling the semantics of synchronous and asynchronous procedures with abstract state machines. In: Raschke, A., Riccobene, E., Schewe, K.-D. (eds.) Logic, Computation and Rigorous Methods. LNCS, vol. 12750, pp. 326–352. Springer, Cham (2021). https://doi.org/10.1007/978-3-030-76020-5_18

Designing Exception Handling Using Event-B

Asieh Salehi Fathabadi[(✉)] [iD], Colin Snook[iD], Thai Son Hoang[iD],
Robert Thorburn[iD], Michael Butler[iD], Leonardo Aniello[iD],
and Vladimiro Sassone[iD]

School of Electronics and Computer Science (ECS), University of Southampton,
Southampton, UK
{a.salehi-fathabadi,cfs,t.s.hoang,robert.thorburn,
m.j.butler,l.aniello,vsassone}@soton.ac.uk

Abstract. The design of exception handling is a complex task requiring insight and domain expertise to ensure that potential abnormal conditions are identified and a recovery process is designed to return the system to a safe state. Formal methods can address this complexity, by supporting the analysis of exception handling at the abstract design stages utilising mathematical modelling and proofs.

Event-B is a state-based formal method for modelling and verifying the consistency of discrete systems. However it lacks explicit support for analysing the handling of exceptions. In this paper, we use UML-B state machines to support the modelling of normal behaviour assisting the identification and handling of exceptions. This is followed by verification of exception handler recovery mechanisms using the built-in model checker and provers of the Event-B tool-set.

1 Introduction

Programming languages offer exception handling for responding to detected failures. Exception handling is a complex and error prone activity, and systematic reasoning is needed to identify and characterise exceptions. The formal analysis of the exceptional control flow provides a means to validate the exception handling design [6]. However, formal methods lack explicit support to specify exception handling behaviour. This paper proposes an approach to systematic reasoning about exception handling at the design level using the Event-B formal method.

Event-B [2] is a formal method to model and verify correctness of safety/security critical systems. While exception handling can be modelled within the existing features of Event-B toolkit, there is no explicit support for it. We use UML-B [9] to visualise the normal expected behaviour of a system and add support for handling exceptions in safety/security systems from the design level to the implementation. Our work is influenced by considering implementations on *capability hardware* which provides hardware level protection against incorrect memory access [11]. Capability hardware blocks unauthorised memory access

S. Bonfanti et al. (Eds.): ABZ 2024, LNCS 14759, pp. 270–277, 2024.
https://doi.org/10.1007/978-3-031-63790-2_22

at runtime, raising hardware exceptions that should be handled by application code. Unauthorised memory access might be caused by unintentional coding errors, e.g., out of bounds array access, or malicious attacks, e.g., buffer overflow exploitation. In principle, code that is developed formally will be free from incorrect memory access. However, we assume the applications we develop will operate in software environments where vulnerabilities remain, e.g., through use of use of untrusted libraries.

We illustrate our approach using a Smart Ballot System (SBB) [1], an integral part of some modern voting systems. Earlier research work [8] presented a correct-by-construction secure SBB system using Event-B. Our proposed approach can address the robustness of SBB model in [8].

The paper, is structured as follows. Section 2 introduces Event-B and the SBB case study. Our proposed approach is outlined in Sect. 3 followed by application of our approach in the SBB case study, Sect. 5 and Sect. 5. Finally Sect. 6 concludes including summarising related works and directions for future works.

2   Background

Event-B [2] is a refinement-based formal method for system development. The mathematical language of Event-B is based on set theory and first order logic. An Event-B model consists of two parts: *contexts* for static data and *machines* for dynamic behaviour. Contexts contain carrier sets, constants, and axioms that constrain the carrier sets and constants. Machines contain variables, invariant predicates that constrain the variables, and events. In Event-B, a machine corresponds to a transition system where *variables* represent the states and *events* specify the transitions. An event comprises a guard denoting its enabling-condition and an action describing how the variables are modified when the event is executed.

Event-B is supported by the Rodin[1] tool set [3], an extensible open source toolkit which includes facilities for modelling, verifying the consistency of models using theorem proving and model checking techniques. In this paper we make extensive use of the UML-B plug-in [10] extend the Rodin. UML-B [9] provides a diagrammatic modelling notation for Event-B in the form of state machines and class diagrams, which automatically generate the Event-B data elements.

SBB (Smart Ballot Box) [1] is to inspect a ballot paper by detecting a barcode, decode it and evaluate if the decoded contents verifies the paper. If the ballot is valid, then it can be cast into the storage box. Otherwise, the SBB rejects the paper, that will be ejected. The key function of the SBB is to ensure that only valid countable summary ballot documents that can be tabulated later are included in ballot boxes.

---

[1] The formal modelling tools used, are available as bundled installation packages via https://www.uml-b.org/Downloads.html.

3   Overview of Approach

This section gives an outline of our suggested approach to analyse exceptions, and their associated recovery mechanisms, during systems modelling.

To consider exceptions at the formal design level, we propose the steps below:

– Build a state-machine to model normal behaviour (without exceptions). External controlled machinery can be modelled by other state-machines that synchronise via guards and synchronised transitions. Additional (ancillary) variables are added to model details maintained by the control system. Safety, security and other consistency properties are expressed as state invariants. Typically, these are expected values of machinery and ancillary variables in each control state.
– verify the normal-behaviour in the absence of exceptions (i.e. prove the invariant properties about the system).
– For each state in the state-machine, identify potential abnormal behaviour resulting in exceptions.
– For each exception, specify a corresponding recovery state to go to when the exception occurs in that occurrence state.
– Attempt to verify that the system invariants still hold even with abnormal behaviour.
– When an invariant cannot be verified it may be because the recovery state is inappropriate. For example, does not allow external machinery to return to an appropriate state. If so, change the recovery state or introduce new recovery states specifically to address this.
– When an invariant cannot be verified it may be because changes to ancillary variables need to be reverted due to the aborted process. If so, add roll-back actions to the exception handler for these specific cases.

These steps are presented through the SBB case study: Sect. 5 presents the normal behaviour model of the SBB as the first step and Sect. 5 presents the proposed exception handling approach within the rest of the above steps.

4   Case Study: SBB Normal-Behaviour

Utilising UML-B, we model the SBB normal behaviour (without exceptions) as a state-machine (Fig. 1).

The normal-behaviour SBB case, presented in Fig. 1, starts in the Waiting state and, in the case of accepting the ballot, progresses through the following sequence of states: Waiting, BarcodeReading, BarcodeProcessing, UserSelection, PrepareAccepting, Accepting, Waiting. There are 2 ancilliary variables which are not shown in the state-machine but contained in the Event-B model. These are a count of the votes cast by the user (incremented by the transition USER_cast) and a count of the papers accepted by the roller (incremented by the transition ROLLER_accept_paper). The Waiting state contains two invariant properties which are expected to hold when the SBB is in the Waiting state:

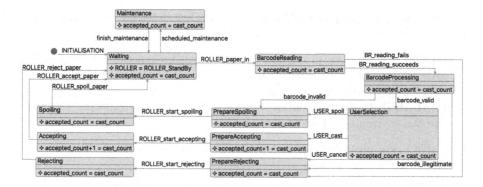

Fig. 1. State Machine, normal-behaviour SBB

- The roller should be in the state ROLLER_Standby so that it is ready to take another paper.
- The count of votes cast by the user should be the same as the count of papers accepted by the roller.

The invariants in the other states are needed to help the provers prove the second of these invariants. The proofs are automatically discharged by the Rodin provers.

In order to encode the state machines in Event-B, the UML-B tools automatically generate sets, constants and axioms in a newly generated context component. The SBB states are an enumeration of a carrier set which is encoded via a generated partition axiom as below. Each state (Waiting, BarcodeReading, ...), is specified as a *constant* and the set of states, SBB_STATES, are specified as an axiom using *carrier sets*:

```
@axm1:  partition(SBB_STATES, {Waiting}, {BarcodeReading}, {BarcodeProcessing},
        {UserSelection}, {Accepting}, {Spoiling}, {Rejecting}, {PrepareRejecting}, {PrepareSpoiling},
        {PrepareAccepting})
```

The dynamic behaviour of the state machine (Fig. 1), is generated as part of the containing machine component. Each event that represents a transition, checks, within its guards, that the current state of the SBB is the transition source state, and changes the state to the transition target state, within its actions. For example:

```
event ROLLER_paper_in when @grd1: SBB =Waiting @grd2: ROLLER =ROLLER_StandBy
then @act1: SBB :=BarcodeReading @act2: ROLLER :=ROLLER_PaperIn end

event BR_reading_succeeds when @grd1: SBB =BarcodeReading @grd2: Exceptions =Normal
then @act1: SBB :=BarcodeProcessing end
```

5 Case Study: SBB Exceptional-Behaviour

We consider two types of exception; an invalid memory access which could be caused by a security attack and a timeout when an external actor or machine does not provide a response. These exceptions are detected by the following interrupt signals:

- SIGPROT: a memory protection exception can be generated by capability hardware [11] when a pointer is used outside of its protected range (representing a possible memory attack).
- SIGALARM: timeout exception can be raised when an expected response from the environment fails to occur within a time limit.

The table below outlines these potential exceptions and their handling mechanisms within the SBB system:

Exception	Signal	States	Handling	Rollback
Memory protection error	SIGPROT	BarcodeReading, BarcodeProcessing, UserSelection	reject ballot	–
User does not enter selection	SIGALRM	UserSelection	reject ballot	–
Roller jammed	SIGALRM	Accepting	maintenance	cast count
Roller jammed	SIGALRM	Spoiling, Rejecting	maintenance	–

An attack on the software resulting in a SIGPROT interrupt is most likely to occur when the barcode reading subsystem is active and the safe handling response is to cancel and reject the ballot. When the user does not respond with a decision a SIGALRM interrupt is generated and again the safe handling response is to cancel and reject the ballot. It is also possible for the roller mechanism to malfunction and not confirm its completion, resulting in a SIGALRM interrupt. However, the ballot cannot be rejected as a response to this exception because it would involve the faulty roller. Instead a maintenance mode is entered to allow human intervention to correct the roller and reject the ballot. In the case where the roller was in the process of accepting a ballot an additional rollback action is needed because the users cast decision has already been counted but the ballot will now be rejected. To maintain consistency (and the invariant of the waiting state), the cast count must be decremented as part of the exception handling before the maintenance state is entered.

We extend our Event-B model to include the abnormal behaviour of exceptions as follows: SIGNAL is a set consisting of the types of interrupting signals (SIGPROT and SIGALRM). For each signal type, we specify a handling state that should be entered in order to recover from each state the signal could occur in. This is a constant partial function from SBB_STATES to SBB_STATES: A further constant function, signalHandling, gives the Handling function to be used for each signal. The values of these signal handling functions for the SBB are defined directly as axioms:

axm3: SIGPROT_Handling ={
    BarcodeReading ↦PrepareRejecting,
    BarcodeProcessing ↦PrepareRejecting,
    UseSelection ↦PrepareRejecting}

axm4: SIGALRM_Handling ={
    UseSelection ↦PrepareRejecting,
    Spoiling ↦Maintenance,
    Accepting ↦Maintenance,
    Rejecting ↦Maintenance}

The event exception_handler represents the occurrence of an exception:

event exception_handler any s
where @grd1: s ∈dom(signalHandling) @grd2: SBB ∈dom(signalHandling(s))
then @act1: SBB :=signalHandling(s)(SBB) end

Since the new event changes the state of the state-machine, the tools generate proof obligations to ensure that the state invariants concerning cast_count and accepted_count are respected. Most of these can be discharged by guiding the prover to show that there are no cases that enter the state containing that invariant or that the property was already true in the occurrence state. (We split the event into the two cases of s (s = SIGPROT and s = SIGALRM) and added theorems concerning the possible values of SBB and signalHandling(s)(SBB) for that case. This enabled the proofs to be automatically discharged). However, there remained one case (s = SIGALRM, SBB = Accepting) that was not proved and this corresponds to the case where we need to add a rollback of the cast_count. Hence the Event-B verification identifies any missing rollback actions and discovers the exact case where they are needed.

Other state invariants may identify inappropriate handling recovery states. For example, initially, we specified a recovery from a SIGPROT exception occuring in BarcodeReading directly to Waiting and imagine a transition from BarcodeReading to Waiting), the ROLLER would be left in the state ROLLER_PaperIn violating the safety invariant. We could not prove this unsafe design (the proof obligation could not be discharged) and we discovered a counter-example using the ProB model checker. Since the Roller is an external system it cannot be easily changed like the cast_count. Changing the recovery state from BarcodeReading to PrepareRejecting allows the ROLLER sub-system to reject the paper before the controller returns to Waiting, thereby maintaining a verified safe system.

6   Conclusion and Future Direction

This paper outlines an approach to analysing systematic exception handling and recovery at a formal systems design level. The proposed approach utilises UML-B state machines augmented by systematic identification and handling of exceptions in Event-B. We extend normal behavioural modelling and formal verification to address exceptional behaviour and recovery responses to bring the system back to a safe state according to system invariant properties. By considering exception handling in an abstract formal model of the complete system (i.e. a closed incorporating the controller and its environment including the controlled subsystems) we are able to verify that the chosen recovery mechanisms do not violate any safety properties. If we were to leave this verification to an implementation level (e.g. code) it would be more difficult to provide this level of verification since the controlled external environment would not be represented in a format that can be analysed.

To address the exception handling mechanism in different domains, related attempts have been presented before. [7] extends ERS (Event Refinement Structure) to introduce the interrupt and retry operators in Event-B. [5] and [4] formally define BPEL (Business Process Execution Language) compensation mechanisms using Event-B, focusing on the role of Event-B invariants during refinement. The research work presented in this paper, elaborates the existing state machine feature and automatic transformation to Event-B model to support explicit exception handling.

It is important to assure that the verified model is reflected in an implementation. Our future aim is to generate C code to implement the application functionality and exception handling based on signals as defined in UNIX systems. The implementation is derivable from our UML-B/Event-B models in a straightforward methodical way that could be mechanised with tool support.

Acknowledgement. This work is supported byHD-Sec project, which was funded by the Digital Security by Design (DSbD) Programme delivered by UKRI to support the DSbD ecosystem.

Competing Interests. The author(s) has no competing interests to declare that are relevant to the content of this manuscript.

References

1. Galois and Free & Fair. The BESSPIN Voting System. https://github.com/GaloisInc/BESSPIN-Voting-System-Demonstrator-2019. Accessed 07 Feb 2024
2. Abrial, J.R.: Modeling in Event-B: System and Software Engineering. Cambridge University Press, Cambridge (2010)
3. Abrial, J.R., Butler, M., Hallerstede, S., Hoang, T.S., Mehta, F., Voisin, L.: Rodin: an open toolset for modelling and reasoning in Event-B. Int. J. Softw. Tools Technol. Transf. **12**(6), 447–466 (2010)
4. Ait-Sadoune, I., Ait-Ameur, Y.: Formal modelling and verification of transactional web service composition: a refinement and proof approach with Event-B. In: Thalheim, B., Schewe, K.-D., Prinz, A., Buchberger, B. (eds.) Correct Software in Web Applications and Web Services. TMSC, pp. 1–27. Springer, Cham (2015). https://doi.org/10.1007/978-3-319-17112-8_1
5. Babin, G., Ameur, Y.A., Pantel, M.: Web service compensation at runtime: formal modeling and verification using the Event-B refinement and proof based formal method. IEEE Trans. Serv. Comput. **10**(1), 107–120 (2017)
6. Brito, P.H.S., de Lemos, R., Rubira, C.M.F., Martins, E.: Architecting fault tolerance with exception handling: verification and validation. J. Comput. Sci. Technol. **24**(2), 212–237 (2009)
7. Dghaym, D., Butler, M.J., Fathabadi, A.S.: Extending ERS for modelling dynamic workflows in Event-B. In: 22nd International Conference on Engineering of Complex Computer Systems, ICECCS 2017, Fukuoka, Japan, 5–8 November 2017, pp. 20–29. IEEE Computer Society (2017)

8. Dghaym, D., Hoang, T.S., Butler, M., Hu, R., Aniello, L., Sassone, V.: Verifying system-level security of a smart ballot box. In: Raschke, A., Méry, D. (eds.) ABZ 2021. LNCS, vol. 12709, pp. 34–49. Springer, Cham (2021). https://doi.org/10.1007/978-3-030-77543-8_3

9. Snook, C.F., Butler, M.J.: UML-B: formal modeling and design aided by UML. ACM Trans. Softw. Eng. Methodol. **15**(1), 92–122 (2006)

10. Snook, C., Butler, M.: UML-B: a plug-in for the Event-B tool set. In: Börger, E., Butler, M., Bowen, J.P., Boca, P. (eds.) ABZ 2008. LNCS, vol. 5238, pp. 344–344. Springer, Heidelberg (2008). https://doi.org/10.1007/978-3-540-87603-8_32

11. Watson, R.N.M., et al.: CHERI: a hybrid capability-system architecture for scalable software compartmentalization. In: 2015 IEEE Symposium on Security and Privacy, SP 2015, San Jose, CA, USA, pp. 20–37. IEEE Computer Society (2015)

Case Study

The Mechanical Lung Ventilator Case Study

Silvia Bonfanti$^{(\boxtimes)}$ and Angelo Gargantini

University of Bergamo, Bergamo, Italy
{silvia.bonfanti,angelo.gargantini}@unibg.it

Abstract. This paper introduces the ABZ 2024 Case Study: Mechanical Lung Ventilator (MLV), inspired by the Mechanical Ventilator Milano developed during COVID-19. The case study reports the specification of the Mechanical Lung Ventilator used to ventilate patients who are not able to breathe on their own or need ventilation support. Expected contributions to the case study include, among others, modeling, validation and verification, management of temporal behavior, modeling of the graphical user interface or automatically generating executable source code.

Keywords: ABZ · State Based Formal Methods · Mechanical Lung Ventilator · Case Study

1 Introduction

At the beginning of the COVID-19 pandemic, the region around Bergamo, where ABZ 2024 took place, was hit very hard by COVID-19, as suggested by the high number of hospitalizations and deaths. During those days, a group of researchers was involved in the design, development, and certification of an electro-mechanical lung ventilator called MVM (Mechanical Ventilator Milano)[1] [1]. The project started from the idea of the physicist Cristiano Galbiati, who was soon joined by dozens of physicists, engineers, physicians, and computer scientists from 12 countries around the world[2]. The team was able to realize a ventilator that is reliable, easily reproducible on a large scale, available in a short amount of time, and at a limited cost [4,7]. The MVM has obtained the FDA (Food and Drug Administration) Emergency Use Authorization (EUA) followed by authorizations issued by Health Canada and the CE marking.

The specification of the mechanical lung ventilator chosen as case study for ABZ 2024, is inspired by MVM, with some simplifications to make it suitable as a case study:

---

[1] https://mvm.care/.

[2] At that period, many projects on mechanical ventilator started, but only a few get certified https://github.com/PubInv/covid19-vent-list.

© The Author(s), under exclusive license to Springer Nature Switzerland AG 2024
S. Bonfanti et al. (Eds.): ABZ 2024, LNCS 14759, pp. 281–288, 2024.
https://doi.org/10.1007/978-3-031-63790-2_23

- we have removed one component, the supervisor which was responsible for monitoring the controller, the GUI, and the hardware. In the case of errors, it raises alarms if not already raised by the controller or the GUI, ensuring patient safety.
- we use only visual alarms, instead of audio and visual alarms.

The requirement specification for the ABZ 2024 Case Study is available here [3]. That document is NOT intended to be used as software requirements specification of a real ventilator.

Note that this case study is one of those proposed by the ABZ conference, all the case studies can be found here: https://abz-conf.org/case-studies/.

2   Mechanical Lung Ventilator

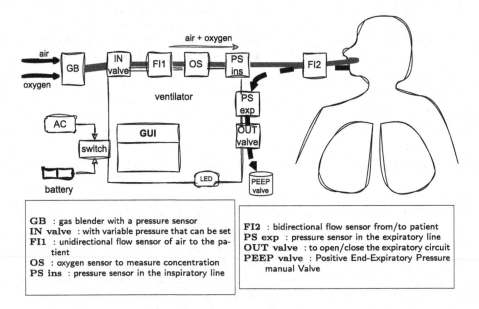

GB : gas blender with a pressure sensor	**FI2** : bidirectional flow sensor from/to patient
IN valve : with variable pressure that can be set	**PS exp** : pressure sensor in the expiratory line
FI1 : unidirectional flow sensor of air to the patient	**OUT valve** : to open/close the expiratory circuit
OS : oxygen sensor to measure concentration	**PEEP valve** : Positive End-Expiratory Pressure manual Valve
PS ins : pressure sensor in the inspiratory line	

Fig. 1. High level view of ventilator sensors

The mechanical lung ventilator is intended to ventilate patients in intensive therapy who require mechanical ventilation [8]. The ventilator proposed for the ABZ 2024 Case Study works in pressure mode, i.e., the respiratory time cycle of the patient is controlled by pressure, and, therefore, this ventilator requires a source of compressed oxygen and medical air readily available in intensive care units.

The overall structure of the ventilator proposed by the case study is depicted in Fig. 1. The pressurized air enters the inspiration circuit (continuous line) and is mixed with the oxygen. Its flux is controlled by a valve (IN) and monitored by several sensors. The air enters the breathing circuit with a flux monitored (by FI2), then, after being inspired by the lungs, it expires and exits the breathing circuit (dashed arrow) with its pressure monitored by a sensor (PS exp) and controlled by two valves, one (OUT valve) is controlled by the machine while the other (PEEP) is manually set to provide a constant Positive End-Expiratory Pressure.

2.1   Ventilation Modes

By alternating the opening and closing of the two valves, the MLV governs the entering/exiting flux and air pressure in the lungs. More precisely, the ventilator has two operative modes: *Pressure Controlled Ventilation* (PCV) and *Pressure Support Ventilation* (PSV). In the PCV mode, the respiratory cycle is kept constant and the pressure level changes between the target inspiratory pressure (P_{insp}) and the positive end-expiratory pressure (PEEP). New inspiration is initiated either after a breathing cycle is over, or when the patient spontaneously initiates a breath. In the former case, the breathing cycle is controlled by two parameters: the respiratory rate (RR) and the ratio between the inspiratory and expiratory times (I:E). In the latter case, a spontaneous breath is triggered when the ventilator detects a sudden pressure drop within the trigger window during expiration. The PSV mode is unsuitable for patients who are not able to start breathing on their own. The respiratory cycle is controlled by the patient, and the ventilator partially takes over the work of breathing. A new respiratory cycle is initiated with the inspiratory phase, detected by the ventilator when a sudden pressure drop occurs. When the patient's inspiratory flow drops below a set fraction of the peak flow, the ventilator stops the pressure support, thus allowing exhalation. If a new inspiratory phase is not detected within a certain amount of time (apnea lag), the ventilator will automatically switch to the PCV mode because it is assumed that the patient is not able to breathe alone.

The ventilator allows the air to enter/exit through two valves, i.e., an input valve and an output valve. When the ventilator is not running, the valves are set to safe mode: the input valve is closed and the output valve is opened. In this configuration, the ventilator does not prevent breathing thanks to some relief valves.

When the inspiration starts, the input valve is opened and the output valve is closed, while during the expiration the input valve is closed and the output valve is opened. Both in PCV and PSV mode, inspiratory pause, expiratory pause, and recruitment maneuver are allowed by user request. Inspiratory/Expiratory pause consists in closing the input and output valves of the ventilator respectively after the inspiration and expiration phases. The inspiratory pause allows measuring the pressure reached inside the alveoli at the end of the inspiratory cycle, while the expiratory pause allows measuring the residual pressure to check possible obstruction in the exhalation channel. The recruitment maneuver is an emergency procedure required after intubation, and it consists of prolonged lung inflation as necessary to reactivate the alveoli immediately; during this maneuver, the input valve is opened and the output valve is closed.

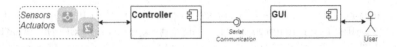

Fig. 2. The high-level software architecture

2.2 Software Architecture

The high-level software architecture, shown in Fig. 2, illustrates the communication among the software components: graphical user interface (GUI) and controller. The GUI is a touchscreen panel that displays the information needed to check the respiratory condition, allows parameter setting, and displays ventilation parameters and alarm settings. When the controller receives operator input from the GUI, it communicates with the valve controllers, serial interfaces, and other subcomponents and sends them commands.

Before starting the ventilation, the ventilator controller passed through three phases. The *start-up* in which the controller is initialized with default parameters, *self-test* which ensures that the hardware is fully functional, and *ventilation off* in which the controller is ready for ventilation when requested. If during ventilation and other phases, the controller detects a severe condition that prevents the ventilator from sustaining the ventilation, the machine is brought to fail-safe mode (in valve closed and out valve open).

3   Structure of the Specification Document

In this section, we explain the structure of the requirement specification document available here [3]. In this article, we do not detail the requirements since there are around 370 requirements.

The chapter 2. System Requirements contains the general high-level specification of the ventilator: functional requirements (2.1), measured and displayed parameters (2.2), values and ranges of parameters (2.3), interfaces between components (2.4), and alarm requirements (2.5).

The chapter 3 GUI Requirements consists of the specifications of the GUI, which is responsible for receiving information from the user and displaying information to the user. It details each mode of operation: Start-up Mode (3.1), Start Mode (3.2), Menu Mode (3.3), Self-Test Mode (3.4), Ventilation Mode (3.5), Show Real Time Data Mode (3.6), Settings Mode (3.7), Frozen Mode (3.8), and Alarm settings Mode (3.9).

The chapter 4 Controller Requirements comprehends the specification of the controller, which is responsible for controlling the phase of the respiratory cycle (inhalation, pause, exhalation) by operating on the valves and receiving information from sensors and commands from the GUI. It details each mode of operation: Start-up Mode (4.1), Self Test (4.2), PCV Mode (4.3), PSV Mode (4.4), and requirements common to multiple modes like inspiratory/expiratory pauses (4.5).

The chapter 5 Alarms presents the specification of the alarm system responsible for raising alarms.

Requirement Numbering Convention

The specification is divided into requirements, and the format of each requirement ID is: XXX.n.y, where: XXX is a three-letter code indicating a requirement type, n is the requirement number, and y is the sub-requirement number (it is empty if a parent). The following table reports the connection between the three-letter code and the type of requirement.

Three-letter code	Description
AL	Alarm requirements
CONT	Controller requirements
FUN	Functional (general) requirements
GUI	GUI requirements
INT	Interfaces requirements
PER	Values and ranges requirements
SAV	Safety requirements

Table 1 reports an example of a GUI requirement:

Table 1. Example of GUI requirement

ID	Requirement
GUI.7	The transition from Menu to Ventilation shall occur when the Self-test is passed if required (new patient connected), and the clinician wants to proceed with the ventilation

Scenario

Besides the requirement specification document, we have released the scenarios for the initialization. Each scenario reports the state of the controller and the GUI and the events that lead to the state change. For example, the scenario in Table 2 refers to the new patient connection: when a new patient is connected, the doctor selects a new patient and runs the self-test. Once the self-test is passed, the ventilation can start.

4   Suggested Outcomes

During the development of the MVM software, no formal method has been applied, mainly because of a lack of developers' skills with any formal method.

Table 2. Scenario example

	event	*powerOn*	*start-up ended*	–	*selfTestPassed*
Controller	state	Start-Up	SelfTest	SelfTest	VentilationOff
	event	*powerOn*	*start-up ended*	*new Patient*	*selfTestPassed*
GUI	**state**	Start-Up	Start	SelfTest	Menu

However, we want to propose this case study to demonstrate the feasibility of developing the ventilator by using a formal method-based approach. Mechanical lung ventilators, as well as other medical devices which incorporate software, must be certified before their use. Several standards for the validation of medical devices have been proposed - as ISO 13485, ISO 14971, IEC 60601-1, EU Directive 2007/47/EC -, but they mainly consider hardware aspects of the physical components of a device, and do not mention the software component. The only reference concerning the regulation of medical software is the standard IEC (International Electrotechnical Commission) 62304. This standard provides a very general description of common life cycle activities of the software development, without giving any indication regarding process models, or methods and techniques to assure safety and reliability.

With this case study, we aim to study the applicability of formal methods in the software development of medical devices to satisfy the standards, in this case, the IEC 62304.

We have envisioned several aspects of the ventilator that could be the object of research activities. In the following, we give a non-exhaustive list of possible outcomes.

- A classical approach consists of modeling the system or part of it and applying the classical V&V activities (as partially done [2]), like formal verification of the correctness or validation of scenarios. One could check that the system behavior is correct, like in case of some errors, the system goes into a fail-safe mode.
- A critical aspect of the system is its temporal behavior. Many properties and constraints have explicit temporal requirements (like after 10 s ...). One could model these aspects and make a temporal analysis of the system.
- After the good experience with ABZ2023, we decided to include the GUI. Research activities could model this critical component and analyze the human-computer interaction.
- Generation of executable source code and implement a prototype of the ventilator on a simple electronic board like Arduino (or part of it).

5   Contributions to ABZ 2024

In this section, we resume (in random order) the contributions accepted for publication in the ABZ 2024 proceedings. All the papers use different formal modeling techniques and contribute to different outcomes.

Paper [9] illustrates the correct-by-construction approach and introduces an Event-B formal model of the MLV controller and part of alarms. Validation and verification techniques are applied using the ProB model checker to validate and verify the specification.

In paper [10] the authors model the controller of the MLV using Timed Algebraic State-Transition Diagrams (TASTD). Then the specification is validated using cASTD compiler to translate the specification into C++ code.

Paper [6] models controller and general requirements using the Formal Requirements Elicitation Tool (FRET) to provide traceability from natural-language requirements to a formal design model. The authors explore the link between formal requirements in FRET and formal specifications in Event-B, presenting how techniques like FRET can be used to guide the development of a formal model in a large case study in a state-based technique (Event-B in this case).

The MLV is modeled in the process algebra mCRL2 in [5]. The functional requirements of the MLV are formalized in the modal μ-calculus, and the model checker is used to analyze whether these requirements hold true in the model. Each scenario provided with the case study has been can be captured in a modal μ-calculus formula and verified that the model satisfies those formulas. Their formalization helped us in revealing a few subtle incomplete or not completely clear requirements in the informal document and we have used the feedback to improve the original specification.

The Clock Constraint Specification Language (CCSL) has been applied to the case-study and the authors report their experience in [11]. CCSL captures the causal and temporal behavior of a system by specifying constraints on logical clocks. Logical clocks are integer counters where the occurrence of an event, a tick, advances the counter and marks the advance in time. The paper introduced some new real-time constructs to directly encode phenomena like clock drift, skew and jitter and these constructs are applied to the case study. Earlier versions of the paper, allowed us to clarify some temporal constraints (e.g., the different phases in the PCV mode).

Competing Interests. The author(s) has no competing interests to declare that are relevant to the content of this manuscript.

References

1. Abba, A., et al.: The novel mechanical ventilator Milano for the COVID-19 pandemic. Phys. Fluids **33**(3), 037122 (2021). https://doi.org/10.1063/5.0044445
2. Bombarda, A., Bonfanti, S., Gargantini, A., Riccobene, E.: Developing a prototype of a mechanical ventilator controller from requirements to code with ASMETA. Electron. Proc. Theor. Comput. Sci. **349**, 13–29 (2021)
3. Bonfanti, S., Gargantini, A.: Mechanical Lung Ventilator Requirements Specification, December 2024. https://github.com/foselab/abz2024_casestudy_MLV
4. Bonivento, W., Gargantini, A., Krücken, R., Razeto, A.: The mechanical ventilator Milano. Nucl. Phys. News **31**(3), 30–33 (2021)

5. van Dortmont, D., Keiren, J.J., Willemse, T.A.: Modelling and analysing a mechanical lung ventilator in mCRL2. In: Rigorous State-Based Methods 10th International Conference, ABZ 2024, Bergamo, Italy, 25–28 June 2024, Proceedings, LNCS, vol. 14759. Springer (2024)

6. Farrell, M., Luckcuck, M., Monahan, R., Reynolds, C., Sheridan, O.: FRETting and formal modelling: a mechanical lung ventilator. In: Rigorous State-Based Methods 10th International Conference, ABZ 2024, Bergamo, Italy, 25–28 June 2024, Proceedings, LNCS, vol. 14759. Springer (2024)

7. Guardo, M.C.D., et al.: When nothing is certain, anything is possible: open innovation and lean approach at MVM. R&D Manag. (2021). https://doi.org/10.1111/radm.12453

8. Lei, Y.: Medical Ventilator System Basics: A Clinical Guide. Oxford University Press, Oxford (2017). https://doi.org/10.1093/med/9780198784975.001.0001

9. Mammar, A.: An Event-B model of a mechanical lung ventilator. In: Rigorous State-Based Methods 10th International Conference, ABZ 2024, Bergamo, Italy, 25–28 June 2024, Proceedings, LNCS, vol. 14759. Springer (2024)

10. Ndounal, A.R., Frappier, M.: Modelling the mechanical lung ventilation system using TASTD. In: Rigorous State-Based Methods 10th International Conference, ABZ 2024, Bergamo, Italy, 25–28 June 2024, Proceedings, LNCS, vol. 14759. Springer (2024)

11. Tokariev, P., Mallet, F.: Real-Time CCSL: application to the mechanical lung ventilator. In: Rigorous State-Based Methods 10th International Conference, ABZ 2024, Bergamo, Italy, 25–28 June 2024, Proceedings, LNCS, vol. 14759. Springer (2024)

Real-Time CCSL: Application to the Mechanical Lung Ventilator

Pavlo Tokariev(✉)⑩ and Frédéric Mallet⑩

Université Côte d'Azur, Inria, CNRS, i3S, Sophia Antipolis, France
Pavlo.Tokariev@inria.fr, Frederic.Mallet@univ-cotedazur.fr

Abstract. This case-study paper reports on our experience in modelling the mechanical lung ventilator using the Clock Constraint Specification Language (CCSL). CCSL captures the causal and temporal behaviour of a system by specifying constraints on logical clocks. Logical clocks are integer counters where the occurrence of an event, a *tick*, advances the counter and marks the advance in time. In this framework, chronometric clocks become logical clocks just with a special external meaning. Encoding chronometric clocks as counters may result in verification inefficiency and hard-to-read specifications.

The paper introduces in the language some real-time constructs to directly encode phenomena like clock drift, skew and jitter. This makes patterns explicit in turn enabling optimizations. To realize these optimizations, we alter the internal symbolic representation of clock constraints. We also introduce an explicit notion of parameters and intervals. While for some constraints it mainly consists of adding syntactic sugar and pre-processing facilities, we believe it improves the readability.

We illustrate the new constructs on the mechanical lung ventilator system. We start with a purely logical specification, we point at the sources of inefficiencies and then we discuss the benefits of the extensions on specific parts.

Keywords: Temporal requirements · Logical time · Real-Time

1 Introduction

As more and more systems become digital or include digital parts, the complexity of systems constantly increases. Thus, it requires revisiting the expressiveness of specification languages to cope with new features that need to be considered. Scientific challenges help compare the various expressiveness of solutions to identify pros and cons. We consider here the modelling of the mechanical lung ventilator provided as a challenge to the ABZ community and report on the experience.

The Clock Constraint Specification Language (CCSL) was defined as a specification language for capturing both timed and temporal aspects of safety-critical systems. Its formal semantics is used to conduct various kinds of analyses for the early detection of potential system flaws. In CCSL, recurring events are captured as logical clocks, i.e. (infinite) streams of ticks, where each tick stands for

© The Author(s), under exclusive license to Springer Nature Switzerland AG 2024
S. Bonfanti et al. (Eds.): ABZ 2024, LNCS 14759, pp. 289–306, 2024.
https://doi.org/10.1007/978-3-031-63790-2_24

an occurrence of this event. Logical clocks provide a generic mechanism to unify untimed events that are linked only by causal relationships and timed events usually related to physical phenomena associated with real-time. Chronometric clocks can measure timed events by associating a date with each occurrence. Logical clocks can both measure the progression of a system by observing the occurrence of an event, but also describe the activation conditions under which something good may happen or something bad must not happen. CCSL constraints serve both purposes, building probes to observe the system and activation conditions to control what should or should not happen.

While logical clocks give an elegant generic modelling framework, encoding everything as a logical clock may lead to some verification inefficiencies or difficult-to-read specifications. We use the example of the mechanical lung ventilator to identify such cases. We also provide new constructs that allow for optimization at the cost of a more complex internal symbolic representation.

Related Work. The challenge of ABZ 2024 is about designing a mechanical lung ventilator [7] using formal methods. This usually includes, but not limited to, defining behaviour in state machines of various expressiveness and performing model checking of required liveness and safety properties (functional or operational).

Synchronous languages, such as Esterel [6] or Lustre [9] (and its industrial development, SCADE [10]), were devised as formal *programming* languages dedicated to the modelling of reactive systems. They rely on the synchronous hypothesis: the system consumes external actions, and may produce reactions in infinite loop, which happens when base clock ticks. This hypothesis is based on two assumptions. The loop body considered instantaneous regardless of actual computations and relation with the inputs and the state. And it requires to process the loop body at an adequate rhythm compared to the input rate so that no input is lost or aged.

Another way to approach the formal description of a system, called *declarative*, is to specify the expected behaviour without necessarily giving a unique operational way to execute it. In that sense, a specification describes possible valid or forbidden behaviours, but not necessary how to achieve actual valid executions. It is also a way to abstract the aspects important to requirement engineers or their customers from implementation details. The examples of specification languages or related formalisms include Timed Automata [2] (with UPPAAL model checker), Z specification language [24], AltaRica [5]. In this paper we shall focus on logical clock specifications, or more specifically, the Clock Constraint Specification Language (CCSL) [16].

Contributions. This paper proposes several extensions to the base language of CCSL and illustrates their application on the use case of the mechanical lung ventilator. We add real-time constraints to the language, which not only extend the expressiveness, but also add the possibility to provide better optimizations during the analysis. We discuss some elements of using this new information to build the analysis using abstract interpretation [11]. Other extensions are mostly syntactic yet important to make the language suitable to describe large systems. An important addition regarding proof relation does require a specialized theoretical work to be implemented. Here we only present the intention and idea but leave the solution for future work.

Structure of the Paper: Section 2 shortly explains the use case from our point of view and classify the requirements by the usage intention and/or nature. Section 3 briefly presents semantics of CCSL followed with the modelling of the system using only logical clocks. Section 4 introduces the real-time extensions to CCSL and show how they enrich the model. Section 5 discusses other extensions, but due to space limitations, only in a short form. Section 6 sums up the ideas we see promising in implementing the desired analyses. Section 7 concludes this exploration paper and discusses the ongoing and future work in supporting the full language with algorithmic solving capabilities.

2   Requirements Classification

A mechanical lung ventilator is a complex interdependent system consisting of several cyber-physical components like mechanical parts, computer-human interfaces and a control. The description of mechanical parts includes oxygen and compressed air lines, their valves, pressure and flow sensors. The computer-human interface consists of a touch screen, buttons, a speaker and visual indicators. The embedded software has to coordinate the other parts according to the safety and functionality requirements.

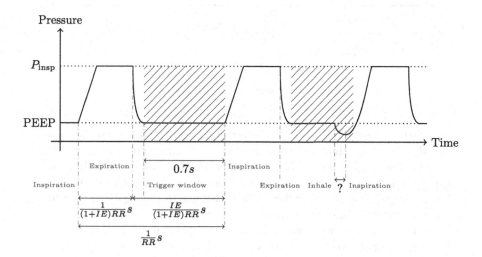

Fig. 1. PCV mode plot with events.

From the provided use case [7], we have built a formal model in RTCCSL (see [27]). We expect to check consistency on them, explore the possible solutions to check what properties hold, and if the code of the system was provided, to check it against the requirements using so-called observers.

Our model refers directly to the identifiers provided (such as FUN.21). Overall we have encoded the following requirements:

- functional (FUN): 4, 19, 20, 21, 23, 24, 25, 27, 27.1, 27.2, 30, 31, 32;
- controller (CONT): 1, 2, 3, 4, 4.2, 5, 6, 8, 9, 10, 19, 21, 22, 25, 26, 30, 32, 36, 36.2, 36.3, 37, 40, 41.2, 56;
- parameter (PER): 4, 5, 11, 12, 13, 21.

We focused on requirements related to events and their time relations, sometimes with parameters. Timing parameters can vary in given intervals or be defined as expressions of other parameters. The subset of requirements is limited due to the functional and data-related expressiveness of CCSL. As such, we leave encoding and reasoning of the rest of the requirements to be complemented by other methods, like Event-B [1], Frama-C [15].

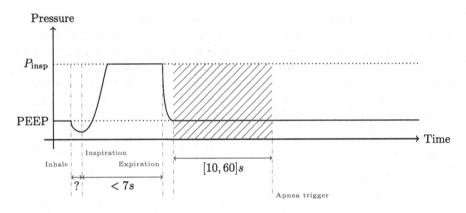

Fig. 2. PSV mode plot with events.

We start by describing the logical events and their relationships, like causality or other abstract time ordering. In Pressure Controlled Ventilation (PCV) mode (FUN.19 and Fig. 1), we have identified the following events: inspiration, expiration, trigger window deadline, detection of patient trying to inhale.

From the plot, we can establish some relationships among those events. For example, inspiration should alternate with expiration. Trigger window starts after expiration occurrence. The cycle should continue until stopped.

Pressure Support Ventilation (PSV) mode is similar (Fig. 2), inspiration and expiration events still alternate. The main difference is the reason to change the mode, it depends on the occurrence of apnea (FUN.27).

We also describe mechanical parts and some safety requirements. Valves can have 2 states: closed and open. When there is no ventilation, out valve should be open and in valve should be closed (CONT.38).

The second class of requirements is timing relations, mostly durations in the procedure of the ventilation. More precisely, some pairs of events have time relations between them: trigger window start and finish, inspiration and expiration, the whole ventilation cycle.

The third class is about ensuring that the specification, and so an implementation satisfying it, shall also satisfy some important properties by construction. Examples of this are the finiteness of memory needed to achieve the behaviour, absence of deadlocks or, to be more specific to the use case, the safety of the patient by ensuring that the exhalation valve is not closed for more than the required amount of time.

The fourth class is not represented widely, but there are some timing ranges that either can be selected by a user or to be computed from the behaviour of the ventilator. These parameters are then used in expressions, which in turn parametrize constraints. The uncertain nature of the parameters from the point of view of specification, requires checking the specification with all their combinations. Examples of such requirements would be recruitment maneuver duration (PER.3.2), PCV respiratory rate (PER.4), inspiration-expiration ratio (PER.5), PSV apnea lag (PER.11).

3 Logical Modelling of the Ventilator

This section shortly introduces the semantics of the Clock Constraint Specification Language and uses it to specify the use case. Refer to [20] for the full semantics and constraint definitions.

3.1 CCSL

The Clock Constraint Specification Language (CCSL) is a language operating with constraints as statements over logical clocks as variables. Each constraint binds ticks of its clocks to appear only in a certain order, effectively reducing the set of possible behaviours.

Tooling. Over the years, CCSL was implemented with an extensive collection of approaches and tools. These include translation into other languages and theories, and then simulation or verification using native tools: VHDL [3], Esterel, Signal and Time Petri Nets [17], Timed Automata [25]. Simulation and some model checking, specific to CCSL, is implemented in TimeSquare [12], checking finiteness of state using graphs [19], finding bounded periodic schedules with SMT [28]. The modelling using CCSL was demonstrated in the following use cases: brake-by-wire subsystem [13], spark ignition control [22], CPU interference [21].

Definition 1. *A specification Spec is defined as a tuple $\langle C, R \rangle$: logical clocks C and constraints R, both are a finite sets.*

Definition 2. *A logical clock c is a finite or infinite sequence of ticks $(c_n)_{n=1}^{\leq\infty}$, where $c_i \prec c_{i+1}$, i.e. totally ordered.*

For example, a clock can be chronometric, like the movement of the second's arm in a wall clock, an electric circuit oscillating and outputting signal at a certain frequency, or sporadic, like user request or start of communication. The real-time difference between two successive ticks of the same clock is not defined and only the time causality between the ticks has to be preserved.

Definition 3. *A schedule is a function $\sigma : \mathbb{N} \to 2^C$. Given an execution step $n \in \mathbb{N}$ and a schedule $\sigma, \sigma(n)$ denotes a set of clocks that tick at step n.*

Figure 3 illustrates the relation between logical clocks and a schedule.

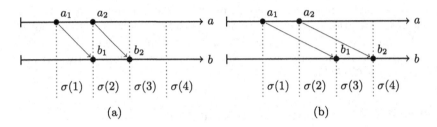

Fig. 3. Some valid schedules for $a \prec b$ constraint, arrows represent order.

Definition 4. *Given a schedule σ, a history over a set of clocks C is a function $H_\sigma : C \times \mathbb{N} \to \mathbb{N}$ defined inductively for all clocks $c \in C$:*

$$H_\sigma(c,0) = 0$$
$$\forall n \in \mathbb{N} : c \notin \sigma(n) \implies H_\sigma(c, n+1) = H_\sigma(c, n)$$
$$\forall n \in \mathbb{N} : c \in \sigma(n) \implies H_\sigma(c, n+1) = H_\sigma(c, n) + 1$$

Informally, for a clock $c \in C$, and step $n \in \mathbb{N}, H_\sigma(c, n)$ denotes the number of times clock c has ticked *before* step n within schedule σ.

CCSL constraints are divided into two groups: relations and expressions. Relations are intended to bound two clocks by some condition, while expressions are seen as a way to combine two clocks into a new clock. Some of the constraints are parametrized with integers. The notations and definitions of the common relations and expressions are defined in Table 1.

Definition 5. *Given a set Φ of constraints, the scheduling problem of CCSL is to compute whether there exists a schedule σ such that σ satisfies all constraints in Φ.*

In CCSL, "nothing happened" or $\sigma(i) = \emptyset$ is always a valid step in any schedule for any specification, so we only consider schedules without such steps, otherwise scheduling problem becomes trivial.

Table 1. Definitions of common CCSL constraints [18,20]. Variables are $a, b, c \in C$, $d, p \in \mathbb{N}$, a schedule σ and its history H_σ.

	Constraint	Notation	Definition, $\forall n \in \mathbb{N}$
Relation	Causality	$a \preccurlyeq b$	$H_\sigma(a, n) \geq H_\sigma(b, n)$
	Precedence	$a \prec b$	$(H_\sigma(a, n) = H_\sigma(b, n)) \Rightarrow b \notin \sigma(n + 1)$
	Exclusion	$a \# b$	$a \notin \sigma(n) \vee b \notin \sigma(n)$
	Coincidence	$a = b$	$a \in \sigma(n) \Leftrightarrow b \in \sigma(n)$
	Subclocking	$a \subseteq b$	$a \in \sigma(n) \Rightarrow b \in \sigma(n)$
Expression	Delay	$c = a \, \$ \, d$	$H_\sigma(c, n) = \max(H_\sigma(a, n) - d, 0)$
	Supremum	$c = \sup(a, b)$	$H_\sigma(c, n) = \min(H_\sigma(a, n), H_\sigma(b, n))$
	Infimum	$c = \inf(a, b)$	$H_\sigma(c, n) = \max(H_\sigma(a, n), H_\sigma(b, n))$
	Intersection	$c = a * b$	$c \in \sigma(n) \Leftrightarrow (a \in \sigma(n) \wedge b \in \sigma(n))$
	Union	$c = a + b$	$c \in \sigma(n) \Leftrightarrow (a \in \sigma(n) \vee b \in \sigma(n))$
	Periodic	$c = a \propto p$	$c \in \sigma(n) \Leftrightarrow (H_\sigma(a, n) = p \cdot H_\sigma(c, n) \wedge a \in \sigma(n))$
	Sampling	$c = \texttt{sample } a \texttt{ on } b$	$c \in \sigma(n) \Leftrightarrow \begin{pmatrix} b \in \sigma(n) \wedge \\ \exists 0 < j \leq n : a \in \sigma(j) \wedge \\ \forall j \leq k < n : b \notin \sigma(k) \end{pmatrix}$

3.2 Usage in the Use Case

First of all, to better express the intention, we make some changes to the way we use the basic language presented above:

- $c = \sup(a, b)$ is $c = \texttt{slowest}(a, b)$ (resp. inf is $\texttt{fastest}$);
- $c = a \, \$ \, 1$ is $c = \texttt{next } a$;
- $a \prec \texttt{next } b$ expands into $a \prec \alpha \wedge \alpha = \texttt{next } b$, where α is a unique anonymous clock name;
- the dot . in *prefix.c1* $\prec$ *prefix.c2* is part of the name of the clock, and is used only for convenience to name and structure clocks, the semantics remains identical;
- $a \texttt{ alternates } b$ rewrites into $a \prec b \prec \texttt{next } a$.

From the provided plot and the requirements (Fig. 2, FUN.19), it is obvious that some of the events are causally related: expiration cannot begin without inspiration, trigger window is activated only after expiration starts. The next cycle, which starts with inspiration, can only begin after the trigger deadline or with inhale detection (whichever is faster; FUN.21):

$$inspiration \prec expiration \prec window.start \prec window.finish$$
$$\texttt{fastest}(window.finish, sensor.inhale) \preccurlyeq \texttt{next } inspiration$$

Then we describe the relevant physical parts, including valves and sensors. Valves are devices which are supposed to open and close, and so have only 2 states, which is precisely what the alternation constraint represents. In the specification, we have decided to alternate close with open. It is so to force the valve to close as soon as possible, which clearly defines the initial state as closed. Next we define a safety check, which is not present in the requirements, that the valves should not be open at the same time. For this, we define an equivalent of a mutex. This mutex mediates the access of valves to the shared resource of the patient mask.

$$in.close \text{ \textbf{alternates} } in.open$$

$$out.close \text{ \textbf{alternates} } out.open$$

$$(in.open + out.open) \text{ \textbf{alternates} } (\textbf{next } in.close + \textbf{next } out.close)$$

For sensors, we model only the detection signalling and not the whole collection and processing of sensor data. For example, inhalation is detected when the pressure drops below the set value (FUN.21.1). The resulting clock is named *sensor.inhale*.

3.3 Gaps in the Requirements

There are two places (Fig. 1 and Fig. 2; marked by "?") for which we could not find a timing requirement. This missing requirements prevent the specification from being fully time-deterministic while ventilating. This means that some phases are permitted to be executed indefinitely, which is against the purpose of the device and will prevent proving functional safety.

The missing requirement should specify what is the maximum latency between actual pressure dropping below target value and the controller making the decision that it *is* an inhalation attempt. How wide is the interval when the decision can be made will influence the solution cost as tighter requirements may imply costlier approaches. For example, the latency depends on the sensor itself, data acquisition architecture or simply the processor frequency.

3.4 Real-Time as Logical Time

Additionally to having logical relations, some events are time-bounded and require a special treatment to be expressed in CCSL. These mostly cover PCV and PSV mode cycle durations and their parts. The basic trick to write real-time relations in logical time is to introduce a clock that is interpreted externally as the progress of physical time with a given period. Let us assume that the precision of one nanosecond (ns) is enough for the ventilator. Then to express the time difference of d seconds, we use the following template:

$$right = left \text{ \$ } n_d \text{ \textbf{on} } ns$$

where $n_d = \frac{d\,s}{1\,ns}$, i.e. the number of nanoseconds in d. If clock *left* always coincides with ns, the delay is exact, otherwise it is approximate. Then, this template should be read as: clock *right* should tick after counting n_d number of nanoseconds.

As it is, there are several problems with this approach. First, one needs to decide on the precision beforehand, and in the case the precision should change, all real-time constraints have to be rewritten or regenerated.

Second, the state grows too fast in the case of using the classic automata approach. Ternary delay constraint $a = b \, \$ \, d$ on *base* is a combination of delay and sampling constraints and requires 2^d of states in the automata representation, in other words, $\lceil \frac{d}{8} \rceil$ bytes. If we would encode this way just 3 constraints and synchronize them into a single automaton, in order to do model checking, we would need $2^{\frac{7\,s}{1\,ns}} \times 2^{\frac{10\,s}{1\,ns}} \times 2^{\frac{6\,s}{1\,ns}} = 2^{77 \times 10^9}$ states, i.e. 9.625 GB of memory.

To tackle it where possible, we need to detect specific patterns of behaviour (see examples in Sect. 6). To simplify this process we opted in to make the behaviour syntactically explicit by introducing new *real-time* constraints.

4   Real-Time Constraints

This section introduces new constraints, explains their meaning and gives semantics as a modified labelled transition system. Just as in most languages dealing with real-time, we assume the existence of a global notion of (physical) time and we use a *special* clock s (for second) to refer to it. This is a major evolution as otherwise all clocks in CCSL are assumed to be independent unless explicitly constrained. With this assumption, all clocks referring to physical time become indeed (implicitly) related. Part of our work to get efficient analysis is therefore to compute this implicit relation and use it whenever possible.

To capture the semantics of these real-time constraints, we introduce a new form of transition systems. We then describe how these transition systems are composed with *classical* CCSL.

4.1   Definition

Syntax. This extension adds three new constraints to the language to capture frequently used timing patterns.

$o_1 =$ **repeat each** p **relative error** e **offset** φ defines a periodic clock o_1 with period p, cumulative error e and offset φ (a clock with jitter). In short, a periodic clock with cumulative error is best suitable for events like ticks of oscillator inside of a computer. Declaring 2 periodic clocks with exactly the same parameters *will* result in desynchronization;

$o_2 =$ **repeat each** p **absolute error** e **offset** φ defines a periodic clock o_2 with absolute or non-cumulative error (a clock with skew), other parameters have the same meaning as with cumulative error. A periodic clock with absolute error can be used to describe ideal processes that are observed thought other non-ideal processes or with unknown influences. For example, it could model the sampling of shaft turns with a sensor, which produces signal earlier or later depending on vibration or temperature. In other words, assuming constant speed of the shaft, frequency of turning *will not* drift indefinitely;

$b =$ **delay** a **by** d defines a clock b that is delayed between d_1 and d_2 seconds relative to the time when a clock ticks.

The parameters $p, \varphi \in \mathbb{R}_{\geq 0}$ are in seconds, error d and e are intervals $[d_1, d_2], [e_1, e_2]$, where $0 \leq d_1 \leq d_2, e_1 \leq e_2 \in \mathbb{R}$ and are in seconds too.

Automata. Each constraint is defined as the corresponding real-time augmented CCSL automaton.

Definition 6. *Real-time augmented automaton A is a tuple $\langle P, p_0 \in P, p_e \in P, C, V, Q, T \rangle$, where:*

- *locations P, clocks C, variables V, queues Q are sets of symbols;*
- *S is a set of possible variable evaluations in a state, $S = (V \to \mathbb{R}_\perp) \times (Q \to \mathbb{N} \to [\mathbb{R}, \mathbb{R}] \cup \{\perp\}))$, where $\mathbb{R}_\perp = \mathbb{R} \cup \{\perp\}$ with $\perp$ as a symbol for nothing;*
- *$p_0 \in P$ is the initial location, $s_0 = (\lambda v. \perp, \lambda q.\lambda i. \perp)$ is the initial evaluation;*
- *p_e is a state that is reachable only if an invariant in some state is violated (for example, time passed certain value);*
- *$T \in P \times S \times \mathbb{R} \times 2^C \to P \times S$ is a transition function from location, its variable evaluation, clock label, current time into the next location and new evaluation.*

We put some syntactic restrictions on *transition functions*. The *guard* (valid arguments) is any boolean expression with atoms being a clock, an inclusion test or a test of queue emptiness.

If clock atom is true in the expression then the related clock has to tick, and vice-versa.

Inclusion tests are expressed as $a \in i$ or equivalently $i_1 \leq a \leq i_1$. In that case, atom a can be either current time η, a variable $v \in V$ or the first value from the queue $\mathrm{head}(q), q \in Q$. i is an interval that can be expressed as a linear combination of atoms. If an expression evaluates to a scalar r we interpret it as an interval $[r, r]$. A queue emptiness test is $\mathrm{head}(q) = \perp, q \in Q$.

The *assignment* is a set of variable assignments and queue updates. A variable assignment $v := e$ contains an expression e, which is a linear combination of atoms described above. A queue update $\mathrm{pop}(q)$ removes the head value and returns a new queue. $\mathrm{push}(q, e)$ adds evaluation of e at the end of the queue and returns the new queue. These operations can be combined, i.e. it is possible to remove and add a value to the same queue within a single transition.

We describe the new constraints as automata in Fig. 4, Fig. 5 and Fig. 6. The guard of the transitions is given above the arrow and the assignment is below.

Definition 7. *A run is an alternating sequence of rules (similarly to Timed Automata [8]):*

- *time elapse: $(p, s, \eta) \xrightarrow{\delta} (p, s, \eta + \delta)$;*
- *transition: $(p, s, \eta) \xrightarrow{l} (p', s', \eta)$ such that $\exists l \in 2^C : T(p, s, \eta, l) = (p', s')$.*

A run $(p_0, s_0, \eta = 0) \xrightarrow{\delta} (p_0, s_0, \eta' = \eta + \delta) \xrightarrow{l} (p', s', \eta) \xrightarrow{\delta'} (p', s', \eta' = \eta + \delta') \xrightarrow{l'} \ldots$ is *valid* if p_e is never visited, and where $\eta, \eta' \in \mathbb{R}$ are the current times, $\delta, \delta' \in \mathbb{R}_{>0}$ are the time evolutions, $l, l' \in 2^C$ are labels or sets of clock ticks.

We then consider a *trace* to be a sequence of clock labels with preceding values of real-time η in a run. Thus we extend the original CCSL schedules (traces) from $\sigma : \mathbb{N} \to 2^C$ to $\mathbb{N} \to 2^C \times \mathbb{R}$.

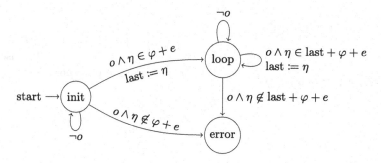

Fig. 4. Relative periodic o = **repeat each** p **relative error** e **offset** φ.

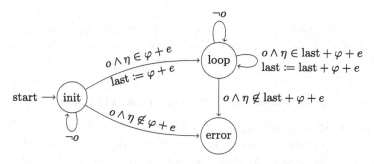

Fig. 5. Absolute periodic o = **repeat each** p **absolute error** e **offset** φ.

Synchronization. We use the classic synchronized product [4] for most of the states and transitions. The only exception is the error states as they should stay unique, thus they are fused across the network of automata and all transitions, meaning pointing to some error state translates to pointing to the new global one.

Definition 8. *Synchronization of transition functions T_1 and T_2 is the new transition function T defined as*

$$T = T_1 \circ T_2 = \lambda((p_1, p_2), (s_1, s_2), \eta, l).$$

$$E\left(\begin{array}{l} (T_1(p_1, s_1, \eta, \Pi_{C_1}(l)) \times P_2 \times S_2) \cap \\ (P_1 \times S_1 \times T_2(p_2, s_2, \eta, \Pi_{C_2}(l))) \end{array}\right)$$

where $\Pi_{C_i} : 2^C \rightarrow 2^{C_i}$ is a projection to labels on clocks $C_i \subseteq C$, E is a mapping of compound and partial error locations to the new error location p_e.

Definition 9. *A synchronized real-time augmented automaton A of automata A_1 and A_2 is the tuple $\langle P \subseteq P_1 \times P_2 \cup \{p_e\}, p_0 = (p_{01}, p_{02}), p_e \in P, C = C_1 \cup C_2, V = V_1 \cup V_2, Q = Q_1 \cup Q_2, T = T_1 \circ T_2 \rangle$.*

To synchronize with the regular CCSL, the automata of CCSL constraints need to be translated into the new representation. The automata stays mostly

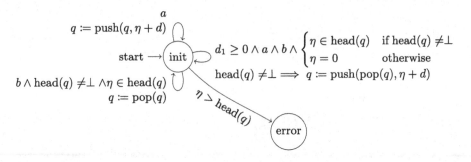

Fig. 6. Real-time delay $b = \texttt{delay}\ a$ by d.

the same as described in [18], with the addition of a disconnected error state, empty sets of variables and queue symbols. The transitions are a subset of real-time transition functions and so can be synchronized as described above.

4.2 Rewriting Real-Time Constraints in the Ventilator

Going back to the timing constraints of the ventilator, we replace previously defined template (Subsect. 3.4) with the real-time delay constraint. Instead of specifying number of ticks on some base clock, we write durations in seconds directly. This way we let the solver figure out the necessary precision, if needed, or reason without discretization at all, when possible.

While there is no precision specified for any values in the requirements, to make the system more realistic we may add some imprecision to the delays. As multiplication is distributive under addition, adding the same precision to all constraints, at least in the PCV mode, will not result in any interesting constraint interaction. Thus we assume that the PCV cycle should be precise up to 1%, inspiration and expiration phases up to 5% and trigger window delay and duration up to 10%.

With such a specification, the controller has more freedom in implementing the exact timings. For example, it could use a precise dedicated timer to measure the cycle and an interrupt to switch execution to prepare for a new cycle, and a general coarse timer and cooperative preemption to execute intermediate tasks.

Additionally, it is possible to model the controller with more details if we know the frequency of the CPU base clock, for instance by assigning a frequency of some MHz plus-minus some error. One then could describe the control as conditions when to sample the inputs and to schedule tasks. As any computation should happen on the base clock, real-time constraints will induce causal relations between real-time related logical clocks. Then the task is to reverse search for conditions when the control would satisfy the higher-level constraints. We discuss this idea more in Subsect. 5.1.

5 Other Extensions

This section briefly discusses other CCSL extensions intended to better convey user intentions. These include modular specifications and their proofs, parameters and constraints, and new logical constraints.

5.1 Modularity

The need for modularity arises from the demand to design and analyse complex specifications, including the one for the use case. We propose several interdependent extensions to make it easier: macros, name binding, specification structuring and proofs.

The central unit of the modular system is a macro. A macro is a list of constraints that has a name, for example `m1(){a < b}`. When the macro name is called in another macro, all constraints and clocks are added to it, but with a specified prefix, for example `m2(){prefix = m1()}` is equivalent to `m2(){prefix.a < prefix.b}`. In the use case, the macros are used to reuse specifications and to separate functionally different parts: environment interaction, modes and control.

As such, it is just a build system and does not make the analysis modular. For that we allow macros to contain not only the body of specification but sections of assumptions, assertions and interface, all of which can be specified as constraints. The interpretation is the following: under the given assumptions, does the specification violate the assertions and if not, does the interface include the specification behaviour? To make an analogy to functions, assumptions are argument types, an interface is a return type and a body is an algorithm. Making such a distinction allows separation of proofs between the body interface, and the specification properties. Proved properties on interfaces become "theorems" later on. This pattern allows scaling of the overall system analysis.

There are several properties that we are interested in, but which cannot be expressed as regular specifications and are only allowed for the top level macro. These include:

- check for deadlocks: deadlock-free specifications do not have a trace prefix that leads to traces that exclude some clocks indefinitely;
- safety: safe specifications have finite memory representation;
- existence of periodic or k-periodic schedules: a periodic schedule is a regular schedule where each clock ticks with a period defined on some global clock, high regularity of periodic schedules provides a compact and performant implementation of the system;
- condition for *some* liveness: being deadlock-free is a strong property, it may be easier to identify which subpart of the specification is live instead of proving that the specification is *exactly* live;
- and any combination of these properties.

For the ventilator, physical and control parts, as well as modes, are described as separate macros which are then connected together in the top level macro.

The top level macro should be checked to satisfy safety and liveness. We add the following general functional safety property: the out valve cannot be closed for too long, otherwise it may result in the death of the patient.

5.2 Parameters and Constants

An orthogonal feature to modules is macro parameters and constants. In the ventilator, the modes have different allowed ranges of parameters and some of them are used in the constraints. In this case, we consider all of them to be constant as they are local to the modes and are not subject to the search for optimization. The constant parameters are declared as scalars or intervals inside the macros and can be algebraically manipulated with usual numerical operators, parametrize constraints, and specify or additionally constrain other parameters. The example of a non-constant parameter is the frequency of the CPU in the ventilator. The intention then is to find a value of this parameter that allows the specification to satisfy the desired properties. Such a scheme is known as parametric verification.

The parametric verification in CCSL is undecidable, but we believe that the specification and its parameters should be kept together, even if it is not possible to solve in general and a strategy to preselect values of parameters has to be provided.

5.3 Extension to Logical Constraints

The final extension introduces some convenient logical constraints to alleviate the reading of the specification.

The first extension is to allow intervals instead of single values to express delays. This makes the delay itself uncertain, but bounded. The proposed syntax is $b = a \$ [d_1, d_2]$, where $d_1 \leq d_2 \in \mathbb{N}$.

We introduce also other extensions. first sampled and last sampled, which produce a new clock when sampling occurs the first or last time in the sampling period. allow and forbid, respectively allows and forbids clocks to occur within a time interval defined by 2 other clocks.

6   Implementation

Any language is hardly useful without the appropriate tooling. This section discusses the already available implementation and several ways to achieve the required analysis for the extended CCSL.

6.1 Simulation

We have implemented a preliminary version of a simulator [26] for the extended language. Not all constraints and features are implemented at this moment, meaning the whole use case is not feasible to express and simulate. Thus we have implemented a fragment that describes the PCV mode. It is able to produce traces of this mode, an example being Fig. 7.

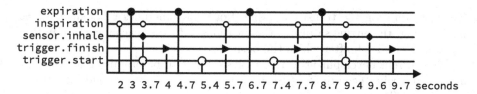

Fig. 7. Trace of specification for PCV mode.

6.2 Specialization

Specialization for Real-time CCSL means that depending on the shape of the specification, it may be beneficial to use or not real-time constraints, or a whole different representation. For example, in a specification with a real-time delay, if at no point it is checked when the ticks occur, the real-time information is irrelevant, and the constraint can be simplified to the causality relation. An example of such specification simplification is:

$$base = \texttt{repeat each } 20\,\text{MHz relative error } \pm 1\% \texttt{ offset } 0$$

$$delayed = \texttt{delay } external \texttt{ by } 5\,\text{ns}$$

$$detected = \texttt{sample } delayed \texttt{ on } base$$

$$\Downarrow \texttt{(erasure of real-time information)}$$

$$external \prec delayed$$

$$detected = \texttt{sample } delayed \texttt{ on } base$$

Another variant of the specialization is algebraic reasoning. For certain type of constraints, it is possible to conclude results without building any automata, only by manipulating relations related to real-time values. An example would be checking that neither of the ventilation modes allows for the valves to be closed or open for too long. Just making sure that the cycle has real-time delays defined or implied should be enough for the check.

6.3 Abstract Interpretation

CCSL is undecidable as it is Turing-complete, thus it is not possible to build a generic model checking. A way around it would be to use abstract interpretation that would trade precision for decidability and efficiency.

It is possible to express CCSL specifications as symbolic transition systems (sort of a program with constrained inputs) which then would be symbolically run by an abstract interpretation engine with a goal to prove that a bad condition is never reached. Generally, it includes partitioning the state of the transition system into locations, which later are complemented by an abstract domain, and specializations of the symbolic transition function from and to these locations. The specialization is made by propagating the reached state in the given location though the transition function and remembering to which locations it leads.

Then by iterating the transition application and sometimes refinement of the partitioning, the engine saturates the locations with the reachable state until a fixpoint is obtained, after which the property is checked.

The current development in the analysis seems to be promising as we managed to describe the core of CCSL with it. More precisely, we made the translation of CCSL into transition systems of NBac ([14], later used in [23]). Unfortunately, important optimizations and features are lacking due to the generic nature of the analysis. It is related both to the domains, optimizations in the application of the transition function and the properties we want to check. We intend to develop and implement the missing components as future work.

7   Conclusion

In this paper, we define a part of the specification that describes timing and causality relations between events of the mechanical lung ventilator, between its software and hardware parts. Missing requirements of the specification are either derived from pressure plots or common sense (different valves should not be opened at the same time) and influenced by the way of modelling in CCSL. We also include the patient safety check, formalized as a proof that under some conditions, the system specification satisfies the safety specification.

To describe the use case, we introduce several new constraints that express real-time relations directly and in turn allow easier reasoning and more consistent usage of real-time in specifications. We added other extensions, like modularity and separation of concern, parameters, as well as expressions and restrictions on the parameters. While this addition may not be theoretically significant, it allows users to better structure and scale the systems. It also includes the possibility to reuse generic specifications in different subsystems or even projects. We conclude the contribution with the addition of logical constraints. Some are just syntactic sugar, some are not. All are of equal importance if the goal is to avoid accidental complexity or cumbersome constructs.

The future work will consist of implementing the proposed extensions and further explore solutions sketched in this paper. We expect that execution of proofs in a proof tree can be produced by dedicated tools. Some work of using abstract interpretation for relevant subsets has been done already, but it needs to be implemented for the new constructs and integrated with relevant optimization rules to produce the main solving engine of CCSL.

Competing Interests. The author(s) has no competing interests to declare that are relevant to the content of this manuscript.

References

1. Abrial, J.R., Butler, M., Hallerstede, S., Hoang, T.S., Mehta, F., Voisin, L.: Rodin: an open toolset for modelling and reasoning in Event-B. Int. J. Softw. Tools Technol. Transf. **12**(6), 447–466 (2010). https://doi.org/10.1007/s10009-010-0145-y

2. Alur, R., Dill, D.L.: A theory of timed automata. Theor. Comput. Sci. **126**(2), 183–235 (1994). 10/bn332s. https://www.sciencedirect.com/science/article/pii/0304397594900108
3. André, C., Mallet, F., Deantoni, J.: VHDL observers for clock constraint checking. IEEE Computer Society, July 2010. 10/bf3jng. https://hal.inria.fr/inria-00587107
4. Arnold, A.: Finite Transition Systems - Semantics of Communicating Systems. International Series in Computer Science, Prentice Hall, Hoboken (1994)
5. Arnold, A., Point, G., Griffault, A., Rauzy, A.: The AltaRica formalism for describing concurrent systems. Fundam. Inform. **40**(2-3), 109–124 (1999). 10/gpb5x8. https://content.iospress.com/articles/fundamenta-informaticae/fi40-2-3-02
6. Berry, G.: The Esterel v5 Language Primer, December 2002
7. Bonfanti, S., Gargantini, A.: The mechanical lung ventilator case study. In: Proceedings of the Rigorous State-Based Methods 10th International Conference, ABZ 2024. LNCS, vol. 14759. Springer, Cham (2024)
8. Bouyer, P., Gastin, P., Herbreteau, F., Sankur, O., Srivathsan, B.: Zone-based verification of timed automata: extrapolations, simulations and what next?, July 2022. https://doi.org/10.48550/arXiv.2207.07479. http://arxiv.org/abs/2207.07479. arXiv:2207.07479 [cs] version: 1
9. Caspi, P., Pilaud, D., Halbwachs, N., Plaice, J.: LUSTRE: a declarative language for programming synchronous systems* (1987). https://www.semanticscholar.org/paper/LUSTRE%3A-A-declarative-language-for-programming-Caspi-Pilaud/893b9e21f01df1f14a922d2e4eb863be9ecb25d2
10. Colaço, J., Pagano, B., Pouzet, M.: SCADE 6: a formal language for embedded critical software development (invited paper). In: 11th International Symposium on Theoretical Aspects of Software Engineering, TASE, pp. 1–11. IEEE Computer Society (2017). https://doi.org/10.1109/TASE.2017.8285623
11. Cousot, P., Cousot, R.: Abstract interpretation: past, present and future. In: Proceedings of the Joint Meeting of the Twenty-Third EACSL Annual Conference on Computer Science Logic (CSL) and the Twenty-Ninth Annual ACM/IEEE Symposium on Logic in Computer Science (LICS), Vienna, Austria, pp. 1–10. ACM, July 2014. https://doi.org/10.1145/2603088.2603165. https://dl.acm.org/doi/10.1145/2603088.2603165
12. DeAntoni, J., Mallet, F.: TimeSquare: treat your models with logical time. In: Furia, C.A., Nanz, S. (eds.) TOOLS 2012. LNCS, vol. 7304, pp. 34–41. Springer, Heidelberg (2012). https://doi.org/10.1007/978-3-642-30561-0_4
13. Goknil, A., DeAntoni, J., Peraldi-Frati, M.A., Mallet, F.: Tool support for the analysis of TADL2 timing constraints using timesquare. In: 2013 18th International Conference on Engineering of Complex Computer Systems, Singapore, Singapore, pp. 145–154. IEEE, July 2013. https://doi.org/10.1109/ICECCS.2013.28. http://ieeexplore.ieee.org/document/6601815/
14. Jeannet, B.: Dynamic partitioning in linear relation analysis: application to the verification of reactive systems. Formal Methods Syst. Des. **23**(1), 5–37 (2003). https://doi.org/10.1023/A:1024480913162
15. Kirchner, F., Kosmatov, N., Prevosto, V., Signoles, J., Yakobowski, B.: Frama-C: a software analysis perspective. Formal Aspects Comput. **27**(3), 573–609 (2015). https://doi.org/10.1007/s00165-014-0326-7
16. Mallet, F.: Clock constraint specification language: specifying clock constraints with UML/MARTE. Innov. Syst. Softw. Eng. **4**, 309–314 (2008). 10/dn4ptd
17. Mallet, F., André, C.: UML/MARTE CCSL, signal and Petri nets. Report, INRIA (2008). https://hal.inria.fr/inria-00283077

18. Mallet, F., Millo, J.V., Romenska, Y.: State-based representation of CCSL operators. Technical report, Inria (2013)
19. Mallet, F., Millo, J.V., de Simone, R.: Safe CCSL specifications and marked graphs, p. 157. IEEE CS, October 2013. https://hal.inria.fr/hal-00913962
20. Mallet, F., de Simone, R.: Correctness issues on MARTE/CCSL constraints. Sci. Comput. Program. **106**, 78–92 (2015). 10/f7qbxg
21. Oueslati, A., Cuenot, P., Deantoni, J., Moreno, C.: System based interference analysis in Capella. J. Object Technol. **18**(2), 14:1 (2019). https://doi.org/10.5381/jot. 2019.18.2.a14. https://hal.inria.fr/hal-02182902
22. Peraldi-Frati, M.A., DeAntoni, J.: Scheduling multi clock real time systems: from requirements to implementation. In: 2011 14th IEEE International Symposium on Object/Component/Service-Oriented Real-Time Distributed Computing, pp. 50–57, March 2011. https://doi.org/10.1109/ISORC.2011.16. iSSN 2375-5261
23. Schrammel, P., Jeannet, B.: Logico-numerical abstract acceleration and application to the verification of data-flow programs. In: Yahav, E. (ed.) SAS 2011. LNCS, vol. 6887, pp. 233–248. Springer, Heidelberg (2011). https://doi.org/10.1007/978-3-642-23702-7_19
24. Spivey, J.M.: The Z Notation: A Reference Manual. Prentice Hall International Series in Computer Science, 2nd edn. Prentice Hall, New York (1992)
25. Suryadevara, J., Seceleanu, C., Mallet, F., Pettersson, P.: Verifying MARTE/CCSL mode behaviors using UPPAAL. In: Hierons, R.M., Merayo, M.G., Bravetti, M. (eds.) SEFM 2013. LNCS, vol. 8137, pp. 1–15. Springer, Heidelberg (2013). https://doi.org/10.1007/978-3-642-40561-7_1
26. Tokariev, P.: Implementation of MRTCCSL. https://github.com/PaulRaUnite/mrtccsl
27. Tokariev, P.: Mechanical lung ventilator specification. https://github.com/PaulRaUnite/mlv_spec
28. Zhang, M., Song, F., Mallet, F., Xiaohong, C.: SMT-based bounded schedulability analysis of the clock constraint specification language, April 2019. https://hal.inria.fr/hal-02080763

An EVENT-B Model of a Mechanical Lung Ventilator

Amel Mammar[(✉)]

SAMOVAR, Télécom SudParis, Institut Polytechnique de Paris, Evry, France
amel.mammar@telecom-sudparis.eu

Abstract. In this paper, we present a formal EVENT-B model of the Mechanical Lung Ventilator (MLV), the case study provided by the ABZ'24 conference. This system aims at helping patients maintain good breathing by providing mechanical ventilation. For this purpose, two modes are possible: *Pressure Controlled Ventilation* (PCV) and *Pressure Support Ventilation* (PSV). In the former mode, respiratory cycles are completely defined by the patient that is able to start breathing on its own. In the latter mode, the respiratory cycle is constant and controlled by the ventilator. Let us note that it is possible to move from a given mode to the other depending on the breathing capabilities of the patient under ventilation. In this paper, we illustrate the use of a correct-by-construction approach, the EVENT-B formal method and its refinement process, for the formal modeling and the verification of such a complex and critical system. The development of the formal models has been achieved under the RODIN platform that provides us with automatic and interactive provers used to verify the correctness of the models. We have also validated the built EVENT-B models using the PROB animator/model checker.

Keywords: Mechanical Lung Ventilator · System modeling · EVENT-B method · Refinement · Verification

1 Introduction

The paper presents the formal modelling of a Mechanical Lung Ventilator (MLV), a case study proposed in the context of the ABZ'24 conference. The goal of this system is to offer a support for patients that are in intensive therapy and thus need a mechanical ventilation. This system includes two ventilation modes: *Pressure Controlled Ventilation* (PCV) and *Pressure Support Ventilation* (PSV). The use of a given mode depends on the breathing capabilities of the patient. Basically, the PCV mode is used for patients that are not capable of breathing on their own. In this case, the breathing cycle (among others, inspiration and expiration) is entirely controlled by the ventilator. The PSV mode is used for other patients that can initiate breathing cycles. To ensure

---

This work was supported by the ANR project DISCONT.

the safety of a patient, the controller can decide to switch from PSV to PCV when it detects that the patient is not able to re-start inspiration. Similarly, the user(technician/doctor) can ask the controller to move to the PSV mode if he/she assesses that the patient is able to breath on its own. The MLV is composed of two main components, the *controller* and the GUI (Graphical User Interface), that interact with each other while having some independent phases/states and some synchronisation points (see Fig. 1): the user sends commands to the controller through the GUI, the controller informs the user about the status of the ventilation using the GUI. According to the requirement document(Requirements **GUI.2** and **GUI.13**), any crash that may happen on the GUI does not affect the controller that continues accomplishing at least the activities that do not require user interactions.

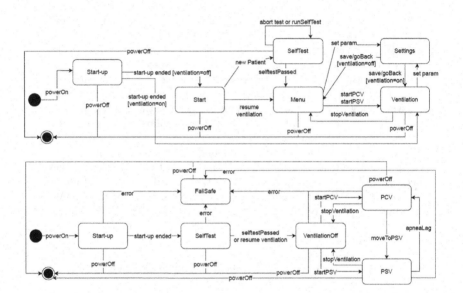

Fig. 1. GUI/Controller state machines taken from [2]

The present paper introduces an EVENT-B formal model of the MLV system built incrementally thanks to the refinement concept of the EVENT-B method. The refinement technique permits to master the complexity of a system by gradually introducing its components and characteristics. The obtained model has been validated by simulating some scenarios using PROB [4] and proved under RODIN [3] that provides us with automatic and interactive provers like AtelierB provers, SMT, etc.

The rest of this paper is structured as follows. A brief description the EVENT-B method is provided in the next section, then Sect. 3 presents our modelling strategy. Section 4 describes our model in more details. The validation and verification of our model are discussed in Sect. 5. Finally, Sect. 6 concludes the paper.

2   EVENT-B Method

Introduced by J-R.Abrial, the formal EVENT-B method [1] is a mathematical concepts-based approach to build correct-by-design discrete systems. An EVENT-B model is made up of components, each of which can either be a *context* or a *machine*. A context models the static part of a system and may define constants and sets (user-defined types) together with axioms that specify their properties. A context is seen by machines that model the dynamic part in terms of variables and a number of events. The type of these variables and the properties that must be satisfied whatever the evolution of the system are specified as invariants using first-order logic and arithmetic.

To master the complexity of a system, EVENT-B defines a refinement technique that allows for an incremental development. Machines are related by a refinement relation (**refines**) whereas the contexts are linked by an extension link (**extends**). By refinement, new variables, events and properties are introduced along with guard strengthening and nondeterminism reduction. A new event introduced in a model M', which refines a model M, is considered to refine a *skip* event of M. Therefore, this new event cannot modify a variable of M. As a result, any event that needs to modify a variable v must be defined in the same model where v is first introduced.

The EVENT-B models presented in this paper have been built, validated and proved within the Rodin platform [3] that provides editors, provers and plugins for various tasks like animation and model checking with PROB [4].

3   Modelling Strategy

3.1   Control Abstraction

Through the formal modeling of the different ABZ case studies [6–9] we have carried out, the use of the concepts described by Parnas and Madey in [10] has proved to be very suitable for the modeling of control systems. This is why we propose to reuse the same paradigm to build the EVENT-B formal models for the MLV.

The MLV system can be considered as a control system that uses sensors to acquire information from the environment elements m, called *monitored* variables (*e.g.*, state/value of the valves but also the different orders sent by the user like starting/stopping ventilation, etc.), and provides these measures to the controller as an *input* variable i. Depending on the information received by the sensors, the controller sends commands via actuators. The objective of these commands, called *output* variable o, is to modify the value of some characteristics of the environment, called a *controlled* variable c. In this particular case study, the controller also sends commands to the GUI to inform the user about the state of the system. These different elements (environment and controller elements) are modelled as variables in EVENT-B. In this paper, we do not model the delays of the sensors/actuators. In other words, we consider such delays are insignificant compared to other actions.

A control system can be viewed from two different perspectives: a control loop that acquires all inputs at once, at a given moment, and then computes all output commands in the same iteration. But, it can be also viewed as a continuous system that can be interrupted by any change in the environment represented by a new value sent by a sensor. In this paper, we adopt the second view where the controller/GUI reacts to each modification of the environment element. From the EVENT-B point of the view, we model each of these modifications as an EVENT-B event.

3.2 Modeling Structure

The EVENT-B specification of the MLV is composed of 6 levels (6 machines and 7 contexts) built iteratively using refinement. Before elaborating this final structure, we have evaluated several alternatives which differ on the following main points:

1. which component, GUI or the controller, should be modelled at first?
2. which level is the best to introduce time?
3. can the controller event error be dealt with like other events?
4. can the events common to the GUI and the controller (powerOn, powerOff, start-up ended, etc.) be represented by a single EVENT-B event?

In the following, we give and justify the choices made for each point:

1. As depicted in Fig. 1, even if the first step of the controller's behavior is independent from that of the GUI, we model the GUI at first because the main functionalities of the controller depend on the orders received from the GUI. Indeed, some events of the controller's state machine are those received from the GUI (startPCV, stopVentilation, etc.).
2. To master the complexity of EVENT-B models, a common practice is to introduce the time aspect as late as possible. For this particular case study, this was not possible because when the controller is on backup battery, its state may change (become Off) when the battery level is null. Thus, we introduce the time aspect starting from the first level by defining the event progress that models time progression.
3. Contrary to the other events, the controller can at any moment raise an error and move to a safe state where no action is possible anymore. As an error may be due to several causes (valve failure, backup battery failure, etc.), we chose to represent this event as the refinement of the event progress that can detect at any time malfunctions in the system.
4. Even if two transitions of the GUI and the controller states machines are labelled with the same event start-up ended, this event does not have the same effect (actions to execute) on the GUI and the controller. Indeed, the GUI may crash and require to be re-initiated from the initial state, but the behaviour of the controller is not affected at all. This is why we defined two different events, startUpEndedGui for the GUI and startUpEndedCont for the controller.

Given the above, the first level (context GuiStates + machine GuiSM) of the EVENT-B specification models the different states and the transitions of the GUI along with the backup/external batteries of the system. Mainly, each transition of the GUI's state machine is translated into an EVENT-B event. In particular, we modelled all the transitions ongoing/outgoing to/from the state Ventilation with a unique event changeMode that is refined later into several events, that is, one event per transition. At this level, we introduce the time progression by specifying that this event can make the system move into the state Off when specific conditions are fulfilled. In the second level, we model the state machine of the controller (context ContStates + machine ContSM). The third level (contexts {ComParams, PCVParams, PSVParams} + machine Ventilation) models the two ventilation modes (PSV and PCV) along with their associated parameters. The next level (context VentilStates + machine VentilationPhases) details the different phases of a respiratory cycle (*inspiratory, expiratory, inspiratory/expiratory pauses*, etc.). In the last level (context Alarms + machine MVLWithAlarms), we model some alarms that can be raised either by the GUI or the controller.

3.3 Considered Requirements

The requirements document [2] is very large and contains a huge number of requirements that are classified according to the related elements (GUI, controller, valves, alarms, etc.). Some of them are even reported in several sections since they depend on several elements. As it will be difficult to enumerate all the properties that have been considered, we give hereafter the main functionalities we have considered for the development of the EVENT-B model:

- the different states of the controller and the GUI as depicted in Fig. 1: we have considered all the states and also all the possible transitions between them,
- the different ventilation modes (PCV and PSV) and the switching from one to the other,
- the ventilation parameters and their update before and during the ventilation,
- the position of the valves (*in* and *out*) during the ventilation and their failures,
- Alarms related to the following failures:
  - the valves (*in* and *out*),
  - patient connection while the system is in the state StartUp,
  - ventilation parameters values that can be outside the allowed values,
  - the backup battery, the switchover, the FI1/FI12/oxygen sensors.

4 Model Details

In this section, we give some excerpts of the EVENT-B specification of the MLV system. The complete archive of the EVENT-B project is available in [5]. Except Section that describes the first abstract level and the first refinement, each subsection will describe a specific refinement level.

4.1 Machines GuiSM + ConSM

Machines GuiSM and ConSM model the state transition machines of the GUI and the controller. For the GUI for instance, we create the context GuiStates that defines a set of all its possible states *ModesG* and a constant *possTransG* that represents the allowed transitions between these states. Even if the state machine of the GUI considers a super state Ventilation, we split it to two sub-states PCV and PSV (see Fig. 1).

axm1: **partition**(*Ventilation*, {*PCV*}, {*PSV*})
axm2: **partition**(*ModesG*, {StartUp}, {*Start*}, {Menu}, {SelfTest},
$\qquad\qquad\qquad\qquad\qquad$ {Settings},Ventilation, {Off})
axm3: *possTransG* ∈ **BOOL** → ℙ(*ModesG* × *ModesG*)
axm4: *possTransG* = {**TRUE** ↦ {*Menu* ↦ *Settings, Settings* ↦ *Menu*, ...} ∪
$\qquad\qquad\qquad\quad$ ({*Menu, Settings*} × *Ventilation*)∪ ...∪
$\qquad\qquad\qquad\quad$ (*Ventilation* × ({*Menu,Settings*}∪ *Ventilation*)),
$\qquad$ **FALSE** ↦ (*ModesG* × {*Off*}))}

The set *possTransG*(**TRUE**) (resp. *possTransG*(**FALSE**)) denotes the allowed transitions when the power is on (the user pushes power button on the ventilator unit), the backup battery or the external power (AC) did not fail and the GUI did not crash. This property, deduced from the state machine of the GUI, is specified in the machine GuiSM by the following invariant:

$modeGP \neq modeG \Rightarrow$
$\quad modeGP \mapsto modeG \in$
$\qquad possTransG(\mathbf{bool}(power=\mathbf{TRUE} \wedge crashed = \mathbf{FALSE} \wedge$
$(onAC = \mathbf{TRUE} \vee (switchover = \mathbf{TRUE} \wedge batLev > 0 \wedge batFail=\mathbf{FALSE}))))$

where the variables are defined as follows:

- *modeG*(resp. *modeGP*) denotes the current (resp. previous) state of the GUI,
- *power*: states whether the power is on or not, that is, whether the user pushes power button on the ventilator unit or not.
- *crashed*: states whether the GUI is crashed or not,
- *OnAC*: states whether the system is powered using the external power AC or not,
- *switchover* (resp. *batFail*): denotes the state of the switchover (resp. backup battery),
- *batLev*: denotes the level of the backup battery.

In the machine GuiSM, we define, among others, the event saveBackAbort that corresponds to the transition labelled save/goBack of the GUI state machine (see Fig. 1). This event is used to store or abort the parameters update performed by the user in the state Settings. As we can remark, this transition has one source state Settings but two possible target states Menu and Ventilation. In fact, the GUI has to come back to its previous state when the user asks for the parameters setting. In the machine GuiSM, this event is specified as follows where *modeg* is an event parameter that denotes the new state of the GUI after the execution of the event:

Event saveBackAbort $\widehat{=}$
   any
      modeg
   where
      grd1: $modeG = $ Settings $\wedge\ modeg \in ModesG$
      grd2: $modeg \in Ventilation \cup \{$Menu$\}$
   then
      act1: $modeG := modeg$
      act2: $modeGP := modeG$
   end

The guard grd1 states that this event is enabled when the GUI is in the state Settings, This event makes the GUI move to a new state *modeg* that may be *Ventilation* or *Menu* (Guard grd2). Indeed, from the state Settings, the system should come back to its previous state. This state can be deduced from the state of the controller: if the controller was ventilating, *modeg* is equal to *Ventilation*, otherwise it is equal to *Menu*. This is modelled by refining the event saveBackAbort in the machine ContSM and adding the following guards with *modeC* and *modec* representing respectively the current and the next state of the controller:

grd1: $modeC \neq FailSafe$
grd2: $modeC \in Ventilation \Rightarrow modec \in Ventilation \wedge modeg = modec$
grd3: $modeC \notin Ventilation \Rightarrow modec = modeC \wedge modeg = Menu$

In order to save/abort the ventilation parameters, the controller should not be in the state *FailSafe* (Guard grd1). After saving/aborting the parameters update, we distinguish the following cases:

- if the controller is ventilating, it will still ventilating and the GUI will be in the same state as the controller. This means that before being in the state Settings, the GUI was in the state Ventilation and the user asks for a parameters update during ventilation: the transition setParam from the state Ventilation to the state Settings. Let us remark that after saving/aborting parameters setting, even if the controller is ventilating, it may change the ventilating mode, moving from PCV to PSV, when asked by the user. This is why the guard grd2 does not state that the current/next states *modeC* and *modec* are equal.
- if the controller is not ventilating (state *VentilationOff*, the controller will stay in the same state and the GUI will move (comes back more precisely) to the state *Menu*. This means that before being in the state Settings, the GUI was in the state Menu and triggered the transition setParam from the state Menu to the state Settings

Machines GuiSM and ContSM also specify a generic event changeMode that permits switching between modes Settings and Ventilation for the GUI and between different ventilation modes (PCV and PSV) for the controller. This event is specified as follows (parts in bold are those added by refinement in the machine ContSM):

Event changeMode $\widehat{=}$
refines changeMode
   any
       $modeg,\ modec$
   where
      grd1: $modeG \in \texttt{Ventilation}$
      grd2: $modeg \in \texttt{Ventilation} \cup \{\texttt{Settings}\}$
      grd3: $\boldsymbol{modeC} \in \texttt{Ventilation} \wedge \boldsymbol{modec} \in \texttt{Ventilation}$
   then
      act1: $modeG := modeg$
      act2: $modeGP := modeG$
      act3: $\boldsymbol{modeC := modec}$
      act4: $\boldsymbol{modeCP := modeC}$
  end

From the GUI point of view, the guards grd1 and grd2 state that when the MLV is ventilating, it is possible either to move to state $\texttt{Settings}$ in order to modify the ventilating parameters or continue to ventilate. Guard grd3 specifies that this event can be enabled when the controller is ventilating. This event makes the controller continue the ventilation ($modec \in \texttt{Ventilation}$) but possibly by changing its ventilation mode.

Finally, we have the event *progress* that models time progression with the possibility of modifying the state of both the GUI and the controller. The main parts of this event are as follows:

Event progress $\widehat{=}$
refines progress
   any
       $step,\ modec,\ l,\ batf,\ \ldots$
   where
      grd1: $step \in \mathbb{N}1 \wedge l \in \mathbb{N}1 \wedge batf \in \textbf{BOOL}$
      grd2: $modec \in \{\texttt{FailSafe},\ modeC,\ \texttt{Off},\ \texttt{StartUp}\}$
      grd3: $(l = 0 \vee batf=\textbf{TRUE} \vee switchover=\textbf{FALSE}) \wedge onAC = \textbf{FALSE}$
           $\Rightarrow$
         $modec=\texttt{Off}$
      grd4: $(batLev > 0 \wedge l > 0) \vee switchover = \textbf{FALSE} \vee onAC = \textbf{TRUE} \vee$
        $power = \textbf{FALSE}$
           $\Rightarrow$
         $modec \in \{modeC,\ \texttt{FailSafe}\}$
        $\ldots$
   then
      act1: $curTime := curTime + step$
      act2: $batLev := l$
      act3: $batFail := batf$
      act4: $modeC := modec$
        $\ldots$
  end

Event progress makes time progress by *step* units of time. It stores the new level of the backup battery (l) and its status (*batf* is true if the backup battery fails). The state of the controller may change as stated by guards grd3 and grd4: if the system is on the backup battery whose level is null or it has a defect, the controller moves to state **Off**. In the conditions specified by the guard grd4, either the controller does not change its states or goes to the state *failSafe* (see Sect. 4.5).

4.2 Machine **Ventilation**

In this machine, we mainly model the ventilation parameters and the switch between the PCV to PSV modes. As the parameters of the GUI and those of the controller may be different before saving the GUI parameters, we have defined a separate set of variables for each. The PSV parameters for instance are modelled by the following invariants:

inv1: $psvParamsValC \in 0..curTime \twoheadrightarrow (psvParams \twoheadrightarrow \mathbb{N}_1)$
inv2: $\forall x.\ x \in \mathrm{ran}(psvParamsValC) \Rightarrow psvParams \setminus \{\texttt{RRAP, PinspAP}\} \subseteq \mathrm{dom}(x)$
inv3: $modeC = \text{PSV}$
$$\Rightarrow$$
$$\mathrm{dom}(psvParamsValC(\mathrm{max}(\mathrm{dom}(psvParamsValC))))=psvParams$$

Invariant inv1 gives the type of the variable *psvParamsValC* that represents the PSV parameters stored in the controller. As one can notice, we use partial function since these parameters may have no values at given moments (when the controller/GUI crashes for instance). Invariant inv2 states that the parameters that should always have values. Finally, invariant inv3 specifies that all the PSV parameters should be valued when the PSV ventilation mode is selected. A similar variable *psvParamsValG* is defined for the GUI. In this machine, we also model the action of the user that wants to change the ventilation mode from PCV to PSV. Thus, we have introduced a Boolean variable *PCV2PSV* with the following invariant that states that when the user asks for moving from PCV to PSV, the possibility of modifying the parameters is given for the user (*modeG* = **Settings**); in that case the controller is either ventilating or in the state **FailSafe**. We have deduced this invariant from the state machines of both the GUI and the controller.

inv1: $PCV2PSV = \textbf{TRUE}$
$$\Rightarrow$$
$$modeG = \texttt{Settings} \wedge modeC \in \{\texttt{PCV, FailSafe}\}$$

In the machine Ventilation, the event changeMode is refined by the event move-ToPSV as follows: we state in the guards that the event is enabled when both the GUI and the controller are in the state PCV, then the GUI moves into the state **Settings** while the controller stays in the same state.

Event moveToPSV $\,\widehat{=}\,$
refines changeMode
    any
        modeg, modec
   where

$$\begin{aligned}
&\texttt{grd1:} \ \dots \\
&\texttt{grd2:} \ \dots \\
&\texttt{grd3:} \ \dots \\
&\texttt{grd4:} \ modeG = \textsf{PCV} \wedge modeC = \textsf{PCV} \\
&\texttt{grd5:} \ modeg = \textsf{Settings} \wedge modec = modeC
\end{aligned}$$

then

$$\begin{aligned}
&\texttt{act1:} \dots \\
&\texttt{act2:} \dots \\
&\texttt{act3:} \dots \\
&\texttt{act4:} \dots \\
&\texttt{act5:} \ PCV2PSV := \textbf{TRUE}
\end{aligned}$$

end

Similarly, the event saveBackAbort is refined by distinguishing the cases where the parameters are saved or not. Mainly, we introduce a new Boolean event parameter sv with the following semantics: if sv is true, the controller parameters become equal to those of the GUI, otherwise (the user aborts the parameters update) the GUI parameters become equal to their previous values that are those of the controller. Moreover, if the variable $PCV2PSV$ is true, the controller should move to the PSV mode. The refinement of the event saveBackAbort is as follows where $\mathbf{max}(\mathbf{dom}(psvParamsValG))$ is used to denote the moment of the last update of the parameters:

Event saveBackAbort $\widehat{=}$
refines saveBackAbort

    any

        $modeg, modec, sv, psvC, psvG,\dots$

    where

$$\begin{aligned}
&\texttt{grd1:} \ \dots \\
&\quad \dots \\
&\texttt{grd6:} \ PCV2PSV = \textbf{TRUE} \wedge modeC = \text{PCV} \Rightarrow modec{=}\text{PSV} \\
&\texttt{grd7:} \ PCV2PSV = \textbf{FALSE} \vee modeC \neq \text{PCV} \Rightarrow modec{=}modeC \\
&\texttt{grd8:} \ psvG{=}\{\textbf{TRUE} \mapsto psvParamsValG(\mathbf{max}(\mathbf{dom}(psvParamsValG))), \\
&\qquad \textbf{FALSE}{\mapsto} psvParamsValC(\mathbf{max}(\mathbf{dom}(psvParamsValC)))\}(sv) \\
&\texttt{grd9:} \ psvC{=}\{\textbf{TRUE} \mapsto psvParamsValG(\mathbf{max}(\mathbf{dom}(psvParamsValG))), \\
&\qquad \textbf{FALSE}{\mapsto} psvParamsValC(\mathbf{max}(\mathbf{dom}(psvParamsValC)))\}(sv) \\
&\texttt{grd10:} \ modec = \text{PSV} \Rightarrow \mathbf{dom}(psvC){=}psvParams
\end{aligned}$$

    then

$$\begin{aligned}
&\texttt{act1:} \dots \\
&\quad \dots \\
&\texttt{act5:} \ psvParamsValG(curTime) := psvG \\
&\texttt{act6:} \ psvParamsValC(curTime) := psvC \\
&\texttt{act7:} \ PCV2PSV := \textbf{FALSE}
\end{aligned}$$

end

4.3   Machine VentilationPhase

In this level, we detail the different breathing phases: *inspiration, inspiration pause, expiration, expiration pause*, etc. To this end, we define a variable *cycles* that denotes the set of the breathing cycles. A new breathing cycle is created for each new inspiration; its current phase and mode are stored in the variables *cycleMode* and *ventilPhase* defined as follows:

axm1: **partition**(*ventSates*,{inspBeg},{inspEnd},{expBeg},{expEnd},...)
inv1: *cycleMode* $\in$ *cycles*$\rightarrow$ *Ventilation*
inv2: *ventilPhase* $\in$ *cycles* $\rightarrow$ *ventSates*

One can wonder why we have to store the mode of each cycle. We do that because the breathing mode may change during any breathing cycle c, but the characteristics of this cycle should not be modified. Let us consider for instance the requirement **CONT.22** for the mode PCV: *The cycle starts with the inspiration phase that lasts an inspiratory time* $I = 60 \times IE_{PCV} \div ((RR_{PCV} * (1 + IE_{PCV})))$. A naive modeling of this requirement would be (RR_{PCV} denotes the Respiratory Rate, IE_{PCV} is the ratio of inspiratory time to expiratory time):

$\forall\ c.\ c \in cycles \wedge modeC = $ PCV $\Rightarrow$
$inspEndT(c)$ - $inspBegT(c)$=10 $* 60 \times (pcvParamsValC(curTime))(IE_{PCV}) \div$
$\quad\quad ((pcvParamsValC(curTime))(RR_{PCV})*$
$\quad\quad\quad\quad (1 + (pcvParamsValC(curTime))(IE_{PCV})))$ $\quad\quad$ **(InspDur)**

where *inspBegT* (resp. *inspEndT*) gives the start (resp. end) time of a cycle. This modeling is inadequate because during a breathing cycle both values of variables *pcvParamsValC* and *modeC* may change. This is why we need to define an expression that depends on the values of the parameters taken at the beginning of the inspiration phase. So, we propose instead the following invariant where t is used to denote the values of the parameters at the moment where the breathing cycle c starts. As one can remark, this invariant uses values *pcvParamsValC*(t) and *cycleMode* that never change even if the PCV parameters and ventilation mode are updated.

$\forall\ c, t.\ c \in cycles \wedge t = $ **max**($\{x \mid x \in $ **dom**($pcvParamsValC$) $\wedge x \leq inspBegT(c)\}$) $\wedge$
$\quad\quad cycleMode(c) = $ PCV
$\quad\quad\quad \Rightarrow$
$inspEndT(c)$ - $inspBegT(c)$=10 $\times 60 * (pcvParamsValC(t))(IE_{PCV}) \div$
$\quad\quad ((pcvParamsValC(t))(RR_{PCV})*$
$\quad\quad\quad\quad (1 + (pcvParamsValC(t))(IE_{PCV})))$

In the machine VentilationPhase we define two events (Start and End) for each ventilation phase. Below, we give the specification of the event inspStart that represents the beginning of a new inspiration. Basically, the event start by creating a new cycle *cy* for which a mode (*modeC*), an inspiration phase (inspBeg), a beginning (curTime) and end (*inspT*) times are assigned. This event can be enabled when the system is ventilating (Guard grd1), all others cycles reach their end states (grd2: **ran**(*ventilPhase*) $\subseteq$ {expEnd,expPauseEnd}). In that case, the end inspiration time is calculated according to the guard grd3 with the last values of *pcvParamsValC* before the inspiration time ($t = $ **max**(**dom**($pcvParamsValC$))). Let us remark that we cannot replace t with *curTime* since *pcvParamsValC* is not updated continuously but only at some moments. Thus, *pcvParamsValC* can be not valued at *curTime*, this is why we take the value of the last update of this variable.

Event inspStart $\widehat{=}$

   any

        $cy,\ inspT,\ t$

   where

        grd1: $modeC \in$ Ventilation $cy \in Cycles \setminus cycles$

        grd2: $t = \mathbf{max}(\mathbf{dom}(pcvParamsValC)) \wedge$

                $\mathbf{ran}(ventilPhase) \subseteq \{\textbf{expEnd},\textbf{expPauseEnd}\}$

        grd3: $modeC=$PCV

         $\Rightarrow$

         $inspT=curTime + 10 \times 60 \times (pcvParamsValC(t))(I : E_{PCV}) \div$

              $((pcvParamsValC(t))(RR_{PCV}) \times$

                    $(1 + (pcvParamsValC(t))$

   then

        act1: $cycles := cycles \cup \{cy\}$

        act2: $cycleMode(cy) :=modeC$

        act3: $ventilPhase(cy):=$**inspBeg**

        act4: $inspBegT(cy):=\ curTime$

        act5: $inspEndT(cy):=inspT$

   end

4.4 Machine Valves

In the machine Valves, we model the state/position of the valves during the different breathing phases. We define two Boolean variables $inValve$ and $outValve$ for in and out valves respectively: **TRUE** (resp. **FALSE**) for an open (resp.closed) valve. Moreover, we define two Boolean variables $inValveF$/$outValveF$ to model the failure of these valves. For each requirement on the position of a given valve during a breathing phase, we define a particular invariant. For instance, the requirement stating that the in (resp. out) valve is open (resp. closed) during the inspiration is modelled by the following invariant:

inv1: $(\exists\ c.\ c \in cycles \wedge ventilPhase(c) \in \{\textbf{inspBeg, inspEnd}\}) \wedge inValveF = \textbf{FALSE} \wedge$
     $modeC =$ Ventilation $\Rightarrow inValve = \textbf{TRUE}$

inv2: $(\exists\ c.\ c \in cycles \wedge ventilPhase(c) \in \{\textbf{inspBeg, inspEnd}\}) \wedge outValveF = \textbf{FALSE} \wedge$
     $modeC =$ Ventilation $\Rightarrow outValve = \textbf{FALSE}$

To maintain these invariants, each event representing the beginning/end of a breathing phase is refined by adding adequate actions that open/close a valve if it is not defective. Event inspStart is refined by adding the following actions:

$inValve := \{\textbf{FALSE} \mapsto \textbf{TRUE}, \textbf{TRUE} \mapsto inValve\}(inValveF)$

$outValve := \{\textbf{FALSE} \mapsto \textbf{FALSE}, \textbf{TRUE} \mapsto outValve\}(outValveF)$

4.5 Machine MVLAlarms

Machine MVLAlarms models the different undesirable situations that may occur on the system. The case study specifies a huge number of such undesirable states. Roughly speaking, when an undesirable situation happens, the controller/GUI emits an alarm and bring the system in a safe state by closing the *in* valve and opening the *out* one. At the time of the submission of this paper, we have mainly modelled alarms related to the valves, the backup battery failure, GUI failure and Controller failure. To this end, we define in a new context the set of all the possible failures we consider as follows:

axm1: **partition**($Alarms$,{guiFailure},{contFailure},
{inValveFailure},{patConnected},...)

Then, in the machine MVLAlarms, we introduce a new varaible *alarmRaised* as a Boolean total function that indicates whether an given alarm is raised or not: $alarmRaised \in Alarms \rightarrow$ **BOOL**. For each type of alarm, we specify the conditions under which it must be raised. For the *in* valve for instance, we specify that the inValveFailure must be raised in the following two conditions:

1. the *in* valve is closed while there is a cycle c in one of the following breathing phase: *inspiration* or *recruitment maneuver*,
2. the *in* valve is open while there is a cycle c in one of the following breathing phase: *expiration* or *inspiratory/expiratory pause*.

These two conditions are modelled using the following invariant:

$alarmRaised($inValveFailure$)=$ **bool**$(\exists\ c.\ (c \in cycles\ \wedge$
$((((ventilPhase(c)=$**inspBeg**$\wedge\ curTime > inspBegT(c))\ \vee$
$(ventilPhase(c) =$ **rmBeg** $\wedge\ curTime > rmBegT(c)))\ \wedge$
$$inValveP =\textbf{FALSE}$$
$))\ \vee$
$(((ventilPhase(c) =$ **expPauseBeg** $\wedge\ curTime > expPauseBegT(c))\ \vee$
$(ventilPhase(c) =$ **expBeg** $\wedge\ curTime > expBegT(c))\ \vee$
$(ventilPhase(c)=$**inspPauseBeg** $\wedge\ curTime > inspPauseBegT(c))\ )\ \wedge$
$$inValveP =\textbf{TRUE}))))$$

Let us remark the use of a new variable *inValveP* introduced in order to express this dynamic property. It is used to store the previous state of the *in* valve. Indeed, when the controller detects a defect on a valve it forces it to move into a safe position. Therefore, it not possible to express this property using the variable *inValve* as its position changes when an alarm is raised on it. To maintain this invariant, the event **progress** is refined by adding the following guards: grd1 defines an event parameter to verify if the conditions to raise the *in* valve alarm are fulfilled. If so, the second guard grd2 puts the controller into the state *FailSafe*.

grd1: $alarmInV=$**bool**$(\exists\ c.\ (c \in cycles\ \wedge($
$(ventilPhase(c) \in \{inspBeg,\ inspEnd,\ rmBeg,\ rmEnd\}\ \wedge\ inValve=$**FALSE**$)$
$\vee$
$(ventilPhase(c) \in \{expPauseBeg,\ inspPauseBeg,\ inspPauseEnd\}\ \wedge$
$$inValve =\textbf{TRUE}))))$$
grd2: $alarmInV =$ **TRUE** $\Rightarrow modec=$FailSafe

We also update the variables *alarmRaised* and *inValveP* in the event progress by assigning true to the alarms to raise. The variable is updated as follows:

$$alarmRaised := alarmRaised \lhd \{..., inValveFailure \mapsto alarmInV\}$$
$$inValveP := inValve$$

5   Validation and Verification

The verification and validation of the built EVENT-B specification have been achieved in three steps detailed hereafter. It is worth noting that these steps are performed in an iterative manner to detect bugs as soon as possible.

5.1   Model Checking of the Specification

For complex systems as the one presented in this paper, model-checking the specification is not only useful for verifying the preservation of the invariant but this task also helps us during the development of the models, that is, finding the adequate invariants/guards/actions. Indeed, when the invariant depends on several variables that are modified by the same event, determining the right actions/guards is sometimes difficult. Basically, we proceed as follows. We write an initial specification for each event, then we use the PROB model checker to ensure that its guards/actions are sufficient for preservation of the invariant. Proceeding like this also avoids providing guards that are too strong. When the invariant is violated, PROB displays a trace (sequence of events), along with the values of each variable, that starting from the initial state of the machine, leads to a state that violates the related invariant. Analysing such a trace allows us to tweak the specification by revising the guards/actions of events but also sometimes the invariants itself that may be too strong. For this particular case study, the use of PROB helps us find the invariants corresponding to the duration of each breathing phase (**InspDur**). Indeed, as stated before (see Sect. 4.2), this invariant must not depend on the current values of the PCV/PSV parameters but on the last values just before the breathing cycle starts. The counterexample in that case is as follows: (1) a breathing cycle starts with a duration fulfilling the invariant **InspDur**; (2) the user updates the parameters; (3) the inspiration phase terminates with the previous value of the parameters making the invariant **InspDur** violated.

5.2   Proof of the Specification

The absence of invariant violation during the model-checking does not ensure that the specification is consistent. Indeed, PROB works with a timeout that may prevent us from finding complex scenarios with more events. Therefore, we need to proceed with the proof of the specification in order to verify that each event does preserve the invariant and that the guard of each refined event is stronger than that of the abstract one. These proof obligations are automatically generated by RODIN: 1322 proof obligations have been generated, of which 23% (312) were automatically proved by the various provers. The interactive proof of the remaining proof obligations took about three weeks since they are more complex and require several inference steps and need the use of external provers (like the Mono Lemma prover, *Dis-prove* with PROB and STM provers). During an interactive proof, users ask the internal prover to follow specific steps to discharge a proof obligation. A proof step consists in applying a deductive rule, adding a new hypothesis that is in turn proved or calling external provers. The external Mono Lemma prover has been very useful for arithmetic formulas. The more complex proofs for this particular case study have been those related to the breathing phase duration since we have to distinguish several cases depending on the ventilation mode.

5.3   Validation with Scenarios

In this step, we ensure that the built models does represent/prevent the desired/undesirable behaviours, that is, we have built the right models that behave as expected. Unfortunately, the requirements document does not contain enough scenarios that can be used as oracles during this task. Indeed, the provided scenarios are only related to some very basic behaviors, mainly some transitions of the state machines of the GUI and the controller. Therefore we have defined our own scenarios based on our understanding of the system. According to the state machines of the GUI and the controller, we have defined the scenarios that permit covering the different paths. Using PROB, we have validated the following functionalities of the system:

- The system permits to proceed with the ventilation of patient when no error is detected by the controller and the GUI never crashes. This corresponds to the *nominal behaviour*.
- The controller continues to work even if the GUI crashes. When the GUI re-initialises, its next state is Ventilation if the controller is ventilating, Start otherwise.
- It is possible to update the ventilation parameters during ventilation, and this does not affect the current cycle if any.
- In case of error, the controller moves into the state FailSafe and no action is possible anymore.
- The position of the valves are appropriate for each breathing phase and any failure makes the controller move into the state FailSafe with the valves in an adequate position.

6   Conclusion

In this paper, we presented an EVENT-B formal model of the Mechanical Lung Ventilator (MLV), the case study provided in the ABZ'2024 conference. Our specification takes most requirements and functionalities into account even if some alarms are not modelled. The main difficulty of this case study in the fact that some data can be modified during the ventilation phase while ensuring that the current breathing cycle continues with the previous values. From a practical point of view, this is reasonable since the cycle duration is very small compared to that of the parameters update. However as we do not model the update duration, we got a counterexample when the parameters are updated during the breathing cycle.

Compared to the previous ABZ case studies [7,9], the present case study is time-dependent as the state of the GUI/controller may change by time progression when the system is powered using the backup battery. This is why we introduced time from the first specification level along with the event **progress** that makes the time evolve. Moreover, PROB fails to find counterexamples on the last 3 refinement levels. This is due probably to the high number of invariants/events to check.

We think that the requirements document should be improved on several points. First, the document is not clear on the conditions under which the controller must move to the state **FailSafe**. For instance, apart from emitting an alert in case of some undesirable situations, the document does not clearly specify for which kinds of alarms the system has to move to the state **FailSafe**. Second, one can wonder whether the controller continuously checks the presence of undesirable events or not. The state machine of the controller specifies that errors may happen in any state, but it is not clear which ones can happen in each specific state. For instance, does the controller continuously checks the communication with the GUI or only in the state **StatUp**?

As future work, we plan to model more alarms to cover more error cases. We think that is not difficult since the remaining alarms are related to values of sensors that are independent of each other. So, we just have to add a variable that monitors the sensor value and raise an alarm if the read value is not in the range of the desired ones. Future improvements also include exploring the use of decomposition plugins available in RODIN for decomposing the models into smaller and thus more manageable units.

Competing Interests. The author(s) has no competing interests to declare that are relevant to the content of this manuscript.

References

1. Abrial, J.: Modeling in Event-B. Cambridge University Press, Cambridge (2010)
2. Bonfanti, S., Gargantini, A.: The mechanical lung ventilator case study. In: Bonfanti, S., et al. (eds.) ABZ 2024. LNCS, vol. 14759, pp. 281–288. Springer, Cham (2024)
3. EB Consortium. http://www.event-b.org/
4. Leuschel, M., Bendisposto, J., Dobrikov, I., Krings, S., Plagge, D.: From animation to data validation: the ProB constraint solver 10 years on. In: Boulanger, J.L. (ed.) Formal Methods Applied to Complex Systems: Implementation of the B Method, chap. 14, pp. 427–446. Wiley ISTE, Hoboken (2014)

5. Mammar, A.: An Event-B Model of Mechanical Lung Ventilator (2024). https://github.com/AmelMammar/MechanicalLungVentilator
6. Mammar, A., Frappier, M., Fotso, S.J.T., Laleau, R.: An Event-B Model of the Hybrid ERTMS/ETCS Level 3 Standard (2018). http://info.usherbrooke.ca/mfrappier/abz2018-ERTMS-Case-Study
7. Mammar, A., Frappier, M., Laleau, R.: An Event-B model of an automotive adaptive exterior light system. In: Raschke, A., Méry, D., Houdek, F. (eds.) ABZ 2020. LNCS, vol. 12071, pp. 351–366. Springer, Cham (2020). https://doi.org/10.1007/978-3-030-48077-6_28
8. Mammar, A., Leuschel, M.: Modeling and verifying an arrival manager using Event-B. In: Glässer, U., Creissac Campos, J., Méry, D., Palanque, P. (eds.) ABZ 2023. LNCS, vol. 14010, pp. 321–339. Springer, Cham (2023). https://doi.org/10.1007/978-3-031-33163-3_24
9. Mammar, A., Laleau, R.: Modeling a landing gear system in Event-B. STTT (2015)
10. Parnas, D.L., Madey, J.: Functional documents for computer systems. Sci. Comput. Program. **25**(1), 41–61 (1995)

Modelling a Mechanical Lung Ventilation System Using TASTD

Alex Rodrigue Ndouna$^{(\boxtimes)}$ (iD) and Marc Frappier (iD)

Université de Sherbrooke, Sherbrooke, QC J1K 2R1, Canada
{Alex.Rodrigue.Ndouna,Marc.Frappier}@USherbrooke.ca

Abstract. For the ABZ2024 conference, the proposed case study consists of modelling an adaptive outdoor mechanical lung ventilation system. The mechanical lung ventilator is intended to provide ventilation support for patients that are in intensive therapy and that require mechanical ventilation. The system under study is made up of two main software components: the graphical user interface (GUI) and the controller, this paper introduces a model for the controller part of the software system using Timed Algebraic State-Transition Diagrams (TASTD). TASTD is an extension of Algebraic State-Transition Diagrams (ASTD) providing timing operators to express timing constraints. The specification makes extensive use of the TASTD modularity capabilities, thanks to its algebraic approach, to model the behaviour of different sensors and actuators separately. We validate our specification using the cASTD compiler, which translates the TASTD specification into a C++ program. This generated program can be executed in simulation mode to manually update the system clock to check timing constraints. The model is executed on the test sequences provided with the case study. The advantages of having modularisation, orthogonality, abstraction, hierarchy, real-time, and graphical representation in one notation are highlighted with the proposed model.

Keywords: ASTD · real-time model · ABZ2024 case study · TASTD · formal method

1 Introduction

The ABZ2024 Conference case study [5] describes an mechanical lung ventilator system. This system is made up of two main software elements: the graphical user interface (GUI) and the controller. The GUI is a touchscreen panel that displays the information needed to check the respiratory condition, allows parameter settings, and displays ventilation parameters and alarm settings. When the controller receives operator input from the GUI, it communicates with the valve controllers, serial interfaces, and other subcomponents and sends them commands. A major

Supported by Public Safety Canada's Cyber Security Cooperation Program (CSCP) and NSERC (Natural Sciences and Engineering Research Council of Canada).

critical aspect of the system is its temporal behavior. Many properties and constraints have explicit temporal requirements (like after 7 s ..)

In this article we present the specification of the controller component for the ABZ2024 case study with TASTD [3] to demonstrate the usefulness of TASTD as a modelling language. We use ASTD tools [6] to generate executable code in C++, which could be deployed in an embedded system. First, we specify our model with the ASTD editor, eASTD [6]. Second, we produce executable code with the ASTD compiler, cASTD [6].

This paper is structured as follows. Section 2 provides a brief introduction to TASTD, its support tools, and highlights the distinctive features of our approach. Section 3 describes our modelling strategy. In Sect. 4, we take into account all the requirements of the controller component, except a minor one which deals with the graphical user interface. Section 5 presents the validation process of the case study model, and the discussion around the verification of the model. We discuss issues and flaws identified in the case study documentation [5] in Sect. 6. Lastly, Sect. 7 concludes the paper.

2 Distinctive Features of Our Approach

2.1 An Overview of TASTD

Timed Algebraic State-Transition Diagrams (TASTD) [3,4] is a time extension for ASTD [9]. ASTD allows the composition of automata using CSP-like process algebra operators: sequence, choice, Kleene closure, guard, parameterized synchronization, flow (the AND states of Statecharts), and quantified versions of parameterized synchronization and choice. Each ASTD operator defines an ASTD type that can be applied to sub-ASTDs. Elementary ASTDs are defined using automata. Automaton states can either be elementary or composite; a composite state can be of any ASTD type. Within an ASTD, a user can declare attributes (i.e., state variables). Actions written in C++ can be declared on automata transitions, states, and at the ASTD level; they are executed when a transition is triggered. These actions can modify ASTD attributes and execute arbitrary C++ code. Attributes can be of any C++ type (predefined or user defined).

TASTD introduces time-triggered transitions, i.e., transitions triggered when conditions referring to a global clock are satisfied. In ordinary ASTDs, only the reception of an event from the environment can trigger a transition. The special event Step labels the timed-triggered transitions. Step is treated as an event; its only particularity is that it is evaluated on a periodical basis. The specifier determines the value of the period according to the desired time granularity required to match system timing constraints. TASTD also introduces new ASTD timing operators that can perform Step transitions: delay, persistent delay, timeout, persistent timeout, and timed interrupt. TASTDs rely on the availability of a global clock called cst, which stands for *current system time*. If the guard of a Step transition is satisfied, the transition can be fired. TASTD is fully algebraic, TASTD operators can be freely mixed with ordinary ASTD operator.

2.2 TASTD Support Tools

TASTD specifications can be edited with a graphical tool called eASTD and translated into executable C++ programs using cASTD. The generated C++ programs can be used as an actual implementation of the TASTD specification. cASTD can generate code for simulation, where a manual clock, which the specifier controls, replaces the system clock. The specifier can decide to advance the clock to a specific time; the simulator will generate the Step events necessary to reach the specified time. Environment events can be submitted at these specified times. We use a simulation to validate the provided scenarios discussed in Sect. 5.

2.3 Distinctive Features of Our Modelling Approach

Modularisation, Hierarchy and Orthogonality. ASTD is an algebraic language, in the sense that an ASTD is either elementary, given by an automaton, or compound, given by a process algebra operator applied to its components. This algebraic approach streamlines modularity. A model can be decomposed into several parts which are combined with the process algebra operators. As it will be described in Sect. 3, the case study is decomposed into several parts which are specified separately and then connected with ASTD types synchronisation or flow. Each ASTD contains a name, parameters, variables, transitions, actions, and states (an initial state is required). An ASTD state may be of any ASTD type, called sub-ASTD, and share its variables, transitions, and states with its nested ASTDs. With this modular and hierarchical structure, isolating an ASTD and modifying its behaviour does not produce side effects in other ASTD. Modularity also makes the specification easier to understand, because each component can be analysed separately.

Time. In TASTD, time is integrated into its syntax and its semantics. As portrayed by the case study requirements, time management is implemented with clock variables or using TASTD operators. That allows us to produce executable code satisfying the time constraints.

Graphical Representation. With the ASTD graphical representation, to understand the behaviour of an ASTD is to reason about its transitions and states. ASTD visualisation is an advantage over other formal methods that only use textual representation, which makes their specification harder to understand.

3 Modelling Strategy

This section describes our modelling strategy and how the model is structured and provides insights into how we approached the formalization of the requirements. The complete model is found in [8].

Model Structure. Our specification mainly uses seven ASTD operators to structure the model. These are the flow operator, denoted by Ψ, the interleaving operator, denoted by $|||$, the sequence operator, denoted by $\rightarrow$, the kleene closure operator, denoted by $\star$, the timeout operator, denoted by $Timeout$, the choice operator, denoted by $|$, and the guard operator, denoted by $\Rightarrow$.

The flow operator is inspired from AND states of Statecharts, which executes an event on each sub-ASTD whenever possible. The interleaving executes two sub-ASTDs in parallel, this operator looks like an exclusive OR: $E_1 ||| E_2$ will execute e on either E_1 or E_2, but on only one of them; if both E_1 and E_2 can execute e, then one of them is chosen nondeterministically. The sequence operator allows for the sequential composition of two ASTDs. When the first ASTD reaches a final state, the second one can start its execution. This enables decomposition of problems into a set of tasks that have to be executed in sequence. The Kleene closure operator comes from regular expressions; it allows for iteration on an ASTD an arbitrary number of times (including zero). When the sub-ASTD is in final state, it enables to start a new iteration. The Timeout operator allows for verifying if a TASTD receives an event in a period of time, if not, then another TASTD has the right to execute. In the Timeout operator, the first transition of the first TASTD has to occur before d time units, otherwise the timeout is executed. The choice operator allows a choice between two sub-ASTDs; once a sub-ASTD has been choosen, the other sub-ASTD is ignored. It is essentially the same as a choice operator in a process algebra. The guard operator guards the execution of its sub-ASTD using a predicate or a function declaration of its parent ASTD. The first event received must satisfy the guard predicate; once the guard has been satisfied by the first event, the sub-ASTD execute the subsequent events without further constraints.

At the start, we divide our model into the elements that the user or the environment can manipulate, such as buttons, and sensors, and the response on the actuators after manipulating those elements. We call the former group the *sensors* and the latter group the *actuators*. Figure 1 shows the ASTD Controller, composed of sensors and actuators. In our case study solution, the notion of sensors covers both the sensor coming from the hardware part of the system and all the system configuration parameters coming from the GUI. The notion of actuators includes both the list of parameters that the controller transmits to the GUI when the request is made by the user, the parameters that the controller sets at the hardware level and the list of parameters resulting from the controller capturing indicators for its own operation.

Each green box is a call to the ASTD of that name. ASTD Sensors combines the various sensor ASTDs using an interleave operator; no synchronisation is needed between the sensors, because each sensor has its own distinct set of events. Operator $|||$ being commutative and associative, ASTD Sensors is shown here as an n-ary ASTD.

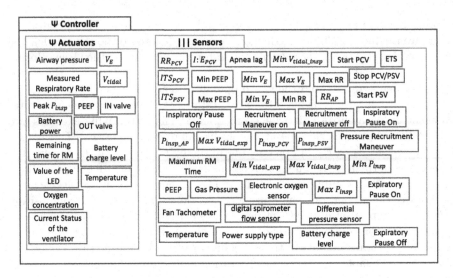

Fig. 1. ASTD Controller composing sensors and actuators

ASTD Main in Fig. 2 is the root (main) ASTD. This ASTD just allows us to start or stop the ventilator. It is mainly made up of the ASTD Controller and two events; the *power_on* event, wich is triggered when the user presses the start button, and the *power_off* event, which is triggered when the user presses the stop button.

The controller's machine state diagram of Fig. 4.1 in [5] is made up of 6 main states: *Start-up*, *FailSafe*, *SelfTest*, *VentilationOff*, *PCV* and *PSV*. To take advantage of the modularisation, hierarchy, originality and above all reusability options offered by ASTDs, we're going to decompose our controller into modules corresponding to each state of the state diagram and, using TASTD operators, link these modules together. The same principle of decomposition has been applied to each of the modules individually. The TASTD of the controller is shown in Fig. 3, where the details of ASTD Sensors and Actuators are hidden, since they are shown in Fig. 1.

Communication with Shared Variables. ASTD allows the use of shared variables, which are called *attributes* in the ASTD notation. An attribute declared in an ASTD may be used in guards and actions of its sub-ASTDs. Attributes are used to communicate the state of a sensor to the other ASTDs; this allows for the reduction of the number of states in automata. Sensor ASTDs update attributes describing the state of a sensor. Other ASTDs read these attributes to determine the acceptance of an event and to compute the actuator response. For flow and synchronisation ASTDs, shared attributes must be used with care, because their sub-ASTDs are executing in sequence. The semantics of the ASTD requires commutativity on the execution of the actions in a flow $E_1 \Psi E_2$, such that it terminates on the same values of the attributes whether

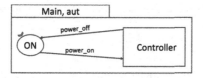

Fig. 2. Main ASTD of Mechanical Lung ventilator controller

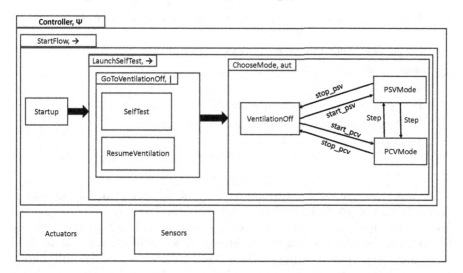

Fig. 3. Controller ASTD of Mechanical Lung ventilator

either E_1 or E_2 is executed first. Commutativity is easily ensured in our specification, because only the sensor ASTDs update the sensor attributes.

In ASTDs, attributes can have primary types, but using the eASTD tool it is also possible to define more complex types in C++ through the notion of class or struct, an option that is very useful depending on the problem to be solved. So our model integrates a new data type called *Parameters* which contains both the sensors coming from the GUI and those coming from the hardware initialised to their default values in accordance with the specification of our case study. The notion of a complex type is even more effective and interesting in this case, as it allows us to associate utility functions with our complex type, which can then be used to update it. In order to comply with the FUN5.1 specification, we have defined a *read_config* utility function associated with our type, which allows us to initialise a *Parameters* object from the values of the attributes saved in the config file. The *readConfig.h* [8] header file in our model contains the definition of our *Parameters* type.

Table 1 presents the attributes declared in each ASTD. Attributes declared in the root ASTD Controller indicate the current state of the sensors. For example, attribute *parameters.start_PCV* indicates whether the user has triggered PCV mode. ASTD *parameters.battery_charge_level* indicates the battery charge level.

Table 1. Shared variable by components

Component	Variables
Main (root)	*parameters, power_status*
Controller	*error_value, paw_drop_in, last_inspiration_time, move_to_pcv, mode, peak_pinsp, ve, rr, peep, fio2, vtidal, updated_parameters*
StartUp	*adc_timeout, pressure_sensor_timeout, error, processes_count*
InspirationPhaseEnd	*inspiration_phase_timer*
Initialization	*attempt, status*
CheckSensors	*pressure_sensor_valid_response*
PCVModeExpiration	*its_trigger_window*
PSVModeExpiration	*its_trigger_window, inspiration_time*
LaunchLoop	*enable_loop*

We want to come back to two important variables in our model, *parameters* and *updated_parameters*. These 2 variables are of the *Parameters* type presented above but with the only difference that *parameters* will contain the values of the attributes at the start of the breathing cycle, values which will be used throughout the current breathing cycle, whereas *updated_parameters* will contain the same values as *parameters* but including the updates made to the attributes during the current cycle. This is because changes made to attributes during the current cycle can only be used by the controller during the next cycle. Attribute *updated_parameters* therefore contains updates made to attributes during the current cycle and will be used to initialise *parameters* at the start of the next cycle so that this cycle can take into account changes made to attributes during the previous cycle. Before the start of the first cycle, *updated_parameters* and *parameters* have the same attribute values, values taken from the configuration file.

The complete model is composed of 73 automata, 5 sequence, 5 synchronisation or interleaving, 4 flow, 28 call, 13 guard, 8 timeout, 15 closure, 7 choice, and 2 delays, for a total of 160 ASTDs.

Formalization of the Requirements. Tables 2 relates ASTDs and requirements listed in [5]. Some requirements are present in several ASTDs because they have to be verified by several components. This is the case, for example, for CONT.42 and CONT.43 functionalities, which must be verified by both the PCVMode and PSVMode ASTDs. However, as ASTDs allow for modular modelling, we are going to implement these functionalities in 2 different ASTDs and they will just be called in the PCVMode and PSVMode ASTDs, thus avoiding duplication of code. Time requirements, such as CONT.37, CONT.36.2 and CONT 25, are covered with the use of event Step, the use of Timeout ASTD or the use of Delay ASTD type.

Table 2. Cross-reference between ASTDs and requirements for mechanical lung ventilator of [5]

ASTD	Requirements
Controller	CONT.1, CONT.2, CONT.3, CONT.4, CONT.5, CONT.6, CONT.7, CONT.8, CONT.9, CONT.10
StartUp	CONT.12, CONT.13, CONT.14, CONT.15, CONT.16
SelfTest	CONT.17, CONT.18, CONT.19
VentilationOff	CONT.38
PCVMode	CONT.20, CONT.21, CONT.22, CONT.23, CONT.24, CONT.25, CONT.26, CONT.27, CONT.28, CONT.39, CONT.40, CONT.41, CONT.42, CONT.43, CONT.44, CONT.45
PSVMode	CONT.29, CONT.30, CONT.31, CONT.32, CONT.33, CONT.34, CONT.35, CONT.36, CONT.37, CONT.39, CONT.40, CONT.41, CONT.42, CONT.43, CONT.44, CONT.45
FailSafe	CONT.38
Main (root)	CONT.11, CONT.38

4   Model Details

This Section shortly describes the main modelling elements of our specification following the structure explained in the previous section.

4.1   Sensors ASTD

The ASTD Sensors, is a component that allows all parameter changes to be listened to in the form of events from the GUI or hardware, with the aim of modifying the controller's behaviour by updating certain attributes of variables shared in the specification. Sensors is an interleave ASTD made up of several sub-ASTDs such as: HWSensors which is an ASTD for listening to changes coming from the hardware, PCVModeSensors, PSVModeSensors and AlarmTresholdsSensors which are ASTDs for listening to changes coming from the GUI concerning the configuration of PCV mode, PSV mode and alarm management respectively. Figure 4 shows the PCVModeSensors ASTD.

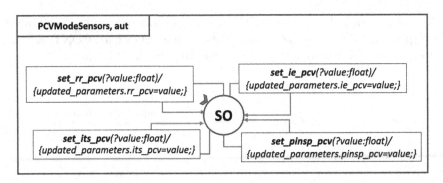

Fig. 4. Automaton ASTD PCVModeSensors

ASTD PCVModeSensors is an automaton with only one state, S0, which is the initial state. This automaton does not have a final state because here we want to listen to updates continuously, so there is no need for an accepting state which would stop listening to these updates. The transitions here represent the update actions coming from the GUI. As transitions we have: *set_rr_pcv* which updates the *rr_pcv* attribute with a float value passed as a parameter, the update is performed using the instruction *updated_parameters.rr_pcv=value*. In the same logic *set_ie_pcv* updates the *ie_pcv* attribute, *set_its_pcv* updates the *its_pcv* attribute and *set_pinsp_pcv* updates the *pinsp_pcv* attribute. Having a single state makes all these transitions reflexive, which means that changes to each attribute can be listened to infinitely. The other sub-ASTDs of the Sensors ASTD follow the same implementation and operating logic as the PCVModeSensors.

4.2   Actuators ASTD

As mentioned in Sect. 3 presenting the structure of our model, we have defined the actuators in our model as elements that enable our model to provide information to external elements. For our model we have detected fourteen main actuators. These actuators are divided into two main groups: actuators enabling communication with the GUI (*PAW, Peak Pinsp, RR, Temperature, V_E, V_{tidal}, FiO_2, PEEP, Battery power, Battery charge level, Remaining time for RM, current status of the ventilator*), and those enabling communication with the hardware which are *IN Valve* and *OUT Valve*. Our ASTD Actuators will only focus on the actuators communicating with the GUI, as the actions or events enabling the actuators to be modified in the direction of the hardware are all actions internal to the fan start-up management process or the breathing cycle management process; thus the updating of the latter will be carried out by the StartFlow ASTD in Fig. 3.

The Actuators ASTD is of type flow and is made up of twelve sub-ASTDs of the closure type, each corresponding to the management of one of the twelve GUI actuators. the sub-ASTDs are of the closure type in order to be able to express the notion of continuously listening to requests for information from the

GUI for each of the actuators. Each of the closure ASTDs is made up of an automaton ASTD with 3 states and 2 transitions; a transition representing the request from the GUI and an automatic Step transition that we use to simulate the controller's response to the request made by the GUI. The Fig. 5 shows the LoopGetPaw ASTD used to process any request for information on the value of *PAW*.

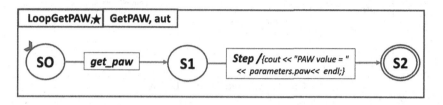

Fig. 5. Automaton ASTD LoopGetPAW

The structure of the LoopGetPAW sub-ASTD follows the general structure described above, with a closure-type LoopGetPAW ASTD for infinite processing of requests, and an automaton-type GetPAW sub-ASTD for processing a request for a PAW value. The GetPAW ASTD has three states S0, S1 and S2, with S0 as the initial state and S2 as the final state. S0 and S1 are linked by a *get_paw* transition which corresponds to a request for a PAW value from the GUI, S1 and S2 are linked by an automatic Step transition which is a simulation of the response from the controller to the *get_paw* request. Here the response simulation only displays the value of the attribute to the console.

4.3   Main(root) ASTD

The general structure of the main ASTD has already been presented in Sect. 3 but here we return to each of the elements making up this ASTD in greater detail. The main ASTD presented in Fig. 6 is made up of two states: the ON state, which is the start state of our model, and the StartUpCall state, which is a Call type ASTD enabling a call to be made to another ASTD contained in another diagram, which enables us to take advantage of the modularity offered by ASTDs. The StartUpCall ASTD is used to call the ASTD Controller, which is responsible for managing the ventilator start-up process and managing the different breathing modes. The two states are linked by two transitions: the *power_on* transition from the ON state to the StartUpCall state, this transition refers to the action of starting the ventilator by pressing the ON button. The second transition *power_off* between the StartUpCall state and the ON state corresponds to the stopping of the ventilator by the user, as shown in Fig. 6. It allows for an important action to be carried out, that of saving the main parameters in the configuration file before stopping the ventilator. The parameter values saved in this way will be used as parameter initialisation values the next time the program is started. This save is made by calling the *save_config* function, which is a utility function of our *Parameters* type that saves certain attribute values in the configuration file.

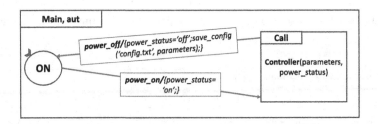

Fig. 6. Automaton ASTD Main

4.4   Controller ASTD

The controller ASTD is the element which contains the implementation of the internal operation of our controller, its overall structure was presented in Sect. 3. It is made up of a StartFlow ASTDs and two ASTDs of type call to Actuators and Sensors. Actuators and Sensors have been described above. Here we will focus on the StartFlow ASTD.

According to Fig. 4.1 of the specification document [5], the controller's state diagram comprises 5 main states: *StartUP*, *FailSafe*, *SelfTest*, *VentilationOff*, *PCVMode*, *PSVMode*. The transition from one state to another takes place in a precise order depending on the triggering of certain events or when the processing carried out on the previous state has been completed successfully. Figure 7 shows our StartFLow ASTD, which is of the sequence type, i.e., an ASTD that allows for moving from one ASTD to another when the first ASTD has reached a final state.

The first ASTD type is a call to the Startup ASTD, which implements the ventilator startup process. Once the startup process has been successfully completed, the StartFlow ASTD allows it to switch to another sequence ASTD called LaunchSelfTest, which in turn allows it to combine in sequence a choice ASTD called GoToVentilationOff and an automaton ASTD called ChooseMode, which triggers the VentilationOff ASTD. This ASTD either executes ASTD SelfTest, represented by an ASTD call, before switching to the VentilationOff ASTD, or switches directly to the VentilationOff ASTD by executing the *resume_ventilation* transition in accordance with the specification. The ASTD ChooseMode permits, after executing the VentilationOff ASTD as its initial state, to switch to the PCV mode, represented here by the call to ASTD PCVMode, by executing the *start_pcv* transition. It also permits to switch to the PSV mode, represented by the call to ASTD PSVMode, by executing the *start_psv* transition. The Choose-Mode ASTD can also be used to toggle back and forth between PSV and PCV modes via time-triggered Step transitions. For example, to switch from PCV-Mode to PSVMode, the user has to trigger the *start_psv* operation while in PCV

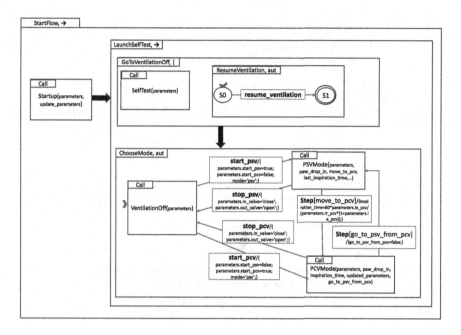

Fig. 7. StartFlow ASTD

mode, so that at the end of the inspiration time in PCV mode, we switch to PSV mode. This is shown in our model in Fig. 7 by the fact that the variable *go_to_psv_from_pcv* is equal to true.

One of the most important aspects of the case study, if not the most important, is the management of breathing cycles. Breathing is done in PCV mode or in PSV mode. Both modes have the same general operating scheme, which consists of a loop of breathing cycles. A breathing cycle generally consists of two stages: an inhalation stage and an exhalation stage.

Figure 8 shows the proposed model for managing breathing in PSV mode. It is made up of six hierachically nested ASTDs. The first PSVMode closure ASTD allows us to model the infinite repetition of the breathing cycle. The second sequence type ASTD PSVBreathCycle enables us to model the notion of a breathing cycle by putting two ASTDS into sequence: the ASTD PSVInspirationAndPawCheck which implements the inspiration logic and a call to ASTD PSVModeExpiration which implements the exhalation management logic. The PSVBreathCycle ASTD can therefore be used to pass from inspiration represented by the PSVInspirationAndPawCheck ASTD to expiration represented by the call to the PSVModeExpiration ASTD, with the PSVMode ASTD simply allowing the cycle to be repeated. It should also be noted that the PSVInspirationAndPawCheck ASTD is a flow, which in certain cases allows it to skip the

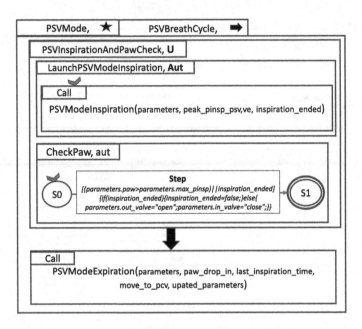

Fig. 8. *PSVMode* ASTD

inspiration phase and trigger the expiration phase when *PAW > MAX PINSP*, a condition which is verified here by the second sub-ASTD of PSVInspirationAnd-PawCheck called CheckPaw.

4.5 Modelling Time Requirements

A critical aspect of the system is its temporal behavior. Many properties and constraints have explicit temportal requirements (like after 10 s ...) [5]. In TASTD, a clock tick is represented by the triggering of a Step event. To manage time constraints, it is therefore important to choose the time difference or time interval between two clock ticks, i.e. the time difference between two consecutive Step events. For this case study, we chose an interval value of 0.1 s. With this step value, we meet all the temporal constraints of our case study. The main temporal constraints are found in the process of managing respiratory cycles (inspiration and expiration): CONT.22, CONT.25, CONT.36.2, CONT.37, CONT.41.2, CONT.42.2, CONT.43.1, CONT.45.

After analysis, we can see that all these temporal constraints are either of ASTD type Timeout or Delay. A Timeout is a temporal constraints where we wait for an event to occur during a period of d units of time, and if the event does not occur, the ASTD stops waiting and goes on to execute another ASTD. A Delay ASTD waits for at least d units of time before accepting the first event. We can also express these constraints using automatic Step transitions guarded with conditions on timers. But for our model we have opted for Delay and Timeout for a more explicit representation of the timing constraints.

Figure 9 shows our solution to the CONT.22 time constraint, which stipulates that in PCV mode, after a given inspiration time, which we will call *inspiration_time*, the controller checks whether the user has manually triggered the inspiration pause or whether he has triggered the recruitment maneuver. Here we'll use a Delay that waits for an *inspiration_time* delay before calling the InspirationPhaseEnd ASTD, which is supposed to check whether the user has triggered the inspiration pause or the recruitment maneuver.

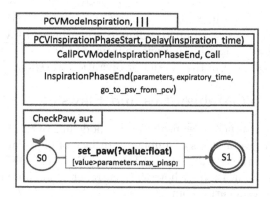

Fig. 9. PCVModeInspiration ASTD

Figure 10 shows our solution for modelling the CONT.42.2 constraint. We have opted to use the Timeout operator via the DetectExpiratoryPauseOff ASTD of type Timeout, which allows the user to wait for *parameters.max_exp_pause* seconds before triggering an *expiratory_pause_off* transition contained in the CheckExpiratoryPauseOff ASTD. If the transition is not triggered, the switch to the StopExpiratoryPause ASTD is triggered to end the inspiration pause and, as StopExpiratoryPause has only one state, which is final, this final state status will allow the user to exit the DetectExpiratoryPauseOff ASTD and start the next inspiration.

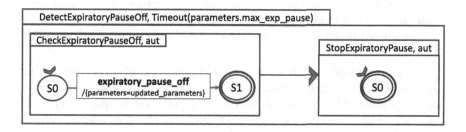

Fig. 10. DetectExpiratoryPauseOff ASTD

5   Validation and Verification

To validate our model, we use interactive animation of the specification with the executable code generated by the cASTD compiler for simulation. The compilation is automatic, and no human modification is necessary after production. We execute the compiled code and compare the results with the provided scenarios [7]. Our model satisfies the scenario given for the case study, although the proposed scenario only covers part of the controller's operating workflow. For the rest of the workflow we have generated test cases in compliance with the specification to validate the PCV mode and PSV mode steps which were not taken into account by the scenario proposed with the case study. We have implemented 12 test cases to test our specification: 5 test cases to simulate different scenarios in PSV mode, 6 test cases to simulate different scenarios in PCV mode and one test case to simulate an execution scenario from ventilator start-up to execution of the VentilationOff step in the ventilator operation workflow.

6   Specification Ambiguities and Flaws

In the ABZ2024 case study, specifically in the modelling of the controller component, we detected several cases of ambiguity or lack of information, particularly in the modelling of the SelfTest step (FUN.6, CONT.17, CONT.18, CONT.19) where there is no indication of how the controller is supposed to receive the results of the self-tests carried out by the controller and the GUI. There is also a lack of information, particularly at the level of the communication verification stage with the sensors, where CONT.15 states that a maximum of 5 connection attempts must be made with the pressure sensor and after these 5 attempts it is deduced that there is an error and the controller switches to FailSafe mode, but there is no mention of how long to wait before being able to attempt a new connection. We have the same situation for CONT.16 with the attempt to initialise the external ADC. To solve the problem we have assumed that this time for each case will be taken as a parameter of our controller.

7   Conclusions

To summary, we have presented a TASTD model for the Controller component of the ABZ2024 case study software system. Our model considers all the requirements. We validate our model through interactive animation and comparison with the validation scenarios proposed in the case study.

The main advantages of modelling with TASTD in comparison with other methods are the following.

- The algebraic approach allows for the decomposition of a specification into very small components which are easier to analyse and understand. In particular, the behavior of an event that affects several components can be separately specified in each component. The synchronisation and flow operators can be used to indicate how these components interact over these events (i.e., hard or soft synchronisation).

- Communication by shared attributes permits to simplify automata of a specification and reduce the number of automaton states.
- The graphical nature of TASTD allows for an easier understanding of a specification. Automata and process algebra operators makes it easier to understand the ordering relationship between events.
- TASTD provides a simple, modular approach to deal with timing requirements.
- TASTD, with its compiler cASTD, can generate C++ code that can be deployed into an embedded system. It is also capable of generating code for simulation, in order to check scenarios.

The development of models for the controller component, as well as their validation and documentation, required approximately two months. The modelling and analysis phase lasted almost 80 h. The validation process took 40 h, during which the model was updated to ensure that all the start-up stages of the system's ventilation were respected, that the system shut down safely for every error that occurred, to ensure that the switchover between PCV and PSV mode was carried out correctly and also that all the required time constraints were respected, as this was defined as one of the main critical aspects.

Currently, TASTD has a number of shortcomings, one of which is the size of the generated C++ code. Each ASTD is represented by a C++ structure, and nested ASTDs generate nested structures. Our specification is large and contains many deeply nested ASTDs, which induces very long prefixes to access variable x in the most nested ASTDs. During the code generation process, inefficient representation of these prefixes generates huge expressions on which several substitutions must be recursively applied. The problem could be solved by generating more modular C++ code. As a result, cASTD is currently unable to compile the main ASTD representing the entire controller system. We thus had to compiled its sub-ASTDs independently and test them individually. In future work, we will be working on the generation of more compact C++ code by cASTD.

TASTD currently also lacks supports for verification. As future work, we intend to extend TASTD with Event-B [1] and CCSL [2]. These extensions will enable us to have in a single specification certain modules modeled in Event-B and others in CCSL or TASTD. These modules will enable us to translate TASTD specifications into Event-B or CCSL and thus take advantage of the verification tools offered by these two languages to be able to verify our TASTD specifications.

Competing Interests. The author(s) has no competing interests to declare that are relevant to the content of this manuscript.

References

1. Abrial, J.: Modeling in Event-B. Cambridge University Press, Cambridge (2010)
2. André, C.: Syntax and Semantics of the Clock Constraint Specification Language (CCSL). Research Report RR-6925, INRIA (2009). https://inria.hal.science/inria-00384077

3. de Azevedo Oliveira, D., Frappier, M.: TASTD: a real-time extension for ASTD. In: Glässer, U., Creissac Campos, J., Méry, D., Palanque, P. (eds.) ABZ 2023. LNCS, vol. 14010, pp. 142–159. Springer, Cham (2023). https://doi.org/10.1007/978-3-031-33163-3_11

4. de Azevedo Oliveira, D., Frappier, M.: Technical report 27 - Extending ASTD with real-time (2023). https://github.com/DiegoOliveiraUDES/astd-tech-report-27

5. Bonfanti, S., Gargantini, A.: The mechanical lung ventilator case study. In: Rigorous State-Based Methods 10th International Conference, ABZ 2024, Bergamo, Italy, 25–28 June 2024, Proceedings, LNCS, vol. 14759. Springer (2024)

6. Frappier, M.: ASTD support tools repo (2023). https://github.com/DiegoOliveiraUDES/ASTD-tools. Accessed 26 Jan 2024

7. Gargantini, A.: SCENARIO VERS 1.5 (2023). https://github.com/foselab/abz2024_casestudy_MLV/blob/main/scenarios_v_1_5.pdf

8. Ndouna, A.R., Frappier, M.: Case Study ABZ 2024 TASTD Model (2024). https://github.com/ndounalex/casestudyABZ2024-tastdmodel

9. Nganyewou Tidjon, L., Frappier, M., Leuschel, M., Mammar, A.: Extended algebraic state-transition diagrams. In: 2018 23rd International Conference on Engineering of Complex Computer Systems (ICECCS), pp. 146–155. Melbourne, Australia (2018)

Modelling and Analysing a Mechanical Lung Ventilator in mCRL2

Danny van Dortmont, Jeroen J. A. Keiren$^{(\boxtimes)}$ ⓘ, and Tim A. C. Willemse ⓘ

Eindhoven University of Technology, Eindhoven, The Netherlands
d.f.m.v.dortmont@student.tue.nl, {j.j.a.keiren,t.a.c.willemse}@tue.nl

Abstract. We model the Mechanical Lung Ventilator (MLV) in the process algebra mCRL2. The functional requirements of the MLV are formalised in the modal μ-calculus, and we use model checking to analyse whether these requirements hold true of our model. Our formalisation of the MLV and its requirements reveal a few subtle imprecisions and unclarities in the informal document and we analyse their impact.

1 Introduction

During the SARS-CoV-2 pandemic, there was a surge in demand for mechanical lung ventilators. Several projects were started to make emergency ventilators,[1] some of which were ultimately certified for emergency use. The Mechanical Ventilator Milano (MVM) [2,11], inspired by the Manly ventilator [26], obtained authorizations from Health Canada, the CE marking, as well as FDA Emergency Use Authorization. It was developed to be quickly producible on large scale using readily available parts.

Although formal methods were not used in the development of the MVM, some of the researchers involved in its initial development followed up with a study using formal methods to develop a controller for the MVM [7]. In particular, they use ASMETA, an abstract statemachine metamodeling framework to develop a prototype of the MVM controller.

The Mechanical Lung Ventilator (MLV) [9] is a simplification of a mechanical ventilator intended for use as a case study for the development of a ventilator using formal methods. It is inspired by the MVM, but the number of components and alarms is limited.

In this paper, we create a model of the MLV system using the mCRL2 modelling language [17]. In our model we include hardware components such as sensors and actuators, the controller, as well as the graphical user interface (GUI) and their communication. We show how to extend the model by including a limited number of alarms. Requirements are formalised using the first-order μ-calculus [16,19], and we verify that our model satisfies the requirements using the symbolic model checking tools [25] in the mCRL2 toolset [12]. The model and requirements are available from Zenodo [30].

---

[1] See https://github.com/PubInv/covid19-vent-list.

S. Bonfanti et al. (Eds.): ABZ 2024, LNCS 14759, pp. 341–359, 2024.
https://doi.org/10.1007/978-3-031-63790-2_27

Related Work. Medical devices are safety critical systems that have been widely studied using formal methods. Well-studied examples are infusion pumps [3] and hemodialysis machines [20,28]. The use of formal methods for regulatory review and forensic analysis of medical devices was studied in [23]. Some work focuses specifically on the verification of user interfaces [27]. Daw *et al.* considered the integration of clinical workflows into the formal verification process of medical devices [13]. For an overview of the use of formal methods in medical software systems the reader is referred to [10]. The use of formal methods to verify medical guidelines was described in, e.g., [21].

Industrial applications of mCRL2 have been described extensively, for instance for the verification of industrial control software [22,29], in the railway domain [5] and to design protocols [18]. Several medical applications have also been analysed using mCRL2, in particular, the firmware of a pacemaker [32], the session setup of the IEEE 11073-20601:2010 standard [1,24], as well as the eXtensible Access Control Markup language, which is an OASIS standard used for access control systems in health care [4].

2   Mechanical Lung Ventilator

The system we study in this paper is the mechanical lung ventilator MLV as described in [8,9]. This is a medical device that supports the breathing of patients requiring mechanical ventilation. The MLV works in pressure mode. This means it uses compressed oxygen and medical air as well as a network of sensors and valves to control the respiratory cycle of the patient.

We recall the high-level overview of the ventilator system from [8] in Fig. 1. It has in inspiratory track, indicated in blue, that shows the airflow when inhaling, and expiratory track, indicated in red, showing the airflow when exhaling.

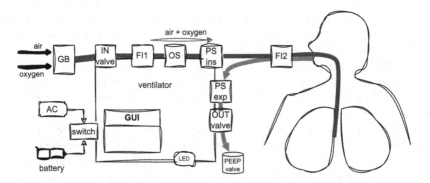

Fig. 1. A high level overview of the ventilator, taken from the case study [8].

The system consists of four valves that control the flow of air to and from the patient. These are as follows (see also Fig. 1). *IN valve* is the inlet valve of the system. This valve can be set to the target inspiratory pressure, depending on the current operation mode, or set to 0, in which case the valve is closed. *OUT valve* is the outlet valve. This valve may be closed or opened, depending on the current operation mode. *GB* is the gas blender that can be set to a desired mixture of air and oxygen. The Positive End Expiratory Pressure valve (*PEEP valve*) can be set to the desired pressure in the expiratory track. Of these four valves, the *IN valve* and *OUT valve* are controlled by the system, whereas the gas blender *GB* and the *PEEP valve* are both set manually.

Six sensors are used by the system to control the flow of air, and to monitor and detect problems in the system or the patient's respiration. The sensors and their functions are as follows. The gas blender is equipped with a pressure sensor *GB (PS)* which can be used to detect whether the flow of air and oxygen into the system is sufficient. Flow indicators *FI1* and *FI2* are used to measure the flow of air to the patient (*FI1*) and to and from the patient (*FI2*). An oxygen concentration sensor (*OS*) is used to measure the concentration of oxygen flowing to the patient. Pressure sensors *PS ins* and *PS exp* measures the air pressure in the inspiratory track and the expiratory track (PEEP), respectively.

The sensors and valves are connected to the controller of the MLV. The GUI is connected to the controller and can be used to visualise parameters retrieved from the controller, as well as set parameters in the controller. These parameters are stored in a memory component that we model explicitly: the controller can read from the memory, while the GUI can read and write to the memory. Several LEDs are connected to the controller. These LEDs can be used to signal problems (and their severity) in the patient's respiration, and can be reset through the GUI. A high-level architecture of the system is depicted in Fig. 2.

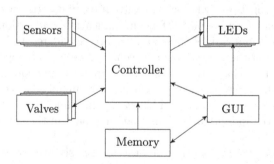

Fig. 2. Architecture of the MLV.

3   mCRL2 Model of the MLV

The language mCRL2 [17] is designed for modelling the behaviour of concurrent systems. It consists of a process algebra based on ACP [6] for the specification of (the behaviour of) concurrent processes, a language for the specification of data types and their operations, as well as a first-order modal μ-calculus for the

specification of requirements [16,19]. In this section we describe our model of
the MLV, and introduce the mCRL2 language concepts we use as needed. For
details about the language and its syntax and semantics we refer to [17]. A more
in-depth introduction to modelling with mCRL2 can be found in [14,15].

Our mCRL2 model of the MLV closely follows the architecture as depicted
in Fig. 2. Sensors, valves, LEDs, GUI, memory and controller are modelled as
mCRL2 *processes*, running in parallel. The structure of the high-level system
model is as follows:

```
init allow({..., setValveValue_c, getValveValue_c, ...,
            loadConfiguration, powerOn, powerOff, ... },
      comm({...,
            setValveValue_s | setValveValue_r -> setValveValue_c,
            getValveValue_s | getValveValue_r -> getValveValue_c,
            ...},
            Controller || GUI || LEDs || Valves || Sensors || Memory
      ));
```

In this high-level system description, || indicates (interleaved) parallel com-
position of processes. Each process is defined in terms of *actions* and operators
such as the sequential composition operator ., the alternative composition operator +, *etcetera*. Processes can communicate by simultaneously executing actions
that are specified to synchronise. Such synchronisation is specified using the *comm*
operator. For instance, the expression setValveValue_s | setValveValue_r
-> setValveValue_c that is part of the *comm* operator in the above system
model indicates that when, *e.g.*, process Controller wants to set the value of
a valve using action setValveValue_s and the Valves process can receive this
value using setValveValue_r at the same time, their simultaneous occurrence
is renamed to setValveValue_c, indicating that both processes communicate.
In our model, we consistently follow the convention that action with suffix _s and
_r are sending and receiving parts of a communication, and actions with _c their
result. Actions without any of these suffixes are considered to be *local* actions,
such as inputs from the environment or sensor reading. The operator *allow* is
used to allow actions that either do not participate in any communication, e.g.,
local actions such as powerOn, or that are the result of a successful communication, such as setValveValue_c. This way, communication between processes
is enforced, and the individual actions that take part in the communication are
removed.

In the remainder of this section we describe the six processes in more detail.

3.1 Modelling the Sensors and Valves

The processes Sensors and Valves, modelling the sensors and valves are structured similarly. For this reason, we focus on process Sensors, depicted below.

```
proc Sensors =
    Sensor(GasBlenderPressure, Working, 4500, [4500])
 || Sensor(FlowIndicator1, Working, 20, [15,20,25])
 || Sensor(FlowIndicator2, Working, 20, [15,20,25])
 || Sensor(InPressure, Working, 15, [5,15,25,35,45,50])
```

```
|| Sensor(ExpPressure, Working, 10, [5,10,15,20])
|| Sensor(Oxygen, Working, FIO2target,
          [FIO2target-4,FIO2target-3,FIO2target,
          FIO2target+3,FIO2target+4]);
```

The Sensors process is again a parallel composition, modelling the behaviour of all sensors described in Sect. 2 running in parallel. Each sensor is modelled as a specific instance of the same generic Sensor process, depicted below:

```
Sensor(id: SensorId, state: SensorState, currVal: Int,
       validValues: List(Int)) =
     sum value: Int . (value in validValues && state == Working)
       -> updateSensorValue(id, value) . Sensor(currVal = value)
  + (state != sFaulty) -> getSensorState_r(id, state) . Sensor()
  + (state == Working) -> error. Sensor(state=Error)
  + (state == Error) -> recover. Sensor(state=Working)
  + (state != sFaulty) -> break. Sensor(state=sFaulty)
  + (state != sFaulty) -> getSensorValue_r(id, currVal) . Sensor();
```

Observe that the Sensor process has four parameters: parameter id of type SensorId, indicating which sensor it is, parameter state of type SensorState, parameter value of (built-in) type Int, indicating the current value reported by the sensor, and parameter validValues of (built-in) type List(Int) that represents the set of valid values the sensor can report. Data types such as SensorState are specified in the data language of mCRL2:

sort SensorState = **struct** Working | Error | sFaulty;

Each value (constructor) of this data type represents a state in which a sensor can be: it can be working correctly, represented by Working, it can be temporarily malfunctioning, represented by Error, and it can be beyond repair, represented by sFaulty. When it is in the latter state, it can also no longer communicate with its environment. Apart from introducing the constructors of the data type, this construction automatically introduces operators such as equality == and inequality !=. The other data types are modelled similarly.

The Sensor process describes the behaviour (and the underlying control flow logic) of a sensor; see also Fig. 3 for a visualisation of the (abstract) transition system induced by this process. If state == Working, an error action causes state to update to Error. When state==Error, the sensor can still recover from the error, indicated by a recover action and resulting in state to update to Working. The sensor can also break irreparably, modelled by the break action, causing state to be updated to sFaulty.

As long as the sensor is in state Working, it can update its value to an arbitrary value, modelled by a parameterised action updateSensorValue, so long as the value with which the action is parameterised is within the range of values it can assume (given by validValues). This is modelled using the *alternative quantification* operator sum, which binds the local variable value of type Int, and assigns, non-deterministically an integer value to value in its subprocess. This subprocess is a conditional process, executing action updateSensorValue (id,value) and updating parameter currVal to value, provided that the condition value in validValues is met. If this condition is not met, then this

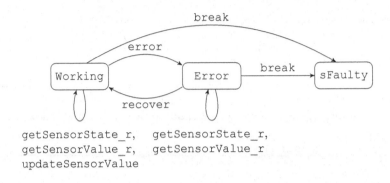

Fig. 3. Abstraction of the labelled transition system described by process Sensor. We omitted the (values of the) parameters of several actions to facilitate readability.

process does not 'do' anything, and the only behaviour can come from any of the other alternative subprocesses, specified using the + operator modelling non-deterministic choice.

Whenever the sensor is not irreparably broken (modelled by condition state != sFaulty) it can report its state to its environment using parameterised action getSensorState_r. In the same way, the sensor can report the latest sensor value through the parameterised getSensorValue_r action. Within the broader context, the communication operator of the high-level process on pp. 4 ensures that the getSensorState_r action and getSensorValue_r action can communicate with counterpart actions getSensorState_s and getSensorValue_s of the Controller process.

The initialisation of the valves is similar to that of the sensors but the control flow logic is simpler since we have assumed that valves cannot break down. However, we distinguish input valves, output valves and manual valves. The input valve can be in a state, modelled by a parameter state that can be set to Open or Closed, and it has a parameter targetPressure that is only used when the valve is Open. The output valve is similar, but does not have the target pressure parameter. The manual valves cannot be opened or closed by the system. Instead they are set to a target value, modelled by a parameter value, manually. To restrict the settings of the manual valves, we again use a parameter validValues similar to the Sensor process.

3.2   Modelling the Configuration Parameters

The MLV has many configuration parameters that define the conditions within which it shall operate. The Memory process models the collection of these configuration parameters. It uses a separate process ConfigurationMemory that keeps track of the current values of all of these parameters, essentially as a shared memory location. The controller can read from the memory, whereas the GUI can read and write to the memory. Technically, one could consider the memory to be part of the controller, and our modelling to be merely a logical decomposition of the latter. However, modelling the memory as a separate process has the advantage that it is easy to ensure that the memory can be read from/written to by the GUI while the controller is busy.

The process Memory initialises the memory with its default values. Note that [8] does not specify default values for some parameters (*e.g.*, parameter RR_{AP}); as every parameter needs to be initialised in mCRL2, default values were chosen arbitrarily for these parameters. The process ConfigurationMemory has parameters representing the parameters of the MLV. For instance, RR_PCV represents the MLV parameter RR_{PCV}, modelling the target respiratory rate in PCV mode, and I'E_PCV represents the MLV parameter $I : E_{PCV}$, the ratio between the inspiratory and expiratory time in PCV mode, as described in [8]. For each parameter, we have introduced a dedicated action to get and set the parameter. For example, using action get_RR_PCV_r the value of parameter RR_PCV is exposed by adding it as a parameter to the action. Exposing the value of a parameter has no impact on the value of that parameter, unlike setting the parameter. For instance, the parameter RR_PCV can be updated to a (non-deterministically chosen) new value using action set_RR_PCV_r: by means of a recursive call to process ConfigurationMemory, the value the parameter this action carries is assigned to the parameter of the process upon executing the action. Note that the values these parameters can be assigned are bounded using conditions; for instance, the condition 4 <= v && v <= 50 ensures that only natural numbers at least 4 and at most 50 are assigned to the RR_PCV parameter. The boundary values are taken from the requirements in [8]. Finally, we have introduced an action load_defaults_r that restores all parameters to their default values when instructed to do so.

The Memory and ConfigurationMemory processes are shown below; for the latter, we only show the first two process parameters, but the invocation in process Memory shows the full list of values for the parameters we have modelled.

```
proc Memory = ConfigurationMemory(12, ratio(1,2), 15, 3, 15, 3, 30, 30,
                    0, ratio(1,2), 0, 40, 50, 990, 10, 990, 10, 2, 0,
                    4, 50, 0, 0, 20, 10, 60, 40, 7/10, 7);

ConfigurationMemory(RR_PCV: Nat, I'E_PCV: Ratio, ...) =
    load_defaults_r . Memory
  + get_RR_PCV_r(RR_PCV) . ConfigurationMemory()
  + get_I'E_PCV_r(I'E_PCV) . ConfigurationMemory()
  + ...
  + sum v: Nat . (4 <= v && v <= 50)
        -> set_RR_PCV_r(v) . ConfigurationMemory(RR_PCV = v)
  + sum e: Nat, v: Ratio . (10 <= e && e <= 40 && v == ratio(1,e/10))
        -> set_I'E_PCV_r(v) . ConfigurationMemory(I'E_PCV = v)
  + ...
```

Most of the parameters we have used are of type natural number (*Nat*). For *ratios* we can use the following user-defined type:

sort Ratio = **struct** ratio(pi1: *Nat*, pi2: *Real*);

This type describes a set of elements consisting of the shape ratio(v,r), where v is a natural number and r is a real number. While this is a valid construction and proper mCRL2, in practice, the type *Real* is problematic since it is not enumerable. As a consequence, the type Ratio is problematic, too, in particular when generating state spaces for the purpose of verification. For this particular case, we can circumvent the issue by redefining the type Ratio as a pair of natural numbers (*i.e.*, replacing the type *Real* by *Nat*), and scaling all conditions accordingly. For instance, we can replace the following subprocess of ConfigurationMemory:

```
sum e: Nat, v: Ratio . (10 <= e && e <= 40 && v == ratio(1,e/10))
  -> set_I'E_PCV_r(v) . ConfigurationMemory(I'E_PCV = v)
```

by the following subprocess:

```
sum e: Nat, v: Ratio . (10 <= e && e <= 40 && v == ratio(10,e))
  -> set_I'E_PCV_r(v) . ConfigurationMemory(I'E_PCV = v)
```

Of course, scaling needs to be done carefully, so as to not introduce any issues.

3.3   Modelling the Alarms

The requirements describe visual alarms using an RGB LED [8, Section 5.2]. Process LEDs models these LEDs, describing their behaviour assuming that initially they are all inactive. For simplicity, we associate one LED to each of the three categories (*viz.*, *low*, *medium* and *high* priority) of alarm severity described in [8]. Process VisualAlarms maintains three Boolean parameters (with names reflecting the three categories), indicating whether an LED in a particular category is active or not. For instance, in case low == *false*, there is no alarm of low priority, whereas when low == *true*, an alarm of low priority *is* active. The full process definitions are as follows:

proc LEDs = VisualAlarms(*false, false, false*);

```
VisualAlarms(low, medium, high: Bool) =
  alarm_r(Low) . VisualAlarms(low = true)
+ alarm_r(Medium) . VisualAlarms(medium = true)
+ alarm_r(High) . VisualAlarms(high = true)
+ snooze_alarm_r(Low) . VisualAlarms(low = false)
+ snooze_alarm_r(Medium) . VisualAlarms(medium = false)
+ snooze_alarm_r(High) . VisualAlarms(high = false)
+ low -> LowAlarm. VisualAlarms()
+ medium -> MediumAlarm. VisualAlarms()
+ high -> HighAlarm. VisualAlarms();
```

An alarm is typically triggered from the controller, by synchronising on the alarm_r action. For instance, a High alarm can be set by the controller when detecting a apnea lag. Snoozing an alarm is initiated via the GUI. As long as an alarm is set, it can report so using the `LowAlarm`, `MediumAlarm` and `HighAlarm`, respectively. These actions can happen independently of any other action; in a way, they could be viewed as output signals of the system.

3.4   Modelling the Controller and GUI

The controller and the GUI are the most complex parts in the MLV. For both, we followed a similar approach when modelling these. We here mainly focus on a few aspects of our model of the controller. The requirements document [8] is actually quite explicit on how the controller should behave by including requirements on the different modes a controller can be in, and a UML State Machine that describes the high-level behaviour for the various modes, see also Fig. 4.

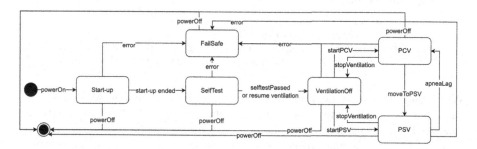

Fig. 4. State Machine describing the behaviour of the controller, taken from [8].

Since the different modes in the controller do not share any information outside the configuration parameters set in the `Configuration` process, we model every mode in the controller using a separate process. Calling the process representing a particular mode is preceded by "announcing" that the controller is moving to that mode. For instance, the Start-up mode is modelled by process `Controller_Startup`. Before entering process `Controller_Startup`, the controller signals that it is moving to this mode using action `emitMode_s`.

The State Machine focusses mainly on the high-level modes and transitions of the controller; the requirements described in [8] impose some further restrictions on the behaviour that is possible or required in each mode. For instance, requirement CONT.38 in [8] requires:

> *"when the ventilator is in Start-up or VentilationOff mode the valve pressure shall be set to close and the out valve shall be open".*

This configuration for the valves is referred to as the *safe mode*, as "In this configuration, the ventilator does not prevent breathing thanks to some relief valves" [8]. To ensure that the model guarantees this requirement, modes may need to move through a `Setup` process before entering the actual mode. For instance, process `Controller_StartUp_Setup` models what should happen before the controller enters Start-up mode:

```
Controller_StartUp_Setup =
  powerOff . ControllerSwitcher(Stop)
+ setValveState_s(In, Closed)
  . setValveState_s(Out, Open)
  . emitMode_s(StartUp)
  . Controller_StartUp(InitialSensorStatus, InitialValveStatus,
                      0, 0, true);
```

One of the options the controller can execute is the powerOff action, which will cause the controller to move to the Stop mode, which is left implicit in the State Machine. Alternatively, before entering the actual Start-up mode, the controller can adjust the In-valve, setting it to Closed and, subsequently setting the Out-valve to Open. Note that we could also have chosen to change both valves simultaneously, using a so-called *multi-action*; these are constructed using the |-operator on actions:

```
Controller_StartUp_Setup =
  powerOff . ControllerSwitcher(Stop)
+ (setValveState_s(In, Closed) | setValveState_s(Out, Open))
  . Controller_StartUp(InitialSensorStatus, InitialValveStatus,
                      0, 0, true);
```

While the latter style of modelling leads to a slightly smaller state space, we chose not to model setting the valves simultaneously since it is unclear (to us) whether this is realistically possible.

Once the valves have been set to safe mode, the controller can move to the actual Start-up mode. The behaviour of this mode is given by process Controller_StartUp, depicted below. We will not discuss all details of this process but instead sketch the high-level idea captured in the model.

```
Controller_StartUp(cs: ConnectedSensors, cv: ConnectedValves,
                   PS_retries, ADC_retries: Int,
                   configLoaded: Bool) =
  (PS_retries < 5 && ADC_retries < 5) ->
    (   powerOff . ControllerSwitcher(Stop)
    + StartUpComplete(cs,cv,configLoaded)
        -> startUpSuccessful . ControllerSwitcher(SelfTest)
    + !configLoaded -> loadConfiguration
                    . Controller_StartUp(configLoaded =true)
    + !GB(cs) ->
        (
            getSensorState_s(GasBlenderPressure, Error)
            . Controller_StartUp(PS_retries = PS_retries + 1)
          + timeout(GasBlenderPressure)
            . Controller_StartUp(PS_retries = PS_retries + 1)
        )
    + sum sID: SensorId, s: SensorState.
        (!SensorChecked(cs,sID)
          && (sID == GasBlenderPressure => s == Working)) ->
          getSensorState_s(sID, s)
          . Controller_StartUp(cs =UpdateSensorStatus(cs,sID,true))
    + sum vID: ValveId, v: ValveState .
        (!ValveChecked(cv,vID)) ->
          getValveState_s(vID,v)
```

```
        . Controller_StartUp(cv =UpdateValveStatus(cv,vID,true))
    )
  <>
    ControllerSwitcher(FailSafe);
```

In the Start-up mode, the controller must check whether it can successfully connect to the sensors, valves and ADC, and load the configuration. This is exactly what our `Controller_StartUp` process checks. For the pressure sensor and the ADC, the controller tolerates a limited number of times these peripherals can indicate they are not working as they should be, or their communication simply hits a timeout. The number of times this happens is tracked using the `PS_retries` and `ADC_retries` parameters. Note that since the ADC appears to be an external component, not further detailed in [8], we have decided not to include the ADC in our model, and also have not included communication with the ADC, so the `ADC_retries` counter is currently without effect. Furthermore, we remark that since our model abstracts from time, the timeouts are modelled as events that can happen non-deterministically, allowing us to qualitatively study the effect of these events happening.

If the number of retries is exceeded, the controller switches to the FailSafe mode. This is achieved using the if-then-else construct in mCRL2, where `c -> p <> q` means that if condition `c` is true process `p` is executed, else process `q` is executed. As long as the number of retries is not yet reached, the controller can be powered off using action `powerOff`, and the configuration can be loaded using action `loadConfiguration` if not done so already. Parameters `cs` and `cv` keep track of whether the controller has successfully communicated with the various sensors. We remark that the types `ConnectedSensors` and `ConnectedValves` essentially model tuples of Booleans. Along with the user-defined functions `UpdateSensorStatus`, `UpdateValveStatus` and `startUpComplete` on these data types, this allows for compactly modelling of the `Controller_StartUp` process, although part of the logic is moved to the definitions of these functions. In particular, using the (user-defined) Boolean function `startUpComplete` the controller can check that the current configuration of sensors and valves is working properly, and whether the configuration is loaded; if so, the function returns *true* and startup was successful, allowing the controller to switch to the `SelfTest` mode. For the remaining sensors and the valves, the status is updated if communication with the sensor/valve is successful.

The other five modes of the controller are modelled in a similar fashion. For the PCV and PSV modes we should point out that we abstract from the actual ventilation control in the model. We do include setting valves, and allow the sensors to report arbitrary values. Depending on the values for the configuration parameters that have been set through the GUI, the controller may trigger an alarm when reading a sensor value that meets the alarm conditions. For instance, if Flow indicator 1 reports a value below the value for parameter $Min\ V_E$, alarm condition AL.22 (which is related to alarm requirement SAV.16 and SAV.18) triggers the controller to issue a high priority alarm. Several other alarm conditions are included in our model in the same way, although we have not implemented all alarm conditions due to some of these requiring checks on parameters that are not fully specified.

To extend the model with additional details regarding the ventilation mode, details on ventilation beyond the requirements provided are needed. Such an extension probably also needs the modelling of continuous dynamics and the inclusion of time, to study the behaviour of the MLV under realistic scenarios. This would likely make the end-to-end verification of the model infeasible using the mCRL2 toolset.

Finally, we remark that the GUI can perform certain actions only if the controller is in a particular mode. For instance, the operator may wish to switch from Pressure Support Ventilation (PSV) mode to Pressure Controlled Ventilation (PCV) mode via the GUI. This is only allowed if the MLV is still in PSV mode. However, first reading the controller mode and only then triggering the switch may result in a race condition: the controller may have switched to PCV mode autonomously after the GUI has read the mode and before it has triggered the switch. We circumvent this by requiring that actions like switching mode through the GUI must happen simultaneously with reading the mode of the controller, using multi-actions. In order to achieve that, we have modelled a separate process ExposeControllerMode.

```
ExposeControllerMode(mode: OperationMode) =
    sum m: OperationMode. emitMode_r(m) . ExposeControllerMode(mode = m)
+ controller_Mode_s(mode) . ExposeControllerMode()
+ emitMode(mode) . ExposeControllerMode();
```

The above process runs in parallel to the controller. It uses action emitMode_r to synchronise with the controller on emitMode_s actions, which are executed by the controller process whenever it updates mode. The GUI process can read the most current mode by synchronising with the controller_Mode_s action. The emitMode action, which will not synchronise with any other action, is added for the purpose of verification, but is not required for the correct functioning of the system.

3.5   State Space Generation

We believe that our model of the MLV system contains the most relevant aspects of the control flow logic and the design requirements listed in [8]. Nevertheless, we have not included the ability to change every configuration parameter or to allow for all possible sensor values in our model. The aspects we have modelled allow us to verify a number of interesting requirements, as we will highlight in the next section, while keeping the state space to manageable proportions. Our model currently induces a labelled transition system that contains $1.5 \cdot 10^{23}$ reachable states; this state space can be generated using a symbolic reachability tool in mCRL2 in 13 s. State space generation and the verification in the next section were run on a 2017 Macbook pro 3.5 GHz Dual-Core Intel Core i7 processor with 16 GB of main memory.

4   Verification

In this section we present a small selection of requirements extracted from [8] and discuss their formalisation in the requirements language of the mCRL2 toolset.

We note that many of the requirements listed in [8] are in fact design requirements rather than functional or safety requirements. While these design requirements have been of great help in obtaining a working model, we expect the design requirements to be guaranteed by construction. Next to the design, functional and safety requirements from [8], we have included a few requirements of our own, which helped to improve the model. Finally, version 5 of [8] comes with a handful of test-scenarios. We also discuss how these can be formalised in mCRL2. We moreover show that all requirements can be verified using symbolic model checker of the mCRL2 toolset [25].

The requirements and scenarios are formalised in the modal μ-calculus; the specific fragments of the language that we use will be introduced when needed. For full details regarding this language, we refer to [16,19].

4.1   Design, Functional and Safety Requirements

Apart from the State Machines, describing how the controller and GUI should operate, several more detailed design requirements are included in [8], restricting the modelling choices of the various components. Requirements CONT.1 and CONT.1.(1-6) specify that the controller should have the modes depicted in Fig. 4. For instance, CONT.1.3 requires that the controller implements the VentilationOff mode. We can assert that this is true by verifying the following formula:

```
<true*. emitMode(VentilationOff)>true
```

This formula essentially asserts the existence of a finite sequence of arbitrary actions ending in an `emitMode(VentilationOff)` action. The way to read this formula is as follows: a construct of the shape `<R>true` specifies that a sequence of actions, described by the language `R` over actions, is possible. This is basically the *may*-operator from Hennessy-Milner logic, extended to sequences. Here the language is described by `true*.emitMode(VentilationOff)`, which is the set of all sequences consisting of zero or more arbitrary actions (described by `true *`), followed by an `emitMode(VentilationOff)` action. Internally, the above language construct is mapped onto a least fixed point, but in practice, many formulae in the modal μ-calculus can be expressed in the more user-friendly syntax we provide here. We note that requirements CONT.1.(1-6) can all be verified in the same way. Using the mCRL2 symbolic model checker [25], all six properties can be verified to hold true; the verification of a single property using the symbolic model checker of mCRL2 takes approx. 3 s.

An example of a safety requirement is the previously mentioned requirement CONT.38, which we will repeat here:

> *"when the ventilator is in Start-up or VentilationOff mode the valve pressure shall be set to close and the out valve shall be open".*

We have formalised this requirement as follows:

```
[true*]
  (<emitMode(VentilationOff) || emitMode(StartUp)>true
  =>
  [emitValveState(In,Open) || emitValveState(Out,Closed)] false
  )
```

A construct of the shape `[true*]f` should be read as *invariantly* `f` holds true. In this case, property `f` asserts that the enabledness of an action matching `emitMode(VentilationOff)` or `emitMode(StartUp)`, implies that no action matching `emitValveState(In,Open)` or `emitValveState(Out,Closed)` is enabled.

Somewhat to our surprise, the requirement was violated in our earlier models. The cause of this violation is a subtle ambiguity in the requirements document. The violating scenario involves entering PCV mode, powering off the controller and again powering on the controller, after which it moves to the Start-up mode. At this point, the valves are not yet in safe mode. As discussed on pp. 9, if the controller reports being in the Start-up mode before it has set the valves to safe mode, requirement CONT.38 is violated. This is nicely reported by the model checker. The fix is, as discussed on pp. 9 to only report that the controller has moved to the Start-up mode after the valves have been set to safe mode. The model checker confirms the requirement holds true on the final model; this requires approx. 4 s. However, it is questionable whether this is the desired fix: a safer solution would probably be to move the valves to safe mode when powering down the system, thus ensuring that upon rebooting no hazardous situations emerge.

In a similar vein, Alarm requirements can be checked. For instance, requirement SAV.16 states that:

> "The system shall raise an alarm when the inspiratory flux is below a user-controlled value ($MinV_E$)."

A "strong" interpretation of this requirement asserts that the high priority alarm is unavoidable. Taking into account that we have introduced various self-loops in our model for the purpose of verification, a formalisation of such a strong interpretation will not hold true for our model. We therefore verify the following "weaker" interpretation of this requirement, asserting that so long as the high priority alarm has not yet been raised or snoozed, it remains possible.

```
[true*]
  (forall v,w:Nat. [getSensorValue_c(FlowIndicator1,v)|get_Min_V_E_c(w)]
                   (val(v < w)
                   =>
                   [!(  alarm_snooze_c(High)
                     || HighAlarm )*]<true*.HighAlarm>true))
  )
```

Verifying this requirement requires approx. 25 s. The requirements shown in this section are representative of other requirements imposed on the MLV. We have additionally formalised and verified requirements SAV.1, 17 and 22 as well as requirements CONT.3-10, 13, 15, 19, 21, 25 and 46 using similar translations.

4.2 Scenarios

In Fig. 5 we give a graphical representation of the scenarios of [8] using activity diagrams. Each scenario can be captured in a modal μ-calculus formula that holds true exactly when the scenario is admitted by our mCRL2 model.

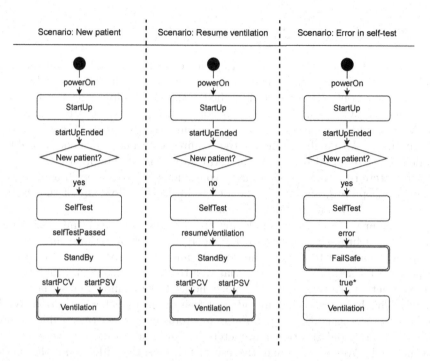

Fig. 5. Activity diagram representation of the scenarios outlined in the attachment to the case study [8].

We show how the new patient scenario can be formalised in the modal μ-calculus. The error in self-test scenarios and resume ventilation scenario are similar to the new patient scenario and can be formalised analogously.

The new patient scenario describes that when a new patient is connected to the MLV and the self-test procedure is successfully completed, it must then be possible to start ventilation. We formalise this scenario as follows:

```
< (!powerOn)* . powerOn .
  (!emitMode(StartUp))* . emitMode(StartUp) .
  (!new_patient)*. new_patient .
  (!startUpSuccessful)* . startUpSuccessful .
  (!emitMode(SelfTest))* . emitMode(SelfTest) .
  (selfTestPassed_c)* . selfTestPassed_c .
  (!emitMode(VentilationOff))*. emitMode(VentilationOff) .
  (!exists m: OperationMode.
     (  startPCV_c|controller_Mode_c(m)
     || startPSV_c|controller_Mode_c(m) ) )*>
```

```
(   < exists m: OperationMode. startPCV_c|controller_Mode_c(m) > true
&& < exists m: OperationMode. startPSV_c|controller_Mode_c(m) > true )
```

The scenario (and also the other two) can be verified to exist in under 20 s using the on-the-fly symbolic model checking optimisations of [25]; the on-the-fly optimisation yields a speed-up of a factor 3–4.

5   Discussion and Conclusions

The MLV system provides an interesting challenge for the mCRL2 language and toolset. The discrete behaviour of components such as the sensors, valves, the GUI and the controller can be described rather faithfully using the language constructs of mCRL2, and their description is straightforward. A full analysis of the MLV would also require taking into account the dynamics of, e.g., the ventilation itself. Although technically the required continuous behaviour could be modelled, the required support for its verification is limited in practice. We therefore abstracted from aspects requiring continuous behaviour, such as detection of breathing phases, and instead nondeterministically allow any of the changes described in the requirements document.

Particularly useful in the modelling are the multi-actions of mCRL2, which allow for synchronising between components on a set of actions, and which a component can use to "read" the state of another component when deciding to perform an action. We observe that due to the large configuration space of the parameters involved, the state space induced by our model grows large very quickly. This has caused us to introduce details in our model with caution. While we have not stretched the boundaries of our tools, we expect that including several additional configuration parameters in our model will put those bounds within reach. We do note that the use of the recently added symbolic model checker for mCRL2 turned out to be essential to analyse our model; using the explicit model checkers would have necessitated the use of more aggressive modelling abstractions. A major drawback of the symbolic model checker is that it currently does not allow to efficiently and effectively construct counterexamples using the approach from [31]. In practice this functionality proves to be essential for identifying and understanding problems in preliminary versions of the model.

Our analysis of the design and safety requirements revealed a few subtleties in [8]. For instance, our initial violation of CONT.38 reveals that it is not completely clear when the controller can be considered to be in a particular mode. Furthermore, it is not entirely clear whether the events depicted in the two State Machines of [8] are intended to synchronise. For instance, we assume in our model that the PowerOn event, which appears in both the State Machine of the GUI and the controller, can happen in isolation and that these events do not need to synchronise. This interpretation allows for both components to start and stop independently, which makes sense if the GUI can, e.g., crash; also, this interpretation is more general and includes studying the system in case such synchronisation had occurred.

Competing Interests. The author(s) has no competing interests to declare that are relevant to the content of this manuscript.

References

1. ISO/IEC/IEEE Health informatics–Personal health device communication–Part 20601: Application profile–Optimized exchange protocol. ISO/IEEE 11073-20601:2010(E), pp. 1–208 (2010). https://doi.org/10.1109/IEEESTD.2010.5703195
2. Abba, A., et al.: The novel Mechanical Ventilator Milano for the COVID-19 pandemic. Phys. Fluids (Woodbury, N.Y.: 1994) **33**(3), 037122 (2021). https://doi.org/10.1063/5.0044445
3. Arney, D., Jetley, R., Jones, P., Lee, I., Sokolsky, O.: Formal methods based development of a PCA infusion pump reference model: generic infusion pump (GIP) project. In: 2007 Joint Workshop on High Confidence Medical Devices, Software, and Systems and Medical Device Plug-and-Play Interoperability (HCMDSS-MDPnP 2007), pp. 23–33 (2007). https://doi.org/10.1109/HCMDSS-MDPnP.2007.36
4. Arshad, H., Horne, R., Johansen, C., Owe, O., Willemse, T.A.C.: Process algebra can save lives: static analysis of XACML access control policies using mCRL2. In: Mousavi, M.R., Philippou, A. (eds.) FORTE 2022. LNCS, vol. 13273, pp. 11–30. Springer, Cham (2022). https://doi.org/10.1007/978-3-031-08679-3_2
5. Bartholomeus, M., Luttik, B., Willemse, T.: Modelling and analysing ERTMS hybrid level 3 with the mCRL2 toolset. In: Howar, F., Barnat, J. (eds.) FMICS 2018. LNCS, vol. 11119, pp. 98–114. Springer, Cham (2018). https://doi.org/10.1007/978-3-030-00244-2_7
6. Bergstra, J.A., Klop, J.W.: Process algebra for synchronous communication. Inf. Control **60**(1), 109–137 (1984). https://doi.org/10.1016/S0019-9958(84)80025-X
7. Bombarda, A., Bonfanti, S., Gargantini, A., Riccobene, E.: Developing a prototype of a mechanical ventilator controller from requirements to code with ASMETA. Electron. Proc. Theor. Comput. Sci. **349**, 13–29 (2021). https://doi.org/10.4204/EPTCS.349.2
8. Bonfanti, S., Gargantini, A.: Mechanical Lung Ventilator (2023). https://github.com/foselab/abz2024_casestudy_MLV/blob/main/Mechanical_Lung_Ventilator%201_5.pdf
9. Bonfanti, S., Gargantini, A.: The mechanical lung ventilator case study. In: Bonfanti, S., et al. (eds.) ABZ 2024. LNCS, vol. 14759, pp. 281–288. Springer, Cham (2024)
10. Bonfanti, S., Gargantini, A., Mashkoor, A.: A systematic literature review of the use of formal methods in medical software systems. J. Softw. Evol. Process **30**(5), e1943 (2018). https://doi.org/10.1002/smr.1943
11. Bonivento, W., Gargantini, A., Krücken, R., Razeto, A.: The Mechanical Ventilator Milano. Nucl. Phys. News **31**(3), 30–33 (2021). https://doi.org/10.1080/10619127.2021.1915047
12. Bunte, O., et al.: The mCRL2 toolset for analysing concurrent systems. In: Vojnar, T., Zhang, L. (eds.) TACAS 2019. LNCS, vol. 11428, pp. 21–39. Springer, Cham (2019). https://doi.org/10.1007/978-3-030-17465-1_2
13. Daw, Z., Cleaveland, R., Vetter, M.: Formal verification of software-based medical devices considering medical guidelines. Int. J. Comput. Assist. Radiol. Surg. **9**(1), 145–153 (2014). https://doi.org/10.1007/s11548-013-0919-2

14. Groote, J.F., Keiren, J.J.A.: Tutorial: designing distributed software in mCRL2. In: Peters, K., Willemse, T.A.C. (eds.) FORTE 2021. LNCS, vol. 12719, pp. 226–243. Springer, Cham (2021). https://doi.org/10.1007/978-3-030-78089-0_15

15. Groote, J.F., Keiren, J.J.A., Luttik, B., de Vink, E.P., Willemse, T.A.C.: Modelling and analysing software in mCRL2. In: Arbab, F., Jongmans, S.-S. (eds.) FACS 2019. LNCS, vol. 12018, pp. 25–48. Springer, Cham (2020). https://doi.org/10.1007/978-3-030-40914-2_2

16. Groote, J.F., Mateescu, R.: Verification of temporal properties of processes in a setting with data. In: Haeberer, A.M. (ed.) AMAST 1999. LNCS, vol. 1548, pp. 74–90. Springer, Heidelberg (1998). https://doi.org/10.1007/3-540-49253-4_8

17. Groote, J.F., Mousavi, M.R.: Modeling and Analysis of Communicating Systems. The MIT Press, Cambridge (2014)

18. Groote, J.F., Willemse, T.A.C.: A symmetric protocol to establish service level agreements. Logical Methods Comput. Sci. **16**(3) (2020). https://doi.org/10.23638/LMCS-16(3:19)2020

19. Groote, J.F., Willemse, T.A.C.: Model-checking processes with data. Sci. Comput. Program. **56**(3), 251–273 (2005). https://doi.org/10.1016/J.SCICO.2004.08.002

20. Harrison, M.D., et al.: Formal techniques in the safety analysis of software components of a new dialysis machine. Sci. Comput. Program. **175**, 17–34 (2019). https://doi.org/10.1016/j.scico.2019.02.003

21. Hommersom, A., Groot, P., Lucas, P.J., Balser, M., Schmitt, J.: Verification of medical guidelines using background knowledge in task networks. IEEE Trans. Knowl. Data Eng. **19**(6), 832–846 (2007). https://doi.org/10.1109/TKDE.2007.190611

22. Hwong, Y.L., Keiren, J.J.A., Kusters, V.J.J., Leemans, S., Willemse, T.A.C.: Formalising and analysing the control software of the Compact Muon Solenoid experiment at the Large Hadron Collider. Sci. Comput. Program. **78**(12), 2435–2452 (2013). https://doi.org/10.1016/j.scico.2012.11.009

23. Jetley, R., Purushothaman Iyer, S., Jones, P.: A formal methods approach to medical device review. Computer **39**(4), 61–67 (2006). https://doi.org/10.1109/MC.2006.113

24. Keiren, J.J.A., Klabbers, M.D.: Modelling and verifying IEEE STD 11073-20601 session setup using mCRL2. In: Proceedings of the Workshop on Automated Verification of Critical Systems (AVoCS 2012), vol. X, pp. 1–15 (2012). http://journal.ub.tu-berlin.de/eceasst/article/view/793

25. Laveaux, M., Wesselink, W., Willemse, T.A.C.: On-the-fly solving for symbolic parity games. In: TACAS 2022. LNCS, vol. 13244, pp. 137–155. Springer, Cham (2022). https://doi.org/10.1007/978-3-030-99527-0_8

26. Manley, R.W.: A new mechanical ventilator. Anaesthesia **16**(3), 317–323 (1961). https://doi.org/10.1111/j.1365-2044.1961.tb13830.x

27. Masci, P., Zhang, Y., Jones, P., Curzon, P., Thimbleby, H.: Formal verification of medical device user interfaces using PVS. In: Gnesi, S., Rensink, A. (eds.) FASE 2014. LNCS, vol. 8411, pp. 200–214. Springer, Heidelberg (2014). https://doi.org/10.1007/978-3-642-54804-8_14

28. Mashkoor, A., Egyed, A.: Analysis of experiences with the engineering of a medical device using state-based formal methods. In: 2018 IEEE International Conference on Software Quality, Reliability and Security (QRS), pp. 75–82 (2018). https://doi.org/10.1109/QRS.2018.00021

29. Stramaglia, A., Keiren, J.J.A.: Formal verification of an industrial UML-like model using mCRL2. In: Groote, J.F., Huisman, M. (eds.) FMICS 2022. LNCS, vol. 13487, pp. 86–102. Springer, Cham (2022). https://doi.org/10.1007/978-3-031-15008-1_7

30. van Dortmont, D., Keiren, J.J.A., Willemse, T.A.C.: Models for: modelling and analysing a mechanical lung ventilator in mCRL2 (2024). https://doi.org/10.5281/zenodo.10978852

31. Wesselink, W., Willemse, T.A.C.: Evidence extraction from parameterised Boolean equation systems. In: Proceedings of the 3rd International Workshop on Automated Reasoning in Quantified Non-Classical Logics (ARQNL 2018) Affiliated with the International Joint Conference on Automated Reasoning (IJCAR 2018), vol. 2095. CEUR-WS, Oxford (2018). https://ceur-ws.org/Vol-2095/paper6.pdf

32. Wiggelinkhuizen, J.E.: Feasibility of formal model checking in the Vitatron environment. Master's thesis, Eindhoven University of Technology, Eindhoven (2008). https://research.tue.nl/en/studentTheses/feasibility-of-formal-model-checking-in-the-vitatron-environment

FRETting and Formal Modelling: A Mechanical Lung Ventilator

Marie Farrell[1]([✉]), Matt Luckcuck[2], Rosemary Monahan[3], Conor Reynolds[1], and Oisín Sheridan[3]

[1] Department of Computer Science, The University of Manchester, Manchester, UK
marie.farrell@manchester.ac.uk
[2] School of Computer Science, University of Nottingham, Nottingham, UK
[3] Department of Computer Science, Maynooth University/Hamilton Institute, Maynooth, Ireland

Abstract. In this paper, we use NASA's Formal Requirements Elicitation Tool (FRET) and the Event-B formal method to model and verify the requirements for the ABZ 2024 case study, the Mechanical Lung Ventilator. We use the FRET requirements to guide the development of a formal design model in Event-B. We provide details about the artefacts produced and reflect on our experience of using these tools in this case study. We focus on the Functional and Controller requirements for the system, as given in the case study documentation. This paper provides a first step towards using Event-B as part of a FRET-guided verification workflow in a large case study.

1 Introduction

We describe a workflow that captures the requirements of the ABZ 2024 case study, the Mechanical Lung Ventilator,[1] using the Formal Requirements Elicitation Tool (FRET) [16]. Our workflow uses the requirements, written in FRET's structured-natural requirements language FRETISH, to guide the development of a formal design in Event-B. We previously proposed this FRET-guided workflow in [22,28,29], and this paper explores how to use FRETISH requirements to guide the development of a formal design in a large case study.

FRET parses FRETISH requirements and translates them into past- and future-time Metric Temporal Logic (MTL) [16], useful for formal verification. MTL extends Linear-time Temporal Logic (LTL) with timing constraints. MTL properties express that a proposition becomes true within a given interval. FRET also produces a *diagramatic* semantics for each requirement that shows the period in which the requirements should hold, and their triggering and stopping conditions. Both representations help to sanity check the requirement's behaviour.

---

[1] ABZ 2024 Case Study: https://abz-conf.org/case-study/abz24/.

All authors (listed alphabetically by surname) contributed equally to this work. This work was partially supported by the Royal Academy of Engineering and EPSRC grant EP/Y001532/1, as well as Maynooth University's Hume Doctoral Award.

S. Bonfanti et al. (Eds.): ABZ 2024, LNCS 14759, pp. 360–383, 2024.
https://doi.org/10.1007/978-3-031-63790-2_28

Software requirements are properties that the software must satisfy; they specify what the system should do, without saying how it should do it [31]. But requirements specifications are usually written in natural-language, not as a *formal* specification. FRETISH enables us to step from natural-language requirements, to formal requirements in MTL.

A software design should be built to obey the system's requirements. The novelty of our work lies in using FRETISH to guide the development of a formal design in Event-B, into which we can trace the requirements and prove that they are preserved. We do not have a formal translation between FRETISH and Event-B, but the formality of these artefacts supports the development of a *formal* design that preserves the properties specified by the FRETISH requirements.

The FRETISH requirements provide an unambiguous representation of the properties that the system must obey, and the formal design modelled in Event-B ensures that these properties hold. The requirements are represented by several artefacts in the Event-B model (Sect. 4), but the formality of both the requirements and design make verification possible.

We begin our description by providing some background prerequisite information in Sect. 2 related to FRET, Event-B and the case study. We also provide a brief overview of related work. In Sect. 3 we describe how we formalised the requirements given in the case study documentation, and in Sect. 4 we discuss how we modelled these in Event-B. We reflect on our approach in Sect. 5, and Sect. 6 concludes.

2   Background and Related Work

In this section, we provide overviews of FRET and the Event-B formal method that we used for the Mechanical Lung Ventilator case study. We also outline the case study itself and provide a short description of related work.

2.1   Formal Requirements Elicitation Tool (FRET)

FRET is supported by a structured natural-language, called FRETISH, with which users can express requirements [16]. For each requirement, FRET generates a formal semantics in past- and future-time MTL. To aid usability, FRET also produces a diagrammatic semantics to help users to understand the meaning of the requirements. FRET is open-source and available on GitHub.[2]

FRETISH requirements are composed of the following five fields:

scope condition component shall timing response

The component and response fields are mandatory (along with the "shall" keyword) for all FRETISH requirements. Using this syntax, users can express requirements for individual components that pertain to a particular scope under some condition where the response (expected behaviour) can be specific to a defined timing. Uses of FRET have typically focused on aerospace use cases [13,25],

---

[2] FRET GitHub Repository: https://github.com/NASA-SW-VnV/fret.

though some studies exist for other domains including robotics [10,14]. This paper reports the first use of FRET for a medical use case.

FRET provides automated translations from FRETISH requirements to CoCoSpec contracts [12], that can be verified with the Kind2 model checker, and Copilot runtime monitors [26]. There is no automated support for translating between FRETISH requirements and theorem proving approaches like Event-B, though previous work has shown that these proof-based methods are useful for verifying requirements that are difficult to verify using the current supported CoCoSpec approach [10].

2.2 Event-B

Event-B is a state-based formal method that has been used in the development of safety-critical systems in a variety of sectors, including rail [20], aerospace [23] and medical [18]. The Event-B language is based on set theory and first-order logic [2]. Event-B is supported by its Eclipse-based IDE, the Rodin Platform [3]. Event-B, like FRET, is open-source. Specifications in Event-B are composed of *machines* and *contexts*. A machine specifies dynamic behaviour via variants, invariants, and events. Static behaviour is typically specified in a context, using carrier sets, constants, and axioms.

Event-B supports formal refinement, enabling users to gradually add more detail to their model and discharge proofs of correctness at each stage [27]. Theorem proving is supported in Rodin with most of the generated proof obligations discharged automatically, although some may need manual interaction with Rodin's provers. The semantics of Event-B models is often thought of in terms of the generated proof obligations [17], and a detailed formal semantics for the Event-B language itself is given in [15].

2.3 Case Study: Mechanical Lung Ventilator

The case study proposed for ABZ 2024 is a mechanical lung ventilator. An Abstract State Machine (ASM) model of this use case is provided in [8] and it provides the basis for the case study documentation.[3]

During the COVID-19 pandemic, mechanical lung ventilators were an essential piece of medical equipment, supporting patients who were unable to breathe on their own [1,9]. The system provides two ventilation modes: Pressure Controlled Ventilation (PCV) and Pressure Support Ventilation (PSV). The case study description includes a diagram of the system, as shown in Fig. 1. We used this architecture as the basis for our first abstract Event-B machine, discussed in Sect. 4. We also used it to inform our understanding of the requirements.

The case study documentation provided a large number of requirements for the system. These were partitioned into Functional Requirements (FUN), Values and Ranges (PER), Sensors and Interfaces (INT), Alarm Requirements (SAV),

---

[3] Mechanical Lung Ventilator Repository: https://github.com/foselab/abz2024_casestudy_MLV.

GUI Requirements (GUI), Controller Requirements (CONT), and Alarms (AL). Some requirements have 'child' requirements; for example, FUN6 is decomposed into FUN6_1–6. Requirements also reference others; for example, CONT4 refers to FUN6. The documentation does not make it clear what these relationships are formally and we will discuss this further later.

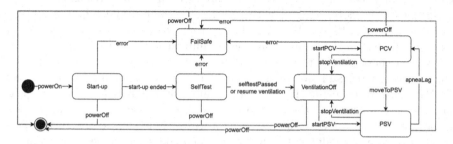

Fig. 1. The controller state machine is labelled as Fig 4.1 in the case study document.

2.4 Related Work

Event-B, and its variants, have been used extensively in ABZ case studies, both in isolation and alongside other tools [6,19,21,23,24]. These case studies, as well as industrial applications of Event-B, emphasise its use in multiple distinct safety-critical domains such as rail, healthcare and aerospace. FRET has not been used for an ABZ case study before; its use has mostly been focused on the aerospace domain [13,25], though some robotics use cases exist [10,14].

One of these robotics use cases made an attempt at linking FRETISH requirements with an Event-B model. This focused on a small part of the robotic system (the planner), and Event-B was chosen because the Kind2 model checker that was used to verify the FRETish requirements timed out on properties concerning the planner [10]. In contrast, our work here seeks to represent more requirements and to specifically examine which parts of the Event-B model were impacted by the FRETISH requirements.

Bonfanti *et al.* [8] describe the experience of modelling the behaviour of a Mechanical Ventilator using a compositional modelling and simulation technique [7]. Their approach is supported by the AsmetaComp tool of the ASMETA toolset for ASMs [5]. Here, separate abstract state machines represent the behaviour of interacting subsystems of the ventilator; where they can communicate with each other through I/O events, and co-operate by a precise orchestration schema.

3 FRETISH Requirements

In this section, we describe our journey from the natural-language requirements given in the case study document to formalised FRETISH requirements. At first, we focused on the functional (FUN) requirements that were identified in the documentation. FRET has been mostly used for functional requirements in the past so this seemed like the logical place for us to start. However, there is a strong relationship between these Functional (FUN) and the Controller (CONT) requirements, so we expanded our scope to also examine the CONT requirements.

We mapped 142 Functional and Controller requirements from their natural-language specification into FRETISH. The requirements are labelled FUN⟨X⟩ and CONT⟨X⟩, respectively ($X \in \mathbb{N}$); the requirement numbers match the documentation, with the dots replaced with underscores in the child requirements for compatibility with FRET. We omit the dot from the top-level requirements; for example, FUN.1 in the natural-language requirements becomes FUN1.

Table 1 shows a subset of the FRETISH requirements that we could formalise; the full set of FRETISH requirements is available in the Appendix. Figure 2 shows FRET's dashboard, displaying the total number of requirements in the project, and the percentage that have been formalised (green circles). Requirements that could not be formalised are indicated by a white circle (see Sect. 3.2). Requirements that are not valid FRETISH are represented as red circles; for example, CONT36, which is an incomplete sentence in the case study document. Circles within other circles indicate a parent-child relationship between requirements.

Figure 3 shows an example of a requirement that we were able to formalise, FUN10_6. The requirement's "Rationale" (top left) captures its natural-language version. FRET produces a diagrammatic semantics (top right) from the FRETISH requirement (text box, bottom left) that is useful for sanity checking the requirement. FUN10_6's timing condition, after 15 minutes, is reflected in both the diagrammatic semantics (top right) and the temporal logic (bottom right). While FRET labels the temporal logic "Future Time LTL" we can see that the formula is MTL, for example it contains "G[0,15]".

Initially, we only included timing in the FRETISH requirements where it was explicitly mentioned in the natural-language version, like in FUN10_6. If a FRETISH requirement has no timing condition, then it defaults to eventually; so, on a second pass, we rechecked the timing conditions and added them explicitly. Each requirement's timing was considered individually, but we usually used: always when the requirement had no conditions, eventually for events that would take an indeterminate amount of time (such as waiting for a process to finish or for user input), and at the next timepoint for a response triggered by an event or button-press. We chose at the next timepoint instead of immediately to represent the time taken to react to the trigger and generate the response.

3.1 Formalising Requirements with FRET

We mapped the requirements into FRETISH in several stages, producing sequential versions of the requirements set. As mentioned above, we initially focused on formalising specifically the Functional requirements from the case study, from FUN1 up to FUN42. These were first compiled in v0.1 and v0.2 of the requirements set. We made revisions and additions as a group, producing v0.3 and v0.3.1. Further edits were made in v0.4 to better align with the case study document and fix model checking errors arising from invalid variable names (e.g. the variable "I:E" in the case study had to be changed to "ItoE" in FRETISH).

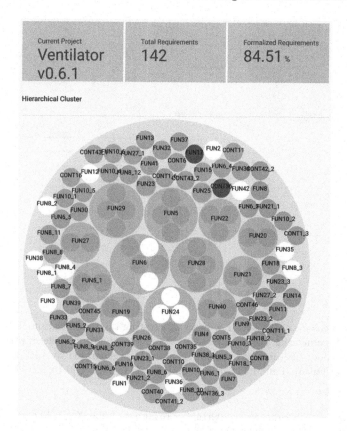

Fig. 2. View of FRET's dashboard for the Ventilator project. Formalised requirements are indicated in green, and those in white have not been formalised. A red circle indicates invalid FRETISH in that requirement. (Color figure online)

Following this, we realised that the Controller requirements provided additional detail that would be helpful during the development of the Event-B model. We expanded the scope of the FRETISH formalisation to include the Controller requirements, from CONT1 up to CONT46. These were formalised in v0.5. v0.5.1 formalised one additional requirement, CONT43_3, that was initially omitted. Finally, we decided to update the FRETISH to include explicit timing conditions in all of the requirements, in v0.6 and v0.6.1.

What follows are some explanations of our methodology when formalising the requirements. For traceability, the names of variables and constants align with those mentioned in the case study, where possible. For example, FUN20:

"In PCV mode, the breathing cycle shall be defined by inspiratory pressure P_{insp_PCV} relative to atmosphere, respiratory rate (RR_{PCV}) and the ratio between the inspiratory and expiratory times ($I{:}E_{PCV}$)."

This natural-language description is accompanied by a note that details how the times are defined. This was formalised in FRETISH as "in **PCVMode**

Fig. 3. A screenshot of the FRET window illustrating the formalisation of requirement FUN10_6 documenting the requirement rationale and FRETISH description, as well as the associated diagrammatic semantics and MTL generated by FRET. While the heading says "Future Time LTL", the formula is MTL (e.g. "G[0,15]").

System shall always satisfy breathingCycleTime = 1/RR_PCV & ExpiratoryTime = breathingCycleTime / (1+ItoE_PCV)".

We created FRETISH requirements for all of the Functional and Controller requirements, even those that could not be formalised in FRET. The main exceptions to this were CONT4 and CONT39. For example, CONT39 states:

> *"When the ventilator is in an Inspiration state, the out valve shall be closed and the in valve pressure shall be set to target inspiratory pressure (P_{insp} of the corresponding mode)."*

and then each of its three child requirements specify the correct pressure for each mode, e.g. CONT39_2 states *"P_{insp_PSV} if current mode is PSV"*. This format does not lend itself well to FRETISH, as none of these are full requirements on their own. Additionally, a conflict would arise between CONT39_1 (*"P_{insp_PCV} if current mode is PCV"*) and CONT39_3 (*"P_{insp_AP} if current mode is PCV from apnea backup"*) if they were translated directly, requiring additional information to be added to CONT39_1. As a result, these requirements were combined into a single CONT39 as shown in Table 1. CONT4 was a similar case.

3.2 Unformalised Requirements

The unformalised requirements often related to capabilities of the overall system, rather than specifiable behaviour. For example, we did not formalise FUN1:

"The system shall provide ventilation support for patients who require mechanical ventilation and weigh more than 40 kg (88 lbs). Rationale: ventilation of children and infants is more challenging",

because it refers to things that are not within the scope of the functioning system. For example, whether patients require ventilation or not should be determined by a medical practitioner and not the system. Similarly, the ventilator has no way to determine or check the weight of a given patient. Perhaps a doctor could input this to the machine and it could then issue a warning to the user if the patient were outside the permitted weight range, but we did not find references to any such functionality in the requirements.

We chose not to translate the "Measured and displayed parameters" requirements from §2.2 of the case study, although they are labelled FUN43–FUN58. These requirements specify parameters that the system should measure and display for the patient, e.g. FUN56: *"Value of the temperature inside the system unit is reported".* There was no meaningful way to capture these requirements in FRET without a more detailed understanding of the sensors and GUI. Since they are in a separate subsection and don't seem to add to the description of the core functionality of the ventilator system, we felt it best to omit them at this time. We chose not to formalise other sections of the case study for this paper, such as the Alarm requirements in §2.5, for similar reasons. These requirements are straightforwardly expressed as boolean conditions in Event-B so they would not have added to our exploration of using FRET to scaffold an Event-B model.

3.3 Analysis

In some cases, once formalised, a CONT requirement matched a FUN requirement exactly, apart from the `component` field. For example, FUN4 and CONT1 both list the operating modes that the system should implement, and were both ultimately formalised as "System/Controller shall always satisfy StartUpMode | SelfTestMode | StandbyMode | PCVMode | PSVMode | FailSafeMode".

An obstacle we encountered in some of these cases was that, even when the (seemingly) same underlying behaviour is being described, the language is not entirely consistent. Here, the mode that comes after the self test has passed and before the system moves to PCV or PSV mode is called "Standby Mode" in the FUN requirements, but is named "VentilationOff" in the CONT requirements. We chose to maintain consistency and use StandyByMode in FRETISH.

In other cases, the Controller requirements contained more detail than Functional requirements that described the same behaviour, or vice-versa, or they were structured differently to put more focus on certain aspects of the behaviour. This sometimes led to requirements gaining extra detail. For example, our initial version of FUN5_1 simply read "in StartUpMode System shall satisfy initStart". However, when formalising CONT13 and CONT14, which list FUN5_1 as their "Input ref.", we realised that the description of FUN5_1 contained more functionality that could be included. As such, FUN5_1 was updated to "in StartUpMode System shall satisfy initStart & checkCommsSensors & checkCommsValves & checkCommsGUI" (with explicit timing also added later).

However, there were also cases where a lack of detail led to an apparent conflict between two requirements. This occurred with CONT24 and FUN22, which both specify the "Recruitment Maneuver (RM)" behaviour. FUN22:

"In PCV mode it shall be possible to initiate with the push of a single button a lung recruitment procedure, termed Recruitment Maneuver (RM)"

We interpreted this to mean that RM begins immediately when the corresponding GUI button is pressed during PCV mode. However, CONT24 states:

"At the end of an inspiration phase, if inspiratory pause is not required and the Recruitment Maneuver is set by the GUI, a Recruitment Maneuver shall start"

Note that CONT24 is found in the subsection of Controller requirements that apply to the PCV mode. The Controller requirements only refer to the recruitment manoeuver starting at the end of the inspiration phase as seen here, leading to an apparent conflict with the earlier requirement.

Formalising requirements in a structured language like FRETISH helps to find cases like these where a requirement lacks important details. A similar case is found with CONT19, which states *"If the SelfTest fails, the Controller shall not be able to proceed to ventilation"*. A naive implementation of this could easily create a deadlock, as there is no stated endpoint where the failure stops applying. We added a timing condition "`until off`" to the FRETISH CONT19 for this reason.

4   Event-B Model

This section describes our Event-B modelling approach using both the FRETISH and natural-language requirements. Our primary focus was to explore how the FRETISH requirements are represented in the corresponding Event-B model.

4.1   Modelling the Architecture

A key feature of Event-B is formal refinement: the stepwise development of a system from an abstract to a concrete specification [27]. Event-B model development thus typically begins with an abstract machine capturing the high-level operation of the system. The case study document provides two useful starting-points for a formal model: Fig. 2.1, a "high-level operation diagram"; and Fig. 4.1, the "controller state machine". The controller state machine at first appears as if it is a refinement of the high-level operation diagram, but there are some inconsistencies.

As mentioned earlier, one such inconsistency is reflected in the requirements themselves. Specifically, the "Standby Mode" in Fig. 2.1 appears to correspond to the "VentilationOff" mode in Fig. 4.1. Figure 2.1 has a transition from "StandBy Mode" to "SelfTest", while Fig. 4.1 has no transition from "VentilationOff" to "SelfTest". This transition does not seem possible and is not described anywhere else in the case study document. After examining the case study documentation, we have concluded that the requirements listed there are more consistent with the controller state machine than with the high-level operation diagram.

Table 1. Selected FRETISH requirements, the full list is in the Appendix.

Req ID	FRETISH
CONT1	Controller shall always satisfy StartUpMode | SelfTestMode | StandbyMode | PCVMode | PSVMode | FailSafeMode
CONT1_3	in StandbyMode Controller shall always satisfy ventilationOff & inValveClose & outValveOpen
CONT1_6	in FailSafeMode Controller shall always satisfy inValveClose & outValveOpen
CONT4	in SelfTestMode if selfTestPassed | GUIResumeRequest Controller shall at the next timepoint satisfy StandbyMode
CONT13	in StartUpMode Controller shall eventually satisfy checkCommsSensors & checkCommsValves
CONT14	in StartUpMode Controller shall eventually satisfy checkCommsGUI
CONT19	in SelfTestMode if SelfTestFail Controller shall until off satisfy !StandbyMode & !ventilating
CONT39	while inspiratoryPhase Controller shall always satisfy outValveClose & (PCVMode & !apnea => P_insp = P_isnpPCV) & (PSVMode => P_insp = P_inspPSV) & (PCVMode & apnea => P_insp = P_inspAP)
FUN4	System shall always satisfy StartUpMode | SelfTestMode | StandbyMode | PCVMode | PSVMode | FailSafeMode
FUN5	when powerButton & (breathingCircuitConnected & !(patientConnected) & airSupplyConnected & powerConnected) System shall at the next timepoint satisfy StartUpMode
FUN5_1	in StartUpMode System shall eventually satisfy initStart & checkCommsSensors & checkCommsValves & checkCommsGUI
FUN5_3	System shall always satisfy (StartUpMode | SelfTestMode) -> !patientConnected
FUN6	in SelfTestMode System shall eventually satisfy selfTestPassed | selfTestFailed
FUN6_1	in SelfTestMode System shall eventually satisfy testPowerSwitchPass | testPowerSwitchFail | testPowerSwitchSkip
FUN7	in SelfTestMode if selfTestFail System shall at the next timepoint satisfy OutOfServiceWarning & FailSafeMode
FUN10	when startUpDone System shall eventually satisfy newPatient | resumeVentilation
FUN10_1	when newPatient System shall eventually satisfy patientAttributesEntered & SelfTestMode & ((testPowerSwitchPass & testLeaksPass & testFl2Pass & testPSExpPass & testOxygenSensorPass & testAlarmsPass) => selfTestPassed)
FUN10_2	when resumeVentilation System shall at the next timepoint satisfy loadLastParams
FUN10_3	when resumeVentilation System shall eventually satisfy SelfTestMode & (((testPowerSwitchPass | testPowerSwitchSkip) & (testLeaksPass | testLeaksSkip) & (testFl2Pass | testFl2Skip) & (testPSExpPass | testPSExpSkip) & (testOxygenSensorPass | testOxygenSensorSkip) & (testAlarmsPass | testAlarmsSkip)) => selfTestPassed)
FUN10_4	when selfTestPassed System shall at the next timepoint satisfy StandbyMode
FUN10_6	when off System shall after 15 minutes satisfy !resumeVentilation
FUN20	in PCVMode System shall always satisfy breathingCycleTime = 1/RR_PCV & ExpiratoryTime = breathingCycleTime / (1+ItoE_PCV)

```
1    MACHINE mac00
2    SEES ctx00                          36    Event StartPSV ≙
3    VARIABLES mode                      37      when
4    INVARIANTS                          38        grd0_1: mode = VentilationOff
5      typeof__mode: mode ∈ Mode         39               ∨ mode = PCV
                                         40      then
6    EVENTS                              41        act0_1: mode := PSV
7    Initialisation
8      then                             42    Event StopVentilation ≙
9        act1: mode := PoweredOff       43      when
                                         44        grd0_1: mode = PCV
10   Event PowerOn ≙                     45               ∨ mode = PSV
11     when                             46      then
12       grd0_1: mode = PoweredOff      47        act0_1: mode := VentilationOff
13     then
14       act0_1: mode := StartUp        48    Event MoveToPSV ≙
                                         49      when
15   Event StartUpEnded ≙               50        grd0_1: mode = PCV
16     when                             51      then
17       grd0_1: mode = StartUp         52        act0_1: mode := PSV
18     then
19       act0_1: mode := SelfTest       53    Event ApneaLag ≙
                                         54      when
20   Event ResumeVentilation ≙          55        grd0_1: mode = PSV
21     when                             56      then
22       grd0_1: mode = SelfTest        57        act0_1: mode := PCV
23     then
24       act0_1: mode := VentilationOff 58    Event Error ≙
                                         59      when
25   Event SelfTestPassed ≙             60        grd0_1: mode ≠ PoweredOff
26     when                             61        grd0_2: mode ≠ Failsafe
27       grd0_1: mode = SelfTest        62      then
28     then                             63        act0_1: mode := Failsafe
29       act0_1: mode := VentilationOff
                                         64    Event PowerOff ≙
30   Event StartPCV ≙                    65      when
31     when                             66        grd0_1: mode ≠ PoweredOff
32       grd0_1: mode = VentilationOff  67      then
33               ∨ mode = PSV           68        act0_1: mode := PoweredOff
34     then                             69 END
35       act0_1: mode := PCV
```

Fig. 4. Abstract Event-B machine corresponding to the ventilator behaviour in Fig. 1.

As a result of these inconsistencies, we chose to use the controller state machine in Fig. 1 (Fig. 4.1 in the case study documentation) as our canonical high-level operation diagram for the system. The initial Event-B model, mac00 in Fig. 4 and its context in Fig. 5, correspond directly to Fig. 1. A single variable *mode* indicates the current mode, and transitions between these modes are triggered by events. This method of modelling state-machine diagrams is similar to the approach taken by the iUML-B plugin (though we do not use iUML-B here) [30]. This initial Event-B model captures requirements FUN4 and CONT1.

By encoding the state machine abstractly and supporting new behaviour via refinement of this state machine, we ensure that the refined models switch modes according to the state-transition diagram.

```
                                    1  CONTEXT ctx01
                                    2     EXTENDS ctx00
   1  CONTEXT ctx00                 3     SETS ValveState, TestResult
   2  SETS  Mode                    4     CONSTANTS
   3  CONSTANTS                     5        ValveOpen, ValveClosed, TestPassed
   4    Failsafe, PoweredOff, VentilationOff    6        TestFailed, TestSkipped
   5    PCV, PSV, SelfTest, StartUp           7     AXIOMS
   6  AXIOMS                        8        axm1_1: partition(ValveState,
   7    axm0_1: partition(Mode, {StartUp},    9                {ValveOpen}, {ValveClosed})
   8            {SelfTest}, {VentilationOff},  10       axm1_2: partition(TestResult,
   9            {PCV}, {PSV}, {Failsafe},      11               {TestPassed}, {TestFailed},
  10            {PoweredOff})                  12               {TestSkipped})
  11  END                          13  END
```

Fig. 5. Context for the abstract machine, capturing FUN4/CONT1.

Fig. 6. Extending context to capture necessary sets and constants related to the selftest process (FUN6_1–6).

4.2 Encoding the Requirements

We encoded the FRETISH requirements into Event-B in different ways, depending on what they specified. Some requirements were easily represented in a context, others became part of the behavioural event specifications, and some became invariant specifications. We outline how the requirements were represented in Event-B in Table 2. Since Event-B does not have direct support for temporal logic, we focused on the FRETISH requirements and associated diagrammatic semantics, rather than attempting to represent MTL directly in Event-B. Hence, we do not provide a systematic translation from FRETISH requirements to Event-B. This is left as future work.

We were curious about the parent-child relationships between requirements that were present in the document. We found that, for FUN10, some of its child requirements were actually specified via event refinement in the Event-B model. For example, FUN10_3 is defined in natural language as

> If "Resume Ventilation" is selected, every step of the self-test procedure FUN.6 can be skipped or optionally rerun individually.

The corresponding FRETISH requirement (Table 1) is straightforward and has a response indicating that each step can either be passed or skipped. This requirement prompted us to add new sets and constants by extending ctx00 using ctx01 as shown in Figs. 5 and 6, respectively. Specifically, we add the TestPassed, TestFailed and TestSkipped constants to allow us to keep track of which tests have passed/failed. In the concrete machine (mac01), we include the variables: testPowerSwitch, testLeaks, testFF12, testPS_EXP, testOxygenSensor and testAlarms; which are updated in the SelfTestPassedOrSkipped (Fig. 7), SelfTestFailed and SelfTestPassed events. The latter directly models the test passing specification of FUN10_1.

In the concrete SelfTestPassedOrSkipped event (Fig. 7), we add the timing parameter, timePoweredOff (line 3), which is an integer (line 12) that is less than 15 (line 13), to capture requirement FUN10_6: when off System shall after 15 minutes satisfy !resumeVentilation. The response part was already captured in the abstract event specification as an action on line 15 of Fig. 7 (parts of the

```
1  Event SelfTestPassedOrSkipped ≙
2    REFINES  SelfTestPassed
3    any timePoweredOff
4      when
5        grd0_1:  mode = SelfTest
6        grd1_1:  testPowerSwitch ∈ {TestPassed, TestSkipped}
7        grd1_2:  testLeaks ∈ {TestPassed, TestSkipped}
8        grd1_3:  testFF12 ∈ {TestPassed, TestSkipped}
9        grd1_4:  testPS_EXP ∈ {TestPassed, TestSkipped}
10       grd1_5:  testOxygenSensor ∈ {TestPassed, TestSkipped}
11       grd1_6:  testAlarms ∈ {TestPassed, TestSkipped}
12       grd1_7:  timePoweredOff ∈ ℤ
13       grd1_8:  timePoweredOff ≤ 15 ∧ is_new_patient = FALSE
14     then
15       act0_1:  mode := VentilationOff
16       act1_1:  in_valve := ValveClosed
17       act1_2:  out_valve := ValveOpen
18 END
```

Fig. 7. `SelfTestPassedOrSkipped` event after the first refinement step. This captures requirements FUN10 and some of it's children, along with FUN6. The components in light gray font are included from the abstract event.

```
1  cont1_3:  mode = VentilationOff  ⇒  in_valve = ValveClosed ∧ out_valve = ValveOpen
2  cont1_6:  mode = Failsafe  ⇒  in_valve = ValveClosed ∧ out_valve = ValveOpen
```

Fig. 8. Invariants for CONT1_3 and CONT1_6.

abstract version of this event are in gray) hence the refinement from FUN10 to FUN10_6 in this case is a *superposition* refinement that constrains the event further [4]. Event-B does not have a native way to address timing properties, in contrast to FRETISH, so we assume the existence of a clock from which the `timePoweredOff` parameter gets its value. Using a clock variable also appears in related work that integrates timing constraints for Event-B [11].

We did not model FUN10_2 explicitly in Event-B since we assume that global variable updates are sufficient to keep the last parameters available. Interestingly, FUN10_4 was already present in the abstract event (line 15, Fig. 7) since `StandbyMode` corresponds to `VentilationOff` mode.

Some of the parent-child relationships between the requirements could be modelled (and verified) via refinement in Event-B. For example FUN10 and FUN10_6 as described earlier. However, not all of these relationships could be easily represented by refinement; for example FUN5 and FUN5_3. These requirements were both captured in the same Event-B machine as they seemed to us to be at the same level of abstraction, FUN5_3 caused us to add functionality related to `SelfTestMode` which was not mentioned in FUN5. FUN5_3 also inspired the addition of an invariant. Exploring the role that refinement plays in the parent-child requirements relationship more generally is left as future work.

Due to time constraints, we did not explore the formalisation of all of the requirements in Event-B. That said, we have identified over 60 of the remaining FUN and CONT requirements that should be formalisable in future refinement steps. These include, for example FUN18 and its children, and CONT40–45. We intend to continue working on this case study and explore this further.

Table 2. Moving between FRETISH and Event-B contexts, events and invariants.

FRETISH Requirement ID	Context(s)	Event(s)	Invariant(s)	Event-B File(s)
FUN4	✓	✓		mac00, ctx00
FUN5		✓		mac01
FUN5_3		✓	✓	mac01
FUN6	✓	✓		mac00, mac01, ctx01
FUN6_1–FUN6_6	✓	✓		mac01, ctx01
FUN7		✓		mac01
FUN10		✓		mac00
FUN10_1	✓	✓		mac01, ctx01
FUN10_3–FUN10_6		✓		mac01
FUN23		✓		mac01
FUN27		✓		mac01
CONT1	✓	✓		mac00, ctx00
CONT1_1		✓		mac01
CONT1_3			✓	mac01
CONT1_6			✓	mac01
CONT3		✓		mac00
CONT4		✓		mac00
CONT12		✓		mac00, mac01
CONT18	✓	✓		mac01, ctx01
CONT19		✓		mac01
CONT38			✓	mac01
CONT46		✓		mac01

4.3 Verification

The Rodin Platform generates proof obligations for Event-B models, which can be discharged automatically or interactively using Rodin's theorem provers. These proof obligations relate to properties including well-definedness, event feasibility, invariant preservation, and refinement [17]. We were able to discharge all 79 proof obligations generated by Rodin automatically.

Some requirements were verified by construction. Specifically, adherence to the controller state machine (Fig. 1) is obtained by constructing an Event-B model that evolves following the mode changes indicated by the arrows in Fig. 1. There is no corresponding proof obligation in Rodin; it is purely a matter of modelling the behaviour according to the document. Thus, we consider requirements referring to this sequence of states, e.g. FUN4, to be correct-by-construction.

Other requirements are verified more directly, by inspecting the guard or action of the event that corresponds to the behaviour described by that requirement. For example, the start-up procedure may only proceed if the system is connected to the breathing circuit, air supply, and power source. The guard of the StartUpProcedure event in mac01 ensures these three things are true and otherwise cannot proceed. This is similar to the correct-by-construction approach above; but it also involves event refinement, so proof obligations related to event refinement (e.g. guard strengthening) were discharged for these requirements.

We modelled some requirements as invariants in mac01. Figure 8 shows the Event-B encoding of the invariants for CONT1_3 and CONT1_6. Invariants must be true before and after every event. This is a classical correctness property in Event-B, and Rodin generates specific invariant preservation proof obligations to ensure that the user considers this property.

5 Discussion

This section discusses how we link requirements with our formal model, and reflects on how some of the functional requirements contain elements related to both the controller and GUI.

Linking Requirements and Formal Specification
One key aim of this work was to examine how the requirements can be integrated into a formal design model. As previously mentioned, the Event-B model captures the requirements in a variety of ways. Table 2 summarises how each FRETISH requirement was captured in the Event-B model; in a context, as an event, as an invariant, or as a combination of these three things.

Modelling the transitions between the states in Fig. 1 was straightforward, and captured FUN4 and other requirements relating to mode changes. These requirements were easily specified using events to describe the required behaviour. In ctx00, the Mode set enumerates the various modes that the system can be in (line 2, Fig. 1). The current mode is represented by the mode variable in mac00 (Fig. 4). The mode is updated when an event triggers a mode change, for example PowerOn on lines 10–14 of Fig. 4.

The refined machine, mac01 (supported by ctx01) captured more requirements; for example FUN6_1, which was added via event refinement. In this refinement step, we were able to directly translate some requirements into a behavioural specification in the Event-B model. For example, a requirement's condition often became part of the guard of an event, and the response often became part of the event's action.

Some requirements were translated into the refined Event-B model as invariants. As outlined in Sect. 1, requirements are properties that the software must satisfy; so we initially suspected that this would be the most common way to express FRETISH requirements in Event-B. However, for this set of requirements at least, Event-B seems to more naturally capture requirements in events. In our future work with this case study, it will be interesting to see if certain classes of requirements are more likely to become invariants. Perhaps the functional and controller requirements were more specific to behaviour than others.

When constructing the Event-B model, we used both the FRETISH and the natural-language requirements as sources of information. Both were useful to help with modelling. First, mapping the natural-language requirements into FRETISH enabled us to clearly express our understanding of the requirements. However, we were unable to clarify some details in the requirements without a domain expert. To help fill gaps in our group's knowledge, we consulted more general guidance on how mechanical lung ventilators work. In previous work [13], we were able to collaborate closely with the authors of the natural-language requirements; we see the benefit of that collaboration through its absence here.

Controller and GUI Attributes in Functional Requirements
Our work focuses on requirements for the Mechanical Lung Ventilator's control software, so we have captured the Functional (FUN) and Controller (CONT)

requirements and used them to build a formal design. We leave the GUI requirements as future work.

We found that some of the FUN natural-language requirements specify functionality for both the Controller and the GUI at the same time. This is not overly surprising, since the FUN requirements are a high-level specification of the system's requirements, which are 'implemented' by the CONT and GUI requirements. However, this means that our translation into FRETISH captures the parts of the FUN requirements that were needed for the controller, but treats parts that seem to relate to the GUI more trivially.

A good example of our approach is FUN7, which says: "*if the self-test mode fails, the user shall be warned that the system is out-of-service. In addition, any other operations shall be not allowed*". When we captured this in FRETISH (see Table 1), the "*if the self-test mode fails*" is the `condition` that triggers the requirement. But the clause after the comma, "*the user shall be warned that the system is out-of-service*", reads like a requirement of the GUI, so it is captured with a boolean that trivially states that there is a warning. The second sentence, however, "*In addition, any other operations shall be not allowed*", reads like a Controller requirement that signals a mode change. The full FRETISH requirement is shown in Table 1. The `FailSafeMode` variable denotes that the system should change to Fail Safe mode; this was our interpretation of "any other operations shall be not allowed" given the state machine in Fig. 1.

Other examples of this are requirements FUN13–17. They all "measure... and display..." a sensor reading. "Measure" seems to suggest there is a sensor, and a variable in the Controller will hold the result of reading the sensor. "Display" seems like a GUI requirement, for which we are not creating a design. Each of these requirements follow a similar pattern, for example FUN14: `System` shall `always` `satisfy measure02% & display02%`.

6   Conclusion

This paper described our use of FRET and Event-B to formalise and model the requirements for the ABZ 2024 Mechanical Lung Ventilator case study.[4] We discuss our approach to providing traceability from natural-language requirements to a formal design model, using the FRETISH structured requirements language as an intermediate step. We reflect on the requirements that we could and could not formalise with FRET. Then we examine how these requirements were specified and subsequently verified in the Event-B model. This work allowed us to explore the link between formal requirements and formal specifications. In this case, requirements became both behavioural specifications and correctness conditions (invariants) in the formal model. This case study provides a basis for linking FRET and Event-B which we intend to explore in future work.

Competing Interests. The author(s) has no competing interests to declare that are relevant to the content of this manuscript.

---

[4] FRET and Event-B artefacts: https://github.com/mariefarrell/abz2024.

A   Formalised Requirements

(See Table 3).

Table 3. FRETISH Requirements.

Req ID	FRETISH
CONT1	Controller shall always satisfy StartUpMode | SelfTestMode | StandbyMode | PCVMode | PSVMode | FailSafeMode
CONT1_1	in StartUpMode Controller shall eventually satisfy initStart & (initDone | (initFail & OutOfServiceWarning & FailSafeMode))
CONT1_3	in StandbyMode Controller shall always satisfy ventilationOff & inValveClose & outValveOpen
CONT1_6	in FailSafeMode Controller shall always satisfy inValveClose & outValveOpen
CONT2	if powerOff & !powerButton Controller shall always satisfy !StartUpMode
CONT3	in StartUpMode when initDone Controller shall at the next timepoint satisfy SelfTestMode
CONT4	in SelfTestMode if selfTestPassed | GUIResumeRequest Controller shall at the next timepoint satisfy StandbyMode
CONT5	in StandbyMode if PSVModeSelected Controller shall at the next timepoint satisfy PSVMode
CONT6	in StandbyMode if PCVModeSelected Controller shall at the next timepoint satisfy PCVMode
CONT7	in PCVMode if inspiratoryPhaseEnd & PSVModeSelected Controller shall at the next timepoint satisfy ventilating & PSVMode
CONT8	in PCVMode if stopVentilation Controller shall at the next timepoint satisfy StandbyMode
CONT9	in PSVMode when breathingTime >= apneaLagTime Controller shall at the next timepoint satisfy PCVMode & RR = RR_AP & P_insp = P_inspAP & ItoE = ItoE_AP
CONT10	in PSVMode if stopVentilation Controller shall at the next timepoint satisfy StandbyMode
CONT11	if powerOff Controller shall at the next timepoint satisfy FinalState
CONT11_1	in FinalState Controller shall eventually satisfy parametersStored & off
CONT12	in StartUpMode Controller shall eventually satisfy defaultParamsLoaded
CONT13	in StartUpMode Controller shall eventually satisfy checkCommsSensors & checkCommsValves
CONT14	in StartUpMode Controller shall eventually satisfy checkCommsGUI
CONT15	in StartUpMode if pressureSensorRetries >= 5 & (pressureSensorConnFailure | pressureSensorError) Controller shall at the next timepoint satisfy FailSafeMode
CONT16	in StartUpMode if ADCRetries >= 5 & (ADCConnFailure | ADCError) Controller shall at the next timepoint satisfy FailSafeMode

(continued)

Table 3. (*continued*)

CONT18	in SelfTestMode Controller shall eventually satisfy selfTestPassed | selfTestFailed
CONT19	in SelfTestMode if SelfTestFail Controller shall until off satisfy !StandbyMode & !ventilating
CONT20	in PCVMode Controller shall always satisfy breathingCycleTime = 1/RR_PCV & ExpiratoryTime = breathingCycleTime / (1+ItoE_PCV)
CONT21	in PCVMode when BreathingCycleStart Controller shall at the next timepoint satisfy inspiratoryPhaseStart
CONT22	in PCVMode Controller shall always satisfy inspiratoryTime = 60*(ItoE_PCV/(RR_PCV * (1 + ItoE_PCV)))
CONT23	while PCVMode & inspiratoryPauseButton when inspiratoryPhaseEnd Controller shall for 40 seconds satisfy (inspiratoryPauseButton => inValveClose & outValveClose)
CONT24	while PCVMode & RMButton when inspiratoryPhaseEnd Controller shall at the next timepoint satisfy RM
CONT25	in PCVMode Controller shall always satisfy (breathingCycleDone | patientBreathingRequest) => (breathingCycleStart & inspiratoryPhaseStart)
CONT26	while PCVMode when dropPAW > ITS_PCV Controller shall at the next timepoint satisfy patientBreathingRequest
CONT27	in PCVMode when expiratoryPauseButton & ExpiratoryPhaseEnd & !patientBreathingRequest Controller shall until buttonUnPressOr60Seconds satisfy expirationPhaseEnd & inValveClose & outValveClose
CONT28	in PCVMode Controller shall always satisfy P_insp = P_inspPCV
CONT30	in PSVMode when BreathingCycleStart Controller shall at the next timepoint satisfy inspiratoryPhaseStart
CONT32	in PSVMode Controller shall until (P_insp >= MaxP_insp | inspClock >= inspiratoryTime) satisfy inspiratoryPhase
CONT33	in PSVMode when V_E < ExpiratoryTriggerSensitivity*PeakV_E Controller shall at the next timepoint satisfy expirationPhaseStart
CONT34	while PSVMode & inspiratoryPauseButton when inspiratoryPhaseEnd Controller shall for 40 seconds satisfy (inspiratoryPauseButton => inValveClose & outValveClose)
CONT35	while PSVMode & RMButton when inspiratoryPhaseEnd Controller shall at the next timepoint satisfy RM
CONT36_1	while PSVMode & expiratoryPhase when dropPAW > ITS_PSV Controller shall at the next timepoint satisfy patientBreathingRequest
CONT36_2	while PSVMode when expiratoryPauseButton & expClock <= apneaLagTime & !patientBreathingRequest Controller shall until buttonUnPressOr60Seconds satisfy expirationPhaseEnd & inValveClose & outValveClose
CONT36_3	in PSVMode Controller shall always satisfy minExpiratoryTime >= 0.4 & minExpiratoryTime <= 2 & (expiratoryPhase => minExpiratoryTime = inspClock/2)

(*continued*)

Table 3. (*continued*)

CONT37	in PSVMode when expClock >= apneaLagTime Controller shall at the next timepoint satisfy apnea & PCVMode & RR = RR_AP & P_insp = P_inspAP & ItoE = ItoE_AP
CONT38	while StartUpMode | StandbyMode Controller shall always satisfy inValveClose & outValveOpen
CONT39	while inspiratoryPhase Controller shall always satisfy outValveClose & (PCVMode & !apnea => P_insp = P_isnpPCV) & (PSVMode => P_insp = P_inspPSV) & (PCVMode & apnea => P_insp = P_inspAP)
CONT40	while expiratoryState Controller shall always satisfy inValveClose & outValveOpen
CONT41	while (PCVMode | PSVMode) when inspiratoryPauseButton Controller shall eventually satisfy inspiratoryPause | !inspiratoryPauseButton
CONT41_1	while (PCVMode | PSVMode) & inspiratoryPauseButton when inspiratoryPhaseEnd Controller shall at the next timepoint satisfy (inspiratoryPauseButton => inspiratoryPause & inValveClose & outValveClose)
CONT41_2	when inspiratoryPause Controller shall after 40 seconds satisfy !inspiratoryPause & expirationPhaseStart
CONT42	while (PCVMode | PSVMode) when expiratoryPauseButton Controller shall eventually satisfy expiratoryPause | !expiratoryPauseButton
CONT42_1	while (PCVMode | PSVMode) & expiratoryPauseButton when expiratoryPhaseEnd Controller shall at the next timepoint satisfy (expiratoryPauseButton => expiratoryPause & inValveClose & outValveClose)
CONT42_2	when expiratoryPause Controller shall after 40 seconds satisfy !expiratoryPause & inspiratoryPhaseStart
CONT43	while (PCVMode | PSVMode) & RMButton & !inspiratoryPauseButton when inspiratoryPhaseEnd Controller shall at the next timepoint satisfy RM
CONT43_1	while RM if !RMButton Controller shall at the next timepoint satisfy !RM & expirationPhaseStart
CONT43_2	when RM Controller shall after 10 seconds satisfy !RM & expirationPhaseStart
CONT43_3	while RM Controller shall always satisfy outValveClose & inValveOpen
CONT44	if P_insp > MaxP_insp Controller shall at the next timepoint satisfy inspiratoryPhaseEnd & expirationPhaseStart
CONT45	when expirationPhaseStart Controller shall after 700 milliseconds satisfy monitorInhaleTrigger
CONT46	after FailSafeMode Controller shall until off satisfy !(StartUpMode | SelfTestMode | StandbyMode | PCVMode | PSVMode)
FUN4	System shall always satisfy StartUpMode | SelfTestMode | StandbyMode | PCVMode | PSVMode | FailSafeMode
FUN5	when powerButton & (breathingCircuitConnected & !(patientConnected) & airSupplyConnected & powerConnected) System shall at the next timepoint satisfy StartUpMode
FUN5_1	in StartUpMode System shall eventually satisfy initStart & checkCommsSensors & checkCommsValves & checkCommsGUI

(*continued*)

Table 3. (*continued*)

FUN5_2	in StartUpMode System shall eventually satisfy initDone | (initFail & OutOfServiceWarning & FailSafeMode)
FUN5_3	System shall always satisfy (StartUpMode | SelfTestMode) -> !patientConnected
FUN6	in SelfTestMode System shall eventually satisfy selfTestPassed | selfTestFailed
FUN6_1	in SelfTestMode System shall eventually satisfy testPowerSwitchPass | testPowerSwitchFail | testPowerSwitchSkip
FUN6_2	in SelfTestMode System shall eventually satisfy testLeaksPass | testLeaksFail | testLeaksSkip
FUN6_3	in SelfTestMode System shall eventually satisfy testFl2Pass | testFl2Fail | testFl2Skip
FUN6_4	in SelfTestMode System shall eventually satisfy testPSExpPass | testPSExpFail | testPSExpSkip
FUN6_5	in SelfTestMode System shall eventually satisfy testOxygenSensorPass | testOxygenSensorFail | testOxygenSensorSkip
FUN6_6	in SelfTestMode System shall eventually satisfy testAlarmsPass | testAlarmsFail | testAlarmsSkip
FUN7	in SelfTestMode if selfTestFail System shall at the next timepoint satisfy OutOfServiceWarning & FailSafeMode
FUN8	System shall always satisfy logParams & saveLog & loadLog
FUN8_5	System shall always satisfy if user = operator then !eraseLog
FUN8_6	when ventilatorSettingsChanged System shall at the next timepoint satisfy logVentilatorSettings
FUN8_7	when alarmSettingsChanged System shall at the next timepoint satisfy logAlarmSettings
FUN8_8	when patientChanged System shall at the next timepoint satisfy logPatientChange
FUN8_9	when powerSupplyChanged System shall at the next timepoint satisfy logPowerSupply
FUN8_10	when preUseCheckDone System shall at the next timepoint satisfy logPreUseCheck
FUN8_11	System shall always satisfy logO2SensorUse
FUN8_12	System shall always satisfy logVentilationParams & logAlarmParams & logCalibrationParams
FUN9	when selfTestPassed System shall at the next timepoint satisfy startMonitoring & startReportingHealthParams & StandbyMode
FUN10	when startUpDone System shall eventually satisfy newPatient | resumeVentilation
FUN10_1	when newPatient System shall eventually satisfy patientAttributesEntered & SelfTestMode & ((testPowerSwitchPass & testLeaksPass & testFl2Pass & testPSExpPass & testOxygenSensorPass & testAlarmsPass) => selfTestPassed)
FUN10_2	when resumeVentilation System shall at the next timepoint satisfy loadLastParams

(*continued*)

Table 3. (*continued*)

FUN10_3	when resumeVentilation System shall eventually satisfy SelfTestMode & (((testPowerSwitchPass | testPowerSwitchSkip) & (testLeaksPass | testLeaksSkip) & (testF12Pass | testF12Skip) & (testPSExpPass | testPSExpSkip) & (testOxygenSensorPass | testOxygenSensorSkip) & (testAlarmsPass | testAlarmsSkip)) => selfTestPassed)
FUN10_4	when selfTestPassed System shall at the next timepoint satisfy StandbyMode
FUN10_5	in StandbyMode System shall always satisfy ventilationOff & ventilationParmsAdjustable
FUN10_6	when off System shall after 15 minutes satisfy !resumeVentilation
FUN11	System shall always satisfy GBPS <= 5.2
FUN13	System shall always satisfy measureRR & displayRR
FUN14	System shall always satisfy measureO2% & displayO2%
FUN15	System shall always satisfy measurePSins
FUN16	System shall always satisfy measureTV & displayTV
FUN17	System shall always satisfy measureF11 & display F11
FUN18	System shall always satisfy (if enableLeakCompensation then leakCompensation) | !leakCompensation
FUN18_1	System shall always satisfy (if enableLeakCompensation then leakCompensation) & (if disableLeakCompensation then (!leakCompensation & !enableLeakCompensation))
FUN18_2	when leakCompensationEnable if MinPEEPAlarm System shall at the next timepoint satisfy leakCompensationActive
FUN20	in PCVMode System shall always satisfy breathingCycleTime = 1/RR_PCV & ExpiratoryTime = breathingCycleTime / (1+ItoE_PCV)
FUN21	in PCVMode System shall always satisfy (breathingCycleDone | patientBreathingRequest) => breathingCycleStart
FUN21_1	when inspiratoryPressure < InhaleTriggerSensitivityPCV System shall at the next timepoint satisfy breathingCycleStart
FUN21_2	when patientBreathTrigger System shall at the next timepoint satisfy breathingTimerReset
FUN22	in PCVMode when RMButton System shall at the next timepoint satisfy RM
FUN23	in PCVMode when PSVModeSelected System shall at the next timepoint satisfy ventilating & PSVMode
FUN23_1	in PCVMode when PSVModeSelected System shall eventually satisfy confirmPSVParameters
FUN23_2	in PCVMode System shall always satisfy ((confirmPSVParameters & PSVMode) | (!confirmPSVParameters & PCVMode)) & ventilating
FUN23_3	in PCVMode when PSVModeSelected System shall at the next timepoint satisfy !(PCVInspTimeEnd & PSVMode)
FUN25	in PSVMode when inspiratoryPressure < InhaleTriggerSensitivityPSV System shall at the next timepoint satisfy breathingCycleStart
FUN26	in PSVMode when F11 < ExpiratoryTriggerSensitivity System shall at the next timepoint satisfy expirationPhaseStart

(*continued*)

Table 3. (*continued*)

FUN27	in PSVMode when breathingTime >= apneaLagTime System shall at the next timepoint satisfy apnea
FUN27_1	if apnea System shall at the next timepoint satisfy apneaAlarm
FUN27_2	if apnea System shall at the next timepoint satisfy PCVMode & RR = RR_AP & P_insp = P_inspAP & ItoE = ItoE_AP
FUN28	when expiratoryPauseButton & (ExpiratoryPhaseEnd) System shall until buttonUnPressOr60Seconds satisfy expirationPhaseEnd & inValveClose & outValveClose
FUN29	while inspiratoryPauseButton when (inspiratoryPhaseEnd) System shall for 40 seconds satisfy (inspiratoryPauseButton => inValveClose & outValveClose)
FUN30	System shall always satisfy if StartUpMode then (if newPatient then SelfTestMode & if !newPatient then StandbyMode) & if SelfTestMode then (if selfTestPassed then StandbyMode) & if StandbyMode then (if startPCV then PCVMode & if startPSV then PSVMode & if runSelfTest then SelfTestMode) & if error then FailSafeMode & if powerOff then off
FUN31	System shall always satisfy patientSafe
FUN32	in FailSafeMode System shall always satisfy patientSafe
FUN33	if powerFailure System shall at the next timepoint satisfy patientSafe
FUN34	if gasSupplyFailure System shall at the next timepoint satisfy patientSafe
FUN37	if powerFailure System shall for 120 minutes satisfy !off
FUN38_1	if param_V > paramMax_V | param_V < paramMin_V System shall at the next timepoint satisfy paramAlarm_V
FUN39	before PSVMode | PCVMode System shall eventually satisfy enterAlarmThresholds
FUN40	if P_insp > MaxP_insp System shall at the next timepoint satisfy inspiratoryPhaseEnd & expirationPhaseStart
FUN41	if GUIFailue | !GUIConnected System shall at the next timepoint satisfy ventilating & highPriorityAlarm

References

1. Abba, A., et al.: The novel mechanical ventilator Milano for the Covid-19 pandemic. Phys. Fluids **33**(3) (2021)
2. Abrial, J.-R.: Modeling in Event-B: System and Software Engineering. Cambridge University Press, Cambridge (2010)
3. Abrial, J.-R., Butler, M., Hallerstede, S., Hoang, T.S., Mehta, F., Voisin, L.: Rodin: an open toolset for modelling and reasoning in Event-B. Int. J. Softw. Tools Technol. Transfer **12**(6), 447–466 (2010)
4. Abrial, J.-R., Hallerstede, S.: Refinement, decomposition, and instantiation of discrete models: application to Event-B. Fund. Inform. **77**(1–2), 1–28 (2007)

5. Arcaini, P., Bombarda, A., Bonfanti, S., Gargantini, A., Riccobene, E., Scandurra, P.: The ASMETA approach to safety assurance of software systems. In: Raschke, A., Riccobene, E., Schewe, K.-D. (eds.) Logic, Computation and Rigorous Methods. LNCS, vol. 12750, pp. 215–238. Springer, Cham (2021). https://doi.org/10.1007/978-3-030-76020-5_13

6. Banach, R.: The landing gear case study in hybrid Event-B. In: Boniol, F., Wiels, V., Ait Ameur, Y., Schewe, K.-D. (eds.) ABZ 2014. CCIS, vol. 433, pp. 126–141. Springer, Cham (2014). https://doi.org/10.1007/978-3-319-07512-9_9

7. Bonfanti, S., Gargantini, A., Riccobene, E., Scandurra, P.: Compositional simulation of abstract state machines for safety critical systems. In: Tapia Tarifa, S.L., Proenca, J. (eds.) FACS 2022. LNCS, vol. 13712, pp. 3–19. Springer, Cham (2022). https://doi.org/10.1007/978-3-031-20872-0_1

8. Bonfanti, S., Riccobene, E., Santandrea, D., Scandurra, P.: Modeling the MVM-adapt system by compositional I/O abstract state machines. In: Glässer, U., Creissac Campos, J., Méry, D., Palanque, P. (eds.) ABZ 2023. LNCS, vol. 14010, pp. 107–115. Springer, Cham (2023). https://doi.org/10.1007/978-3-031-33163-3_8

9. Bonivento, W., Gargantini, A., Krücken, R., Razeto, A.: The mechanical ventilator Milano. Nucl. Phys. News **31**(3), 30–33 (2021)

10. Bourbouh, H., et al.: Integrating formal verification and assurance: an inspection rover case study. In: Dutle, A., Moscato, M.M., Titolo, L., Muñoz, C.A., Perez, I. (eds.) NFM 2021. LNCS, vol. 12673, pp. 53–71. Springer, Cham (2021). https://doi.org/10.1007/978-3-030-76384-8_4

11. Cansell, D., Méry, D., Rehm, J.: Time constraint patterns for Event B development. In: Julliand, J., Kouchnarenko, O. (eds.) B 2007. LNCS, vol. 4355, pp. 140–154. Springer, Heidelberg (2006). https://doi.org/10.1007/11955757_13

12. Champion, A., Gurfinkel, A., Kahsai, T., Tinelli, C.: CoCoSpec: a mode-aware contract language for reactive systems. In: De Nicola, R., Kühn, E. (eds.) SEFM 2016. LNCS, vol. 9763, pp. 347–366. Springer, Cham (2016). https://doi.org/10.1007/978-3-319-41591-8_24

13. Farrell, M., Luckcuck, M., Sheridan, O., Monahan, R.: FRETting about requirements: formalised requirements for an aircraft engine controller. In: Gervasi, V., Vogelsang, A. (eds.) REFSQ 2022. LNCS, vol. 13216, pp. 96–111. Springer, Cham (2022). https://doi.org/10.1007/978-3-030-98464-9_9

14. Farrell, M., Mavrakis, N., Ferrando, A., Dixon, C., Gao, Y.: Formal modelling and runtime verification of autonomous grasping for active debris removal. Front. Robot. AI (2022)

15. Farrell, M., Monahan, R., Power, J.F.: Building specifications in the Event-B institution. Logical Methods Comput. Sci. **18** (2022)

16. Giannakopoulou, D., Mavridou, A., Rhein, J., Pressburger, T., Schumann, J., Shi, N.: Formal requirements elicitation with FRET. In: International Conference on Requirements Engineering: Foundation for Software Quality (2020)

17. Hallerstede, S.: On the purpose of Event-B proof obligations. In: Börger, E., Butler, M., Bowen, J.P., Boca, P. (eds.) ABZ 2008. LNCS, vol. 5238, pp. 125–138. Springer, Heidelberg (2008). https://doi.org/10.1007/978-3-540-87603-8_11

18. Hoang, T.S., Snook, C., Ladenberger, L., Butler, M.: Validating the requirements and design of a hemodialysis machine using iUML-B, BMotion studio, and co-simulation. In: Butler, M., Schewe, K.-D., Mashkoor, A., Biro, M. (eds.) ABZ 2016. LNCS, vol. 9675, pp. 360–375. Springer, Cham (2016). https://doi.org/10.1007/978-3-319-33600-8_31

19. Hoang, T.S., Snook, C., Salehi, A., Butler, M., Ladenberger, L.: Validating and verifying the requirements and design of a Haemodialysis machine using the Rodin toolset. Sci. Comput. Program. **158**, 122–147 (2018)
20. Kiss, T., Jánosi-Rancz, K.T.: Developing railway interlocking systems with session types and Event-B. In: International Symposium on Applied Computational Intelligence and Informatics, SACI, pp. 93–98. IEEE (2016)
21. Ladenberger, L., Hansen, D., Wiegard, H., Bendisposto, J., Leuschel, M.: Validation of the ABZ landing gear system using ProB. Int. J. Softw. Tools Technol. Transfer **19**, 187–203 (2017)
22. Luckcuck, M., Farrell, M., Sheridan, O., Monahan, R.: A methodology for developing a verifiable aircraft engine controller from formal requirements. In: IEEE Aerospace Conference, pp. 1–12 (2022)
23. Mammar, A., Laleau, R.: Modeling a landing gear system in Event-B. Int. J. Softw. Tools Technol. Transfer **19**, 167–186 (2017)
24. Mammar, A., Leuschel, M.: Modeling and verifying an arrival manager using Event-B. In: Glässer, U., Creissac Campos, J., Méry, D., Palanque, P. (eds.) ABZ 2023. LNCS, vol. 14010, pp. 321–339. Springer, Cham (2023). https://doi.org/10.1007/978-3-031-33163-3_24
25. Mavridou, A., et al.: The ten lockheed martin cyber-physical challenges: formalized, analyzed, and explained. In: Proceedings of the 28th IEEE International Requirements Engineering Conference (2020)
26. Perez, I., Mavridou, A., Pressburger, T., Goodloe, A., Giannakopoulou, D.: Automated translation of natural language requirements to runtime monitors. In: Fisman, D., Rosu, G. (eds.) TACAS 2022. LNCS, vol. 13243, pp. 387–395. Springer, Cham (2022). https://doi.org/10.1007/978-3-030-99524-9_21
27. Schneider, S., Treharne, H., Wehrheim, H.: The behavioural semantics of Event-B refinement. Formal Aspects Comput. **26**, 251–280 (2014)
28. Sheridan, O.: Exploring a methodology for formal verification of safety-critical systems. In: Glässer, U., Creissac Campos, J., Méry, D., Palanque, P. (eds.) ABZ 2023. LNCS, vol. 14010, pp. 361–365. Springer, Cham (2023). https://doi.org/10.1007/978-3-031-33163-3_26
29. Sheridan, O., Monahan, R., Luckcuck, M.: A requirements-driven methodology: formal modelling and verification of an aircraft engine controller. In: ter Beek, M.H., Monahan, R. (eds.) IFM 2022. LNCS, vol. 13274, pp. 352–356. Springer, Cham (2022). https://doi.org/10.1007/978-3-031-07727-2_21
30. Snook, C., Butler, M.: UML-B and Event-B: an integration of languages and tools. In: IASTED International Conference on Software Engineering, pp. 336–341 (2008)
31. Sommerville, I.: Software Engineering. International Computer Science Series. Addison-Wesley (1982)

Doctoral Symposium

From Event-B to Lambdapi

Anne Grieu$^{(\boxtimes)}$

IRIT, Université de Toulouse, CNRS, INP, UT3, Toulouse, France
`anne.grieu@irit.fr`

Abstract. B, Event-B and TLA+ are modelling notations based on set theory. Dedukti/Lambdapi is a logical framework based on the λΠ-calculus modulo rewriting in which many theories and logics can be expressed. In the context of ICSPA (ANR project), Lambdapi will be used to exchange models and proofs between the set theory-based formal methods B, Event-B and TLA+. They will rely on the encoding of the respective set theories in Lambdapi. Our current work focuses on translating the mathematical language of Event-B and proof trees obtained with the Rodin platform for Event-B.

1 Context

Deductive formal methods are used to improve confidence in software development, especially for critical systems. The purpose of the ICSPA[1] ANR project is to formally verify proofs performed in B [2], Event-B [3] and TLA+ [13] environments, all based on set theory, and to exchange proofs and models developed with their respective platforms Atelier B [9], Rodin [4] and TLAPS [8]. The framework chosen to express this interoperability is Dedukti/Lambdapi [6] [10], a logical framework making easy the definition of various logics. It is based on Martin-Löf's type theory and supports modulo reasoning through rewrite rules. We will here focus on Event-B and the Rodin Platform, an Eclipse-based IDE and logical framework.

Other works on Atelier B, like the BWare project [11] and its recent development [14] or reconstruction of TLAPS proofs [5], share this objective of interoperability with Dedukti/Lambdapi but have different approaches. For example, in the BWare project, Atelier B proof obligations are translated to Why3 [1] platform which submits it to different SMT provers and then to Dedukti. However the proof effort and the structure of the proof realised in Atelier B is lost. It is expected that the proof can be entirely performed by an SMT tool. Here we propose to translate not only proof obligations but also the user provided proofs so we are able to verify proofs realised with the Rodin toolbox and its connected SMT-solvers. In this first work, our aim is to be able to check in the Lambdapi framework, proof-trees restricted to Rodin basic deduction rules, thus excluding calls to automatic provers.

---

[1] https://icspa.inria.fr.

Supported by the ICSPA french ANR project.

2   Current Work

A Rodin proof contains a proof tree annotated by intermediate sub-goals defined by Event-B formulas, the applied deduction rule and its parameters (expressions, hypotheses, positions in the term, ...). To be able to check proofs made with Rodin in Lambdapi, we have to translate the mathematical language of Event-B and its deduction rules to Lambdapi. The formalism of Event-B is based on first order classical logic with equality extended with arithmetic and set theory. The embedding to Lambdapi relies on Lambdapi standard library of first order logic and equality[2], to which we have added the *classic* axiom $(P \lor \neg P)$. Next we have to express the typed set theory of B/Event-B [2] in Lambdapi and then, when we are able to fully express predicates, we have to perform the translation of the deduction rules of Rodin in Lambdapi. In the following, we present some elements of the Lambdapi syntax and the outline of our work.

2.1   Elements of the Lambdapi Syntax

Lambdapi is a proof assistant, an interactive version of the proof system Dedukti based on $\lambda\Pi$-calculus modulo rewriting [7]. Here are examples of its syntax, as found in the file Prop.lp. First, we see how to declare the type Prop of propositions and the function π which associates to a proposition the type of its proofs. The type-checking of Lambdapi is performed between objects of type TYPE. The command symbol declares typed identifiers with an optional definition.

```
constant symbol Prop: TYPE;    injective symbol π: Prop → TYPE;
```

We can declare as well the logical connectors, for example, the conjunction, with its signature and its introduction rule:

```
constant symbol ∧: Prop → Prop → Prop;
symbol ∧ᵢ p q: π p → π q → π(p ∧ q);
```

We have also at our disposal the rule command to give rewriting rules between terms formed using already declared symbols, separated with the curved arrow ↪. The two parts of the rewriting rule will be considered as identical, thus allowing reasoning inside the quotient space. It is illustrated by the rule for implication saying that the proof of an implication is a function associating a proof of the conclusion to the proof of the hypothesis:

```
rule π ($p ⇒ $q) ↪ π $p → π $q;
```

2.2   Some Design Alternatives

An important part of our work is to complete the implementation we began, taking into account the different possibilities to express constructs in Lambdapi.

---

[2] https://github.com/Deducteam/lambdapi-stdlib.

For example, we thought about different ways to express the negation in Lambdapi. The connector can be defined with its signature and some rewriting rules, as seen in the left of Fig. 1. Or it could be a definition, with the command `symbol`, using the implication already declared. Then the properties of negation must be proved as theorems as seen in the right of Fig. 1.

```
symbol ¬ :Prop → Prop;              symbol ¬ p ≔ p ⇒ ⊥;
rule ¬ ($P ∧ $Q) ↪ ¬ $P ∨ ¬ $Q      symbol not_or [P Q: Prop]:
with ¬ ($P ∨ $Q) ↪ ¬ $P ∧ ¬ $Q          π (¬ (P ∨ Q) ⇒ ¬ P ∧ ¬ Q) ≔
with ¬ ($P ⇒ $Q) ↪ $P ∧ ¬ $Q        begin
with ¬ ⊤ ↪ ⊥                          assume P Q h;
with ¬ ⊥ ↪ ⊤                          apply ∧ᵢ _ _ _
with ¬ (¬ $P) ↪ $P                    {assume p; apply h;
with ¬ (∃ (λ x, $P.[x]))               apply ∨ᵢ₁; apply p}
          ↪ ∀ (λ x, ¬ ($P.[x]))       {assume q; apply h;
with ¬ (∀ (λ x, $P.[x]))               apply ∨ᵢ₂; apply q}
          ↪ ∃ (λ x, ¬ ($P.[x]));      end;
```

Fig. 1. Different alternatives to define negation.

The choice will have consequences on the upcoming proofs and on the contents of the proof term as rule application is implicit. However rule-based specifications will not be close to the usual formalization of classical logic. For now, we use rules but it makes the kernel logic diverge from that of Rodin. We are modifying our encoding, which makes negation elimination much more complex, but closer to what is performed by the Rodin prover.

Another part is to take into account the peculiarities of Rodin. For instance, some Rodin operators and thus some proof nodes are n-ary, while Lambdapi's operators are of a fixed arity. Currently the Java plug-in generates n-ary proof schemes to match the structure of Rodin proof trees (for instance **And** nodes). An improvement could be to do that processing in Lambdapi, so it could be used by other systems, like TLA+, with n-ary operators.

2.3   Cantor's Theorem

To guide the beginning of our work, we made a user guided proof of Cantor's theorem[3] in Rodin, without using internal or SMT provers, and we worked on checking the translation of our proof with Lambdapi. Figure 2 (left) shows the beginning of the proof tree made with Rodin and the right part shows the four first steps of the translated proof. The gray boxes, with rule details extracted from the Rodin proof tree, are not part of the Lambdapi script. In the comments (lines beginning with //), we can read the nodes exported by Rodin and between the comments and the gray boxes, the Lambdapi tactics.

---

[3] The Cantor's theorem has been proposed as a case study in ICSPA.

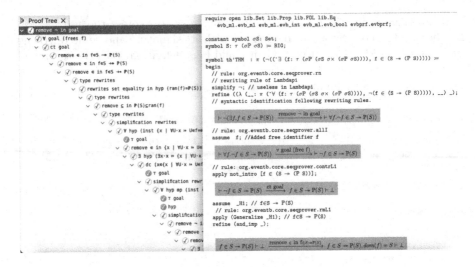

Fig. 2. Rodin proof tree and its Lambdapi translation.

3   Future Work

There is still a significant work ahead to perform the complete translation of Event-B proofs to Lambdapi.

The development is still at its beginning and no prototype is available yet. As it was suggested in the previous section, the choices of the representations are not fixed and are meant to move to answer future needs. We have also to complete the translation of all the deduction rules of Rodin.

Furthermore, the automated provers are a strength of Rodin. They are provided by integrated (deduction or rewriting-based) tools or external SMT solvers Fig. 3 for which Rodin removes set constructs. After treatment, the SMT solver gives its result to Rodin. Then Lambdapi terms or tactics should be built from internal

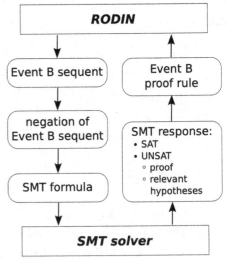

Fig. 3. Rodin and SMT solvers [12].

provers and SMT proof traces and incorporated to the current proof. Then, we will have to express the full formalism of Event-B, to define machines, events and the mechanisms of proof obligations, some of the major features of the formal method to be able to export Event-B developments.

Competing Interests. The author(s) has no competing interests to declare that are relevant to the content of this manuscript.

References

1. Why3, a tool for deductive program verification, GNU LGPL 2.1. https://www. why3.org/
2. Abrial, J.R.: The B-Book - Assigning Programs to Meanings. Cambridge University Press, Cambridge (1996)
3. Abrial, J.: Modeling in Event-B - System and Software Engineering. Cambridge University Press, Cambridge (2010)
4. Abrial, J.R., Butler, M., Hallerstede, S., Hoang, T.S., Mehta, F., Voisin, L.: Rodin: an open toolset for modelling and reasoning in Event-B. STTT **12**(6), 447–466 (2010)
5. Alessio, C.: Reconstruction of TLAPS proofs solved by VeriT in Lambdapi. In: Glässer, U., Creissac Campos, J., Méry, D., Palanque, P. (eds.) ABZ 2023. LNCS, vol. 14010, pp. 375–377. Springer, Cham (2023). https://doi.org/10.1007/978-3-031-33163-3_29
6. Assaf, A., et al.: Expressing theories in the $\lambda\Pi$-calculus modulo theory and in the Dedukti system. In: TYPES: Types for Proofs and Programs. Novi SAd, Serbia (2016). https://minesparis-psl.hal.science/hal-01441751
7. Boespflug, M., Carbonneaux, Q., Hermant, O.: The $\lambda\Pi$-calculus modulo as a universal proof language. In: Pichardie, D., Weber, T. (eds.) Proceedings of the Second International Workshop on Proof Exchange for Theorem Proving, PxTP 2012, Manchester, UK, June 30, 2012. CEUR Workshop Proceedings, vol. 878, pp. 28–43. CEUR-WS.org (2012). http://ceur-ws.org/Vol-878/paper2.pdf
8. Chaudhuri, K., Doligez, D., Lamport, L., Merz, S.: Verifying safety properties with the TLA + proof system (2010). https://doi.org/10.1007/978-3-642-14203-1_12
9. CLEARSY: Atelier B Tool (2024). https://www.atelierb.eu/en/
10. Cousineau, D., Dowek, G.: Embedding pure type systems in the Lambda-Pi-calculus modulo (2023)
11. Delahaye, D., Dubois, C., Marché, C., Mentré, D.: The BWare project: building a proof platform for the automated verification of B proof obligations. In: Ait Ameur, Y., Schewe, K.D. (eds.) ABZ 2014. LNCS, vol. 8477, pp. 290–293. Springer, Heidelberg (2014). https://doi.org/10.1007/978-3-662-43652-3_26
12. Déharbe, D., Fontaine, P., Guyot, Y., Voisin, L.: Integrating SMT solvers in Rodin. Sci. Comput. Program. **94**, 130–143 (2014)https://doi.org/10.1016/j.scico.2014. 04.012, https://www.sciencedirect.com/science/article/pii/S016764231400183X. Abstract State Machines, Alloy, B, VDM, and Z
13. Lamport, L.: Specifying Systems, The TLA+ Language and Tools for Hardware and Software Engineers. Addison-Wesley, Boston (2002). http://research. microsoft.com/users/lamport/tla/book.html
14. Stolze, C., Hermant, O., Guillaumé, R.: Towards Formalization and Sharing of Atelier B Proofs with Dedukti (2024). https://hal.science/hal-04398119. working paper or preprint

Proof Construction and Checking
on Evolving Abstract State Machines

Edward Sabinus[✉][ID]

Institut für Informatik, Martin-Luther-Universität Halle-Wittenberg,
06120 Halle (Saale), Germany
edward.sabinus@informatik.uni-halle.de

Abstract. Abstract State Machines (ASMs) are widely used in the formalization and verification of the semantics of software or hardware. However, tools for assisting this process for evolving specifications are still lacking. With evolving we denote adding extensions without refactoring. We want to create a tool assisting in the verification of evolving specifications. Our approach is to translate ASM specifications into the language of an existing proof checker, construct the proofs as far as possible automatically, and check the proofs with the proof checker. Further, we want proofs of evolvable specifications also to be evolvable. This paper gives a brief overview of the approach and discusses the first step of this work, namely the translation of ASM specifications into the language of an existing proof checker, with consideration of automation possibilities.

Keywords: Abstract State Machines · Automatic Proof
Construction · Proof Checking

1 Introduction

Today, specifications evolve rapidly or are developed incrementally, as in [14–16]. So their verification is usually done mechanically with a proof checker. However the verification systems that support Abstract State Machines (ASMs) [16], do not support their clean evolution.

By evolution of a specification, we mean the addition of extensions without refactoring. The evolution of static functions is analogous to evolution in software engineering. Evolution of dynamic functions means adding new update rules with guard ϕ without changing previous update rules with guard ψ. In particular, when $\phi \rightarrow \psi$. No existing tool supports proofs with the evolution property for dynamic functions (see Sect. 2).

Our research question is: Can a verification system support the evolution of ASMs without revising previous proofs? Since specifications are evolvable, we assume this concept also applies to their proofs, i.e., proofs of evolvable specifications should also be evolvable. Previous proofs have to be replayed after evolving the specification. If an error occurs, we assume it is due to the extension.

Our goal is to assist in the verification of evolving ASMs. The approach is to translate ASM specifications into the language of an existing proof checker

S. Bonfanti et al. (Eds.): ABZ 2024, LNCS 14759, pp. 392–396, 2024.
https://doi.org/10.1007/978-3-031-63790-2_30

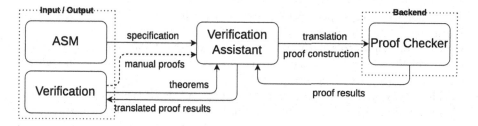

Fig. 1. The Verification Assistant

like Coq [4], Pvs [10], Isabelle/HOL [9], or KIV [5], construct as many proofs
for given theorems as possible, check the proofs with that proof checker, and let
humans complete proofs manually, that could not be finished automatically, as
seen in Fig. 1. This should support evolving ASMs with their evolving proofs.

2 Related Work

For ASMs as described in [16], there is the interpreter AsmGofer [13]. It introduces an extension to the Haskell sublanguage: Gofer, which allows executable
ASM specifications in Haskell. However, AsmGofer does no verification on ASMs.

KIV [5] is the closest verification system to our goal that supports ASMs with
data types. The difference to [16] is that the data types are not abstract, and
[16] includes subtypes. This is required for static semantic functions. Another
problem with KIV is that it does not support evolution of ASMs: Update rules
must be performed simultaneously. KIV achieves this by requiring that all update
rules with the same guard are merged. This violates the evolution property.

Asmeta [7] is a toolset for ASMs, containing multiple tools like a simulator, a
model checker, and much more, but it does not contain a verifier. It is intended to
use the model checker [2] to verify the properties of an ASM specification, which
gets automatically translated into the NuSMV model checker language. The
problem is that NuSMV supports only finite state model checking, as described
in [11], but ASM specifications often have an infinite number of states. So the
Asmeta model checker is not suitable for verification on ASMs. Furthermore, it
has the same problem with evolving ASMs as KIV.

There are many other tools for ASMs: XASM [1] can only execute ASMs.
AsmL [3] and CoreASM [6] do not support explicitly specifying the dynamic
functions, so they do not support the evolution of classic dynamic functions.

The traditional proof checkers Coq [4], Pvs [10], and Isabelle/HOL [9] do
neither support ASMs nor their evolution.

3 Approach for Verification Assistance

One possibility would be to extend an existing tool, but we are confident it is
less complex to use an existing tool in the backend than to extend the source
code of it. As we need to support the evolution of ASMs, we need to create a

translation from ASM specifications to the language of an existing proof checker. We need to find principles in the translation for each concept so that we can use these principles to automate the translation from ASM to the proof checker language. We also need to check if the proofs can be made simple enough for automation with the given translation.

Then we will try how to make proofs over ASMs in the proof checker and then again find principles for automation. The goal is to automatically generate proofs with the principles found in the proof checker using its tactics. While doing that, we have to consider the extensibility of the proofs to not revise all the proofs after the next extension of the specification.

We provisionally decided to experimentally try Coq as the proof checker for our approach, as our focus is to help with compiler verification in [15], and Coq has already been successfully involved in the large compiler verification project CompCert [8]. Thus in the following, we describe this experiment.

3.1   Translating ASM to the Coq Language

The formal definition of an ASM can be found in [16]. The main concepts of ASMs are an abstract data type, states, and update rules that transfer the ASM into the next state. Figure 2 shows the approach how ASM specifications can be translated into the Coq language.

All sorts can be translated into inductive types, defined by their constructor operations. However, Coq's type system does not support real inheritance [12], so subtypes must be managed explicitly: For each subtype, the upper type gets a constructor that manages coercion from the lower to the upper type, storing information about what type it is.

The other operations can be translated into recursive fixpoint or non-recursive functions, where also their axioms and variables are translated into. Since Coq only supports total functions, partial operations $f : t_1 \times \cdots \times t_n \rightarrow ?t$ require translation into total functions with partial types, which allows the unde-

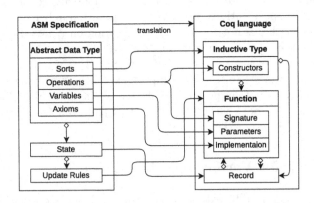

Fig. 2. Translation Approach from ASM to Coq

fined value $f : t_1 \times \cdots \times t_n \to t?$. All occurrences of t must be replaced by $t?$ in all functions. Things get more complicated with conditional axioms.

While it is possible to translate operations and axioms directly in Coq, this reduces the complexity of translation but makes proofs more complicated. Also, Coq cannot say anything about the validity of such translated operations and axioms, while defining functions allows many automated tactics like `simpl` or `auto` and verifies the termination and completeness of these functions.

One key proof strategy is induction. In order to make the induction on a function provable, it must be defined by matching the constructors of the input parameters. The advantage of this is that making an induction over one of these parameters is equivalent to the cases of the definition of the function. This makes all proofs over it much simpler.

However, transforming arbitrary conditional axioms into such functions can lead to a complex engineering process. One idea is to create helping functions with all conditions as parameters and check the conditions by constructor matching. This should also be the approach for translating the update rules.

4   Current Results

We are still experimenting with translating ASM specifications into the Coq language. We encountered many problems with the translation of axioms since many of them are not defined as a matching over constructors in our ASM specification.

The approach of transforming all axioms into functions, matching over constructors of the input parameters combined with induction proving, promises the extensibility of the proofs: Adding new functions is trivially extensible. Adding new constructors to existing types requires new induction cases to be proved, while the cases for the previous constructors remain proved. Only changing existing functions for existing constructor cases leads to a revision of previous proofs, which violates the extension property of not refactoring existing semantics.

The problem, however, is that translating arbitrary conditional axioms into terminating and well-defined functions defined by a matching over constructors of input parameters can lead to a complex engineering process. Some problems, such as completeness or rewriting conditions, may be automatable, but it may remain hard to transform everything into a constructor matching.

5   Future Work

Since we are in the early stage of our research we plan to examine the suitability of other tools, e.g. KIV, for our purpose. After completing our current experiment with Coq and making the final decision for the tool of our backend, we will analyze how to make proofs in ASMs and then transform those proofs to get them proved by the proof checker. We will start by proving simple invariants, and continue with invariants expressed in temporal logic. It is important to find principles for automation of the proofs and keep the proofs extensible. We also need to consider back-translation of the proof results.

Competing Interests. The author(s) has no competing interests to declare that are relevant to the content of this manuscript.

References

1. Anlauff, M.: XASM- an extensible, component-based abstract state machines language. In: Gurevich, Y., Kutter, P.W., Odersky, M., Thiele, L. (eds.) ASM 2000. LNCS, vol. 1912, pp. 69–90. Springer, Heidelberg (2000). https://doi.org/10.1007/3-540-44518-8_6
2. Arcaini, P., Gargantini, A., Riccobene, E.: AsmetaSMV: a way to link high-level ASM models to low-level NuSMV specifications. In: Frappier, M., Glässer, U., Khurshid, S., Laleau, R., Reeves, S. (eds.) ABZ 2010. LNCS, vol. 5977, pp. 61–74. Springer, Heidelberg (2010). https://doi.org/10.1007/978-3-642-11811-1_6
3. Barnett, M., Schulte, W.: The ABCs of specification: AsmL, behavior, and components. Informatica 25(4), 517–526 (2001)
4. Bertot, Y., Castéran, P.: Interactive Theorem Proving and Program Development: Coq'Art: The Calculus of Inductive Constructions. Springer, Heidelberg (2013)
5. Ernst, G., Pfähler, J., Schellhorn, G., Haneberg, D., Reif, W.: KIV: overview and VerifyThis competition. Int. J. Softw. Tools Technol. Transfer 17(6), 677–694 (2015)
6. Farahbod, R., Gervasi, V., Glässer, U.: CoreASM: An extensible ASM execution engine. Fundam. Inf. 77(1–2), 71–103 (2007)
7. Gargantini, A., Riccobene, E., Scandurra, P.: Model-driven language engineering: the ASMETA case study. In: 2008 The Third International Conference on Software Engineering Advances, pp. 373–378 (2008)
8. Leroy, X., Blazy, S., Kästner, D., Schommer, B., Pister, M., Ferdinand, C.: CompCert – a formally verified optimizing compiler. In: ERTS 2016: Embedded Real Time Software and Systems. SEE (2016)
9. Nipkow, T., Wenzel, M., Paulson, L.C. (eds.).: Isabelle/HOL. LNCS, vol. 2283. Springer, Heidelberg (2002). https://doi.org/10.1007/3-540-45949-9
10. Owre, S., Rushby, J.M., Shankar, N.: PVS: a prototype verification system. In: Kapur, D. (ed.) CADE 1992. LNCS, vol. 607, pp. 748–752. Springer, Heidelberg (1992). https://doi.org/10.1007/3-540-55602-8_217
11. Pakonen, A.: Model-checking infinite-state nuclear safety i&c systems with nuXmv. In: 2021 IEEE 19th International Conference on Industrial Informatics (INDIN), pp. 1–6 (2021)
12. Saïbi, A.: Coq reference manual: Implicit coercions (2018)
13. Schmid, J.: Introduction to AsmGofer (2001)
14. Stärk, R.F., Schmid, J., Börger, E.: Compilation of Java: The Trustful JVM, chapter 9-12, pp. 139–163. Springer, Heidelberg (2001)
15. Zimmermann, W., Kühn, T., Sabinus, E., Weißbach, M.: Small step incremental verification of compilers. In: 10th International Conference on Rigorous State Based Methods (ABZ'24). Springer (2024)
16. Zimmermann, W., Weißbach, M.: A framework for modeling the semantics of synchronous and asynchronous procedures with abstract state machines. In: Raschke, A., Riccobene, E., Schewe, K.-D. (eds.) Logic, Computation and Rigorous Methods. LNCS, vol. 12750, pp. 326–352. Springer, Cham (2021). https://doi.org/10.1007/978-3-030-76020-5_18

Correction to: Formal Methods and Tools Applied in the Railway Domain

Maurice H. ter Beek

Correction to:
Chapter 1 in: S. Bonfanti et al. (Eds.): *Rigorous State-Based Methods*,
LNCS 14759,
https://doi.org/10.1007/978-3-031-63790-2_1

In the originally published version of chapter 01, minor typos in references 5, 7, 16, 40, 41, 42, 48, 52, 66 and 80 were present. Surname of the authors in references 60 and 66 in the reference list were incorrect. Sentence on page 6 related to table 1 citation was incorrect. The minor typos,the surname of the authors in the references and the sentence on page 6 related to table 1 citation has been corrected.

The updated version of this chapter can be found at
https://doi.org/10.1007/978-3-031-63790-2_1

Author Index

S. Bonfanti et al. (Eds.): ABZ 2024, LNCS 14759, pp. 397–398, 2024.
https://doi.org/10.1007/978-3-031-63790-2

Printed in the United States
by Baker & Taylor Publisher Services